Method and Analysis
in Organizational Research

Method and Analysis in Organizational Research

Edited by

THOMAS S. BATEMAN
GERALD R. FERRIS

Texas A & M University

RESTON PUBLISHING COMPANY, INC.
A Prentice-Hall Company
Reston, Virginia

Library of Congress Cataloging in Publication Data

Main entry under title:

Method and analysis in organizational research.

Includes bibliographies.
1. Organization—Research—Addresses, essays,
lectures.   I. Bateman, Thomas S.   II. Ferris, Gerald R.
HD30.4.M48   1984   302.3'5   83-27009
ISBN 0-8359-4339-9

Editorial/production supervision and
interior design by Camelia Townsend

© 1984 by Reston Publishing Company, Inc.
A Prentice-Hall Company
Reston, Virginia 22090

10   9   8   7   6   5   4   3   2   1

Contents

Preface

The study of organizations today includes a broad range of topics and levels of analysis, from a concern with individual behavior and attitudes of employees to a more "macro"-analytic focus on how organizations interact with their environments. Such diversity of topical interests is essential in our movement toward more informed understanding of organizational functioning. One major element that most organizational scientists share cuts across this wide array of interests: an appreciation of the need for a solid foundation in the essentials of research methods and scientific inquiry. It is this element, this striving for validity in the execution of organizational research, that serves as the focus of this book.

Our interest in putting together this volume was prompted by our concerns with the usual, dysfunctional segregation of research design and data-analytic strategies found across most methodology courses and books, and by the relatively few volumes in existence which deal explicitly with organizational research. We believe the present volume has notable features relatively unaddressed, or absent, in other related books. First, the book takes a fairly comprehensive approach in coverage of both research design and data analysis techniques. Many of the articles provide exemplary studies illustrating the application of a certain approach or technique which makes the concept "come to life," as opposed to just an abstract description. It is too often the case in statistics courses that we learn the important principles and become good technicians but lose sight of the larger picture of what the technique is actually doing, how it is applied, and under what conditions one procedure is preferred over another.

A second feature of the book, congruent with the attempt at reasonably broad coverage, is the inclusion of five especially prepared papers. These invited papers cover topics we felt could be better presented with new statements than with existing publications. Traditional topics including psychometrics and laboratory experimentation are given fresh, succinct treatments, and newer and/or controversial issues including multiple regression as a general analytic system, moderator analysis, and exploratory data analysis are discussed in chapters that may be as useful to experienced researchers as to the graduate student just beginning a research career.

Another timely feature of the book is the

sizable section devoted to qualitative research methods. While the predominant thinking for many years has been that collecting quantifiable data and subjecting it to rigorous statistical tests is the way organizational science should be conducted, we are beginning to see a re-emergence of interest in "qualitative" research methods such as interviewing, unobtrusive measures, and participant observation. To be sure, tradeoffs exist in the exclusive use of either qualitative or quantitative approaches, but the data richness and depth of understanding potentially achieved through the appropriate use of qualitative methods should not be overlooked or understated. As the readings in this section suggest, perhaps we should more often employ multiple approaches.

The collection of readings does not, of course, exhaust all of the possible research issues and techniques. Although many useful articles presented themselves, length limitations prevented their more wholesale inclusion. We do feel, however, that the domain of organizational research methods and analysis has been representatively sampled.

The book is divided into six chapters. Each chapter consists of a number of readings, some introductory paragraphs, and a list of suggested further readings. Readings were chosen for their contributions as lucid descriptions of research processes or techniques, or as exemplary illustrations of actual applications. Suggested readings then broaden the range of exploration into other important or illustrative statements about the design and conduct of organizational research.

Chapter 1 presents several readings about some of the early considerations in the launching of a research project. The section begins by identifying some of the features which characterize significant research ideas, thus aiding the researcher in deciding whether or not to pursue an idea. The second reading then provides an overview of how the idea might be pursued, laying out the strengths and weaknesses of various general approaches to research. The remaining readings in the first chapter explore more specific topics of hypothesis creation and testing.

Chapter 2 includes papers addressing issues and techniques of data analysis. Readings about psychometric properties of data, exploratory data analysis, and techniques of multivariate analysis provide the reader with a broad base of information helpful for understanding research data.

Chapters 3 and 4 discuss the design of research, including numerous examples of well-conceived ideas and applications of statistical techniques. Chapter 3 concerns research in laboratory settings, including simulations. Chapter 4 moves into field settings, and includes experimental, quasi-experimental, and nonexperimental designs.

Chapter 5 also concerns field research, but the emphasis is on "qualitative" rather than "quantitative" approaches. This chapter significantly broadens the traditional research perspective which is sometimes rather constraining, and should provide some inspiration toward creativity in approach and the "mixing" of methods. Finally, Chapter 6 contains some concluding (though by no means parenthetical) thoughts about ethics, imperfect rigor, and a challenge for future learning.

We wish to express our gratitude to a number of people who provided various forms of contributions at different stages in the development of this book. We are grateful to Rick Mowday and Lyman Porter for their encouragement and support in the very early phases, when we were struggling with the decision of whether or not to "press onward."

A readings book on such a narrow topic, targeted primarily toward small graduate seminars and faculty libraries, would be accurately construed as having a fairly small market. Publishers are often a bit cautious in their receptivity to such volumes. Despite such valid concerns, Reston Publishing Company developed a keen interest early on.

The assistance of our editors, Ted Buchholtz and Greg Woods, is acknowledged and appreciated.

Our sincerest thanks go to our colleagues who devoted their time, energies, and considerable skills to the preparation of the invited papers. Each paper appropriately meets a need and strengthens the book significantly. Particularly considering the deadline pressures and other demands on their time, we were doubly pleased by their interest in and contributions to the final product.

Finally, we acknowledge the spirit of research that surrounds us in our Department of Management and College of Business Administration at Texas A&M. We continue to learn about and enjoy research, both directly and vicariously, through the faculty and administrators with whom we interact on a regular basis. Their varied pursuits and skills as organizational scientists provide a climate from which we have benefited in many ways, including the development of this collection.

Thomas S. Bateman
Gerald R. Ferris
College Station, Texas
July, 1983

Method and Analysis
in Organizational Research

Fundamental Considerations in Organizational Research

The first selection of readings presents some discussion of a number of basic considerations in the conduct of research. Topics range from the early identification of research ideas which may prove most (and least) fruitful, through the generation and testing of research hypotheses. These and other considerations in this chapter constitute some of the crucial, early decisions in the planning and execution of research projects.

To be sure, proper research planning entails explicit consideration of many choice points along the route from idea conception to the reporting of results. Ideally, these choices are made prior to the actual implementation of the study. In practice, though, contingencies may arise which necessitate (sometimes ultimately for the better) departure from plans. The ability to adapt to unexpected constraints (and opportunities) is an important asset to the investigator.

Nonetheless, certain preliminary decisions often set the parameters within which the research process must unfold. Many of these key issues are represented in Chapter 1. Unfortunately, they are so basic (as in foundational, not as in simple) that they are often not as salient to the researcher as, for example, decisions concerning data-analytic

strategies. As such, these considerations are sometimes given relatively little attention, when in fact their explicit incorporation into the research plan can only strengthen the final product.

The opening piece by Daft provides information useful in making that crucial decision about an idea: whether or not to pursue it. Daft suggests that too much organizational research is dull, uninteresting, and insignificant, and he seeks to identify and thereby promote the process by which scholars become engaged in truly significant pursuits. Significant research, he concludes, is characterized by an important duality of mechanistic and organic processes. Daft's piece is not only about research, it *is* research tackling an open question and ending up with useful guidelines toward maximizing the probabilities of making important contributions to knowledge. The message is both practical and inspirational.

Scientific thinking causes one to question statements proposed as truth, not accept things on blind faith, consider alternative explanations of events and relationships, and appreciate and use valid means of acquiring new knowledge. Scott's paper provides a general, solid overview of research strategies, from naturalistic observation to care-

1

fully controlled experimentation. He nicely describes the role of language in science, and then introduces fundamental concepts including operational definitions, independent and dependent variables, confounding variables and control, factorial designs, within-and between-subjects designs, main and interactive effects, and the examination and interpretation of data. Descriptions and examples of such concepts, and delineation of the major strengths and weaknesses of various methods, provide a good foundation for more detailed analyses of specific topics later in the book.

After this general treatment of research methods, the remaining articles become much more topic-specific. Two readings address aspects of hypothesis-generation. Lundberg describes, among other things, various sources of hypotheses and the basic forms they can assume. Platt then describes a systematic approach to generating alternative hypotheses and sequential hypotheses in a continuous research program. Although Platt's field(s) are different from ours, and some might argue that the "crucial experiment" is impossible for us to attain, we can benefit from much of Platt's thinking. His article provides insight into such conceptual arenas as the power of alternative hypotheses, scientific advancement through disproof, deduction and induction, symptoms of false science, method and problem orientations, the value of the notebook method, the importance of *thinking*, and the potential utility of modeling other sciences. There is also a source of comfort to go with some of Platt's inspirational messages in his statement that success is often due to a systematic approach to research "as much as to rare and unattainable intellectual power." Taken together, these two articles about hypothesis creation nicely address a topic that receives relatively little attention in print. The reader might also consider the contributions which Lundberg's and Platt's recommendations might make to the generation of significant research as defined by Daft.

Once hypotheses are generated they must, if deemed significant, be tested. Lykken addresses some important issues in hypothesis-testing. Statistical significance, he rightly suggests, is not as important as effect size. He goes on to suggest ways in which statistical tools are misused or misinterpreted. He also discusses the importance of replication/crossvalidations. On balance, Lykken succeeds in "raising consciousness" toward increased skepticism in reading and evaluating research reports.

SUGGESTIONS FOR FURTHER READING

Bakkan, D. "The Test of Significance in Psychological Research." *Psychological Bulletin*, 1966, 66, 423–437.

Burrell, G., & Morgan, G. *Sociological Paradigms and Organizational Analysis*. London: Heinemann Educational Books, 1979.

Dubin, R. *Theory Building*. New York: The Free Press, 1978.

Dunnette, M. D. "Fads, Fashions, and Folderol in Psychology." *American Psychologist*, 1966, 21, 343–352.

Greenwald, A. G. "Consequences of Prejudice Against the Null Hypothesis." *American Psychologist*, 1975, 82, 1–20.

Kaplan, A. *The Conduct of Inquiry: Methodology for Behavioral Science*. New York: Thomas Y. Crowell, 1964.

Mackenzie, K. D., & House, R. "Paradigm Development in the Social Sciences: A Proposed Research Strategy." *Academy of Management Review*, 1978, 3, 7–23.

Mowday, R. T., & Steers, R. M. *Research in Organizations: Issues and Controversies*. Santa Monica, CA: Goodyear, 1979.

Roberts, K. H., Hulin, C. L., & Rousseau, D. M. *Developing an Interdisciplinary Science of Organizations*. San Francisco: Jossey-Bass, 1978.

Webb, W. B. "The Choice of the Problem." *American Psychologist*, 1961, 16, 223–227.

Antecedents of Significant and Not-So-Significant Organizational Research[1]

Richard L. Daft

What is the process by which scholars become engaged in significant organizational research? How can a researcher identify innovative research ideas that will result in substantial increments to knowledge? These are difficult questions. They deal with the very essence of organizational research. Indeed, definitive answers to these questions may not be possible. Significant research may be the result of chance, or luck, or experience and judgment. Significant research projects may originate in the intuitive, nonlinear processes deep in the minds of investigators. We simply don't know. The purpose of this paper is to at least raise these questions, and to begin the search for answers about the origins of significant research.

Understanding how we become engaged in significant research also means understanding how we become engaged in not-so-significant research. And a substantial amount of not-so-significant research is available for examination. A common criticism of organizational behavior research is that it is dull. Research outcomes too often are neither interesting nor significant. The problems chosen for investigation often are already well researched and trivial.

The notion of research significance affects us all. We have to make choices about which research projects to undertake, and our decisions often weigh the eventual outcomes and publishability of the research. And after the research is undertaken, there are endless evaluations: by colleagues who read drafts and provide criticisms; by journal referees; perhaps by journal editors; by department heads; by promotion and tenure committees; by readers of the journal; and by other scholars doing research in the same field. Various devices are employed to assess the research, which include journal quality, number of citations, and creativity. We are continuously involved in the evaluation of research significance. And these evaluations typically are very imperfect. They do not occur until after the research act is completed, and they provoke a great deal of uncertainty and dissatisfaction because research quality is poorly understood.

[1] This paper is adapted from chapter four in John P. Campbell, Richard L. Daft, and Charles L. Hulin, *What to Study: Generating and Developing Research Questions* (Beverly Hills, CA: Sage Publications, Inc, 1982). Readers are encouraged to consult the book and the series in which it was published: *Studying Organizations: Innovations in Methodology* (Beverly Hills, CA: Sage 1983).

Special thanks to John Campbell, Chuck Hulin and Vic Vroom who collaborated on the research design and data collection for this project. This research was supported by the Office of Naval Research and the National Institute of Education as part of the "Innovations in Methodology" project, J. Richard Hackman, Principal Investigator.

The research described in this paper has two goals. The first is to directly compare significant and not-so-significant research projects along a number of specific dimensions. This comparison may help identify characteristics of significant organizational research. Improved clarification and definition of significant research may result. The second goal of this paper is to develop criteria for predicting significant research *in advance*. In other words, what should an investigator look for when choosing a research project in order to enhance the probability that it will make a significant contribution to knowledge. To meet this end, research projects were traced back to their origins. The antecedents of significant organizational research is something about which we know almost nothing, and this is the activity we must begin to understand. An "early warning" system of sorts may be helpful if we are to improve the significance of organizational research undertaken and eventually submitted for publication.

THEORY

Good research papers might be characterized by such things as good writing, novel ideas, a clever methodology, or the integration of different concepts into a single study. These characteristics make sense, and two recent papers offer particularly useful perspectives about characteristics of research outcomes. These two papers are the theoretical starting point for the study described here.

In 1971, Murray Davis proposed an intriguing idea. He argued that sociological theories which have significant impact are those that are "interesting." Davis claimed that impact and significance have little to do with truth or empirical proof. Indeed, verifiable theories are soon forgotten. A theorist or a piece of work is considered great simply because the work is interesting.

In order to be interesting, Davis said the theory has to deny certain assumptions of the audience. If all assumptions are denied, then the theory will be seen as unbelievable or irrelevant. If no assumptions are denied, the theory will be seen as obvious, as replowing old ground. The theory must be in the middle. The theory must differ moderately from readers' assumptions in order to surprise and intrigue them. From an analysis of the sociological literature, Davis developed 12 propositions that described when theories would deny some assumptions of the audience and hence be perceived as interesting. Example theories are when the assumed independent variable in a causal relationship is shown to be a dependent variable, when assumed covariation in a positive direction between phenomena is shown to be in a negative direction, when a phenomena which appears to be ineffective is shown to be effective, or when unrelated phenomena actually are found to have a single underlying theme, and so on. Theories which have one of these characteristics will tend to be noticed and will have impact. The contribution of Davis, then, is that he went beyond the notion of "newness" in research, and described 12 explicit characteristics of research ideas that might be considered in advance. If a study is simply designed to reaffirm the assumption set of the audience, then it is not likely to be very significant.

The other study is from psychology. Stephen Gottfredson (1978) examined the peer evaluation system by collecting opinions about articles from psychology journals. This was an empirical, cross-sectional study that included 83 statements describing attributes of journal articles, evaluations by 299 qualified scholars, and articles from 9 psychology journals. His research provided a comprehensive list of article characteristics, and the results indicated that judges are highly reliable when estimating the quality of articles. The 83 items were summarized in 9 scales. Key characteristics were called originality, stylistic/compositional qualities, ho-hum research, whether the paper provided direction for new research, and the type of substantive contribution.

The work of both Davis and Gottfredson dealt with evaluation after the fact. Their research explained the success of already published papers. But one comes from sociology and one from psychology, one pertains to theories and the other to empirical papers. Within these two studies is a beginning from which to start exploring the antecedents as well as the characteristics of significant research. From this starting point we may be able to identify criteria that predict early in a project whether research is likely to be perceived as original, whether it denies the assumptions of the audience, or whether it will be simply more of the same ho-hum research that is now being published.

METHOD

The purpose of the methodology was to develop a direct comparison between significant and not-so-significant research at two stages—(1) the initial circumstances under which the research was undertaken, and (2) the published research outcomes. This meant measuring the beginning and ending of research projects. Learning about the research beginnings required personal interviews. Controlling for differences in research experience and creativity was also important, so a "within person" research strategy was adopted. Each investigator would be interviewed twice, once for a project considered significant, and once for a project considered not-so-significant.

Criterion of Significance

The first problem concerns the definition of significant and not-so-significant research. The researcher was asked to select a research project in each category (significant and not-so-significant), using acceptance by colleagues in the field as the criterion. Investigators are aware of feedback in the form of journal reviews, acceptance by colleagues, citations, and whether the work has been recognized as making a significant contribution to the field. Likewise, the researcher would know that a not-so-significant project had not been accepted in a positive manner by colleagues, had not received recognition, and perhaps was never published even though submitted to journals. Thus respondents chose the research projects about which they were interviewed, and they used acceptance by other scholars in the discipline as the criterion of significance.

Closed-ended Questions

The next step was to develop a list of specific dimensions along which to compare the research projects. This involved two steps. The first step was a literature search for dimensions along which successful projects might be discriminated from non-successful projects. This search included both the literature on research (Davis, 1971; Gottfredson, 1978), and the literature on organizational innovation which had used the method of comparing successful and unsuccessful projects (Zand and Sorensen, 1975; Science Policy Research Unit, 1972). The second step was a survey of colleagues, who were asked to provide their description of what characterized exceptionally good research papers and exceptionally poor research papers. From these sources a pool of 38 questionnaire items was developed which seemed to capture most characteristics by which significant and not-so-significant research projects would differ from one another.

Open-ended Questions

The open-ended questions were designed to trace each project back to its beginning. The formal interview was only semistructured. Since the antecedents of research is a poorly understood topic, open-ended questions provided an opportunity to explore and discover important differences between the early stages of significant and not-so-significant research outcomes. General questions were asked, and then the interviewer probed until he understood the history of the project. Example questions included: How did the project originate? Where did the idea come from? How was it developed? What attracted you to the project? What contextual factors facilitated or inhibited development of the research? Responses to these questions were written down by the interviewer for later content analysis.

Sample and Procedure

The respondents were a convenience sample of 29 scholars. The sample included all participants in the Innovations in Methodology Conference working sessions at the Center for Creative Leadership in Greensboro, N.C., August 1980. Additional researchers were interviewed at the University of Minnesota and Texas A&M University. The criterion for selection was that the scholar had done organizational research, was recognized as a capable scholar, and had completed research projects that could be considered significant and not-so-significant. Respondents were interviewed face-to-face for the open-ended questions, and then they completed the 38 closed-ended items by themselves.

Caveat

After examination of the set of 29 written pairs of interviews, it became clear that the interview team had not maintained rigorous consistency. In a few cases respondents selected projects they especially liked or disliked as the criterion of significance, with only secondary regard for acceptance or rejection by the larger academic community. Different kinds of studies also were included. Most were oriented toward theory development, but a few were oriented toward methodology. These problems reflected the exploratory nature of the research. On balance, the interviews yielded robust informa-

tion. Most interviews did pertain to research that was theoretical rather than methodological, and the definition of significance in most cases was influenced by the response of the academic community rather than by the respondent's own taste. And the field interview team did conduct the interviews in a sufficiently coordinated way so that initial comparisons and insights were possible.

RESULTS

Open-ended Responses

SIGNIFICANT RESEARCH PROJECTS. Excerpts from the open-ended interviews about the origin of significant research projects are in Table 1. The paraphrases provide examples of the imagery associated with significant research projects as described by the respondents. *The reader is urged to read the items in Table 1 before reading the author's interpretation that follows.* Content analysis of the descriptions suggest several antecedents to successful research.

1. *Activity.* Significant research was an outcome of investigator activity and exposure. Frequent interactions, being in the right place at the right time, chance, and contact with management and with colleagues are related to the beginning of good research ideas. Investigator solitude and isolation probably would be less likely to result in significant research outcomes.

2. *Convergence.* There is a sense that several activities or interests converge at the same time. This convergence might include an idea with a method, or the interest of a colleague or student with exposure to an organizational problem or a new technique. Convergence seems related to the notion of activity because it is through activity and exposure that the investigator is able to be at the convergence point of several events.

3. *Intuition.* The importance of the research and the interest in it seem to be

TABLE 1
Origins of Significant Research Projects

I threw out an idea in a doctoral seminar to which a student responded. Sense of great excitement, engagement in task, reading, thinking, interacting. Continuous interaction to test ideas against one another—couldn't let go. Original idea came from interaction with executives and learning the problems they faced.

Study evolved from 2–3 streams; libertarian view, visit with _____ who had similar ideas or conclusions, endless informal discussion, previous studies I had done, observation of people.

Wanted to develop theoretical rationale and interpretation for the seemingly confusing and contradictory empirical results concerning _____. Wanted to clarify and make sense of it, and colleagues agreed with importance.

Theoretically eloquent. Idea originated in a seminar where diverse backgrounds led to stimulating clashes. Connections plus enthusiasm.

Novel combination—new theoretical idea with interesting way to test it. Also did pilot study and boom, discovered a new factor that limited previous research.

Worked in _____, and personal experience contrasted with academic theory. Findings were politically relevant for understanding motivations of poor people.

We were playing bridge with a couple from marketing. He mentioned a problem, and I said that sounds like _____ theory. We got very excited. Solved an applied problem.

I was perplexed by some results, and at the same time I read a paper by someone else who had observed the same thing and was perplexed. Tested ideas to show that conventional wisdom was erroneous and provided much simpler strategy for prediction models.

I was the entrepreneur. I perceived the need and felt it was timely. I listened to clients and sensed their careers.

Real world problems that could have policy implications. Also personal values—concern over Viet Nam war. Came from real life experience and reflection and not from literature.

The intent was to discover correct dimensions of the concept and clarify it for the literature. The concept was poorly conceptualized and was relevant to management.

Student had done an excellent paper. Decided spontaneously to collaborate with student, and was not an outgrowth of long term interests.

The idea occurred as a result of studying literature relevant to this problem. Also playful, exploratory intellectual climate—lots of "what if" conversation.

Chance. It was a matter of being in a place that did this kind of work and having the right previous experience. Had both applied and theoretical implications.

Convergence of several things. Previous book, interest in this industry, interest in _____, wife's career, and ability to use new technique.

Grew from literature review, work over previous years, interaction with Ph.D student, mathematical model developed previously, and the situation in which all this could be chunked.

From frustration over issues of motivation; from wondering how to motivate employees; from previous study of supervisors; from current literature.

A colleague walked in one day and tried to explain a new concept from operations research. Suddenly I realized significance for organizations. Multiple implication blossomed right in front of us. We talked for a year, were very excited, and finally wrote everything down.

It was a plight. I didn't believe in _____ and wanted to show it. I could use a high-powered methodology I had been taught. I meshed all my interests—small groups, personality, creativity, applied.

Dramatic topic and of interest to my associates. Methodology was of long standing interest to me. Current events influenced thinking, as did one or two key books.

guided by intuition and feeling rather than by logical analysis. Investigators often expressed a feeling of excitement or commitment, a perceived certainty, as if they "knew" at a deeper level they were doing the right thing. A great deal of intrinsic interest is also present. Logical decision processes

or planning were typically not used to select research that turned out to be significant.

4. *Theory.* A concern with theory also seems to be important. A primary goal often was to understand or explain something about organizational behavior. The investigator was curious, was concerned with a

TABLE 2
Origins of Not-So-Significant Research Projects

My heart was in other things. The research concerned demographic questions (age) and there was no reason or theory behind it.

Wanted to do a quick and dirty study for publication.

The topic was timely and new at the time and I thought I could mesh practical and theoretical issues. But the project was skewed to satisfy the funding agency, not me. A new car for me, but no theoretical contribution.

Low grade interest in the project. Easy access to student population and had to show something for a year's sabbatical. Expedient. Mechanical giving of questionnaire. No novelty, no theory, no application to anyone. Have questionnaire, will travel.

Gathered data to try a statistical technique. I was fascinated by quantitative measurement techniques. It worked, but no theory.

The concept I tried to develop a measure for was of little use. I did not think through the conceptual foundations of the study very well.

Persuaded by a colleague to look at the question. Not theoretically motivated. Little attention to the process being studied.

Instrument development was shortchanged. Theoretical model was not well developed so the study became descriptive rather than model testing.

The theory was not complex enough—too mainstream, meat and potatoes. Data were just dull.

The data were cheap and easy to obtain. The idea came up because I was specifically thinking, "How can I get a publication out of this activity." Didn't think through problem or talk about it with colleagues.

Did it for money! Contract research. Nothing intrinsically interesting about the problem. Problem was nonexistent.

Colleagues wanted to do joint paper for presentation at national meetings. Several sections of students were available so we distributed personality tests and questionnaires to them. Typology was not carefully developed.

Insufficient thought about research.

No real conceptual anchor or goals because there was no theory. Methods were adopted by analogy. Let analysis do thinking.

Convenient location. Proximity facilitated the study. Questionnaire was available for other research.

While doing dissertation, I discovered data base in government office. But the study dealt with minor modification of same old questions already in literature.

It was a replication of earlier project. Easy to do. Strictly mechanical. Reviewers recognized this, and it was never published. Method wasn't very good either.

I needed some research activity and a business student game was there to be used. Only reason for study was that it was "convenient."

puzzlement, or wanted to clarify something that was poorly understood. Theoretical understanding of some aspect of organizations seems to be the primary goal of significant research.

5. *Real World.*   Often the research problem has an applied, real world flavor to it. Significant projects were not simply elaborations of abstract, academic ideas unrelated to real organizations. The ideas often were tangible, useful, and pertained to ongoing organizational activities. Often the idea arose from contact with laymen in organizations. Many significant investigations were about something real within organizations rather than about something imaginary as seen from outside of organizations.

NOT-SO-SIGNIFICANT RESEARCH.   The paraphrases drawn from the discussion of not-so-

significant research are in Table 2. Not-so-significant projects are characterized by quite different imagery. *The reader is urged to read the items in Table 2 before reading the author's interpretation that follows.* The content of the Table 2 responses suggest the following patterns.

1. *Expedience.*   A frequent theme is that the investigator undertook the research project because it was cheap, quick, or convenient. The explicit motivation for many not-so-significant research projects is the opportunity to do the research easily. A significant contribution to knowledge, by contrast, takes extensive thought and effort. Based on Table 2, expedient short cuts tend to be associated with insignificant outcomes.

2. *Method.*   Often a statistical technique or the method to be employed took priority

over theory and understanding. The purpose of the not-so-significant studies was simply to try out a methodological technique. The techniques of science took priority over theoretical knowledge. In these projects, the method or technique may have been successfully completed and published, but the final outcome was not very important.

3. *Motivation.* In not-so-significant projects, the investigators were not motivated by a desire for knowledge and understanding of some organization phenomenon. They did the research because they were motivated toward a possible publication, or money, or they were more interested in other research projects. The absence of personal interest in and commitment to the research problem tends to distinguish research that produces little new knowledge from research that has impact on the field.

4. *Lack of Theoretical Effort.* Another common theme is that the investigator did not provide enough thought to make the study work. Complex theoretical issues had not been carefully worked through in advance. Theoretical development requires extensive intellectual effort. Without well developed theory, the research may be completed easily and quickly, but the outcome may often be insignificant.

SUMMARY. Interesting differences between significant and not-so-significant research have emerged from the open-ended interviews. An entirely different pattern of activities and motivations seem to distinguish significant from not-so-significant research. Significant research tends to be the result of broad exposure and activity, the convergence of several streams of thinking and ideas, an intuitive decision process, and a concern with theoretical understanding and real world problems. Not-so-significant research tends to result from expedience, from method dominating theory as the goal of the research, and from investigator motivation for such things as money or publication rather than new knowledge.

An alternative explanation is that self report descriptions bias the statements about research antecedents. Respondents may ascribe successful outcomes to themselves and unsuccessful outcomes to external circumstances. This does not appear to be the case in the descriptions in Tables 1 and 2. Respondents indicated that internal motivations and personal decisions were the antecedents of not-so-significant research outcomes. Respondents attributed the causes of failure to themselves as often as they did success. Indeed, respondents often attributed significant research outcomes to factors outside themselves, such as interactions with colleagues and students, good luck, and the convergence of real world activities. Although the findings are very tentative, they suggest clear differences between significant and not-so-significant research that cannot be explained by respondent bias. The findings may mean that research significance is influenced by antecedent activities and decisions.

Closed-ended Responses

The closed-ended responses which seemed to discriminate between significant and not-so-significant research projects are listed in Table 3. These items are listed in rough order of the absolute score (on a five-point scale) combined with the difference from the score for not-so-significant projects. The imagery in Table 3 contains some overlap with the patterns observed in Tables 1 and 2, and also suggests additional ideas that were not covered in the open-ended discussions. *The reader is again urged to read the items in the table before reading the author's interpretation that follows.*

SIGNIFICANT RESEARCH. Significant research was rated substantially higher than not-so-significant research on fourteen questionnaire items. These differences reflect the average scores for 29 research projects in each category.

1. *Rigor.* One frequent image in Table 3 is that of intellectual and empirical rigor.

TABLE 3

Characteristics That Differentiate Successful from Not-So-Successful Research

Item	Score for Significant Research (5 point scale)	Difference from Not-So Significant Research
.... would you say the methodology and argument were systematic, sound, rigorous, tight and relatively error free ...(31)	4.3	1.7
.... have implications that apply to the real world, such as being useful to managers or to teachers of introductory O.B. and I/O psychology courses ...(23)	3.7	1.5
.... clarify a poorly understood or cloudy issue ...(28)	3.9	1.3
.... would you say the methodology might be perceived as complex and sophisticated by the intended audience ...(33)	4.0	1.2
.... reflected your personal interest and curiosity rather than acceptability and interest to the discipline ...(11)	42.	.8
.... the variables of interest were quantifiable in an objective rather than subjective fashion (e.g., size easily quantifiable as counting # of employees; power is illusive and intangible ...(37)	4.0	.9
.... help resolve a controversial or disputed issue in the literature ...(27)	3.4	1.4
.... did you have firm expectations about the empirical outcomes ...(30a)	3.6	1.0
.... was to apply a new research method or technique as a way to shed light on a well-established research problem ...(1)	3.3	1.1
.... apply to organization settings or individuals in general (rather than to limited type or to limited population within organizations) ...(24)	3.4	.9
.... was to test directly competing theories or models about a phenomenon ...(10)	3.0	1.2
.... was to use an improved, more rigorous method than was previously used to study an established phenomenon (greater internal validity) ...(4)	3.3	.9
.... determine that diverse phenomena are united by a single explanation (simplification or integration) ...(18)	2.9	1.2
.... identify a relationship between variables that previously were believed not to be related ...(15)	3.0	1.0

Methodology and argument were systematic, sound, and relatively error free in significant projects. Variables often were quantifiable and the methodology complex. The purpose of the study may have been to bring a research method that was new or more rigorous to bear on a problem.

2. *Importance to the Discipline.* Another image seems to be the relevance to theoretical problems in the discipline. Significant research clarifies a poorly understood issue, helps resolve a controversial issue, tests directly competing theories, or may show that diverse phenomena are united by a single explanation compared to not-so-signifi-

cant research. The outcome of significant research thus makes a contribution to the theoretical knowledge base of the discipline.

3. *Personal Interest and Motivation.* Significant research is more likely to be undertaken because of personal interests of the investigator rather than because the research is acceptable to the discipline (and publishable), and the investigator is likely to have strong beliefs about the expected outcomes.

4. *Real World Implications.* The final image in Table 3 concerns problems that are related to the real world, such as being useful to managers or to teachers. Significant

TABLE 4

Characteristics for Which Not-So-Significant Research Received a Higher Score than Significant Research

Item	Score for Not-So-Significant Research	Difference
. . . . was the opportunity to use a method that was convenient for you to execute (familiarity, expense, facilities, etc.) . . .(12)	3.0	.6
. . . . was the discovery or availability of a data base that enabled you to test ideas that were interesting to you . . .(13)	2.4	.3
. . . . was to add a new variable or new combination of variables to the study of an established phenomenon . . .(2)	2.3	.3

research has practical as well as theoretical value. Significant research findings also apply to a wide range of organizational situations rather than to a very limited or narrowly defined population.

NOT-SO-SIGNIFICANT RESEARCH. The significant research projects scored slightly higher or about the same as the not-so-significant projects on most other (nineteen) questionnaire items. For three questions, however, there was a reversal, and the not-so-significant research received a higher score. Those three items are in Table 4. The differences are not large, but they are especially interesting because each of the items represented a legitimate reason for undertaking a research project.

1. *Expedience.* Undertaking research because it was convenient or because of the availability of the data was given a higher score for not-so-significant research. This finding reflects a pattern similar to what we saw in the open-ended responses. Expedient and convenient research apparently is not associated with significant research outcomes.

2. *Lack of Theoretical Effort.* The third item in Table 4 pertains to the mechanical combination of variables rather than effort to achieve theoretical understanding. Routinely combining new variables in a study of traditional phenomena apparently is associated more often with not-so-significant than with significant research.

DISCUSSION

The above findings must be treated as extremely tentative. They are based upon an exploratory study, a convenience sample, and subjective recollections of research processes. Despite the limitations of the study, some interesting and potentially useful patterns have emerged. At this point, we can once again raise the questions from the beginning of the paper: What is the process by which scholars become engaged in significant organizational research? How can a researcher identify an innovative research project that will result in a substantial increment to knowledge? Based upon the findings described so far in this paper, some tentative answers can be proposed. The answers are summarized in the Guidelines for Significant Research which follow. These guidelines summarize the activities and processes that seem to distinguish significant from not-so-significant research outcomes.

Guidelines for Significant Research

SIGNIFICANT RESEARCH IS AN OUTCOME OF INVESTIGATOR INVOLVEMENT IN THE PHYSICAL AND SOCIAL WORLD OF ORGANIZATIONS. The implications for scholars is clear: Make contacts. Leave your office door open. Look for wide exposure and diverse experiences. Go into organizations. Discuss ideas with students and colleagues. Look for new methodologies. Listen to managers. Activity and exposure are important because significant research often results from the chance convergence of ideas and activities from several sources. Investigators who remove themselves from these streams, who stay isolated, who do research based upon the next logical step from a recent journal article, are less likely to undertake projects that make outstanding contributions.

SIGNIFICANT RESEARCH IS AN OUTCOME OF INVESTIGATOR INTEREST, RESOLVE, AND EFFORT. Significant research is not convenient. Significant research is not designed to achieve a quick and dirty publication. Significant research is not expedient. A great deal of effort and thought is required to transform difficult research problems into empirical results that are clear, useful and important. For most of us, there is no easy path. Genuine interest and great effort are needed to achieve significant outcomes.

SIGNIFICANT RESEARCH PROJECTS ARE CHOSEN ON THE BASIS OF INTUITION. When a project has the potential for high payoff, investigators feel good about it, they are excited, and that feeling seems to be an accurate indicator of future significance. Investigators typically are emotionally involved and committed to the project. The project is not chosen on the basis of hard logic or certainty of publication.

SIGNIFICANT RESEARCH IS AN OUTCOME OF INTELLECTUAL RIGOR. Although the project may begin in a fuzzy state, it must end up well understood if it is to have impact. Substantial effort goes into theoretical development and clarification. The research method may be complex and sophisticated, which also requires careful thought and application. When a study turns out to be not-so-significant, it is often because the theory was not thought out. Theory development may be the hardest part. Often a research technique can be applied quickly and easily, but without theoretical depth, although the study may be publishable, it probably will not be considered outstanding or have impact.

SIGNIFICANT RESEARCH REACHES INTO THE UNCERTAIN WORLD OF ORGANIZATIONS AND RETURNS WITH SOMETHING CLEAR, TANGIBLE, AND WELL UNDERSTOOD. Good research takes a problem that is not clear, is in dispute or out of focus, and brings it into resolution. Rigor and clear thinking are needed to make this transformation. Significant research begins with disorder, but ends with order. Successful research often reaches out and discovers order and understanding where none was perceived previously. The result is something specific and tangible which can be understood and used. Logic and certainty do not begin the process, but are an outcome of the research process.

SIGNIFICANT RESEARCH FOCUSES ON REAL PROBLEMS. Significant research does not simply build abstract concepts onto a purely academic structure. Significant research deals with the real world, and the findings have relevance for colleagues, teachers and managers. Research that deals exclusively with the strains of intellectual life created solely through scholarly activity is less likely to be significant.

SIGNIFICANT RESEARCH IS CONCERNED WITH THEORY, WITH A DESIRE FOR UNDERSTANDING AND EXPLANATION. An important antecedent of significant research is curiosity and excitement associated with understanding and discovery. Studies which are mechanical, which simply combine variables or use established data bases, seldom provide significant outcomes. When the primary motivation is publication, or money, or a research contract rather than theoretical understanding of organizations, then not-so-significant outcomes tend to emerge.

CONCLUSION

One important idea to emerge from this exploratory study of significant and not-so-significant research is that the selection of innovative research questions is not a single act or decision. *Significant research is the outcome of a process, an attitude, a way of thinking.* Significant research is accomplished by people who are motivated to do significant research, who are willing to pay the cost in time and effort. Significant research is motivated by curiosity, by the desire to discover and understand. Investigators apparently can make conscious choices necessary to achieve significant outcomes. Among the scholars surveyed for this study, nearly all had been involved in both significant and not-so-significant research. Thus researchers can involve themselves in the types of activities conducive to significant research, and can select problems based upon their own interest and excitement. When they do, they are more likely to attain significant research outcomes.

A second important idea from this study is that significant research is characterized by a *duality.* This interpretation goes beyond the data, but significant research seems to be characterized by both organic and mechanistic processes, by both linear and nonlinear thinking. Organic processes characterize the investigator's immediate world, and include widespread contacts, involvement in many streams of research, and letting things happen that can converge and be exciting. The choice process for selecting significant research is often nonlinear and based on intrinsic interest and intuition. The significant research outcome, on the other hand, can be characterized as well understood and mechanistic. The successful project thus begins in an organic way, but concludes as a clearly defined, logical, rational product for diffusion to colleagues or managers. Perhaps this is why so much theoretical effort is required to produce significant research. Translating poorly understood phenomena into well understood phenomena requires intensity and commitment. It is a high order activity. The research product clearly defines and illustrates some aspect of organizational reality for other people.

When research in organizational behav-
ior is dull, one reason is that it fails to capture the duality. Too much O.B. research starts with mechanistic, linear thinking, and ends there as well. Investigators choose topics that are frequently studied and well defined, and make minor adjustments to them. Mechanistic processes dominate. Journal evaluations are concerned with logic and rationality in both the beginning and ending of the project. By contrast, significant research often is characterized by uncertainty, fuzziness, and ambiguity in the initial stages. To achieve significant research, we must take chances, we must probe beyond what we already know.

We hear so much about scientific rigor, experimental control, measurement precision, and the anticipation and removal of uncertainties as the norm for good research. Our research training encourages us to get rid of anything that could upset the research blueprint, to be sure of what we are doing, to define the problem precisely. The findings from this study suggests that we rethink this approach. The shortcoming of a mechanistic, predictable research beginning is that it assumes investigators know a substantial amount about the phenomenon under investigation. Knowledge beforehand makes for tidy research, but the significance will typically be small. If we know in advance what the research answer will be, if we understand the phenomenon well enough to predict and control what happens, then we are not allowing for chance convergence or intuition. We probably have not reached into the real organizational world to learn something new. If we are to acquire genuinely new knowledge, then we won't know the answer in advance. We won't even be sure there is an answer. The significant discoveries require us to go outside the safe certainty of mechanistic research ideas and designs.

The notion that we must begin with uncertainty, even build uncertainty into our research, may be the key. It is important to ask research questions without knowing the answer in advance. The only requirement is that we end up with some level of certainty. In one sense, then, scientific progress requires both the organic and mechanistic. We must begin with the organic and finish with the mechanistic. To some extent we must bring organic processes into our research lives in order to be exposed to the exciting, unanticipated convergence of ideas that has the potential to be outstanding. If our research starts out neat and tidy and mechanistic, and the results come out as expected, then the outcome will be insignificant, and the project was probably a waste of time.

REFERENCES

Davis, Murray S. "That's Interesting: Toward a Phenomenology of Sociology and a Sociology of Phenomenology." *Philosophy of Social Science*, 1971, *1*, 309–344.

Gottfredson, Stephen D. "Evaluating Psychological Research Reports: Dimensions, Reliability, and Correlates of Quality Judgments." *American Psychologist*, 1978, *33*, 920–934.

Science Policy Research Unit, University of Sussex. *Success and Failure in Industrial Innovation*. London: Center for the Study of Industrial Innovation, 1972.

Zand, Dale E. and Richard E. Sorensen. "Theory of Change and the Effective Use of Management Science." *Administrative Science Quarterly*, 1975, *20*, 532–545.

The Development of Knowledge in Organizational Behavior and Human Performance[1]

W. E. Scott, Jr

Within the past few years, researchers have been able to develop useful knowledge about the behavior of individuals in organizations to replace the human relations saws of an earlier time. It is comprised of a body of theory as well as empirical generalizations which possess sufficient reliability and generality to be worthy of critical study. While our knowledge of organizational behavior is incomplete, it is clear that we are no longer required to rely upon anecdotal evidence and speculation as our primary source of information. Rather, it is empirical knowledge based upon systematic study and experimentation which needs to be emphasized. That being the case, it may prove helpful to consider the nature and function of knowledge and the methods by which it is produced.

A number of practical benefits are gained from a study and development of knowledge of organizational behavior and human performance. First, systematic studies of this subject are being conducted at a rapidly increasing rate. Administrators and educators will soon become outdated unless they equip themselves to read, understand,

and evaluate the reports of these studies. Second, interest in sponsoring research of all kinds of organizations has been increasing. Specialized research units in many large organizations have presented a number of unresolved, difficult organizational problems. Perhaps, an improved understanding of scientific goals and methods would lead to more satisfactory solutions to these problems. Finally, more interaction between researchers and practitioners is needed. The researcher who seeks to establish relationships between organizational variables and behavior under controlled settings also seeks to apply his findings to an expanding set of conditions. Administrators sensitive to the goals and methods of the behavioral scientist can provide feedback to researchers about the generality of these relationships in complex organizations. This feedback often can raise additional questions which are significant from both a practical and scientific viewpoint. While the popular misconceptions that research is simply a way of solving problems or that the so-called scientific method is applicable to all or most of the complex problems facing the administrator

[1] Reproduced by permission of the American Institute for Decision Sciences, *Decision Sciences*, 1975, 6, 142–165.

must be rejected, a better understanding of empirical knowledge and its development would enhance the administrator's ability to use and to contribute to the systematic study of organizational behavior.

CHARACTERISTICS OF KNOWLEDGE

An individual may acquire knowledge about objects and events in his environment through direct encounter or first-hand experience. Nearly all of us have observed the behavior of others in complex organizations. However, knowledge based solely upon direct encounters with natural phenomena is limited. Some insist that these encounters cannot make the individual knowledgeable at all unless he is able to verbally describe or represent that experience to himself and to others. This is a complex psychological issue not to be pursued here, but raising the issue does provide an opportunity to emphasize two points. First, most of our scientific knowledge is received from significant others by means of conversation, lectures, newspapers, books, and other such media. Second, this process is so ubiquitous that we often forget that verbal symbols, concepts or terms are different from that to which they refer. The term organizational behavior, for example, is a verbal stimulus distinguishable from the phenomena which it signifies. Unfortunately, some concepts from the everyday vernacular signify different meanings to different individuals. To avoid confusion and misunderstanding, the researcher is typically forced to develop a specialized vocabulary which employs precise and invariant meanings, but which lacks appeal until the user gains familiarity with it.

This paper focuses on that knowledge which enables an individual to describe objects and events specifically and to state relationships between objects and events. Several advantages accrue to those who possess this knowledge. First, the knowledgeable individual gains a viewpoint by which to examine and assess behavioral events, especially those in which the significance is not obvious. He is also sensitive to antecedent or causal variables which might not otherwise be perceived either because they are embedded in a complex setting or because they are not a part of the current stimulus field. Second, this kind of knowledge provides the individual with a set of expectancies regarding behavioral outcomes given the occurrence of or variations in certain environmental and individual difference variables. Therefore, when one has possession of empirical propositions reflecting relationships between antecedent events and behavioral outcomes, that person understands and is able to predict organizational behavior, thereby avoiding uncertainty, surprises, and frustration. Finally, if an individual knows propositions stating relationships between behavior and environmental events which can be changed or varied, then he is able to influence behavior.

BELIEFS AND OPERATING ASSUMPTIONS OF THE RESEARCHER

The researcher believes in reality. Unlike the solipsist, the scientist assumes that the objects and events which he observes do exist apart from himself.

The researcher also believes that organizational behavior, like other natural phenomena, shows certain consistencies which can be anticipated and explained. He believes that organizational behavior is determined, but he does not assume that there is a single determinant or cause. Rather, he believes that there are multiple determinants which act alone and with other determinants to produce behavior. Yet, he posits *finite* causality. He does not believe that *all* events in nature can influence all other events.

The researcher is an empiricist. He believes reliable knowledge of organizational behavior can best be developed by means of firsthand, controlled observations. He would disagree with the philosophical doctrine which advocates that knowledge may be acquired or developed *solely* through reasoning processes and intuition. For the modern empiricist, reasoning is required for purposes of organizing knowledge and is indispensible to the process of inductive generalization, but the emphasis is upon direct observation and experimentation as the source of knowledge.

The researcher has learned to be skeptical for he has learned that man, as an observer, is subject to error. Consequently, he does not readily agree with a propositional statement simply because it was uttered by a person of recognized status or because it appears intuitively to be true. He does not reject such statements as necessarily false since an empirical test may ultimately lead him to conclude otherwise. He merely asks (1) whether or not they are true, and (2) how could one go about demonstrating their truth or falsity [6, p. 9].

THE RESEARCHER AND HIS LANGUAGE

As stated above, the researcher believes that organizational behavior is a reality apart from himself and that reliable knowledge can be developed about it by means of direct encounter. However, he is aware of the sociolinguistic nature of all scientific endeavor. While linguistic symbols can be distinguished from the objects and events they are meant to represent, few observations of any consequence can be communicated to others without the use of symbols. Direct experience is private and of little social value until it is communicated to others.

The researcher, sensitive to the problems of conceptualization and communication, sets about to construct an objective language which will accurately convey his observations. This language will never be totally independent of the vernacular. Nor

should it be. Many terms in the common, everyday language are reasonably precise and unambiguous, in which case they are taken over by the researcher without modification. However, there are also terms in the common language which do not always refer to something out there, or if they do, the "something" is so vague and amorphous that confusion and misunderstanding are rampant. In these cases the researcher is confronted with the necessity of either reconstructing the common language or coining new terms. He will often do both by defining his concepts operationally.

To define a concept operationally means to specify precisely the procedures or operations which are associated with its use. In making a concept synonymous with a set of concrete, reproducible operations, the researcher is able to clarify the phenomenon under investigation and to communicate his observations in an unambiguous manner. For example, to test the proposition that democratic leadership results in (is functionally related to, produces, causes) higher productivity than autocratic leadership, the researcher will have to develop a set of operations defining the terms democratic leadership, autocratic leadership, and productivity. How will the researcher do this?

First of all, the terms are taken from the common language and may require some logical explication[2] before operational definitions can be developed. Upon reflection, the researcher might conclude that the terms autocratic and democratic leadership refer to specific behavioral patterns exhibited by leaders in formal organizations. But what is the nature of these patterns and how do they differ? Further analysis might lead to the conclusion that autocratic leadership can be characterized by an individual who (1) unilaterally decides what tasks are to be performed by each subordinate, (2) directs subordinates to perform those tasks without

---

[2] Mandler and Kessen [3, pp. 98–104] describe logical explication as a process by which terms in the common language are more precisely defined or redefined.

deviation, and (3) makes punishment or threats of punishment contingent upon not performing those tasks as directed. The researcher may also decide that democratic leadership can be characterized by an individual who (1) consults with and takes into account the suggestions and preferences of his subordinates in deciding what tasks are to be performed, (2) does not specifically direct his subordinates to perform the tasks, or having elicited task performance, permits deviations in the manner in which they are performed, and (3) makes rewards or promises of rewards contingent upon successful task accomplishment.

If the researcher has not become discouraged at this point, he may attempt to develop a set of operations which he hopes will be somewhat reflective of the explicated concepts. For example, he might develop a behavioral questionnaire which requires organizational leaders to describe how they typically behave with regard to task decisions, methods of eliciting task performance, deviations from task performance, and administration of rewards and punishment. Several analyses and refinements of the questionnaire might enable him to set up a continuum and to classify high scorers on the questionnaire as democratic leaders and low scorers as autocratic leaders. This public and repeatable set of operations is synonymous with and defines the two concepts.[3] After analyzing and defining productivity in the same manner, the researcher is able to investigate the relationship between leadership styles and productivity to be operationally defined in a similar way.

Many concepts in the common, everyday language are rendered less vague and ambiguous by the use of the foregoing procedure. New concepts are also introduced by making them equivalent to a set of operations which others can reproduce. However,

the operational analysis of the concepts must not be considered a panacea. Spence [9] points out that the formulation of operational definitions is merely one faltering step in building a body of empirical knowledge. If the operationally defined concept is not subsequently found to be related to other concepts, then, it has no scientific significance and should be discarded. The number of digits on the left foot multiplied by the number of freckles on the face divided by two is a perfectly acceptable set of operations defining a concept we shall label Welles, but it is highly improbable this would be of any interest to the behavioral scientist.

Another consideration of the researcher is the complexity or "size" of a concept. He may choose to work with concepts referring to a complex of empirical events treated as a syndrome, or he may prefer to work with molecular, unidimensional concepts. Yet, more important than the size or complexity of concepts is the continued persistence of the researcher in conducting research which utilizes a variety of conceptual approaches and which establishes systematic relationships between a syndrome of environmental events and behavioral variables. If these relationships are not found to hold up in every instance, the researcher should break up the syndrome in search of the one or a more limited sub-set of characteristics which may be responsible for the relationship.

RESEARCH VARIABLES IN ORGANIZATIONAL BEHAVIOR AND HUMAN PERFORMANCE

Most concepts contained in empirical propositions refer to things which vary or can be varied in amount, degree, or kind. The researcher seeks to establish relationships between *independent* and *dependent variables*.

---

[3] Perhaps the defining operations should be referred to as "ZIZ" and "ZAZ". Democratic and autocratic leadership are common terms which have already acquired a variety of meanings. It is doubtful that the reader will readily dismiss those ingrained meanings in favor of the defining operations described here. It is for this reason that it is often a good idea to coin new terms to represent operational definitions.

A dependent variable is anything which is changed or modified as a consequence of a change or a modification in something else. The dependent variable is nearly always some observable aspect of behavior or the consequences of behavior. For example, a researcher may be interested in learning why individuals become members of an organization or do *not* become members, why they remain as members for a long period of time or leave the organization. He may be interested in learning why some individuals or groups are more creative than others, or why some individuals appear to be more satisfied with their jobs than others. He may be interested in learning why some individuals cooperate with each other, while others conflict; why some individuals often contribute far more than is prescribed, while others perform their jobs in the prescribed manner but rarely go beyond that; and, why some individuals engage in behavior that is judged to be organizationally disruptive.

Obviously, there are a number of dependent variables which are interesting and significant not only because they are functionally related to organizational success, but also because they remain as scientific curiosities, not yet fully explained or predictable. The lives of researchers and managers would be considerably less complicated if they could say that dependent variables were all related and that those factors which lead to high productivity also produce satisfaction, cooperation, and creative contributions. Unfortunately, such is not the case. At least, the relationship between satisfaction and productivity is obscure. Moreover, it is possible that under certain circumstances, such behavioral variables as individual productivity and interpersonal cooperation are inversely related. The researcher will frequently direct his attention to these complexities in order to investigate the relationships between behavioral variables or to search for more basic dependent variables.

The independent variable is anything which when changed or modified induces a change or a modification in some aspect of organizational behavior. When a person seeks explanations for turnover, variations in productivity, cooperation, satisfaction, and so on, he is really inquiring about those factors (independent variables) which are functionally related to or cause variations in behavior.

Independent variables in organizational behavior may be viewed as falling into one of two broadly defined classes. There are *environmental* variables, such as task design, magnitude or quality of rewards and punishments and the manner in which they are scheduled, the presence and behavior of significant others, temperature, noise, illumination, group size, and variations in organizational structure. The second class of independent variables is known as *subject* or *individual-difference* variables. These are relatively enduring behavioral characteristics of the individual and include intelligence, aptitudes, propensity to take risks, characteristic energy level, motor skills, and motives.

OBSERVATIONAL STRATEGIES

Empirical propositions depend upon first hand observation for their development, but past experience has made it quite clear that all humans are subject to a variety of observational errors. Consequently, researchers have developed strategies for observing phenomena so that such errors are reduced to a minimum.

Observational strategies may be viewed as falling on a continuum between naturalistic observation and experimentation. As a researcher progresses along the continuum, he exerts increasingly greater control over the phenomena which he is observing.

Naturalistic Observation

Utilizing this strategy, the researcher observes the behavior of individuals as it occurs in a natural setting, namely, in formal organizations. He does not control and manipulate independent variables in order to note their effects on behavior. Rather, he attends to be-havior as it ordinarily occurs, watching for apparent covariation betwen environmental events and behavioral episodes. The re-searcher may attempt to record those events which seem to be relevant, and he emerges from his study with a verbal description of his observations.

Because naturalistic observation has a number of limitations, a researcher should maintain a cautious attitude towards knowl-edge based solely upon this strategy. Signifi-cant behavioral events may not occur frequently, and since the researcher exerts no control over those events, he may not be prepared to observe them when they do occur. More importantly, the observer makes few attempts to reduce the sources of human error that are attributable to his own act of perceiving. He would not worry much about this source of error if he could depend upon the fact that his sense organs furnish the brain with exact replicas of the real world. However, such is not the case. Illusions are common. Unaided perceptions of physical objects rarely correspond exactly with those resulting from a direct encounter with the object by means of various kinds of measure-ment techniques.

When the events observed are behav-ioral, and thus more variable and ambiguous than physical objects, the emotions, expec-tancies, and past experiences of the observer may become as prominent in determining what is perceived as the behavioral events themselves. Similarly, our perceptions of cause and effect relationships are often inac-curate, especially when the cause and the ef-fect do not always occur together or when the effect does not immediately follow the cause in time [2]. Temporal contiguity be-tween events *is* a compelling factor in draw-ing cause and effect conclusions [11]. How-ever, there are a number of events occurring concomitantly with behavior when we ob-serve it in a natural setting. Perhaps the ob-server could logically dismiss the fly unobtrusively crawling along the sill in an-other building as a determiner of the behav-ior of an operative employee on a production line. Yet, which of the several events that are present *will be* selectively attended to? The answer to the question is that the observer will usually arrive on the scene with certain preconceived notions or tentative ideas as to what are the relevant and irrelevant factors, and he will direct his attention to those fac-tors which he believes to be relevant. If he observes a relationship between those events he chooses to concentrate upon, does he do so because there is a relationship which could be confirmed by others, or is the ob-served relationship attributable to the fact that he expected to find one? Suppose, for example, that the observer suspected that group productivity is higher when the super-visor is physically present than when he is physically absent. Let us further assume (1) that group productivity did not invariably change with the presence or absence of the supervisor, (2) that the supervisor was more often present than absent, (3) that there is *no* inherent relationship between the super-visor's presence and group productivity, and (4) that the observer could accurately dis-criminate between high and low group pro-ductivity and between supervisory presence and non-presence.[4]

Figure 1 shows a record of a series of ob-servations that might have been made under these circumstances.

The naturalistic observer in this situa-

---

[4] Point four is not a very valid assumption. Changes in group productivity are not easily discernible, and in the absence of an objective means of assessing significant variations in group output, the observer may "see" changes in the direction of his expectations. Naturalis-tic observers attempt to sharpen the definitions of the concepts they use in reporting their ob-servations, but they rarely define their dependent and independent variables in terms of a reproducible set of measurement operations. An attempt to develop operational definitions of the terms "supervisory presence" and "group productivity" could prove to be humorous, if not enlightening for the reader.

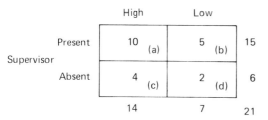

Figure 1. A Record of Observations Made in Organization X Group Productivity

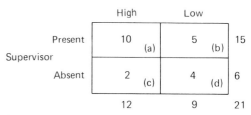

Figure 2. A Record of Observations Made in Organization Y Group Productivity

tion might perceive only a limited set of instances which would tend to verify his expectation. For example, Figure 1 shows that group productivity was high during 10 of the 15 times the supervisor was present and that group productivity was low only 5 of the 15 times he was present. Alternatively, the supervisor was present during 10 of the 14 times that group productivity was observed to be high and was absent only 4 times during which group productivity was observed to be high. In the event the observer was astute enough to look for *all* confirming and disconfirming cases during the observational period, he would note that there was a total of 12 confirming cases (cells a and d) and only 9 disconfirming ones, (cells b and c). Again, however, the observer might erroneously conclude that the supervisor's presence enhances group productivity since his expectation is verified more often than it is not.

Only the observer who has an abstract appreciation of correlation [2, pp. 14–15] would come to the correct conclusion. He would do so by comparing the probability of high group productivity given the supervisor's presence (10/15 or .67) with the probability of high group productivity given his absence (4/6 or .67). Since the probabilities are identical, he would conclude that in this situation, variations in group productivity appear to be independent of the presence or absence of the supervisor.

Let us assume that all the conditions described above are the same except that the observations were made in a different organization in which there *is* a relationship between supervisory presence and group productivity. An example of a series of observations made under these circumstances is shown in Figure 2.

This set of observations would reinforce the observer's expectations in the same manner as those made in Organization X. In this case, however, the probability of high group productivity when the supervisor is present is .67, while the probability of high group productivity when he is not present is only .33.

Although the conclusion that the supervisor's presence caused higher group productivity seems to be supported by the observations made in Organization Y, we must consider the possibility that *other* events were operating in this situation to cause the changes in group productivity. While repeated observations would rule out some of them on the basis that they were never present or always present (and nonvarying) when changes in group productivity occurred, perhaps not all of them could be so readily dismissed. Several events may occur together so that it is difficult to say which one is the cause of higher productivity. For example, suppose that the supervisor tended to appear only when production pressure was intense. Then, increased productivity could have resulted because of the varying backlog of visible materials, partially completed assemblies, work orders, etc., rather than the supervisor's presence. The above is an example of *confounding*, a situation in which any variable other than the dependent variable changes along with the independent variable of primary concern.

Confounding is always a danger no matter what the observational strategy, but it is most likely to occur when the observer exercises little control over the events he observes.

One often hears that knowledge stemming from naturalistic observation is more relevant to real-life behavior, and hence more valuable to the administrator. But the possibility of confounding places limitations on this knowledge. Different supervisors may not show up only during those times when production pressure increases. Therefore, the results of this study would be of limited generality and quite erroneous if it could be established by more rigorous methods that production pressure rather than supervisory presence was the cause of changes in group productivity.

Despite the limitations of naturalistic observation, a researcher should remain open to knowledge that comes from observers utilizing this strategy. A significant portion of what we know or what we think we know about organizational behavior has been generated by astute individuals who have spent their lives observing behavior as it naturally occurs in formal organizations. Oppenheimer, the physicist, [5] has made a plea not to treat too harshly those who tell a story without having established the completeness or the generality of that story. That plea should not go unheard. In many cases, an observation that has been made in the field has been verified in the laboratory where the observer can exercise the necessary controls over the independent variable and other potentially confounding variables.

Systematic Assessment

In all probability, the individuals in the production departments of organizations X and Y were not responding as one. Some were undoubtedly producing more than others during the presence *and* absence of the supervisors. Furthermore, both the direction and amount of change may have varied from one individual to another as the supervisors were alternately present and absent. Behavioral scientists have grown to expect significant differences in behavior when several individuals are placed in a common environmental setting, and have approached the problem of explaining those differences by postulating that they are attributable to certain enduring characteristics of the individual. This postulate has led to the development of a wide variety of individual-difference measures, the most common of which are standardized tests. Thus, the term "systematic assessment" has come to be applied to that observational strategy in which events existing in varying degrees in nature are operationally defined, and the relationships between events, so defined, are investigated. The observer does not purposefully manipulate the independent variable as in the experimental strategy, but he typically exercises greater control than the naturalistic observer. An example will serve to illustrate the kinds of control that are exercised when the systematic assessment strategy is employed.

Noting that some employees are consistently more productive than others in the same situation, the observer might hypothesize that the differences are due to variations in aptitude.

The first step in testing the hypothesis is to select or construct operational definitions of the aptitudes which are important in determining productivity. In this case, let us assume that a researcher selects rather than constructs a measure of Closure Flexibility.[5] Then, he assembles all the employees in a

---

[5] The Closure Flexibility Test is a standardized measure of the ability to hold a configuration in mind despite distraction. This aptitude has been found to be related to certain personality traits and has also been found to differentiate among individuals in various occupational groups.

room in which noise levels, illumination, and other features of the environment are held constant, and administers the test according to the instructions specified by the test manual. Since the observer has controlled environmental stimulation, he assumes that individual scores are representative of the ability which is measured rather than a function of environmental events. If the observer finds reliable differences in scores, he is ready for the next important step. He must now devise an operational definition of productivity so that he might investigate the relationship between the attribute presumably measured by his test and productivity back at the work site. He may decide to define productivity as the number of acceptable units completed by each individual during a specified period of time. He might also choose to introduce some *additional controls* such as having the supervisor always present and holding the quality and quantity of materials constant for each individual during the observing period.

Having observed and recorded the output of each individual, the researcher is now ready to assess the relationship between scores on the Closure Flexibility Test and productivity. A relationship that might have been obtained is depicted by the scatter diagram in Figure 3.

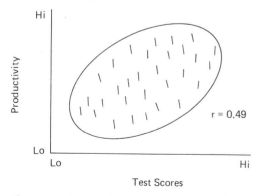

Figure 3. The Relationship Between Scores on the Closure Flexibility Test and Individual Productivity

Utilizing the Pearson product-moment correlation coefficient, one of several techniques for assessing relationships between variables, the observer finds a statistically significant correlation of .49. He concludes, therefore, that there is a functional relationship between scores achieved on the Closure Flexibility Test and the level of individual productivity in this situation.

There is a curious mixture of inference and empiricism in this and in all studies utilizing the systematic assessment strategy. It is empirical in the sense that the variables are operationally defined. Since concepts refer to observable events, the observations are capable of being repeated by another individual. Also, the proposition asserting the relationship between Closure Flexibility Test scores and productivity is relatively clear and unambiguous. However, it seems absurd to remain at a strictly empirical level and state that the individual's responses in the test-taking situation caused his subsequent behavior on the production line. Rather, a researcher *infers* some sort of characteristic from the score, and it is that characteristic which is believed to determine the behavioral outcome. In addition to finding that the inferred characteristic is somewhat obscure, a researcher has difficulty specifying and defending the direction of causality. In the above case, it was implicitly assumed that the characteristic measured by the test determined the level of productivity, but variations in task behavior *preceding* the test administration may have determined the score achieved on the test.

The observer utilizing the systematic assessment strategy takes advantage of differences which already exist in nature rather than deliberately creating those differences. As a consequence, the observer does not provide very convincing evidence for causal relationships, whatever the direction. While knowing that individuals differ with regard to closure flexibility, researchers do not know in what other respects the subjects might differ. Perhaps, those who score high on this test also have higher needs for achievement, and the latter characteristic, rather than a high degree of closure flexibility, results in high levels of productivity. The now-familiar problem of confounding is evident here as in every study in which systematic assessment is used.

Nevertheless, functional relationships established by means of systematic assessment can be very useful. Our Closure Flexibility Test, for example, could be used to select from an applicant population those who are most likely to be high producers. However, the possibility of confounding makes it difficult to understand why the relationship exists and places limitations on the generality of the relationship. If the tasks were different and were performed by a different group of individuals in another organization, the same relationship might not hold.

The use of the systematic assessment strategy is not restricted to psychological tests and individual differences. One can also establish operational definitions of organizational characteristics, and then investigate the relationships between differences in those characteristics and behavioral variables. Indik [1], for example, has reviewed a number of studies in which organizational size was found to be related to member satisfaction, absenteeism, and individual output. Size was operationally defined as the number of individuals who are members of the organization, and size was systematically assessed rather than deliberately manipulated as in the experimental strategy. Interestingly enough, Indik offered a set of theoretical postulates to account for the observed relationships between organizational size and behavior (and to account for contradictory findings as well). He speculated that as size increases, communications problems among members tend to increase, task complexity tends to decrease, the need for supervision and coordination increases, and the use of impersonal controls tends to increase. What Indik has done is to ask the reader to consider a variety of *confounding* variables which may be the real causes of dissatisfaction, absenteeism, and productivity. In other words, he seems to be saying that communications problems, task complexity, etc. may often, though not necessarily, vary concomitantly with size to cause the behavior. When they do not vary with size, the relationships will not be observed.

Experimentation

The observer who utilizes the experimental strategy deliberately produces the event he wishes to observe. He systematically varies one event (the independent variable), while controlling the influence of others (potentially confounding variables). Then, he notes the effects of the varied event on behavior (the dependent variable). The experimental strategy is by no means a foolproof procedure for producing reliable and generalizable knowledge, but it does provide more convincing evidence for cause and effect relationships than other approaches.

Weick [12] prefers to discuss the experimental strategy without reference to a distinction between settings. However, there is some merit in distinguishing between *field experiments* and *laboratory experiments*. The observer may utilize the experimental strategy to study behavior in an on-going organization, or he may choose to bring behavior into the laboratory where more control can be exercised. Seashore [7] has described the problems which an observer may encounter in conducting a field experiment. They arise primarily because the experiment is incidental to the pursuit of organizational goals and because some loss of control over the appropriate experimental variable is inevitable.

Assume that the observer has decided to conduct a field experiment in order to test the hypothesis that the supervisor's physical presence has a significant effect on group productivity. His first problem is to find an organization which will allow him to conduct the experiment. Having gained entry into an organization, the observer is now faced with

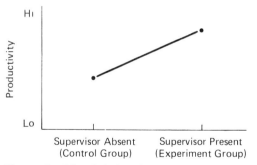

Figure 4. The Relationship Between Supervisory Presence and Group Productivity

a series of experimental design decisions. The experimental strategy, whether employed in the field or in the laboratory, requires at least two different values of the independent variable. Therefore, the observer's first decision is whether to have one group perform the task while the supervisor is present and the other group perform while he is absent (the between-subjects design), or to have *all* employees perform the task under *both* conditions (the within-subjects design). Should the former course of action be chosen, the observer must take care in assigning the subjects to each group so that both groups are approximately equal with respect to confounding variables. He may accomplish this goal by randomly assigning individuals to each group, and then tossing a coin to decide which group will perform with the supervisor present.

A series of observations in which both groups performed the task under identical conditions except the presence and absence of the supervisor may have yielded the data shown in Figure 4.

As the data indicate, the presence of the supervisor seems to affect group productivity. This conclusion assumes that other variables were controlled either by holding them constant or by randomization. If, for example, those who score high on the Closure Flexibility Test are typically the most productive, the random assignment of individuals to the experimental and control groups

tends to insure that the average test scores of both groups will be approximately equal before the observations were begun.

The various organizational constraints are likely to prevent the observer from randomly assigning individuals to either the experimental or the control group. Furthermore, it would be nearly impossible to achieve a "pure" condition of supervisory absence for any length of time in a formal organization. A consideration of these and other problems with the implementation of a between-subjects design might have led the observer to adopt the within-subjects design.

The observer is faced with a different kind of problem when he adopts the within-subjects design. He must anticipate the possibility of a progressive error [11, p. 32], a change in behavior that may occur as a function of performing the task over time. In this case, it would not be wise to have the supervisor present during the first four hours of the day and absent during the remaining hours because fatigue effects may confound the results. While there are a number of methods for controlling progressive error, probably the most appropriate one in this experiment would be randomization. The observer would have the supervisor appear at random times throughout the observing period.

The results of the within-subjects experiment may have been quite similar to those obtained from the between-subjects design. However, in both cases, the conclusion that the supervisor's presence enhances group productivity may only hold true in this isolated situation. The observer is dealing with a specific supervisor and a specific work group, and neither is likely to be representative of supervisors and work groups in general. The patterns of interaction between the workers and the relationships between this supervisor and the work group have developed over a period of time. The nature of the interaction history peculiar to this group may be determined by the effects of the supervisor's presence. Moreover, production pressure, which may have affected group productivity and which could not be easily controlled by the observer, may have been significantly higher or lower when the supervisor was present than when he was absent.

The lack of control and the attendant probability of confounding may lead the observer to choose the laboratory as the site for conducting his observations. Here, he might be able to repeat his observations using different supervisors and different work groups while holding interaction histories, production pressure, and other factors constant. Under these circumstances, the observer is most likely to be able to make a general causal statement about the effect of the supervisor's presence on productivity. However, he is also most likely to be criticized by the laymen on the grounds that the knowledge he had provided is too "theoretical" or has no relevance for the administrator. After all, work groups in organizations have an interaction history. They are not *ad hoc* groups who have never seen each other before, nor are they inexperienced at the task. Furthermore, supervisors come and go at will, and production pressures are variable rather than constant. What the critic really means in this case is that he is not likely to comprehend the influence of the supervisor's presence on behavior in a natural setting because there are other determining factors operating simultaneously there. The effect of the supervisor's physical presence observed in the laboratory may not be observed in the formal organization because that effect is swamped by the effects of other factors which could be controlled in the laboratory. But, a researcher will never know whether a supervisor's presence has an effect on behavior until he observes it when the influences of other factors are controlled. If the effect *is* swamped by other variables in a natural setting, then they too need to be observed under controlled conditions.

As we have seen, the observer, sus-

pecting that production pressure has an effect on behavior, could have controlled its influence either by holding it constant at some value or by allowing it to vary randomly. He could just as well have investigated its effects at the same time that he observed the effects of the supervisor's presence. This possibility brings us to a discussion of the *factorial* experiment in which the simultaneous effects of *two* or *more* independent variables are observed.

If production pressure could be defined in a manner that permitted the observer to systematically vary it from a normal value to a high value, the *main* effects of each of the two independent variables could then be examined. The primary influence of the supervisor's presence could be ascertained by contrasting average group productivity when he is present with average group productivity when he is absent, the average being obtained in both cases by summing across both levels of production pressure. This result is shown in Figure 5.

The main effect of variations in production pressure could be examined in a similar fashion, as shown in Figure 6.

The most significant feature of the factorial experiment is that it allows the observer to investigate the *interaction* effects of the independent variables. An interaction effect is said to exist when the relationship between the dependent variable (productivity)

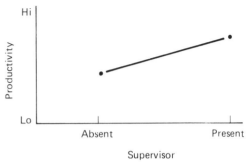

Figure 5. The Main Effect of the Supervisor's Presence on Group Productivity

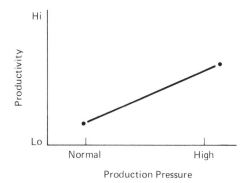

Figure 6. The Main Effect of Production Pressure on Group Productivity

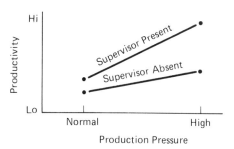

Figure 7. The Effects of Production Pressure and Supervisor's Presence on Group Productivity

and one independent variable (supervisor's presence) varies as a function of the value of another independent variable (production pressure). To clarify the notion of interaction effects, let us assume that the results of the observer's factorial experiment were as illustrated in Figure 7.

The data suggest[6] that the main effect of production pressure is significant since both curves slope upward. The main effect of the supervisor's presence also appears to be significant since group productivity is generally higher when he is present than when he is absent. However, there appears to be a significant interaction effect as well. That is, the effect of the supervisor's presence on group productivity varies with the value of production pressure. At normal levels of production pressure, the supervisor's presence does not seem to have a large effect on group productivity, but when production pressure is high, his presence has a considerable effect.

One is now able to understand the negative attitude toward knowledge that is produced by the experimental strategy in which the influence of all variables except one is controlled. One observer might have unwittingly or deliberately observed the effects of

the supervisor's presence only when production pressure was high, in which case he would have concluded that the physical presence of the supervisor has a very significant effect on group productivity. The response that this bit of knowledge is either irrelevant or theoretical is undoubtedly based upon the subjective feeling that the relationship would only hold under certain conditions which are not typically obtained in nature.

Further observations might support the critic's premise, but such support does not mean that the single factor experiment produced knowledge that is irrelevant or theoretical. That the supervisor's presence has an effect on productivity under certain specifiable circumstances represents a bit of knowledge which we did not possess before the experiment was conducted. Furthermore, researchers seek to extend the generality of their findings by repeating their observations under different conditions. A failure to observe the same relationship under different conditions inevitably stimulates speculation and additional studies until the contradictory findings are resolved. Finally, interaction effects are not always found. If the two productivity curves shown in Figure 7 were parallel or approached that condition, one would have to conclude that

---

[6] Needless to say, we cannot discern significant differences in productivity merely by inspection of the data. There are available a number of statistical tests for determining the significance of main and interaction effects.

the effects of the supervisor's presence were similar whether production pressure was normal or high.

The experimental strategy is most frequently employed by those who seek to establish behavioral propositions which hold for all individuals. Individual differences are deliberately masked or treated as experimental error when changes in behavior, if they occur as a consequence of a change in an environmental event, are shown as changes in group averages. The attempt to establish general behavioral laws is a perfectly legitimate and useful enterprise. However, researchers often observe the behavior of two individuals to be both quantitatively and qualitatively different at the same value of the independent variable. The attempt to explain individual differences in response to constant environmental events and to changes in environmental events has led to the development of a factorial experiment in which at least one of the independent variables is an individual-difference variable systematically assessed [4].

As an example, let us assume that the observer administered the Closure Flexibility Test to his group of subjects and then observed the effects of the supervisor's presence on the productivity of those who scored high and those who scored low on the test. If the observer programmed the supervisor to appear in a randomized sequence, the influence of variations in production pressure would tend to be randomized, and progressive error would similarly be controlled. The results of this hypothetical experiment are shown in Figure 8.

The main effects of both independent variables appear to be significant, but there is also an interaction effect. In this case, the degree to which the supervisor's presence affects productivity depends upon the level of closure flexibility inherent in an individual.

Since behavior is widely held to be a function of the *interaction* between the individual and his environment, the observational approach which combines systematic

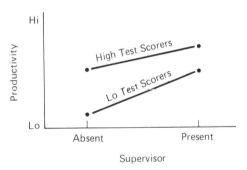

Figure 8. The Effects of Closure Flexibility and the Supervisor's Presence on Productivity

assessment and experimental manipulation is perhaps the most appropriate one yet devised.

THE RELIABILITY AND GENERALITY OF KNOWLEDGE

As has been previously noted, researchers seek to establish a body of knowledge comprised of empirical propositions. However, an awareness of the kinds of errors to which observers are prone should lead us to be skeptical about the *reliability* and *generality* of those propositions.

When raising the question of reliability, we are simply asking whether a repetition of the observations by the same observer would yield the same results. Therefore, the basic test of the reliability of an empirical proposition is provided by replicating the observations under the same conditions.

When a person questions the generality of a proposition, he is asking whether he can expect the relationship stated by it to hold when different observers conduct the study utilizing different subjects in a wide variety of settings.

Direct replication of an experiment in order to test the reliability of an observation is rare unless the results are in conflict with other widely held generalizations. Even then, the researcher may not duplicate his study in all its details. Perhaps, his subjects are now experienced so exact replication may be impossible. A more important reason, however, is that evidence for both the reliability *and* the generality of a proposition can be obtained by conducting the observations under conditions which differ from those prevailing in the initial experiment. Thus, the researcher might utilize different subjects, different values of the independent variables, or add new independent variables to those initially studied.

This strategy is somewhat risky because a failure to replicate the initial observations means either that they were unreliable or that the relationships observed will only be found under certain restricted conditions. The experienced researcher is willing to take this risk because he usually has some subjective estimates of the reliability of his observations. Furthermore, there is a much greater pay-off in taking the risk. If the results observed in the initial study are observed again under conditions which differ significantly from those in the initial study, then the evidence for the generality of the initial observations is much stronger.

When he uses his initial observations as the bases for testing new hypotheses logically deduced from or otherwise suggested by his earlier observations and when the new hypotheses are supported, then a *body* of related empirical propositions begins to form. As one increases the number of empirical propositions that are consistent with each other, then the probability of the whole system being true is considerably enhanced. This strategy of *systematic* replication is simply a reflection of the scientist's primary goal. He is not interested in isolated events. Rather, he seeks to establish a body of reliable and generalizable knowledge which will help predict and explain the behavior of many individuals performing under all manner of organizational circumstances.

If the results of subsequent observations do not prove to be consistent with the initial ones, then the researcher has no choice but to back up and directly replicate his observa-

tions. If an acceptable degree of reliability is found, then it is quite likely that the new conditions which were introduced interacted with the original independent variables. That being the case, the generalization becomes more complicated although no less valid. It would be convenient to be able to state that the supervisor's presence increases the performance of all individuals no matter what the circumstances. However, if the relationship holds for some individuals and not for others or if it holds only under certain conditions, the researcher does not know less. He actually knows more, but his generalizations are now complex, reflecting, perhaps, the complexity of human behavior.

A misleading impression would be that researchers always conduct their observations and then perform additional studies to check the reliability and generality of their findings before reporting them. On the contrary, they typically report their initial observations and immediately offer generalizations which extend far beyond the particular observations they have made. This inductive leap from a limited set of observations to an indefinite universe of similar events may be startling to the interested layman, but again the reasons are clear. The researcher is not terribly interested in single, isolated events, but rather in the development of a body of generalizable knowledge.

One would think that after centuries of knowledge development, scientific logicians would have developed a set of explicit rules for generalizing, but neither philosophy nor the study of inductive behavior has provided formal guidelines which tell researchers how to generalize. A scientist may generalize as far as he dares, but he should remember that other members of the scientific community will be viewing his generalizations in a critical manner. Interestingly enough, the generalizations offered by one researcher are remarkably consistent with those offered by others viewing the same data; yet, the consistency is not attributable to a fear of one's peers or to some sort of scientific conspiracy. Rather, it is the consequence of evaluating the proposed generalization on the basis of its plausible relationships with other widely-held generalizations about behavior. If the proposed generalization seems to fit with what else is known, then it is typically accepted without further confirmatory evidence. If the new generalization appears to be at odds with other widely-held generalizations, then (1) the observations upon which the generalization was based may be unreliable, (2) the generalization could be more restricted in scope, or (3) some of the generalizations currently held to be true may be in error. Whatever the case, inconsistencies in propositional statements set the occasion for additional experiments, and the self-corrective nature of science continues.

The researcher would be much more limited in his ability to appropriately generalize from limited observations if the existing body of knowledge were equivocal or of questionable reliability. Consequently, a researcher may spend a great deal of time conducting studies which may appear trivial or of no pragmatic value in order to establish a body of reliable and generalizable knowledge against which future generalizations can be evaluated.

THE ROLE OF THEORY IN KNOWLEDGE DEVELOPMENT

A final consideration is the role of theory in knowledge development. The fact that this subject seems to be treated as an afterthought does not imply that theory is of nominal importance. Most behavioral scientists take the position that theories are indispensable in knowledge development although there is controversy regarding their essential nature and proper role.

Theory is a term that belongs to the vernacular, and its varying meanings have resulted in a great deal of misunderstanding and confusion. It may be useful, therefore, to indicate the manner in which the term theory has been variously used before some of the features of a fully-developed theory are described.

In the researcher's world, sensory contact with overt behavior may lead to speculations about the determinants of the behavior followed by more carefully controlled observations. When those speculations take the form of tentative propositional statements which assert relationships between causal variables and observed behavior, are such speculations to be called theories? The answer is that they often are, and there is little doubt that they provide direction for empirical observations whether or not the researcher makes his speculations public. However, when the terms in the single proposition refer to potentially observable variables, we would prefer to call such provisional statements *hypotheses.*

When appropriate evidence has been gathered and is consistently supportive of an hypothesis, then the propositional statement becomes an empirical generalization or a law. Empirical generalizations have also been called theories for reasons that may be readily understood. As was indicated above, a researcher will often make an inductive leap from a limited set of observations to a universe of similar events. Furthermore, even with additional experimental evidence, the absolute truth of a generalization is not guaranteed. One *can* say that its truth range has been extended, but it is altogether possible that under certain conditions, not yet observed, the generalization may not hold. As a consequence of this uncertainty about the range of application of empirical generalizations, one could infer that they should be considered theories.

Possibly another reason for considering empirical generalizations as theories is that, like fully-developed theories, empirical generalizations are utilized as explanatory systems. However, it is useful and perhaps necessary to distinguish between empirical generalizations and theories and between lawful explanations and theoretical explanations.

The most common distinction between a theory and an empirical generalization is that the former is an unsubstantiated, quite speculative statement, whereas the latter is factual, believed to be true beyond reasonable doubt. There is a sense in which the distinction has some validity. In the above discussion it was implied that the more speculative or uncertain the propositional statement, the greater the likelihood the statement will be termed theoretical. There are, however, some hazards in accepting this distinction as the final word. In the first place, there is a penumbra of uncertainty surrounding even the most widely held generalization. Thus, the distinction is relative and not absolute as it is so often assumed. Secondly, a fully-developed theory is not a singular statement of conjecture, but is comprised of a connected *set* of statements including, but not restricted to, statements which are speculative and not amenable to direct test. Finally, the popular distinction unduly fosters and tends to reinforce a negative evaluation of theories.

The fully-developed or ideal theory contains a number of initial statements called *postulates*. Unlike empirical generalizations, the terms in the postulates do not have an empirical referent. In other words, the terms in the postulates refer to one or more events or processes which are not directly observable and are not susceptible to operational definition. In the behavioral sciences, the terms in the postulates typically refer to events or processes assumed to be taking place beneath the skin. It should be clearly understood that the terms *may* refer to events or processes which may be directly observed some time in the future, but for the time being, they are inaccessible and their exact nature is a matter of speculation.

Since a basic function of a theory is to explain and predict observable behavioral events, and since the postulates themselves can not be directly verified, the fully-developed theory must include a set of deductive rules which spell out the logical implications of the postulates. When these rules are stated, one is able to derive hypotheses which are amenable to empirical test. When hypotheses deduced from the postulates are empirically tested and found to be supported, they are called the theorems (empirical generalizations or laws) of the theory. Thus, a fully-developed theory embodies an internally consistent *system* of postulates, theorems, and rules for deducing statements about potentially observable events.

When the postulates of a theory as well as the rules for deduction are explicitly stated, then it becomes possible to derive unequivocal, consistent, and confirmable hypotheses. The theory not only then becomes capable of summarizing and integrating a group of empirical generalizations, but it also can be used to deduce new hypotheses for test, hypotheses that might not otherwise be suggested by experience or naturalistic observation.

When viewed from this lofty perch, a fully explicit theoretical system encompassing a broad range of phenomena has not yet been achieved in the behavioral sciences. Occasionally, one may find the postulates to be crudely stated. More often, according to Mandler and Kessen [3, pp. 237–240] the basic postulates of behavioral theories are not ambiguous. Rather, it is the absence of explicit guidelines for deducing unequivocal, experimental hypotheses that is characteristic of most current theories. These deductive rules need not be highly formal. All that is necessary is that competent peers be able to deduce the same hypotheses without having to consult with the theorist. Otherwise, the theory permits the derivation of contradictory hypotheses. Under those circumstances, it becomes incapable of refutation, and it cannot offer much in the way of a synthesis of a large number of empirical generalizations.

Although current behavioral theories fall short of the ideal, they are not useless. In spite of their inadequacies, they play a crucial role in summarizing empirical observations. This role is of no little consequence in knowledge development. One needs some framework to assist in the recall and integration of empirical generalizations and to remind us of the inconsistencies in our body of knowledge. Current theories also serve to generate new research, sometimes because contradictory hypotheses are deduced. But one must be careful not to conclude that the theory is necessarily valuable unless the research it stimulates also proves to be valuable.

Scientific Explanation

Given the occurrence of an environmental event that has attracted attention, children and adults, alike, seek an explanation for it. An individual might ask why an employee group seems to be more productive at certain times and not at others, and one explanation that might be offered is that people work harder when the supervisor is present than when he is not. The curiosity of the inquirer may rest upon hearing such an explanation because it refers to a causal variable which seems to make sense. But why, others may ask, do employees work harder when the supervisor is around? The response to that question brings us a little closer to a scientific explanation as contrasted with a common-sense one.

An explanation is said to be scientific if the statement of the event to be explained can be shown to be a logical consequence of (can be deduced from) a general statement. The general statement can be an empirical generalization in which case we are dealing with a *lawful explanation* [10, pp. 271–274]. A lawful explanation includes an empirical generalization along with statements of antecedent conditions such that the event to be explained can be logically deduced from or recognized as an instance of the generalization. For example, in a wide variety of circumstances, the performance of a well learned task by any given individual is

enhanced by the presence of others whether the others are passive spectators or co-workers. This change in behavior in the presence of others is called the social facilitation effect, and the statement describing the effect is fundamentally an empirical generalization. If the antecedent conditions now are supplied (e.g., the task was well learned, the supervisor was a passive spectator or a coworker or both), one could view performance increases in the presence of a supervisor as an instance of the more general social facilitation effect.

An individual could very well ask why the presence of other members of the same species enhances the performance of a well learned task. The explainer might then supply a higher order or *theoretical explanation*. In this case, the more general statement is a postulate or a set of interrelated postulates from which can be deduced the social facilitation principle as well as other empirical generalizations. Thus, the event to be explained, the effect of the supervisor's presence on task performance, is recognized as an instance of the social facilitation principle which itself can be deduced from the postulates of a theory.

One theory which has been advanced to explain the social facilitation effect has come to be known as activation theory [13]. In that theory, a theoretical construct known as activation level is defined as the degree of excitation of a neural system in the brain stem. Since excitation of this neural system is presumed to vary from essentially no activity to a very high degree of activity, activation level is correspondingly viewed as a continuum. The relationship between activation level and behavior efficiency is postulated to be an inverted U function in which very low and very high levels of activation result in low performance, whereas an intermediate activation level results in optimal performance. Changes in activation level are postulated to be a function of variation in the external environment. A relatively novel or absolutely novel stimulus is assumed to increase activation level, whereas an unchanging environment will produce a low level of activation. Also, a stimulus that is a reward or punishment or is one that has been associated with a reward or a punishment will, when intermittently introduced, increase activation level.

All of the above are postulates since no one has directly viewed the level of excitation in the brain stem reticular formation. However, one can deduce from these postulates a number of hypotheses which are amenable to empirical test. For example, if a task were routine and unchanging, the intermittent introduction and withdrawal of a stimulus object such as another person would be expected to increase activation level from some low level to a level approaching optimal, in which case performance would be facilitated. If the social stimulus were also a person who had previously been associated with rewards and/or punishments, then the activation level might rise and be sustained over a longer period than would be the case if the person had never been associated with the mediation of rewards and punishments. One could also deduce from this set of postulates the hypothesis that the social facilitation effect would be short-lived (performance would drop back to its original level) if the person remained in view all of the time and was not associated with rewards and punishments. Another hypothesis that can be deduced from the postulates of activation theory is that the introduction of another

person would impair performance if the activation level is already high as it may be if the task were complex or if performance were not yet asymptotic. Most of the above hypotheses have some empirical support [13] and could, therefore, be viewed as theorems of the theory. However, the empirical consequences of the postulates have been deduced more through informal argument, hunch, and intuition than by means of explicit deductive rules. It should also be understood that while activation theory seems to provide a plausible explanation for a number of empirical generalizations, many empirical propositions regarding behavior remain beyond its purview.

Since current behavioral theories fall short of the ideal and may, furthermore, produce wasteful research if any at all, it has been contended that theoretical explanations are unnecessary. Skinner [8], the most notable proponent of this view, prefers to pursue the business of developing empirical generalizations and, when necessary, to advance lawful explanations rather than theoretical ones. His view is well taken. One should be skeptical of explanations which refer to hypothetical inner events or processes as the sole determinants of behavior and which do not permit the derivation of empirical hypotheses. On the other hand, one should not reject a theoretical explanation simply because it does not meet all the criteria of a fully deductive system.

REFERENCES

1. Indik, Bernard P., "Some Effects of Organizational Size on Member Attitudes and Behavior." *Human Relations*, 1963, *16*, pp. 369–384.

2. Jenkins, Herbert M., and William C. Ward, "Judgment of Contingency Between Responses and Outcomes." *Psychological Monographs: General and Applied*, 1965, *79*, pp. 1–17.

3. Mandler, George, and William Kessen, *The Language of Psychology*. New York: Wiley and Son, 1959.

4. McGuigan, F. J., *Experimental Psychology: A Methodological Approach* (2nd. ed.). Englewood Cliffs, N.J.: Prentice-Hall, 1968.

5. Oppenheimer, Robert, "Analogy in Science." *American Psychologist*, 1956, *11*, pp. 127–135.

6. Scott, William, and Michael Wertheimer, *Introduction to Psychological Research*, New York: Wiley and Sons, 1962.

7. Seashore, Stanley E., "Field Experi-

ments with Formal Organizations."
Human Organization, 1964, *23,* pp.
164–170.

8. Skinner, B. F., "Are Theories of Learning Necessary?" *Psychological Review,* 1950, *57,* pp. 193–216.

9. Spence, K. W., "The Nature of Theory Constructions in Contemporary Psychology." *Psychological Review,* 1944, *51,* pp. 47–68.

10. Turner, Merle B., *Philosophy and the Science of Behavior.* New York: Appleton-Century-Crofts, 1967.

11. Underwood, Benton J., *Experimental Psychology* (2nd. ed.). New York: Appleton-Century-Crofts, 1966.

12. Weick, Karl E., "Laboratory Experimentation with Organizations," In J. G. March (ed.), *Handbook of Organizations.* Skokie, Illinois: Rand McNally, 1965.

13. Zajone, Robert B., "Social Facilitation," *Science,* 1965, *149,* pp. 269–274.

Hypothesis Creation in Organizational Behavior Research[1]

Craig C. Lundberg[2]

In the development of any field or discipline, there comes a period where "respectability" insidiously reigns. During this period, the earlier spokespersons for the field are increasingly supplanted by a cadre of influential younger researchers who are usually sophisticated in methodology as well as ambitious. Subtly, choices are made which profoundly affect the field; methodological rigor and precision become prized over phenomenological significance, researching over scholarship, conceptual edifices for scientists only, and reification over elucidation. The field of organizational behavior appears to be slipping into such a period at the present time.[3]

Why is this so? The position taken here is straightforward and, therefore, probably an oversimplification. The contemporary nature of organizational behavior knowledge is primarily the product of how researchers are trained for their craft. This paper comments primarily on the growing emphasis attributed to hypothesis testing as opposed to hypothesis creation or generation. It secondarily takes note of a variety of approaches for discovering new ideas for research questions and hypotheses, thereby modestly contributing to a portion of the literature that is at present meager and uneven.

CONTEMPORARY RESEARCH THOUGHT IN ORGANIZATIONAL BEHAVIOR

Contemporary organizational behavior researchers have misplaced their attention in the research process, resulting in a dysfunctional emphasis on hypothesis testing over hypothesis creation. Just a couple of decades ago the field of organizational behavior was a diffuse amalgam of applied sociology, applied psychology and human relations, before coalescing as organizational behavior. Being "well-trained" as a researcher in organizational behavior meant beginning with cases and/or clinical work. A considerable portion of one's early research apprenticeship was spent "in the field," gaining what Henderson (8) has called, "an intimate, habitual,

---

[1] Reprinted by permission of the Academy of Management Review.

[2] The author wishes to acknowledge the challenging critique of John W. Hennessey, Jr. as well as the provocative discussions with Barbara Karmel and Kurt Motamedi in the preparation of this paper.

[3] An eloquent appraisal which concludes that many of these same trends are occurring for industrial and organizational psychology is made by Bass (1).

intuitive familiarity with things" of everyday experiences. After being well grounded in one's chosen phenomenon, one judiciously acquired more systematic and rigorous methodologies (11). Theoretically speaking, these extensive field experiences prompted low and middle-range, conservative conceptual schemes.

To contrast the above with a caricature of contemporary organizational behavior research, the problems selected today as worthy of investigation most often are derived from review essays and abstract models. Wide-band research approaches are forsaken for a preoccupation with precision in measurement. Basic paradigms are likewise forsaken for methods, and external validity is widely ignored. An alternative characterization is the stereotype that has developed among both scientists and practitioners as to what constitutes "serious" organizational behavior research. It goes (somewhat ironically) like this: crucial studies growing out of previous findings are performed with precision and elegance. The results are subjected to the closest scrutiny and analysis, with all alternative interpretations judiciously considered, and accepted or rejected in accordance with the canons of scientific rigor. Finally, the now confirmed discovery is inserted in a systematized lattice of already available knowledge to complete a forward step toward humanity's mastery of the unknown.

The imagery promoted above contrasts in both the style and the strategy of research. On the one hand, research is seen to be a messy affair, a meandering, blundering, often serendipitous adventure, with the objective of ever more adequate descriptions of reality. On the other hand, research is seen as a highly formal, preplanned and programmed activity in the quest of certainty. Von Mises (17) provides a label of this in the extreme; "apodietic certainty" is when there is absolutely certain certainty. This latter image is seemingly based on the assumption that the more formal and sophisticated the

methodological preparation one has for research, the more productive and creative one will be in performing the research: an assumption which clearly depends on the nature of the preparation.

There are two primary reasons why contemporary research preparation for organizational behavior is inadequate and therefore contributes to an enactment of the stereotype noted above. The first is that the research training offered today lacks effectiveness in several ways. Basic methods tend to be relatively ignored, basics such as interviewing and observation, and how to cull data from documents. Methods that are taught are probably obsolescent procedures. For example, methodology courses continue to emphasize or maintain a rigorous distinction between dependent and independent variables. Examples with two variable or few variable designs are used, and the assumption of continuous variables is constantly reinforced, as is the setting of equal numbers in equal intervals, etc. Yet it seems that the complexity of individuals and social systems requires not only more use of multivariate time-series designs, but also more attention to parallel processing, bi-directional relationships and feedback circuits as well as a much stronger attention to time. (A similar argument for psychology is made eloquently by McGuire (12)). Lastly, some techniques which have led to progress are mistakenly taken as a kind of master key to inquiry in general; that is, some successful technique is assumed to be generally fruitful, as Handy and Harwood note,

> when inquiry is understood as beginning with a "well-formulated" hypothesis and then searching for evidence, or when mathematical transformations are assumed to be the essence of scientific inquiry, or when logical deductions are emphasized (6, p. 3).

The second detracting influence in the training of researchers comes from the literature itself. Reading vast numbers of research reports and studies can be grossly misleading, not because of their content but because of their structure. This applies to both quantitative (15) and qualitative (10) reports. Research reports are, of course, the context of justification and use logic for proof or what Kaplan calls "reconstructed logic" (9). Both the context and the logic which are by custom the proper format for reporting have little to do with the initiation of research projects. In initiating research, one is interested in the context of discovery, not justification; and one's intuition (logic-in-use) is more prominent than one's rational logic. Intuition here is something preconscious and outside the preferred inference structure. Attempting to be overly formal or trying to make phenomena or reality fit preconceptions of order and construction too early (i.e., to resemble research reports) has obvious dysfunctional consequences for discovery. At the extreme this is termed "ratiocination": the belief that important knowledge can be obtained independently of observation or experience.

The above lament does not imply that the training of organizational behavior researchers should regress; rather the plea is simply that this training reintroduce some of the basic phenomena-grounding activities of earlier days, as well as promote the acquisition of systematic and rigorous methodologies, and that the latter be more compatible with the phenomena to be understood. In other words, all that is urged is that an old epistemological caveat be recalled—in successful inquiry, neither measurement nor conceptual work exists in isolation from one another nor has primacy over the other.

ON IDEA GENERATION AND HYPOTHESIS CREATION

The conventional initiation of research in behavioral science tends to use one or more of the bases succinctly noted by Webb.

> Curiosity, confirmability, compassion, cost, cupidity, and conformability—or, more sim-

ply, "Am I interested," "Can I get an answer," "Will it help," "How much will it cost," "What's the payola," "Is everyone else doing it?" (18, p. 223).

Webb then goes on to show that:

> . . . these bases, used alone or in combination although perhaps correlated positively with a "successful" piece of research, will probably have a zero or even negative correlation with a "valuable" piece of research.

Research depends on ideas, and valuable research comes from ideas for really new questions and hence new hypotheses. Experienced scientists would agree with Taylor's contention that:

> . . . worthwhile ideas do not come fullblown in all their glorious maturity out of an empty void. The process of getting and developing ideas is undoubtedly a confused mixture of observation, thinking, asking why, cherishing little unformed notions, etc. (16, p. 172)

New research questions seem to result from examining our assumptions and a combination of passive observation, putting questions to nature and active observation. Weick (19) argues that what is vital for stimulating research is the transformation of our assumptions into questions. By assumption he means that which we "know" is there in reality. Thus, for example, instead of studying the relationship of an individual's utility function to another construct, one would ask: is it the case that individuals have utility functions? If utilities don't exist, what, if anything, is guiding preference ordering and decisioning? Suppose that what occurs is that goals get progressively clarified in decisioning. If anything like this is going on in people, researchers are missing it; and the reason they are missing it is because they assume that individuals have utilities.

Observation is neither a mysterious nor an erudite process. Basically, it boils down to keeping one's eyes and ears open and making a record. Passive observation occurs by chance or spontaneously. Active observation is induced by some sort of preconceived idea, however roughhewn it may be (2, p. 7). Questions put to nature then stimulate active observation. One must poke into all sorts of silly things and risk looking foolish, even stupid, at times. Active observation often comes down to a simple playfulness, having fun with ideas, theories and oneself. Weick, for example, prescribes the following ways to discover new questions of organizations: fondle building blocks, burn caribou bones, count statues, communicate non-verbally, and construct flimsy objects (19). Playfulness is necessary to counteract the fact that we are all brought up to think we know our own minds and what they are up to at any given moment (7, p. 77).

While we obviously cannot list the questions put to nature, we can speak to their form. There seem to be six basic question forms as follows:

What is an X?

X is asserted. Is it so?

Where does X occur; what is the distribution of X?

What are the similarities and differences between X_1 and $X_2 \ldots X_n$?

What is associated with X?

What causes X, or what does X cause?

In these questions, X is a descriptor of some phenomenon. Actually, these questions indicate two quite different kinds of research work. The first four define descriptive efforts (the identification and classification of various elements). The last two define theoretical work (discovering the relationships among elements).

Before discussing hypothesis creation, there are four prerequisites for such activity: acquiring a "knowledge of acquaintance" of the phenomena, really knowing the subject, possessing an ingrained paradigm, and the ability to "galumph." Acquiring and reac-

quiring a knowledge of acquaintance (14, p. 7), that is a firsthand familiarity, of one's focal phenomenon offers a grasp of it, useful for countervailing more abstract and analytical knowledge. Possessing a thorough knowledge of the subject may appear obvious, although it is often side-stepped by the more eager researcher. There is an old saying that a discovery is an accident finding a prepared mind. Clearly creative insight occurs more frequently with a thorough knowledge of one's subject area than as a bolt from the blue. The third prerequisite, possessing an ingrained paradigm, is less well appreciated. What is suggested here is the ability to think unconsciously in accord with a fundamental model. For example, many sociologists are structural functionists, whether they are aware of it or not. Perhaps in organization behavior the paradigm is that of a cybernetic open system. "Galumphing" (13), the last prerequisite, is the psychological process of voluntarily placing obstacles in one's own path, where such deliberate complication of a process becomes interesting for itself and not under the dominant control of goals. Galumping as a prerequisite to hypothesis creation implies a strict avoidance of task-oriented efficiency.

When a question put to nature is formalized by specification of constructs or concepts and their supposed relationship, this conjecture is called a hypothesis, and hypothesis formulation or generation can come about in many ways. In the listing which follows, the emphasis will be on approaches other than theory testing. The approaches will be discussed in three sets: first, those that are most clearly exploratory efforts; then those approaches that exhibit an intentional search; and lastly, those efforts that extend antecedent research, that is, by the coupling of one project to another.

Exploratory Approaches

The first approach is probably improperly termed exploratory, for it concerns happenstances or *accidents.* Accidents are not just the unexpected, but include those events resulting from a failure or a blunder in a process which provides an opportunity for seeing some phenomenon in another way. Accidents have been dignified in science by the term "serendipity."

The *paradoxical incident* offers another opportunity for arriving at an interesting hypothesis. Something is noted that does not make sense according to our general understanding of social events; that is, it appears paradoxical and efforts to account for it can lead to new discoveries. For example, the problem of performance decline was unsatisfactorily "explained" by motivation models and this led to the recognition of activation/arousal.

The *intensive case study* is an approach long acknowledged as a fruitful source of hypotheses. The case need not be an unusual or exceptional one, for it seems that almost any case studied intensively might serve. The early history of organizational behavior, i.e. its "human relations" phase, held numerous examples. One wonders what the impact on the field would be if another period of such case studies occurred.

The *analyzing of a practitioner's or craftsman's rule of thumb* is another source of hypotheses. The procedural rule of thumb is assumed to work, and the research task is to think of theoretical implications for its effectiveness. Of course, they may be as suggestive by their failures as by their successes. Many prominent ideas in the field, e.g. "satisficing", came about in this way.

The last truly exploratory approach can be labeled "thinking around". This refers to the activity of letting go of one's focus on whatever problem or specific phenomenon one is working on and permitting oneself to speculate and fantasize about any related matters that come to mind. A deliberate cessation of effort to solve a problem often leads unexpectedly to a new perception. More pertinent to the discussion, it sometimes leads

to the discovery of new problems or questions that are likewise surprising.

Intentional Search Approaches

Prior research efforts often provide the opportunity for hypothesis creation from their *byproducts.* Anyone who searches his or her own research or the research of others will find unexpected behaviors or patterns. How often research reports contain phrases which begin "In addition . . ." or "It was also noted that . . ." These incidental observations or those recorded by others can often be mined for new questions or hypotheses. Similarly, there are methodological by-products, such as the idea of using a technique in a different context or with a different problem, or new ways of assessing or controlling variables in the often hard and ingenious work of research.

The *intentional use of analogy* is another approach. Here one simply takes the properties, patterning or functioning of some familiar subject and asks whether some other topic exhibits any similarity. Well-known examples include the computer as an analogy to cognitive processes, the biological analogies to organizational growth and development, and the economic transaction as an analogy to social exchange.

Less in evidence in organizational behavior is the approach called *hypothetico-deductive.* This approach involves putting together two or more common sense principles or empirical findings and deriving from their conjunction some predictions of interest. This hypothesis generating procedure has become increasingly popular and possible with the advent of computer simulation.

The *contextual twist* is one approach that seems underappreciated in organizational behavior. Thinking about replicating a study in a very different context can often point to new interactions or condition general findings. Moving research into the laboratory from the field or vice versa, as well as replicating a project in a different business function, industry, institution or culture, can be provocative of new ideas.

Seldom do research findings lend themselves to single explanations. Thus, another source of hypotheses is by thinking through the possible *additional interpretations* of any set of data. A closely related technique for provoking new hypotheses is to try to *account for conflicting results*. Another creative method is to attempt to *account for the exceptions to general findings*. Still another approach related to these efforts of developing new hypotheses by examination of prior work is to attempt to *reduce observed complex relationships* to simpler component relationships.

Finally, in the cataloguing of intentional search approaches to hypothesis creation, *the manipulation of scientific statements* must be mentioned—specifically, the two forms of questions listed earlier, defined as theoretical, and their more complex kin. Scientists tend to put their knowledge in the form of statements, and any untested statements are hypotheses. The manipulation of statements of association simply involves substituting some new factor or variable for one already established (including the specification of new conditioning variables). For "causative" statements, manipulation could consist of reversing the statement (e.g., satisfaction and productivity), substituting variables, the postulation of intervening variables, etc. This approach, called the manipulation of statements, is close to the next set of approaches to be discussed, the explicit coupling of research to research.

Extending-Coupling Approaches

Research often evolves from research. The two prior sections have emphasized the more obviously creative approaches. This section notes approaches to hypothesis generation which most explicitly build on previous research, forming a well-defined line of investigation (5). In general, this means extending research by *making a finding (or tech-nique) interactive with the findings, observations or capabilities of others* (18). Actually these approaches can be rather quickly identified. Independent variables can be substituted, added to, controlled better or differently, or reduced in number. Similarly, dependent variables may be replaced, added to or otherwise modified (i.e. altering the level of measurement or refining the selected behavior). There are also the obvious surplus or additional relationship variables, the so called intervening variables. The point here is that these changes in statements deliberately reflect other research and therefore "couple" prior research to that being initiated.

AN AMENDMENT ON IMPLEMENTING NEW RESEARCH IDEAS

Assuming the discovery of a new and interesting idea for either a question to put to nature or for a hypothesis: then what? While experienced researchers will exhibit stylistic uniqueness, the following advice seems to have wide acceptance.

Any new idea must be examined in light of a critical requirement—for while any new idea may produce a doable or even a successful research project, to increase the probability that it will result in a valuable project, one must ask of it, will the results be generalizable? That is, in how many and what kind of specific circumstances will the relationship expected to be confirmed in the research be likely to hold? This is the requirement of "extensity." If the idea produces findings applicable to a vast heterogeneity of events in time and space, the findings are likely to have a great value.

If a question or hypothesis seems to possess extensity, two activities are urged: professional encounter and the mental experiment. The professional encounter takes the two forms of talking with colleagues and searching the relevant literature. Such talk can generate leads to other investigators working on the same or similar problems, pertinent parts of the literature, alternative explanations, etc.

An extensive literature search, an arduous and often dull task which is often done inadequately, is more than collecting citable references. It is also a place to test questions and hypotheses without going into the field or the laboratory. How does this occur? One way is to go to the classical pieces of research in one's field, which may or may not have any apparent relationship to one's focus, and then read those research reports carefully once again, trying to see whether the phenomenon that one is interested in was in fact in that previous research. It just didn't happen to be of direct interest. Second, if one takes key terms and asks what the synonyms are and then goes to the literature and looks up those synonyms, one may find all kinds of things hidden away that would not have been otherwise noticed, especially what Blumer calls additional "sensitizing concepts" (3, p. 5)

The second activity urged is called the mental experiment. It consists of putting one's feet up and staring at the ceiling and imagining the research project in some detail—envisioning in a detailed and descriptive way what is involved and what one finds. The phrase "mental experiment" is appropriate because the project is best fantasized as an experiment: if I did or didn't do something, what phenomena would appear? This kind of mental work lets one get a better hold, not only on the phenomena but also on the processes and the implicit model.

The last suggestion relates to time. There is a great pressure to rush into print these days, particularly among younger researchers. This can be dangerous. A caricature of an older style of scholarship makes the point. Here a researcher talked to colleagues, carefully and thoroughly looked at the literature, thought through one after another mental experiment and then, and only then, wrote down a set of notes, roughly defining the research, probably slighting methodology and the finer details, concentrating on the phenomena and the questions. The key activity at this point is to put those notes away for a while. Go on and do something else; then after the passage of time, pull out the notes and read them with somewhat fresher eyes as well as pass them around to colleagues. Then, if it still seems reasonable and makes sense, formalize the research proposal.

CONCLUDING COMMENTS

Organizational behavior research today is fast becoming complex, costly and overly formalized. Some redirections in research training and a renewed emphasis on hypothesis creation are called for. While it is likely that we cannot all construct basic paradigms or initiate crucial experiments, we can at least try to be less trivial. When it comes to doing research that is enduring and critical, we can, paraphrasing Webb, learn as much as we can, believe in new ways, more effectively discover new ideas, seek as great extensity in our variables as we can, and never lose sight of the phenomenon (18). Doing research in organizational behavior is just like doing science in general; and that, according to Bridgman, is simply "doing one's damnedest with one's mind" (4, p. 460).

REFERENCES

1. Bass, B. M. "The Substance and the Shadow," *American Psychologist*, Vol. 29 (1974), 870–886.

2. Bernard, C. *An Introduction to the Study of Experimental Medicine* (New York: Dover Publications, 1957).

3. Blumer, H. "What is Wrong with Social Theory," *American Sociological Review,* Vol. 19 (1954), 3–10.

4. Bridgman, P. W. *Yale Review* (1954), 444–461.

5. Cartwright, Dorwin. "Determinants of Scientific Progress: The Case of Research on the Risky Shift," *American Psychologist,* Vol. 28 (1973), 222–231.

6. Handy, Rollo, and E. C. Harwood. *Useful Procedures of Inquiry* (Great Barrington, Mass.: Behavioral Council, 1973).

7. Hebb, D. O. "What is Psychology All About," *American Psychologist,* Vol. 29 (1974), 71–79.

8. Henderson, L. J. Introductory lectures. Unpublished lectures in "Concrete Sociology," 1938.

9. Kaplan. A. *The Conduct of Inquiry* (San Francisco: Chandler Publishers, 1964).

10. Lofland, John. "Styles of Reporting Qualitative Field Research," *The American Sociologist,* Vol. 9 (1974), 101–111.

11. Lundberg, C. C. "New Directions for Personnel Research," *Personnel Journal,* Vol. 41 (1962), 497–504.

12. McGuire, W. J. "The Yin and Yang of Process in Social Psychology: Seven Koan," *Journal of Personality and Social Psychology,* Vol. 26 (1973), 446–456.

13. Miller, S. "Ends, Means, and Galumphing: Some Leitmotifs of Play," *American Anthropologist,* 1973, 87–98.

14. Roethlisberger, F. J., et al. *Training for Human Relations* (Division of Research, Graduate School of Business Administration, Harvard University, 1954).

15. Signorelli, Anthony. "Statistics: Tool or Master of the Psychologist?" *American Psychologist,* Vol. 29 (1974), 774–777.

16. Taylor, D. W., et al. "Education for Research in Psychology," *American Psychologist,* Vol. 4 (1959), 167–179.

17. von Mises, Ludwig. *Human Action: A Treatise on Economics* (New Haven: Yale University Press, 1949).

18. Webb, W. B. "The Choice of the Problem," *American Psychologist,* Vol. 16 (1961), 223–227.

19. Weick, K. "Methodology and Systems Theory." Unpublished paper, 1974.

Strong Inference[1]

John R. Platt

Scientists these days tend to keep up a polite fiction that all science is equal. Except for the work of the misguided opponent whose arguments we happen to be refuting at the time, we speak as though every scientist's field and methods of study are as good as every other scientist's, and perhaps a little better. This keeps us all cordial when it comes to recommending each other for government grants.

But I think anyone who looks at the matter closely will agree that some fields of science are moving forward very much faster than others, perhaps by an order of magnitude, if numbers could be put on such estimates. The discoveries leap from the headlines—and they are real advances in complex and difficult subjects, like molecular biology and high-energy physics. As Alvin Weinberg says (1), "Hardly a month goes by without a stunning success in molecular biology being reported in the Proceedings of the National Academy of Sciences."

Why should there be such rapid advances in some fields and not in others? I think the usual explanations that we tend to think of—such as the tractability of the subject, or the quality or education of the men drawn into it, or the size of reseach contracts—are important but inadequate. I have begun to believe that the primary factor in scientific advance is an intellectual one. These rapidly moving fields are fields where a particular method of doing scientific research is systematically used and taught, an accumulative method of inductive inference that is so effective that I think it should be given the name of "strong inference." I believe it is important to examine this method, its use and history and rationale, and to see whether other groups and individuals might learn to adopt it profitably in their own scientific and intellectual work.

In its separate elements, strong inference is just the simple and old-fashioned method of inductive inference that goes back to Francis Bacon. The steps are familiar to every college student and are practiced, off and on, by every scientist. The difference comes in their systematic application. Strong inference consists of applying the following steps to every problem in science, formally and explicitly and regularly:

1. Devising alternative hypotheses;

2. Devising a crucial experiment (or several of them), with alternative possible outcomes, each of which will, as nearly as possible, exclude one or more of the hypotheses;

3. Carrying out the experiment so as to get a clean result;

[1] Reproduced by permission of *Science*, 1964, *146*, 347–353.

This is the text of an address given before the Division of Physical Chemistry of the American Chemical Society in September 1963, under the title "The New Baconians."

4. Recycling the procedure, making subhypotheses or sequential hypotheses to refine the possibilities that remain; and so on.

It is like climbing a tree. At the first fork, we choose—or, in this case, "nature" or the experimental outcome chooses—to go to the right branch or the left; at the next fork, to go left or right; and so on. There are similar branch points in a "conditional computer program," where the next move depends on the result of the last calculation. And there is a "conditional inductive tree" or "logical tree" of this kind written out in detail in many first-year chemistry books, in the table of steps for qualitative analysis of an unknown sample, where the student is led through a real problem of consecutive inference: Add reagent A; if you get a red precipitate, it is sub-group alpha and you filter and add reagent B; if not, you add the other reagent, B'; and so on.

On any new problem, of course, inductive inference is not as simple and certain as deduction, because it involves reaching out into the unknown. Steps 1 and 2 require intellectual inventions, which must be cleverly chosen so that hypothesis, experiment, outcome, and exclusion will be related in a rigorous syllogism; and the question of how to generate such inventions is one which has been extensively discussed elsewhere (2, 3). What the formal schema reminds us to do is to try to make these inventions, to take the next step, to proceed to the next fork, without dawdling or getting tied up in irrelevancies.

It is clear why this makes for rapid and powerful progress. For exploring the unknown, there is no faster method; this is the minimum sequence of steps. Any conclusion that is not an exclusion is insecure and must be rechecked. Any delay in recycling to the next set of hypotheses is only a delay. Strong inference, and the logical tree it generates, are to inductive reasoning what the syllogism is to deductive reasoning, in that it offers a regular method for reaching firm inductive conclusions one after the other as rapidly as possible.

"But what is so novel about this?" someone will say. This is *the* method of science and always has been; why give it a special name? The reason is that many of us have almost forgotten it. Science is now an everyday business. Equipment, calculations, lectures become ends in themselves. How many of us write down our alternatives and crucial experiments every day, focusing on the *exclusion* of a hypothesis? We may write our scientific papers so that it looks as if we had steps 1, 2, and 3 in mind all along. But in between, we do busywork. We become "method-oriented." We say we prefer to "feel our way" toward generalizations. We fail to teach our students how to sharpen up their inductive inferences. And we do not realize the added power that the regular and explicit use of alternative hypotheses and sharp exclusions could give us at every step of our research.

The difference between the average scientist's methods and the methods of the strong-inference users is somewhat like the difference between a gasoline engine that fires occasionally and one that fires in steady sequence. If our motorboat engines were as erratic as our deliberate intellectual efforts, most of us would not get home for supper.

MOLECULAR BIOLOGY

The new molecular biology is a field where I think this systematic method of inference has become widespread and effective. It is a complex field; yet a succession of crucial experiments over the past decade has given us a surprisingly detailed understanding of hereditary mechanisms and the control of enzyme formation and protein synthesis.

The logical structure shows in every experiment. In 1953 James Watson and Francis Crick proposed that the DNA molecule—the "hereditary substance" in a cell—is a long two-stranded helical molecule (4). This suggested a number of alternatives for crucial test. Do the two strands of the helix stay together when a cell divides, or do they separate? Matthew Meselson and Franklin Stahl used an ingenious isotope-density-labeling technique which showed that they separate (5). Does the DNA helix always have two strands, or can it have three, as atomic models suggest? Alexander Rich showed it can have either, depending on the ionic concentration (6). These are the kinds of experiments John Dalton would have liked, where the combining entities are not atoms but long macromolecular strands.

Or take a different sort of question: Is the "genetic map"—showing the statistical relationship of different genetic characteristics in recombination experiments—a one-dimensional map like the DNA molecule (that is, a linear map), as T. H. Morgan proposed in 1911, or does it have two-dimensional loops or branches? Seymour Benzer showed that his hundreds of fine microgenetic experiments on bacteria would fit only the mathematical matrix for the one-dimensional case (7).

But of course, selected crucial experiments of this kind can be found in every field. The real difference in molecular biology is that formal inductive inference is so systematically practiced and taught. On any given morning at the Laboratory of Molecular Biology in Cambridge, England, the blackboards of Francis Crick or Sidney Brenner will commonly be found covered with logical trees. On the top line will be the hot new result just up from the laboratory or just in by letter or rumor. On the next line will be two or three alternative explanations, or a little list of "What he did wrong." Underneath will be a series of suggested experiments or controls that can reduce the number of possibilities. And so on. The tree grows during the day as one man or another comes in and argues about why one of the experiments wouldn't work, or how it should be changed.

The strong-inference attitude is evident just in the style and language in which the papers are written. For example, in analyzing theories of antibody formation, Joshua

Lederberg (8) gives a list of nine propositions "subject to denial," discussing which ones would be "most vulnerable to experimental test."

The papers of the French leaders François Jacob and Jacques Monod are also celebrated for their high "logical density," with paragraph after paragraph of linked "inductive syllogisms." But the style is widespread. Start with the first paper in the *Journal of Molecular Biology* for 1964 (9), and you immediately find: "Our conclusions . . . might be invalid if . . . (i) . . . (ii) . . . or (iii). . . . We shall describe experiments which eliminate these alternatives." The average physicist or chemist or scientist in any field accustomed to less closely reasoned articles and less sharply stated inferences will find it a salutary experience to dip into that journal almost at random.

RESISTANCE TO ANALYTICAL METHODOLOGY

This analytical approach to biology has sometimes become almost a crusade, because it arouses so much resistance in many scientists who have grown up in a more relaxed and diffuse tradition. At the 1958 Conference on Biophysics, at Boulder, there was a dramatic confrontation between the two points of view. Leo Szilard said: "The problems of how enzymes are induced, of how proteins are synthesized, of how antibodies are formed, are closer to solution than is generally believed. If you do stupid experiments, and finish one a year, it can take 50 years. But if you stop doing experiments for a little while and *think* how proteins can possibly be synthesized, there are only about 5 different ways, not 50! And it will take only a few experiments to distinguish these."

One of the young men added: "It is essentially the old question: How *small* and *elegant* an experiment can you perform?"

These comments upset a number of those present. An electron microscopist said,

"Gentlemen, this is off the track. This is philosophy of science."

Szilard retorted, "I was not quarreling with third-rate scientists: I was quarreling with first-rate scientists."

A physical chemist hurriedly asked, "Are we going to take the official photograph before lunch or after lunch?"

But this did not deflect the dispute. A distinguished cell biologist rose and said, "No two cells give the same properties. Biology is the science of heterogeneous systems." And he added privately, "You know there are *scientists;* and there are people in science who are just working with these oversimplified model systems—DNA chains and in vitro systems—who are not doing science at all. We need their auxiliary work: they build apparatus, they make minor studies, but they are not scientists."

To which Cy Levinthal replied: "Well, there are two kinds of biologists, those who are looking to see if there is one thing that can be understood, and those who keep saying it is very complicated and that nothing can be understood. . . . You must study the *simplest* system you think has the properties you are interested in."

As they were leaving the meeting, one man could be heard muttering, "What does Szilard expect me to do—shoot myself?"

Any criticism or challenge to consider changing our methods strikes of course at all our ego-defenses. But in this case the analytical method offers the possibility of such great increases in effectiveness that it is unfortunate that it cannot be regarded more often as a challenge to learning rather than as a challenge to combat. Many of the recent triumphs in molecular biology have in fact been achieved on just such "oversimplified model systems," very much along the analytical lines laid down in the 1958 discussion. They have not fallen to the kind of men who justify themselves by saying, "No two cells are alike," regardless of how true that may ultimately be. The triumphs are in fact triumphs of a new way of thinking.

HIGH-ENERGY PHYSICS

This analytical thinking is rare, but it is by no means restricted to the new biology. High-energy physics is another field where the logic of exclusions is obvious, even in the newspaper accounts. For example, in the famous discovery of C. N. Yang and T. D. Lee, the question that was asked was: Do the fundamental particles conserve mirror-symmetry, or "parity" in certain reactions, or do they not? The crucial experiments were suggested; within a few months they were done, and conservation of parity was found to be excluded. Richard Garwin, Leon Lederman, and Marcel Weinrich did one of the crucial experiments. It was thought of one evening at suppertime; by midnight they had rearranged the apparatus for it; and by 4 A.M. they had picked up the predicted pulses showing the nonconservation of parity (10). The phenomena had just been waiting, so to speak, for the explicit formulation of the alternative hypotheses.

The theorists in this field take pride in trying to predict new properties or new particles explicitly enough so that if they are not found the theories will fall. As the biologist W. A. H. Rushton has said (11), "A theory which cannot be mortally endangered cannot be alive." Murray Gell-Mann and Yuval Ne'eman recently used the particle grouping which they call "The Eightfold Way" to predict a missing particle, the Omega-Minus, which was then looked for and found (12). But one alternative branch of the theory would predict a particle with one-third the usual electronic charge, and it was not found in the experiments, so this branch must be rejected.

The logical tree is so much a part of high-energy physics that some stages of it are commonly built, in fact, into the electronic coincidence circuits that detect the particles and trigger the bubble-chamber photographs. Each kind of particle should give a different kind of pattern in the electronic counters, and the circuits can be set to exclude or include whatever types of events are desired. If the distinguishing criteria are sequential, they may even run through a complete logical tree in a microsecond or so. This electronic preliminary analysis, like human preliminary analysis of alternative outcomes, speeds up progress by sharpening the criteria. It eliminates hundreds of thousands of the irrelevant pictures that formerly had to be scanned, and when it is carried to its limit, a few output pulses, hours apart, may be enough to signal the existence of the antiproton or the fall of a theory.

I think the emphasis on strong inference in the two fields I have mentioned has been partly the result of personal leadership, such as that of the classical geneticists in molecular biology, or of Szilard with his "Midwest Chowder and Bacteria Society" at Chicago in 1948–50, or of Max Delbrück with his summer courses in phage genetics at Cold Spring Harbor. But it is also partly due to the nature of the fields themselves. Biology, with its vast informational detail and complexity, is a "high-information" field, where years and decades can easily be wasted on the usual type of "low-information" observations or experiments if one does not think carefully in advance about what the most important and conclusive experiments would be. And in high-energy physics, both the "information flux" of particles from the new accelerators and the millon-dollar costs of operation have forced a similar analytical approach. It pays to have a top-notch group debate every experiment ahead of time; and the habit spreads throughout the field.

INDUCTION AND MULTIPLE HYPOTHESES

Historically, I think, there have been two main contributions to the development of a satisfactory strong-inference method. The first is that of Francis Bacon (13). He wanted a "surer method" of "finding out nature" than either the logic-chopping or all-inclusive theories of the time or the laudable but crude attempts to make inductions "by simple enumeration." He did not merely urge experiments, as some suppose; he showed the fruitfulness of interconnecting theory and experiment so that the one checked the other. Of the many inductive procedures he suggested, the most important, I think, was the conditional inductive tree, which proceeded from alternative hypotheses (possible "causes," as he calls them), through crucial experiments ("Instances of the Fingerpost"), to exclusion of some alternatives and adoption of what is left ("establishing axioms"). His Instances of the Fingerpost are explicitly at the forks in the logical tree, the term being borrowed "from the fingerposts which are set up where roads part, to indicate the several directions."

Many of his crucial experiments proposed in Book II of *The New Organon* are still fascinating. For example, in order to decide whether the weight of a body is due to its "inherent nature," as some had said, or is due to the attraction of the earth, which would decrease with distance, he proposes comparing the rate of a pendulum clock and a spring clock and then lifting them from the earth to the top of a tall steeple. He concludes that if the pendulum clock on the steeple "goes more slowly than it did on account of the diminished virtue of its weights . . . we may take the attraction of the mass of the earth as the cause of weight."

Here was a method that could separate off the empty theories!

Bacon said the inductive method could be learned by anybody, just like learning to "draw a straighter line or more perfect circle . . . with the help of a ruler or a pair of compasses." "My way of discovering science goes far to level men's wit and leaves but little to individual excellence, because it performs everything by the surest rules and demonstrations." Even occasional mistakes would not be fatal. "Truth will sooner come out from error than from confusion."

It is easy to see why young minds leaped to try it.

Nevertheless there is a difficulty with this method. As Bacon emphasizes, it is necessary to make "exclusions." He says, "The induction which is to be available for the discovery and demonstration of sciences and arts, must analyze nature by proper rejections and exclusions; and then, after a sufficient number of negatives, come to a conclusion on the affirmative instances." "[To man] it is granted only to proceed at first by negatives, and at last to end in affirmatives after exclusion has been exhausted."

Or, as the philosopher Karl Popper says today, there is no such thing as proof in science—because some later alternative explanation may be as good or better—so that science advances only by disproofs. There is no point in making hypotheses that are not falsifiable, because such hypotheses do not say anything: "it must be possible for an empirical scientific system to be refuted by experience" (14).

The difficulty is that disproof is a hard doctrine. If you have a hypothesis and I have another hypothesis, evidently one of them must be eliminated. The scientist seems to have no choice but to be either soft-headed or disputatious. Perhaps this is why so many tend to resist the strong analytical approach—and why some great scientists are so disputatious.

Fortunately, it seems to me, this difficulty can be removed by the use of a second great intellectual invention, the "method of multiple hypotheses," which is what was needed to round out the Baconian scheme. This is a method that was put forward by T. C. Chamberlin (15), a geologist of Chicago at the turn of the century, who is best known for his contribution to the Chamberlin-Moulton hypothesis of the origin of the solar system.

Chamberlain says our trouble is that when we make a single hypothesis, we become attached to it.

"The moment one has offered an original explanation for a phenomenon which seems satisfactory, that moment affection for his intellectual child springs into existence, and as the explanation grows into a definite theory his parental affections cluster about his offspring and it grows more and more dear to him. . . . There springs up also unwittingly a pressing of the theory to make it fit the facts and a pressing of the facts to make them fit the theory. . . .

"To avoid this grave danger, the method of multiple working hypotheses is urged. It differs from the simple working hypothesis in that it distributes the effort and divides the affections. . . . Each hypothesis suggests its own criteria, its own means of proof, its own method of developing the truth, and if a group of hypotheses encompass the subject on all sides, the total outcome of means and of methods is full and rich."

Chamberlin thinks the method "leads to certain distinctive habits of mind" and is of prime value in education. "When faithfully followed for a sufficient time, it develops a mode of thought of its own kind which may be designated the habit of complex thought. . . ."

This charming paper deserves to be reprinted in some more accessible journal today, where it could be required reading for every graduate student—and for every professor.

It seems to me that Chamberlin has hit on the explanation—and the cure—for many of our problems in the sciences. The conflict and exclusion of alternatives that is necessary to sharp inductive inference has been all too often a conflict between men, each with his single Ruling Theory. But whenever each man begins to have multiple working hypotheses, it becomes purely a conflict between ideas. It becomes much easier then for each of us to aim every day at conclusive disproofs—at *strong* inference—without either reluctance or combativeness. In fact, when there are multiple hypotheses which are not anyone's "personal property" and when there are crucial experiments to test them, the daily life in the laboratory takes on an interest and excitement it never had, and the students can hardly wait to get to work to see how the detective story will come out. It seems to me that this is the reason for the development of those "distinctive habits of mind" and the "complex thought" that Chamberlin described, the reason for the sharpness, the excitement, the zeal, the teamwork—yes, even international teamwork—in molecular biology and high-energy physics today. What else could be so effective?

When multiple hypotheses become coupled to strong inference, the scientific search becomes an emotional powerhouse as well as an intellectual one.

Unfortunately, I think, there are other areas of science today that are sick by comparison, because they have forgotten the necessity for alternative hypotheses and disproof. Each man has only one branch—or none—on the logical tree, and it twists at random without ever coming to the need for a crucial decision at any point. We can see from the external symptoms that there is something scientifically wrong. The Frozen Method. The Eternal Surveyor. The Never Finished. The Great Man With a Single Hypothesis. The Little Club of Dependents. The Vendetta. The All-Encompassing Theory Which Can Never Be Falsified.

Some cynics tell a story, which may be apocryphal, about the theoretical chemist who explained to his class,

"And thus we see that the C-Cl bond is longer in the first compound than in the second because the percent of ionic character is smaller."

A voice from the back of the room said, "But Professor X, according to the Table, the C-Cl bond is shorter in the first compound."

"Oh, is it?" said the professor. "Well, that's still easy to understand, because the double-bond character is higher in that compound."

To the extent that this kind of story is accurate, a "theory" of this sort is not a theory at all, because it does not exclude anything. It predicts everything, and therefore does not predict anything. It becomes simply a verbal formula which the graduate student repeats and believes because the professor has said it so often. This is not science, but faith; not theory, but theology. Whether it is hand-waving or number-waving or equation-waving, a theory is not a theory unless it can be disproved. That is, unless it can be falsified by some possible experimental outcome.

In chemistry, the resonance theorists will of course suppose that I am criticizing *them*, while the molecular-orbital theorists will suppose I am criticizing *them*. But their actions—our actions, for I include myself among them—speak for themselves. A failure to agree for 30 years is public advertisement of a failure to disprove.

My purpose here, however, is not to call names but rather to say that we are all sinners, and that in every field and in every laboratory we need to try to formulate multiple alternative hypotheses sharp enough to be capable of disproof.

SYSTEMATIC APPLICATION

I think the work methods of a number of scientists have been testimony to the power of strong inference. Is success not due in many cases to systematic use of Bacon's "surest rules and demonstrations" as much as to rare and unattainable intellectual power? Faraday's famous diary (*16*), or Fermi's notebooks (*3, 17*), show how these men believed in the effectiveness of daily steps in applying formal inductive methods to one problem after another.

Within 8 weeks after the discovery of x-rays, Roentgen had identified 17 of their major properties. Every student should read his first paper (*18*). Each demonstration in it is a little jewel of inductive inference. How else could the proofs have gone so fast, except by a method of maximum effectiveness?

Organic chemistry has been the spiritual home of strong inference from the beginning. Do the bonds alternate in benzene or are they equivalent? If the first, there should be five disubstituted derivatives; if the second, three. And three it is (19). This is a *strong*-inference test—not a matter of measurement, of whether there are grams or milligrams of the products, but a matter of logical alternatives. How else could the tetrahedral carbon atom or the hexagonal symmetry of benzene have been inferred 50 years before the inferences could be confirmed by x-ray and infrared measurement?

We realize that it was out of this kind of atmosphere that Pasteur came to the field of biology. Can anyone doubt that he brought with him a completely different method of reasoning? Every 2 or 3 years he moved to one biological problem after another, from optical activity to the fermentation of beet sugar, to the "diseases" of wine and beer, to the disease of silkworms, to the problem of "spontaneous generation," to the anthrax disease of sheep, to rabies. In each of these fields there were experts in Europe who knew a hundred times as much as Pasteur, yet each time he solved problems in a few months that they had not been able to solve. Obviously it was not encyclopedic knowledge that produced his success, and obviously it was not simply luck, when it was repeated over and over again; it can only have been the systematic power of a special method of exploration. Are bacteria falling in? Make the necks of the flasks S-shaped. Are bacteria sucked in by the partial vacuum? Put in a cotton plug. Week after week his crucial experiments build up the logical tree of exclusions. The drama of strong inference in molecular biology today is only a repetition of Pasteur's story.

The grand scientific syntheses, like those of Newton and Maxwell, are rare and individual achievements that stand outside any rule or method. Nevertheless it is interesting to note that several of the great synthesizers have also shown the strong-inference habit of thought in their other work, as Newton did in the inductive proofs of his *Opticks* and Maxwell did in his experimental proof that three and only three colors are needed in color vision.

A YARDSTICK OF EFFECTIVENESS

I think the evident effectiveness of the systematic use of strong inference suddenly gives us a yardstick for thinking about the effectiveness of scientific methods in general. Surveys, taxonomy, design of equipment, systematic measurements and tables, theoretical computations—all have their proper and honored place, provided they are parts of a chain of precise induction of how nature works. Unfortunately, all too often they become ends in themselves, mere time-serving from the point of view of real scientific advance, a hypertrophied methodology that justifies itself as a lore of respectability.

We praise the "lifetime of study," but in dozens of cases, in every field, what was needed was not a lifetime but rather a few short months or weeks of analytical inductive inference. In any new area we should try, like Roentgen, to see how fast we can pass from the general survey to analytical inferences. We should try, like Pasteur, to see whether we can reach strong inferences that encyclopedism could not discern.

We speak piously of taking measurements and making small studies that will "add another brick to the temple of science." Most such bricks just lie around the brickyard (20). Tables of constants have their plane and value, but the study of one spectrum after another, if not frequently re-evaluated, may become a substitute for thinking, a sad waste of intelligence in a research laboratory, and a mistraining whose crippling effects may last a lifetime.

To paraphrase an old saying, Beware of the man of one method or one instrument, either experimental or theoretical. He tends to become method-oriented rather than problem-oriented. The method-oriented man is shackled; the problem-oriented man is at least reaching freely toward what is most important. Strong inference redirects a man to problem-orientation, but it requires him to be willing repeatedly to put aside his last methods and teach himself new ones.

On the other hand, I think that anyone who asks the question about scientific effectiveness will also conclude that much of the mathematicizing in physics and chemistry today is irrelevant if not misleading.

The great value of mathematical formulation is that when an experiment agrees with a calculation to five decimal places, a great many alternative hypotheses are pretty well excluded (though the Bohr theory and the Schrödinger theory both predict exactly the same Rydberg constant!). But when the fit is only to two decimal places, or one, it may be a trap for the unwary; it may be no better than any rule-of-thumb extrapolation, and some other kind of qualitative exclusion might be more rigorous for testing the assumptions and more important to scientific understanding than the quantitative fit.

I know that this is like saying that the emperor has no clothes. Today we preach that science is not science unless it is quantitative. We substitute correlations for causal studies, and physical equations for organic reasoning. Measurements and equations are supposed to sharpen thinking, but, in my observation, they more often tend to make the thinking noncausal and fuzzy. They tend to become the object of scientific manipulation instead of auxiliary tests of crucial inferences.

Many—perhaps most—of the great issues of science are qualitative, not quantitative, even in physics and chemistry. Equations and measurements are useful when and only when they are related to proof; but proof or disproof comes first and is in fact strongest when it is absolutely convincing without any quantitative measurement.

Or to say it another way, you can catch phenomena in a logical box or in a mathematical box. The logical box is coarse but strong. The mathematical box is fine-grained but flimsy. The mathematical box is a beautiful way of wrapping up a problem, but it will not hold the phenomena unless they have been caught in a logical box to begin with.

What I am saying is that, in numerous areas that we call science, we have come to like our habitual ways, and our studies that can be continued indefinitely. We measure, we define, we compute, we analyze, but we do not exclude. And this is not the way to use our minds most effectively or to make the fastest progress in solving scientific questions.

Of course it is easy—and all too common—for one scientist to call the others unscientific. My point is not that my particular conclusions here are necessarily correct, but that we have long needed some absolute standard of possible scientific effectiveness by which to measure how well we are succeeding in various areas—a standard that many could agree on and one that would be undistorted by the scientific pressures and fashions of the times and the vested interests and busywork that they develop. It is not public evaluation I am interested in so much as a private measure by which to compare one's own scientific performance with what it might be. I believe that strong inference provides this kind of standard of what the maximum possible scientific effectiveness could be—as well as a recipe of reaching it.

AIDS TO STRONG INFERENCE

How can we learn the method and teach it? It is not difficult. The most important thing is to keep in mind that this kind of thinking is not a lucky knack but a system that *can* be taught and learned. The molecular biologists today are living proof of it. The second thing is to be explicit and formal and regular about it, to devote a half hour or an hour to analytical thinking every day, writing out the logical tree and the alternatives and crucial experiments explicitly in a permanent notebook. I have discussed elsewhere (3) the value of Fermi's notebook method, the effect it had on his colleagues and students, and the testimony that it "can be adopted by anyone with profit."

It is true that it takes great courtesy to teach the method, especially to one's peers—or their students. The strong-inference point of view is so resolutely critical of methods of work and values in science that any attempt to compare specific cases is likely to sound both smug and destructive. Mainly one should try to teach it by example and by exhorting to self-analysis and self-improvement only in general terms, as I am doing here.

But I will mention one severe but useful private test—a touchstone of strong inference—that removes the necessity for third-person criticism, because it is a test that anyone can learn to carry with him for use as needed. It is our old friend the Baconian "exclusion," but I call it "The Question." Obviously it should be applied as much to one's own thinking as to others'. It consists of asking in your own mind, on hearing any scientific explanation or theory put forward, "But sir, what experiment could *dis*prove your hypothesis?"; or, on hearing a scientific experiment described, "But sir, what hypothesis does your experiment *dis*prove?"

This goes straight to the heart of the matter. It forces everyone to refocus on the central question of whether there is or is not a testable scientific step forward.

If such a question were asked aloud, many a supposedly great scientist would sputter and turn livid and would want to throw the questioner out, as a hostile witness! Such a man is less than he appears, for he is obviously not accustomed to think in terms of alternative hypotheses and crucial experiments for himself; and one might also wonder about the state of science in the field

he is in. But who knows?—the question might educate him, and his field too!

On the other hand, I think that throughout most of molecular biology and nuclear physics the response to The Question would be to outline immediately not one but several tests to disprove the hypothesis—and it would turn out that the speaker already had two or three graduate students working on them!

I almost think that government agencies could make use of this kind of touchstone. It is not true that all science is equal, or that we cannot justly compare the effectiveness of scientists by any method other than a mutual-recommendation system. The man to watch, the man to put your money on, is not the man who wants to make "a survey" or a "more detailed study" but the man with the notebook, the man with the alternative hypotheses and the crucial experiments, the man who knows how to answer your Question of disproof and is already working on it.

There are some really hard problems, some high-information problems ahead of us in several fields, problems of photosynthesis, of cellular organization, of the molecular structure and organization of the nervous system, not to mention some of our social and international problems. It seems to me that the method of most rapid progress in such complex areas, the most effective way of using our brains, is going to be to set down explicitly at each step just what the question is, and what all the alternatives are, and then to set up crucial experiments to try to disprove some. Problems of this complexity, if they can be solved at all, can be solved only by men generating and excluding possibilities with maximum effectiveness, to obtain a high degree of information per unit time—men willing to work a little bit at thinking.

When whole groups of us begin to concentrate like that, I believe we may see the molecular-biology phenomenon repeated over and over again, with order-of-magnitude increases in the rate of scientific understanding in almost every field.

REFERENCES

1. A. M. Weinberg, *Minerva* 1963, 159 (winter 1963); *Phys. Today* 17, 42 (1964).

2. G. Polya, *Mathematics and Plausible Reasoning* (Princeton Univ. Press, Princeton, N.J. 1954), vol. 1, *Induction and Analogy to Mathematics;* vol. 2, *Patterns of Plausible Inference.*

3. J. R. Platt, *The Excitement of Science* (Houghton Mifflin, Boston, 1962); see especially chapters 7 and 8.

4. J. D. Watson and F. H. C. Crick, *Nature* 171, 737 (1953).

5. M. Meselson and F. Stahl, *Proc. Natl. Acad. Sci. U.S.* 44, 671 (1958).

6. A. Rich, in *Biophysical Science: A Study Program*, J. L. Oncley *et al.*, Eds. (Wiley, New York, 1959), p. 191.

7. S. Benzer, *Proc. Natl. Acad. Sci. U.S.* 45, 1607 (1959).

8. J. Lederberg, *Science* 129, 1649 (1959).

9. P. F. Davison, D. Freifelder, B. W. Holloway, *J. Mol. Biol.* 8, 1 (1964).

10. R. L. Garwin, L. M. Lederman, M. Weinrich, *Phys. Rev.* 105, 1415 (1957).

11. W. A. H. Rushton, personal communication.

12. See G. F. Chew, M. Gell-Mann, A. H. Rosenfeld, *Sci. Am.* 210, 74 (Feb. 1964); *ibid.* 210, 60 (Apr. 1964); *ibid.* 210, 54 (June 1964).

13. F. Bacon, *The New Organon and Related Writings* (Liberal Arts Press, New York, 1960), especially pp. 98, 112, 151, 156, 196.

14. K. R. Popper, *The Logic of Scientific Discovery* (Basic Books, New York, 1959), p. 41. A modified view is given by T. S. Kuhn, *The Structure of Scientific Revolutions* (Univ. of Chicago Press, Chicago, 1962), p. 146; it does not, I believe, invalidate any of these conclusions.

15. T. C. Chamberlin, *J. Geol.* 5, 837 (1897). I am indebted to Professors Preston Cloud and Bryce Crawford, Jr., of the University of Minnesota for correspondence on this article and a classroom reprint of it.

16. M. Faraday, *Faraday's Diary 1820–62* (Bell, London, 1932–36).

17. H. L. Anderson and S. K. Allison, *Rev. Mod. Phys.* 27, 273 (1955).

18. E. C. Watson [*Am. J. Phys.* 13, 281 (1945)] gives an English translation of both of Roentgen's first papers on x-rays.

19. See G. W. Wheland, *Advanced Organic Chemistry* (Wiley, New York, 1949), chapter 4, for numerous such examples.

20. B. K. Forscher, *Science* 142, 339 (1963).

Statistical Significance in Psychological Research[1]

David T. Lykken

In a recent journal article Sapolsky (1964) developed the following substantive theory: Some psychiatric patients entertain an unconscious belief in the "cloacal theory of birth" which involves the notions of oral impregnation and anal parturition. Such patients should be inclined to manifest eating disorders: compulsive eating in the case of those who wish to get pregnant and anorexia in those who do not. Such patients should also be inclined to see cloacal animals, such as frogs, on the Rorschach. This reasoning led Sapolsky to predict that Rorschach frog responders show a higher incidence of eating disorders than patients not giving frog responses. A test of this hypothesis in a psychiatric hospital showed that 19 of 31 frog responders had eating disorders indicated in their charts, compared to only 5 of the 31 control patients. A highly significant chi-square was obtained.

It will be an expository convenience to analyze Sapolsky's article in considerable detail for purposes of illustrating the methodological issues which are the real subject of this paper. My intent is not to criticize a particular author but rather to examine a kind of epistemic confusion which seems to be endemic in psychology, especially, but by no means exclusively, in its "softer" precincts.

One would like to demonstrate this generality with multiple examples. Having just combed the latest issues of four well-known journals in the clinical and personality areas, I could undertake to identify several papers in each issue wherein, because they were able to reject a directional null hypothesis at some high level of significance, the authors claimed to have usefully corroborated some rather general theory or to have demonstrated some important empirical relationship. To substantiate that these claims are overstated and that much of this research has not yet earned the right to the reader's overburdened attentions would require a lengthy analysis of each paper. Such profligacy of space would ill become an essay one aim of which is to restrain the swelling volume of the psychological literature. Therefore, with apologies to Sapolsky for subjecting this one paper to such heavy handed scrutiny, let us proceed with the analysis.

Since I regarded the prior probability of Sapolsky's theory (that frog responders unconsciously believe in impregnation per os) to be nugatory and its likelihood unenhanced by the experimental findings, I undertook to check my own reaction against that of 20 colleagues, most of them clini-

[1] Reprinted by permission of *Psychological Bulletin*, 1968, 70, 151–159.

cians, by means of a formal questionnaire. The 20 estimates of the prior probability of Sapolsky's theory, which these psychologists made before being informed of his experimental results, ranged from 10^{-6} to 0.13 with a median value of 0.01, which can be interpreted to mean, roughly, "I don't believe it." Since the prior probability of many important scientific theories is considered to be vanishingly small when they are first propounded, this result provides no basis for alarm. However, after being given a fair summary of Sapolsky's experimental findings, which "corroborate" the theory by confirming the operational hypothesis derived from it with high statistical significance, these same psychologists attached posterior probabilities to the theory which ranged from 10^{-5} to 0.14, with the median unchanged at 0.01. I interpret this consensus to mean, roughly, "I still don't believe it." This finding, I submit, *is* alarming because it signifies a sharp difference of opinion between, for example, the consulting editors of the journal and a substantial segment of its readership, a difference on the very fundamental question of what constitutes good (i.e., publishable) clinical research.

The thesis of the present paper is that Sapolsky and the editors were in fact following, with reasonable consistency, our traditional rules for evaluating psychological research, but that, as the Sapolsky paper exemplifies, at least two of these rules should be reconsidered. One of the rules examined here asserts roughly the following: "When a prediction or hypothesis derived from a theory is confirmed by experiment, a nontrivial increment in one's confidence in that theory should result, especially when one's prior confidence is low." Clearly, my 20 colleagues were violating this rule here since their confidence in the frog responder-cloacal birth theory was not, on the average, increased by the contemplation of Sapolsky's highly significant chi-square. From their comments it seems that they found it too hard to accept that a belief in oral impregnation could lead to frog responding merely because the frog has a cloacus. (One must, after all, admit that few patients know what a cloacus is or that a frog has one and that those few who do know probably will also know that the frog's eggs are both fertilized and hatched externally so neither oral impregnation nor anal birth are in any way involved. Hence, *neither* the average patient *nor* the biologically sophisticated patient should logically be expected to employ the frog as a symbol for an unconscious belief in oral conception.) My colleagues, on the contrary, found it relatively easy to believe that the observed association between frog responding and eating problems might be due to some other cause entirely (e.g., both symptoms are immature or regressive in character; the frog, with its disproportionately large mouth and voice may well constitute a common orality totem and hence be associated with problems in the oral sphere; "squeamish" people might tend both to see frogs and to have eating problems; and so on.)

Assuming that this first rule *is* wrong in this instance, perhaps it could be amended to allow one to make exceptions in cases resembling this illustration. For example, one could add the codicil: "This rule may be ignored whenever one considers the theory in question to be overly improbable or whenever one can think of alternative explanations for the experimental results." But surely such an amendment would not do. ESP, for example, could never become scientifically respectable if the first exception were allowed, and one consequence of the second would be that the importance attached to one's findings would always be inversely related to the ingenuity of one's readers. The burden of the present argument is that this rule is wrong not only in a few exceptional instances *but as it is routinely applied to the majority of experimental reports in the psychological literature.*

CORROBORATING THEORIES BY EXPERIMENTAL CONFIRMATION OF THEORETICAL PREDICTIONS[2]

Most psychological experiments are of three kinds: (a) studies of the effect of some treatment on some output variables, which can be regarded as a special case of (b) studies of the difference between two or more groups of individuals with respect to some variable, which in turn are a special case of (c) the study of the relationship or correlation between two or more variables within some specified population. Using the bivariate correlation design as paradigmatic, then, one notes first that the strict null hypothesis must always be assumed to be false (this idea is not new and has recently been illuminated by Baken, 1966). Unless one of the variables is wholly unreliable so that the values obtained are strictly random, it would be foolish to suppose that the correlation between any two variables is identically equal to 0.0000 ... (or that the effect of some treatment or the difference between two groups is exactly *zero*). The molar dependent variables employed in psychological research are extremely complicated in the sense that the measured value of such a variable tends to be affected by the interaction of a vast number of factors, both in the present situation and in the history of the subject organism. It is exceedingly unlikely that any two such variables will not share at least some of these factors and equally unlikely that their effects will exactly cancel one another out.

It might be argued that the more complex the variables the smaller their average correlation ought to be since a larger pool of common factors allows more chance for mutual cancellation of effects in obedience to the Law of Large Numbers. However, one knows of a number of unusually potent and pervasive factors which operate to unbalance such convenient symmetries and to produce correlations large enough to rival the effects of whatever causal factors the experimenter may have had in mind. Thus, we know that (a) "good" psychological and physical variables tend to be positively correlated; (b) experimenters, without deliberate intention, can somehow subtly bias their findings in the expected direction (Rosenthal, 1963); (c) the effects of common method are often as strong as or stronger than those produced by the actual variables of interest (e.g., in a large and careful study of the factorial structure of adjustment to stress among officer candidates, Holtzman & Bitterman, 1956, found that their 101 original variables contained five main common factors representing, respectively, their rating scales, their perceptual-motor tests, the McKinney Reporting Test, their GSR variables, and the MMPI); (d) transitory state variables such as the subject's anxiety level, fatigue, or his desire to please, may broadly affect all measures obtained in a single experimental session.

This average shared variance of "unrelated" variables can be thought of as a kind of ambient noise level characteristic of the domain. It would be interesting to obtain empirical estimates of this quantity in our field to serve as a kind of Plimsoll mark against which to compare obtained relationships predicted by some theory under test. If, as I think, it is not unreasonable to suppose that "unrelated" molar psychological variables share on the average about 4% to 5% of common variance, then the expected correlation between any such variables would be about .20 in absolute value and the expected difference between any two groups on some such variable would be nearly 0.5

---

[2] Much of the argument in this section is based upon ideas developed in certain unpublished memoranda by P. E. Meehl (personal communication, 1963) and in a recent article (Meehl, 1967).

standard deviation units. (Note that these estimates assume zero measurement error. One can better explain the near-zero correlations often observed in psychological research in terms of unreliability of measures than in terms of the assumption that the true scores are in fact unrelated.)

Suppose now that an investigator predicts that two variables are positively correlated. Since we expect the null hypothesis to be false, we expect his prediction to be confirmed by experiment with a probability of very nearly 0.5; by using a large enough sample, moreover, he can achieve any desired level of statistical significance for this result. If the ambient noise level for his domain is represented by correlations averaging, say, .20 in absolute value, then his chances of finding a statistically significant confirmation of his prediction with a reasonable sample size will be quite high (e.g., about 1 in 4 for $N = 100$) even if there is no truth whatever to the theory on which the prediction was based. Since most theoretical predictions in psychology, especially in the areas of clinical and personality research, specify no more than the direction of a correlation, difference or treatment effect, we must accept the harsh conclusion that a single experimental finding of this usual kind (confirming a directional prediction), no matter how great its statistical significance, will seldom represent a large enough increment of corroboration for the theory from which it was derived to merit very serious scientific attention. (In the natural sciences, this problem is far less severe for two reasons: (a) theories are powerful enough to generate point predictions or at least predictions of some narrow range within which the dependent variable is expected to lie; and (b) in these sciences, the degree of experimental control and the relative simplicity of the variables studied are such that the ambient noise level represented by unexplained and unexpected correlations, differences,

and treatment effects is often vanishingly small.)

THE SIGNIFICANCE OF LARGE CORRELATIONS

It might be argued that, even where only a weak directional prediction is made, the obtaining of a result which is not only statistically significant but large in absolute value should constitute a stronger corroboration of the theory. For example, although Sapolsky predicted only that frog responding and eating disorders would be positively related, the fourfold point correlation (phi coefficient) between these variables in his sample was about .46, surely much larger than the average relationship expected between random pairs of molar variables on the premise that "everything is related to everything else." Does not such a large effect therefore provide stronger corroboration for the theory in question?

One difficulty with this reasonable sounding doctrine is that, in the complex sort of research considered here, *really large* effects, differences, or relationships are not usually to be expected and, when found, may even argue *against* the theory being tested. To illustrate this, let us take Sapolsky's theory seriously and, by making reasonable guesses concerning the unknown base rates involved, attempt to estimate the actual size of the relationship between frog responding and eating disorders which the theory should lead us to expect. Sapolsky found that 16% of his control sample showed eating disorders; let us take this value as the base rate for this symptom among patients who do not hold the cloacal theory of birth. Perhaps we can assume that all patients who do hold this theory will give frog responses but surely not all of these will show eating disorders any more than will patients who believe in vaginal conception be inclined to show coital or urinary disturbances); it seems a reasonable assumption that no more than 50% of the believers in oral conception will therefore manifest eating problems. Similarly, we can hardly suppose that the frog response *always* implies an unconscious belief in the cloacal theory; surely this response can come to be emitted now and then for other reasons. Even with the greatest sympathy for Sapolsky's point of view, we could hardly expect more than, say, 50% of frog responders to believe in oral impregnation. Therefore, we might reasonably predict that 16 of 100 nonresponders would show eating disorders in a test of this theory, 50 of 100 frog responders would hold the cloacal theory and half of these show eating disorders, while 16% or 8 of the remaining 50 frog responders will show eating problems too, giving a total of 33 eating disorders among the 100 frog responders. Such a finding would produce a significant chi-square but the actual degree of relationship as indexed by the phi coefficient would be only about .20. In other words, if one considers the supplementary assumptions which would be required to make a theory compatible with the actual results obtained, it becomes apparent that the finding of a really strong association may actually embarrass the theory rather than support it (e.g., Sapolsky's finding of 61% eating disorders among his frog responders is *significantly larger* ($p < .01$) than the 33% generously estimated by the reasoning above).

MULTIPLE CORROBORATION

In the social, clinical, and personality areas especially, we must expect that the size of the correlations, differences, or effects which might reasonably be predicted from our theories will typically not be very large relative to the ambient noise level of correla-

tions and effects due solely to the "all-of-a-pieceness of things." The conclusion seems inescapable that the only really satisfactory solution to the problem of corroborating such theories is that of *multiple corroboration*, the derivation and testing of a number of separate, quasi-independent predictions. Since the prior probability of such a multiple corroboration may be on the order of $(0.5)^n$, where n is the number of independent[3] predictions experimentally confirmed, a theory of any useful degree of predictive richness should in principle allow for sufficient empirical confirmation through multiple corroboration to compel the respect of the most critical reader or editor.

THE RELATION OF EXPERIMENTAL FINDINGS TO EMPIRICAL FACTS

We turn now to the examination of a second popular rule for the evaluation of psychological research, which states roughly that "When no obvious errors of sampling or experimental method are apparent, one's confidence in the general proposition being tested (e.g., Variables A and B are positively correlated in Population C) should be proportional to the degree of statistical significance obtained." We are following this rule when we say, "Theory aside, Sapolsky has at least demonstrated an empirical fact, namely, that frog responders have more eating disturbances than patients in general." This conclusion means, of course, that in the light of Sapolsky's highly significant findings we should be willing to give very generous odds that any other competent investigator (at another hospital, administering the Rorschach in his own way, and determining the presence of eating problems in whatever manner seems reasonable and convenient for him) will also find a substantial

---

[3] Tests of predictions from the same theory are seldom strictly independent since they often share some of the same supplementary assumptions, are made at the same time on the same sample, and so on.

positive relationship between these two variables.

Let us be more specific. Given Sapolsky's fourfold table showing 19 of 31 frog responders to have eating disorders (61%), it can be shown by chi-square that we should have 99% confidence that the true population value lies between 13/31 and 25/31 (between 42% and 81%). With 99% confidence that the population value is at least 13 in 31, we should have .99(99) = 98% confidence that a new sample from that population should produce at least 6 eating disorders among each 31 frog responders, assuming that 5 of each 31 nonresponders show eating problems also as Sapolsky reported. That is, we should be willing to bet $98 against only $2 that a replication of this experiment will show *at least as many* eating disorders among frog responders as among nonresponders. The reader may decide for himself whether his faith in the "empirical fact" demonstrated by this experiment can meet the test of this gambler's challenge.

THREE KINDS OF REPLICATION

If, as suggested above, "demonstrating an empirical fact" must involve a claim of confidence in the replicability of one's findings, then to clearly understand the relation of statistical significance to the probability of a "successful" replication it will be helpful to distinguish between three rather different methods of replicating or cross-validating an experiment. *Literal replication*, of course, would involve exact duplication of the first investigator's sampling procedure, experimental conditions, measuring techniques, and methods of analysis; asking the original investigator to simply run more subjects would perhaps be about as close as we could come to attaining literal replication and even this, in psychological research, might often not be close enough. In the case of *operational replication*, on the other hand, one strives to duplicate exactly just the sampling and experimental procedures given in the first author's report of his research. The purpose of operational replication is to test whether the investigator's "experimental recipe"—the conditions and procedures he considered salient enough to be listed in the "Methods" section of his report—will in other hands produce the results that he obtained. For example, replication of the "Clever Hans" experiment revealed that the apparent ability of that remarkable horse to add numbers had been due to an uncontrolled and unsuspected factor (the presence of the horse's trainer within his field of view.) This factor, not being specified in the "methods recipe" for the result, was omitted in the replication which for that reason failed. Operational replication would be facilitated if investigators would accept more responsibility for specifying what they believe to be the minimum essential conditions and controls for producing their results. Psychologists tend to be inconsistently prolix in describing their experimental methods; thus, Sapolsky tabulates the age, sex, and diagnosis for each of his 62 subjects. Does he mean to imply that the experiment will not work if these details are changed?—surely not, but then why describe them?

In the quite different process of *constructive replication*, one deliberately avoids imitation of the first author's methods. To obtain an ideal constructive replication, one would provide a competent investigator with *nothing more than* a clear statement of the empirical "fact" which the first author would claim to have established—for example, "psychiatric patients who give frog responses on the Rorschach have a greater tendency toward eating disorders than do patients in general"—and then let the replicator formulate his own methods of sampling, measurement, and data analysis. One must keep in mind that the data, the specific results of a particular experiment, are only seldom of any real interest in themselves. The "empirical facts" which we value so highly consist usually of confirmed conceptual or constructive (not operational) hypotheses of the form "Construct A is positively related to Construct B in Population C." We are interested in the *construct* "tendency toward eating disorders," not in the *datum* "has reference made to overeating in the nurse's notes for May 15th." An operational replication tests whether we can duplicate our findings using the same methods of measurement and sampling; a constructive replication goes further in the sense of testing the validity of these methods.

Thus, if I cannot confirm Sapolsky's results for patients from my hospital, assessing eating disorders by means of informant interviews, say, or actual measurements of food intake, then clearly Sapolsky has *not* demonstrated any "fact" about eating disorders among psychiatric patients in general. I could then revert to an operational replication, assessing eating problems from the psychiatric notes as Sapolsky did and selecting my sample to conform with the age, sex, and diagnostic properties of his, although I might not regard this endeavor to be worth the effort since, under these circumstances, even a successful operational replication could not establish an empirical conclusion of any great generality or interest. Just as a reliable but invalid test can be said to measure something, but not what it claimed to measure, so an experiment which replicates operationally but not constructively could be said to have demonstrated something, but not the relation between meaningful constructs, generalizable to some broad reference population, which the author originally claimed to have established.[4]

RELATION OF THE SIGNIFICANCE TEST TO THE PROBABILITY OF A "SUCCESSFUL" REPLICATION

The probability values resulting from significance testing can be directly used to measure one's confidence in expecting a "successful" literal replication only. Thus, we can be 98% confident of finding at least 6 of 31 frog responders to have eating problems only if we reproduce all of the conditions of Sapolsky's experiment with absolute fidelity, something that he himself could not undertake to do at this point. Whether we are entitled to anything approaching such high confidence that we could obtain such a result from an operational replication depends entirely upon whether Sapolsky has accurately specified all of the conditions which were in fact determinative of his results. That he did not in this instance is suggested by the fact that, investigating the feasibility of replicating his experiment at the University of Minnesota Hospitals, I found that I should have to review several thousand case records in order to turn up a sample of 31 frog responders like his. Although he does not indicate how many records he examined, one strongly suspects that the base rate of Rorschach frog responding must have been higher at Sapolsky's hospital, either because of some difference in the patient population or, more probably, because an investigator's being interested in some class of responses will tend to subtly elicit such responses at a higher rate unless the testing procedure is very rigorously controlled. If the base rates for frog responding are so different at the two hospitals, it seems doubtful that the response can

---

[4] This distinction between operational and constructive replication seems to have much in common with that made by Sidman (1960) between what he calls "direct" and "systematic" replication. However, in the operant research context to which Sidman directs his attention, "replication" means to run another animal or the same animal again; thus, direct replication involves maintaining the same experimental conditions in detail whereas in systematic replication one allows all supposedly irrelevant factors to vary from one subject to the next in the hope of demonstrating that one has correctly identified the variables which are really in control of the behavior being studied.

have the same correlates or meaning in the two populations and therefore one would be reckless indeed to offer high odds on the outcome of even the most careful operational replication. The likelihood of a successful constructive replication is, of course, still smaller since it depends on the additional assumptions that Sapolsky's samples were truly representative of psychiatric patients in general and that his method of assessing eating problems was truly valid, that is, would correlate highly with a different, equally reasonable appearing method.

ANOTHER EXAMPLE

It is not my purpose, of course, to criticize statistical theory or method but rather to suggest ways in which these tools are sometimes misused or misinterpreted by writers or readers of the psychological literature. Nor do I mean to abuse a particular investigator whose research report happened to serve as a convenient illustration of the components of the argument. An abundance of articles can be found in the journals which exemplify these points quite as well as Sapolsky's but space limitations forbid multiple examples. As a compromise, therefore, I offer just one further illustration, showing how the application of these same critical principles might have increased a reader's— and perhaps even an editor's—skepticism concerning some research of my own.

The purpose of the experiment in question (Lykken, 1957) was to test the hypothesis that the "primary" psychopath has reduced ability to condition anxiety or fear. To segregate a subgroup in which such primary psychopaths might be concentrated, I asked prison psychologists to separate inmates already diagnosed as psychopathic personalities into one group that met 14 rather specific clinical criteria specified by Cleckley (1950, pp. 355–392) and to identify another group which clearly did not fit some of these criteria. The normal control subjects were comparable to the psychopathic groups in age, IQ, and sex. Fear conditioning was assessed using the GSR as the dependent variable and a rather painful electric shock as the unconditioned stimulus (UCS). On the index used to measure rate of conditioning, the primary psychopathic group scored significantly lower than did the controls. By the usual reasoning, therefore, one might conclude that this result demonstrates that primary psychopaths are abnormally slow to condition the GSR, at least with an aversive UCS, and this empirical fact in turn provides significant support for the theory that primary psychopaths have defective fear-learning ability (i.e., a low "anxiety IQ").

But to anyone who has actually participated in research of this kind, this seemingly straightforward reasoning must appear appallingly oversimplified. It is quite impossible to obtain anything resembling a truly random sample of psychopaths (or of nonpsychopathic normals either, for that matter) and it is a matter of unquantifiable conjecture how a sample obtained by a different investigator using equally defensible methods might perform on the tests which I employed. Even with the identical sample, no two investigators are likely to measure the GSR in the same way, use the same conditioned stimulus (CS) and UCS or the same pattern of reinforced and CS-only trials. Given even the same set of protocols, there is no standard formula for obtaining an index of degree or rate of conditioning; the index I used was essentially arbitrary and whether it was a good one is a matter of opinion. My own evaluation of the methods used, together with a complex set of supplementary assumptions difficult to explicate, leads me to believe that these results increase the likelihood that primary psychopaths have slower GSR conditioning with an aversive UCS; I might now give odds of two to one that this empirical generalization is true and odds of three to two that another investigator would be able to confirm it by means of a constructive replication. But this already biased claim is far more modest than the one which is implicit in the significance testing operation, namely, "such a mean difference would only be expected 5 times in 100 if the [generalization] is not true."

This empirical generalization, about GSR conditioning, is derivable from the hypothesis of interest, that psychopaths have a low anxiety IQ, by a chain of reasoning so complex and elliptical and so burdened with accessory assumptions as to be quite impossible to spell out in the detail required for rigorous logical analysis. Psychologists knowledgeable in the area can evaluate whether it is a reasonable derivation but their opinions will not necessarily agree. Moreover, even if the derivation could pass the scrutiny of some "Certified Public Logician," confirmation of the prediction about GSR conditioning should add only very slightly to our confidence in the hypothesis about fear conditioning. Even if this confirmation were made relatively more firm by, for example, constructive replication of the generalization, "aversive GSR conditioning is retarded in primary psychopaths," the hypothesis that these individuals have a low anxiety IQ could still be said to have passed only the weakest kind of test. This is so because such simple directional predictions about group differences have nearly a 50–50 chance of being true a priori even if our particular hypothesis is false. There are doubtless many possible explanations for low GSR conditioning scores in psychopaths other than the possibility of defective fear conditioning. Indeed, some of my subjects whose conditioning scores were nearly as low as those of the most extreme primary psychopaths seemed to me to be clearly neurotic with considerable anxiety and I attempted to account for their GSR performance with an ad hoc conjecture involving a kind of repression phenomenon, that is, a denial that a low GSR index implied poor fear conditioning in their cases.

A redeeming feature of this study was that two other related but distinguishable predictions from the same hypothesis were tested at the same time, namely, that primary psychopaths should do as well as normals on a learning task involving positive reward but less well on an avoidance learning problem, and that they should be more willing than normals to choose embarrassing or frightening situations in preference to alternatives involving tedium, frustration, physical discomfort, and the like. Tests of these predictions gave affirmative results also, thus providing some of the multiple corroboration necessary for the hypothesis to claim the attention of other experimenters.

Obviously, I do not mean to criticize the editor's decision to publish my (1957) paper. The tendency to evaluate research in terms of mechanical rules based on the results of the significance tests should not be replaced by equally rigid requirements concerning replication or corroboration. This study, like Sapolsky's or most others in this field, can be properly evaluated only by a qualified reader who can substitute his own informed judgment and scientific intuition for the rigorous reasoning and experimental control that is usually not achievable in clinical and personality research. As it happens, subsequent work has provided some encouraging support for my 1957 findings. The two additional predictions mentioned above have received operational replication (i.e., the same test methods used in a different context) by Schachter and Latené (1964). The prediction that psychopaths show slower GSR conditioning with an aversive UCS has been constructively replicated (i.e., independently tested with no attempt to copy my procedures) by Hare (1965a). Finally, two additional predictions from the theory that the primary psychopath has a low anxiety IQ have been tested with affirmative results (Hare, 1965b; 1966). All told, then, this hypothesis can now boast of having led to at least five quasi-independent predictions which have been experimentally confirmed and three of which have been replicated. The hypothesis is therefore entitled to serious consideration although one would be rash still to regard it as proven. At least one alternative hypothesis, that the psychopath has an unusually efficient mechanism for inhibiting emotional arousal, can account equally well for the existing findings so that, as is usually the case, further research is called for.

CONCLUSIONS

The moral of this story is that the finding of statistical significance is perhaps the least important attribute of a good experiment: it is *never* a sufficient condition for concluding that a theory has been corroborated, that a useful empirical fact has been established with reasonable confidence—or that an experimental report ought to be published. The value of any research can be determined, not from the statistical results, but only by skilled, subjective evaluation of the coherence and reasonableness of the theory, the degree of experimental control employed, the sophistication of the measuring techniques, the scientific or practical importance of the phenomena studied, and so on. Ideally, all experiments would be replicated before publication but this goal is impractical. "Good" experiments will tend to replicate better than poor ones (and, when they do

not, the failures will tend to be informative in themselves, which is not true for poor experiments) and should be published so that they may stimulate replication and extension by others. Editors must be bold enough to take responsibility for deciding which studies are good and which are not, without resorting to letting the *p* value of the significance tests determine this decision. There is little real danger that anything of value will be lost through this approach since the unpublished investigator can always resort to constructive replication to induce editorial acceptance of his empirical conclusions or to multiple corroboration to compel editorial respect for his theory. Since operational replication must really be done by an independent second investigator and since constructive replication has greater generality, its success strongly implying that an operational replication would have succeeded also, one should usually replicate one's own work constructively, using different sampling and measurement procedures within the purview of the same constructive hypothesis. If only unusually well done, provocative, and important research were published without such prior authentication, operational replication of such research by others would become correspondingly more valuable and entitled to the respect now accorded capable replication in the other experimental sciences.

References

Baken, D. "The Test of Significance in Psychological Research." *Psychological Bulletin,* 1966, 66, 423–437.

Cleckley, H. *The Mask of Sanity.* Saint Louis: C. V. Mosby, 1950.

Hare, R. D. "Acquisition and Generalization of a Conditioned Fear Response in Psychopathic and Nonpsychopathic Criminals." *Journal of Psychology,* 1965, 59, 367–370. (a)

Hare, R. D. "Temporal Gradient of Fear Arousal in Psychopaths." *Journal of Abnormal Psychology,* 1965, 70, 442–445 (b)

Hare, R. D. "Psychopathy and Choice of Immediate versus Delayed Punishment." *Journal of Abnormal Psychology,* 1966, 71, 25–29.

Holtzman, W. H., & Bitterman, M. E. "A Factorial Study of Adjustment to

Stress." *Journal of Abnormal and Social Psychology,* 1956, *52,* 179–185.

Lykken, D. T. "A study of Anxiety in the Sociopathic Personality." *Journal of Abnormal and Social Psychology,* 1957, *55,* 6–10.

Meehl, P. E. "Theory-testing in Psychology and Physics: A Methodological Paradox." *Philosophy of Science,* 1967, *34,* 103–115.

Rosenthal, R. "On the Social Psychology of the Psychological Experiment: The Experimentor's Hypothesis as Unintended Determinant of Experimental Results." *American Scientist,* 1963, *51,* 268–283.

Sapolsky, A. "An Effort at Studying Rorschach Content Symbolism: The Frog Response." *Journal of Consulting Psychology,* 1964, *28,* 469–472.

Schachter, S., Latené, B. "Crime, Cognition and the Autonomic Nervous System." *Nebraska Symposium on Motivation,* 1964, *12,* 221–273.

Sidman, M. *Tactics of Scientific Research.* New York: Basic Books, 1960.

(Received March 8, 1967)

Data Properties and Analytical Strategies

TWO

This chapter includes readings that stress the importance of using sound research tools or instruments, of understanding your data, and of becoming familiar with several statistical data-analytic strategies which are useful in much organizational research today. The importance of these issues is reflected in the too frequently adopted practice among researchers of moving too quickly to the hypothesis testing and statistical analysis phase without first attempting to "get a feel for the data," its properties, and distributions. A second pitfall for many researchers is using sophisticated statistical techniques which they do not thoroughly understand for data analysis. With the advances made in computer software packages and "canned" statistical programs, it becomes a relatively easy matter to perform almost any type of analysis available. Researchers should educate themselves properly in the principles of such advanced techniques as well as in the situations where they should most appropriately be used.

The first article, prepared especially for this book by Lyle Schoenfeldt, discusses the psychometric properties of organizational research measuring instruments. It stresses the importance of determining the reliability of measurement devices, since if acceptable levels of consistency cannot be demonstrated, such an instrument can never exhibit predictive validity. Schoenfeldt also discusses the usefulness of incorporating multiple methods of measurement to establish convergent and discriminant validity (Campbell & Fiske, 1959). Furthermore, the issue of construct validity, which has become a prominent concern in organizational research (Schwab, 1980), is presented in detail. Finally, implications of research employing exclusively self-report measures are discussed relative to claims of method variance or response-response bias, the conclusions that can be drawn from such research, and the influence this may have on the design of future investigations.

The important but often neglected practice of attempting to better understand one's data is the topic of the article by Mitchell Fields. In reaction to the too frequent approach of researchers to move quickly to the application of statistical data analysis techniques before truly gaining an understanding of the properties of their data, Fields presents a discussion of several Exploratory Data Analysis approaches advocated by Tukey (1977). While many of the techniques discussed represent essentially nothing new to the field (e.g., use of scatter plots, histograms, etc.), the appeal to researchers to develop a routine of examining the properties of their data before proceeding too quickly to hypothesis testing is a compelling one which would seem to serve the field well.

The next two articles by David Weiss concern a data analysis technique, factor analysis, which has enjoyed considerable usage in organizational research. The first article discusses some of the problems in factor analysis, the distinction between factor analysis and cluster analysis, and conditions, when one technique is preferred over the other. The second article focuses on the series of decisions the researcher must make in order to effectively use factor analysis, such as communality estimation, the type of factor rotational scheme needed, and the criteria used for determining the number of factors to be extracted.

Two statistical techniques widely used in the analysis of organizational research data are analysis of variance (ANOVA) and least squares linear regression. In recent years, statisticians have demonstrated the similarity between ANOVA and regression when viewed as components of the general linear model (e.g., Cohen & Cohen, 1983). The article by Stuart Youngblood, prepared for this book, presents a synthesis and an update of work in this area. He also demonstrates, through example, issues such as the use of dummy coding to treat categorical variables in a regression framework and how interaction effects are analyzed using a regression model.

Peters, O'Connor, and Wise focus their discussion on strategies for handling moderator variables. While the moderated regression technique has been increasing in usage as a mechanism for examining interaction effects within a regression model, the authors suggest that deciding whether moderated regression or subgroup correlational analysis is used to test for moderator effects should be a function of the researcher's interest in either the form or the degree of relationship between two variables at different levels of a third variable.

The issue of causation is as prevalent in organizational research as it is in other fields of research. As we will see in Chapter 4, causal determinations are less problematic in well-designed and controlled laboratory research. However, in most field research, we are forced to temper the conclusions we reach and the strength of the statements we can make about our research results. Indeed, one of the first principles we learn about the concept of correlation is that it can never be equated with causation. There are data-analytic techniques available, however, that permit somewhat stronger statements concerning causal priorities albeit still not allowing definitive cause-effect determinations. In the article by Billings and Wroten, the authors review some of the principles underlying one of these techniques, path analysis, discuss some problems with the procedure, and make suggestions for its effective use.

The final article in this chapter deals with a statistical technique which has received little use in organizational research to date, although it provides a quite powerful mechanism for understanding complex relationships among variables of interest. Canonical correlation permits two vectors to be examined for their covariation. Wood and Erskine provide a readable introduction to this reasonably complex procedure and discuss applications of this approach to behavioral data.

REFERENCES AND SUGGESTIONS FOR FURTHER READING

Arnold, H. J. Moderator Variables: "A Clarification of Conceptual, Analytic, and Psychometric Issues." *Organizational Behavior and Human Performance,* 1982, *29,* 143–174.

Campbell, D. T., and Fiske, D. W. "Convergent and Discrimination Validation by the Multitrait-multimethod Matrix," *Psychological Bulletin,* 1959, *56,* 81–105.

Cohen, J., and Cohen P. *Applied Multiple Regression Correlation Analysis for the Behavioral Sciences.* (Second Edition). Hillsdale, NJ: Lawrence Erlbaum, 1983.

Feldman, J. "Considerations in the Use of Causal-Correlational Techniques in Applied Psychology." *Journal of Applied Psychology,* 1975, *60,* 663–670.

Ghiselli, E., Campbell, J. P. and Zedeck, S. *Measurement Theory for the Behavioral Sciences.* San Francisco: Freeman, 1981.

Johns, G. "Difference Score Measure of Organizational Behavior Variables: A Critique." *Organizational Behavior and Human Performance,* 1981, *27,* 443–463.

Kenny, D. A., and Harackiewicz, J. M. "Cross-lagged Panel Correlation: Practice and Promise." *Journal of Applied Psychology,* 1979, *63,* 372–379.

Price, J. L., and Mueller, C. W. "A Causal Model of Turnover for Nurses." *Academy of Management Journal,* 1981, *24,* 543–565.

Schwab, D. P. "Construct Validity in Organizational Behavior." In B. M. Staw and L. L. Cummings (eds.), *Research in Organizational Behavior* Vol. 2. Greenwich, CT: JAI Press, 1980.

Tukey, J. W. *Exploratory Data Analysis.* Reading, MA: Addison-Wesley, 1977.

Psychometric Properties of Organizational Research Instruments

Lyle F. Schoenfeldt

Organizational research typically involves the conceptualization of a problem and the development of procedures for acquiring and analyzing data to address the salient issues. Other readings in this book speak to the approaches one might take to develop relevant hypotheses, to conceive of experiments, both laboratory and field, and to examine various conceptualizations. The purpose of the present paper is to look at characteristics of the measuring instruments and measurements that affect the research.

The goal in all measurement is the documentation of differences among individuals and/or organizations. New knowledge is gained through the development of relationships, such as the relationship between work attitudes and attendance studied by Smith (1977), in an article that appears later in this book. In that well-conceived study, variations in job satisfaction among 27 groups of managers were related to attendance on a particular day. The point is, this very successful study was dependent upon meaningful job satisfaction differences between groups of managers, differences in attendance between these same groups, and the relationship between these two sets of data.

THE NATURE OF SCALES

Research is not simply a few items in a survey or observations recorded in the course of an experiment. The resulting numbers have properties, which in turn dictate manipulations that can be undertaken with the numbers. The problem is one of understanding the rules used in the assignment of numbers

TABLE 1

Scale	Basic Empirical Operations	Mathematical Group Structure	Permissible Statistics (invariantive)
NOMINAL	Determination of equality	Permutation group $x' = f(x)$ $f(x)$ means any one-to-one substitution	Number of cases Mode Contingency correlation
ORDINAL	Determination of greater or less	Isotonic group $x' = f(x)$ $f(x)$ means any monotonic increasing function	Median Percentiles
INTERVAL	Determination of equality of intervals or differences	General linear group $x' = ax + b$	Mean Standard deviation Rank-order correlation Product-moment correlation
RATIO	Determination of equality of ratios	Similarity group $x' = ax$	Coefficient of variation

to objects or events, and then matching the statistical operations to those appropriate to the resulting scale.

The seminal work in the area of the theory of scales of measurement was done by S. S. Stevens (1946). Stevens defined four sets of scales representing the basic empirical operations and resulting permissible statistics. These operations are described in Table 1.

The simplest form of quantification involves the assignment of numbers to individuals or objects. The resulting measurement is preferred to as being on a *nominal scale.* An example of this type of measurement would be the assignment of numbers to members of a football team. The only rule is that no two individuals have the same number. Also, in the case of football, players of certain categories have similar numbers, as for example offensive backs have numbers in the 20's, 30's or 40's. Smith (1977) used a nominal scale to represent the 27 functional groupings to which the 3,010 salaried employees belonged. The only rule was that all individuals in the same functional area be assigned the same number, and no two individuals belonging to different areas be given the same number. With nominal scaling, the major type of mathematical operation permitted is that of counting.

A second level of sophistication is the *ordinal scale.* An ordinal scale involves the assignment of numbers to individuals or groups on the basis of rank. For example, if we know that someone was ranked first in terms of height, and another individual second, this would be an example of an ordinal scale. We know nothing about the height of either individual, or the amount of difference. We only know the rank in relation to those compared. In addition to the permissible statistics indicated in Table 1, procedures developed especially for use with ranked data, such as Kendall's tau, are possible.

The *interval scale* is the result of equal units of measurement, but no absolute zero. For example, temperature is typically measured on an interval scale. In a given location, we may know that the usual high temperature in the summer is 70 degrees, and in the winter 35 degrees. We know that a summer day tends to be 35 degrees warmer than in the winter, but can not say that it is twice as warm since the zero point is arbitrary. As is indicated in Table 1, the interval scale is useful in terms of the permissible statistical operations.

The most sophisticated level of quantification, one virtually never achieved in organizational research, is through the *ratio scale.* Ratio scales require an absolute zero as well as equal units of measure throughout the scale. The measure of height or weight would be indicative of a ratio scale.

It should be pointed out that the issue of permissible statistical operations applicable to various levels of scaling is a matter of some debate. Of course, numbers are just that, and do not complain if the arithmetical operations performed are impermissible. The question concerns the legitimacy of inferences drawn and conclusions made, and the possibility that the result of impermissible operations might be misleading. Over the years since Stevens' work, other discussions have appeared in the literature. In a book of selected readings, Mehrens and Ebel (1967) reprinted the Stevens article along with those by Burke (1953), Senders (1953), and Baker, Hardyck, and Petrinovich (1966) dealing with the issues surrounding weak measurements versus strong statistics.

MEASUREMENT OF CONCEPTS

A relevant question which cuts to the core of any research is the extent to which a particular set of measurements (e.g., the measures of work attitudes used by Smith) actually represent the theoretical concept (e.g., job satisfaction) indicated. There are potentially a large number of properties of measurements that need to be considered. However, at the most general level, the two basic properties of measurements are reliability and validity. Reliability has implications for the stability of measurements. A thermometer that measured 80 degrees one minute and 74 degrees shortly thereafter would be said to be unreliable, assuming similar conditions. Validity has implications for the inferences one might draw from the measurement. A thermometer that measured a consistent 80 degrees while snow was falling would be reliable, but invalid.

Both of these concepts are multifaceted. In other words, the calculation and interpretation of reliability and validity can be approached in various ways. Further, the specifics of the research being initiated have implications for our interests in understanding the reliability and validity of the measurements involved. Finally, both reliability and validity have implications for the development and refinement of questionnaires or scales. It is the purpose of this paper to define and examine the concepts of reliability and validity, and the utility these concepts have in the planning and execution of organizational research.

RELIABILITY

Reliability Defined

Reliability is the consistency of an experiment, test, observation, or any measuring procedure over a series of trials. Reliability information is an indication of the amount of confidence we can place in a measurement. Measurements (or scores) vary from one trial to another. In organizational research, behavioral studies, or most any area involving measurements, no procedure of measurement is totally free of error. For this reason, the theoretical true score is defined as follows:

$$T = X - e$$

where:

    T = the "true" score,
    X = the observed score,
    e = error.

Procedures for determining the reliability of a measuring procedure are, in part, a function of what one defines as noise or error. Thorndike (1949) defined the five sources of variation in scores given below. The examples are in terms of variation that might be expected in job satisfaction, as measured by the Index of Organizational Reactions (IOR) used in the study by Smith (1977).

1. Lasting and general characteristics of each individual responding to the IOR. This source of variation is virtually always defined as part of the true score (i.e., what is intended to be measured). In the example of the IOR, this would consist of an individual's general regard for the organization.

2. Lasting and specific characteristics of the individual. This source of variation is typically defined as part of the true score. Again using IOR as an example, the lasting and specific variation would be related to an individual's regard for his/her unit of the larger organization (i.e., satisfaction related to the specific unit of the organization).

3. Temporary and general characteristics of the individual systematically affecting performance on various scales of the IOR at a particular time. This would include such things as health, fatigue, motivation, and survey conditions (light, ventilation, etc.). In the case of the IOR, as well as most other measures, this would be regarded as error.

4. Temporary and specific characteristics of the individual. This would include, among other things, fluctuations in attention and changes in fatigue. Again, in the case of the IOR, this source of variation would be regarded as error.

5. Random error. This would include such events as mismarking the answer sheet (clerical errors) and scanner errors in processing the responses.

The point is, reliability is consistency over a series of trials. It is also the aggregate result of the extent to which error is a component of the observed score for a series of individuals. In this context, the reliability is the ratio of the true score variance to the total (observed) variance (or the difference of the observed variance minus the error variance divided by observed variance).

Types of Reliability

There are various ways of determining reliability. For example, in the case of six work-related areas covered by the IOR, one procedure would be to have separate "identical" forms of each scale, and administer these forms to each individual in a *parallel forms* design. Ideally the administrations would be at the same session (or very close in proximity) to eliminate the possibility that the dimensions of job satisfaction would not fluctuate (temporary and general characteristics). The result would be two (or possibly more) scores for each individual on each scale of the IOR. The reliability would be the correlation between these parallel measures.

Alternately, the scales of the IOR could be readministered at a later date, the fairly standard *test-retest* design. In this design, sources (3), (4), and (5) of variation would be allocated to error. Again, the reliability would be the correlation between the test-retest scores.

It is not always possible, and is seldom convenient, to readminister a survey to the same individuals. The *split-half* approach allows the administration of a single test (or survey), and the subsequent division of the items into two equivalent parts, each half the length of the original test, and each scored separately. The correlation between the scores obtained from the two halves of the test represent a measure of equivalence or reliability. Although there are a number of ways of splitting a test into two halves, typically odd items constitute one score, and even items the other. The resulting reliability includes temporary and general, as well as lasting, characteristics of the individual. For this reason split-half reliability is generally regarded as the upper bound estimate.

In other words, including an additional source of variance as part of the true score is likely to result in an estimate that is greater than or equal to the true reliability.

As will be discussed, reliability is related to test length. One problem with the split-half method is the resulting reliability is for a test or survey half the length of the original. To correct the reliability found between scores on two halves of a test, the Spearman-Brown procedure is used. The specific formula is given in a later section.

Internal Consistency Reliability

One problem with the split-half procedure is that it does not produce a unique value for the reliability. There are 126 different ways of dividing a test of 10 items into two halves, and 92,378 ways of dividing a test of 20 items. The logical extension of the split-half method is one of the several methods of calculating internal consistency reliability. The internal consistency reliability is equivalent to the mean of all split-half coefficients resulting from different splits of a test. Viewed this way, the internal consistency reliability is really a measure of item (test) homogeneity, that is, the degree to which the test is a relatively pure measure of a single trait or construct.

The mathematical derivation of the internal consistency reliability was developed by Kuder and Richardson (1937). The formula for cognitive items, that is, items regarded as either correct (scored 1) or incorrect (scored 0), is as follows:

$$r_{xx} = \left(\frac{n}{n-1} \right) \left(\frac{\sigma_x^2 - \sum_{j=1}^{n} p_j q_j}{\sigma_x^2} \right)$$

where:

r_{xx} = reliability of the test,
n = number of the items in the test,
σ_x^2 = the variance of the test scores,
p = the proportion of persons correct on item j,
q = $1 - p$.

The formula for internal consistency reliability of an instrument with continuous items, such as an attitude survey, would be as follows:

$$r_{xx} = \left(\frac{n}{n-1} \right) \left(\frac{\sigma_x^2 - \sum\limits_{j=1}^{n} \sigma_j^2}{\sigma_x^2} \right)$$

where:

$\sum \sigma_j^2$ = the sum of the item variances.

The difference between these formulas is in the term for the item variance.

It should be pointed out that these formulas are in the form of true score variance (i.e., observed variance minus error variance) divided by observed variance, with a correction to adjust for a small sample. Error is defined as the sum of item variances, a definition likely to produce a lower-bound estimate of reliability. Other internal consistency conceptualizations, such as Cronbach's (1951) Coefficient Alpha are essentially the same in the definition of reliability.

The internal consistency procedure is valuable in that only one administration of the test or survey is required. At the same time, it is not particularly appropriate unless the items are a relatively pure measure of a single trait or characteristic.

Standard Error of Measurement

An alternate way of looking at consistency (i.e., reliability) is in terms of the standard deviation of the errors of measurement. The initial formulation of a test or survey score was in terms of both true and error components. For a given individual, true score is infallible, that is, it does not change over a series of administrations of the same test. Thus all the variation from the successive administrations is a result of error of measurement. The standard error of measurement (SEM) represents an estimate of the standard deviation of the errors obtained in repeated testing.

Since the SEM is a function of reliability, the usual procedure is to use reliability to estimate the SEM. The formula for SEM is:

$$s_e = s_x \sqrt{1 - r_{xx}}$$

where:

s_e = standard error of measurement,
s_x = standard deviation of the observed scores,
r_{xx} = estimated reliability.

The advantage of the SEM is that the reliability is given in terms of test score units. For example, a 39 item test had a test-retest reliability of 0.872 and the observed standard deviation of 5.077. In this case the SEM was 1.816. This SEM can be considered as the band of error around test scores. In this example, a person's score may be expected, in two cases out of three, to be within ±1.82 raw score points of his/her true score. Thus one has a feel for the stability of individual scores in terms of test score units. It should be noted that it is not possible to compare the SEM's from one test to another.

Factors Influencing Reliability

As has been seen, each approach to estimating reliability defines error in a slightly different way and thus results in different outcomes. It is important that the researcher purposefully select the approach (or approaches) to be used in terms of sources of variation to be allocated to true score versus error. In addition, other factors will influence the estimate of reliability.

TEST LENGTH.   A major factor influencing the reliability of a test is its length. As explained by Helmstadter (1964),

Perhaps the easiest explanation will result from considering any set of items which are organized into a test as but a sample of all possible items which represent a given content universe. If the entire universe could be used, the test would be one of infinite length, and a person's score on it would be his true score. Because only a sample is taken in a practical situation, the score observed is only an estimate of the true score. From principles of sampling design it is known that the larger the sample (and therefore the longer the test), the more precise the estimate and the smaller the error is likely to be on any particular testing. (p. 75–76)

The Spearman-Brown prophecy formula has been developed to estimate the effect of length on a test. The formula is expressed as:

$$r'_{xx} = \frac{mr_{xx}}{1 + (m-1)\ r_{xx}}$$

where:

r_{xx} = reliability obtained from the original calculation,

m = the multiple of the original test length,

r'_{xx} = the estimated reliability of a test m times as long.

In the case of the 39 item test described previously, if the test were doubled, m would equal 2, and the reliability of the 78 items would be 0.93. This assumes that the additional 39 items would be equivalent to the previous items. If the goal were to shorten the test to 20 items, m would equal 0.51, and the reliability of the new test would be 0.78. It should be pointed out that the Spearman-Brown formula is always used (m=2) in the process of estimating reliability by the split-half procedure. Since the split-half procedure is based upon a correlation between scores obtained on only half the test, the Spearman-Brown correction is needed to determine the reliability of the entire test.

GROUP HETEROGENEITY. The range of scores on the trait being measured in the analysis group also influences reliability. This problem is a result of the fact that, by definition, reliability is the ratio of true score variance to observed score variance. As a relative measure, the reliability will vary as a function of the group.

One way of overcoming this problem is to use the standard error of measurement (SEM). The SEM gives an index of variable error which is not affected by the heterogeneity of the group involved.

Desired Reliability

The reliability can be interpreted as the proportion of true score variation. Thus a test-retest reliability of 0.45 indicates that 45% of the score distribution is a function of information, while 55% is a result of error of measurement. When the amount of error exceeds the level of information, use of the measure is problematic.

As has been seen, the estimated reliability varies as a function of the procedure used to calculate it and as a function of certain characteristics of the analysis group. Reliability also varies according to the content of the measuring device. In a survey of 183 studies involving six types of tests, Helmstadter (1964) observed that the median reliability of achievement batteries was 0.92, ability tests had a median reliability of 0.90, aptitude tests a median of 0.88, personality surveys (objective) a median of 0.85, interest inventories a median of 0.84, and attitude scales (similar to the Index of Organizational Reactions) a median of 0.79. Although there are no absolute standards of reliability, these medians provide good guidance as to the values that would be both useful and generally acceptable in most research and applied situations.

VALIDITY

The term validation implies the assessment of some entity (individuals, organizations, etc.), and the relationship of this assessment to a relevant criterion of performance. The success of a validation effort, or the lack thereof, has implications for the value of the assessment and for the utility of the procedures. More than any other area, the validation study is where the "rubber meets the road" in the construction and usage of measuring instruments.

Validity Defined

Validity is the degree to which inferences from scores on tests or other assessments are supported or justified on the basis of actual evidence. Validity is not a characteristic of a test; rather it is a characteristic of inferences that result from a test, assessment, or observation. Thus, validity determines the degree of relatedness between inferences made and actual events.

Traditionally the two accepted approaches to validation have been the criterion-related and content-oriented procedures. Of these, the former, criterion-related validation, has been the standard procedure whereby inferences were validated. However, during the last 30 years, it has become increasingly accepted that validation should be extended to understanding the underlying dimensions or attributes being measured with any test or observation process, construct validation. This type of validation is less concerned with specific performance inferences, but instead considers the relationship of scores to possible underlying attributes. Details surrounding these three approaches to validation are covered in the sections that follow.

Criterion-Related Validity

As previously noted, criterion-related validity provides evidence to support the interpretation of a test score or assessment by demonstrating a relationship between the score, on one hand, and some behavior or criterion on the other. The relationship between assessment and criterion performance can be expressed in several ways, but usually involves a measure of association such as the correlation coefficient.

It is possible to distinguish two alternate approaches within the criterion-related procedure. Concurrent validation involves the relationship of tests to criterion measures obtained at the same time as the test data. Predictive validity involves the assessment of individuals followed by the collection of criterion information at some subsequent time. In some designs, the time factor can be an important consideration; whereas in other instances it is not. For example, in predicting job success, concurrent validation inevitably involves existing employees whose motives for performing well on the test may differ from the motivation of applicants. In other instances, concurrent validity is used to demonstrate, for example, that a paper and pencil assessment is an adequate substitution for a more cumbersome, more costly, or inefficient assessment procedure.

The Smith (1977) study referred to earlier, is essentially an empirical (i.e., criterion-related) validation. Attendance on a specific day (April 3, 1975) is the criterion, that is the dependent variable, against which elements of job satisfaction are correlated. Interestingly, the goal is not a means to predict attendance or to substitute a more efficient procedure for a less efficient procedure. If attendance is needed for administrative or salary purposes, measures of job satisfaction are not likely to be an acceptable substitute. Rather the goal is to learn more about job satisfaction and the relationship it bears to work-related behavior when the latter is under the control of the individual.

Relationship of Validity to Reliability

The previous section discussed the importance of reliability and procedures for determining this psychometric characteristic. Both the assessment and the criterion can be evaluated in terms of their reliability. Reliability is important because it establishes the upper limit of validity. More specifically, the maximum possible validity of an assessment is equivalent to the square root of the reliability. For example, a test or assessment procedure with a reliability of 0.50 could not have a validity greater than 0.71, and this assumes that the reliability of the criterion is 1.00. (In the case of the Smith study, it is relevant to inquire as to the reliability of the attendance measure. Clearly there is room for error in recording of attendance, especially "since attendance data are not systematically collected for salaried people" in the organization under study.) Since such criterion reliabilities are never achieved in practice, the importance of having reliable survey/measurement tools can not be overstated. The value of reliable measurement is that it removes the possibility of imposing a low ceiling on potential validity coefficients.

Interpreting Validity Coefficients

The question of interpreting validity coefficients is an important one. There are two broad approaches. First, it is possible to determine the amount of error which would be made if the test were used to predict a criterion score for an individual. Second, it is possible to determine the kinds of errors made when using an assessment device. At the same time, there is no standard to be used as guidance in determining the value of a validity. Obviously, those undertaking studies of criterion-related validity seek high coefficients, say values of 0.60 or 0.70. However, it is entirely possible that, given the appropriate circumstance, a relatively low validity, for example a value of 0.30, may be of value in improving prediction. This would be the case if applicants were numerous (providing a favorable selection ratio) and existing procedures were even poorer.

Prediction of an individual criterion score is accomplished by converting the validity relationship into a scatterplot, and drawing the estimated criterion score for an individual with a given predictor (test) score. The standard error of estimate can be used to compute a confidence interval around the estimated criterion score.

There are several procedures to determine the amount of selection errors that would be made using a given test. A scatterplot can be used to locate successful individuals in the validation sample that would have been predicted to fail, and vice versa. The expectancy chart is also of value in indicating the overall improvement that can be expected in comparison to previous prediction procedures.

Content-Oriented Validity

Another traditional approach to the validation of tests is the content-oriented procedure. This approach is applicable when empirical investigation is not possible, and involves validation on the basis of assumed or hypothesized relationships. The legitimacy of the content-oriented procedure lies in the degree to which the hypothesis itself is well grounded in carefully controlled observations and prior research results (Guion, 1976). Although mentioned in various texts and in the *Standards for Education and Psychological Tests* (American Psychological Association, 1974), content-oriented validation has always been the step-child of testing. Until quite recently information about procedures for demonstrating content-oriented validity have been perfunctory, contradictory, or unavailable. The emergence of content-oriented validity has been largely a result of a series of conferences (Guion, 1974a; *Proceedings*, 1975), articles (Guion, 1974b, 1977; Schoenfeldt, Schoenfeldt, Acker, & Pearlson, 1976; Tenopyr, 1977), and manuals (American Psychological Association, 1974, 1975, 1980; Mussio & Smith, 1973). The steps involved in a study of content-oriented validity are summarized in Table 2.

Again, using the Smith (1977) study as an example, it is possible to consider the six scales of the Index of Organizational Reactions (Supervision, Kind of Work, Amount of Work, Career Future and Security, Financial Rewards, and Company Identification) in terms of the content validity. For example, in developing the scale on Financial Rewards, it

TABLE 2
Steps in Content Validation

1. Task Analysis
2. Definition of Performance Domain
3. Survey of Performance Domain
4. Development of Items
5. Demonstration that Items Constructed Are Representative of the Performance Domain
6. Development of Cut-Off Score

would be important to consider all the elements of the financial package (salary, bonus, profit sharing, medical coverage, vacation, and so forth). Content-related validity would be in terms of appropriate representation of all elements of the domain. Financial rewards are not a performance domain or skill, but the steps in Table 2 can be redefined in terms of coverage of attitudes in this area.

Construct Validity

CONSTRUCT VALIDITY DEFINED. Construct validity is concerned with understanding the underlying dimensions or attributes being measured through any test or observation process. This type of validation is less concerned with specific performance inferences, but instead considers the relationship of test scores to possible underlying attributes.

Construct validity has always existed, at least at an implicit level, but was only formally defined and discussed in the last 30 years. The first formal proposal for consideration of constructs in the behavioral/social sciences was in the "Technical Recommendations for Psychological Tests and Diagnostic Techniques" (1954). A number of articles in the literature further defined and developed the notion of construct validity. The revised standards (American Psychological Association, 1974), as well as the revision of these same standards currently underway, have further elevated the role of construct validity in the behavioral sciences.

Many researchers have conducted validation studies, but a number of these same individuals tend to show little concern for construct validation. Construct validity is more in the nature of determining the scientific basis of a particular measure. By relating particular measures to a wide variety of possible other test scores or performance outcomes, a network of research data is developed from which inferences can be drawn about the nature of the original test and the constructs that underlie it. Construct validations form the basis for new scientific learning about specific measures in particular and individuals and/or organizations in general.

The Smith (1977) study is a perfect example of an effort which speaks more to the construct of job satisfaction than to other areas of validity. In its simplest form the study is a series of six sets of two correlations, one set from the experimental site, Chicago, and a second from the control site, New York. However, the lessons learned are in terms of job-related attitudes and their relationship to behavior that is substantially under the control of the employee.

MULTITRAIT-MULTIMETHOD APPROACH. In terms of providing a methodology to verify construct validity, the article with by far the greatest impact has been "Convergent and Discriminant Validation by the Multitrait-Multimethod Matrix" by Campbell and Fiske (1959). In this seminal work, Campbell and Fiske (1959) advocated a procedure for triangulating a construct, utilizing a matrix of intercorrelations among tests representing at least two traits, each measured by at least two methods. Construct validity is the degree to which measures of the same trait correlate higher with each other than they do with measures of different traits involving separate methods.

The multitrait-multimethod (MTMM) procedure could be used to establish the construct validity of job satisfaction. The several dimensions or scales, as for example the six scales constituting the Index of Organizational Reactions, could be measured by questionnaire and by interview. In a successful use of the MTMM procedure, attitudes toward Supervision, for example, as measured by survey and interview, should correlate more highly with each other than attitudes toward Supervision, as measured by the survey, correlate with attitudes toward Kind of Work, also measured by the survey. The same scales measured by different methods should converge while a method should be capable of discriminating different attitude scales.

OTHER APPROACHES TO CONSTRUCT VALIDITY. The multitrait-multimethod procedure has clearly become a standard for the establishment of construct validity. At the same time, given the definition of construct validity discussed previously, it is obvious that researchers are not limited in the number of procedures employed to establish its existence. In fact, given the nature of content validity, it is somewhat heretical to focus on methods rather than models, although to a large extent the two are closely linked in the context of this topic.

Historically, factor analysis has been associated with the establishment of constructs. Many applications of factor analysis are in the nature of data reduction, and as such the results have little in the way of implications for the establishment of construct validity. However, in conjunction with an appropriate model, factor analysis can play a valuable role in the validation of constructs. Guilford's (1967; Guilford & Hoepfner, 1971) extensive work on the structure of in-

tellect is one of many examples that could be cited illustrating how a model and appropriate factor-analytic procedures can come together in the establishment of construct validity. A comparable body of research in the organizational area is involved with the Ohio State Leadership Behavior Description Questionnaire (LBDQ). This questionnaire has been used extensively, with much of the analyses by way of factor analysis (see Kerr, Schreisheim, Murphy, & Stogdill, 1974, for a review of the LBDQ research). The factor-analytic results of the LBDQ have been reported at various levels, with the higher order factors of consideration and initiating structure being the best known results in leadership research.

Other analytic procedures, although less well known, define what might be considered further approaches to construct validity. For example, the person-process-product model by Campbell, Dunnette, Lawler, and Weick (1970) provides a theoretical framework for viewing job performance as a product of the person impacting with various organizational forces. The aptitude by treatment interactions approach articulated by Cronbach (1975; Cronbach & Snow, 1976) as well as the assessment-classification model (Schoenfeldt, 1974) represent still further attempts to permit the possibility of identifying constructs that underlie performance in various domains.

APPLICATIONS OF CONSTRUCT VALIDITY. In its simplest form, construct validity could be as straightforward as a factor analysis or an application of the multitrait-multimethod procedure. More generally it is as involved as the years of research behind the LBDQ. For example, the Smith (1977) study, by itself, would probably not be sufficient to serve as the validation of the job satisfaction questionnaire. However, in combination with previous research, especially previously developed models, this study does contribute to the construct validity of the work attitudes involved.

Some of the most recent work was reported in a conference on *Construct Validity in Psychological Measurement* (U.S. Office of Personnel Management, 1980). The conference involved several important themes. First was a call for more clearly defined professional standards for construct validity. The development of these standards is currently underway. Second was a discussion of the realization of the role construct validity plays, in conjunction with other types of validity, in the scientific study of relationships. Included in this theme was the singularly unique application of a construct model in the validation of the Federal Government's Professional and Administrative Career Examination (McKillip & Wing, 1980). What became clear was that as a part of a scientific undertaking, the study of constructs should be pursued by diverse research strategies.

SCALE DEVELOPMENT

If nothing else, it should be clear that the development of questionnaires, interviews, or observation protocols requires a great deal of forethought and care. The construction of the measuring devices is perhaps the most important segment of any study. Many well-conceived research studies have never seen the light of day because of flawed measures. The idea of relating work satisfaction to attendance, as was done by Smith (1977), on a day that required extraordinary effort to be at work would certainly rate as a creative experiment. Had the measurement of either work attitudes or attendance been wanting, the reported correlations would never have materialized.

A number of authors have specified rules for constructing questionnaires and interviews, including Erdos (1970) and Kornhauser and Sheatsley (1959). The result of these efforts is a checklist evaluating the necessity of each question, possible repetition, question clarity, and so forth. Another consideration is the possibility that the informa-

tion being sought might be available from a more reliable source. For example, Smith (1977) collected attendance information administratively rather than by asking participants.

Any questionnaire or interview should be piloted, that is, tried with a sufficient sample to be sure that the questions are clear, and that they can be answered unambiguously. An example of such an effort with respect to an interview is provided by Brush (1979). It is also a good idea to code responses and evaluate the reliability of scales, at least on a preliminary basis. Typically the Coefficient Alpha, or other procedure producing an estimate of reliability from a single administration, is used to evaluate consistency.

SUMMARY

The legitimacy of organizational research as a scientific endeavor is dependent on the psychometric properties of the measuring instruments. Past efforts have frequently paid lip service to this need.

Foremost concern should be for the consistency or reliability of measurements. A measurement that does not correlate with itself (as for example, from time one to time two) can not correlate with anything else. There are a number of approaches to estimating reliability, and the specific procedure used should depend on the sources of variance to be allocated to error versus true score. The internal consistency procedures, such as Coefficient Alpha, have been most popular in organizational research, probably because of the fact that reliability can be estimated from a single administration.

Measurements result in inferences. A high score on a Financial Rewards scale tells the researcher something about individual or group attitudes on this subject. This cognitive process is the result of drawing an inference from the score, and the validation process is one of verifying these inferences. Several potentially interdependent procedures are typically delineated for determining validity. Criterion-related validity, by far the most frequently used approach, is concerned with the relationship of the measurement to some criterion. This relationship is typically expressed in terms of a correlation coefficient. Content-oriented validity is a logical (rather than statistical) process of insuring that a measuring procedure is representative of a given performance domain. Content-oriented validity is particularly important in verifying the coverage of measuring instruments.

The ultimate goal of organizational research is the understanding of concepts or constructs, the goal of construct validity. Typically construct validity is demonstrated by a variety of procedures and is the result of all validity evidence, including that obtained by criterion and content procedures. Construct validity is demonstrated through a network of performance outcomes from which converging inferences are drawn about the nature of the original measurement and the concepts that underlie it. The multitrait-multimethod approach and use of factor analysis are two popular procedural vehicles contributing to the construct validity of measurements.

Sound organizational research requires attention to the psychometric properties of the measurement involved. The present paper has defined and examined the concepts of reliability and validity, and the utility these concepts have in carrying out organizational research.

REFERENCES

American Psychological Association, American Educational Research Association, & National Council on Measurement in Education. *Standards for Educational and Psychological Tests.* Washington, D.C. American Psychological Association, 1974.

American Psychological Association, Division of Industrial-Organizational Psychology. *Principles for the Validation and Use of Personnel Selection Procedures.* Dayton, OH: Author, 1975.

American Psychological Association, Division of Industrial-Organizational Psychology. *Principles for the Validation and Use of Personnel Selection Procedures.* (Second edition) Berkeley, CA; Author, 1980.

Baker, B. O., Hardyck, C. D., & Petrinovich, L. F. "Weak Measurements vs. Strong Statistics: An Empirical Critique of S. S. Stevens' Proscriptions on Statistics." *Educational and Psychological Measurement,* 1966, 26, 291–309.

Brush, D. H. "Technical Knowledge or Management Skills? Recruiting Graduates Who Have Both." *Personnel Journal,* 1979, 32, 369–384.

Burke, C. J. "Additive Scales and Statistics." *Psychological Review,* 1953, 60, 73–75.

Campbell, D. T. & Fiske, D. W. "Convergent and Discriminant Validation by the Multitrait-Multimethod Matrix." *Psychological Bulletin,* 1959, 56, 81–105.

Campbell, J. P., Dunnette, M. D., Lawler, E. E., III, & Weick, K. E., Jr. *Managerial Behavior, Performance, and Effectiveness.* New York: McGraw-Hill, 1970.

Cronbach, L. J. "Coefficient Alpha and the Internal Structure of Tests." *Psychometrika,* 1951, 16, 297–334.

Cronbach, L. J. "Beyond the Two Disciplines of Scientific Psychology." *American Psychologist,* 1975, 30, 116–127.

Cronbach, L. J. & Snow, R. E. *Aptitudes and Instructional Methods.* New York: Irvington, 1976.

Erdos, P. L. *Professional Mail Surveys.* New York: McGraw-Hill, 1970.

Guilford, J. P. *The Nature of Human Intelligence.* New York: McGraw-Hill, 1967.

Guilford, J. P. & Hoepfner, R. *The Analysis of Intelligence.* New York: McGraw-Hill, 1971.

Guion, R. M. "Content Validity Conference." *The Industrial-Organizational Psychologist,* 1974, *12,* (1), 18. (a)

Guion, R. M. "Open a New Window: Validities and Values in Psychological Measurement." *American Psychologist,* 1974, *29,* 287–296. (b)

Guion, R. M. "Recruiting, Selection and Job Placement." In M. D. Dunnette (Ed.) *Handbook of Industrial and Organizational Psychology.* Chicago: Rand McNally, 1976.

Guion, R. M. "Content Validity—the Source of My Discontent." *Applied Psychological Measurement,* 1977, *1,* 1–10.

Helmstadter, G. C. *Principles of Psychological Measurement.* New York: Appleton-Century-Crofts, 1964.

Kerr, S., Schriesheim, C. A., Murphy, D. J., & Stogdill, R. M. "Toward a Contingency Theory of Leadership Based upon the Consideration and Initiating Structure Literature." *Organizational Behavior and Human Performance,* 1974, *12,* 62–82.

Kornhauser, A. & Sheatsley, P. "Questionnaire Construction and Interview Procedure." In C. Selltiz, M. Johoda, M. Deutsch, & S. Cook (Eds.) *Research Methods in Social Relations.* New York: Holt, Rinehart and Winston, 1959.

Kuder, G. F. & Richardson, M. W. "The Theory of the Estimation of Test Reliability." *Psychometrika,* 1937, *2,* 151–160.

McKillip, R. H. & Wing, H. "Application of a Construct Model in Assessment of Employment." In U.S. Office of Personnel Management & Educational Testing Service. *Construct Validity in Psychological Measurement: Proceedings of a Colloquium on Theory and Application in Education and Employment.* Princeton, NJ: Educational Testing Service, 1980.

Mehrens, W. A. & Ebel, R. L. *Principles of Educational and Psychological Measurement: A Book of Selected Readings.* Chicago, IL: Rand McNally, 1967.

Mussio, S. J. & Smith, M. K. *Content Validity: A Procedural Manual.* Chicago, IL: International Personnel Management Association, 1973.

Proceedings of Content Validity II. Bowling Green, OH: Bowling Green State University, 1975.

Senders, V. L. "A Comment on Burke's Additive Scales and Statistics." *Psychological Review,* 1953, *60,* 423–424.

Schoenfeldt, L. F. "Utilization of Manpower: Development and Evaluation of an Assessment-Classification Model for Matching Individuals with Jobs." *Journal of Applied Psychology,* 1974, *59,* 583–595.

Schoenfeldt, L. F., Schoenfeldt, B. B., Acker, S. R., & Perlson, M. R. "Content Validity Revisited: The Development of a Content-Oriented Test of Industrial Reading." *Journal of Applied Psychology,* 1976, *61,* 581–588.

Smith, F. J. "Work Attitudes as Predictors of Attendance on a Specific Day." *Journal of Applied Psychology,* 1977, *62,* 16–19.

Stevens, S. S. "On the Theory of Scales of Measurement," *Science,* 1946, *103,* 677–680.

"Technical Recommendations for Psychological Tests and Diagnostic Techniques." *Psychological Bulletin Supplement,* 1954, *51,* (Part 2), 1–38.

Tenopyr, M. L. "Content-Construct Confusion." *Personnel Psychology,* 1977, *30,* 47–54.

Thorndike, R. L. *Personnel Selection.* New York: Wiley, 1949.

U.S. Office of Personnel Management & Educational Testing Service. *Construct Validity in Psychological Measurement; Proceedings of a Colloquium on Theory and Application in Education and Employment.* Princeton, NJ: Educational Testing Service, 1980.

Exploratory Data Analysis in Organizational Research

Mitchell W. Fields

The data analysis phase in organizational research is susceptible to a myriad of problems, resulting mainly from omission. Readily accessible canned computer programs, universally accepted statistical techniques, and new technologies for data entry may contribute to restricting the range of possibilities researchers consider when selecting statistical procedures for the analysis of their data. The following example illustrates this point:

John is a Ph.D. candidate in Organizational Behavior at a major university. He is currently in his fourth year of graduate school and is about to begin the statistical analysis of his dissertation data. John has spent approximately the last year religiously reading and summarizing the relevant research in his topic area. Based on his review of the literature, John has developed several hypotheses which he intends to test as the goal of his dissertation. For the last six months of this process, John has been collecting, from the employees of a nearby organization, the attitudinal and behavioral data necessary to test his hypotheses. He spent extensive time developing the study, and has conducted the methodology with an appropriate degree of experimental rigor. John selected survey research as the most appropriate method of generating the proper information on the variables of interest. The actual survey instruments were established

from previous research with particular attention paid to the issues of reliability, content, and construct validity.

Because John has received his graduate training from a department with a heavy quantitative emphasis, he feels quite capable of applying the correct statistical techniques to test his hypotheses. On his own, John has pursued additional training in the applications of computers to social sciences data. This has enabled him to supplement his graduate stipend by assisting other students with analyses of their data through the readily available canned statistical programs. Because of his experience with statistical programs and the rigors of his academic training in statistics and methodology, John considers himself as having considerable expertise regarding the possibilities for the analysis of his data. As part of his statistical consulting, John has gained hands-on experience correcting the mistakes resulting from the flaws present in the quantitative aspects of several different research projects. As a result, John designed the methodology of his research to overcome potential obstacles. First, to facilitate data entry, he developed his survey instruments for direct keypunching. This process eliminates the need for separate data coding and reduces the likelihood of errors because one step is eliminated when data are entered directly from the surveys into the computer. Second, to save considerable time, John subcontracted the data entry to a private keypunching service which transferred information from the original questionnaires directly into a computer file. As an additional safeguard against errors, all keypunching was verified to insure an accurate transfer of information.

Up to this point, John has used his time very effectively. In addition to time savings from subcontracting the keypunching, John recruited several new graduate students to assist with the data collection. In return for their assistance, he provided these students with the opportunity to benefit from experience in on-site data collection. As a result, prior to the actual analysis John did not even have to examine the raw data, which he perceived as a very efficient time savings.

Concurrently, with data entry by the keypunching service, John began preparing an SPSS (Statistical Package for the Social Sciences) program. This program applies specified statistical analyses to a set of data with a minimum number of control commands. Statistical packages like SPSS, BMDP (BMDP statistical software), and SAS (Statistical Analysis Systems) have made complicated analyses possible without having to learn a great deal of computer programming. These programs have so simplified the statistical analysis of data that a multivariate analysis of variance may require 15 or fewer lines of program information. John's program was ready at about the same time the data was entered into the computer and verified. The next step for John was to actually conduct the analysis. He entered the commands necessary to execute the program into the computer. He then checked the results to insure there were no logical errors and routed the results to an online printer at the university computing center.

The next day John picked up his printouts and was shocked to find that none of his hypotheses were confirmed! First, John predicted a significant relationship between two variables which the research literature sug-gests should be related. The Pearson correlation coefficient is so small that John is too embarrassed to show the results to his doctoral committee. John also predicted the presence of significant effects in a factorial analysis of variance (ANOVA) design, none of which were confirmed. John is at a loss of what to do. After a year of literature review, data collection, and analysis, no positive results were found. After three sleepless nights, John arrives at what he feels is the most sensible solution: He will approach his major advisor and ask for permission to reconceptualize and recollect his data.

This story, although purely fictitious, is representative of some of the shortcomings inherent in the popular approaches to data analysis in organizational research. An emphasis is placed on expedient analyses with a number of universally accepted statistical techniques. In the example above, although nothing is technically wrong with John's analytic plan, the first commandment of data analysis is overlooked: Know Thy Data. This is typical of most research efforts in the social sciences: Get the data analyzed in as expedient a manner as possible. Although frighteningly common, John's response—to collect new data—is both uncalled for and unnecessary. A more appropriate alternative would have been to assume that the data contained the sought after answers to his research questions. Once this assumption is accepted, logically the next step becomes an application of Exploratory Data Analysis (EDA).

This does not suggest, however, that the only reason to explore data arises from problems with the analysis. Over and above concerns connected with the non-confirmation of research hypotheses, the results of research should be explored as part of all data analytic plans. It has become too easy, as is illustrated in the above example, to collect, keypunch, and analyze data without directly examining the information. This problem is exacerbated by new, high speed computers and increasingly complex, yet user friendly, canned statistical programs. With these technological changes, it is now more important than ever to return a qualitative component to the data analysis phase of research. It is the purpose of this paper to examine a set of techniques introduced by Tukey (1977) in order to supplement traditional statistics by allowing researchers to acquaint themselves with their data. These procedures, referred to as Exploratory Data Analysis, will be the subject of some brief discussion accompanied by a description of their application to the types of data collected in organizational research.

Computers, mechanization, and advanced software have all contributed to increasing the distance between researchers and the data they collect. Complicated analyses, previously thought impossible, are now available to researchers with a minimal level of statistical competence. Canned statistical programs allow the analysis of the most complex multivariate designs. Analyses can be achieved by researchers without even a rudimentary knowledge of the assumptions and/or the derivations of the statistics they are generating. This raises the dangers associated with the computation of potentially inappropriate statistics (e.g., regression analyses with nominal criteria). Therefore, this increased statistical capacity, although certainly beneficial, provides a greater potential for misuse. Not only will conducting an inappropriate analysis invalidate the conclusions derived from one's research, but increased statistical capacity leads to an increase in the number of statistical tests to which a set of data are subjected. As the number of distinct statistical tests increases, the probability of a type I error (i.e., the probability of rejecting a true null hypothesis) increases. This results in an inflation of the specified level of significance or alpha level. Thus, caution must be exercised so as to avoid increasing the likelihood of rejecting a true null hypothesis simply because of an increase in the number of significance tests conducted. EDA displays promise as a potential method for avoiding abuses resulting from technological improvements, because

when it is applied prior to, and as a part of analytic plans, it adds a conservative element. Researchers are afforded the opportunity to become more intimately familiar with their data. It must be considered inappropriate for a set of data to be analyzed and conclusions drawn without any sort of investigation into the properties of the data set. In other words, by restoring a degree of intimacy between the researcher and his/her data, a qualitative component is restored to the quantitative analysis of data.

HINGES AND MEDIANS

Most of the techniques of EDA were first proposed by Tukey (1977) as an alternative and supplement of traditional statistical analyses of data. Traditional analyses, with the exception of factor analytic procedures, focus on hypothesis testing. Factor analysis represents the exception because the most commonly employed factor analytic algorithms are exploratory in nature. With the exception of the relatively new confirmatory factor analysis procedures, most popular approaches to factor analysis investigate a data set to determine the underlying patterns of intercorrelations among variables. Whether it be an experimental or non-experimental design, the goal of most other statistical analyses concerns the testing of specific hypotheses. The techniques of EDA are not meant to replace these analytic procedures; rather, they allow researchers to choose the most appropriate analysis by developing a more intimate relationship between researcher and data. With an improved awareness of their data, researchers will be more able to select those analyses best suited to the structure of their data as an alternative to selecting an expedient and marginally acceptable analysis.

According to Barnett and Lewis (1978), an outlier may be defined as ". . . an observation (or subset of observations) which appears to be inconsistent with the remainder of that set of data." In other words, an outlier represents an extreme score (or scores) which does not belong with the remaining observations. In small and some large data sets, uncorrected outliers can have a substantial impact on the most commonly used descriptive statistics. Suppose we have the set of numbers:

5,6,7,7,8,8,9,75.

The mean and standard deviation for the above numbers are 15.6 and 22.9 respectively. Notice what the presence of 75 does to both of these statistics. Removing the 75 changes the mean to 7.1 and the standard deviation to 2.2. This is central to Tukey's (1977) argument when he suggests that alternative measures of central tendency and dispersion of scores should be employed in data analysis. This is not to argue that we simply abandon the mean as a measure of central tendency. Rather, in certain instances there may be measures of central tendency which are psychometrically superior to the mean.

Two explanations for this phenomenon both focus on the psychometric properties of the data under investigation. The first concerns the adverse impact outliers may have on these indices. The second centers on the shape of the distribution of scores. The mean and standard deviation are only valid when a set of scores is normally distributed. As the distribution deviates from normality, these statistics become increasingly inappropriate. With Poisson or skewed distributions, these measures do not provide an accurate representation of the distribution. Tukey proposes employing hinges and medians as supplements to the traditional computations of variance and means, respectively.

Medians are already a somewhat familiar concept. The median is the middle score in a distribution of scores, the 50th percentile score, and that value which separates the highest half of the scores from the lowest half. In the case of an odd number of scores, the median becomes the exact middle score. In situations where there is an even number

of observations, the median is computed by adding the two middle scores together and dividing by two. One advantage of the median derives from its lowered susceptibility to the presence of extreme scores because it is essentially non-distributional in form. In the above example, the median (with the 75 included) is 7.5. Excluding the extreme value of 75 changes the median to 7.0, resulting in a less severe change than that which was experienced when the mean served as a measure of central tendency.

As an alternative to standard deviation, to accompany the median, Tukey proposes the use of hinges. These are data points which divide a distribution of scores into quartiles. Thus, there are two hinges in a data set, one which denotes the first quartile (or twenty fifth percentile) and one which denotes the third quartile (or seventy fifth percentile). As with the median, the advantage of the hinge over the standard deviation is that it is relatively unaffected by the magnitude of scores. As an example, suppose the following scores were derived from an instrument which measures the intrinsic motivation of 18 employees on a scale of 1 (low) to 100 (high):

20,20,30,30,34,36,38,40,43,50,50,50,50,55,-55,58,59,60

The median for the above set of scores is 50 and the two hinges are 34 and 55. Had there been extreme scores on either the high or low end of the distribution, these results would have remained largely unaffected. However, with the addition of extreme scores, the mean and standard deviation would change drastically.

STEM AND LEAF

Most readers are probably already familiar with another technique of EDA, namely histograms. A histogram is a two dimensional representation of a frequency distribution.

Histograms present a graphic representation of the frequency with which scores are repeated within a distribution. Typically the x-axis represents the different scores and the y-axis represents the frequency of their occurrence. By definition, the normal distribution is a probability density distribution. This implies that the normal bell shaped curve is nothing more than a plot of the expected frequency of scores within a population. Although histograms are presented in virtually every statistics text, Tukey (1977) and Hartwig and Dearing (1982) present an alternative to the histogram, the stem and leaf display. According to Mosteller and Tukey (1977), the stem and leaf display is a useful method of presenting and summarizing large batches of numbers. Suppose the following set of numbers are collected from the use of a new performance appraisal instrument:

91	200	242	300
93	201	246	300
96	201	249	325
120	201	249	326
124	226	265	327
126	228	268	328
133	239	291	329
185	239	294	340
187	241	296	341

Through the application of a stem and leaf display, these numbers could be rewritten as:

```
0|91 93 96
1|20 24 26 33 85 87
2|00 01 01 01 26 28 39 41 42 46 49 49 65 68 91 94 96
3|00 00 25 26 27 28 29 40 41
```

According to Hartwig and Dearing (1981), numbers to the left of the vertical line represent the highest power, which in this case is hundredths. In other words, the number on the left of the vertical line is the first digit of the highest order of the numerical scores. Numbers to the right of the line represent the remaining values after the first digit is removed. Thus, the 00 in the '2' row represents the number 200. One advantage of the stem and leaf technique is that, similar to the histogram, it provides an excellent pictorial representation of the shape of the distribution. Unlike the histogram, the stem and leaf requires minimal drawing. More importantly, because a variety of different manipulations are available, it tends to provide a greater breadth of information. The stem and leaf display can be even further reduced to provide the following results without any significant loss of information:

```
1*   0002233
1⌐   99
2*   0000334444
2⌐   5557799
3*   0003333344
```

According to Hartwig and Dearing, the above reduction is accomplished in three steps. First, all scores are rounded to two decimal places and the third decimal is dropped. Thus 093 becomes 10 and 341 becomes 34. Second, each line of data from the initial display is split into two, represented by lines beginning with either a '*' or a '⌐'. In lines beginning with a * the second digit (after rounding) varies from 1 to 4. When the line begins with a ⌐ the second digit can take on any value from 5 to 9. Finally, physical spaces between the numbers are eliminated resulting in a very compact representation of the original data set.

There are many different variations for the stem and leaf display. Readers who are interested in further information or who want to investigate additional possibilities for the stem and leaf data display are urged to consult Tukey (1977) for additional information.

BOX AND WHISKER PLOTS

Box and Whisker plots represent another method of displaying data to maximize the information transmitted. Whereas most statistical computations are complex and require the use of a computer, computation of

the EDA procedures are simple, often accomplished with perhaps graph paper and a
pencil. However, the information accessible
from these techniques may even surpass the
most complex statistical anayses.

Box and Whisker plots are representative of this simplicity of form. A rectangular
box is drawn with the longer sides in a vertical position. The top of the box is denoted as
the top hinge (i.e., the twenty-fifth percentile). The bottom side of the box is denoted
as the bottom hinge (the seventy-fifth percentile). Somewhere in the box, scaled to proportion of course, a horizontal line is drawn
to represent the median. Suppose the following scores are collected from a job satisfaction survey administered to 11 employees:

38,40,50,51,56,70,76,77,78,81,82

A simple calculation will determine that the
median is equal to 70. The top hinge is 78
and the bottom hinge is 50. The box which
represents this pattern is displayed in Figure 1.

Point 1 represents the upper hinge, point 2-
the lower hinge, and point 3-the median.

The next step is to sketch in the whiskers. In the basic box and whisker plot, the
whiskers are vertical lines extending from
each hinge to the point representing the

Figure 1.

most extreme score at each end of the distribution. Thus, adding the whiskers to the
above box would generate:

Figure 2.

Points 1 and 2 in this figure represent the
extension of the whiskers from the top and
bottom ends of the box (i.e., the hinges) to
the most extreme scores in the data set. In
the case of point 1, the whisker is extended
to the point representing the observation
with the highest value. At point 2, the
whisker extends to the point with the lowest
value in the distribution. This technique
contains several advantages. First, it builds
upon the hinge and median approach. The
advantages associated with the hinge and
median technique are automatically realized
through applications of the box and whisker
plots. Second, with only slight modification,
this procedure can be altered to directly display extreme observations. This allows the
researcher to determine whether these observations belong in the distribution. If not,

they can be treated and corrected as outliers. As with the stem and leaf display, the box and whisker plot presents a useful mechanism to investigate the range and form of a distribution of observations. Tukey (1977) provides examples of the combination of stem and leaf displays with box and wisker plots and other exploratory techniques to maximize the information transmitted from a visual display of data.

SCATTER PLOTS

One of the most useful and most common of the exploratory data analytic techniques is the simple scatter plot. In correlational studies, the Pearson product-moment correlation coefficient is the most commonly employed index of relationship between two variables. To review, the Pearson correlation provides a measure of the degree of the linear relationship between two variables. Although in many cases researchers specifically examine their data for linear relationships, situations exist when investigations of linearity are not the purpose of the research. In many situations, as in John's dissertation, hypotheses merely concern themselves with testing a relationship between two variables without specifying the form of that relationship. Researchers who are unconcerned regarding the form of a relationship often use only the Pearson statistic, because of its popularity and accessibility. This limits the pattern of relationships tested to linearity. Therefore, it is to be expected that some researchers will find themselves in the same situation as John, left with unconfirmed hypotheses because of potentially inappropriate statistics.

All computations involving correlation coefficients should be accompanied by a scatter plot. Scatter plots present a graphic illustration of each data point in a set of data. Traditionally, the information is presented on a graph where the independent variable (or predictor) is plotted on the x-axis and the dependent variable (or criterion) is dis-

played on the y-axis. Each data pair (x,y) is specified as a point on the graph, thus providing a visual display of the relationship. The advantage of the scatter plot lies in the information readily available from this simple yet essential technique. A visual examination of the plot provides information regarding the scope and pattern of the relationship between the x and y variables. Whereas the Pearson correlation coefficient provides only information concerned with the linearity of data, the scatter plot will indicate many nonlinear (e.g., curvilinear) patterns of association. If John had accompanied or preceded his correlation analysis with a scatter plot, he might have been able to avoid those sleepless nights because he would have realized that the conclusions derived from his data regarding poor conceptualization of variables may have been erroneous. Actually, the nonsignificant correlation coefficients may have been attributed to a nonlinear pattern of association as an alternative to conclusions regarding poor data conceptualization. Adopting this point of view opens many additional possibilities for data investigation.

Figures 3 and 4 both provide examples of scatter plots which contain information that would have been overlooked had one (e.g., John) relied exclusively on the Pearson product moment correlation coefficient. Determinations of a linear relationship for the data displayed in Figure 3 would provide low results, masking a very strong bivariate relationship. The strong 'U' or curvilinear trend evident in this example would be obscured when computing a measure of linear association. Although more robust indices of relationship exist (i.e., eta; Cohen and Cohen, 1975), the scatter plot serves as an indicator to researchers, suggesting whether these alternative correlational statistics are appropriate.

Figure 4 represents different information entirely. This diagram exhibits information which would be obscured by all traditional correlation analyses of any shape

```
X   X   XXX X  X          X    X   X   XXX XX
  XX   XX X X X                XX XX XX
  X   X   X   X   X            XX   X  X
  ZZ XXXXX   X X X       X     XX   XX X
XXX XX XX X  X X               XXXXX
      X   X   X               XX   X X XX
        XX XXXX               XX X X XX
                           XX XX XX
         XXXX        X        XX XX XX  X XX XX X  X
  X     X    XXX X          XX   XX   XX X   XX XX X X
        XX   X X          XX   XXX XXX XX XX X
      X   X   X X X      X X X X X X X X X
          X X   X             XXX   X XX   X
```

Figure 3. Hypothetical curvilinear scatter plot

or pattern and would be devastating to the accuracy of these computations. The dispersion of some of the extreme scores in this example points to the presence of outliers in the data set. Points 1 and 2 on Figure 4 represent outliers. These extreme scores, if not accounted for, can have a substantial effect on the resulting correlation coefficient. In their book, Barnett and Lewis (1978) discuss several different techniques for detecting and treating outliers. Observation of these scores is only a beginning. They must be detected and treated statistically. The scatter plot functions as a useful detection device by providing an alert that outliers may be present in a set of data. Once detected, a host of procedures are available to remove their confounding effects. The scope of this

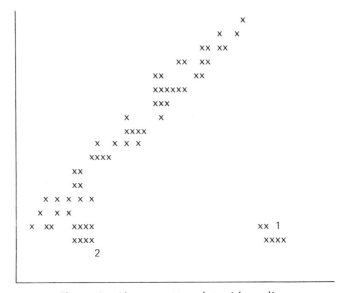

Figure 4. Linear scatter plot with outliers

paper does not permit a treatment of the various techniques for the detection and correction of outliers (For a more detailed treatment of this topic, see Barnett and Lewis, 1978.)

BIVARIATE RELATIONSHIPS

Of all the techniques associated with EDA, the most useful to the organizational sciences concerns the manipulation and investigation of bivariate relationships. EDA provides mechanisms for extracting information from bivariate relationships which supplements the information provided from traditional analyses. Many research designs consist of establishing a relationship between two variables. These studies attempt to establish a scheme which will provide a prediction of performance on one variable given knowledge only of performance on the second variable. Typically, these designs contain both predictor and criterion variables. The intent of these studies is to predict criterion performance from knowledge of predictor performance. This is the basic design employed in the development of selection systems. The goal is to select individuals who will be successful on the criterion when knowledge of certain predictors are available.

Regression analyses stand out as the most commonly employed technique for deriving these prediction systems. Most regression equations attempt to predict y from x. Mathematically, regression equations take the following form:

$$Y'=bX+a+e$$

In the above, a represents the y intercept (the y value in the system when x is assumed to be zero), b represents the slope of the line, and e comprises the error of prediction. Without indulging in an elaborate explanation, the method employed to derive the regression line incorporates a least squares algorithm. The least squares solution for generating the regression line capitalizes on the variability in a distribution of scores. The distance from all data points to the regression line is minimized.

One problem inherent in all prediction systems concerns the inability of prediction schemes to generate perfect predictions. A system of perfect prediction is theoretically impossible because for each point of x there are always y scores of differential values. Some points will fall above and others below the regression line. The least squares procedure fits a line which results in points above and below the line falling at approximately the same distance from the regression line.

Obviously, with data falling both above and below the regression line, this procedure results in a certain degree of inaccuracy when the correlation falls short of unity. This necessitates the use and computation of the standard error of regression. This is a statistic which provides an index of the accuracy of predictions. Whereas correlation indicates the strength of a relationship between two variables, standard error provides a measure of the variability of scores around the regression line. Returning to the above equation for predicting y from x:

$$Y'=bX+a+e$$

Errors of prediction can be computed from:

$$e=Y-Y'$$

This treats errors as the difference between the predicted y scores (Y') and the actual y scores (Y).

Normally in regression analyses, the standard error statistic is rarely used or even computed. EDA procedures provide a use for the component of the y score not predicted (i.e., the residual) to extract additional information concerning the relationship between x and y. Tukey (1977) implies that because of these errors of prediction, regression analyses result in an "incomplete description" of the bivariate relationship. The EDA contribution involves a plot of the residual information $(Y-Y')$ to extract remaining knowledge. Instead of error, $Y-Y'$ is reformulated as variable R (residual):

$$R=Y-Y'$$

If the residual is plotted on the y-axis, against the independent variable on the x-axis, a wealth of information is available. Tukey (1977, p. 113) discusses two important reasons for examining residuals. First, they provide an index of the ". . . successive step-by-step improvement in our analyses." Thus, when exploring a bivariate relationship for the appropriate pattern of association, residuals become increasingly smaller as the fit improves. With increases in the adequacy of fit, as measured by the magnitude of the residuals, it is necessary to determine when the appropriate degree of fit has been achieved. This is diametrically opposed to the typical treatment of residuals within ordinary linear regression. Linear models treat residuals as unavoidable errors of prediction as contrasted to an index of error which may be improved upon with subsequent models. This is the second advantage of plotting residuals. The researcher can determine when an acceptable degree of "incomplete description" has been attained. In other words, residuals will turn ". . . an investigator's eye toward the adequacy of current analyses."

In addition, when computed and plotted, residuals can be subjected to any one of a number of axis transformations (discussed later) to straighten the plot. If any additional patterns of association exist, these provide information concerning additional relationships between the variables of interest. These procedures emphasize that a simple regression equation does not provide an adequate explanation of the data. Needed are more thorough investigations which include an examination of residual information.

Accompanying his discussion on plots of relationship, Tukey (1977) presents a host of techniques which are designed to deal with a problem discussed earlier, the issue of linearity. Most regression procedures investigate a linear format. They attempt to fit linear plots to describe bivariate relationships. Obviously, the regression process is subject to the same shortcomings as that of linear statistics applied to nonlinear data. The EDA solution to this problem is simple. Find the actual form of the relationship and apply the proper description. In the regression paradigm, this is accomplished through testing various nonlinear components. The x term in the regression equation can be squared, cubed, or subjected to any other transformation the researcher so desires. Canned statistical programs provide transformation algorithms permitting new variables to be created and added to the regression procedure. These allow tests of nonlinear trends. In addition, the regression procedures in many of these programs accommodate testing of various weighted orthogonal components, provided the appropriate degrees of freedom are available. For example, if investigations are to focus on a quadratic trend, a regression equation of the following form will accomplish this end:

$$Y=b_1x^2+b_2x+a+e$$

The addition of the x^2 component to the general linear equation will allow the test of one additional form of relationship. It is also possible to develop sets of orthogonal weights to test for many different patterns of association.

If the research is exploratory in nature, EDA offers a useful substitute. If a relationship between two variables is predicted, an approach testing many different forms will be cumbersome, will use degrees of freedom indiscriminantly, and will rapidly inflate the probability of a type I error. EDA provides a more expedient solution which can be accomplished with graph paper, a calculator, and a pencil. Tukey (1977) calls this procedure Straightening. It is approximately the same as testing different forms of relationship without indulging in unnecessary statistical analyses. This approach begins with the generation of the simple bivariate scatter plot. It is then the responsibility of the researcher to investigate the pattern displayed in the plot. If the shape of the plot assumes a straight line pattern, then the simple linear regression will suffice. However, if the pattern indicates a more powerful trend, Tukey recommends testing various transformations of the x-axis until a linear trend is apparent. The scaling of the x-axis can be altered with any one of a number of transformations. Possibilities include logarithmic transformations, squaring, cubing, square roots, and almost any other alternative. The plots are developed by rescaling the x-axis according to the new transformation imposed upon the data. The y-axis meanwhile, remains unaffected. More advanced forms of straightening allow transformations of the y-axis as well. As transformations are applied to the axis, researchers may examine the emerging patterns for a straightening of the plot of the relationship. When a transformation straightens out the plot so that the scatter of data appears linear, this indicates the appropriate form of the relationship.

Normally this might be thought of as a simplistic form of "shotgun empiricism" because the researcher is superimposing a host of transformations until an appropriate fit is determined. However, applications of EDA allow exploration of the results of research efforts with the final product resulting in a more appropriate application of traditional statistics. Researchers are afforded the opportunity to seek potentially more powerful alternatives to the traditional statistics we have come to rely on so heavily.

CONCLUSIONS

The preceding pages should in no way be construed as an exhaustive explanation of EDA. An elementary introduction to these techniques is provided, accompanied by some ideas concerning their uses with the types of data collected in the organizational sciences. These procedures are certainly not new. Researchers will perhaps recognize that many of the tenets of EDA involve old statistical principles which are packaged under a new label. For example, plots of residuals are recommended by most advanced statistics texts. Certainly, no one well versed in statistics is unfamiliar with the median and mode as alternative measures of central tendency. However, the use of these measures in the published literature represents a low baseline phenomenon.

John, in the opening example to this paper, would have benefited from an application of these techniques. His original emphasis on expediency and "efficiency" no doubt cost more than it saved. In his attempt to facilitate data collection, entry, and analysis John lost a necessary familiarity with his research results. Restricting himself to an examination of computer printouts caused John to reach possibly erroneous conclusions at what should have been a preliminary stage in the data analysis. With the procedures of EDA available, John could have investigated a greater breadth of potential possibilities for finding the answers to his research questions within the data he collected.

The gains to be realized from EDA are not derived from radically new statistical techniques with which to analyze data. What EDA offers is a different philosophical orientation to the implementation of data analysis. It is advantageous because it encourages a shift in how data are perceived. Hypothesis testing will always be an integral part of research designs. However, there will always be the need to apply the correct techniques to a well understood set of data. It is here that EDA displays the most potential. An orientation to analysis which approaches data with fewer assumptions, a broader perspective, and a more open attitude concerning different possibilities, can only represent a positive addition to the arsenal of data-analytic approaches we now possess.

REFERENCES

Barnett, V. and Lewis, T. *Outliers in Statistical Data.* Chinchester: John Wiley & Sons, 1978.

Cohen, J. and Cohen, P. *Applied Multiple Regression/Correlation Analysis for the Social Sciences.* Hillsdale, N.J.: Lawrence Erlbaum Assoc., 1975.

Hartwig, F. and Dearing, B. E. *Exploratory Data Analysis.* Beverly Hills: Sage Publications, 1979.

Mosteller, F. and Tukey, J. W. *Data Analysis and Regression: A Second Course in Statistics.* Reading, Mass.: Addison Wesley, 1977.

Tukey, J. W. *Exploratory Data Analysis.* Reading, Mass.: Addison Wesley, 1977.

Factor Analysis and Counseling Research[1]

David J. Weiss[2]

Factor analysis has been an important tool in counseling psychology research. Frequently, factor-analytic techniques have been used to develop, refine, and study the interrelationships of instruments used in client evaluation (e.g., Baruch, Segal, & Handrick, 1968; Stinson, 1968). Factor analysis recently has been applied in the development of instruments used directly in counseling research to measure dimensions of empathic judgments (Greenberg, Kagan, & Bowes, 1969), linguistic structure in small group discussions (Cope, 1969), clients' perceptions of therapists (Walker & Little, 1969), empathic aspects of counselor behavior (Zimmer & Anderson, 1968), and problems appropriate for discussion at various counseling centers (Ogston, Altmann, & Conklin, 1969). Predictors of counseling outcomes (Barry, Dunteman, & Webb, 1968) as well as criterion measures of counseling effectiveness (Hause & Miller, 1968) also have been submitted to factor analysis, as have the interindividual profile correlations of change scores (Elton & Rose, 1968) and therapists' Q sort descriptions of client personality (VanAtta, 1968).

As psychometricians and statisticians continue to do research on factor-analytic methods, the domain of factor analysis becomes more complex. A variety of factor-analytic models and techniques have arisen, as a result of the increasing availability of computers, combined with the development of new knowledge in factor analysis. Each factor-analytic model makes different assumptions of the data and requires different decisions from its user. The interpretations of the results also differ somewhat, depending on the decisions made by the investigator in choosing a solution (Harris, 1967). In precomputer days, the range of decisions in doing a factor analysis was limited by the computational difficulty of many theoretical solutions. Now, an adequate factor analysis requires a more sophisticated set of decisions on the part of the researcher to arrive at a meaningful solution for the problem under investigation. Prior to the choice of a specific factor-analytic method, however, the investigator first must determine whether his problem is appropriate for factor analysis. Second, he must decide whether his particular data are worth factor analyzing.

WHEN TO FACTOR ANALYZE

Factor Analysis Versus Cluster Analysis

Factor analysis and cluster analysis are the two major methods available for analysis of covariation matrices. While the two tech-

---

[1] Reproduced by permission of the *Journal of Counseling Psychology* 1970, *17*, 477–485.

[2] The author gratefully acknowledges the careful review of this paper by Robert M. Thorndike. His many helpful comments resulted in several important clarifications.

niques frequently have been used almost interchangeably, they are designed for different purposes.

The primary distinction between factor-analytic techniques and most cluster-analytic techniques is in their treatment of the variance of a variable. In factor analysis, the variance of a variable usually is "partitioned" among several sources. The total variance of a variable usually is not factor analyzed, and the variance which is analyzed is distributed among the factors extracted. Rather than analyzing "total" variance of a variable, factor analysis is concerned only with the "common" variance, or that portion of the variance which correlates with other variables in the matrix. The "unique" variance, including both specific reliable variance and "error" variance, does not correlate with other variables and hence is not analyzed in most factor-analytic methods. In factor analysis, common variance becomes fractionated, or distributed among the factors. Factor analysis, therefore, is indicated when a researcher desires to study the *structure* of a set of variables in terms of how the common variance of a variable distributes itself across a number of "basic" dimensions. Factor analysis should be used when the investigator wants to reduce his variables to a smaller set by essentially decomposing the original variables into a new subset of variables composed of linear combinations of parts of the variance of the original variables.

Cluster analysis, on the other hand, typically treats the *total* variance of each variable. Rather than fractionating the variance of each variable among a set of "basic" variables, cluster analysis assigns the total variance of the variable to a group of other variables which are highly correlated with it. In this way, cluster analysis yields a set of new "category" variables, each set (or cluster) defined by the inclusion of a subset of variables and by the exclusion of all other variables. The results of a factor analysis are rarely so clear, since in factor analysis parts of the variance of each variable may be attributable to each of the "subsets" or factors.

The unique application of most cluster-analytic methods, then, is to the situation where a categorical decision is required. That is, where the investigator is interested in *classifying* a set of variables in relation to each other to identify subgroups of variables that are similar; this situation should be kept distinct from the factor-analytic question of whether *portions* of the common variance of variables are highly related to each other. Choice of cluster versus factor analysis depends, then, on the objectives of the study in relation to the characteristics of the two techniques in terms of their treatment of variance components.

Q Correlation Analysis

Cluster analysis usually is to be preferred to factor analysis in the case of "people typing" as operationalized by Q correlation analysis. The goal of Q analysis is to develop "people types" by analyzing the Q correlations among the multivariable profiles for a group of individuals. For example, the counselor might wish to identify subgroups of profiles in the Minnesota Multiphasic Personality Inventories of a group of rehabilitation clients. If identifiable subgroups exist, a subsequent study might investigate the differential effect of certain counseling techniques for the different groups.

To investigate this question, the investigator would compute a matrix of Q correlations among all possible pairs of Minnesota Multiphasic Personality Inventory profiles for the group under study. The next step is to develop people types by some sort of co-variation analysis. Here the researcher must question the objectives of factor analysis in relation to the question at hand. He should concern himself with the question of whether he wishes to know what proportion of the variance of individual A's profile is in common with individual B, individual C, individual D, and so on. By looking at the question in this way, it becomes obvious that factor analysis is not the appropriate technique for most Q correlation studies. People typing is better accomplished by cluster analysis, since "all" of each individual is assigned to clusters with "all" of other individuals. The use of factor analysis for the development of people types frequently leads to a large number of "factors," each having a small number of individuals representing the factors. Such analysis also frequently results in individuals who are factorially "complex" in that the variance of their profiles distributes across a number of factors, thus making assignment to types difficult and rather arbitrary.

Q correlation matrices should not, in general, be factor analyzed since they rarely meet the specifications indicated by Guilford (1952) in his classic article, "When Not to Factor Analyze." Q correlations are unlikely to meet Guilford's criteria of "good" correlations as normally distributed—unimodal and symmetric. In addition, squared multiple correlations, often used to estimate common variance in factor analysis, cannot be computed from Q correlations, nor can Q correlation matrices be tested for statistical significance to see if the matrix is worth factor analyzing.

In general, cluster analysis is preferred to factor analysis when the index of covariation used is not an R type product-moment correlation (Cattell, 1952). Most factor-analytic methods should not be used on Q correlations, on "distance measures," or "proportions of agreement." Nor should factor analyses usually be done on such correlation coefficients as tetrachoric and biserial, since these correlations are not product-moment correlations and hence do not meet the assumptions of the factor-analytic model. Factor analysis also is contraindicated where an intercorrelation matrix is composed of sections of correlation matrices derived from different groups. Such matrices usually do not permit the computation of reasonable communality estimates and hence are not appropriate for most factor-analytic methods.

Furthermore, factor analysis assumes linear relationships among variables and between variables and factors. Deviations of the bivariate relationships from linearity also contraindicate the use of almost all methods of factor analysis.

Unique Applications of Factor Analysis

Factor analysis is the method of choice when an investigator wishes to analyze a set of variables to discover a new set of variables which are uncorrelated with each other. This would be the case where a psychologist wants to construct measures of some aspects of human functioning which comprehensively cover a domain of behavior and wants to spend minimum time in the measurement process. Since correlated variables tend to duplicate parts of each other, thus spending duplicate time in assessment, the use of uncorrelated measures gives maximal information in a specified amount of time.

Orthogonal or uncorrelated variables frequently are desirable for theoretical purposes. Since a variable which is defined operationally to be uncorrelated with other variables is not "contaminated" by the actions of other variables, the influence of manipulated experimental variables may be clearer on the orthogonal variable. Thus, in the experimental situation it may be easier to discern or identify causal relationships between independent and dependent variables if the measuring instruments used to operationalize the dependent variables are factorially pure. Factorial purity of measures in this situation also will permit the development of more specific and testable hypotheses than would be possible with dependent variable measures that represent a conglomerate of dependent variables.

Uncorrelated variables also have advantages in applied prediction situations. Thorndike (in Guilford, 1965, p. 407) has shown that linear multiple-regression techniques operate most effectively with uncorrelated predictor variables. For example, given a fixed predictor-criterion correlation for each of nine predictor variables of .30, the multiple correlation of the nine predictors with the criterion can vary from a low of .37, when all predictors intercorrelate .60 with each other, to .90 when all predictors intercorrelate .00 with each other. Thus, for the psychologist who is attempting to predict a single outcome variable from a set of continuous predictors, the same number of predictors can account for 67% more criterion variance if the predictors are uncorrelated with each other than if they have moderately high intercorrelations. Similar reasoning would hold true for predictions derived from linear multiple discriminant function and canonical correlation analysis, since both techniques are closely related to linear multiple regression. Such a potential gain in predictability well might be worth the investment of time necessary to develop uncorrelated measures of relevant predictor variables in counseling research. Since cluster analysis usually does not result in uncorrelated variables, factor analysis is the method of choice.

Factor analysis is, of course, the method of choice where the investigator is concerned with the structure of his variables in terms of an underlying set of dimensions. Factor analysis, therefore, can be used to generate hypotheses of structure and to verify hypotheses of structure derived from earlier studies. In addition, factor analysis is indicated rather than cluster analysis when less than total variance of a variable is to be analyzed as it distributes across the underlying factor dimensions.

Ipsativity

While Guilford (1952) cautioned researchers against factor analyzing ipsative or partially ipsative data, in the almost 20 years since Guilford's paper, several aspects of the question have become clarified. (A future paper in this series will treat the general problem of ipsativity in greater detail). First, "ipsative" must be differentiated from "partially ipsative" (Smith, 1967). A purely ipsative measure is one in which the total score, across all subscales, is the same for all individuals. Among instruments commonly used in counseling, the Edwards Personal Preference Schedule, raw scores on the 1967 Revision of the Minnesota Importance Questionnaire, and the Allport-Vernon-Lindzey Study of Values meet this criterion. Both the Edwards Personal Preference Schedule and the Minnesota Importance Questionnaire are applications of the method of pair comparisons; hence the total score for an individual is equal to the number of choices he has to make. Most data obtained from Q sorts also are purely ipsative. Purely ipsative measurement is completely intraindividual.

Partially ipsative data do not meet the criterion of pure ipsativity; partially ipsative data would be better referred to as "artificially correlated." Partially ipsative scores result from scoring items on two or more scales such as is done in the Kudor Preference Record and other instruments. In these instruments the total score, across all scales, for any individual is *not* a constant.

Both purely and partially ipsative R-type correlations can be factor analyzed. The problem arises in the interpretation of the resulting factors. If the investigator is factor analyzing to obtain uncorrelated factors for use in some applied situation (e.g., multivariate prediction), interpretation of the factors is not necessary. If, however, the factor analysis was done to generate or verify a hypothesis about the structure of the variables, extreme care must be taken in interpreting the results from purely or partially ipsative measurements (Atkinson & Lunneborg, 1968).

Purely ipsative intercorrelation matrices are characterized by intercorrelations that are half positive and half negative, with a median close to $r = .00$. Factor analysis of these data typically yields a set of bipolar factors. The bipolarity is a result of the forced-choice character of the measuring instrumcnt and not necessarily a reflection of the "true" structure of the variables. Interpretation of ipsative factors involves the interpretation of the "relativistic" nature of intraindividual measurement. Hence, an Allport-Vernon-Lindzey Study of Values factor loaded high positive on Theoretical and high negative on Religious would imply a preference for the former *versus* the latter type of activity, rather than just high or low preferences for either.

Partially ipsative data do not yield the characteristic correlation matrix of purely ipsative data. When factor analyzed, the interpretation of the factors resulting from partially ipsative data is also less clear. Since an undetermined amount of each correlation in the matrix is artificial as a result of the scoring method, no characteristic types of factors emerge from this type of data. Interpretation of the factor analysis of partially ipsative data must be approached cautiously and the investigator must attempt somehow to avoid over-interpreting the results by considering the role of the scoring method in artificially causing correlations to be high positive or high negative. To identify the "true" structure of a set of variables measured ipsatively or partially ipsatively, replication of the analysis with the artificial covariance removed would be desirable. Such "deipsatizing" would require that items not be scored on more than one scale.

SHOULD A SPECIFIC DATA MATRIX BE FACTOR ANALYZED?

Given that factor analysis is not contraindicated for a specific set of data, and prior to a choice of the most appropriate type of solution for the question at hand, the investigator should determine whether his correlation matrix is worth factor analyzing. Most frequently the psychologist simply assumes that the intercorrelation matrix contains meaningful information beyond that which would be obtained from the intercorrelation of random data, hence making factor analysis worthwhile. By making this assumption, the psychologist implicitly assumes that the factor analysis of random data will yield a factor matrix with defined characteristics, such as uninterpretability, which indicate that only error variance was being analyzed.

Armstrong and Soelberg (1968) addressed themselves to this assumption. They generated sets of random numbers for 50 observations across 20 variables, and intercorrelated the random numbers. They then factor analyzed the correlation matrix using a principal components solution with 1.0 in the diagonal. Contrary to what might be expected under these circumstances, they obtained nine factors with loadings as high as .88; each factor had one or more loadings greater than .50. The factor matrix, therefore, was similar to the results that frequently appear in the literature based on "real" data. The data used in that study, however, were only random numbers.

Such results indicate the need for a method of testing intercorrelation matrices for significance before factor analyzing. If this is not done, the psychologist well may be interpreting and using factor analyses which appear to be meaningful, but are no more meaningful than the factor analyses of random numbers generated by Armstrong and Soelberg.

An infrequently used test for the statistical significance of a correlation matrix was developed some years ago by Bartlett (1950). Bartlett's test is concerned with the null hypothesis of no significant deviation of an observed correlation matrix from an identity matrix (a matrix with 1s in the diagonal and 0s in all the off-diagonal elements). In other words, Bartlett's test could be interpreted as determining whether the intercorrelation matrix contains "enough" common variance to make factor analysis worth pursuing. The test might be construed as answering the question of whether "enough" statistically significant correlations are in the matrix to yield factors that represent something other than the intercorrelations of random data. Essentially, Bartlett's formula tests the correlation matrix for randomness.

In applying Bartlett's test to the random correlation matrix generated by Armstrong and Soelberg (1968), Tobias and Carlson (1969) found that they were unable to reject the null hypothesis of no significant deviation from an identity matrix. An investigator using Bartlett's test on the Armstrong and Soelberg data, then, would have been forced to conclude that his correlation matrix was *not* worth factor analyzing and would have avoided generating a factor matrix which, while appearing reasonable, represented the factor analysis of meaningless data.

Since most factor analyses now are done on computers, the computation of Bartlett's test is relatively simple, requiring in most cases the addition of only a statement or two in an existing program. The test statistic can also be computed by hand given the determinant of the correlation matrix, which is (or easily can be) standard output in many factor analysis programs. The formula for Bartlett's test is as follows:

$$\chi^2 = -\left[N - 1 - \frac{2p + 5}{6}\right] \log_e |R|$$

where N = number of individuals
  p = number of variables
  $|R|$ = the absolute value of the determinant of the correlation matrix

The resulting statistic is the familiar chi-square statistic, with $p(p - 1)/2$ degrees of freedom. As can be seen by the formula, the test is based primarily on the relationship between number of observations (individuals) and number of variables, as these relate to the amount of "information" in the correlation matrix (as reflected in the determinant of the matrix). The chi-square value, in conjunction with its degrees of freedom, indicates the probability of error in rejecting the null hypothesis of no deviation from an identity matrix. As with all chi-square statistics, the higher the chi-square value (with a given number of degrees of freedom) the lower the probability of error in rejecting the null hypothesis, and the more confident the investigator can be that his correlation matrix is not an identity matrix.

While it is frequently assumed that large numbers of individuals in relation to the number of variables will yield a factor analysis that is meaningful, consideration of Bartlett's test suggests that this may not be the case, since even large numbers of individuals can yield identity matrices. Hence, any investigator using factor analysis as part of his research design first should apply Bartlett's test to his correlation matrix and proceed only if the results permit him to reject the null hypothesis at an acceptable level of statistical significance. In this way, counseling research will not fall into the trap of interpreting and using factor-analytic results based on essentially meaningless data.

CHOICE OF A METHOD FOR FACTOR EXTRACTION

With the development of many new methods of factor analysis within the last decade, the researcher must be able to choose meaningfully among the alternatives. While most choices of methods were, in the past, based primarily on computational ease (the principal reason for the use of the "centroid" method of factor analysis), in most cases this basis for choice is no longer defensible since computer programs exist for virtually all the new methods of factor analysis.

Choice of factor-analytic method should be made on the basis of the objectives of the study and the hypotheses being investigated. If the investigator is concerned with studying the factorial composition of the total variance of each of a number of variables, the method of choice is principal components analysis (with unities in the diagonal). If the researcher is unwilling to assume perfect reliability in all his measures—a frequent occurrence in psychological research—the method of principal factors is appropriate. The latter method basically is the principal components solution, but it uses a reduced correlation matrix with an estimate of communality (often the squared multiple correlation) in the diagonal.

If the decision is to analyze only the common variance of a set of variables, however, the researcher must further examine his assumptions to determine the appropriate solution for his factor-analytic problem. Jones (1964) presents a convenient way of helping the investigator determine the appropriate method for a specific problem. Two of the common assumptions frequently made in factor analysis concern the characteristics of either "subjects" or "variables" as populations or samples. The investigator may wish to assume that his group of subjects is a sample from some defined population and that his variables represent a population of variables. In this case, the purpose for doing the factor analysis would be to develop a set of factorially pure variables which can be generalized to a population of subjects, with some assurance that the factors measured in the sample will also be similarly measured in the population of subjects. In other words, the researcher will be doing a factor analysis in order to "measure" the factored variables on samples of subjects, from the same population of subjects, by means of factor scores.

Canonical Factor Analysis

When subjects are a sample and variables are assumed to be a population, Rao's canonical factor analysis (Rao, 1955) is an appropriate method. This method requires the investigator to specify, in advance, the number of factors expected from the solution. Given the number of factors and the number of individuals on whom the solution is being obtained, canonical factor analysis is one of the class of "maximum likelihood" solutions in that the resulting factor solution is the "best estimate" of the given number of factors for a sample of the size used. The method is an iterative procedure which converges on observed communalities until they stabilize. In canonical factor analysis the correlation matrix is rescaled so that variables with high communalities receive more "weight" in the solution than those with low communalities.

The outcome of a canonical factor analysis solution is a set of factor loadings which maximize the canonical correlations between the original variables and the common parts of those variables as reflected in the scores on the common factors. In other words, this method enables the investigator to develop factor scores which correlate as highly as possible with the original variables, and thus permit maximal "prediction" of the original variables from the factor measurements. This, then, permits the researcher to generalize the factor scoring weights to the larger population of individuals with some confidence that the factor scores will be representative of the original variables. Canonical factor analysis is, therefore, an appropriate method to be used when the purpose of factor analysis is to derive factor measurements for use in describing individual differences in the factored variables.

Alpha Factor Analysis

If the purpose of the factor analysis is to generalize from a subset of variables to a population of variables, Kaiser's alpha factor analysis (Kaiser & Caffrey, 1965) is indicated. Alpha factor analysis assumes that subjects represent a population (versus a sample) and that the variables are a sample from a population of variables. The method yields a solution which maximizes the generalizability of the obtained factors to the population of variables from which the variables in the study were obtained. This method, then, is most appropriate for the factor-analytic problem where the investigator is concerned with drawing general conclusions about the structure of a "domain"—for example, vocational interests, normal "personality," values—from measures of a sample of variables which are assured to be representative of that domain.

Since alpha factor analysis assumes that subjects represent a "population," results of this method are most generalizable for large numbers of subjects. Furthermore, the variables to be included in the analysis should be carefully defined, via appropriate theory, to be representative of the domain under investigation. Only under these two conditions can the alpha factor analysis solution yield the generalizability for which it was designed.

Principal Factors

This method is differentiated from the principal components solution in terms of its use of an estimate of communality of the variables in the diagonal. It is closely related to image covariance analysis which rescales the original correlation matrix into an "image" of the original matrix which can then be submitted to a principal components solution. Image covariance analysis (Guttman, 1953) and principal factors yield similar results if only those variables with positive eigenvalues are used in the principal factors solution (Jones, 1964).

Image covariance analysis and principal factors analysis assume that both subjects and variables are populations. The results, therefore, permit no generalizability to either other individuals or other variables in a domain. The method yields purely descriptive factor analyses with the results applicable only to the subjects and instruments involved in the particular study. While the investigator need not do the careful sampling of either subjects or variables required by the two previous methods, results of image and principal factors analyses must be interpreted with extreme caution due to the possible influence of sample-specific sources of covariation. Results of these types of factor

analysis require replication before generalizations can be made to other groups of individuals. The methods are most appropriately used for large numbers of subjects with large numbers of variables, or with variables which implicitly define a population (e.g., all scales scored on a specified instrument).

Other Factor-Analytic Solutions

Some investigators might desire a solution which treats both subjects and variables as samples from defined populations. Such a factor-analytic solution would permit maximum generalizability of the factors obtained to the population or domain of variables, in addition to simultaneous generalizability of the factor scores to the population of subjects. Unfortunately, however, because of the complexities involved in the mathematical solution for all these simultaneous parameters, no solution has yet been proposed which permits this degree of generalizability.

On occasion, the counseling psychologist is concerned with studying the factors common in two multivariable psychometric instruments. Such analysis permits the user of these instruments to understand the common aspect of the two instruments and hence better utilize them in client evaluation. However, factor analysis of this sort presents a major problem.

Method variance can play an important part in determining the intercorrelations of variables in specific instruments. As indicated above, factor analysis of the Edwards Personal Preference Schedule yields factors characteristic of ipsative measures. Factor analysis of the Minnesota Multiphasic Personality Inventory yields factors which are somewhat artifactually overdetermined by the common items scored in its subscales. Such method variance, in a combined factor analysis of the two instruments, tends to yield factors which reflect primarily the method variance of the two instruments, thereby concealing the factors common to the two instruments (Siess & Jackson, 1970).

Jackson (1969) has presented a method for eliminating method variance in this type of factor analysis. In his multimethod factor analysis, Jackson eliminates method variance simply by setting the intrainstrument correlation submatrix equal to an identity matrix. Thus, for each of the instruments in the factor analysis, the intercorrelations in the total matrix which represent correlations of scales in that instrument are set at zero. Factor analysis then proceeds using only the cross-correlations of the instruments, which are the correlations of the scales on one instrument with the scales on the other.

In an illustration of multimethod factor analysis, Siess and Jackson (1970) showed that this method, as expected, uncovered common factors between instruments which might otherwise not have appeared in the application of regular factor-analysis techniques due to method variance. Such results only can serve to emphasize the necessity, for the counseling researcher, of choosing the method of factor analysis appropriate to the research question, in terms of the hypotheses being investigated and the assumptions the researcher is willing to make.

An article will appear in a forthcoming issue on communalities, number of factors, rotation, and factor scoring.

REFERENCES

Armstrong, J. S., & Soelberg, P. "On the Interpretation of Factor Analysis." *Psychological Bulletin*, 1968, 70, 361–364.

Atkinson, J., & Lunneborg, C. E. "Comparison of Oblique and Orthogonal Simple Structure Solutions for Personality and Interest Factors." *Multivariate Behavioral Research*, 1968, 3, 21–35.

Barry, J. R., Dunteman, G. H., & Webb, M. W. "Personality and Motivation in Rehabilitation." *Journal of Counseling Psychology*, 1968, 15, 237–244.

Bartlett, M. W. "Tests of Significance in Factor Analysis." *British Journal of Psychology*, 1950, 3, 77–85.

Baruch, R., Segal, S., & Handrick, F. A. "Constructs of Career and Family: A Statistical Analysis of Thematic Material." *Journal of Counseling Psychology*, 1968, 15, 308–316.

Cattell, R. B. "The Three Basic Factor-analytic Designs—Their Interrelations and Derivatives." *Psychological Bulletin*, 1952, 49, 499–520.

Cope, C. S. "Linguistic Structure and Personality Development." *Journal of Counseling Psychology Monograph*, 1969, 16, (4, Pt. 2).

Elton, C. F., & Rose, H. A. "The Face of Change." *Journal of Counseling Psychology*, 1968, 15, 372–375.

Greenberg, B. S., Kagan, N., & Bowes, J. "Dimensions of Empathic Judgment of Clients by Counselors." *Journal of Counseling Psychology*, 1969, 16, 303–308.

Guilford, J. P. "When Not to Factor Analyze." *Psychological Bulletin*, 1952, 49, 26–37.

Guilford, J. P. *Fundamental Statistics in Psychology and Education.* New York: McGraw-Hill, 1965.

Guttman, L. "Image Theory for the Structure of Quantitative Variates." *Psychometrika*, 1953, 18, 277–296.

Haase, R. F., & Miller, C. D. "Comparison of Factor-analytic Studies of the Counseling Evaluation Inventory." *Journal of Counseling Psychology*, 1968, 15, 363–367.

Harris, C. W. "On Factors and Factor Scores." *Psychometrika*, 1967, 32, 363–379.

Jackson, D. N. "Multimethod Factor Analysis in the Evaluation of Convergent and

Discriminant Validity." *Psychological Bulletin*, 1969, 72, 30–49.

Jones, K. J. *The Multivariate Statistical Analyzer.* Cambridge, Mass. Harvard Coop., 1964.

Kaiser, H. J., & Caffrey, J. "Alpha Factor Analysis." *Psychometrika*, 1965, 30, 1–14.

Ogston, D. G., Altmann, H. A., & Conklin, R. D. "Problems Appropriate for Discussion in University Counseling Centers." *Journal of Counseling Psychology*, 1969, 16, 361–364.

Rao, C. R. "Estimation and Tests of Significance in Factor Analysis." *Psychometrika*, 1955, 20, 93–111.

Siess, T. F., & Jackson, D. N. "Vocational Interests and Personality: An Empirical Integration." *Journal of Counseling Psychology*, 1970, 17, 27–35.

Smith, L. H. *Some Properties of Ipsative, Normative and Forced Choice Normative Measures.* Philadelphia, Pa.: The Franklin Institute Research Laboratories, 1967.

Stinson, R. C. "Factor Analytic Approach to the Structured Differentiation of Description." *Journal of Counseling Psychology*, 1968, 15, 301–307.

Tobias, S., & Carlson, J. E. "Brief Report: Bartlett's Test of Sphericity and Chance Findings in Factor Analysis." *Multivariate Behavioral Research*, 1969, 4, 375–377.

VanAtta, R. E. "Concepts Employed by Accurate and Inaccurate Clinicians." *Journal of Counseling Psychology*, 1968, 15, 338–345.

Walker, B. S., & Little, D. E. "Factor Analysis of the Barrett-Lennard Relationship Inventory." *Journal of Counseling Psychology*, 1969, 16, 516–521.

Zimmer, J. N., & Anderson, S. "Dimensions of Positive Regard and Empathy." *Journal of Counseling Psychology*, 1968, 15, 417–426.

(Received May 13, 1970)

Further Considerations in Applications of Factor Analysis[1]

David J. Weiss[2]

Choice of a method for factor extraction (Weiss, 1970) is only the first of a series of decisions to be made by the psychologist who plans to factor analyze an intercorrelation matrix. Subsequent decisions include (*a*) the portion of variance to be analyzed, (*b*) the number of factors to extract and retain, (*c*) whether rotation of the factor matrix is necessary, (*d*) how to rotate if rotation is indicated, and (*e*) how to compute factor scores if it is necessary to measure individual differences in the factored variables. The problem also frequently arises as to what data and information are necessary in reporting the results of a factor analysis so that others may properly understand and replicate the procedures followed in a given application of factor analysis.

TOTAL VERSUS COMMON VARIANCE

The general factor-analysis model assumes that the total variance of a variable is composed of three components: common variance, unique variance, and error variance. For each variable included in the factor analysis of a correlation matrix, the mix of these three components may be different, but the sum of the components is the same—1.0. The model further assumes that error variance is "unreliable" variance, or variance which is sample-specific for a given variable measured on a given group of subjects at a given point in time. Common variance and unique variance, on the other hand, are assumed to represent reliable variance, or variance likely to be stable from sample to sample.

Total Variance

Principal components analysis (a principal axis solution of a correlation matrix with 1.0 in the diagonal) is the only method of factor analysis which analyzes the total variance of each variable. Since the variables submitted to principal components analysis sometimes have low reliabilities (and therefore low common variance), analyses of these kinds of variables may lead to principal components matrices in which some of the factors represent correlated error variance. These factors would be unlikely to replicate in another sample of individuals measured on the same variables and, therefore, might lead the

[1] Reproduced by permission of the *Journal of Counseling Psychology* 1971, *18*, 85–92

[2] While the author takes complete responsibility for the contents of this paper, thanks are due to Robert M. Thorndike for his careful review and many helpful comments.

researcher to draw unwarranted conclusions about the structure of his variables. Because of the possibility of the appearance of such spurious factors, applications of unreplicated principal components analysis are rarely justified in psychological research.

Common Variance

With the exclusion of the method of principal components, most factor-analytic methods are concerned only with common variance, which is that portion of the reliable variance of a variable which correlates with other variables in the matrix. Because common variance is a subset of reliable variance, factor analysis of common variance should lead to the identification of factors most likely to be stable from one sample to another.

In factor analyzing only common variance, the investigator puts an estimate of common variance in the principal diagonal of the correlation matrix to be factor analyzed. Several solutions have been proposed for this problem, including the use of reliability estimates, squared multiple correlations, and the highest correlation of a variable with one of the other variables in the matrix.

Reliability coefficients are the most liberal of the three estimates of common variance since the reliability of a variable may include unique variance as well as common variance. The use of reliability coefficients as estimates of communality is complicated by the variability in results obtained by application of the different formulas available for the computation of internal consistency reliability coefficients, as well as the conceptual and practical differences obtained from using internal consistency, parallel forms, and stability estimates of reliability. Because of these problems, reliability estimates should rarely be used as estimates of common variance.

The highest correlation of a variable with the other variables in the matrix is a moderately conservative estimate of the common variance of a variable. Use of this estimate of common variance is based on the assumption that a variable cannot correlate with another variable higher than its reliability. Hence, the highest correlation estimate is a simple way to estimate the minimum reliability of a variable. While it avoids some of the problems in the choice of reliability coefficients, this method of estimating communalities generally has been replaced by the use of squared multiple correlations.

The squared multiple correlation of a variable with all other variables in the matrix is the most conservative and most used of the communality estimates. Squared multiple correlations are used in the majority of factor-analytic solutions, although sometimes as only an initial estimator. The squared multiple correlation is referred to as the lower-bound estimate of common variance (Guttman, 1956), since it gives directly the proportion of variance of each variable that is in common with all other variables in the matrix. Because use of the squared multiple correlation as an initial communality estimate excludes most unique and error variance (in comparison with other communality estimates) it should be used in the majority of factor-analytic studies designed to investigate the structure of common variance.

Occasionally, however, use of the squared multiple correlation is inappropriate as an estimate of communality. A recent study (Navran & Posthuma, 1970) reports a principal factors analysis of the Strong Vocational Interest Blank (SVIB). While an estimate of the common variance of each variable was appropriate for use as the diagonal of the matrix to be factor analyzed in this study, use of the squared multiple correlation may actually represent an overestimate of the actual communalities in this case. This would result from the fact that most scales on the SVIB are scored on a large number of common items. As a result, squared multiple correlations predicting scale scores on one scale from those of all other scales would yield values of the squared multiple correlation that were artificially inflated by the scoring procedure. In the extreme case of purely ipsative data (the logical extreme of the artificially correlated scores of the SVIB) the squared multiple correlation of any one scale as predicted from all other scales is 1.0. In both these cases, factor analyses with squared multiple correlations in the diagonal may lead the unwary researcher to analyze artificial common variance resulting in the identification of common factors derived from spurious communality estimates. Factor analysis of instruments possessing the artificially correlated characteristics of the SVIB might better proceed with reliability estimates as the diagonal elements of the reduced correlation matrix to minimize the possible appearance of artificial common factors.

NUMBER OF FACTORS

Perhaps the most controversial problem faced by the user of factor analysis is that of the number of factors to extract or retain. The problem is basically one of defining a residual or error factor, a factor which has no practical, psychological, or statistical significance. Failure to identify a residual factor results in extracting too many factors, one or more of which are essentially error factors that are meaningless or would be unlikely to replicate in other analyses of the same variables. Extracting too few factors, the result of identifying nonresidual factors as residuals, leads to misidentification of the true factor structure with additional important factors likely to appear in subsequent factor analyses of the same variables.

A variety of solutions have been proposed to the "number of factors" problem. Some solutions are appropriate only for specified methods of extraction; others may be used with more than one model. Most of the common methods, however, are based to some extent on the value of the eigenvalue of

a factor. In an unrotated principal axis analysis, the eigenvalue of a factor corresponds to the sum of its squared loadings. Eigenvalues are also sometimes equated with the roots of a matrix, there being one root to correspond to each eigenvalue. A more general term for the sum of the squared factor loadings is the factor contribution. This term reflects the idea of the amount of information in the matrix attributable to a given factor, and has the added advantage of being applicable to both unrotated and rotated solutions, as well as the occasional solutions appearing in the literature which are not based on the principal axis model.

Kaiser Criterion

The Kaiser criterion is the most widely known decision rule for the number of factors problem. The Kaiser criterion specifies that only factors with factor contributions (eigenvalues) of 1.0 or greater should be retained in a factor analysis. According to Kaiser (1960), such factors have positive alpha reliabilities and hence are generalizable factors under the assumptions of Alpha Factor Analysis. When the Kaiser criterion is applied within other factor-analytic models, however, it underestimates the number of "real" factors in the matrix. This is especially true when the analysis is done on a reduced correlation matrix, such as factor analyses of matrices with squared multiple correlations as the diagonal elements (Humphreys & Ilgen, 1969). Since underfactoring is generally considered to be a more serious error than overfactoring, use of the Kaiser criterion should be confined to Kaiser's Alpha Factor Analysis.

Statistical Tests

Statistical tests for residual factors are used primarily in conjunction with the maximum likelihood models of factor analysis, since these methods assume a population of variables measured on a sample of subjects. In general, the statistical tests test the significance of each factor contribution to determine if it deviates significantly from the factor contribution expected under a specified random error model. Bartlett's chi-square test for the significance of a correlation matrix (Bartlett, 1950) can be used (with minor modifications of the basic formula for a zero-order correlation matrix) to test each successive residual matrix until the investigator is unable to reject the hypothesis of no significant deviation from an identity matrix. This test, however, is limited to principal components analysis of total variance. Lawley (1940), Rao (1955), and others have developed statistical tests for the significance of factors which are applicable to the analysis of reduced correlation matrices; these tests are designed for use on correlation matrices derived from large samples of individuals. Because these statistical tests for the significance of factors have been developed within the framework of the statistical approaches to factor analysis, their applications should be confined to the situation in which a given factor-analysis problem meets those assumptions.

Cattell's Scree Test

Cattell (1966) proposes that error factors are those which have equal and low factor contributions. He appears to reason that, as a matrix becomes residual, succeeding factors extracted from that matrix will represent only error factors, and that the contributions of these factors will represent only minor and random fluctuations from some constant value. Accordingly, Cattell suggests that an appropriate procedure for determining the number of factors to retain in a factor analysis may result from an inspection of the factor contributions of all factors extracted in the analysis. Cattell recommends that the investigator make a two-dimensional plot with factors numbered in order of extraction on the horizontal axis and size of factor contribution on the vertical

axis. The investigator plots the factor contributions for each factor and connects the points with a curve. Since principal axis solutions always yield factors in decreasing order of contribution, the curve will decrease rapidly at first, and then level off. According to Cattell, eventually the curve will define a scree, or a point at which it becomes horizontal, or nearly so. To determine the number of factors, the researcher finds the break in the curve at the point of leveling off. All factors to the left of this point are real factors; those to the right are error or residual factors.

While one Monte Carlo study supports the scree test as an appropriate criterion for the number of factors (Linn, 1968), the method has obvious problems which limit its applicability in some situations. First, it may be difficult for different investigators to agree on when a scree has appeared. Visual methods of inspecting curves are likely to yield different results for different people, particularly when some plots of factor contributions do not have a sharp break. Secondly, some factor contributions appear to have several screes. The problem of which scree is the correct one has yet to be resolved. While mathematical methods of curve analysis may indicate the point at which a curve straightens out, such analytic methods have not yet been demonstrated to be satisfactorily applicable to the number of factors problem. In general, while the scree test may be applicable to some factor-analytic results, it should be used in combination with other information to assure an appropriate resolution.

Other Decision Rules

Some factor analysts define a factor as residual if its factor contribution accounts for only a small percentage of total variance extracted. Such decision rules usually are based on such definitions as a factor which accounts for 10%, 5% or 1% of either common or total variance. Because these rules are not firmly grounded in either empirical results or sound theoretical reasoning, they should not be used without other supporting evidence.

Cliff and Hamburger (1967) report studies of the statistical significance of factor loadings by means of Monte Carlo experiments. Their results indicate that the standard error of a factor loading is about $1/\sqrt{N}$, similar to the standard error of a correlation coefficient. This suggests that a factor analyst may declare a factor to be residual if it has no significant loadings (loadings greater than 2 or 2½ times their standard error). In common factor analysis a factor may be essentially residual (or, practically, a unique factor) if it has only one significant factor loading. This approach, however, has the disadvantage of all tests of significance, namely that as the sample size (N) gets very large, very small factor loadings will become statistically significant. As a result, few residual factors will be identified in this way unless some arbitrary criterion of practical significance is also taken into account, such as a minimum specified portion of variance of the factor accounted for by a variable (as reflected in the squared factor loading).

An interesting approach to the number of factors problem was proposed recently by Humphreys and Ilgen (1969). These writers suggest that at the same time a factor analyst submits real data to factor analysis, he do a parallel factor analysis with the same method, on a sample of individuals and variables of the same size, using random data as the basis for the correlation matrix. The factor analysis of the random data will yield a set of factor contributions of a given size, with only minor fluctuations around a central tendency value. Comparison of the factor contributions from the real data analysis with the factor contributions from the random data analysis can assist the investigator in determining which factors in the real data do not contribute more than those derived from factor analysis of random data. These factors can then be rejected as residual. While this approach requires two factor analyses rather than only the factor analysis of the real data matrix, it has substantial logical appeal and avoids many of the problems of the other methods. At the same time it takes into account both number of individuals and number of variables, both of which can affect the size of factor contributions.

Harris (1967), while not addressing himself directly to the number of factors problem, proposes that a factor be considered a real factor if it appears as a result of more than one type of solution. According to Harris, the investigator should submit the same data matrix to several methods of factor analysis and retain only those factors that appear in at least more than one method. Such an approach, however, raises the problem of matching factors from various studies, in itself a complex problem.

Summary

While some methods of factor analysis imply specific solutions to the number of factors problem (i.e., the Kaiser criterion for Alpha Factor Analysis and statistical tests in the maximum likelihood methods) the usual descriptive methods of factor analysis lack a clear answer to the problem. The most promising approach seems to be the parallel analysis method of Humphreys and Ilgen, since it requires the fewest arbitrary decisions on the part of the investigator and takes into account more of the parameters of a given solution.

All these solutions, however, have one characteristic in common—the decision about the number of factors to retain is made *prior* to rotation. Since the rotation process redistributes the factor contributions among the factors, it would seem appropriate to decide on the number of factors *after* rotation (Thorndike, 1970). On occasion, a factor with a low factor contribution prior to rotation may "pick up" the variance of other factors; what was apparently a residual factor prior to rotation becomes a factor with meaningful contribution. Thus, it is suggested that the specification of a factor as residual be made following rotation using decision rules appropriate to the investigator's purpose and hypotheses.

ROTATION OF FACTOR MATRICES

Why Rotate?

Almost all methods of factor extraction now use the basic principal axis solution to obtain the unrotated factor matrix. Principal axes solutions, however, have several undesirable characteristics in terms of psychological interpretability. First, the principal axis method of factoring is designed to remove as much variance as possible with each successive factor. In order to do this, the technique simultaneously extracts general factors which have high loadings on all variables. Second, the principal axis factors, following the first factor, tend to be both general and bi-polar factors, with high loadings for most variables of both positive and negative sign. Because of these mathematical characteristics of the unrotated solution, the factors are not clearly interpretable or psychologically meaningful.

Because the mathematical solution is a maximization procedure, results of unrotated factor analyses tend to be somewhat unstable in replication. A recent study by Rosenblatt (1969) shows that unrotated factor matrices are less stable across samples from the same population than are rotated matrices. By rotating his matrix, then, the analyst obtains a solution less dependent upon a specific maximization procedure and more likely to be representative of the structure in other samples from the same population.

In addition, if factor analysis has been done to verify a hypothesis of the structure of a set of variables or to locate variables with respect to one or more reference variables, specific methods of rotation are necessary to accomplish these goals.

Simple Structure

The vast majority of rotational methods are designed to approach Thurstone's concept of simple structure. Thurstone's simple structure concept is based on the idea of parsimony in that it specifies a set of criteria for the parsimonious simultaneous description of both the factors and variables in a factor matrix. According to Thurstone (1947, ch. 14), a factor matrix approaches simple structure when each factor is loaded highly by only a few variables (the rest loading essentially zero) and each variable loads highly on only one factor. When these conditions are achieved (in addition to a few corollary conditions) a most parsimonious hypothesis can be used to explain a factor or to describe the structure of a variable.

The controversy over orthogonal versus oblique rotations results from attempts to better approximate the ideal of simple structure. In general, oblique rotational solutions, in which factors are permitted to be correlated with each other, appear to be better representations of simple structure than the orthogonal solutions. However, in using oblique solutions the researcher pays the price of having to generate a more complex hypothesis concerning the nature of his factors, since such hypotheses must take into account both the common variance among variables loading high on a factor, and the variance common among factors. Because of this complexity of explanation, orthogonal solutions appear to be more relevant for the present status of hypothesis construction and verification in counseling psychology research.

Among the orthogonal rotations, Varimax and Quartimax are the two methods most frequently used to approximate simple structure. Since they operationalize the simple structure concept by different mathematical formulas, they have differing applications in specific factor-analysis problems.

The Varimax solution (Kaiser, 1958)

finds the rotational position that simplifies the description of each factor by maximizing the variance of its factor loadings. It accomplishes this by finding the solution that has the most divergent factor loadings for each factor, as reflected in factor loadings that are nearest the extremes of 1.0 and 0.0. As a result, Varimax should be used if the objective of the factor analysis is to understand the nature of the factors as opposed to understanding the variance composition of the variables.

Quartimax (Harman, 1967, P. 298), on the other hand, is designed to simplify the description of variables. While Varimax operates on the columns of the factor matrix, Quartimax operates on the rows by finding the solution that has the most divergent factor loadings for each variable. The result is a set of loadings for each variable that are nearest the extremes of 1.0 and 0.0. Quartimax rotation should be used where the objective is to identify the variance composition of variables or to classify variables in terms of the factor which is most representative of each variable.

Because the Quartimax solution sometimes gives general factors whereas Varimax is less likely to yield general factors, Varimax seems to be a better approximation to simple structure. The problem is further complicated by the fact that there is no clear way of determining whether simple structure has been achieved or how closely it has been approximated, although some promising steps in this direction have been taken by Thorndike (1970).

Other Rotational Objectives

Factor matrices may be rotated to objectives other than simple structure. In some cases the investigator may wish to locate his variables with reference to some specific variable or variables which can be considered a criterion. In this case, Eysenck's (1950) method of criterion rotation is appropriate, in which one of the orthogonally rotated axes is run through the criterion variable or variables. The researcher may wish to rotate his matrix to be maximally similar to a target matrix. For this purpose, a variety of Procrustes solutions have arisen, typified by the oblique Procrustes solution of Browne (1967) and the orthogonal solution of Schoneman (1968). Comrey (1967) has proposed a rotational method which yields a cluster-like solution in that the resulting rotated factors are defined by variables which are related to each other and not to the other variables in the matrix. The choice of the specific rotational solution, of course, depends on the purpose of the factor analysis and the objectives the researcher desires to achieve by rotation.

FACTOR SCORES

In order to measure an individual's status on a factor by means of linear combinations of his scores on the variables included in the factor analysis the researcher must compute factor scores. The first step in computing factor scores is to transform all raw scores to Z scores or some form of standard scores so that scores on different variables may be added together.

The major decision in computing factor scores is how to weight the variables in computing the linear combination comprising the factor score. Three approaches to the problem are commonly used. The simplest approach is simply to unit weight all salient variables and zero weight all others. The major problem with this method, of course, is the definition of salient. If an arbitrary minimum cutoff value is used (e.g., .30) all variables above that value receive equal weight regardless of whether their loadings are as different as .31 or .97. The arbitrariness of the minimum cutoff is also a serious fault of this method since different investigators may make different decisions.

A second method of factor scoring is to weight each variable by the magnitude of the factor loading. In this method, each variable is scored on every factor in deriving the weighted linear composite but the weights applied to an individual's standardized score vary with each factor's loadings. While this method avoids the arbitrary weighting problem of the unit weighting method it is computationally somewhat more complex.

The third type of factor scoring method, which can only be done with computers, also differentially weights all variables on each factor. This class of methods includes several regression solutions which are the "best" approximations to the true factor scores. In these methods, the weights derived to be multiplied by the standard scores on the original variables are the least-squares partial regression weights for predicting the "true" factor scores from the observed variable scores.

Harman (1967, ch. 16) presents computing procedures for various types of factor scores. However, to choose meaningfully among the alternatives the researcher should be aware of other characteristics of the three types of factor scoring approaches. While little research has been done on the characteristics of the three types of solutions, the research evidence available (Horn, 1965; Weiss, Dawis, England, & Lofquist, 1966) supports the following conclusions: While unit weighted factor scoring procedures yield scores of highest internal consistency reliability (and, therefore, greater interindividual discrimination) they do so at the expense of the independence of factor scores. Regression solutions yield factor scores most nearly uncorrelated with each other, but they are less reliable (internally consistent) than the unit weighted factor scores. Factor scores derived from factor loading weights fall between the other two methods in terms of both reliability and independence.

If the researcher requires factor scores that are most nearly uncorrelated with factor scores of other factors, the regression solutions are most appropriate. As Harris (1967)

indicates, factor scores derived from a complete regression solution following canonical factor analysis will be uncorrelated. The low correlation, however, is obtained at the expense of reliability. On the other hand, highly reliable factor scores obtained from unit weighting may be desirable in a given study if the independence of the factor scores is not an important consideration.

REPORTING A FACTOR ANALYSIS

Since the decisions made in doing a factor analysis may importantly affect the obtained results, it is important that reports of factor-analytic investigations carefully detail the decisions made at each step. In addition, because reanalysis of a correlation matrix or rerotation of a factor matrix by different methods of factor analysis may yield across-methods replication, thereby implying some generality for the results (Harris, 1967), certain basic matrices should be made available to other researchers.

In reporting a factor analysis a paper should include the following items of information: (a) size, composition, and method of selection of both variables and subjects, (b) method of correlation used to generate the matrix, (c) value of Bartlett's chi-square (or other) test for the significance of the correlation matrix, (d) specification of the communality estimate, (e) method of extraction (e.g., principal axis, centroid) and indication of whether the matrix has been rescaled by a specific procedure (e.g., alpha, canonical), (f) an explanation of the criterion for retaining factors and an indication of whether the decision was prior to or following rotation, (g) specific method of rotation, and (h) if factor scores are computed, the method of computation.

So that other researchers may reanalyze an investigator's data, the intercorrelation matrix should be available in most cases through supplementary documentation services. If an estimate of the communality was used in the solution, that value should appear in the diagonal of the correlation matrix. In general, there is no necessity to publish the unrotated factor matrix unless the decision to retain factors was based on that matrix; in that case, the unrotated matrix should also be available by supplementary documentation.

Unless the final rotated factor matrix is too large for direct publication in the article, it should be included as primary data. Rotated matrices should be bordered by the variable communalities and by the factor contributions. In addition, it is helpful to compute both proportion of common variance and proportion of total variance for each rotated factor. If factor scores are computed by a solution other than unit weights or factor loading weights, it is necessary for those who wish to apply factor measurements to other subjects that the factor scoring matrix be made available by supplementary documentation.

By complete, but concise and accurate, reporting of the decisions made in factor analyzing his data, the counseling investigator can assist others in understanding and utilizing his findings. In addition, complete reporting may stimulate cross-fertilization among counseling psychologists by permitting reanalysis of obtained results by other methods (sometimes yet to be developed), which may lead to new and valuable insights into previously reported data.

REFERENCES

Bartlett, M. W. "Tests of Significance in Factor Analysis." *British Journal of Psychology, Statistical Section,* 1950, *3,* 77–85.

Browne, M. W. "On Oblique Procrustes Solution." *Psychometrika,* 1967, *32,* 125–132.

Cattell, R. B. "The Screen Test for the Number of Factors." *Multivariate Behavioral Research,* 1966, *1,* 245–276.

Cliff, N., & Hamburger, C. D. "The Study of Sampling Errors in Factor Analysis by Means of Artificial Experiments." *Psychological Bulletin,* 1967, *68,* 430–445.

Comrey, A. L. "Tandem Criteria for Analytic Rotation in Factor Analysis." *Psychometrika,* 1967, *32,* 143–154.

Eysenck, H. J. "Criterion Analysis—An Application of the Hypothetico-Deductive Method to Factor Analysis." *Psychological Review,* 1950, 57, 38–53.

Guttman, L. " 'Best Possible' Systematic Estimates of Communalities." *Psychometrika,* 1956, *21,* 273–285.

Harman, H. H. *Modern Factor Analysis* (2nd ed.) Chicago: University of Chicago Press, 1967.

Harris, C. W. "On Factors and Factor Scores." *Psychometrika,* 1967, *32,* 363–379.

Horn, J. L. "An Empirical Comparison of Methods for Computing Factor Scores." *Educational and Psychological Measurement,* 1965, 25, 313–322.

Humphreys, L. G., & Ilgen, D. R. "Note on a Criterion for the Number of Common Factors." *Educational and Psychological Measurement,* 1969, 29, 571–578.

Kaiser, H. F. "The Varimax Criterion for Analytic Rotation in Factor Analysis." *Psychometrika,* 1958, *23,* 187–200.

Kaiser, H. F. "The Application of Electronic Computers to Factor Analysis." *Educational and Psychological Measurement,* 1960, 20, 141–151.

Lawley, D. N. "The Estimation of Factor Loadings by the Method of Maximum Likelihood." *Proceedings of the Royal Society of Edinburgh,* 1940, 60, 64–82.

Linn, R. L. "A Monte Carlo Approach to the Number of Factors Problem." *Psychometrika,* 1968, *33,* 37–71.

Navran, L., & Posthuma, A. B. "A Factor

Analysis of the Strong Vocational Interest Blank for Men Using the Method of Principal Factors." *Journal of Counseling Psychology,* 1970, *17,* 216–223.

Rao, C. R. "Estimation and Tests of Statistical Significance in Factor Analysis." *Psychometrika,* 1955, *20,* 93–111.

Rosenblatt, S. M. "Empirical Study of the Sampling Error of Principal Components and Varimax Rotation Factor Loadings." *Proceedings of the 77th Annual Convention of the American Psychological Association,* 1969, *4,* 115–116.

Schoneman, P. H. "On Two-sided Orthogonal Procrustes Problems." *Psychometrika,* 1968, *33,* 19–33.

Thorndike, R. M. "Method of Extraction, Type of Data and Accuracy of Solutions in Factor Analysis." Unpublished doctoral dissertation, University of Minnesota, 1970.

Thurnstone, L. L. *Multiple factor analysis.* Chicago: University of Chicago Press, 1947.

Weiss, D. J. "Factor Analysis and Counseling Research." *Journal of Counseling Psychology,* 1970, *17,* 477–485.

Weiss, D. J., Dawis, R. V., Lofquist, L. H., & England, G. W. "Instrumentation for the Theory of Work Adjustment." *Minnesota Studies in Vocational Rehabilitation,* 1966, *21.*

(Received July 9, 1970)

Analysis of Variance and Multiple Regression: Application Issues for Organizational Research

Stuart A. Youngblood

The flexibility of multiple regression as a general data-analytic system was introduced to psychologists and other organizational researchers by Cohen's (1968) classic *Psychological Bulletin* article. Since that time a number of applied regression texts have incorporated these basic ideas in their discussion of analysis of variance (ANOVA) and multiple regression (MR), notably Cohen and Cohen (1975), Kerlinger and Pedhazur (1973), and Neter and Wasserman (1974). The impact of these writings, however, is not fully appreciated by students of organizational research. One reason may be that analysis of variance and its use was developed primarily by those engaged in experimental research rather than in correlational field studies which are frequently used by organizational researchers (Rucci & Tweney, 1980). Although organizational research is interdisciplinary in many respects, paradoxically the analytic tools are often peculiar to specific disciplines. Thus, students of psychology are taught experimental design and analysis of variance, while students of business administration are taught correlation and regression analysis.

The purpose of this paper is to provide a better understanding and perspective on the use of multiple regression as a general data-analytic strategy and to highlight several an-

alytic issues that are common to the interdisciplinary study of organizations. A major theme of this paper is that researchers need to be aware of the statistical models they use to analyze their data and the corresponding estimation and hypothesis testing issues associated with a given model. By examining the similarity of ANOVA and MR approaches to data analysis, these issues can be highlighted. To accomplish this, we begin with a hypothetical organizational research problem and then examine this problem in four ways: the ANOVA approach, the MR approach, the analysis of covariance approach, and the moderator approach. For the latter three approaches the general linear model will be used to illustrate analytical issues peculiar to each approach. Finally, several special issues common to ANOVA and MR approaches to organizational research are discussed.

A HYPOTHETICAL ORGANIZATIONAL PROBLEM

Suppose that an organizational researcher selects an organization in which to study the relationship between a generalized expectancy measure of role force (Mobley, Griffin, Hand, & Meglino, 1979) and turnover intention. The researcher devises a survey instrument to assess worker perceptions of the valence and instrumentality associated with outcomes in either the current role or an alternative role (external to the organization). In addition to the expectancy based measures, the survey assesses demographic information and turnover intention. A random sample of 120 company employees is selected and the survey is administered. Based on previous experience, the researcher learns that males and females experience different rates of turnover. Therefore, a design is used whereby turnover intention is the criterion and sex and relative role force are the independent variables of interest.

THE ANOVA APPROACH

This researcher elects to organize the data for an analysis of variance. Thus, the measures are presented as follows:

THE CRITERION: TURNOVER INTENTION

Factor A: Sex

- level 1   male
- level 2   female

Factor B: Relative Role Force

- level 1   alternative role force greater than company role force
- level 2   alternative and company role force are equal

- level 3   company role force greater than alternative role force

The design is a 2×3 factorial ANOVA whereby Factor A, sex, contains two levels and Factor B, relative role force, contains three levels. For Factor B the researcher has trichotomized the measure by comparing alternative and company role forces constructed from the survey based measures. The researcher is primarily interested in the relative strength of these two forces in relation to turnover intention. Because of theoretical considerations, the researcher has hypothesized that turnover intention will differ significantly between employees with a strong company role force relative to the alternative role force versus employees who exhibit a strong alternative role force relative to the company role force.

If the design were presented in tabular form, it would appear as a 2×3 cross-classification table as shown below.

The means for each cell are shown (M_{ij}) as well as the marginal means for the two levels of Factor A $(\bar{A}_1, \bar{A}_2,)$ and Factor B $(\bar{B}_1, \bar{B}_2, \bar{B}_3)$. The model that underlies this design can be stated as:

$$X_{IJK} = \mu + \alpha_I + \beta_J + \alpha\beta_{IJ} + e_{IJK,} \qquad (1)$$

where:

X_{IJK} = An observation on the criterion, turnover intention, for an individual (K) at a given level I of Factor A, sex and at a given level J of Factor B, relative role force

μ = An effect common to all observations

Factor B: Relative Role Force

	(−) Alternative Role	(0) Neutral	Company (+) Role	
Male	M_{11}	M_{12}	M_{13}	$\bar{A}_1$
Female	M_{21}	M_{22}	M_{23}	$\bar{A}_2$
	$\bar{B}_1$	$\bar{B}_2$	$\bar{B}_3$	

Factor A: Sex

α_I = An effect common to observations at level I of Factor A, I = 1,2

β_J = An effect common to all observations at level J of Factor B, J = 1,2,3

$\alpha\beta_{IJ}$ = Joint effect of Factor A and Factor B for an observation at level IJ.

e_{ijk} = The error or random sources of variation for observation K at level IJ, K = 1, 2 . . . 120.

Thus, each survey participant's observed turnover intention score is decomposed into four components: a mean common to all observations, an effect due to Factor A (being male or female), an effect due to Factor B (relative role force), and a nonadditive or joint effect due to a particular combination of a Factor A level with a Factor B level (for example, being male and having a relatively strong alternative role force).

The effects α_I and β_J are called main effects while $\alpha\beta_{IJ}$ is known as the interaction effect. Intuitively, main effects are estimated by the deviation of the row means (Factor A) or the column means (Factor B) from the grand mean of all the observations. If the design is balanced (that is, the cell sizes are equal), then the main effects (the deviation of row or column means around the grand mean) will sum to zero by definition. This is a scaling constraint associated with classical ANOVA. The greater the variation in either the row or column means, the greater the main effect of either Factor A or B, respectively. Similarly, the interaction effect is estimated by the deviation of a given cell mean (e.g., M_{11}) from its corresponding row and column effect (e.g., $\bar{A}_1$ and $\bar{B}_1$). The greater these deviations, the greater the interaction effect.

Given this design three hypotheses can be tested. First if Factor A does influence turnover intention, then the variance of the row means should be greater than zero. An alternative way of saying this in the null hypothesis form is

H_0: $\bar{A}_1 = \bar{A}_2 = M$, the grand or overall mean. Similarly, if Factor B influences turnover intention then the null hypothesis is

H_0: $\bar{B}_1 = \bar{B}_2 = \bar{B}_3 = M$, the grand mean, and for the interaction effect the null hypothesis is

H_0: $\alpha\beta_{11} = \alpha\beta_{12} = \alpha\beta_{13} = \alpha\beta_{21} = \alpha\beta_{22} = \alpha\beta_{23} = 0$

where $\alpha\beta_{ij} = M_{ij} - \bar{A}_i - \bar{B}_j + M$

The F tests used to test these hypotheses are constructed from special measures of variance called mean squares or, in other words, the average of squared measures. Thus, the variation in the main and interaction effects are compared to the variation of observations within cell as a way to estimate an F statistic. The F statistics for the main and interaction effect hypotheses would take the following form:

$$F_A = \frac{MS_A}{MS \text{ within cell}}$$

$$F_B = \frac{MS_B}{MS \text{ within cell}}$$

$$F_{AB} = \frac{MS_{AB}}{MS \text{ within cell}}$$

Although this has been an oversimplification of ANOVA (for details, see Winer, 1971), several additional comments are in order. Note that the model guiding the ANOVA approach (equation 1) decomposes an observation into main and interaction effects due to the two proposed factors sex and relative role force. The levels of each factor are usually determined by the researcher. If the entire range of levels of each factor is selected (e.g., assume that male and female levels comprehensively represent the factor sex) then the factor is said to be fixed. If only a subset of levels that make up the factor are used then the factor is said to be random. When this occurs the F tests are constructed differently because random variability has been introduced not only from random sampling but also because the levels of the factor have likewise been sampled. Intuitively, one can see that ANOVA results can be influenced by the researcher's decision as to what factors to include in the design as well as how many levels of each factor are to be represented in the design.

The researcher is also making inferences from the sample, randomly drawn for the ANOVA, to some population. In our example, the researcher is attempting to generalize the study findings to the focal organization from which the sample is drawn. Whether inferences can be accurately drawn to the entire organization is a function of the sampling plan used to collect the basic data as well as the design of the survey measures (see Fisher's paper in this volume for a discussion of generalizability issues). An important consideration, then, is whether the researcher planned this type of analysis *before* the data were collected and the model (equation 1) underlying the analysis was specified. Planning before the data collection could ensure, for example, that equal numbers of observations for each cell of the design would be obtained. Designs with equal cell sizes are said to be orthogonal; the factors that make up the design are independent of each other. When cell sizes are not equal, a number of complications arise, which will be discussed in more detail later.

Finally, the model expressed in equation 1 deserves an additional clarification. In the classical ANOVA designs as expressed in equation 1 the interaction term in the model is assumed to be nonsignificant (i.e., equal to 0), yet the term is included in the model for estimation purposes as a check on this assumption. As will be seen in the next section, the classical ANOVA approach to testing main and interaction effects partitions

the sums of squares due to the main effect(s) in the design. The test of the interaction term, however, is adjusted for all the main effects included in the design. This approach to partitioning "explained variance" differs somewhat from the approach used in multiple regression. The significance of the classical ANOVA design is that a model is estimated that includes an interaction term, but presumes that this term will be nonsignificant. In the absence of a significant interaction the main effects can be interpreted unambiguously. Where an interaction is present, further examination of the data is necessary, because the influence of one factor on the criterion will be a function of the levels of the other factor(s) in the design.

To see the identity of the classical ANOVA approach with the multiple regression or ordinary least squares approach, we can take the same two-factor turnover intention study that our organizational researcher began with and reconstruct it from a general linear model framework. The general linear model can then be used to explore alternative analytical approaches to the same set of data, but different model assumptions are made. But first, let's see how the classical ANOVA approach to our problem can be addressed identically through a multiple regression approach.

THE MULTIPLE REGRESSION APPROACH

To see how the turnover intention problem is addressed from a multiple regression framework, a full model can be written to represent the same effects shown in equation 1. The full model could be written as:

$$X_{IJK} \quad \mu \quad \alpha_1 \quad \alpha_2 \quad \beta_1 \quad \beta_2 \quad \beta_3 \quad \alpha\beta_{11} \quad \alpha\beta_{12} \quad \alpha\beta_{13} \quad \alpha\beta_{21} \quad \alpha\beta_{22} \quad \alpha\beta_{23}$$
$$Y = B_0 X_0 + B_1 X_1 + B_2 X_2 + B_3 X_3 + B_4 X_4 + B_5 X_5 + B_6 X_6 + B_7 X_7 + B_8 X_8 + B_9 X_9 + B_{10} X_{10} + B_{11} X_{11} + e \quad (2)$$

Main effects Due to Factor A, Sex

Main effects Due to Factor B, Relative Role Force

Interactions Due to Joint effect of Factors A and B

A dummy variable coding scheme could be used such that each observation would be coded with either a 1 or 0 for the dummy variables X_0 through X_{11}. The upper half of Table 1 illustrates how one observation from each cell of the 2 x 3 design would be coded using the full model shown in equation 2.

The design matrix in Table 1 using dummy variable coding cannot be used to estimate the ANOVA effects because the matrix is singular. That is, some of the columns are linearly dependent (column 1 = columns 2 + 3, or column 1 = columns 4 + 5 + 6), therefore this matrix cannot be inverted for a solution of the ANOVA parameters. The design matrix, however, can be adjusted in two ways so that the parameters can be estimated and identical constraints used by classical ANOVA are incorporated into the multiple regression framework. First, only p − 1 dummy variables are needed to represent p levels of Factor A and q − 1 variables to represent q levels of Factor B. Thus, one dummy variable (X_1) would be needed for Factor A and two dummy variables would be needed for Factor B (X_3, X_4). The interaction terms are then formed by the cross products of X_1 with X_3 and X_4 respectively yielding X_6 and X_7. The second issue is how to incorporate the classical ANOVA constraints such that the sum of main and joint effects (e.g., $\Sigma_j\alpha_i = \Sigma_j b_i = \Sigma_j\alpha\beta_{ij} = 0$) equal zero. This result is easily obtained by using effect coding (Cohen, 1975) to adjust the design matrix as follows.

If an observation is observed under a level of Factor A, level i, and the corresponding vector associated with level i has been *removed* from the design matrix (for the purpose of achieving linearly independent columns in the design matrix), then that observation receives a −1 code in the remaining p − 1 respective vectors. Similarly, for Factor B, if an observation falls under a level of Factor B, level j, and the corresponding vector associated with level j has been eliminated from the design matrix, then code that observation as a −1 in the remaining

q − 1 respective vectors. An observation in either of the (p − 1) or q − 1 categories associated with a vector that appears in the design matrix is coded as a 1 in the vector associated with the specific level that the observation appears under. The same observation receives a code of 0 in the remaining (p − 2) or (q − 2) vectors which appear in the design matrix. The (p − 1) (q − 1) vectors associated with the interactions are found by simply taking the product of the vectors associated with the main effects due to Factor A and Factor B. In the lower half of Table 1, effect coding has been used to code the observations for a reduced model. This model now becomes:

$$Y = \overset{\mu}{B_0X_0} + \overset{\alpha_1}{B_1X_1} + \overset{\beta_1}{B_3X_3} + \overset{\beta_2}{B_4X_4} + \\ \overset{\alpha\beta_{11}}{B_6X_6} \, \overset{\alpha\beta_{12}}{B_7 + X_7} \qquad (3)$$

or

$$Y = \overset{\mu}{B_0X_0} + \overset{\alpha_2}{B_2X_2} + \overset{\beta_1}{B_3X_3} + \overset{\beta_2}{B_4X_4} + \\ \overset{\alpha\beta_{21}}{B_9X_9} \, \overset{\alpha\beta_{22}}{B_{10} + X_{10}} \qquad (4)$$

If you are wondering how α_2, β_3 and $\alpha\beta_{13}$ parameters can be recovered from the model shown in equation 3, remember that classical ANOVA imposes the constraint that $\Sigma_i\alpha_i = \Sigma_j\beta_j = \Sigma_{ij}\alpha\beta_{ij} = 0$. Therefore, once you know the estimate of α_1 (β_1) then the estimate of α_2 can be obtained as $\alpha_2 = \alpha_1$. Similarly, the estimate of β_3 is obtained as $\beta_3 = -\beta_1 - \beta_2$. For the interaction effects, the estimate of $\alpha\beta_{13}$ is obtained as $B_8 = -B_6 - B_7$. Note, that to estimate interaction effects $\alpha\beta_{21}$ $\alpha\beta_{22}$, and $\alpha\beta_{23}$, equation 4 can be estimated using the effect coded variable for parameter α_2 in place of α_1. The design matrix would be similarly adjusted for this alternative model.

To see that all the information needed to estimate the cell means of the 2 x 3 factorial design has been obtained, the conditional

TABLE 1
Design Matrices for a Multiple Regression Approaches to ANOVA

	Effect:	M	A_1	A_2	B_1	B_2	B_3	AB_{11}	AB_{12}	AB_{13}	AB_{21}	AB_{22}	AB_{23}
Cell	Y	X_0	X_1	X_2	X_3	X_4	X_5	X_6	X_7	X_8	X_9	X_{10}	X_{11}

Dummy Variable Coding for Equation (1)

Cell	Y	X_0	X_1	X_2	X_3	X_4	X_5	X_6	X_7	X_8	X_9	X_{10}	X_{11}
ab_{11}	X_{111}	1	1	0	1	0	0	1	0	0	0	0	0
ab_{12}	•	1	1	0	0	1	0	0	1	0	0	0	0
ab_{13}	•	1	1	0	0	0	1	0	0	1	0	0	0
ab_{21}	•	1	0	1	1	0	0	0	0	0	1	0	0
ab_{22}		1	0	1	0	1	0	0	0	0	0	1	0
ab_{23}	X_{23k}	1	0	1	0	0	1	0	0	0	0	0	1

Effect Coding (1, -1, 0) for Equation (3)

Cell	Y	X_0	X_1	X_3	X_4	X_6	X_7
ab_{11}	X_{111}	1	1	1	0	1	0
ab_{12}	•	1	1	0	1	0	1
ab_{13}	•	1	1	-1	-1	-1	-1
ab_{21}	•	1	-1	1	0	-1	0
ab_{22}		1	-1	0	1	0	-1
ab_{23}	X_{23k}	1	-1	-1	-1	1	1

Note: For ease of presentation only one observation per cell has been coded.

expectations of Y with respect to Factors A and B can be taken (see Equation 2):

$$E(Y|ab_{11}) = B_0 + B_1 + B_3 + B_6 = M_{11}$$
$$E(Y|ab_{12}) = B_0 + B_1 + B_4 + B_7 = M_{12}$$
$$E(Y|ab_{13}) = B_0 + B_1 + B_5 + B_8 = M_{13}$$
$$E(Y|ab_{21}) = B_0 + B_2 + B_3 + B_9 = M_{21}$$
$$E(Y|ab_{22}) = B_0 + B_2 + B_4 + B_{10} = M_{22}$$
$$E(Y|ab_{23}) = B_0 + B_2 + B_5 + B_{11} = M_{23}$$

In summary, the classical ANOVA can be accomplished within a multiple regression framework. The complete ANOVA model as expressed in equation (2) was reparameterized into the restricted models of expressions (3) and (4) by imposing the traditional classical ANOVA scaling constraints. The method of ordinary least squares for the models given by (3) or (4) will yield estimates of a subset of the complete set of ANOVA parameters. The remaining parameter estimates are easily obtained from the scaling constraints and the information provided by the least squares solution to the model given by 3 or 4. It is important to note that the least squares solution was obtained using the 1, −1, 0 effect

coding rules for construction of the design matrix such that the classical ANOVA linear restraints were explicitly incorporated into the models given by equations 3 and 4. For a more comprehensive discussion of the use of dummy variables and alternative representations of dummy variable coding the interested reader is directed to Bogartz (1975), Cohen (1975, pp. 183–199), Overall, Spiegel, and Cohen (1975, pp. 182–183), Wolf and Cartwright (1974), and Wolf and Cartwright (1975).

Some authors (Carlson and Timm, 1974; Searle, 1971; Timm & Carlson, 1975) have suggested a full rank linear model be used to estimate a vector of *cell means* instead of the vector of main and interaction effects given in expressions (3) and (4). A full rank model, as such, does not require the usual ANOVA scaling constraints to obtain a unique solution. From the estimates of cell means, the traditional ANOVA parameters can be obtained. This approach has much to recommend it, particularly to those already familiar with the general linear model. The interested reader may wish to consult the aforementioned references for alternative ordinary least squares treatment of the classical analysis of variance model.

Test of Hypotheses in the MR Framework

Test of hypotheses concerning main and interaction effects in the MR framework are easily understood as a method of model comparisons. In a single factor design the congruence between ANOVA and MR hypotheses can be shown as:

$$H_O: \mu_1 = \mu_2 = \mu_3 = \ldots \mu_k = \mu..,$$

which is, in fact, equivalent to the multiple regression hypothesis;

$$H_O: R^2_{Y.12\ldots(k)} = 0$$

where R^2 is the square of the population multiple correlation or that amount of the Y variation that can be accounted for in a system containing 1, 2, 3 to K dummy variables.

To illustrate the equivalence of the two approaches for our 2x3 factorial design for the turnover intention study, it is convenient to show the F ratios and associated sums of squares for the ANOVA approach and the

corresponding MR approach for the estimating sums of squares used in the F ratios. Using a multiple regression or ordinary least squares approach for the turnover intention data, let $R^2_{Y.a,b,ab}$ represent the square of the multiple correlation coefficient or the proportion of total Y variation that can be accounted for by the model containing main effects due to Factor A (sex), main effects due to factor B (relative role force), and the joint effects due to Factors A and B. Similarly, $R^2_{Y.a,b}$ is that amount of Y variance that can be accounted for by a linear model containing main effects due to Factors A and B. $R^2_{Y.a}$, $R^2_{Y.b}$ and $R^2_{Y.ab}$ are analogously defined. In general, for equal cell designs, the sums of squares of the classical ANOVA can be defined as:

$$
\begin{aligned}
& && df \\
SS_a &= SS_{Total}[R^2_{Y.a,b} - R^2_{Y.b}] && p-1 \\
SS_b &= SS_{Total}[R^2_{Y.a,b} - R^2_{Y.a}] && q-1 \\
SS_{ab} &= SS_{Total}[R^2_{Y.a,b,ab} - R^2_{Y.a,b}] && (p-1)(q-1) \\
SS_{Error} &= SS_{Total}[1 - R^2_{Y.a,b,ab}] && N-pq.
\end{aligned}
$$

The corresponding F ratios for testing interaction and main effects then become:

		1 ANOVA F Ratios		*2* MR estimates		*3* MR estimates
Interaction Effect Factors A and B	$F_{ab} =$	$\dfrac{(SS_{a,b,ab} - SS_{a,b})/df}{SS_{error}/df}$	$=$	$\dfrac{SS_{Total}[R^2_{Y.a,b,ab} - R^2_{Y.a,b}]/df}{SS_{Total}[1 - R^2_{Y.a,b,ab}]/df}$	$=$	$\dfrac{(R^2_{Y.a,b,ab} - R^2_{Y.a,b})/df}{(1 - R^2_{Y.a,b,ab})/df}$
Main Effect Factor A	$F_a =$	$\dfrac{(SS_{a,b} - SS_b)/df}{SS_{error}/df}$	$=$	$\dfrac{SS_{Total}[R^2_{Y.a,b,ab} - R^2_{Y.b}]/df}{SS_{Total}[1 - R^2_{Y.a,b,ab}]/df}$	$=$	$\dfrac{(R^2_{Y.a,b,ab} - R^2_{Y.b})/df}{(1 - R^2_{Y.a,b,ab})/df}$
Main Effect Factor B	$F_b =$	$\dfrac{(SS_{a,b} - SS_a)/df}{SS_{error}/df}$	$=$	$\dfrac{SS_{Total}[R^2_{Y.a,b,ab} - R^2_{Y.a}]/df}{SS_{Total}[1 - R^2_{Y.a,b,ab}]/df}$	$=$	$\dfrac{(R^2_{Y.a,b,ab} - R^2_{Y.a})/df}{(1 - R^2_{Y.a,b,ab})/df}$

The various R^2 measures encountered in the above definition are really measures of explained variation for *different* linear models. The numerators of the above F ratios are, in fact, squared part correlations. For example, the numerator of F_a is the squared part correlation between the main effects due to Factor A and Y with the linear effect

of the main effects due to Factor B removed from Factor A. (Because the design is balanced, that is, contains equal cell sizes, this is a pseudo adjustment because $R^2_{Y.a} + R^2_{Y.b} = R^2_{Y.a,b}$). The unique property of the classical ANOVA hypothesis tests is the manner in which each F ratio is constructed. For tests of main effects, the specific test of each main effect is "adjusted" or corrected for the effect of all other *main* effects. The adjustment to the numerator for the test of interaction is likewise adjusted for the influence of all other main effects in the model. In the classical ANOVA model, tests on main effects due to a specific factor are always adjusted for the effects of all other main effects due to the other factors. Interactions are omitted from this adjustment by the assumption that the variation due to interactions is negligible.

The complete model given by equation (3) appears as:

$$Y = B_0 X_0 + B_1 X_1 + B_3 X_3 + B_4 X_4 + B_6 X_6 + B_7 X_7$$

This model is said to be saturated because main effects due to Factors A and B and the joint (not additive) effects due to the covariation of A with B are completely accounted for by the model. The F tests for main effects and interactions can be constructed by comparing the results of a given linear model with a reduced linear model. For example, the numerator for F_a is found by taking the difference of the two R^2 values from the two linear models. For a balanced two factor design the test for main effects due to factor A asks whether the model:

$$Y_{ij} = \mu + \alpha_i + \beta_j + e$$

can account for a significantly greater amount of the Y variation than the reduced model:

$$Y_j = \mu + \beta_j + e$$

The test for main effects due to factor B is actually testing if the increase in explained Y variation for the model:

$$Y_{ij} = \mu + \alpha_i + \beta_j + e \text{ as compared to}$$
$$Y_i = \mu + \alpha_i + e$$

is significantly different from zero. The test for interactions in the two-factor balanced case compares two slightly different models.

The F ratio tests whether the increase in explained variation is significantly different from zero when the linear model
$Y_{ij} = \mu + \alpha_i + \beta_j + \alpha\beta_i; + e$ is used instead of
$Y_{ij} = \mu + \alpha_i + \beta_j + e$.

When significant interactions are present in the saturated linear model, the least squares approach provides a convenient method for testing pairs of cell means to assess the nature of the interaction. To test, for example, whether the mean at cell ab_{11} differs significantly from the mean at ab_{21}, recall the model given by equation (3) will yield:

$$E(Y|ab_{11}) = B_0 + B_1 + B_3 + B_6 = M_{11}$$
$$\text{and} \quad E(Y|ab_{21}) = B_0 + B_2 + B_3 + B_9 = M_{21}$$

The differential effect of A at b_1 is $E(Y|ab_{11}) - E(Y|ab_{21}) = B_1 + B_6 - B_2 - B_9$. To test whether $B_1 + B_6 - B_2 - B_9$ is significantly different from zero, the hypothesis becomes:

$$H_0: B_1 + B_6 - B_2 - B_9 = 0$$

$$\text{where: } t_{(1)} = \frac{(B_1 + B_6 - B_2 - B_9) - 0}{\sqrt{SS_{error}}} \quad \text{and}$$

$$SS_{error} = (1 - R^2_{Y.a,b,ab}) SS_{total}$$

The above t statistic is appropriate when Factors A and B are fixed and when the cell comparisons are planned before the data are collected. The denominator uses data from all cells in the experiment, not just those from which the numerator has been computed. If the experimental error is homogeneous, use of this pooled estimate is appropriate (Winer, 1971, pp. 385–387).

A caution is in order when either the multiple regression approach or the classical ANOVA approaches are used. Individual tests on dummy variable coefficients are to be generally avoided unless hypothesized a priori. Inferences made from single t-tests on each coefficient when the set of coefficients to be tested is large will increase the probability of falsely rejecting at least one of the null hypotheses for the set of variables. For any one t-test the α level is the risk that the researcher accepts for making a type I error. Assuming each t-test to be independent of one another, then the probability of falsely rejecting at *least* one of the null hypotheses associated with the set of dummy variables is $[1 - p\,(\text{not rejecting on all K tests})]$ or $[1 - (1 - \alpha)^K]$. For our 2x3 design, the individual tests on Factor A for each level of Factor B alone sets $K = 3$. If $\alpha = .05$, then the probability of falsely rejecting at least one of the three hypotheses associated with Factor A at levels b_1, b_2, or b_3 is $[1 - (.95)^3] = .1426$, which is nearly triple the original α of .05 set for each test. Cohen (1975, pp. 155–160, 195–207), Kerlinger and Pedhazur (1973, pp. 128–140), and Winer (1971, pp. 196–201) discuss alternatives for conducting a priori or a posteriori tests that maintain a desired α level.

To summarize, the multiple regression approach can easily be applied to research problems to estimate the same parameters and test the same hypotheses as in a classical ANOVA approach. The multiple regression approach, however, offers additional flexibility in terms of the ease in incorporating categorical and continuous variables in the same analysis. In addition, tests of hypotheses in the MR framework are seen as really model comparisons. Given the flexibility of the MR framework, alternative analytical approaches can be examined within this framework. In the sections that follow, the turnover intention study will be examined from these alternative approaches. For the purpose of discussion these approaches are addressed in the following order: (a) the analysis of covariance approach, (b) the moderated regression approach, and (c) the regression approach to nonorthogonal designs.

THE ANALYSIS OF COVARIANCE APPROACH

In the turnover intention study posed earlier two factors were proposed for study, sex and relative role force. The sex factor was pro-posed due to prior observation that males and females experience different turnover rates. Because behavioral intentions are viewed as a precursor to the actual turnover decision, it seems reasonable to include sex in the present study as a factor or independent variable capable of accounting for variation in turnover intentions. If we assume further that the hypothesized relationship between the expectancy based measure of relative role force and turnover intention operates in the same fashion for males and females, then we have accorded sex as nothing more (or less) than a covariate.

To paraphrase Cohen (1968) a covariate is simply an independent variable that assumes priority among a set of independent variables. Covariance analysis as typically presented in ANOVA texts appears both tedious and complex (see, for example, Winer, 1971, p. 952). It need not be, especially when viewed from within the multiple regression framework. In our turnover intention study, the strategy for analysis would be to adjust (or residualize) turnover intention scores with the sex factor prior to assessing the effect of relative role force on turnover intention. The sequence of the hypothesis testing procedure would be as follows:

1. Test the significance of the covariate, sex:

$$F_a = \frac{SS_a/df}{SS_{error}/df} = \frac{R^2_{Y.a}/df}{(1-R^2_{Y.a,b})/df}$$

2. Test the significance of relative role force,

$$F_b = \frac{SS_b/df}{SS_{error}/df} = \frac{R^2_{Y.a,b}-R^2_{Y.a})/df}{(1-R^2_{Y.a,b})/df}$$

3. Test the assumption of same slope relationships between Factor B and Y for all levels of Factor A:

$$F_{ab} = \frac{SS_{ab}/df}{SS_{error}/df} = \frac{R^2_{Y.a,b,ab}-R^2_{Y.a,b})/df}{(1-R^2_{Y.a,b,ab})/df}$$

The three steps for testing these hypotheses are actually comparisons of different models. Note that the partitioning of explained variance in covariance analysis differs from classical ANOVA, because a hierarchy has been established among the independent variables represented in the multiple regression. Step number 3 is included as a check on the covariance assumption of equal slopes of the covariate. Because sex, the covariate factor is nominal, this assumption can be visualized as a *parallel* plot of the means for the relative role force levels (Factor B) for males and females, respectively (hence, no interaction). If the interaction is significant, then the sex factor cannot be considered a covariate. When the interaction is nonsignificant, and the sex factor is significant, then sex is seen to covary with turnover intention. As such, the covariate reduces the error sum of squares and increases the power associated with the design.

Covariance analysis can easily be generalized to include multiple covariates. Although covariates as discussed in experimental design texts are usually viewed as continuous rather than nominal variables, they can be either. If the covariate is nominal and includes more than two categories, then a set of dummy variables can be used to represent the covariate and the steps of hypothesis testing would proceed as described above.

Although beyond the scope of this paper, the hierarchical nature of covariance analysis raises the issue of causal assumptions that underlie the statistical model used. Linn and Werts (1969), Rock (1974), Werts and Linn (1971), and Youngblood (1979) elaborate on the causal assumptions associated with a variety of ordinary least squares models. In a more general context, James, Mulaik, and Brett (1982) discuss causal assumptions and the use of linear models in causal analysis.

One final issue concerning covariance analysis within the multiple regression framework is the generalization of this procedure whereby several independent variables are being studied simultaneously. Gulliksen and Wilks (1950), Johnston (1971), and Snedecor and Cochran (1967) discuss procedures for testing the homogeneity of slope and intercept coefficients across several groups of observations where the groups naturally occur and are unambiguously identified. Suppose we conducted the turnover intention study in ten different organizations. A reasonable question is whether we could pool the data from the ten organizations for greater precision in our estimates of the effect of relative role force and sex on turnover intention. If the underlying relationship among sex and relative role force with turnover intention varies across the ten organizations, then it would be inappropriate to pool the data. Johnston (1972) and Kerlinger and Pedhazur (1973) contain very readable presentations of these procedures for conducting homogeneity of slope and intercept tests.

In conducting a covariance analysis for our turnover intention study we tested the assumption of same slopes of the covariate on turnover intention. Assuming no interaction, the tests described in steps 1 and 2 above are appropriate. There may be instances, however, where the researcher may hypothesize a priori an interaction. In this case, a moderated regression approach could be useful, to which we turn next.

MODERATED REGRESSION APPROACH

Interactions within the classical ANOVA approach to data analysis, from a hypothesis testing viewpoint, are unwelcome complications to the analysis and interpretation of results. The implicit assumption of the classical ANOVA approach is that by randomization and equal cell sizes interactions will not be present; hence, their exclusion from the test of main effects. Some researchers of organizations, however, may posit an interaction from a theoretical basis and thus may want to explicitly test for their effects. To coin a phrase, just as one person's main effect may be another's covariate, one person's covariate could be another person's moderator.

Examples of such phenomena are easily found from various areas of organizational research. In the job design literature, individual differences such as growth need strength (Hackman and Oldham, 1976) were proposed as moderators of the relationship between job scope and outcomes such as job satisfaction, work performance, absenteeism, and turnover. In personnel selection, the situational validity or differential validity hypotheses embody the moderator notion. The basic question in the instance of situational validity is whether a test (or a battery of tests) used for selection in one plant of an organization can be used in other plants. That is, if the tests predict performance in plant A, will they also predict performance in plant B, and in the same manner. The issue of differential validity, a concept that although lacking empirical support is adopted by the current *Uniform Guidelines for Employee Selection Procedures,* proposes that tests may predict one way for minority applicants and quite another way for majority applicants. An employer who adopts a common decision role for selection purposes may then adversely affect the probability of selection of one of these groups (presumably, the minority group) without taking the difference in the test score-job performance relationship into account. Moderator analysis provides a means of testing for these hypothesized effects.

To return to our original problem of the turnover intention study, we may, for example, hypothesize that sex moderates the relationship between relative role force and turnover intention due to the historical occupational segregation of male and female jobs which in turn provide more choices to males than females. The nature of this hypothesized relationship is depicted in Figure 1. The relationship between relative role force and turnover intentions is hypothesized as inverse and linear for males, but inverse and curvilinear for females. Turnover intentions are also hypothesized to differ between males and females, with males exhibiting higher turnover intentions regardless of relative role force. A moderated regression analysis would proceed with a hierarchical test of effects similar to covariance analysis. To test the moderating effect of sex on the

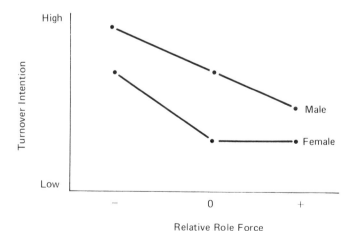

Figure 1.   Sex as a Moderator of the Relative Role Force—
Turnover Intention Relationship

relative role force-turnover intention relationship, the incremental contribution of the moderator is assessed. In terms of model comparisons the following squared multiple correlations are differenced to assess the incremental contribution of the moderator:

$$F_{ab} = \frac{(R^2_{Y.a,b,ab} - R^2_{Y.a,b}) / df}{(1 - R^2_{Y.a,b,ab}) / df}$$

Peters, O'Connor, and Wise (the next paper in this chapter) provide an extensive discussion of moderator issues, so we will conclude this section with an observation and a speculation. Once again, it can easily be seen that the multiple regression framework provides considerable flexibility for the analysis of organizational problems from a variety of viewpoints. Although moderated regression provides a straightforward means of examining the moderator hypothesis, there is some question whether single studies using this technique are capable of adequately assessing this hypothesis. Other techniques such as meta-analysis developed and applied by others such as Fisher and Gitelson (1983), Glass (1977), Osborn, Callender, Greener, and Ashworth (1983), and Schmidt and Hunter (1977) may be an alternative way to assess the moderator hypothesis by using considerably more data drawn from numerous studies.

The final section of this chapter addresses two additional issues that deserve attention regardless of whether one adopts an ANOVA or MR approach to organizational research. These two issues are the problem of nonorthogonal designs and the effective use of measures of association as related to the purpose of the research.

ADDITIONAL ISSUES FOR FURTHER CONSIDERATION

The Nonorthogonal Design Problem

Throughout the previous discussion, with the use of the turnover intention study, a convenient assumption of equal cell sizes has been made. The assumption provides for a balanced or orthogonal design which is convenient for hypothesis testing purposes because of the nonoverlapping sums of squares associated with the main and interaction effects. Frequently, though, studies of organizational problems will result in unbalanced designs either by accident, lack of planning, or forces beyond the control of the researcher. Nonorthogonal or unbalanced designs introduce multicollinearity among the independent variables used to represent main and interaction effects. The question frequently debated in the literature on ANOVA approaches to experimental designs is whether a classical ANOVA approach to hypothesis testing is appropriate under these conditions.

Basically, four alternative methods for testing ANOVA hypotheses have been suggested: a) the classical ANOVA approach whereby each effect is adjusted for all effects at the same or lower level, b) the general linear model ANOVA approach whereby every effect is adjusted for every other effect regardless of level, c) the hierarchical approach whereby the effects are ordered and then each effect is adjusted sequentially for only those effects that precede the given effect in the hierarchy, and d) an approach proposed by Applebaum and Cramer (1974) whereby alternative models are formulated and tested ranging from complex (main and interaction effects) to simple (main effect only).

The latter strategy suggested by Applebaum and Cramer has provoked quite a controversy (Overall, Lee, & Hornick, 1981; Spector, Voissem, & Cone, 1981). The Applebaum and Cramer approach is basically one of letting the data dictate what the appropriate model is with the idea that if a simpler model (i.e., fewer terms, especially higher order terms) fits the data, use it. Overall, Spiegel and Cohen (1975) argue that for nonorthogonal designs the general linear model ANOVA approach is preferred because this solution provides unbiased estimates of the same ANOVA main effects and interactions as would be tested in an orthogonal design. The basic difference in approach is that Overall et al. (1981) strongly believe the model underlying the analysis should be specified prior to conducting the data analysis. Monte Carlo simulations conducted by Overall et al. (1981) and Spector et al. (1981) generally support the general linear model ANOVA approach, especially in the presence of a true but nonsignificant interaction. Moreover, in the presence of a significant interaction the general linear model ANOVA yields estimates with higher accuracy. Unless the research is highly exploratory in nature, the Overall et al. (1981) approach has much to recommend it. This approach is also consistent with an underlying theme of this paper; it is important to specify and understand the type of statistical model that will be used for an organizational study. A better understanding of the problem as well as an appropriate test of hypotheses is fostered when the researcher explicitly states the model underlying the data analysis *before* the data are collected.

Measures of Association

One clear advantage of the multiple regression data-analytic strategy over the ANOVA approach is the ease of obtaining measures of strength of association between the hypothesized effects and the criterion. Measures of strength of association familiar to the ANOVA designs are eta, epsilon, and omega squared; for multiple regression the estimator of the squared population multiple correlation (R^2, the measure of explained variance), estimates of the population cross-validated multiple correlation, and the shrunken or adjusted R^2 are commonly used. Measures of strength of association in either approach permit the researcher to move beyond the significance level and assess whether a hypothesized factor or independent variable accounts, in a relative sense, for a meaningful proportion of variation in the criterion of interest.

Maxwell, Camp, and Arvey (1981) provide an excellent summary and comparison of a variety of measures of strength of association used in ANOVA and regression approaches. They show the identity between the epsilon squared and the Wherry (1931) shrunken R^2 estimate of the population squared multiple correlation, as well as the functional relationship between the sample multiple R^2 and the omega squared measure frequently used with ANOVA designs. Maxwell et al. also caution against the overconfidence placed on a sample estimate of a measure of strength of association when the researcher's purpose is inferential rather than descriptive. The interested reader seeking more information on the rationale and computation of measures of strength of association for both ANOVA and regression approaches should consult Cattin (1980), Dodd and Schultz (1973), Fleiss (1969), Schmitt, Coyle, and Rauschenberger (1977), and Vaughn and Corballis (1969).

Finally, consistent with the Maxwell, et al. caution of placing too much emphasis on measures of strength of association, O'Grady (1982) provides a psychometric, methodological, and theoretical critique of measures of explained variance. When the purpose of the research is to account for the largest possible proportion of the variance, or prediction, or to assess the relative predictive ability of two or more independent variables then measures of strength of association can be useful aids for interpretation. When the purpose of the research is explanation or understanding, then the size of the measure of explained variance should be evaluated against what the theory (and prior research) would suggest.

CONCLUDING REMARKS

In this paper the identity of the classical ANOVA approach with the multiple regression approach to data analysis has been illustrated. The flexibility of the multiple regression approach within the general linear model framework has been examined using a hypothetical organizational research problem. Within this framework, classical analysis of variance, analysis of covariance, and moderated regression approaches to data analysis were examined. Hypothesis testing associated with each of these approaches employs a comparison of linear models for the computation of the appropriate test statistics.

A major theme of this paper is the importance of understanding the type of statistical model used to test hypotheses associated with the research problem. Similar to issues of experimental design (see Fisher's paper in the next chapter of this volume), analytical strategies need to be planned prior to conducting the research. Moreover, planning of the experimental design and data collection will influence decisions regarding

the type of statistical model used to analyze the data. Although the topic is beyond the scope of this paper, another important issue is the preliminary examination of the data to ensure that assumptions underlying the statistical model employed are met (see Field's paper in this chapter). Conducting organizational research thus requires a multitude of conceptual and methodological skills. Regardless of how the organizational researcher has been trained (e.g., the ANOVA school or the multiple regression school), the process of inquiry should result in a research question posed, the hypothesis stated, an experimental design for the data collection devised, a statistical model consistent with the design constructed, and finally an analysis conducted that is consistent with the foregoing steps.

References

Applebaum, M. I., & Cramer, E. M. "Some Problems in the Nonorthogonal Analysis of Variance." *Psychological Bulletin*, 1974, *81*, 335–343.

Bogartz, W. "Coding Dummy Variables Is a Waste of Time: Reply to Wolf and Cartwright, among Others." *Psychological Bulletin*, 1975, *82*, 180.

Carlson, J. E. & Timm, N. H. "Analysis of Nonorthogonal Fixed-Effects Designs." *Psychological Bulletin*, 1974, *81*, 563–570.

Cattin, P. "Estimation of the Predictive Power of a Regression Model," *Journal of Applied Psychology*, 1980, *65*, 407–414.

Cohen, J. "Multiple Regression As a General Data-Analytic System." *Psychological Bulletin*, 1968, *70*, 426–443.

Cohen, J. & Cohen, P. *Applied Multiple Regression/Correlation Analysis for the Behavioral Sciences.* Hillsdale, NJ: Erlbaum, 1975.

Dodd, D. H. & Schultz, R. F. "Computational Procedures for Estimating Magni-

tude of Effect for Some Analysis of Variance Designs." *Psychological Bulletin*, 1973, *79*, 391–395.

Fisher, C. D., & Gitelson, R. "Meta-Analysis of Role Stress Correlates." *Journal of Applied Psychology*, 1983, *68*, 320–333.

Fleiss, J. L. "Estimating the Magnitude of Experimental Effects." *Psychological Bulletin*, 1969, *72*, 273–276.

Glass, G. V. "Integrating Findings: The Meta-Analysis of Research." *Review of Research in Education*, 1977, *5*, 351–379.

Gulliksen, H., & Wilks, S. S. "Regression Tests for Several Samples." *Psychometrika*, 1950, *15*, 91–114.

Hackman, J. R., & Oldham, G. R. "Motivation through the Design of Work: Test of a Theory." *Organizational Behavior and Human Performance*, 1976, *16*, 250–279.

James, L. R., Mulaik, S. A., & Brett, J. M. *Causal Analysis: Assumptions, Models, and Data.* Beverly Hills: Sage Publications, 1982.

Johnston, J. *Econometric Methods* (2nd ed.) New York: McGraw-Hill Book Company, 1972.

Kerlinger, F. N., & Pedhazur, E. J. *Multiple Regression in Behavioral Research*. New York: Holt, Rinehart and Winston, Inc. 1973.

Linn, R. L., & Werts, C. E. "Assumptions in Making Causal Inferences from Part Correlations, Partial Correlations, and Partial Regression Coefficients." *Psychological Bulletin* 1969, 72, 307–310.

Maxwell, S. E. Camp, C. J., & Arvey, R. D. "Measures of Strength of Association: A Comparative Examination." *Journal of Applied Psychology*, 1981, 66, 525–534.

Mobley, W. H., Griffeth, R. W., Hand, H. H., & Meglino, B. M. "Review and Conceptual Analysis of the Employee Turnover Process." *Psychological Bulletin*, 1979, 86, 493–522.

Neter, J., & Wasserman, W. *Applied Linear Statistical Models*. Homewood, IL: Richard D. Irwin, Inc. 1974.

O'Grady, K. E. "Measures of Explained Variance: Cautions and Limitations." *Psychological Bulletin*, 1982, 92, 766–777.

Osborn, H. G., Callender, J. C., Greener, J. M., & Achworth, S. "Statistical Power of Tests of the Situational Specificity Hypothesis in Validity Generalization Studies: A Cautionary Note." *Journal of Applied Psychology*, 1983, 68, 115–122.

Overall, J. E., Lee, D. M., & Hornick, C. W. "Comparison of Two Strategies for Analysis of Variance in Nonorthogonal Designs." *Psychological Bulletin*, 1981, 90, 367–375.

Overall, J. E., Spiegel, D. K., & Cohen, J. "Equivalence of Orthogonal and Nonorthogonal Analysis of Variance." *Psychological Bulletin*, 1975, 82, 182–186.

Rock, D. A. "Appropriate Method for the Least Analysis of Categorical Data." *Psychological Bulletin*, 1974, 81, 1012–1013.

Rucci, A. J., & Tweney, R. D. "Analysis of Variance and the 'Second Discipline' of Scientific Psychology: A Historical Account." *Psychological Bulletin*, 1980, 87, 166–184.

Schmitt, N., Coyle, B. W., & Rauschenberger, J. A. "Monte Carlo Evaluation of Three Formula Estimates of Cross-Validated Multiple Correlation." *Psychological Bulletin*, 1977, 84, 751–758.

Schmitt, F. C., & Hunter, J. E. "Development of a General Solution to the Problem of Validity Generalization." *Journal of Applied Psychology*, 1977, 62, 529–540.

Searle, S. R. *Linear Models*. New York: Wiley, 1971.

Snedecor, G. W., & Cochran, W. G. *Statistical Methods*. Ames, University of Iowa Press, 1967.

Spector, P. E., Voissem N. H., & Cone, W. L. "A Monte Carlo Study of Three Approaches to Nonorthogonal Analysis of Variance." *Journal of Applied Psychology*, 1981, 66, 535–540.

Timm, N. H. & Carlson, J. E. "Analysis of Variance through Full Rank Models." *Multivariate Behavioral Research Monographs*, 1975, no. 75–1.

Vaughan, G. M., & Corballis, M. C. "Beyond Tests of Significance: Estimating Strength of Effects in Selected ANOVA Designs." *Psychological Bulletin*, 1969, 72, 204–213.

Werts, C. E., and Linn, R. L. "Causal Assumptions in Various Procedures for the Least Squares Analysis of Categorical Data." *Psychological Bulletin*, 1971, 75, 430–431.

Winer, B. J. *Statistical Principles in Experimental Design* (2nd ed.). New York: McGraw-Hill, 1971.

Wolf, G., and Cartwright, B. "Rules for Coding Dummy Variables in Multiple Regression." *Psychological Bulletin*, 1974, 81, 173–179.

Wolf, G., and Cartwright, B. "A Timely Reply to Bogartz." *Psychological Bulletin*, 1975, 82, 181.

Youngblood, S. A. "Analysis of Variance or Ordinary Least Squares: A Synthesis and Review." *Psychological Documents*, 8, (MS. No. 1831) May, 1979.

The Specification and Testing of Useful Moderator Variable Hypotheses[1]

Lawrence H. Peters

Edward J. O'Connor

Steven L. Wise

Theories prevalent within behavioral research often imply that the magnitude of relationship between two variables is "moderated" by the values observed on some third variable. Such theories have become increasingly popular during the past 25 years and are evident in a diversity of content areas including leadership, motivation, turnover, selection and job design. A belief in the inadequacy of two variable systems is typically implied in theoretical formulations which specify moderated relationships. Improvement in understanding is, therefore, sought through these more complex moderator theories.

A variety of conceptual definitions of "moderator variables" have been proposed in the behavioral literature during the past twenty-five years (Zedeck, 1971). In fact, a variety of terms including moderator, interaction, and differential prediction appear to have been used to convey a similar, but not precisely the same meaning (see Frederiksen & Melville, 1954; Saunders, 1956; Wiggins, 1973). In addition, alternative statistical tests which include subgroup correlational comparisons and hierarchical moderated regression procedures have been proposed and utilized to identify moderator variables (Zedeck, 1971).

Recent articles by Arnold (1982) and Peters and Champoux (1979a, 1979b) have attempted to clarify alternative moderator variable hypotheses which may be meaningfully postulated and to specify the statistical approaches appropriate to testing such hypotheses. These authors correctly point out that two "different" types of hypotheses *can* be made with regard to moderators. One type of hypothesis indicates that a third, moderator variable will impact on the "magnitude" or "strength" of association between two other variables. The other type of hypothesis indicates that the "form" or "pattern" of the

---

[1] This manuscript is an elaboration of ideas presented by L. H. Peters and E. J. O'Connor at the 1983 Southwest Academy of Management meetings, Houston, TX, March, 1983. We would like to thank Don Brush, Mitch Fields and John Pohlmann for their reactions to and comments on an earlier version of this manuscript. Since we did not follow all of their suggestions, we accept responsibility for all errors. Steven L. Wise is now at the University of Nebraska-Lincoln.

association between a predictor and a criterion will differ depending upon the score values of the moderator. We, however, believe that both Arnold (1982) and Peters and Champoux (1979a, 1979b) have greatly overstated the potential value of testing hypotheses involving differing "strengths of association" by examining differences in subgroup correlation coefficients. The present discussion is therefore directed toward further clarifying these issues. Specifically, attention will be directed toward (a) examining the usefulness of the information resulting from testing these two alternative hypotheses (differing strengths versus differing forms of association), (b) pointing out the greater utility of results from hypotheses aimed at testing both differing forms of association and accuracy and prediction, and (c) presenting the analytical strategies (hierarchical moderated regression and differential accuracy tests) appropriate for testing these more useful hypotheses.

USEFUL INFORMATION REGARDING MODERATOR VARIABLES

Peters and Champoux (1979a) have argued that hypotheses involving differing strengths of association and hypotheses involving differences in the form of relationships each serve different scientific purposes. They state that moderator hypotheses aimed at specifying different response patterns in predictor-criterion associations tend to serve the purpose of "prediction", whereas moderator hypotheses involving differing magnitudes of relationship involve "differential validity." That is, when one is interested in examining whether different predicted criterion score patterns result at different levels of a moderator variable, then the emphasis is clearly one of prediction. On the other hand, these authors indicated that if the researcher is primarily interested in knowing whether a given independent variable is differently (i.e., more or less strongly) related to a given

criterion variable depending upon the score values of the moderator variable, the question of interest involves differential validity.

Arnold (1982) has also argued that moderator hypotheses involving differing strengths of relationships (i.e., differential validity) represent legitimate hypotheses for scientific investigation. He stated that hypotheses involving differing strengths of relationships "answer the question does X account for as much of the variance in Y in group E as in group F?" (Arnold, 1982, p. 146).

As would be expected from the fact that different hypotheses can be made, both Arnold (1982) and Peters and Champoux (1979a, 1979b) go on to specify different statistical tests corresponding to each of these different moderator hypotheses. With regard to moderator hypotheses involving the strength of relationships between two other variables, these authors recommend the use of subgroup correlational comparisons. This test involves the statistical comparison of correlation coefficients computed within the two (or more) subgroups which are formed based on scores on the hypothesized moderator variable. With regard to moderator hypotheses involving the form of relationships between two other variables, hierarchical moderated regression is advocated. This latter test involves examining slope differences across regression lines.

We disagree with the contention that moderator variable hypotheses involving differing *strengths* of relationships across the values of a moderator variable are scientifically meaningful. Specifically, we will argue that such hypotheses do not provide particularly "useful" information for persons interested in understanding, predicting and influencing behavior in organizational settings.

One can always test the hypothesis that the shared variance in predictor-criterion relationships will be greater for one group than for others. It is relevant, however, to ask what meaningful purpose the information resulting from testing such a correlational hypothesis will serve. We contend that the meaningfulness of knowledge about predictor-criterion relationships comes from being able to *use* that information effectively to make more accurate predictions concerning the criterion. Knowing that a given predictor is more strongly related to a given criterion in one setting or for one group of people than in other settings or for other groups of people, at best, suggests that different strategies for prediction *might* be needed, but does not simultaneously specify the useful information necessary to make those better predictions. Additional analyses, those reflecting differing response "patterns" for the different settings or groups of people, would be necessary for that purpose (see O'Connor, Wiorkowski, & Peters, 1981).

We are not suggesting that prediction is a more important goal than understanding. Indeed, we believe that understanding should be the goal of our science, and further, that understanding and prediction are not mutually exclusive goals. In effect, we contend that "understanding" a phenomenon only occurs when one is able to successfully *predict* future outcomes regarding that phenomenon based on predictor information which is currently available. That is, evidence pertaining to how well one really understands a particular phenomenon would necessarily involve being able to predict future score values relevant to that phenomenon. Knowing that one variable accounts for more variance in another in one subgroup as compared to another subgroup provides little useful information in that one cannot utilize that information *directly* to meaningfully make predictions or specify intervention strategies designed to improve organizational effectiveness.

We recognize that simply being able to predict an outcome does not necessarily imply an understanding of it. Raw empiricism has been used successfully within our field to predict important outcomes when very limited understanding has existed. Empirically keyed biographical forms represent

an example of this phenomenon. However, the fact that prediction does not prove understanding does not take away from the fact that true understanding does imply the capacity to predict.

Instead of developing information regarding the relative strengths of relationships across values of a moderator variable (i.e., differential validity), it appears that researchers should be interested in identifying differences in prediction equations and in estimating how good their predictions are. Differences in predicted criterion scores would be reflected by significant main and/or interactive effects in moderated regression equations. Thus, if one were testing a moderator variable hypothesis involving gender, for example, and found a significant interaction between gender and the predictor, then different criterion scores would be predicted from the independent variable depending upon the gender of the person whose score was being predicted. In like manner, a significant main effect (in the absence of an interaction) for gender would result in different predicted scores, constant across sex groups, for males and females whose score is being predicted. While it is only in the former case that gender would be considered to be a moderator variable (i.e., where it has an impact on the relationship between two other variables), in both cases useful information is provided concerning predicted criterion scores, and therefore, better decisions can follow from the information collected.

In addition to being able to predict an outcome, we, as do others (see, for example, Zedeck, 1971), believe that it is also important for researchers to be aware of the accuracy of their predictions. In this regard, accuracy of prediction can be evaluated by examining the standard deviation of the prediction errors, or standard error of estimate (SE_{est}). As with all standard deviations, SE_{est} can be used to compute a confidence interval (e.g., ± 2 SE_{est}'s) within which the actual criterion score can be expected to lie at some stated level of probability (see

Cohen & Cohen, 1975). When the SE_{est} is small, the confidence intervals around predicted scores are also small, and one can have some confidence in the accuracy of those predictions. On the other hand, if the SE_{est} is large, the confidence bound will also be large, leaving one with little confidence that resulting predictions will be useful for organizational decision making. Imagine trying to place persons in an appropriate job given that the confidence interval around their predicted criterion scores ranged from the effective end of that criterion dimension all the way to the ineffective end. One could not meaningfully use this information to select new employees for the organization.

In summary, we have attempted to argue that researchers can only truly know how well they understand a particular phenomenon by seeing how well they can predict it, that testing for differential validity does not provide such useful information, and that more appropriate alternatives exist for investigating moderator effects. These alternatives focus on both criterion score predictability and the accuracy of those predictions. Our emphasis on prediction and prediction accuracy, therefore, reflects an interest in "differential prediction" as opposed to differential validity.

IMPLICATIONS FOR RESEARCH

The field of personnel selection provides a useful arena for exemplifying these issues. Since selection involves making decisions (e.g., hire/not hire) about people based on information obtained in the predictor data set, it follows that "useful" information would necessarily have to be that which allows us to make better selection decisions. *With regard to hypotheses involving moderator effects, this implies the need to incorpo-* *rate the hypothesized moderator variable within a predictive framework.* Thus, knowing that a given test (i.e., predictor) is differentially valid across sex subgroups does not, in and of itself, lead to better selection decisions. Such information, at best, *suggests* that different prediction equations *might* be necessary to optimize correct decisions within each of the sex subgroups, or possibly that the test should not be used for selection purposes for one or more groups of applicants.

This, of course, is the crux of the issue—differential validity does not necessarily imply that different prediction lines must be developed. That is, knowledge that differential validity exists is not invariably synonymous with the need to develop separate prediction equations! As discussed by Arnold (1982), O'Connor et al. (1981), and Peters and Champoux (1979a), differences between subgroup correlations can occur in the absence of slope differences if the ratio of SD_x to SD_y differs markedly across subgroups. Since a correlation coefficient can be rewritten as a raw score slope coefficient times the ratio of variabilities in x over y (i.e., $r_{xy} = (b_{yx})(SD_x/SD_y)$), then a test for the difference between two correlations can be rewritten as an omnibus test comparing $(b_{yx})(SD_x/SD_y)$ in one group to the other. In this form, it is clear that the b's can be exactly equal to one another, across groups, and yet the correlations will differ to the extent that SD_x/SD_y in one group is markedly different from its counterpart in the other group.[2] In effect, knowledge of differential validity (a moderator hypothesis involving differing "strengths" of relationships), at most, signals that different prediction strategies (a moderator hypothesis involving differing "forms" of relationships) might be necessary. Thus, a follow-up step, involving the development of prediction equations per

---

[2] In like manner, significant slope differences, across groups, might be masked by offsetting ratios of standard deviations (O'Connor et al., 1981). This latter result might lead to an incorrect conclusion that separate prediction strategies are unnecessary. Thus, unless SD_x/SD_y are equal, across subgroups, differential validity results are difficult to meaningfully interpret.

se, would be necessary in order to meaningfully assess the need for differential prediction systems across subgroups.

To the degree that it is relevant for researchers to actually predict and influence behavior in organizational settings (e.g., improving performance, reducing stress), their efforts should be directed toward the development of effective prediction and intervention strategies. The effectiveness of such strategies can only be judged in terms of criterion outcomes, not in terms of the magnitude of predictor to criterion associations. Therefore, whenever a researcher wishes to meaningfully consider whether the relationship between a particular variable and relevant organizational outcomes is affected by some third variable, this question can best be examined in terms of the impact of these variables upon the relevant criterion or outcome scores.[3]

Peters and Champoux (1979a) pointed out that when one is interested in response differences, one should employ moderated regression techniques and abandon subgroup correlation comparisons. Our point is that industrial and organizational researchers should always be interested in just that—understanding, predicting, and influencing *response differences*.

ANALYTICAL STRATEGIES

Since the application of knowledge in organizational settings necessitates predicting criterion scores and estimating the accuracy of those predictions, it follows that useful hypotheses and useful statistical procedures should focus on these goals. As implied in the discussion above, and as clearly stated in the papers by Arnold (1982) and Peters and Champoux (1979a, 1979b), such procedures already exist for predicting criterion scores. In particular, we are referring to hierarchical moderated regression techniques. In like manner, procedures exist to compare the accuracy of predictions, across subgroups. We will now turn to describing and exemplifying these analytical procedures.

Testing for Differential Prediction of Criterion Scores

Hierarchical moderated regression is the analytical procedure which allows one to determine the extent to which the potential moderator variable "interacts" with predictors in the prediction of the criterion.[4] In effect, when using moderated regression, we are concerned with the extent to which predicted responses on the criterion depend jointly on the predictor and moderator variables. In so doing, the focus of the moderator variable test is on the equality of the form or pattern of the association relating a criterion to a predictor for different score values (or with qualitative moderator variables, with different subgroups) of a moderator.

Let us first consider the case of a single quantitative predictor variable and a dichotomous moderator variable (represented by a single dummy variable). In this case, if the form of the relationship between the predictor and criterion depends upon the moderator variable, then the slopes of the within-subgroup regression lines will be sig-

---

[3] Peters and Champoux (1979a) suggest that where "the moderating variable is continuous, subgroup analysis should be viewed, at best, as a useful preliminary to applying a moderated regression model" (pp. 94–95). We acknowledge that such procedures might be useful as a preliminary test, but even then, only during the *early* stages of theory development when no theoretically compelling propositions exist regarding the causal direction among the variables under study. However, even in these instances, one must be sure that observed correlational differences do not solely reflect differences, across subgroups, in the variances on either or both the predictors or criteria (O'Connor et al., 1981).

[4] In addition, in the absence of a significant interaction, we can also determine the main effect of the potential moderator variable on the criterion.

nificantly different. This is equivalent to a significant interaction between the predictor and moderator variables (Cohen & Cohen, 1975), and can be tested via the hierarchical moderated regression model. In the case described, the regression equation is given by:

$$\hat{Y} = a + b_1X_1 + b_2X_2 + b_3X_3,$$

where $\hat{Y}$ is the predicted criterion score, X_1 is the dummy variable representing the subgroups of the moderator variable, X_2 is the predictor score, and X_3 is the interaction term (defined as the cross-product of X_1 and X_2).[5] The a and b terms are the understandardized least-squares regression weights.

The presence of a moderator-predictor interaction is evaluated by testing the significance of the regression weight associated with the cross-product term (i.e., b_3) in the regression equation. This, in effect, tests the null hypothesis that $\beta_3 = 0$, where β_3 is the population regression weight for X_3. The most common, of many, methods for performing this test (see Kerlinger & Pedhazur, 1973) is to compare the R^2 for the full regression model (which contains X_1, X_2, & X_3) with the R^2 for the reduced regression model (which deletes X_3 and therefore contains only X_1 & X_2). If the increment in R^2 due to the cross-product term is found to be significant, then X_1 and X_2 are said to interact, and X_1 would be considered to be a moderator variable.

The general test for the increment in R^2 due to the cross-product term is given by:

$$F = \frac{(R_F^2 - R_R^2) / (k_F - k_R)}{(1 - R_F^2) / (N - k_F - 1)},$$

where R_F^2 and R_R^2 are the squared multiple correlations for the full and restricted models, respectively, k_F and k_R are the number of b weights in the full and restricted models, respectively, and N is equal to the sample size. The degrees of freedom for the F-test are $(k_F - k_R)$ and $(N - k_F - 1)$.

The significance test described above in (2) can be used when testing for multivalued categorical moderator variables (requiring the formation of more than one dummy variable) and continuous moderator variables as well. In like manner, more than one predictor and/or more than one moderator variable may be tested using this analytical technique. The significance test requires only the formation of the appropriate number of cross-product terms, the prior partialing of all independent variables which define those cross-product terms, and the appropriate full and restricted models on which the F-tests rest. Detailed reviews of these procedures can be found in Cohen (1978), Cohen and Cohen (1975), and Kerlinger and Pedhazur (1973).

The hierarchical moderated regression model also contains other information useful to the researcher. Returning to our two subgroup example, if the interaction between the moderator and predictor is found to be nonsignificant, then the significance test for the first term entered into the model (X_1) is equivalent to a test for mean differences, across subgroups, on the criterion. Thus, even if X_1 is not found to be a moderator (i.e., the interaction term is nonsignificant), knowledge of subgroup membership may improve our ability to predict outcome scores.

---

[5] The specification of the order of entry of the moderator and predictor variables into the regression equation should correspond to the specific research questions being asked. The second variable entered, naturally, is tested for significance after the effects due to the first have been removed. Thus, different orders of entry will answer different questions regarding these variables. In the present case, we have chosen to follow the examples given in Cohen and Cohen (1975) and Kerlinger and Pedhazur (1973). In no case, however, do we wish to imply that it is a matter of discretion as to when the cross-product term is entered into the model. In all instances, the cross-product term is entered only after its constituent variables have been entered (see, specifically, Cohen, 1978).

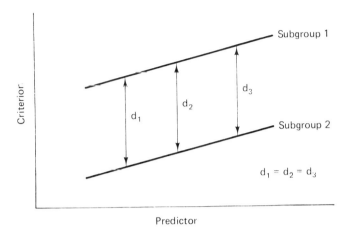

Figure 1.   Hypothetical Regression Results Depicting a Significant Subgroup Main Effect and No Interaction

Note that the lack of an interaction implies parallel within-subgroup regression lines, and therefore, subgroup differences in criterion scores which are constant across all values of the predictor. Figure 1 depicts a significant main effect for group membership in the absence of a group membership x predictor interaction. However, when a significant interaction is found, as exemplified in Figure 2, subgroup differences on the criterion vary across values of the predictor, reflecting within-subgroup regression lines which are not parallel.

When within-subgroup regression lines

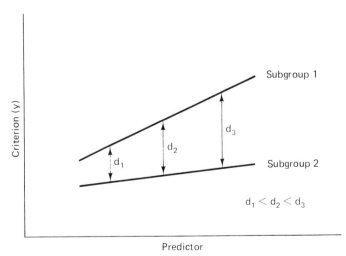

Figure 2.   Hypothetical Regression Results Depicting a Significant Interaction

are not parallel, the situation is analogous to the presence of an interaction in an analysis of variance. With analysis of variance, one would not try to interpret the main effects, but rather, explore the simple effects (see Winer, 1971). In the regression case, this translates into evaluating "regions" along the predictor continuum in which differences in the criterion, across subgroups, are significant. Use of the Johnson-Neyman technique (see Kerlinger & Pedhazur, 1973) allows one to establish such significance regions. In any case, plotting the within-subgroup regression equations further allows the visual inspection of all significant interactions. It is one thing to find a significant interaction and quite another to find a pattern of results which turns out to be consistent with the theoretical model which generated the investigation in the first place!

The within-subgroup regression equations are easily obtained from the moderated regression equation (see Cohen & Cohen, 1975). When the moderator is a continuous variable, the researcher will have to choose values of the moderator for which "within-subgroup" regression lines will be plotted. Of course, caution should always be used when artificially transforming a continuous variable into two or more discrete subgroups. Such decisions should be based on the "range of interest" of the variables under investigation (Kerlinger & Pedhazur, 1973), and result in theoretically meaningful subgroups.

Example: The following hypothetical example is provided to demonstrate the use of hierarchical moderated regression analysis. For this purpose, data are analyzed for 53 persons who provided information on Y (a continuous criterion variable), X_1 (a dichotomous moderator variable, dummy coded) and X_2 (a continuous predictor variable). According to the theory underlying the research, reason exists to expect that X_1 will interact with X_2 in the prediction of Y such

that X_2 will predict Y differently in subgroup 1 than in subgroup 2. Specifically, it was predicted that X_2 would be positively associated with the criterion within subgroup 1, but negatively related to it within subgroup 2. Thus, we hypothesize that X_1 will moderate the $X_2 - Y$ association.

Descriptive statistics for this data set are provided in Table 1. Means, standard deviations and the zero-order correlation matrix for all study variables, including the cross-product term, are displayed. Note that the correlation between the cross-product term and the criterion is uninterpretable. This is because the cross-product term, taken at face value, is an arbitrarily scaled variable, and as such cannot be directly interpreted (Cohen, 1978; Schmidt, 1973). While this cross-product term "carries" the interaction, it cannot be interpreted as an interaction term until X_1 and X_2 have been partialed from it (see Cohen, 1978). As indicated in Table 1, both the X_1 and X_2 variables bear a significant zero-order relationship with the criterion. The question of their interaction in the prediction of that criterion, however, requires the use of hierarchical regression procedures, as discussed above.

The results of the hierarchical moderated regression for this hypothetical data set are given in Table 2. The test for an interaction between X_1 and X_2 is given by the F-value for the increment in R^2 after the addi-

TABLE 1
Descriptive Statistics, and Correlation Matrix for Example Data (n = 53)

		r		
	y	x_1	x_2	x_3
X_1	−.468*			
X_2	.354*	−.103		
X_3	−.139	.647*	.650*	
Mean	22.11	0.28	3.11	3.94
S.D.	11.53	0.45	1.10	1.89

* p < .01

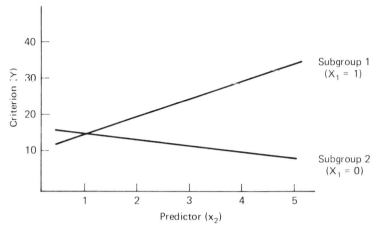

Figure 3.   Within Subgroup Regression Lines for Predicting Y from X_2 for Example Data

tion of the cross-product term (X_3). In this case, the significant R^2 increment of .053 indicates significant differences in the slopes of the within-subgroup regression lines (see Figure 3).

At this point we know that a significant interaction between X_1 and X_2 exists. Further, because of the presence of the interaction, the significant "main effects" for X_1 and X_2 (see Table 2) cannot be directly interpreted. An understanding of the results given in Table 2 now requires an exploration of the individual regression lines of Y on X_2 for each subgroup and the identification of the regions of significance across these subgroups using the Johnson-Neyman technique. The reader is referred to Kerlinger and Pedhazur (1973) for a concrete example

involving the use of this technique. For the present purposes, we need only note that the criterion differences, across subgroups, get increasingly larger as the predictor score increases. Further, an inspection of Figure 3 suggests that for low scores on the predictor, the subgroups are not significantly different on the criterion. However, for high scorers on the predictor, the subgroups appear to differ substantively on the criterion. As predicted, the relationship between Y and X_2 tends to be positive within subgroup 1 and negative within subgroup 2. Note that the moderator variable hypotheses was cast in a way that allows us to better understand the relationship between X_2 and Y. As such, use of the predictor information for decision making purposes is clarified by inclusion of

TABLE 2

Hierarchical Moderated Regression Analysis for Example Data

Independent Variables	cum R^2	F	df	Independent Variable Added	R^2 Increment	F(step)	df
X_1	.219	14.30**	1,51	X_1	.219	14.30**	1,51
X_1, X_2	.314	11.44**	2,50	X_2	.095	6.89**	1,50
X_1, X_2, X_3	.367	9.47**	3,49	X_3	.053	4.11**	1,49

* $p < .05$
** $p < .01$

information provided by the moderator variable.

Testing for Differential Accuracy of Prediction

Computation of the standard error of estimate (SE_{est}) allows one to evaluate the accuracy of prediction for a single group of subjects. When testing for *differential* accuracy in prediction, across the two or more groups formed on a moderator variable, the appropriate test involves comparing standard error terms, across subgroups.

An unbiased estimate of the population SE_{est} using sample data, is given by

$$SE_{est} = S_y\sqrt{(1-r_{xy}^2)\left(\frac{N-1}{N-2}\right)}, \quad (3)$$

where S_y is the standard deviation of the observed criterion scores, r_{xy}^2 is the squared validity coefficient, and N is the sample size on which r_{xy} is based. When there are two subgroups under consideration, the appropriate *test for differential accuracy* (Reynolds, 1982) is given by

$$F = \frac{SE_{est_1}^2}{SE_{est_2}^2}, \quad (4)$$

where $SE_{est_1}^2$ and $SE_{est_2}^2$ are the variance errors of estimate for groups 1 and 2, respectively. This test statistic is compared to an F distribution with $N_1 - 2$ and $N_2 - 2$ degrees of freedom.[6] When one is considering more than two subgroups, significance tests such as the Box-Scheffe test can be used (see Kirk, 1982). With a continuous moderator variable, one would need to form two or more subgroups by breaking up the moderator continuum into discrete "blocks" and then compute SE_{est} for each of these artificially created subgroups. This is directly analogous to the formation of "regions" to be tested for significance when exploring a significant interaction in the case of a continuous moderator variable (see discussion, above). Again, the subgroups formed by this procedure should lie within the range of interest and, if possible, reflect a construct valid distinction.

If a significant F is observed, it would indicate that one cannot have the same degree of confidence in the predictions made about persons in each of the two or more subgroups, even if all have the *same* predicted score. For example, in predicting the scores of both men and women who have an identical predicted criterion score of 80, we might observe that the standard error of prediction is 2 for the male subgroup and 4 for the female subgroup. This would result in a 95 percent confidence interval for males ranging from 76 to 84. For females, the same confidence bound would range from 72 to 88. The impact of such a difference in confidence intervals becomes increasingly clearer as (a) the difference in the size of the standard errors of estimate becomes larger and (b) as the decision to be made becomes more critical.

While it is true that, for a given sample in which S_y is held constant, increases in the correlation between a predictor and a criterion will be associated with a smaller standard error of estimate, it is not true that testing for the difference between correlations is synonymous with testing for differences in prediction accuracy. Not only do correlations affect SE_{est}'s, but just as importantly so do the standard deviations of the criterion scores in each of the subgroups (See formula 3). Hence, unless the standard deviations of criterion scores are equal across subgroups, the tests for differential validity and differential accuracy of prediction will not be equivalent. For example, assume that for N = 200 males, r_{xy} = .60 and

---

[6] In testing for differences between standard errors of estimate, it is assumed that the joint distribution of predictor and criterion scores is bivariate normal within each subgroup, an assumption shared with tests for differences between correlation coefficients.

$SD_y = 15$, and for a sample of N = 200 females, $r_{xy} = .50$ and $SD_y = 25$. The test for differential validity (see Arnold, 1982; Peters & Champoux, 1979a, among others) would yield a value of z = 1.43, which at the .05 confidence level is nonsignificant. Utilizing these same data in a test for differential accuracy, however, yields very different results. In this case, the SE_{est} for the male and female groups are 12.00 and 21.66, respectively. Using formula 2 to test for differential accuracy of prediction, the result (F(198, 198) = 3.26) is highly significant. In this case, the strength of relationships did not differ across subgroups, but the accuracy of prediction did. Thus, it is evident that differences in prediction accuracy involve both the relative dispersion of subgroup criterion scores and the degree of relationship between the predictor and criterion.

CONCLUSION[7]

The theme of this paper has been that researchers should evaluate the usefulness of hypotheses against the real world consequences which result from employing the resulting information in applied decision-making situations. With regard to moderator variable hypotheses, abstract information concerning the amount of variance shared between a predictor and criterion in one group as compared to another group simply does not contribute to advancing our "understanding" of such relationships. In contrast, we contend that moderator hypotheses involving differing patterns of relationships between predictors and criteria, depending on the score values of a third, moderator variable, contribute to both prediction and understanding. Therefore, we conclude that

---

[7] One issue not deal with to this point concerns the accumulation of results across studies. While no method currently exists to accumulate raw score regression weights, such procedures do exist for accumulating correlation coefficients (see Hunter, Schmidt & Jackson, 1982). Since it is the accumulated evidence on any issue which should be considered in reaching general conclusions concerning that issue, this would appear to argue for the use of correlational, as opposed to regression-based, methodologies. We, however, see no inconsistency between the validity generalization cumulation techniques for correlations (as opposed to differences between correlations) and our position advocating the use of moderated regression to test moderator variable hypotheses within any given study.

This conclusion reflects two related issues. First, validity generalization cumulation techniques (see Hunter, Schmidt, & Jackson, 1982) do not initially attempt to directly test hypotheses regarding particular moderator variables. The purposes of such cumulation techniques are to estimate whether or not a moderator variable might be needed to account for the distribution of observed effects across studies, and if none seems warranted, to estimate the strength of the effect in the population. Such techniques help estimate the percentage of variance in observed effects, across studies, which is due to various statistical artifacts (e.g., sampling error, differential reliability or range restriction). Based on this information, the researcher is better able to judge whether or not any substantial variance in the observed effects remains for which one or more moderator variables might be hypothesized as explanations. If most of the variance in the observed effects is "accounted for" by the artifacts, then obviously there is little variance left to be explained by a moderator. If that residual variance is large, it signals that one or more moderators may indeed be operating.

Second, such procedures regard differential range restriction as a primary artifact which requires "control." Such procedures recognize that correlations are affected by the amount of variance available in a particular research setting. Since such differences, across studies, will have the effect of producing a distribution of observed correlations, those differences need to be controlled when determining whether meaningful subgroup correlation differences actually exist. In this same sense, within a given study, we have argued for the need to control for differences in variability, across subgroups, in both the predictor and criterion variables through the use of hierarchical moderated regression. Thus, the meta-analytic cumulation techniques "control" for the same source of variance that we argue warrants against the use of correlational comparisons within any single study. In this manner, both cumulation techniques and the position we have taken are similar.

the "tradition" within industrial and organizational research of testing the moderator effects involving differing strengths of relationships, such as has been done in the differential validity area, does not serve a useful scientific goal. Rather, such goals are best served by the investigation of more precise, theoretically derived prediction equations. As such, we advocate the use of the analytical techniques described in this paper as being more appropriate for testing hypotheses involving both (a) the differential prediction of criterion scores and (b) the differential accuracy of those predictions.

References

Arnold, H. J. "Moderator Variables: A Clarification of Conceptual, Analytic, and Psychometric Issues." *Organizational Behavior and Human Performance,* 1982, *29,* 143–174.

Cohen, J. "Partialed Products Are Interactions; Partialed Powers Are Curved Components." *Psychological Bulletin,* 1978, *85,* 858–866.

Cohen, J., & Cohen, P. *Applied Multiple Regression/Correlation Analysis for the Behavioral Sciences.* Hillsdale, New Jersey: Erlbaum, 1975.

Fredericksen, N., & Melville, S.D. "Differential Predictability in the Use of Test Scores." *Educational and Psychological Measurement,* 1954, *14,* 647–656.

Hunter, J. E., Schmidt, F. L., & Jackson, G. B. *Meta-Analysis: Cumulating Research Findings Across Studies.* Beverly Hills, CA: Sage Publications, Inc., 1982.

Kerlinger, F. N., & Pedhazur, E. J. *Multiple Regression in Behavioral Research.* New York: Holt, Rinehart, & Winston, 1973.

Kirk, R. E. *Experimental Design: Procedures for the Behavioral Sciences.* Belmont, CA: Brooks/Cole Publishing Co., 1982.

O'Connor, E. J., Wiorkowski, J., & Peters, L. H. "The Identification of Moderator Variables: Clarification of the Appropriateness of Alternative Analytical Techniques." Paper presented at the National Meetings of the Academy of Management, San Diego, CA, August, 1981.

Peters, W. S., & Champoux, J. E. "The Use of Moderated Regression in Job Redesign Decisions." *Decision Sciences,* 1979, *10,* 85–95. (a)

Peters, W. S., & Champoux, J. E. "The Role and Analysis of Moderator Variables in Organizational Research." In R. T. Mowday and R. M. Steers (Eds.). *Research in Organizations: Issues and Controversies.* Santa Monica, California: Goodyear Publishing Company, 1979, 239–253. (b)

Reynolds, C. R. "Methods for Detecting Construct and Predictive Bias." In R. A. Berk (Ed.), *Handbook of Methods for Detecting Test Bias.* Baltimore: Johns Hopkins University Press, 1982.

Saunders. D. R. "Moderator Variables in Prediction." *Educational and Psychological Measurement,* 1956, *16,* 209–222.

Schmidt, F. L. "Implications of a Measurement Problem for Expectancy Theory Research." *Organizational Behavior and Human Performance,* 1973, *10,* 243–251.

Wiggins, J. S. *Personality and Prediction: Principals of Personality Assessment.* Reading, Massachusetts: Addison-Wesley, 1973.

Winer, B. *Statistical Principles in Experimental Design.* New York: McGraw-Hill, 1971.

Zedeck, S. "Problems with the Use of 'Moderator' Variables." *Psychological Bulletin,* 1971, *76,* 295–310.

Use of Path Analysis in Industrial/ Organizational Psychology: Criticisms and Suggestions[1]

Robert S. Billings

Steve P. Wroten[2]

Path analysis is a technique that uses ordinary least squares regression to help the researcher test the consequences of proposed causal relationships among a set of variables. Used most specifically, path analysis can test an a priori causal hypothesis against a set of observed correlations. At the most general level, path analysis can be used to test a number of alternative causal sequences against one another. In any application of path analysis, very specific and important assumptions underlie the technique; if any of these assumptions are violated, the causal inferences will very possibly be incorrect.

This article explores these assumptions in detail and offers specific advice about how to deal with them. Our purpose is not to add to the techniques of path analysis, but rather to translate the procedures, problems, and possible solutions into operational terms that can be more easily understood and used by industrial/organizational researchers. In doing so, examples of the use of path analysis from the industrial/organizational psychol-

ogy literature are examined. These examples resulted from a comprehensive search for path analytic studies appearing in the *Journal of Applied Psychology, Personnel Psychology,* the *Academy of Management Journal,* and the *Organizational Behavior and Human Performance* from 1970 to 1978.

BRIEF SUMMARY OF THE PROCEDURES IN PATH ANALYSIS

What follows is a very brief summary of procedures, condensed from other more extensive and quantitative treatments (e.g., Duncan, 1975; Heise, 1975; Kerlinger & Pedhazur, 1973; Land, 1969), to provide an overview and to set the stage for the criticisms and suggestions that follow, not necessarily to enable the reader to conduct a path analysis.

It should be noted that some issues in causal analysis are not dealt with here because they do not affect the points made. For

[1] Reproduced by permission of the *Journal of Applied Psychology* 1978, 63, 677–688.

[2] The authors would like to thank Tony Greenwald and two anonymous reviewers for very useful comments.

example, this article assumes the use of standardized regression coefficients, which are most useful when variables are measured in different units or when the purpose is to compare the relative amount of variance accounted for by different predictors in a single population. Alternatively, unstandardized coefficients are appropriate when comparing structured equations across different populations (Blalock, 1967; Hargens, 1976; Kim & Mueller, 1976).

The first step in path analysis is to order a set of variables so that the direction of causality can plausibly flow only in one direction. That is, if the variables are numbered 1–5, a variable numbered lower than another variable might be a cause of that variable but cannot be affected by that variable, even indirectly through other variables. This causal ordering, which produces a model called *recursive,* is a key assumption that is discussed in more detail as follows.

One-way causal ordering need not hold for variables labeled *exogenous.* Exogenous variables are one or more variables whose causes lie outside of the system. If there are two or more exogenous variables, they may be correlated, with no causal direction specified. Only the *endogenous* variables, whose causes lie within the system, must be ordered. The variance of an endogenous variable is accounted for by the effects of other endogenous and exogenous variables prior to it in the ordering (although some paths may be deleted because of theory or the data) and a *residual* term.

A central assumption in path analysis is that a given residual affects only one variable and is correlated neither with other system variables nor with other residuals. This assumption allows the researcher to create, for each endogenous variable, a causal model

that is a weighted function of variables prior to this variable and an error term (the residual) that is unrelated to other system variables or other residuals. Multiple regression is used to determine the actual weights, with each endogenous variable being treated as the criterion and the variables hypothesized to directly affect it being entered as predictors. The standardized beta weights that result are generally called *path coefficients,* with P_{CB}, for example, standing for the direct effect of variable B on C. Indirect effects occur when (a) a third variable affects both variables in question, either directly or indirectly through other variables, (b) correlated exogenous variables affect the variables directly or indirectly, or (c) one of the two variables affects a third variable, which directly or indirectly affects the second variable. Computationally, an indirect path is computed by multiplying together all of the direct path coefficients making it up.

If the researcher is testing a theory that predicts the absence of one or more direct paths (e.g., leader structuring affects subordinate satisfaction only through role ambiguity and not directly), then those variables having only indirect effects (here, leader structuring) are deleted from the regression for that dependent variable (here, satisfaction). In order for the data to support the theory, the paths that are predicted to exist should be statistically greater than zero (or be deemed "meaningful," usually greater than .05).[3] In addition, the reduced causal model must be consistent with the correlation matrix, as explained below. An alternative to theory testing is *theory trimming* (Heise, 1969). Here, all variables prior to a given variable are entered as predictors, and paths are deleted that do not differ from zero or are not deemed meaningful.

---

[3] There are several potential problems with the use of ordinary F tests for regression coefficients that led to the convention of deleting paths if less than .05. With large samples, trivially small paths may be statistically significant. If extreme multicollinearity exists, then the F test may produce incorrect conclusions. Finally, a direct effect may be nonsignificant and thus deleted, whereas an indirect effect of the same size may be retained because the direct effects making it up are all significant.

Using either approach, if the final model has eliminated one or more direct paths, then the model must be tested against the data by attempting to reproduce the correlation matrix. Given all of the necessary assumptions (recursive system, uncorrelated residuals, plus others discussed below) and given that all paths are left in the model, each correlation is a sum of the direct effect and all indirect effects. If some paths are now deleted (because of one's theory or theory trimming), then the model is only consistent with the data if the observed correlations can still be reproduced with the appropriate direct and indirect paths set equal to zero. In the simplest example, if theory says that $A \rightarrow B \rightarrow C$, then r_{AC} should equal the indirect effect of A on C through B or $P_{RA} P_{CR}$.

In summary, the researcher must assume causality in order to use path analysis. In particular, the causal sequence of the variables must be specified in advance (although, as discussed below, alternative orderings may be tested against one another). In all cases, however, the assumption of uncorrelated residuals applies, meaning that third-variable explanations are eliminated by assumption. Once these two major assumptions are made, then alternative causal sequences can be tested against the data.

PATH ANALYSIS AND MULTICOLLINEARITY

When testing causal models, special problems may arise due to intercorrelations among the variables. Consider a situation in which the effects of A and B on C are being examined. If A and B are completely orthogonal, then the individual effects of the two variables on C can be easily separated (and path analysis loses its value). As A and B become correlated, it becomes more difficult to cleanly separate their effects on C. Here path analysis is most useful, in that the implica-

tions of the different causal models relating A and B to C can be evaluated using the data. However, as A and B become highly correlated (a condition referred to as multicollinearity), problems emerge, for it becomes increasingly difficult to separate the effects of A and B.

Multicollinearity produces several interrelated problems. Computational errors in determining the least squares solution are possible, unless the computer carries many digits. When the multicollinearity is extreme (above .80), the standard error of the regression weight becomes large, making it difficult to reject the null hypothesis that the regression weight (and hence the direct effect) is zero. In addition, the actual size of the regression weight may vary greatly from sample to sample. This has a greater impact on stepwise regression (since the order in which highly correlated variables are brought into the equation depends mostly on sampling error) than on hierarchical regression, upon which path analysis relies. However, if the researcher is disregarding statistical tests and using the .05 rule of thumb discussed earlier, then multicollinearity may result in incorrect causal inference because of instability of the estimation of the regression weights. (See Cohen & Cohen, 1975, pp. 115, 117, for a discussion of these issues.)

Several partial solutions to the problems of multicollinearity exist. A large sample size is useful in decreasing the standard error (Heise, 1975, p. 187). Replication with a different sample is often suggested (e.g., Cohen & Cohen, 1975, p. 116). If the highly correlated variables are conceptually similar, it may be best to combine them into one measure of a broader concept. Alternatively, the intercorrelated variables may be treated as a block, with the relationships among them not analyzed (Namboodiri, Carter, & Blalock, 1975, pp. 526–530). Finally, it may be possible to delete the variable(s) of least interest, although this may violate the assumption of uncorrelated residuals.

PATH ANALYSIS AND CROSS-LAGGED CORRELATION

Despite some recent statements (Feldman, 1975: Young, 1977) path analysis and cross-lagged correlation are entirely different techniques with different purposes and different assumptions. As best articulated by Kenny (1973, 1975), cross-lagged correlation is a technique for testing the null hypothesis that the observed correlation between two variables is spurious. That is, that two variables are correlated only because each is related to a third variable, which may be unknown to the researcher and unmeasured. The technique rests upon very specific and rather stringent assumptions (e.g., synchronicity, stationarity, homogeneous stability) that differ from the assumptions necessary for path analysis.

Cross-lagged correlation can only be conducted when the same set of variables is measured at two (or more) points in time. Path analysis does not require such a design. Although time may be a useful ingredient, a path analysis may be conducted on variables that are all measured at the same time. Even if they are used on the same data, path analysis and cross-lagged correlation would be answering different questions. These two techniques, therefore, should not be lumped under the general heading of "causal correlational techniques" and treated as interchangeable.

Path analysis and cross-lagged correlation can complement each other in an important way. A major assumption of path analysis is that the correlation between observed variables is not due to some unmeasured third variable. Given that the data are available, this assumption can be checked using cross-lagged correlation. Once a nonspurious causal relation is verified, path analysis can be applied to determine the relative size of all direct and indirect effects. In fact, as Kenny (1975) suggests, one can imagine a hierarchy of designs: simple correlation to establish a relationship, cross-lagged correlation to eliminate the third variable explanation, and path analysis to imbed the relationship in a larger causal network.

ASSUMPTIONS OF PATH ANALYSIS

Uncorrelated Residuals

A primary assumption in path analysis is that the residuals of endogenous variables are not correlated with one another or with other endogenous variables. The consequences of disregarding this assumption may be severe; the size of a path coefficient may be either over- or underestimated, leading to incorrect causal inference. For example, consider the simple system.

$$A \to B \to C,$$

with the observed $r_{AB} = .30$. If one accepts the assumption that the residuals of A and B are uncorrelated, then the conclusion is that $P_{BA} = .30$ or that A has a direct effect on B. But, if an unknown variable, D, is correlated with A at .60 and B at .50, then the true direct effect of A on B is zero, because $r_{AB} = P_{BA} + P_{DA} P_{DB}$ or $P_{BA} = r_{AB} - P_{DA} P_{DB} = .30 - (.60) (.50) = 0$.

This crucial assumption is often not dealt with adequately in the industrial/organizational psychology literature. In many of the studies reviewed, plausible unmeasured variables may have been responsible for the observed relationship between two system variables. For example, Sims and Szilagyi (1975) examined the relationship between performance-reward expectancy and work satisfaction, finding a direct effect of expectancy on satisfaction of .28 for associate nursing directors. A plausible, unmeasured third variable is performance level; assuming some rewards were connected to performance, those performing better might perceive a higher expectancy and might also be more satisfied with the work.

Because the failure to consider potential

third variables often stems from inadequate theorizing before the data are collected, theory and other empirical studies should be closely examined. In essence, the researcher should consider the following questions. For each variable in my system, what causes or correlates have others suggested and/or found? Are any of these outside variables suspected causes or correlates of more than one variable in my system? If so, what assumptions can I make about these possible third variables in this study? If such a variable is controlled at one level (either artificially, through selection of subjects or direct control of the variable, or naturally), then it presents no problem (except to note its possible role when discussing the generalization of findings). However, if it is uncontrolled and could conceivably be related to two or more system variables, then the variable should be measured and brought into the system.

This procedure is obviously difficult to carry out and may lead to long lists of variables that must be either examined or controlled. However, the number may be kept more manageable by beginning with a single "dependent" variable, whose causes you wish to examine, and working backward from that variable.

Along with properly specifying the variables in the causal network in advance, there are several other ways of dealing with the third variable problem. The usefulness of cross-lagged correlation was discussed earlier. Likewise, one could conduct a true experiment to demonstrate that there is an effect of A and B.

However, with both of these approaches generalization can be questionable. Even if an effect of A and B can be shown in a controlled experiment, this does not rule out the possibility that in a particular field setting an uncontrolled, unmeasured third variable— one that was held constant or randomized in the experiment—causes both A and B. Likewise, the conclusion of cross-lagged correlation cannot be generalized blindly to a different population or setting because an important third variable may be "controlled" in one setting but not another. As an illustration, assume that A is a minor cause of B but that C strongly affects both A and B. If a cross-lagged analysis is conducted in a setting in which C does not vary, the conclusion might be that the relationship between A and B is causal and not spurious. However, this does not mean that the assumption of uncorrelated residuals is valid in other settings, for C might vary and be a cause of both A and B. Thus, the most powerful way to combine cross-lagged correlation and path analysis is to conduct both analyses on the same sample in the same setting.

Hall and Foster (1977) used this strategy of measuring variables over time and conducting both path analysis and cross-lagged correlations, although they did not use either technique to full advantage. They propose the following model: goals → effort → performance → attitudes (psychological success, self-esteem, involvement) → goals. Each variable is measured at two times, 3 months apart, on subjects competing in a business simulation. Path coefficients are reported for the variables in the order above for (a) all measures at Time 1 (T_1) plus goals at Time 2 (T_2), (b) all measures at T_2, (c) T_1 goals, effort, performance and T_2 attitudes, and (d) T_1 attitudes and T_2 goals, effort, and performance. In addition, cross-lagged correlations between performance and the three attitudes measures are reported. The authors do not mention the assumption of uncorrelated residuals and so do not tie the results of the cross-lagged analysis to the path analysis. Further, it is not clear why only the performance → attitudes portion of the model is examined with the cross lags. Although the path analysis is consistent with their conclusion that goals affect effort and involvement affects goals, the alternative explanation of a spurious relationship is not examined with cross-lagged analysis.

Ordering of Variables

Although path analysis can be used to test alternative orderings of variables (see Kerlinger & Pedhazur, 1973, pp. 327–330, for an example), within each model the direction of causality must be assumed to be one-way. That is, an endogenous variable cannot both affect and be affected by the same endogenous variable, and no variable can feed back upon itself through other variables (Duncan, 1975). Exogenous variables may be allowed to reciprocally cause each other, as explained above.

This may seem to present problems when testing one of the many theories in industrial/organizational psychology, which include feedback loops (e.g., Lawler's, 1973, expectancy theory model). Upon closer examination, most such feedback loops actually hypothesize something like the following: A at Time 1 affects B at Time 2, which then affects A at Time 3. Because the same variable measured at two points in time is actually two different variables, path analysis can be used to test such cyclical models, if the data are collected at different points in time.

Models that actually do involve reciprocal causation (which are probably rarer than the cyclical models) can be dealt with through more complex models, such as two-stage least squares (see Duncan, 1975, or Duncan, Haller, & Portes, 1968). The important point here is that the researcher must clearly articulate the nature of any hypothesized feedback, specifying how time enters into the thinking, and design the research accordingly.

One additional issue concerning the ordering of variables involves the large number of alternative models that would be generated if all possible orders are examined. As Young (1977) points out, even four or five variable systems have more possible configurations than can be reasonably tested. Specifically, an a priori ordering of variables

greatly reduces the number of alternative models; operationally, theory and logic can aid in eliminating some models, as advocated by Young.

A useful, but limited strategy, is that of measuring variables at different times. For example, if a researcher wishes to test $A \to B \to C$ against

$$A \to B \quad C,$$

then measuring A, B, and C sequentially over time will automatically eliminate the alternative explanation that B at Time 2 affects A at Time 1, C at time 3 affects B at Time 2, and so forth. However, it should be noted that these alternative orderings are rejected only for the specific data set examined; measuring the data in the order above cannot eliminate other possibilities, such as C at Time 1 affecting both B at Time 2 and C at Time 3. This argument suggests that the ideal is to measure each variable at each time period, so that all possible orders can be examined, a strategy that becomes more difficult as the number of variables increases.

If sequential measurement across time is used, then it is important that the time period chosen conform to the speed of the causal effects suggested by the theory. Unfortunately, industrial/organizational theorists are not often concerned with the time it takes for an effect to occur. One virtue of causal analyses (e.g., cross-lagged correlations, path analysis over time) and quasi-experimental designs (e.g., interrupted time series) is that they encourage attention to time as a variable (see Billings, Klimoski, & Breaugh, 1977, for an example).

Hall and Foster (1977) provide an example of path analysis with variables measured at different times. Goals, effort, performance, and three attitudes were measured at two times 3 weeks apart. Different combinations of measures were then examined to test their cyclical model. Although not enough time periods were available to order all six variables unambiguously, time was useful in providing a strong test of several implications of their cyclical model. As pointed out earlier, these rich data could have been used to better advantage. For example, the hypothesis that effort affects performance was always tested with the same time period; perhaps it takes time for effort to be translated into performance (implying that effort at Time 1 → performance at Time 2) or perhaps feedback on performance affects efforts in the next round.

In most other uses of path analysis in the industrial/organizational psychology literature, the issue of the correct ordering of variables seems to be disregarded. Most authors put the variables in the order suggested by their theory and neither defend that order nor examine plausible alternative orders. For example, Schermerhorn (1977) suggests that tenure of administrators affects hospital task accomplishment, which affects information sharing between hospitals. It also seems plausible that information sharing affects task accomplishment and that hospital task accomplishment affects the tenure of its administrators. Path analyses testing path-goal theory (Dessler & Valenzi, 1977; Sims & Szilagyi, 1975) assume that structuring behavior of the leader affects role ambiguity of the employee, without examining the alternative model that inherently ambiguous jobs cause a supervisor to attempt more structuring.

In summary, when variables are measured at one point in time, either alternative orders are examined for fit with the data (which can become unwieldy) or a single ordering is assumed to be correct. This assumption should be made explicit and defended against plausible alternatives. Measuring variables across time can provide a limited defense of a given order, as, to some extent, does applying path analysis to data from an experiment (see below).

Linearity, Additivity, and Interval Measures

Because path analysis makes use of ordinary least squares regression, those assumptions necessary for regression apply to path analysis. First, the relationship among variables is assumed to be linear. The major consequence of unrecognized nonlinearity is the possibility of incorrect causal inference. If A is related to B, but in a curvilinear fashion, the path coefficient (and the overall correlation) between A and B may be zero, leading to a conclusion that there is no effect. For example, Dessler and Valenzi (1977) found that the direct path coefficient between leader structuring behavior and employee satisfaction was not significantly different from zero. However, there is the possibility of a curvilinear relationship (low satisfaction when structuring is either very low or very high; Yukl, 1971) that if found would alter the conclusion of no direct effect.

If nonlinearity is suggested by previous research or by visual examination of scatterplots, then the researcher can test for significant nonlinear relationships by computing the correlation ratio, sometimes called eta squared (Hays, 1973, p. 683). Alternatively, exponential terms can be added to the equation and tested for significant increases in variance accounted for (Kerlinger & Pedhazur, 1973, p. 209). When nonlinearity is found, it may be possible to represent the proper relationship by either treating the predictor as a categorical variable and using dummy coding or by using exponential terms in the path analysis (Kerlinger & Pedhazur, 1973, pp. 199–218). However, it is best if the exact form of the relationship can be specified in advance, so that the results do not capitalize on chance fluctuations in the data.

A second assumption, additivity, means that there are no significant interaction effects. If two variables interact in affecting a third variable, then causal inference based on ordinary path analysis may be incorrect. Oliver (1977) implicitly assumed additivity in examining the relationships among level of income, pay satisfaction, and importance of pay. However, there is some evidence (e.g., Hackman & Lawler, 1971) that satisfaction with work outcomes is a function of an interaction between importance and amount of the outcome. Thus, Oliver's conclusion that income affects satisfaction, while correct, may be somewhat incomplete.

As with other important assumptions, one should be alert for theory and previous research that suggests the likelihood of interaction. If interaction is plausible, then the data should be examined. The cross-product term can be entered into the regression equation and the increase in variance accounted for checked statistically (Kerlinger & Pedhazur, 1973). If this procedure suggests significant interaction, then path analysis models developed specifically for interaction terms can be applied (see Nygreen, 1971).

It should be noted that this use of interaction terms in path analysis does not require data with ratio scale properties. Schmidt (1973) correctly argues that zero-order correlations involving an interaction term may lead to erroneous conclusions if the measures do not have true zero points. That is, linear transformations of the measures that change the assumed zero points will alter the zero-order correlations. However, the standardized regression weights used in path analysis are unaffected by linear transformations.

As a further example of the potential usefulness of interactive path analysis, consider the work of Sims and Szilagyi (1975) and Dessler and Valenzi (1977). Both sets of authors examined the way in which job level moderated the relationship between initiating structure and job satisfaction by conducting separate path analyses on groups varying on level. A more powerful approach would be to treat job level (or the underlying variable of task structure) as a continuous variable, obtain a score for each participant, and examine the effects of the cross-product of structure and job level.

Finally, the assumption that measures have interval scale properties is often questionable, given the primitive state of measurement of many variables in industrial/organizational psychology. For example, Oliver (1977) used a single 7-point scale to measure valence of pay and a single 5-point scale for satisfaction with pay. Assuming that using single items increases the probability of noninterval properties, those measures might best be thought of as ordinal.

Fortunately, it appears that the consequences of assuming equal intervals are not severe. Boyle (1970) discusses this problem and concludes that several errors must occur at the same time and that the nonequality of intervals must be great before problems result. Thus, it would appear that carefully constructed measures employing a reasonable number of values and containing multiple items will yield data with sufficient interval properties. If the data clearly contain unequal intervals, then techniques for ordinal data that rely on dummy coding of variables may be used (e.g., Boyle, 1970; Lyons, 1971).

REPRODUCING THE CORRELATION MATRIX

One of the most powerful applications of path analysis involves breaking correlations into direct and indirect effects. If a set of path coefficients among variables is consistent with the data, then each correlation will be approximately equal to the direct effect plus the total indirect effects between the two variables. A rule of thumb has evolved that the observed and recomputed correlation must differ by no more than .05 (Kerlinger & Pedhazur, 1973, p. 318). If a correlation cannot be reproduced, then something is amiss: A path was deleted when it should have been retained, residuals are correlated, or the ordering of variables is incorrect. Unless a path coefficient can be shown to be consistent with the observed correlation, it may totally misrepresent the causal relationship and should not be accepted.

Most examples of path analysis in the industrial/organizational psychology literature do not attempt to reproduce the correlation matrix (e.g., Dessler & Valenzi, 1977; Hall & Foster, 1977; Oliver, 1977; Schermerhorn, 1977; Sims & Szilagyi, 1975). One study that did compare estimated and actual correlations (Lord, 1976) was able to show that the hypothesized model was consistent with the data. Specifically, the leader behavior of developing an orientation to the problem affected group performance only indirectly through the adequacy of the group's problem conceptualization and not through a direct effect.

Although Oliver (1977) did not attempt to reproduce the observed correlations, he did provide the data needed to conduct such an analysis.[4] The present authors computed the direct and indirect effects for the final causal network Oliver reported and found acceptable agreement between the original and recomputed correlations for most of the variables. However, there were two reasonably large discrepancies, both involving income. The observed correlation of tenure and income was .28, while the correlation as recomputed from the final causal model was .12. Likewise, pay plan and income correlated .25, with a recomputed correlation of only .06.

These discrepancies question one aspect of Oliver's (1977) model. Specifically, he concludes that tenure affects pay plan and that tenure also affects job level which af-

fects income. Thus, tenure and pay plan affect income only indirectly through job level (and age, which affects both tenure and job level). The additional analyses reported above suggest that the causal model may be insufficient; the relation between tenure, pay plan, and income goes beyond the indirect paths implied by Oliver's model.

Possible explanations and remedies for this lack of fit include the following. Variables outside the system should be examined (conceptually and, in a follow-up study, empirically) to try to account for discrepancies. In Oliver's (1977) study, the larger than predicted correlation between tenure and income may be due to more competent salesmen staying on the job longer and also earning more money. Although probably not applicable here, an inability to reproduce correlations may also be due to an incorrect ordering of variables (see Kerlinger & Pedhazur, 1973, pp. 327–330, for an example). In general and when logic allows, a reordering and reexamination of system variables may be useful. Finally, additional paths may have to be deleted from or added back to the model. Again from Oliver, tenure and/or pay plan may have had a direct effect on income. Although neither direct effect reached significance at an alpha level of .05, both were of moderate size (.26 and .14, respectively) and might have to be retained in order to make the model fit the data.

MEASUREMENT ERROR

Common Measurement Error or Method Variance

Although errors of measurement create problems in much industrial/organizational psychology research, the problems are magnified in path analysis. When a subset of system variables are measured by the same

---

[4] The authors wish to thank R. L. Oliver for supplying the necessary data and informing us that the original article contained an error. The actual correlation between tenure and valence is −.38.

method (e.g., multiple items from a questionnaire, ratings on more than one outcome variable by the same supervisor), the observed paths connecting those variables can be expected to be larger than the actual paths and also large relative to paths among variables not sharing a method. For example, Schermerhorn (1977) measured both hospital task accomplishment and information-sharing activity through a questionnaire given to administrators. The significant direct effect between these two variables (.41) might be at least partly due to shared method variance.

The ideal way to eliminate shared method variance as a potential alternative explanation is to use different measurement devices for each variable. In the Schermerhorn example, ratings of performance could have been made by local health officials or information sharing rated by administrators of other hospitals. Even when different variables must be measured on the same questionnaire, techniques such as varying format and separating items can still be useful.

Random Measurement Error

In bivariate analyses, random measurement error gives a conservative estimate of the true relationship between variables, increasing Type II error (failing to reject an incorrect null hypothesis), but not Type I error (falsely rejecting a true null hypothesis). However, in path analysis random error can actually produce inflated estimates of path coefficients, leading to an increase in Type I error.

The following is the equation for the direct path from variable B to C in the model $A \rightarrow B \rightarrow C$:

$$P_{CB} = b_{CB.A} = \frac{r_{BC} - (r_{AB})\,(r_{AC})}{1 - r_{AB}^2} \times \frac{SD_C}{SD_B}.$$

Assuming all correlations are positive, P_{CB} is obtained by adjusting r_{BC} downward by a factor which depends mostly on the correlations r_{AB} and r_{AC}. If variable A were to contain a large amount of random error, then r_{AB} and r_{AC} would appear to be smaller than their true values and r_{RB} would not be adjusted downward as much as it should. This would result in an inflated estimate of p_{CB} and might produce the incorrect inference that B is a direct cause of C, when in fact it is not (Duncan, 1975, pp. 119–121). This bias in estimating an effect is of particular concern when reliabilities of the measures vary greatly and has been shown to be of less concern when comparable levels of measurement error exist in all variables (Heise, 1970).

Studies in the industrial/organizational psychology literature may suffer from this problem. For example, Oliver (1977, p. 23) notes that job level, pay plan, and salary lack "precision." Given this measurement error, the direct path between income and satisfaction may be overestimated because job level is treated as a cause of both variables.

The measurement error problem in path analysis should be dealt with by one or more of the following. Error should be minimized by careful construction of items, the use of multiple items or indicators, and adequate pretesting of measures. At a minimum, the reliability of all measures should be assessed and reported. If significant levels of measurement error exist, then several techniques are available to adjust the estimate of the path coefficient for the degree of error present (Duncan, 1975, chap. 9). A useful procedure commonly used in industrial/organizational psychology is to obtain an estimate of reliability and adjust all correlations for attenuation before conducting the path analysis, although large sample sizes and good measures of reliability are needed (Nunnally, 1967, pp. 217–220).

PATH ANALYSIS IN EXPERIMENTS

There are several ways in which path analysis can be useful even when a true experiment is conducted. One is a case in which the researcher wants to verify that the manipulation affected the dependent variable through the conceptual variable that was hypothesized. Otherwise, the dependent variable may have been affected by some other variable that unintentionally covaried with the manipulation (Costner, 1971). In many experiments, the conceptual independent variable is a state of mind, which is only indirectly created by manipulating some event that may also affect other perceptions, beliefs, or feelings. A well-known example in the industrial/organizational psychology literature is the early laboratory research on equity theory. Making a subject feel underpaid by belittling his or her qualifications for the job might also affect self-esteem, which could be responsible for the effects on performance, rather than feelings of inequity (see Goodman & Friedman, 1971, for a discussion of this point).

Operationally, the model that is tested is manipulation → manipulation check → dependent variable, with the manipulation typically a dummy-coded, dichotomous variable. If the manipulation is affecting the dependent variable through a variable other than that measured by the manipulation check, then the correlation between the manipulation and the dependent variable will not equal the products of the two indirect paths in the model. Conceivably, two causal mechanisms could be operating, leading to a significant indirect path and also to a significant direct effect. In this case, the conclusion would be that the experiment is partially confounded, but that there is still evidence of the hypothesized causal mechanism. Further, the size of each effect could be estimated by comparing the proportion of variance accounted for.

Path analysis may also be applied to experiments in which more than one dependent variable is examined. If a chain of events is hypothesized, the alternative models can be identified and tested. For example, does the manipulation affect both variables directly, or does it affect one variable only through the other? A similar, although weaker application would exclude the manipulation and involve only measured dependent variables. Using this approach, Lord (1976) was able to provide support for his hypothesis that the behavior of developing an orientation to the problem affects performance through the adequacy of the conceptualization of the problem.

Path analysis with experimental data may be particularly powerful because several assumptions may be more easily accepted. The ordering of variables is less problematic because the manipulated variable cannot be caused by the other variables and because the manipulation check and various dependent variables can be measured across time in the order of interest. If subjects are randomly assigned to conditions, then the residuals for the manipulations will be independent of other residuals and other system variables. (However, the residuals for other variables may be related and must be dealt with as discussed above.) In the typical example involving three variables—a manipulation, a self-report manipulation check, and a behavioral dependent variable—shared method variance presents few problems. Alternatively, the problems created by random measurement error may apply here. In the typical example just cited, the measure of the manipulation will have no error and the measure of the behavioral dependent variable may also be relatively clean. However, if the manipulation check consists of only one or two questionnaire items, as is typical, it may contain large amounts of random error. As was explained above, this pattern of measurement error would inflate the estimate of the direct path between the manipulation and the dependent variable and might lead to an incorrect causal inference. Therefore, applying path analysis to experiments requires more concern for reliability of measures than is typically the case.

A CONCLUDING NOTE

A major theme of this article has been that path analysis makes the researchers articulate the causal model underlying the research, ideally in advance of data collection. The technique causes one to explicate the relationships among variables, explore possible outside variables causing spurious correlations, specify and defend the causal order of variables, and check for problems stemming from shared and random measurement error. Path analysis discourages the researcher from selectively reporting a few correlations out of a larger correlation matrix. Rather, the entire causal network must be examined.

In reviewing the industrial/organiza- tional psychology literature for examples of path analysis, many correlational studies were found that would have benefited greatly from path analysis, in that one or more of these issues were not dealt with. Of even greater concern are some studies found (e.g., Caplan, Cobb, & French, 1975; Fhaner & Hane, 1974; Mahoney & Frost, 1974) that presented results in a "path diagram," often using correlations in place of path coefficients. Such an approach leads the authors to phrase their conclusions in terms of causal paths and a causal system, without demanding attention to the assumptions explored in this article. Even more serious, the logical implications of the path system presented are not explored and tested against data. Although path analysis cannot prove causality, rigorous application of the proper techniques does allow the researcher to conclude that the causal model is consistent with the data available, which is an important step in the development of tenable multivariate causal theories.

REFERENCES

Billings, R. S., Klimoski, R. J., & Breaugh, J. A. "The Impact of a Change in Technology on Job Characteristics: A Quasi-experiment." *Administrative Science Quarterly,* 1977, 22, 318–339.

Blalock, H. M. "Causal Inferences, Closed Populations, and Measures of Association." *American Political Science Review,* 1967, 61, 130–136.

Boyle, R. P. "Path Analysis and Ordinal Data." *American Journal of Sociology,* 1970, 75, 461–480.

Caplan, R. D., Cobb, S., & French, J. R. P., Jr. "Relationships of Cessation of Smoking with Job Stress, Personality, and Social Support." *Journal of Applied Psychology,* 1975, 60, 211–219.

Cohen, J., & Cohen, P. *Applied Multiple Regression/Correlation Analysis for the Behavioral Sciences.* Hillsdale, N.J.: Erlbaum, 1975.

Costner, H. L. "Utilizing Causal Models to Discover Flaws in Experiments." *Sociometry,* 1971, 34, 398–410.

Dessler, G., & Valenzi, E. R. "Initiation of Structure and Subordinate Satisfaction: A Path Analysis Test of Path-goal Theory." *Academy of Management Journal,* 1977, 20, 251–259.

Duncan, O. D. *Structural Equation Models.* New York: Academic Press, 1975.

Duncan, O. D., Haller, A., & Portes, A. "Peer Influences on Aspirations: A Reinterpretation." *American Journal of Sociology,* 1968, 74, 119–137.

Feldman, J. "Considerations on the Use of Causal-correlation Techniques in Applied Psychology." *Journal of Applied Psychology,* 1975, *60,* 663–670.

Fhaner, G., & Hane, M. "Seat belts: Relation Between Beliefs, Attitude, and Use." *Journal of Applied Psychology,* 1974, *59,* 472–482.

Goodman, P. S., & Friedman, A. "An Examination of Adams' Theory of Inequity." *Administrative Science Quarterly,* 1971, *16,* 271–288.

Hackman, J. R., & Lawler, E. E., III. "Employee Reactions to Job Characteristics." *Journal of Applied Psychology Monograph,* 1971, *55,* 259–286.

Hall, D. T., & Foster, L. W. "A Psychological Success Cycle and Goal Setting: Goals Performance and Attitudes." *Academy of Management Journal,* 1977, *20,* 282–290.

Hargens, L. L. "A Note on Standardized Coefficients as Structural Parameters." *Sociological Methods and Research,* 1976, *5,* 247–256.

Hays, W. L. *Statistics for the Social Sciences* (2nd ed.). New York: Holt, Rinehart & Winston, 1973.

Heise, D. R. "Problems in Path Analysis and Causal Inference." In B. F. Borgatta (Ed.), *Sociological Methodology, 1969.* San Francisco: Jossey-Bass, 1969.

Heise, D. R. "Causal Inference from Panel Data." In D. F. Borgatta & G. W. Bohrnstedt (Eds.), *Sociological Methodology, 1970.* San Francisco: Jossey-Bass, 1970.

Heise, D. R. *Causal Analysis.* New York: Wiley, 1975.

Kenny, D. A. "Cross-lagged and Synchronous Common Factors in Panel Data." In A. S. Goldberger & O. D. Duncan (Eds.), *Structural Equation Models in the Social Sciences.* New York: Seminar Press, 1973.

Kenny, D. A. "Cross-lagged Panel Correlation: A Test for Spuriousness." *Psychological Bulletin,* 1975, *82,* 887–903.

Kerlinger, F. N., & Pedhazur, E. J. *Multiple Regression in Behavioral Research.* New York: Holt, Rinehart & Winston, 1973.

Kim, J., & Mueller, C. W. "Standardized and Unstandardized Coefficients in Causal Analysis: An Expository Note." *Sociological Methods and Research,* 1976, *4,* 423–438.

Land, K. C. "Principles of Path Analysis. In E. F. Borgatta (Eds.), *Sociological Methodology.* San Francisco: Jossey-Bass, 1969.

Lawler, E. E. III. *Motivation in Work Organizations.* Monterey, Calif.: Brooks/Cole, 1973.

Lord, R. G. "Group Performance as a Function of Leadership Behavior and Task Structure: Toward an Explanatory Theory." *Organizational Behavior and Human Performance,* 1976, *17,* 76–96.

Lyons, M. "Techniques for Using Ordinal Measures in Regression and Path Analysis." In H. L. Costner (Ed.), *Sociology Methodology, 1971.* San Francisco: Jossey-Bass, 1971.

Mahoney, T. A., & Frost, P. J. "The Role of Technology in Models of Organizational Effectiveness." *Organizational Behavior and Human Performance,* 1974, *11,* 122–138.

Namboodiri, N. K., Carter, L. F., & Blalock, H. M., Jr. *Applied Multivariate Analysis and Experimental Designs.* New York: McGraw-Hill, 1975.

Nunnally, J. C. *Psychometric Theory.* New York: McGraw-Hill, 1967.

Nygreen, G. T. "Interactive Path Analysis." *The American Sociologist,* 1971, *6,* 37–43.

Oliver, R. L. "Antecedents of Salesmen's Compensation Perceptions: A Path Analysis Interpretation." *Journal of Applied Psychology,* 1977, *62,* 20–28.

Schermerhorn, J. R., Jr. "Information Sharing as an Interorganizational Activity." *Academy of Management Journal,* 1977, *20,* 148–153.

Schmidt, F. L. "Implications of a Measurement Problem for Expectancy Theory Research." *Organizational Behavior and Human Performance,* 1973, *10,* 243–251.

Sims, H. P., Jr., & Szilagyi, A. D. "Leader Structure and Subordinate Satisfaction for Two Hospital Administrative Levels: A Path Analysis Approach." *Journal of Applied Psychology*, 1975, 60, 194–197.

Young, J. W. "The Function of Theory a Dilemma of Path Analysis. *Journal*

of Applied Psychology, 1977, 62, 108 110.

Yukl, G. "Toward a Behavioral Theory of Leadership." *Organizational Behavior and Human Performance*, 1971, 6, 414–440.

Received April 3, 1978

Strategies in Canonical Correlation with Application to Behavioral Data[1]

Donald A. Wood

James A. Erskine

Canonical correlation is a relatively new multivariate tool in the behavioral sciences. Although the mathematical and conceptual developments have been inventive and made readily available through computer programming, the heuristic value of canonical methodology in assessing behavioral data is not yet complete. Some researchers seem to be guided, somewhat indiscriminantly, with raw statistical significance, yet, have been unwilling or unable to offer meaningful interpretation of the canonical dimensions obtained. This paper will first present a brief overview of the historical and current perspectives, some recent refinements, and a review of some applications of canonical correlation. Following this, a detailed application of the method is offered to help demonstrate the full utility of this technique in behavioral analysis.

HISTORICAL AND CURRENT PERSPECTIVES

The canonical technique was first introduced in 1935 by Hotelling in a paper entitled "Relations Between Two Sets of Variates." The problem was to derive a best predictor function from among all possible linear functions in a set of predictor variables while simultaneously deriving a criterion function from among all possible linear functions in a set of criterion variables which the other set predicts most accurately. Hotelling (1935) showed that the number of pairs of weighted linear functions was equal to the number of variables in the smallest set and called the function relationships within these pairs canonical correlation.

Wilks (1935), Roy (1961) and Horst (1961) have since developed generalized solutions for the simultaneous relationships obtained between more than two data sets. Anderson (1958) and Morrison (1967) have explored in detail the statistical properties necessary in canonical analysis. Meredith (1964), Rozeboom (1965) and Green and Tull (1970) have considered the scaling characteristics required of the data inputs. Bartlett (1941) was the first to provide a generalized chi square approximation needed to test the significance of the canonical correlations in cases where the data sets have more than two variables.

Beyond these methodological and statis-

---

[1] Reproduced by permission of *Educational and Psychological Measurement*, 1976, *36*, 861–878.

tical developments, researchers enjoy the advantage of not having to select any one criterion variable from a set of variables (as in R analysis) nor having to arbitrarily assign weights to a set of criterion variables. Furthermore, the data sets do not have to necessarily conform to the predictor criterion model; the relationships between any two sets of variables may be studied using canonical analysis (Koons, 1962). However, high correlations between two variables across sets will be capitalized on in the derivation of weights and the resulting canonical correlations may be spuriously high (Gullikson, 1950).

Despite the power of the method, the ready access to high speed computing machinery, and the necessary programs being readily available, the major difficulty faced by researchers is the interpretation of the results obtained (Cooley, 1965). Two analytical refinements have recently been offered to assist these interpretation difficulties.

REFINEMENTS

One such refinement is the analysis of variance redundancy (Stewart and Love, 1968; Miller and Farr, 1971), through use of a general canonical correlation index. Such an analysis has been proposed because a squared canonical correlation represents only the variance shared by a canonical variate pair, *not* the actual variance shared by two data sets. Even though a canonical variate pair may not extract significant variance from their respective sets, a significant canonical correlation may obtain. However, this paper will not explore this index further since the index appears to include an improper term for the variance of a canonical variate (Nicewander and Wood, 1974).

A second refinement is the canonical cross-validation analysis (Thorndike, Weiss

and Dawis, 1968a, b; and Thorndike and Weiss, 1970). These researchers recognized that the "bouncing beta" problem in multiple regression replications and the shrinkage in cross-validation tests resulting from the variations in sample-specific error (McNemar, 1962) may be even greater in canonical solutions since two weightings are generated simultaneously. Thus, it would seem plausible that only when canonical solutions are cross-validated is there evidence for a meaningful interpretation.

Based on the developments of the refinements noted above, the following analytical procedures are considered necessary, in this order, in a complete analysis of canonical solutions: (1) testing the significance of all canonical correlations calculated, (2) testing the cross-validated stability of the canonical solution, (3) identifying and interpreting the underlying dimensions within the joint space, and (4) testing the bi-directional predictability within the dimensions identified. The predictive potential within canonical solutions has not received the attention it deserves. This neglect is probably due to insufficient analyses prerequisite to this final procedure.

REVIEW OF APPLICATIONS

These analytical procedures provided the authors with the criteria needed for reviewing some behavioral applications of canonical analysis. Cooley (1965) suggested that the number of applications had not kept pace with conceptual and mathematical canonical developments. A review of the literature subsequent to Cooley's (1965) assessment produced over thirty[2] applications of the method. These applications would appear to attest to the increased use and the wide variety of situations studied via canonical analysis.

---

[2] A summary of these applications showing the authors, the study objectives and the procedural steps reported, is available upon request from the authors of this paper.

The following conclusions were drawn from this literature review: (a) Most of the studies have reported canonical correlation magnitudes with associated significance levels; (b) Several studies have estimated canonical variate and total set redundancies; (c) Only two studies reported a cross-validation analysis; (d) Only a few studies have clearly identified labels to reflect the underlying canonical constructs or dimensions; (e) Only two studies have furthered the interpretation of significance with a cross-validation analysis; (f) No study has offered the significance and cross-validation analyses prerequisite to the interpretation of meaningful dimensions; (g) No study has directly tested the bi-directional predictability within canonical dimensions even though some authors have illustrated how such an analysis could be performed.

From this review of applications, it becomes apparent that many of the important methodological concerns in canonical analysis are either ignored or relegated to the incidental. Not one study reviewed directed itself to *all* of the vital areas enumerated above, namely the determination regarding significance levels of all canonical correlations computed, the cross-validation of both canonical correlations and canonical weights, the interpretation of canonical dimensions, and the predictability possible within such dimensions.

The authors do not contend that all such analyses are crucial in every canonical study, especially when the investigator is testing for the independence rather than the dependence between data sets. However, in the absence of any exhaustive application of a canonical solution within a single study, comprehensive appraisals of the method's merits for behavioral research are at best disjointed and inconclusive. This makes it impossible, at present, to make any overall statement regarding the method's potential contribution to or detraction from such research.

In addition, because of the number of analytical steps found within the technique, each providing a significant conclusion in its own right, researchers tend to restrict their interests to only one or at most two of the steps involved. As a result, canonical analyses manifest a glaring void of any semantic continuity from the initial step of canonical correlation estimation through the final step of intra-dimensional prediction. For example, one researcher's canonical loading becomes another's canonical weight; canonical dimension to one is a canonical variate to another; and, canonical correlation is the relationship between data sets for one, but only the relationship between variates for another. It would seem that continued splintering of applicatory interests across researchers using this method will only serve to perpetuate these disparities in descriptive terminology.

It will be the intent of this study to present a detailed and more complete account of the analytical sequences involved in an actual canonical solution so that in all of its complexity, the method can be properly evaluated as a research tool. A secondary objective will be to provide a working vocabulary pertaining to the analytical intricacies related to each procedural step. Only after the successful completion of both objectives can the full potential of the method be ascertained.

ANALYTICAL PROCEDURES IN CANONICAL ANALYSIS

Determining Canonical Correlations $(R_c's)$

The first step in any canonical solution is to establish a series of weights, here called a function, for each of two data sets so that the linearly combined variable vectors using such weights are maximally correlated. This means that if the first pair of the resulting weights are multiplied by the response vectors for each subject in turn for each set, derived score vectors generated by each function will correlate higher than is possible with any other paired weighting scheme. This correlation between the derived score vectors is defined as the first canonical correlation (R_{c1}). That is, if a and b are the first weight vectors and x and y are variable vectors (standardized), then the new derived score vectors are:

$$c = \alpha_1 \chi \text{ and } d = b_1 y \text{ where } R_{C1} =$$
$$\frac{1}{N} \sum_{l=1}^{N} c_l d_l \text{ maximum}$$

If this derived score vector association represented by R_{c1} proves to be zero, the analysis is complete and total independence between data sets has been demonstrated. Since the usual test concerns hypothesized dependence, the null hypothesis of no inter-set dependence would have to be accepted.

Two factors, however, would tend to make data set dependence a more common occurrence. First, behavioral data from the same subjects, even though allocated to different sets thought to be conceptually or psychologically distinctive, will nearly always display non-zero inter-set correlations for at least some of the items. As Gullikson (1950) and others have noted, these are just the relationships which are emphasized in canonical solutions. A second related factor is the optimization involved in the derivation of weights which can serve to exaggerate the actual dependence between sets. Consequently, rarely, if ever, will an initial canonical correlation (R_{c1}) of zero appear. In the more typical case, the number of non-zero R_c's will equal the number of variables in the smaller data set.

In the estimation of multiple R_c's, an important intra-set constraint is imposed. Subsequent weighted score vectors must be orthogonal to all others previously extracted from that particular set. This permits the enhancement of between-set correspondence

that would not be possible if covariation existed within sets. Despite within-set derived score vector orthogonality, vector complements in the opposing set are all, in turn, maximally related. Canonical programs capable of generating all such weights have been reviewed by Roskam (1966).

Testing the Significance of R_c's

The amount of confidence in claiming inter-set dependence after computing a series of non-zero R_c's is best determined by significance tests specifically written for the canonical method. The test nearly universally accepted for such analyses is that offered by Bartlett (1941) involving a chi square for each canonical root extracted. Successive computations of chi square for each R_c is accomplished by eliminating all prior roots associated with R_c's occurring previously in the series and then analyzing the remainder. Bartlett's primary contribution was to extend significance testing beyond the two variable case (Wilks, 1935) while capitalizing on the derivations of the simultaneous distribution of correlations generated by Fisher (1939) and Hsu (1939). Although Lawley (1959) and Marriott (1952) have offered slight refinements in the testing of residual canonical roots, the theoretical justifications have not been made clear and Bartlett's original test still stands and will be employed in a later example.

Cooley and Lohnes (1971) and Hughes and Yost (1971) cite canonical programs in FORTRAN which do provide a chi square test for each R_c computed. This is an extremely helpful addendum to any such program, since the hand calculations for determining significance are quite laborious.

A statistically significant R_c at the designated level of confidence (convention seems to prevail claiming meaningfulness at the .05 level or below) identifies the error level in stating that two data sets are in fact similar to each other.

A canonical loading is the correlation

coefficient between responses for a given item and a derived score vector using the weighted scores. For the first items in each set and the first derived vectors, this would be r_{x1c1}, r_{y1d1}. The higher the coefficient, the more the vector and item have in common. The square of the coefficient depicts the amount of variance shared by both the item and the vector. Consequently, the item coefficient or loading is used when the canonical dimension is ultimately interpreted. The item weight should not be used for this purpose since it is calculated to maximize the derived score covariances across data sets and does not in itself relate to item or derived score variance. A vector of correlation coefficients between all items in a data set and a weighted vector defines a canonical variate.

Determining Canonical Cross-Validation

Cross-validation efforts in a canonical sense seem justified only if R_c significance has been demonstrated. With R_c significance, the concern is whether the magnitude of R_c can be maintained in a second comparable subject sample using the identical data sets and the original weights. Cross-validation is an essential follow-up step here since paired weight functions are involved instead of the single function as estimated in multiple regression (R).

CROSS-VALIDATING R_c. The concern with respect to the R_c itself is whether derived score vectors can be generated in a sample where canonical weighting has not occurred so that the inter-vector correlation or R_c cross-validated (R_{Ccv}) is still statistically significant. It is, of course, preferred that the R_c-R_{Ccv} shrinkage difference be small or zero. In any event, R_{Ccv} will be judged to be the best approximation of derived score relationships for both samples.

An R_{Ccv} can be estimated after the establishment of a set of canonical weights (representing a significant R_c) and an independent or holdout sample having had the same variable administration. The two previously derived weighting schemes are multiplied by the respective standardized response vectors for the first holdout subject yielding a derived score from each data set. Two scores are in turn computed for each remaining subject. The intercorrelation (r) between the resulting derived score vectors is R_{Ccv} (the previously cited algebra is still appropriate here. The only difference is that the a and b weight vectors are predetermined).

This process is continued until all significant R_c's from the original group have been represented in the replication attempt. R_c-R_{Ccv} comparisons provide invaluable insight as to the utility of the weights employed and assist in determining the confidence one would have in any future implementation of the solution. Canonical functions not represented by significant R_{Ccv}'s (traditional r significance tests are employed) are eliminated from further consideration.

CROSS-VALIDATION OF CANONICAL FUNCTIONS. Since the stability inherent in an R_{Ccv} is naturally dichotomized into two canonical functions, the consistency contribution of each must be independently assessed. Such evaluation involves testing the integrity of each function with respect to deciding which of the two sets should receive the interpretive edge when canonical dimensions are named, a process to be discussed later.

Function cross-validation is accomplished by first summing across the standard scores for all variables in each set separately for each holdout subject providing two obtained or actual score vectors. Second, a holdout group derived score vector is estimated using the original group's first canonical weight scheme from the first set (see cross-validation of R_c). This is then correlated with the corresponding obtained score vector. Third, the same process is repeated for the vectors associated with the second set. Therefore, function cross-validation is the correlation between a derived or predicted score vector and the corresponding obtained or actual score vector. All subsequent weighting schemes extracted are similarly analyzed. The predetermined weights that generate a holdout derived score vector most correlated with actual scores from that set is judged to be the most stable function for that pair.

The separate cross-validating of paired canonical functions seems essential for several reasons. First, actual response data is employed *directly* in the process which is not the case when obtaining R_{Ccv}. Second, and related to the first point, is the possibility that R_{Ccv} may be significant, while at the same time, either one or both of the pertinent cross-validated derived score vectors are not significantly associated with actual scores taken from sets they represent (i.e., canonical functions may not be stable). Derived score vector relationships in a cross-validated sense (R_{Ccv}) cannot be authenticated unless the weights in question can demonstrate a more fundamental affinity with observed data in a new group. Consequently, canonical cross-validation necessarily includes not only a demonstration of derived score vector correspondence embodied in R_{Ccv}, but function fidelity with the holdout group data as well. Third, the assessment of function stabilities within a pair provides needed cues as to the interpretive leverage one may well have over the other when the canonical dimension is named. It would appear unrealistic to assume that both functions would be equally vital in every pair extracted.

Naming Canonical Dimensions

Naming canonical dimensions involves identifying the constructs which best describe the way(s) in which two data sets are alike. More specifically, this process concerns the separate appraisal of each canonical variate pair as constituted by original group *loadings* which in turn are represented by significant R_{Ccv}'s. Of course, if an original R_c cannot be cross-validated and/or function stability is minimal, no canonical dimension is indicated. An insignificant R_{Ccv} indicates that the a priori weights cannot generate

dual scores which yield significance when correlated across all new subjects. Instability associated with one or both functions demonstrates partial or complete infidelity of the "dimensions" to new responses for the same variables. When these prerequisites to dimensional labeling are met, however, it appears mandatory to make some attempt to appreciate the inter-set construct involved so that the solution's meaning can be better appreciated.

The ultimate label for a dimension should reflect a "higher-order" construct incapable of emerging from either set taken alone. It may well be, as implied above, that one variate is the more stable of the pair, a cue indicating the appropriateness of emphasizing one set over the other in the identificatory problem. However, the very act of dimensional pursuit attests to the presence of acceptable stability for *both* variates and thus cognizance of variables from both sets is demanded even though partiality toward one set may be justified.

Insensitivity to the common space established by a significant R_c may result in a canonical "dimension" stemming from variables in only one set—a genuine bastardization of the canonical solution. In vain attempts to avoid this, some authors faintly imply a dimension by stating, for example, "those scoring high (low) on variables A, B, and C from set one also tend to be high (low) on variables 1, 2, and 3 from set two." This certainly indicates an awareness of both sets, but it is still very difficult to appreciate what that particular subset of six items shares in a construct sense. The highly desired "higher-order" effect is lost and greatly mitigates the interpretive impact that canonical analysis can provide.

Testing Canonical Prediction

Once the veracity of a canonical dimension has been established, a legitimate concern may arise as to the capability of predicting from one variate to another. This would be especially critical when there is a natural time lag between the administration of data sets prompting one to predict a "later" variate or when it is not feasible for time or money reasons to administer both sets of variables.

Canonical prediction can only be justified, therefore, when the researcher finds, for whatever reasons, the absence of a variate constituting a previously identified canonical dimension. Without such saliency being predetermined, there is no way of determining why prediction is important. However, with proper dimension naming, a subsequent missing counterpart to a *known* variate can be legitimately sought. Only with some predictive knowledge of the absent complement can there be any hope of dimensional restoration in such an abbreviated analysis.

Since any given weighting scheme nearly always involves only a prominent subset of variables from each set, partial function scores must be calculated prior to prediction. This is accomplished by summing across the products of item canonical weights multiplied by the item standard score for each subject on all items surpassing a *loading* cut-off employed on that variate. The predicted partial function score for each subject is defined as the product of the summed score on the known function multiplied by the predetermined R_C for that dimension. It should be emphasized that item loading magnitudes determine the constituency of a canonical dimension while the corresponding weights are used to predict within a dimension.

Since an already established R_C is required in canonical prediction, it may be worthwhile to establish whether prediction is superior from the X to the Y function or vice versa. With differences in function stability, inequality in predictiveness within the pair would also be likely. If a dimension is best complemented by predicting from the X to Y function, for example, then subsequent administration of battery X would be preferred. Also, if prediction between functions

is extremely high in either direction, then one would be permitted in the future to administer either one or the other set. Thus, it is important to determine intradimension prediction trends so that the comparative need for both data sets in the reconstruction of a dimension can be determined.

A CANONICAL APPLICATION

A comprehensive canonical solution will be presented in order to portray the full extent of analytical power to be found using this multivariate technique. The data employed consisted of two distinct data sets generated by 309 skilled factory employees. The first set measured 35 worker value responses concerning the importance placed on various work referents such as job recognition, supervision, company policies, the job itself, etc. The second set measured to what extent the same 35 worker referents characterized the present job setting as perceived by the incumbents.

The canonical question to be examined here is whether there is any substantive relationship between the sample's complex work *value* structure and the perceptions of the organizational climate within which the respondents operate.

Following the random extraction of 105 cases from the total sample to be later used as a cross-validation group (CVG), a canonical program (Urry and Reid, 1968) was modified to analyze the remaining 204 validation group (VG) cases.

R_c Significance

The VG canonical solution disclosed 15 R_c's significant at the .05 level or less as determined by chi square estimates. Since the ultimate desire was for much greater dimensional parsimony, only VG R_c's at the .01 level are reported (see Table 1). The R_c range at this confidence level was from .86 for the first pair of derived canonical functions to .67 for the twelfth pair. Even with the high significance cut-off employed, 12 potential dimensions exist for data sets comprised of only 35 items each.

Canonical Cross-Validation

As outlined above, CVG analyses involve attempts to replicate the original R_c's employing VG weights as well as the independent assessment of function stability. The prerequisite for such efforts, namely high initial R_c significance, has been confirmed for the first 12 VG R_c's.

The $R_{c_{cv}}$'s estimated in the CVG are also presented in Table 1. Although only the seventh $R_{c_{cv}}$ proved insignificant, considerable shrinkage was found ranging from .23 for R_{c11} to .66 for R_{c7}. The seventh R_c demonstrates the possibility of generating a very high R_c using paired weighting schemes incapable of generating, in turn, CVG derived scores that are appreciably related. Also, despite the finding that the highest $R_{c_{cv}}$ occurred for weights associated with R_{c1}, the second highest $R_{c_{cv}}$ was R_{c11}. Thus, there seems to be no necessary relationship be-

tween the order of R_c computation and the capacity of the weights involved to produce new derived score vectors related commensurately with the original R_c ranking. It would also appear as Gullikson (1950) noted that weight optimizations in the VG can highly exaggerate the paired function correlations. In this case, instead of occupying the .70's and .80's, the more realistic range would appear to be in the .20's through .40's.

The results of the function cross-validation analyses are also given in Table 1. It must be concluded that when CVG derived scores based on VG weights are correlated with actual CVG scores from the corresponding set, only sporadic function fidelity is found. Only five of the values functions displayed significant associations while just half of the perception functions could be so classified.

It may also be observed that such functions did not always match. Though both functions were significant for R_{c1}, R_{c2}, R_{c5}, and R_{c7}, only one significant function could be found for R_{c4}, R_{c6}, and R_{c8}. For the remaining five R_c's, neither the values nor per-

TABLE 1

Validation Group (VG) Canonical Correlations (R_c), Cross-Validated Canonical Correlation (R_{CCU}) Shrinkage from Original R_c, and Weight Stability Correlations for the First Twelve Pairs of Canonical Functions

Function Pair	VG-R_C	R_{CCU}	Shrinkage	Weight Stability Correlations Values	Perceptions
1	.859**	.475**	.384	.47**	.61**
2	.846**	.402**	.444	.18*	.32**
3	.826**	.272**	.554	.02	.03
4	.814**	.259**	.555	−.12	.21*
5	.798**	.328**	.416	.22**	.21*
6	.784**	.263**	.521	.13	.23**
7	.760**	.103	.657	.29**	.25**
8	.741**	.199**	.542	.22**	.02
9	.722**	.323**	.399	.04	.01
10	.716**	.359**	.357	.05	.02
11	.676**	.447**	.229	−.01	.09
12	.665**	.385**	.280	.10	.09

* p < .05.
** p < .01.

ception functions were meaningfully related to CVG responses.

Again, there appears to be no relationship between $R_{c_{cv}}$ significance and function stability. For example, the greatly shrunken seventh $R_{c_{cv}}$ is constituted by functions both of which are significant in the CVG. Conversely, the second highest $R_{c_{cv}}$ relating to R_{c11} disclosed instability for both functions concerned. In the former instance, cross-validated derived scores do not correlate with each other, but do align with their respective data sets. In the latter case, derived scores do highly intercorrelate, but lack fidelity to either "new" response set in the CVG. With $R_{c_{cv}}$ significance only, weightings appear too idiosyncratically related to VG responses. With function stability or fidelity only, the desired "between-set" congruence is absent. It seems essential that both conditions be met before one engages in dimension identification.

Naming Canonical Dimensions

With the aforementioned constraints, only three dimensional candidates emerge from the first 12 R_c's—R_{c1}, R_{c2}, and R_{c5}. Although R_{c4}, R_{c6}, and R_{c8} did cross-validate and demonstrate reasonable stability for at least one variate, the questionable status of the opposing variate would leave the integrity of any potential dimension still in doubt.

Table 2 presents the items most correlated with the three pairs of canonical functions. Five of the 35 items surpassed a .40 loading cut-off on the first values function (Set X). These same items also correlated above this .40 level on the first perceptions function (Set Y). It is interesting to note that the more stable Y function offers three additional items for dimension naming. Since the items are judged to represent a general concern for recognition and since both values and perceptions pertaining to

TABLE 2
Item Canonical Loadings for Dimensions Identified

Paired Function Named	Items	Set X (Value) Loadings	Set Y (Perception) Loadings
First Pair: Recognition Compatibility (R_{c1})	Work on challenging problems	.57	.56
	Chance to enhance social status	.59	.64
	Treated as an individual	.40	.41
	Job security from accomplishments	.44	.45
	See ideas put to use	.41	.55
	Working in an organization with a good image		.44
	Having a boss who delegates responsibility		.49
	Work in desirable geographic location		.56
Second Pair: Perceived Job Security (R_{c2})	Have a secure future	.46	
	Advance economically		.43
	Receive needed support for doing work		.41
	Have clear work responsibilities		.42
	Chance to influence work		.44
	Have work variety		.44
	Chance to enhance social status		.40
	No great fear of mistakes		.40
Fifth Pair: Job Autonomy (R_{c3})	Manage own work	.41	
	Free of supervision		.49

Note.—Only loadings of .40 or above are reported.

this concern are generally present, the first canonical dimension has been named Recognition Compatibility. The complementary nature of such a label is meant to suggest the congruency between the job recognition desired or valued and the extent to which that desire is met, as perceived by job incumbents. Such a construct emerges only after careful consideration of pertinent items from *each* data set. It should be reemphasized that the necessary higher-order effect, potential within the canonical method, is lost without such joint contributions acknowledged in the naming process.

For the second pair of functions, only one of the eight relevant items concerns worker values, namely, the importance of a secure employment future. It should be recalled, however, that this single item is part of a function represented by a significant $R_{c_{cv}}$ and which in turn, manifested appreciable stability. Consequently, the associated perceptual items are interpreted as an elaboration of what is necessary, organizationally, to satisfy the value of a secure future. These perceptions include a sense of advancement, having varied and well-defined work tasks, little concern for making job errors, and a chance to increase status and to influence one's work. This dimension is named Perceived Job Security with the security specified by the value item and the perception of that value portrayed by the relevant job characteristic items. Again, it should be noted that the more stable Y function contributes more items to this dimension.

With respect to the fifth pair of functions

in Table 2, only one item exceeded the .40 loading cut-off on each function. This most likely resulted from the lower stability estimates here when compared to R_{c1} and R_{c2}. This dimension is named Job Autonomy which reflects not only the expressed value to manage one's own work but also the perceived job characteristic to be free of supervision. Describing this underlying construct seems very obvious when these two associated items are given. What is not so obvious is that it takes only these two items to represent cross-validated significance, proven function stability and high loadings.

These three dimensions and especially the fifth pair of functions demonstrate the potential power in canonical solutions to reduce multiple items to a selected few which in turn allow meaningful interpretation.

Canonical Prediction

Since interpretable and substantive dimensions have been identified in this example, prediction comparisons were conducted between functions for each construct. Again, it is important to emphasize that whereas the loading magnitudes determine the constituency of a canonical dimension, the corresponding weights are used to predict within a dimension. In this respect, prediction estimates were made within each dimension using partial function scores comprised of only those items and their weights which identified that construct.

The prediction findings summarized in Table 3 disclose highly significant prediction

TABLE 3
Within-Dimension Prediction Correlations

Dimension Name	Prediction from Values to Perceptions	Prediction from Perceptions to Values
Recognition Compatibility	.56*	.57*
Perceived Job Security	.58*	.56*
Job Autonomy	.35*	.33*

Note.—Prediction equations are available upon request from the authors.
* $p < .001$.

of partial function scores for either data set across all three constructs. The rather large prediction decrements for R_{c5} are not too surprising in light of the stability comparisons with R_{c1} and R_{c2}.

Given these prediction successes in this sample, it would appear that dimensional restoration in the absence of a data set can be accomplished regardless of which set is missing. Concerning Recognition Compatibility, for example, the prediction of Perceived Job Recognition from knowledge of job values or vice versa would be possible with equally high precision. The same bi-directional strength can be found in predicting Perceived Job Security from the importance of that value or in predicting the importance of security from corresponding perceptions. The same alternatives hold for Job Autonomy, but with precision suffering somewhat.

The primary advantage from predicting within a known canonical dimension is that one can well anticipate a subject's standing on the unknown complement to the construct with information on only a single data set. Thus, future fidelity to the dimension can conceivably be maintained through parsimoniously approximating it by employing the most expediently administered data set. In fact, it could well be argued that with regard to R_{c1} and R_{c2} in the above example, only one set would be required in perpetuating the dimensions initially identified.

CONCLUSIONS

Several evaluative conclusions are in order based on the authors' extensive employment of the canonical correlation method:

1. Many if not most of the highly significant R_c's estimated proved to be inconsequential with respect to understanding and interpreting the final canonical solution. As a result, only a minority of the R_c's proved to represent a substantive dimension or construct.

2. The majority of items remain unaccounted for in the final canonical solution. Rather, only approximately one-third of the variables across both data sets proved to be crucial. The present findings would seem to justify depicting canonical dependencies dimensionally through concentration on selected item subgroups rather than offering total "set-against-set" propositions that are more expedient, but too often misleading.

3. The large amount of shrinkage in the canonical correlations, detected after cross-validation, would indicate the spurious inflation of the initial estimates and the dangers involved in interpreting the solution directly from them. It would seem that with the large number of weighting schemes computed, one is particularly susceptible to attaching meaning to correlations that will not generalize to comparable samples and which may, to a large extent, be products of error optimization.

4. Not until the canonical dimensions were finally identified did the canonical solution begin to assume substantive relevance and meaning—a procedural step rarely accomplished in the past. It would seem virtually impossible to appreciate the intent and product of a canonical analysis unless the method culminates in a construct that is definable only when items in both data sets are jointly considered. The dimensional names of Recognition Compatibility, perceived Job Security and Job Autonomy offered in this study do reflect a simultaneous consideration of both expressed work values and perceived job characteristics.

5. Intra-dimensional prediction between paired functions was virtually the same in either direction. This equality was not expected since stability figures across associated functions were often quite different. With the prediction success noted in this study, especially for Recognition Compatibility and Perceived Job Security, it would seem feasible to predictively reconstitute these dimensions when only one data set is available.

It is conceivable, for example, that one would want to predict worker job perceptions concerning Recognition Compatibility or Perceived Job Security on the basis of the knowledge of worker job values alone. If such compatibilities were important for organizational admission, the presence or absence of such congruencies could be anticipated with confidence with only partial information. Thus, an effective canonical prediction scheme may make future administration of both data sets unnecessary, offering a desirable simplification not only to facilitate data collection but also to reduce the analyses required of the very complex canonical technique.

It is obvious from the above statements that cautious appraisal of each procedural step in a canonical solution is mandatory. In many cases, researchers can too easily fall prey to an over-abundance of very high canonical correlations that flaunt significance in a statistical sense only. It would seem that the analytical refinements required in a complete canonical application have been neglected in the past prompting an over-dependence on mathematical artifacts which in turn produce weakly substantiated interpretations. This is not to suggest that in the final analysis, a canonical solution cannot overcome these concerns with its more redeeming qualities. Certainly with the analytical complexity offered by the simultaneous presentation of two data sets, canonical strategies can offer a very useful approach in deciphering the vast milieu of variable interdependencies. This has been shown by the fact that the significance of the derived dependencies between data sets can be tested, the stability of canonical functions can be assessed, meaningful dimensions can be identified, and canonical prediction can be accomplished.

When these canonical strategies are completely integrated and implemented, the power and the merits of canonical analysis can be more fully appreciated.

References

Anderson, T. W. *An Introduction to Multivariate Statistical Analysis.* New York: Wiley, 1958.

Bartlett, M. S. "The Statistical Significance of Canonical Correlations." *Biometrika,* 1941, *32,* 29–38.

Cooley, W. W. "Canonical Correlation. "Paper presented at the annual meeting of the American Psychological Association," Chicago, September 1965.

Cooley, W. W. and Lohnes, P. R. *Multivariate Data Analysis.* New York: Wiley, 1971.

Fisher, R. A. "The Sampling Distribution of Some Statistics Obtained from Non-linear Equations." *Annals of Eugenics,* 1939, *9,* 238–249.

Green, P. E. and Tull, D. S. *Research for Marketing Decisions.* Englewood Cliffs, N.J.: Prentice-Hall, Inc., 1970.

Gullikson, H. *Theory of Mental Tests.* New York: Wiley, 1950.

Horst, P. "Relations among Sets of Measures." *Psychometrika,* 1961, *26,* 129–149.

Hotelling, H. "Relations between Two Sets of Variates." *Biometrika,* 1935, *28,* 321–377.

Hsu, P. L. "On the Distribution of Certain Determinantal Equations." *Annals of Eugenics,* 1939, *9,* 250–258.

Hughes, E. F. and Yost, M., Jr. "Complete Canonical Solutions on Small Computers." *Behavioral Science,* 1971, *16,* 571–572.

Koons, P. B., Jr. "Canonical Analysis." In H. Borko (Ed.), *Computer Applications in the Behavioral Sciences.* Englewood Cliffs, N.J.: Prentice-Hall, Inc., 1962.

Lawley, D. N. "Tests of Significance in Canonical Analysis." *Biometrika*, 1959, *46*, 59–66.

Marriott, F. H. C. "Tests of Significance in Canonical Analysis." *Biometrika*, 1952, *39*, 58–64.

McNemar, Q. *Psychological Statistics.* (3rd ed.) New York: Wiley, 1962.

Meredith, W. "Canonical Correlations with Fallible Data." *Psychometrika*, 1964, *29*, 55–65.

Miller, J. K. and Farr, S. D. "Bimultivariate Redundancy: A Comprehensive Measure of Interbattery Relationship." *Multivariate Behavioral Research*, 1971, *6*, 313–324.

Morrison, D. F. *Multivariate Statistical Methods.* New York: McGraw-Hill, 1967.

Nicewander, W. A. and Wood, D. A. Comments on "A general canonical correlation index." *Psychological Bulletin*, 1974, *8*, 92–94.

Roseboom, W. W. "Linear Correlations between Sets of Variables." *Psychometrika*, 1965, *30*, 57–71.

Roskam, E. "A Program for Computing Canonical Correlations on IBM 1620." *Educational and Psychological Measurement*, 1966, *26*, 193–198.

Roy, S. N. *Some aspects of Multivariate Analysis.* New York: Wiley, 1961.

Stewart, D. and Love, W. "A General Canonical Correlation Index." *Psychological Bulletin*, 1968, *20*, 160–163.

Thorndike, R. M. and Weiss, D. J. "Stability of Canonical Components." *Proceedings of the 75th Annual Convention of the American Psychological Association*, 1970, 107–108.

Thorndike, R. M., Weiss, D. J., and Dawis, R. V. "Multivariate Relationships between a Measure of Vocational Interests and a Measure of Vocational Needs. *Journal of Applied Psychology*, 1968, *52*, 491–496 a.

Thorndike, R. M., Weiss, D. J., and Dawis, R. V. "Canonical Correlation of Vocational Interests and Vocational Needs." *Journal of Counseling Psychology*, 1968, *15*, 101–106 b.

Urry, V. W. and Reid, J. C. "Canonical Analysis Program." Lafayette, Indiana: Measurement and Research Center and Instructional Media Unit and Educational Research Center, respectively, Purdue University, 1968.

Wilks, S. S. "On the Independence of *k* Sets of Normally Distributed Statistical Variables. *Econometrika*, 1935, *3*, 309–326.

THREE

Laboratory Research and Simulations

The set of readings comprising Chapter 3 is small, yet of central importance. Laboratory research has for many years been the methodological cornerstone of progress in experimental and social psychology. It has also been used extensively and with much success for advancing our understanding of behavior in organizations. Simulations also hold great potential when used appropriately, although their use has been much less extensive.

Research in the laboratory is criticized by some for its overreliance on homogeneous samples of subjects (i.e., college undergraduates), artificiality of situations, simplicity of design relative to the complexities of the "real world," and other characteristics which may tend to limit the generalizability of findings to employed adults working at real jobs in real organizations. But many of the considerations in designing laboratory studies are equally pertinent to the design of studies in the field; knowledge and skills in laboratory experimentation provide a strong and useful background even for the researcher who works exclusively in the field. Furthermore, the laboratory provides a convenient and inexpensive setting for testing hypotheses prior to more extensive investigation in real organizations. Finally, laboratory studies are useful in their own right; they have advantages not generally available in field research techniques, and have provided much information and many insights which might not otherwise have become known.

The invited paper by Fisher provides a general overview of the execution of experimentation in the laboratory. While Scott's article in Chapter 1 introduced the reader to some basic concepts in experimental design, Fisher explores these and other issues in greater detail. Examples of creative laboratory experiments illustrative of one of the laboratory's major advantages (i.e., identifying cause and effect sequences) are followed by discussions of numerous decisions regarding design and execution. Validity threats, procedures, tasks, subjects, statistical power, and other considerations are highlighted. The information in Fisher's paper will give the reader a firm grounding in regard to the generation of useful data from the laboratory.

The second article, by Staw, not only provides a good example of a well-designed laboratory experiment, but it also explicitly demonstrates a key strength of the labora-

167

tory. Whereas self-report correlational data from field settings are ambiguous regarding the specification of cause and effect, the laboratory can test different causal directions. Staw tested a reversal of a usual causal assumption—a general approach good for generating hypotheses (Lundberg, Chapter 1) and for having an impact (Daft, Chapter 1). His findings provide a major alternative explanation for cross-sectional findings, thereby cautioning the researcher against too quickly drawing single-minded causal interpretations. Staw investigated a single hypothesis via numerous test statistics and performed an additional validation with a second study presented in the same article.

Such thoroughness is as uncommon as it is convincing.

The third piece discusses the "research playground" of simulation. McCall and Lombardo describe the development and advantages of their simulation for the study of leadership. They and others view simulations as a compromise between naturalistic observation (Scott, Chapter 1) and the tight research control of laboratory experimentation. They see the role of simulations as one of "asking questions, generating hypotheses, and collecting data that can be verified using other methods." As such, simulations represent important tools in the repertoire of research methods.

Suggestions for Further Reading

Chapanis, A. "The Relevance of Laboratory Studies to Practical Situations." *Ergonomics,* 1967, *10,* 557–577.

Cohen, K. J., & Cyert, R. M. "Simulation of Organization Behavior." In J. G. March (ed.), *Handbook of Organizations.* Chicago: Rand McNally, 1965.

Dipboye, R. L., & Flanagan, M. F. "Research Settings in Industrial and Organizational Psychology: Are Findings in the Field More Generalizable Than in the Laboratory?" *American Psychologist,* 1979, *34,* 141–150.

Drabeck, T. E., & Haas, J. E. "Realism in Laboratory Simulation: Myth or Method?" *Social Forces,* 1967, *45,* 338–346.

Evan, W. M. (ed.). *Organizational Experiments: Laboratory and Field Research.* New York: Harper & Row, 1971.

Fromkin, H. L., & Struefert, S. "Laboratory Experimentation." In M. D. Dunnette (ed.). *Handbook of Industrial and Organizational Psychology.* Chicago: Rand McNally, 1976.

Mook, D. G. "In Defense of External Validity." *American Psychologist,* 1983, *38,* 379–387.

Orne, M. T. "On the Social Psychology of the Psychological Experiment: With Particular Reference to Demand Characteristics and Their Implications." *American Psychologist,* 1962, *17,* 776–783.

Rosenthal, R., & Rosnow, R. L. "The Volunteer Subject." In R. Rosenthal & R. L. Rosnow (eds.), *Artifact in Behavioral Research.* New York: Academic Press, 1969.

Weick, K. E. "Laboratory Experimentation with Organizations." In J. G. March (ed.), *Handbook of Organizations.* Chicago: Rand McNally, 1965.

Laboratory Experiments

Cynthia D. Fisher

An *experiment* is a procedure in which the researcher attempts to test causal hypotheses by *manipulating* one or more independent variables (hypothesized causes) and measuring one or more dependent variables (hypothesized effects) while controlling all other variables. If done properly, the researcher may be able to conclude that varying levels of the independent variable *caused* the observed differences in the dependent variable, since nothing in the situation, procedure, or subjects was systematically different across groups *except for* the independent variable.

Experiments can be done in either laboratory or field settings. Field experiments take place in ongoing organizations whose primary goal is not to test the researcher's hypotheses, but to produce a good or service, make a profit, or the like. It is very difficult to conduct good research in field settings for a number of reasons, most of which revolve around the ideas of cooperation and control.

Typically, a suitable organization must be found and "sold" on the purpose of the study, or on some side benefit such as an attitude survey, free consulting, etc. This is harder than it sounds. Then the organization must further cooperate by allowing a manipulation to be made, and agreeing *not* to make any other changes during the course of the experiment. This is an ideal seldom realized in practice. Field experiments tend to use fairly simple designs, investigating one or at most two independent variables, again because of the difficulty of gaining cooperation from ongoing organizations. Control is difficult because individuals usually come in intact groups and cannot be randomly assigned to treatment conditions. In addition, field experiments usually run for weeks or months, and precise control is quite difficult to maintain for this long a period in a complex ongoing system.

When done well, field experiments are extremely helpful in understanding the behavior of people in organizations. As an example, see Griffin (1983) for an experiment in which both actual job design and supervisor's social cues concerning job design were manipulated in two manufacturing plants. However, if all organizational research was deferred until a field setting could be found, very little would be accomplished. For many types of research, the laboratory setting is equally or even more appropriate, and it is certainly more readily available.

Laboratory settings are created by the researcher specifically for the purpose of testing hypotheses. There are few problems with cooperation, aside from locating individuals to serve as subjects and dealing with one's local committee-to-assure-that-human-subjects-are-treated-ethically. Control is also much less of a problem. By careful planning the experimenter can assure that extraneous variables are held constant or randomized so that only the independent variables differ systematically across conditions. More complex designs with three or more independent variables are easily used in the lab, and a *series* of experiments refining a theory by testing successively revised hypotheses can be conducted fairly quickly.

In addition, the laboratory experiment allows the researcher to break into the cause and effect cycle to determine exactly what comes first. For example, correlations between leader behavior and subordinate performance had often been observed and were usually attributed to leader behavior *causing* subsequent subordinate performance. In 1968, Lowin and Craig suggested that perhaps the reverse could happen also and conducted an experiment to find out. They hired students to serve as supervisors of one subordinate who was a confederate of the experimenters and who performed either well or poorly. They then observed the closeness of supervision, consideration, and structuring behaviors emitted by their "supervisors". As predicted, supervisors of high performers were more considerate, less structuring, and engaged in less close supervision than supervisors of low performers. It would have been impossible to do this pioneering research in the field, since actual leaders and subordinates come equipped with pre-existing levels of both leader style and performance whose etiology cannot be unraveled. Furthermore, manipulating an individual's performance is just not feasible in a real organization.

A second example of a clever and very edifying laboratory experiment that could not have been done in the field is a study by Cherrington, Reitz, and Scott (1971). These researchers established three reward contingency conditions: 1) better performance results in higher pay, 2) no relationship between pay and performance, 3) lower performance leads to higher pay. They then observed the correlations between satisfaction and performance within each condition, and were able to verify an earlier prediction by Lawler and Porter (1967) that performance causes satisfaction only to the extent that it also causes rewards, which are the more immediate determinant of satisfaction. This excellent study was one of the final nails in the coffin of the satisfaction causes performance school of thought.

There are some obvious criticisms of laboratory research, and the astute reader can undoubtedly already list several—that subjects usually know that they are in an experiment and may act differently than they do in "real life", that the short duration of lab studies makes findings of questionable relevance to longer-duration events, like ongoing jobs and organizations, or that events are so simplified and controlled in the lab that results are not generalizable to the much more dynamic and complex environments found in organizations. Actually, these criticisms are not nearly as serious as they sound, as will be explained later under the heading "Generalizability."

For the researcher who wants the best of both worlds (lab and field), there is one other setting in which experiments can be conducted. It is the simulation, in which participants are placed into a simulated organization which may go on for several days. One type of simulation is described by McCall and Lombardo later in this book. Alternatively, subjects can be hired for what they *think* is a real part-time or temporary job. The experimenter proceeds to control and manipulate variables just as in the lab, but must be careful that dependent variable data collection methods are consistent with the "cover story" given to participants. Most real employees are not handed a job satisfaction scale to fill out every hour on the hour! An excellent experimental simulation was conducted by Umstot, Bell, and Mitchell (1976), in which job enrichment and goal setting were manipulated and their impact on productivity and satisfaction assessed. Much of the research on equity theory has also involved the use of experimental simulations in which subjects believe they have been hired for a real job (c.f. Vecchio, 1981). One caveat is in order—simulations of this sort are almost prohibitively expensive. If participants are to believe that they are real employees, then they must be paid at least the minimum wage, and even a simple design would require 40 or more participants for several hours each (more on how to determine sample size later).

In summary, an experiment is a controlled procedure in which a few variables are intentionally manipulated by the researcher, and their effect on other variables is measured. It is the surest way of determining whether or not causal relationships exist between independent and dependent variables. Experiments can take place in field, simulation, or laboratory settings. Over the years, laboratory research has added a great deal to our understanding of organizational phenomena. It is through experiments, usually in the lab, that the causal mechanics underlying correlations first observed in the field can be discovered, and that new theories can be refined before verification in more expensive and time consuming field settings. However, throughout the history of organizational research, laboratory experiments have been underrepresented and underutilized (Fromkin and Streufert, 1976; Weick, 1969). There is a great deal still to be learned from intelligently planned laboratory research.

DESIGNING EXPERIMENTS

Simple Designs

The simplest experimental design involves only two groups. One group, the "treatment" group, receives a manipulation, such as a training program, a persuasive communication, or a drug. The other group, the "control" group, is treated the same way but does *not* receive the actual manipulation (no training, no message, a placebo). Both groups are then assessed on the dependent variable of interest. The researcher is looking for significant differences in the means of the dependent variable between the treatment and control group.

In interpreting any differences between groups on the "post test," one is making the assumption that the groups were equivalent prior to the treatment. There are three ways in which this assumption can either be made legitimately, or can be verified. In a "true" experiment, subjects are randomly selected

```
R    X    0
R         0
```

Figure 1. Simple Experimental Design, Post-test Only

from a population of interest, and randomly assigned to either the treatment or the control group. Note that the mean of a large random sample will provide a quite accurate and statistically unbiased estimate of the true population mean on any variable. This is called "the law of large numbers." Thus, *two* large random samples from the same population should be quite similar, and differences between them on the post test may be assumed to be a function of something (though not necessarily the intended manipulation) which happened to the groups during the course of the experiment. Thus, the first way of assuming that the groups are equivalent at the outset is through random sampling. If the samples really are randomly selected (this is rare) *and* are quite large (say, several hundred), then the experimenter can assume equivalence and use the simple design shown in Figure 1, where R means random selection, X is the manipulation, and 0 is the post test.

Tversky and Kahnman (1971) criticize researchers for mistakenly believing in the "law of small numbers," or believing that randomly selected *small* samples are also 1) good estimates of population values and 2) equivalent to each other at the outset. This is simply not true and can lead to invalid conclusions. Suppose that an experiment is conducted to compare the efficiency of a new work design to an old design, and subjects are randomly assigned to work under either the new or old design. Upon measuring work output, it is found that individuals working under the new design produced more. Can one conclude that the new design is more efficient? Maybe . . . or the designs could be equally effective but the people assigned to the new design group just happened to be more skilled, or more experienced, or more motivated from the very beginning than those assigned to the old design. Or, suppose there are no differences in efficiency—the designs could either be equally effective, *or* either one could be more effective, but differences in initial skill level could have enabled the less efficient design group to compensate. This type of non-equivalence is called a *selection* problem, and it can occur because randomization does not guarantee equivalence in small samples, or because of a consistent bias in the way subjects are assigned to conditions. For instance, if the experimental subjects are run earlier in the semester than the control subjects, or if experimental subjects are run in the afternoon and control subjects in the evening, there might be systematic differences in the kind of subjects who choose to sign up at the various times. In the case of a new training program, training may be given to those who volunteer for it while the nonvolunteers form the untrained control group. There are quite likely to be some important differences between these groups before the treatment is given!

For the sample sizes typically used in organizational research, it is probably not safe to assume that groups are equivalent merely because of more or less random assignment of people to groups. Thus, one of two other ways of verifying or creating equivalence must be used. One of these is simply to add a pre-test on the dependent variable of interest, as shown in Figure 2. A pre-test allows one to measure change in individual subjects from before to after the treatment, rather than just presumed *aggregate* change, as in a post-test only design.

In some laboratory experiments a pre-test will not be possible since the dependent variable may not really exist at the beginning of the experiment. For example, much recent research has focused on how socially provided information or cues from co-workers and superiors can affect individuals' perceptions of task characteristics and task satisfaction. Yet one cannot ask subjects how much autonomy or feedback or satisfaction a laboratory task provides *before* they have worked on the task, so research on this issue

R	O	X	O
R	O		O

Figure 2. Simple Experimental Design with Pre-test

has typically employed post-test only designs.

When pre-tests can be obtained meaningfully, there may still be problems with their use. Unless pre-tests are unobtrusive, they may create "pre-test sensitization" effects (Lana, 1969) in which people 1) react to the treatment differently because they have been "primed" for it by the pre-test, or 2) respond on the post-test differently simply because they have been pre-tested. An example of the former might be collecting data on perceived job characteristics (autonomy, variety, feedback, etc.) then redesigning the job, then later measuring perceptions again. It is possible that respondents would not notice the job changes, or not associate positive labels (like autonomy) with those changes unless they had been tipped off about the researcher's intent or reminded of the supposed universal desirability of these job characteristics by the pre-test. This "testing effect" could lead the researcher to conclude that job design changes are perceived positively and should be implemented widely. Yet it is possible that this conclusion will not accurately generalize to subsequent groups of workers who have not been sensitized by a pre-test.

Testing effects can also occur in control groups. The mere fact of answering a questionnaire on a given topic may cause one to think more about the topic and perhaps modify one's attitudes before being given the same questionnaire again. Also, it does not take tremendous insight on the part of the subject to realize that if the researcher measures, does something (even if that something is *supposed* to be a placebo), then measures again, a change of some sort is expected. Cues that tell subjects what response seems to be desired are called "demand characteristics," and will be discussed in more detail later.

It is possible to use a more complex de-

```
R   O   X   O
R   O       O
R       X   O
R           O
```

Figure 3. Solomon Four Group Design

sign, called a Solomon four group design (Figure 3), in order to control for and assess the amount of pre-test sensitization. If the post-test mean of the third group is different from that of the first group, then the pre-test must have changed the impact of the treatment in some way. If the post-test mean of the last group is different from that of the second group, then merely receiving a pre-test must have changed post-test replies. Note that the Solomon four group design requires twice as many subjects as the basic two group pre- and post-test design, so it should only be used when one has good reason to suspect that the pre-test is reactive.

A third and final way to equate the experimental and control group is by *matching*. In matching, a large number of subjects are pre-tested on either the dependent variable of interest or on other characteristics which are assumed to affect the dependent variable in some way (e.g., age, intelligence, experience, skill, etc). Then, experimental and treatment groups are constructed to be identical, with each person in the experimental group having a control subject with the same score on the matching variable. (See Plutchik, 1982, p. 143–148 for a more detailed description of matching.) This strategy is not widely used at the individual level in organizational behavior research, but is sometimes used at the group, department, or firm level in organizational theory research.

Internal Validity

The issues we have been discussing (selection and testing) are aspects of a construct called *internal validity* (Campbell, 1957). A study is internally valid if one can draw correct conclusions concerning the impact of the independent variable on the dependent

variable by ruling out competing explanations for the observed results. That is, did the *treatment* cause the results, or did some artifact of the procedure, environment, measuring instruments, or the like cause the results. A number of "threats" to internal validity have been identified by various researchers (Campbell and Stanley, 1963; Cook and Campbell, 1976). In addition to selection and testing, one must worry about *history, maturation, mortality, instrument decay, demand characteristics,* and *experimenter effects.*

History refers to something that happens to one or both groups between the pre- and post-test which is not part of the treatment. For example, one group of subjects may be interrupted by a fire drill or power failure, while others are not. Or, both treatment and control groups may be affected by the same external event which occurs during the course of the study. Suppose a group of managers is receiving weekly training sessions on non-discrimination. At the end of training, their attitudes toward minorities will be compared to an untrained control group. However, while the training is going on, the Watts riots occur, or there is a highly publicized trial of a minority rapist, or the like. Both groups are likely to be affected by this outside event, in unpredictable ways. The treatment effect may be either swamped or exaggerated, the upshot being that the researcher is uncertain of what effect the independent variable had on the dependent variable.

Maturation is the process of gradual, natural growth or decline in an individual over time. Suppose a four month long experiment is done with first graders. Regardless of any particular treatment, first graders will be taller, heavier, stronger, and better readers in a post-test given four months after a pre-test. Careful use of a control group can aid in determining which changes from pre- to post- are due to maturation and which are due to the treatment.

Mortality occurs when individuals drop out of the experiment; thus they contribute to the pre-test mean but not to the post-test mean. If people drop out for reasons totally unrelated to the treatment, then mortality is only a minor annoyance. However, if those who leave do so because of some aspect of the treatment, the results will be biased. For instance, suppose employee satisfaction is measured before and after enriching a job, and is found to be higher after than it was before. *But* suppose a number of workers disliked the enrichment and quit before the post-test was administered. Obviously, the results and conclusions would be different had their data been included.

History, maturation, and mortality are less likely to cause problems in a laboratory setting where subjects participate for a few hours, than in field research that may run for several months. *Instrument decay* (Campbell, 1957) can be a problem in either setting. It occurs when the measuring instrument is not reliable between pre- and post-tests, or even within a single testing period. If one is using human observers or interviewers to record data, they may become more skilled (or more careless) with experience, or more fatigued over the course of a long session. One can minimize skill variation by carefully training raters to a criterion of high inter-rater reliability prior to beginning data collection, and periodically computing reliability and providing feedback and additional training as needed between data collection sessions.

Demand characteristics are clues to the subject about what kind of responses are desired or expected. The earlier example of change apparently being requested when the same questionnaire is administered twice is an example. The threat to internal validity is that any differences or changes may be due to demand characteristics of the experimental situation rather than to the treatment itself. After the experiment is over, subjects should be interviewed to see if they guessed the researcher's hypothesis. If a greater percent of the treatment group than the control group is able to guess, then demand characteristics may be responsible for the results. Orne (1969) gives additional ways of assessing and controlling for demand characteristics.

Experimenter effects are a broad class of problems which include some kinds of demand characteristics. For example, if the researcher knows how he or she expects certain subjects to behave, given the hypothesis, then the experimenter may unintentionally elicit or cue that type of behavior from subjects. In other words, experimenter expectancies could actually *change* subject behavior by leading the experimenter to subtly reinforce hypothesis confirming behavior from subjects (Rosenthal, 1976). Certain fixed characteristics of the experimenter may also tend to affect subject behavior. For instance, experimenter sex, age, and race have been shown to affect subject responses in some cases (Rosenthal, 1976).

Another type of experimenter effect does not change subject behavior, but contaminates the experimenter's observation, recording, or interpretation of that behavior. Even when trying hard to be objective, experimenters tend to see what they expect or want to see. A way of overcoming this problem, as well as the problem of communicating desired behavior to subjects, is to use a "double blind" procedure. This means that neither the experimenter (or data observer/coder) *nor* the subject knows what treatment condition the subject is in. Neither the doctor nor the patient knows if the pill is a drug or a placebo (though obviously *some one* is keeping track of who is in what condition!)

Other ways of controlling experimenter effects are to minimize contact between the experimenter and the subjects and to standardize that contact as much as possible, by use of a script or tape recorded instructions (Fromkin and Streufert, 1976, Rosenthal, 1976). If several experimenters are used, each should run the same number of subjects in each experimental condition, so that effects of experimenter age, sex, attractiveness, demeanor, and the like are equal across groups. See Rosenthal (1976) for much more detail on experimenter effects and how to control them.

Factorial Designs

Thus far, very simple designs with only two groups and one treatment have been presented. In practice, such simple designs are seldom used. Most laboratory experiments use *factorial* designs, in which there are one or more *factors,* and several *levels* of each factor. Figure 4 shows a one factor design with three levels. The factor is pay amount and the levels are $4, $6, and $8 per hour. Each box is called a cell, and is made up of several people who all receive the same pay amount. This design would be analyzed by one-way analysis of variance, to test whether the cell means on the dependent variable (perhaps quality of output) are different from each other.

If different people are in each cell (each subject experiences only one pay level), this is called a "between person" design. Most organizational research uses between person designs. However, it is also possible to use "within person" designs, in which each subject is measured more than once (as in a pre- and post-test) and may receive more than one treatment. For instance, the same subjects could spend time working at *each* level of pay. When subjects are exposed to different treatments serially, it is usually a good idea to *counterbalance* the order of treatments. That is, one sixth of the subjects would work for $4, then $6, then $8, one sixth for $4, $8, $6, one sixth for $6, $8, $4, one sixth for $6, $4, $8, one sixth for $8, $6, $4, and one sixth for $8, $4, $6. Then it is possible to assess the effect of pay level un-

confounded by pay level order. If one is interested in the effect of order, this could also be analyzed as a factor.

Laboratory experiments usually employ multifactor designs. Figure 5 provides a common example. This is a two-factor design, with the factor "subordinate authoritarianism" having two levels (high and low) and the factor "leader style" having three levels (autocratic, democratic, and laissez-faire). This would be called a "two by three" factorial design. Suppose that the dependent variable is satisfaction with the leader. Two-way analysis of variance on this design would answer the questions: 1) Are there mean differences in satisfaction with the leader as a function of subordinate authoritarianism? 2) Are there mean differences in satisfaction with the leader as a result of leader style?, and 3) Is there an interaction between leader style and subordinate authoritarianism (Is the effect of leader style different for different levels of subordinate authoritarianism)? Using the cell, row, and column means shown in Figure 5, the answers to these questions are: 1) No, 2) Yes—laissez-faire is less satisfying over all, and 3) Yes—high authoritarians are more satisfied by autocratic leaders while low authoritarians prefer democratic leaders.

In this example, the researcher manipulated leader style by training confederates to display different styles as they led different groups of subjects. However, the researcher could not directly manipulate subordinate authoritarianism. This is a "demographic" factor that is attached to subjects already (like age, sex, intelligence, smoker-nonsmoker). In working with a demographic factor, the researcher simply measures the subjects and assigns each to a level on the basis of his or her score on the demographic

Figure 4. One Factor Design with Three Levels

Leader Style

		Autocratic	Democratic	Laissez-faire
Subordinate Authoritarianism	High	8	4	3
	Low	4	8	3
		6	6	3

Figure 5. Two by Three Factorial Design

factor. One should generally avoid using more than one demographic factor in a design, since demographic factors may be correlated (for instance, intelligence and education) and thus 1) create difficulty in filling some cells (low intelligence, high education), and 2) violate the assumption of factor independence needed for analysis of variance.

Figure 6 shows a three factor design. Occasionally, studies with four or five factors are published, but these are not common. The reason for using primarily two or three factor designs is that otherwise extreme difficulty of interpreting the interactions may occur. A three-way interaction is difficult enough to comprehend and explain; imagine the difficulty of explaining a five-way interaction. A five-factor design would also include five four-way interactions, ten three-way interactions, and ten two-way interactions. If more than three factors are theoretically of interest, the researcher should run several simpler experiments rather than one extremely complex design. Alternatively, the

researcher could do correlational research in order to weed out variables with little predictive power and then use an experimental design to manipulate the remaining variables.

There are two ways of picking the values or *levels* of each factor. Most organizational researchers arbitrarily select levels, such as the $4, $6, and $8 pay levels discussed earlier. This results in what is called a "fixed factor." Strictly speaking, the results of research with fixed factors can only be generalized to cases where those *exact* levels occur. Thus, the results of the design shown in Figure 4 would have no implications for a pay rate of $5. If the levels which appear in an experiment are randomly chosen from the universe of all possible values of interest, then one has a "random factor." If the researcher is interested in drawing conclusions about all pay levels between the minimum age and $8 per hour, then the three levels to appear in the experiment should be randomly selected from this universe, and the values actually appearing

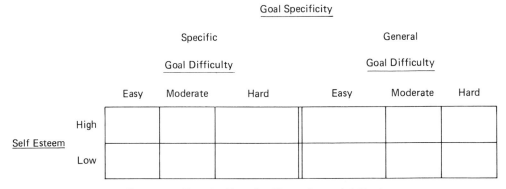

Figure 6. Two by Two by Three Factorial Design

might be $3.98, $6.53, and $7.25. Results could then be generalized to all levels in the universe. Nonetheless, in practice researchers almost always used fixed factors and act as if they can generalize to all possible intervening levels.

CONDUCTING LABORATORY EXPERIMENTS

The preceding section dealt with experiments in general. This section will focus on aspects of experimentation which are more specific to the laboratory setting, such as planning the manipulation, coming up with a "task", and dealing with humans who know they are experimental subjects. In addition to reading this chapter, the fledgling experimenter should read the methods sections of a number of laboratory studies on organizational topics. Suggested journals are *Organizational Behavior and Human Performance, Journal of Applied Psychology,* and *Journal of Personality and Social Psychology.*

What to investigate and how to formulate hypotheses are topics discussed elsewhere in this book. However, the reader should realize that the laboratory is an excellent setting for conducting "crucial experiments" as recommended by Platt (1964). In the lab, one can create conditions which might never occur naturally, but which allow two opposing explanations to by pitted against each other. If this is done, then no matter what the results are, something valuable is learned. Throughout the rest of the chapter it will be assumed that the researcher has already formulated testable hypotheses firmly grounded in theory.

Procedure

The "procedure" (what is done to subjects, when) is obviously tailor-made for each experiment, but a fairly typical procedure is as follows. Subjects arrive at the experiment and may be given a pre-test or a measure of any demographic or personality variables of interest. The researcher then gives the subjects some instructions about what to do and tells them a little about the purpose of the experiment. Frequently, the latter is not true; it is part of a deception or "cover story" intended to make the rest of the procedure make sense to the subjects without revealing the hypothesis to them. Everything the experimenter tells the subjects should follow a prepared script, so that all subjects in the same condition are treated identically, and subjects in different conditions receive different instructions *only* as specified by the manipulation. Subjects then work on a "task" of some sort (group decision making, paper and pencil task, assembling or sorting task, etc.) and dependent variable data is collected during or after the task. The manipulation is given to groups either by the instructions from the experimenter or by some aspect of the task setting (e.g., interesting or dull task, helpful or obstructive coworkers [confederates], false feedback on task performance, etc.) or both. When data collection is completed, subjects are "debriefed" or told the *true* purpose of the experiment, and dismissed. Further detail on many of these steps is presented below.

Manipulating the Independent Variables

Turning a theoretical construct into a concrete set of procedures or manipulations is called *operationalizing* the construct. Some constructs are very straightforward to operationalize, such as group size. Others, such as group cohesiveness, may be much harder to manipulate reliably. To be successful, a manipulation must have two characteristics. First, it must embody the desired construct and not any other construct; and second, it must be strong enough to allow a fair test of the hypotheses. Each of these will be discussed in turn.

Recall that the manipulation (or the levels of various factors to which subjects are exposed) should be the *only* thing different between groups in the experiment. If the manipulation accidentally results in the groups being different on something other than or in addition to the construct that one intends to manipulate, then the manipulation is *confounded*. For example, the early equity theory research induced over-reward inequity by telling subjects that they were underqualified, but would be paid the same rate as fully qualified employees. The feelings of inequity supposedly induced by this manipulation were predicted to cause subjects to perform better as they restored equity by increasing their inputs. These subjects did indeed outperform the "equitably" paid control subjects. Later researchers (Lawler, 1968; Pritchard, 1969) criticized these findings by noting that the inequity inducing manipulation *also* threatened subjects' self esteem, by implying that they were not able to do the job. Subjects may have worked harder to restore their self esteem or to prove to the researcher that they were qualified, rather than to restore equity in payment. Thus, concluding that the results were due to inequity is not justified.

Another example concerns a hypothetical study of pay system and pay satisfaction. Suppose one wishes to find out whether pay satisfaction is greater under an hourly pay system or a piece rate incentive system. In setting up the hourly and piece rates, the experimenter must try to assure that final mean pay is similar in both groups; otherwise any satisfaction differences could be due to total dollars earned rather than to the pay system. The experimenter will probably run a *pilot group* of subjects on an incentive system to get an idea of approximate productivity. If the average person on an incentive makes 8 pieces per hour, then the piece rate could be put at 50¢ per piece, and the hourly pay rate at $4, ensuring similar total pay in both groups. (See Campbell, 1969, for more on confounds.)

How can one avoid problems with manipulations not tapping the "pure" construct of interest? One way is to simply think long and hard about what the manipulation does and what *other* feelings or states it might arouse in individuals instead of or in addition to the desired states. Secondly, experiments should ideally be repeated using *different* manipulations of the same construct. Cook and Campbell (1976, p. 239) note that "Such 'multiple operationalism' allows tests of whether a particular cause-effect relationship holds even though a variety of different theoretical irrelevancies are present in each operation." For instance, over-reward inequity could be induced by telling subjects that they were being paid a higher than usual rate in order to use up grant money that would otherwise have to be returned to the granting agency; or that the rate was mistakenly advertised too high, but the experimenter feels honor bound to pay what the ad promised, etc. If the results consistently support the hypothesis through different operationalizations, then one can have more faith that the hypothesis is correct.

The second requirement of a successful manipulation is that it be strong enough to allow a fair test of the hypothesis. If inequitably paid subjects behave just like equitably paid subjects, either the theory is wrong or the manipulation was not successful in arousing *enough* inequity to influence behavior. In order to develop a manipulation which does what it is supposed to do, one should usually conduct a pilot test. Suppose one wants to develop two laboratory tasks, one that is interesting and one that is boring. Pilot subjects would work on the tasks and rate how interesting they are. It may be necessary to try several tasks before two which are suitably different from each other in level of interest are found. A still more difficult manipulation to develop might be to make a newly formed group of subjects develop high or low group cohesiveness (in order to test the effect of cohesiveness on some dependent variable). One might experiment with increasing cohesiveness by telling subjects that they were selected on the basis of a pretest because of their compatibility with each other, or that they are in competition with an "enemy" group to earn a reward, or that they have done well on a task they worked on together.

In addition to pilot tests, one should also include manipulation check items in the post-test of the actual study. Because pilot samples are usually small and thus tend to give unstable results, it is important to assess whether the manipulation worked as intended in the larger study sample. Manipulation checks are critical in interpreting hypothesis tests. If the hypothesis was not supported and the manipulation was effective, then something is wrong with the hypothesis or theory. The same conclusion, however, could be reached if the hypothesis were supported, but the manipulation was ineffective (i.e., the two groups behaved as predicted, but there were no differences in cohesiveness)! If the hypothesis was not supported and the manipulation was not successful, then it's back to the drawing board for the researcher and his or her still-viable hypothesis. An ideal outcome, of course, is that the hypothesis is supported and the manipulation check shows that the researcher successfully manipulated the desired independent variable construct.

An additional use of the manipulation check is to exclude or reclassify subjects who failed to be influenced by the manipulation as intended (Fromkin and Streufert, 1976). For instance, if subjects are told at the outset that they will be paid an hourly rate of $6, and at the end of the experiment some of them think they are being paid by the piece, these subjects should probably be dropped from the hourly rate condition. Similarly, if some subjects in the "no goal setting" condition say that they set their own goals while working on the task, they could be dropped or reclassified into the goal setting cell. Obviously, these methods are a bit suspect and completely destroy randomization. They should be used only in post hoc analyses in an effort to understand why the hypotheses were not fully supported in the experiment as originally conducted.

A few other cautions with regard to developing a manipulation are in order. First, subjects do not perfectly recall what they are told. If a manipulation is being made via oral instructions (i.e., telling subjects that they are overpaid), it should probably be repeated or highlighted in some other way in order to have sufficient strength. Festinger (1953) suggests that at most only one independent variable be manipulated via instructions, lest the instructions become too confusing and subjects miss the point. Other variables can be manipulated in a more unmistakable fashion (i.e., the experimenter enters between trials and administers positive or negative feedback, the tasks are objectively different, or the confederates behave in prearranged ways).

Second, if a manipulation is accomplished by assigning subjects to high/low groups on the basis of pre-test measures of personality, attitude, or abilities, additional problems with manipulation strength may occur. If pre-test measures are less than perfectly reliable, a phenomenon called "regression toward the mean" will occur. The mean of high scorers will tend to be a bit lower, and the mean of the low scorers a bit higher, and thus both means closer to the grand mean upon retesting (see Cherulnik, 1983, p. 69–77 for a fuller discussion). Regression toward the mean can cause two problems. First, the manipulation based on the high/low split might not be as powerful as it appears, since the "true score" means of the groups are closer to each other than the means on the pre-test. That is, the groups are more similar than they looked. Second, interpreting changes from pre- to post-test is complicated by the fact that some change is probably due to regression while some change may be due to the other treatment(s) received by the groups.

The Experimental Task

The "task" is what the subjects do during the bulk of the time they are in the lab. In some experiments, task variations are important manipulations, whereas in other experiments, all subjects perform the same task while they are exposed to a non-task manipulation. An example of the former would be job design experiments in which some groups work on an enriched task and others on an unenriched task. Another example is the "paper people" experiments in which subjects act as recruiters and make decisions about applicants. The task materials (resumes) embody the manipulation by varying the sex, age, or race of the applicant, or the order of presentation of positive and negative information, or the like. The other end of the spectrum would be a leadership or social influence or reinforcement schedule experiment in which all subjects work on the same task while being exposed to different leader styles, social cues, or reinforcement schedules.

In addition to carrying a manipulation, tasks may also provide dependent variable measures directly, such as quantity or quality of performance, or indirectly such as satisfaction with the task. In the case of performance, tasks should be designed to have easily and objectively measurable output. If differences in task satisfaction are predicted as a result of some nontask manipulation, then a task which is near the middle of the satisfaction scale for pilot subjects should be chosen. This will allow sufficient "top" and "bottom", that is, sufficient room for the manipulation to either inflate or depress satisfaction without running out of range on the scale.

Other considerations in picking a task are whether it makes sense in the context of the cover story being employed and how much it costs. Many lab studies use some sort of paper and pencil task because the cost is low and performance can be scored at a later date. Other researchers have opted for "building something" tasks using electrical components, tinker toys, or erector sets. Prime considerations are 1) are the materials reusable? 2) can we obtain enough sets of material to allow several subjects to be run at the same time? and 3) can performance be quickly and accurately scored before

products are disassembled for the next subjects?

Subjects

TYPE OF SUBJECTS.   A great deal of laboratory research has been done on nonvoluntary subjects, usually college students who are required to participate in experiments for course credit. Much has been written on how such coerced subjects may respond differently from volunteer subjects, on how college student subjects differ from the people-in-general to whom we hope the research generalizes, and finally on how volunteer subjects differ from individuals who are asked to volunteer for research but do not do so. (See Rosenthal and Rosnow, 1975, for a complete discussion of differences between types of subjects.) There are reliable differences across these types of people, but the extent to which such differences interfere with research results depends on what is being researched. If very basic learning, memory, or physiological processes are being studied, then nonvoluntary college student subjects are probably quite a lot like all other human beings and type of subject is irrelevant. For instance, Pavlov did not have to experiment with a random sample of all ages, breeds, and sizes of dogs in order to generalize his findings on classical conditioning.

On the other hand, if one is interested in investigating executive decision making under varying levels of uncertainty, then using college sophomores is not ideal. Night MBA students who are employed full time would provide a more appropriate sample, and executives on campus for a development program still a better sample. However, as will be discussed later, there are still a great many interesting processes that can be studied with nonvoluntary student subjects.

NUMBER OF SUBJECTS.   A crucial aspect of planning any experiment is deciding how many subjects to use, because the *power* of an experiment to detect a given effect size at a particular level of significance is a direct function of sample size. Power refers to the likelihood of detecting an effect as significant if the effect actually exists. In other words, if the null hypothesis (of no relationship or no differences) is *false*, then power is the probability of being able to reject the null hypothesis.

It is pointless to conduct an experiment with low power, because even if one's theorizing is correct, the data are unlikely to support it. The result will be a "type II error"—erroneously failing to reject the null hypothesis. One is left with the conclusion that either the theory was wrong, or the theory was not given a fair test. Why bother to conduct the experiment when this is the most likely result?

A bit of forethought and reference to a book by Cohen (1969) during the planning phase of the experiment can help to assure adequate power. "Adequate" is often considered to be about .80—four chances in five that if an effect exists, it will be detected as significant. Power depends on three things: significance level (customarily set at $\alpha = .05$), effect size, and sample size. Power can be increased by making do with a less-stringent alpha level (say, .10), but journal editors and reviewers may be hard to convince. Alternatively, power can be increased by increasing effect size—that is, the magnitude of the differences between groups which is expected to occur. In laboratory experiments, employing a stronger manipulation should increase effect size a bit, though in many settings effect size cannot be increased. For example, the true relationship between leader consideration and subordinate satisfaction may be .25, period.

This leaves sample size as the easiest and most practical determinant of power to manipulate. Cohen (1969) gives tables which allow one to read off the power of a test given a certain effect size, sample size, and significance criterion. For example, suppose one is conducting a two group (treatment and control) post-test only design (see Figure 1), and will be assessing the results with a one-tailed t-test with $\alpha = .05$. One

must then estimate the expected effect size, which is the expected difference between the means of the two groups, expressed in standard deviations. In much organizational research, effect sizes are small—a single independent variable has some effect on the dependent variable, but not a lot. Cohen defines a "small" effect size as means that differ by .2 standard deviations from each other. (A "medium" effect size is .5, and a "large" one is .8.) Using the table on page 28 of Cohen (1969), one can find that in order to have power = .80, one needs approximately 300 subjects in *each* group to detect a small effect size. If a medium sized effect is expected, 50 subjects per cell will give the same power.

THE PSYCHOLOGY OF BEING A SUBJECT. In laboratory experiments, subjects are aware of their role as participants in research. Their reactions are not due solely to the independent variables carefully presented to them by the experimenter, but also to their expectations and beliefs about laboratory research in general (Orne, 1962; 1969). That is, human laboratory subjects are not "naive" in the same sense as rats or monkeys are, or as human subjects are observed unobtrusively in their natural environment. Laboratory subjects may devote considerable attention to guessing at the experimenter's hypotheses, trying to see through a real or imagined deception, or trying to impress the experimenter with "well-adjusted" or "intelligent" behavior. All of these activities can compromise the validity of the experiment.

Weber and Cook (1972) list four types of subject roles. First, there is the "Good Subject" role, in which the subject tries to cooperate fully with the researcher by complying with demand characteristics. In other words, good subjects may unconsciously slant their responses to verify the hypothesis which they *think* the research is trying to test. A second role is the "Faithful Subject" role, in which subjects bend over backwards to be totally honest. This may occur when demand characteristics are so blatant that subjects become consciously aware of them and of their responsibility to respond as accurately as they can (Orne, 1962). In fact, they may go too far in the opposite direction. A third type is the "Negativistic Subject," who is hostile, resentful, and usually nonvoluntary, and who may try to guess the hypothesis in order to sabotage it (Argyris, 1968). Fortunately, this type of reaction seems to be rare (Schuler, 1982).

The final role which subjects may adopt is the "Apprehensive Subject" role (Schuler, 1982). Evaluation apprehension is the driving force behind the responses of subjects who take this role. Subjects may give "socially desirable" reponses in an effort to obtain a favorable evaluation from the experimenter, particularly if they believe that their personality is being assessed (Rosenberg, 1969). This effect can be minimized by convincing subjects that the task and measures being used are not diagnostic of any valued skills or characteristics, and that the experimenter is only interested in means across a group, not individual responses (Fromkin and Streufert, 1976). The latter is usually true, but subjects mistakenly tend to believe that experimenters are very interested in their individual responses (Schuler, 1982).

Some critics maintain that the laboratory experiment is not a useful way of studying human behavior because of the possible biases listed above. However, Fromkin and Streufert (1976) point out that these biases are found in "real life" as well as in the laboratory. Favorable self-presentation and efforts to read and then comply with the expectations of others are common phenomena, especially in organizational settings. Nevertheless, the experimenter should make every effort to minimize demand characteristics and avoid arousing evaluation apprehension or a negativistic set.

ETHICAL USE OF HUMAN SUBJECTS.   There are a number of ethical issues which must be considered when doing research on human subjects. However, most boil down to the fact that the experimenter is responsible for the physical and mental health of his or her subjects both during the experiment and after it if the treatment effects may be lasting. A general rule is that "Subjects should not feel worse after an experiment than before." (Schuler, 1982, p. 121). (See pages 637–638 of the *American Psychologist,* 1981, volume 36 for the latest version of the American Psychological Association's "Ethical Principles for Research with Human Participants.")

Prior to beginning an experiment, the researcher should consider any possible risks or costs to the participants. These should be weighed against the potential gain in useful knowledge. More than minimal risk to the subject is only acceptable if the gains may be great. The researcher is seldom alone in these deliberations. Most universities have an institutional committee which must review and approve any human experimentation with more than minimal risk, and university departments which sponsor subject pools or require research participation by students often have their own review committees.

The "risks" involved in medical research are obvious, while risks to participants in organizational research are less visible and are usually quite minor. Examples of such risks are 1) damage to self-esteem if subjects are caused to experience failure (via unrealistically high goals, impossible tasks, or false feedback), or 2) unpleasant changes in the self-concept if subjects are induced to behave unethically or counter-attitudinally. Most organizational research involves even less risk than these examples, but there are still two safeguards the researcher should observe. First, the subjects' "informed consent" should be obtained in writing. That is, subjects should be told as much as possible about the experiment and its purpose as is feasible before hand, should be advised of any significant risks, should be guaranteed a complete debriefing after the experiment, should be told that they can leave at any time if the experiment is offensive to them, and should sign a statement to this effect. The second safeguard involves debriefing following any kind of deception or other procedure which may have damaged self-esteem or changed self concept. For instance, subjects should be told that performance feedback was false, or that any atypical behavior they may have displayed was coerced and has no relevance for the way they act in real life. In addition, subjects should be told about the hypotheses and theory during debriefing, since nonvoluntary participation in research is usually justified as an educational experience ostensibly linked to classroom study of psychology or organizational behavior.

There has been an interesting debate on the role of deception in social research with a few investigators maintaining that deception is always morally wrong (Seeman, 1969), and most others holding that deception is both necessary and acceptable when used appropriately (see Beckman and Bishop, 1970). Schuler (1982) provides an extensive discussion of the ethical issues surrounding deception. Obviously, one cannot tell subjects ahead of time that their "co-workers" are confederates who will drop cues about task characteristics at predetermined times throughout the experiment on social information processing! On the other hand, one can debrief subjects thoroughly either after their participation has ended, or after the whole experiment is over. The latter should be done if there is reason to believe that debriefed subjects will tell subjects who have not yet participated about the deception and hypotheses.

GENERALIZABILITY

With the information provided in this paper and the guidance of an experienced colleague, the reader should now be able to design and conduct a respectable laboratory experiment. If carefully planned, the experiment will have acceptable internal validity, that is, the researcher will be justified in concluding that the results were due to the independent variable(s) and not to any contaminating factors. One question remains—that of *external validity* or *generalizability*.

These terms refer to the correctness or accuracy with which a discovery made in one setting applies to or describes a second setting. In the case of laboratory research, the question is whether lab findings hold true in field or "real life" settings.

Laboratory research is so often criticized for being "unreal", or unlike actual organizations. However, Fromkin and Streufert (1976, p. 441) note that "It is unlikely that any single experiment will resemble a large number of organizations because there is as much variation from one real-life situation to another real-life situation as occurs between the laboratory and real life." Weick (1967) states that it is not necessary to reproduce all the props and accoutrements of real organizations to have a valid laboratory organization. Reproducing or simulating only a few of the most salient characteristics is often sufficient (i.e. co-workers, hierarchical relationships, etc.).

Mook (1983) points out that since exactly what one wishes to generalize may vary from study to study, the criteria for determining external validity should also vary. Sometimes one may wish to generalize a sample mean or proportion to a population, as when an opinion poll concludes that "76% of the population (plus or minus 3%) favors passage of the Equal Rights Amendment." When this kind of generalization is intended, then the sample must very closely represent the population. One would not bring college sophomores into the lab and assess their job satisfaction if one desired to reach conclusions about the mean satisfaction level of employed adults! However, we very rarely do laboratory research in order to make this kind of generalization.

One can also be interested in generalizing the effect of a specific manipulation. Mook (1983) calls this the "agricultural model" for the early agricultural research statisticians who were interested in finding out if fertilizer A, which produces effect X on a test plot, will also produce effect X when applied widely in commercial farming. If one is evaluating a training program which will later be widely implemented, then it will be important to use fairly representative subjects and the exact same training program in the lab as will later be used in the field if one is to have confidence in its generalizability. Some organizational laboratory research does have this kind of generalization as its goal, but most work probably falls into the next category.

Finally, laboratory experiments may have the goal of generalizing *theory* or knowledge of *processes* rather than specific values or manipulations (Mook, 1983). A laboratory setting does not have to look anything like a real setting in order to have this kind of generalizability. For instance, one may have a hypothesis about how anxiety affects behavior, and may experimentally induce anxiety by telling subjects that they will receive a painful electrical shock as part of the experiment. This is not a common everyday occurrence, but it will probably induce a state of anxiety which is indistinguishable from the anxiety provoked by many "real life" events (Mook, 1983). Weick (1967) calls this "psychological representation of variables". Since one is not trying to generalize about the manipulation (threat of shock), but about the state created (anxiety) and the processes that ensue, the apparent artificiality of the manipulation is irrelevant.

As stated at the beginning of the paper, laboratory experiments are particularly good for testing hypotheses derived from theory. A theory may make a number of predictions, one of which is "under condition A, B will occur." Perhaps condition A would never occur in nature, but can be created in the lab. One does so, and B occurs (or does not occur). The results have implications for the entire theory, *whether or not* A would ever occur in real life. As Mook (1983) notes, this is using the lab to test "what can happen" as opposed to "what does happen" ordinarily.

Deciding on generalizability is a matter of judgment rather than statistics. Thus, one must ask exactly *what* is being generalized, and to what extent the subjects, manipulation, and setting permit that kind of generalization. The best way to ascertain whether a particular theory is correct and generalizable is to conduct experiments in both the lab and the field, to use various manipulations all intended to get at the same construct or create the same mental state in subjects, and to use multiple measures of the dependent variable(s) of interest. If a theory stands up under this regimen of experimentation (assuming the various experiments have sufficient power), then one can have a great deal of faith in the results.

REFERENCES

Argyris, C. "Some Unintended Consequences of Rigorous Research." *Psychological Bulletin,* 1968, 70, 185–197.

Beckman, L. and Bishop, B. R. "Deception in Psychological Research: A Reply to Seeman." *American Psychologist,* 1970, 25, 878–880.

Campbell, D. T. "Factors Relevant to the Validity of Experiments in Social Settings." *Psychological Bulletin,* 1957, 54, 297–312.

Campbell, D. T. "Prospective: Artifact and Control." In R. Rosenthal and R. L. Rosnow (Eds.) *Artifact in Behavioral Research.* New York: Academic Press, 1969.

Campbell, D. T. and Stanley, J. C. *Experimental and Quasi-Experimental Designs for Research.* Chicago: Rand McNally, 1963.

Cherrington, D. J., Reitz, H. J., and Scott, W. E. Jr. "The Relationship Between Job Performance and Job Satisfaction." *Journal of Applied Psychology,* 1971, 55, 531–536.

Cherulnik, P. D. *Behavioral Research.* New York: Harper & Row, 1983.

Cohen, J. *Statistical Power Analysis in the Behavioral Sciences.* New York: Academic Press, 1969.

Cook, T. D. and Campbell, D. T. "Experiments in Field Settings." In M. D. Dunnette (Ed.), *Handbook of Industrial and Organizational Psychology.* Chicago: Rand McNally, 1976.

Festinger, L. "Laboratory Experiments." In Festinger and D. Katz (Eds.) *Research Methods in the Behavioral Sciences.* New York: Holt, Rinehart and Winston, 1953.

Fromkin, H. L. and Streufert, S. "Laboratory Experimentation." In M. D. Dunnette (Ed.), *Handbook of Industrial and Organizational Psychology.* Chicago: Rand McNally, 1976.

Griffin, R. W. "Objective and Social Sources of Information in Task Redesign: A Field Experiment." *Administrative Science Quarterly,* 1983, *28,* 184–200.

Lana, R. E. "Pretest Sensitization." In R. Rosenthal and R. L. Rosnow (Eds.), *Artifact in Behavioral Research.* New York: Academic Press, 1969.

Lawler, E. E. III. "Equity Theory as a Predictor of Productivity and Work Quality." *Psychological Bulletin,* 1968, *70,* 596–610.

Lawler, E. E., and Porter, L. W. "The Effect of Performance on Job Satisfaction." *Industrial Relations,* 1967, *1,* 20–28.

Lowin, A. and Craig, J. R. "The Influence of Level of Performance on Managerial Style: An Experimental Object-lesson in the Ambiguity of Correlational Data." *Organizational Behavior and Human Performance,* 1968, *3,* 440–458.

Mook, D. G. "In Defense of External Invalidity." *American Psychologist,* 1983, *38,* 379–387.

Orne, M. T. "On the Social Psychology of the Psychological Experiment." *American Psychologist,* 1962, *17,* 776–783.

Orne, M. T. "Demand Characteristics and the Concept of Quasi-controls." In R. Rosenthal and R. L. Rosnow, (Eds.). *Artifact in Behavioral Research.* New York: Academic Press, 1969.

Platt, J. R. "Strong Inference." *Science,* 1964, *146,* 347–353.

Plutchik, R. *Foundations of Experimental Research,* New York: Harper & Row, 1983, 3rd edition.

Pritchard, R. D. "Equity Theory: A Review and Critique." *Organizational Behavior and Human Performance.* 1969, *4,* 176–211.

Rosenberg, M. J. "The Conditions and Consequences of Evaluation Apprehension." In R. Rosenthal and R. L. Rosnow (Eds.). *Artifact in Behavioral Research.* New York: Academic Press, 1969.

Rosenthal, R. *Experimenter Effects in Behavioral Research.* (Enlarged Edition), New York: Irvington Publishers, 1976.

Rosenthal, R. and Rosnow, R. L. *The Volunteer Subject.* New York: Wiley, 1975.

Schuler, H. *Ethical Problems in Psychological Research.* New York: Academic Press, 1982.

Seeman, J. "Deception in Psychological Research." *American Psychologist,* 1969, *24,* 1025–1028.

Tversky, A. and Kahneman, D. "Belief in the Law of Small Numbers." *Psychological Bulletin,* 1971, *76,* 105–110.

Umstot, D. D., Bell, C. H. Jr., and Mitchell, T. R. "Effects of Job Enrichment and Task Goals on Satisfaction and Productivity: Implications for Job Design." *Journal of Applied Psychology,* 1976, *61,* 379–394.

Vecchio, R. P. "An Individual-Differences Interpretation of the Conflicting Predictions Generated by Equity Theory and Expectancy Theory." *Journal of Applied Psychology,* 1981, *66,* 470–481.

Weber, S. J. and Cook, T. D. "Subject Effects in Laboratory Research: An Examination of Subject Roles, Demand Characteristics, and Valid Inferences." *Psychological Bulletin,* 1972, *77,* 273–295.

Weick, K. E. "Organizations in the Laboratory." In V. Vroom (Ed.), *Methods of Organizational Research.* Pittsburgh: University of Pittsburgh Press, 1967.

Weick, K. E. "Laboratory Organizations and Unnoticed Causes." *Administrative Science Quarterly,* 1964, *14,* 294–303.

Attribution of the "Causes" of Performance: A General Alternative Interpretation of Cross-Sectional Research on Organizations[1]

Barry M. Staw[2]

Although much of the research in organizational behavior is devoted to understanding the causes of performance, the findings in the field are still largely based upon correlational data in which the direction of causation is unknown. At present, the research supporting most organizational theories contains hypothesized independent variables which can either be the causes of performance, the effects of performance, covariates of third variables, or the result of a network of reciprocal causation. Therefore, it could be argued strongly that, in terms of both theory and application, resolving ambiguity in causal inference is one of the field's most pressing issues.

Previously, there have been two empirical studies specifically designed to demonstrate problems in interpreting correlational data derived from cross-sectional surveys.[3] In the first of these studies, Lowin and Craig (1968) experimentally manipulated the performance of subordinates and measured the

leadership style of persons hired to perform a real supervisory role. The results of this study showed that closeness of supervision may be a function of subordinate performance rather than a causal determinant of performance, as previously believed. In a somewhat parallel study, Farris and Lim (1969) compared the leadership style of work group supervisors after knowledge of subordinate performance had been experimentally manipulated. This research involved a role playing exercise in which one student was designated as a foreman and three other students acted as a three-person work group in an industrial conflict situation. Each group worked with its foreman toward the solution of the "Change in Work Procedure Case" (Maier, Solem, & Maier, 1957), and then completed a postexperimental questionnaire on the foreman's behavior. Knowledge of performance was manipulated by providing information to the foreman (before the work session) that his

[1] *Organizational Behavior and Human Performance 13*, 414–432 (1975). Copyright © 1975 by Academic Press, Inc.

[2] The author is indebted to Greg R. Oldham for his comments on an earlier version of this paper, and to Ramamoorthi Narayan for serving as an experimenter in this research.

Requests for reprints should be sent to Barry M. Staw, Organizational Behavior Program, 104 Commerce West, University of Illinois, Urbana, Illinois 61801.

[3] The term "cross-sectional" is used in this paper to refer to survey data collected from one point in time (cf. Campbell & Katona, 1953) as opposed to longitudinal or panel studies in which there are several time-dependent measures.

group was one of the highest or lowest groups in terms of previous performance. The results showed that, for high performing groups, the foreman was perceived to be more supportive of the workers, higher in goal emphasis, and more facilitative of interaction than was the foreman of low performing groups.

By showing that changes in performance can cause changes in other behavioral variables, both the Lowin and Craig (1968) and Farris and Lim (1969) studies represent efforts to stimulate more causal research on organizations. The approach represented by their research is a step-by-step demonstration of the plausibility of reversals in causal order. In fact, from this approach, one might advocate measuring the effects of performance upon an array of individual, group, and organizational variables, and the construction of a thorough inventory of plausible causal reversals. With this information, researchers eventually would know where to invest substantial resources on research with methods more conducive to causal inference (i.e., field experimentation, longitudinal analysis, and laboratory simulations of organizational processes).

The step-by-step demonstration of causal reversals is no doubt a worthwhile procedure to help budge the field of organizational behavior from its near total reliance on cross-sectional (correlational) data. However, it is believed that this procedure is neither sufficiently speedy nor now necessary to encourage a significant increase in causal research. The reason for this conjecture is a new alternative interpretation of cross-sectional data which is both parsimonious and of general applicability to correlational findings, linking performance data to self-report measures of individual, group, and organizational characteristics. This alternative interpretation of correlational findings is derived from previous work on attribution theory.

Attribution theory is specifically concerned with how individuals assign enduring traits or dispositions to themselves and other persons (Heider, 1957; Jones & Davis, 1965; Kelley, 1971, 1973; Nisbett & Valins, 1971). It assumes that individuals have a need to understand and explain the events around them, and that based upon this need, individuals will develop a lay or "naive" psychology of behavior (Heider, 1958). To date, most of the research in attribution theory has studied the perception of personal characteristics under varied environmental conditions (e.g., Bem, 1965; Calder & Staw, 1975a, 1975b; Deci, 1971; Jones, Davis & Gergen, 1961; Jones & Harris, 1967; Schachter & Singer, 1962; Staw, 1974a, 1974b; Strickland, 1958). However, in its broadest context, attribution theory is concerned with the ascription of characteristics to any entity. As Kelley (1973) has noted, all of the judgments of the type, "Property X characterizes Entity Y" can be viewed as causal attributions. Thus, it seems reasonable to assume that the organizational participant, in a desire to understand and control his particular environment, may develop a lay psychology of individual, group, and organizational functioning. Just as individuals may possess an implicit personality theory to guide their impressions of others (Bruner & Tagiuri, 1954), the organizational participant may possess a theory of the relationships between organizational characteristics and subsequent performance

The specific attribution hypothesis posited here is that individuals utilize knowledge of performance as a cue by which they ascribe characteristics to an individual, group, or organizational unit. The attribution hypothesis posits that performance is a potent independent variable, and that many of the correlations between performance and self-report data may be accounted for by the following causal sequence: Level of Performance → Attribution of Characteristics → Self-report of Characteristics. That is, performance data may cause persons to assign an entire set of characteristics (i.e., a stereotype) to individuals, groups, and organizations, and this attributed set of characteristics may underlie many of the correlations derived from cross-sectional studies of organizational processes.[4]

The attribution hypothesis can be illustrated by a questionnaire developed by Likert (1967) to support his System 4 theory of management. Likert asked several hundred managers to "think of the most productive department, division, or organization (they) have known well." The managers were then asked to rate this entity in terms of organizational processes such as motivation, influence, communication and cooperation. Subsequently, these same managers were also asked to rate their least productive department, division, or organization on each of these dimensions. As expected, a high degree of motivation, mutual influence, cooperation, and communication were associated with the highest producing units. Although it is not yet clear whether the processes seen by managers as being associated with high performance actually contribute to performance, Likert's data do illustrate that, *perceptually,* individuals will distinguish between high and low producing units. Moreover, the existence of distinct stereotypes of successful versus unsuccessful organizations points to the very possibility that significant correlations between performance and self-report data may only be reflecting the respondents' "theories" of organizational performance rather than actual events. And as Heider (1958) has noted in his now classic analysis of interpersonal perception, a lay or "naive" psychology of behavior may or may not be correct.

Clearly, if knowledge of performance causes one to attribute particular characteristics to individuals, groups, or organizations, it may therefore be risky (and certainly unscientific) to posit that self-report data on these characteristics accurately represent the causal determinants of performance. In essence, questionnaire measures considered by organizational researchers to be indicators of the determinants of performance, may actually constitute the consequences of performance. This possibility is of substantial importance to organizational research since individual, group, and organizational characteristics are rarely observed directly, but are generally measured by respondents' perceptions within a field setting.

A laboratory experiment was conducted to test the relevance of the attribution interpretation to some important correlational findings. Specifically, it seemed desirable to test whether this alternative interpretation is applicable to Tannenbaum's (1968) replicated finding that high mutual influence is associated with high performance. Likert's (1961) finding that group cohesiveness is associated with high performance, and Evan's (1965) finding that interpersonal conflict (but not task conflict) is related to performance. In addition, the relationships of performance to motivation (Galbraith & Cummings, 1967), communication, and openness to change (Likert, 1961) were investigated by this research.

METHOD

Subjects

Subjects for this experiment were undergraduate students enrolled in the College of Commerce and Business Administration at the University of Illinois, Urbana-Champaign. Sixty students were randomly assigned to three-man groups and each group

---

[4] Farris and Lim (1969) interpreted their data as knowledge of performance affecting actual supervisory behavior. However, these data can also be alternatively interpreted by an attribution effect. Persons playing subordinate roles in the study may have learned from their leaders that they were members of a high or low performing work group, attributed this past performance to the foreman's leadership capabilities, and then reported these characteristics on the postexperimental measures of perceived leadership behavior. It is therefore possible that knowledge of performance did not affect actual supervisory behavior but only subordinates' perceptions of it.

was asked to participate in a "Financial Puzzle Task." Group members were given copies of the 1969 annual report of a medium-sized (but not well known) electronics company. The report contained a description of the company, a letter from the president on the firm's prospects, and five preceding years of financial data. The group members were told that their task was to estimate company sales and earnings per share for 1970, taking into consideration any knowledge they might have of the electronics industry or state of the economy at that time. Each group was given 30 min. to discuss the issue and make any necessary calculations in formulating a group estimate of sales and earnings per share. Subjects were told that the purpose of the experiment was to evaluate the performance of groups of various sizes and that previous research had been conducted on three-, four-, and five-man groups.

Manipulation of Performance

After each group presented its estimates of sales and earnings per share, the experimenter stated that "it would be interesting to see how well this group had performed relative to previous three-man groups." The experimenter then took the group's estimates of sales and earnings per share and searched through several file cabinets in the next room. On returning to the (randomly assigned) *High Performance* groups, the experimenter announced that the group had "done quite well," that their sales figure was off by only $10,000, earnings per share was accurate within $.05 a share, and that the group's overall performance was clearly in the top 20% of three-man groups. On returning to the (randomly assigned) *Low Performance* groups, the experimenter announced that they had "not done too well," that their estimate for sales was off by $10,-000,000, their estimate for earnings per share was off by $1.00, and that the group's overall performance was in the lowest 20% of previous three-man groups. No subjects expressed strong doubts about their group's

performance. However, it should be noted that the annual report used in this experiment was selected specifically on the basis of its ambiguity and could be interpreted in either a positive or negative manner.

Dependent Variables

After being told of their group's performance, subjects were led to separate rooms and asked to complete a short questionnaire about, "what went on in the group." On the questionnaire were items to measure group cohesiveness, influence, communication, task conflict, openness to change, motivation, ability, and clarity of instructions. Although the questions were randomly ordered on the questionnaire, they are listed below under the appropriate variable headings.

I. *Cohesiveness*
   a. To what extent did you enjoy working with your teammates?
      (11 point scale from "not at all" to "to a great extent")
   b. In working on the financial puzzle task, what were your personal feelings about your teammates?
      (11 point scale from "I disliked them" to "I liked them")
   c. How would you rate the cohesiveness or group spirit of your team?
      (11 point scale from "extremely low" to "extremely high")

II. *Influence*
   a. How much influence did you have on final solution of the task?
      (11 point scale from "very little" to "a great amount")
   b. How much influence did your teammates have on the final solution of the task?

III. *Communication*
   a. How would you rate the quantity of communication between you and your teammates?
      (11 point scale from "very low" to "very high")
   b. How would you rate the quality of

communication between you and your teammates?

(11 point scale from "very low" to "very high")

IV. *Task Conflict*

  a. To what extent did you and your teammates each have different ideas about methods to solve the financial puzzle task?

  (11 point scale from "not at all" to "to a great extent")

  b. If you and your teammates had different ideas about solving the task, to what extent did you have an open confrontation of ideas?

  (11 point scale from "not at all" to "to a great extent")

V. *Openness to Change*

  a. How open were your teammates to your ideas and suggestions about solving the financial puzzle task?

  (11 point scale from "not open at all" to "extremely open")

  b. In solving the task, to what extent did your teammates ever attempt to impose or force their position(s) on you?

  (11 point scale from "not at all" to "to a great extent")

VI. *Satisfaction*

  a. To what extent did you enjoy working on the Financial Puzzle Task?

  (11 point scale from "not at all" to "to a great extent")

VII. *Motivation*

  a. To what extent were you interested in performing well on the financial puzzle task?

  (11 point scale from "not at all" to "to a great extent")

  b. To what extent were your teammates interested in performing well on the financial puzzle task?

  (11 point scale from "not at all" to "to a great extent")

VIII. *Ability*

  a. In general, how would you rate your ability in solving financial puzzles?

(11 point scale from "very low" to "very high")

  b. In general, how would you rate your teammates' ability in solving financial puzzles?

  (11 point scale from "very low" to "very high")

IX. *Role Clarity*

  a. Were the instructions for solving the financial puzzle made clear to you?

  (11 point scale from "not at all" to "very clear")

RESULTS

Check on the Performance Manipulation

Subjects randomly assigned to High Performance groups rated their ability in solving financial puzzles as higher than did subjects in Low Performance groups ($t(58) = 5.64$, $p < .001$). Subjects in the High Performance groups also rated their teammates' ability as higher than did those in Low Performance groups ($t(58) = 2.60$, $p < .01$). These data support the hypothesis that subjects believed the information provided by the experimenter on their group's performance.

It should be noted that, in actuality, the groups assigned to the High Performance condition performed no better than those assigned to the low Performance Condition (see Table 1). In fact, in terms of predicting corporate sales and earnings, groups told that they had performed well actually performed (nonsignificantly) worse than those told they had performed poorly (For sales: $t = -.48$, N.S.; for earnings: $t = -.23$, N.S.). Thus, any reported differences in the perception of group characteristics are likely to be due to manipulated knowledge of performance rather than to any actual differences in the behavior of the groups. Again, it should be stressed that the financial data comprising the group task was specifically selected (in terms of ambiguity) so as to allow a credible manipulation of knowledge of performance.

TABLE 1

**Estimated 1970 Sales and Earnings Per Share for Low Performance Group,
and Actual Company Data for 1970**

	Low performance group			High performance group			Actual company performance in 1970
	$\bar{x}$	SD	Range	$\bar{x}$	SD	Range	
Estimated 1970 sales (in millions of dollars)	44.93	3.21	39.50–49.00	45.63	3.22	40.00–50.00	40.45
Estimated 1970 earnings per shares (in dollars)	.69	.37	.10–1.25	.74	.44	.10–1.50	(Net loss)

Effect of Knowledge of Performance on Perceptions of Interpersonal Behavior

The perceptions of several dimensions of interpersonal behavior for subjects in both High and Low Performance groups are displayed in Table 2. One-tailed t tests are shown in the table since the statistical contrasts are based on a priori predictions. When more than one item was used to measure a particular variable, and where these items were significantly intercorrelated, a combined score and resulting t value is also reported. As shown in Table 2, individuals who were randomly assigned to High Performance groups rated their groups as more cohesive ($t(58) = 1.68$, $p < .05$) and enjoyed working with their teammates to a greater extent ($t(58) = 1.81$, $p < .05$) than did individuals assigned to Low Performance groups. Persons in High Performance groups also rated their groups higher in quality and quantity of communication ($t(58) = 1.77$, $p < .05$), higher in total influence ($t(58) = 1.86$, $p < .05$), and marginally higher in openness to change ($t(58) = 1.49$, $p < .10$). It is interesting to note that the effect of performance on total influence was due primarily to the large effect of performance on the perception of one's own influence ($t(58) = 2.47$, $p < .01$), and that there was no effect of performance on the perception of teammates' influence on the group task. No clear relationship to performance was shown by the two indicators of task conflict and these two scales were not significantly intercorrelated.

Effects of Knowledge of Performance on Satisfaction, Motivation, Ability, and Role Clarity

Table 3 shows that subjects assigned to High Performance groups enjoyed working on the experimental task to a greater extent than did subjects assigned to Low Performance groups ($t(58) = 5.93$, $p < .001$). In addition, subjects in High Performance groups rated their own interest in performing well on the task as greater than subjects assigned to Low Performance groups ($t(58) = 5.33$, $p < .001$). Similarly, these same subjects rated their teammates' interest in performing well on the task higher than did subjects in Low Performance groups. Finally, as previously reported, feedback on performance affected the subjects' rated ability ($t(58) = 5.64$, $p < .001$), his perception of his teammates' ability ($t(58) = 2.60$, $p < .01$), and also the rated clarity of instructions for the task ($t(58) = 2.20$, $p < .05$).[5]

---

[5] In each of the above analyses, the individual was regarded as the appropriate unit of analysis. This assumption was based on the fact that individuals were randomly assigned to

TABLE 2

Effect of Knowledge of Performance Upon Perceptions of Intragroup Processes

		Low performance	High performance	t Value
Cohesiveness				
Cohesiveness of group	$\bar{x}$	6.70	7.83	1.68**
	SD	3.06	2.07	
Enjoy working with teammates	$\bar{x}$	7.23	8.28	1.81**
	SD	2.65	1.48	
Liking for teammates	$\bar{x}$	8.77	9.23	1.04
	SD	2.10	1.30	
Combined cohesiveness score	$\bar{x}$	7.57	8.43	1.72**
	SD	2.36	1.42	
Influence				
Teammates influence on task solution	$\bar{x}$	7.57	7.43	−.24
	SD	2.62	1.45	
Own influence on task solution	$\bar{x}$	6.00	7.73	2.47**
	SD	3.27	2.03	
Combined influence score	$\bar{x}$	6.78	7.58	1.86**
	SD	1.91	1.37	
Communication				
Quality of communication	$\bar{x}$	6.77	7.93	1.75**
	SD	3.11	1.91	
Quantity of communication	$\bar{x}$	6.47	7.30	1.33
	SD	2.71	2.12	
Combined communication score	$\bar{x}$	6.62	7.61	1.77**
	SD	2.49	1.82	
Task conflict				
Differences in ideas about methods to solve problem	$\bar{x}$	4.83	4.93	.17
	SD	2.38	2.03	
Confrontation of ideas with teammates	$\bar{x}$	5.34	7.03	1.97**
	SD	3.38	3.19	
Openness to change				
Openness of teammate to ideas and suggestions about solving problem	$\bar{x}$	7.73	8.55	1.52*
	SD	2.36	1.72	
Extent teammate attempted to force his position on you (scale reversed)	$\bar{x}$	8.53	9.21	1.02
	SD	2.84	2.19	
Combined openness score	$\bar{x}$	8.14	8.88	1.49*
	SD	2.12	1.69	

   * $p < .10$, one-tailed test.
  ** $p < .05$, one-tailed test.
 *** $p < .01$, one-tailed test.

DISCUSSION

As illustrated by the data of Tables 2 and 3, knowledge of performance had a marked effect on the self-report measures of intragroup processes. As expected, individuals who were told that they had participated in a high-performing group rated their groups higher in cohesiveness, influence, communication, openness to change (marginally sig-

high and low performance conditions, and that the theoretical hypotheses tested by this research lie at the individual level. Specifically, the research reported here deals with how individuals attribute particular characteristics to their work groups rather than the analytic properties of groups, *per se* (see Lazarfeld & Menzel, 1969, for discussion of the relationship between individual and collective variables).

TABLE 3
Effect of Knowledge of Performance on Satisfaction, Motivation Ability, and Role Clarity

		Low performance	High performance	t Value
Motivation				
Teammates' interest in performing well	$\bar{x}$	4.97	7.47	3.87***
	SD	2.79	2.18	
Own interest in performing well	$\bar{x}$	4.73	7.90	5.33***
	SD	2.64	1.90	
Combined motivation score	$\bar{x}$	4.85	7.68	5.24***
	SD	2.26	1.91	
Ability				
Teammates' ability	$\bar{x}$	5.50	7.13	2.60***
	SD	3.01	1.65	
Own ability	$\bar{x}$	3.57	6.80	5.64***
	SD	2.33	2.11	
Combined ability score	$\bar{x}$	4.54	6.96	5.00***
	SD	2.03	1.72	
Satisfaction				
Enjoyed working on financial task	$\bar{x}$	3.47	7.20	5.93***
	SD	2.43	2.44	
Role clarity				
Clarity of instruction for the task	$\bar{x}$	7.23	8.70	2.20***
	SD	2.90	2.23	

* $p < .10$, one-tailed test.
** $p < .05$, one-tailed test.
*** $p < .01$, one-tailed test.

nificant) and motivation as compared to individuals who were told that they had participated in a low performing group. As a whole, these data provide support for the notion that individuals attribute one set of characteristics to a work group they believe is effective and another, different, set of characteristics to an ineffective work group. As a whole, these data also offer support for an attributional interpretation of correlations between self-report data and measures of group performance.

The data on cohesiveness and task conflict provide a particularly interesting test of the attribution hypothesis. Previously, Evan (1965) had hypothesized that the impact of intragroup conflict upon performance may not necessarily be negative, and that the effects of conflict might depend on the type of conflict involved. Specifically, Evan postu-

lated that interpersonal conflict should have a negative effect on work group performance, while task conflict might prove beneficial. By correlating self-report measures of conflict to the performance of R & D groups. Evan's data showed a significant negative relationship between interpersonal conflict and performance, but no clear relationship between task conflict and performance. As shown in Table 1, quite similar results were obtained in this study when knowledge of performance was the manipulated independent variable. Knowledge of high performance caused subjects to perceive less interpersonal conflict (as evidenced by greater interpersonal liking and cohesion), while there was a tendency (significant on one of two measures) to rate a high performing group higher in task conflict.[6] Evan's relatively complex relationship between

[6] It should be noted that the questions used to measure interpersonal and task conflict in Evan's 1965 study were quite similar to those used to measure interpersonal cohesiveness and task conflict in this research.

conflict and performance was thus replicated when knowledge of performance was the manipulated independent variable.

A second test of the attribution hypothesis is provided by the data on intragroup influence. Within several organizational settings, Tannenbaum (1968) has found that the amount of total control of influence is significantly related to organizational effectiveness. In each of these studies (Smith & Tannenbaum, 1963; Tannenbaum, 1962, Tannenbaum, 1968), self-report measures of influence are correlated with objective measures of organizational performance. Although Tannenbaum has interpreted these findings as indicating that greater total influence causes improved performance, an attribution interpretation is also plausible. In fact, the hypothesis that individuals attribute greater influence to high rather than low producing groups is generally supported by the data of this experiment.

The data on quality and quantity of communication also provide support for the attribution hypothesis. Although communication has previously been found to correlate with organizational effectiveness (see Price, 1967), the direction of causation has not been clear. In this experiment, however, members of high producing groups inferred higher quality communication to their groups and tended also to infer a greater quantity of communication. In addition, persons with knowledge of high performance tended to rate their teammates as being more open to change (see Likert, 1961, 1967, for concomitant correlation), and perceived both themselves and their teammates as being higher in motivation (see Galbraith & Cummings, 1967, for concomitant correlation).

Although the data of this experiment are generally supportive of the attribution hypothesis, it should be noted that some of the data can be explained by alternative processes. For example, one indicator of group cohesiveness (enjoyed working with teammates) may have been higher among persons assigned to High Performance groups due to the reinforcement associated with task success. Although this explanation would also clearly apply to the measure of task satisfaction, it would not, however, be as applicable to other intragroup processes measured on the questionnaire (e.g., influence, conflict, communication, motivation, and openness to change).

A second alternative interpretation is suggested by the data on intragroup influence and motivation. Because persons assigned to Low Performance groups attributed less influence to themselves and rated themselves as lower in task motivation than persons in High Performance groups, an ego-defensive process is suggested (Weiner, 1971). One problem with the ego-defensive explanation, however, is that subjects also rated their teammates' motivation as lower under the Low Performance condition, and this result would not be predicted by an ego-defensive process. A second problem with the ego-defensive explanation is that subjects rated their own ability under Low Performance conditions as significantly lower than that of their teammates. Clearly, if an ego-defensive process were operating, one would expect subjects to depreciate their teammate's ability under low group performance, while keeping their own rated ability intact.

In sum, the results of this experiment support the contention that knowledge of performance is a relatively potent independent variable. Moreover, the overall pattern of results can be more parsimoniously explained by an attribution theory than by either a reinforcement or ego-defensive process. The attribution process posited here is that individuals hold distinct stereotypes of high versus low performing groups, and that persons will attribute these characteristics to a group based upon mere knowledge of its performance. So as to provide additional vali-

TABLE 4
Effect of Knowledge of Performance for Interpersonal Stimulation

		Low performance	High performance	t Value
Cohesiveness				
Cohesiveness of group	$\bar{x}$	3.00	8.67	17.18***
	SD	1.31	1.24	
Enjoy working with teammates	$\bar{x}$	4.10	8.10	10.62***
	SD	1.52	1.40	
Liking for teammates	$\bar{x}$	4.93	7.50	7.17***
	SD	1.44	1.33	
Combined cohesiveness score	$\bar{x}$	4.01	8.09	15.46***
	SD	.94	1.10	
Influence				
Influence of each member	$\bar{x}$	5.17	6.97	3.49***
	SD	2.31	1.63	
Influence of "most influential" member	$\bar{x}$	8.90	8.90	.00
	SD	2.01	1.88	
Influence of "least influential" member	$\bar{x}$	2.60	4.03	2.74**
	SD	2.33	1.67	
Combined influence score	$\bar{x}$	5.75	6.47	2.21*
	SD	1.42	1.07	
Communication				
Quality of communication	$\bar{x}$	2.93	8.80	17.08***
	SD	1.33	1.32	
Quantity of communication	$\bar{x}$	4.50	8.37	8.22***
	SD	2.08	1.52	
Combined communication score	$\bar{x}$	3.72	8.58	14.47***
	SD	1.32	1.29	
Task conflict				
Differences in ideas about methods to solve problem	$\bar{x}$	6.80	6.50	−.53
	SD	2.48	1.89	
Confrontation of ideas with teammates	$\bar{x}$	5.30	7.03	2.98***
	SD	2.55	1.92	
Combined task conflict score	$\bar{x}$	6.05	6.77	1.53+
	SD	2.19	1.35	
Openness to change				
Openness of ideas and suggestions about solving problem	$\bar{x}$	4.27	8.07	7.27***
	SD	2.26	1.76	
Extent group members ever attempted to force their positions (scale reversed)	$\bar{x}$	4.03	4.30	.40
	SD	2.51	1.95	
Combined openness score	$\bar{x}$	4.65	6.68	5.04***
	SD	1.85	1.21	
Motivation				
Group members' interest in performing well	$\bar{x}$	3.33	8.30	11.84***
	SD	1.75	1.49	
Ability				
Rated ability of group on task	$\bar{x}$	2.90	8.93	19.13***
	SD	1.42	.98	
Role clarity				
Clarity of instructions for the task	$\bar{x}$	6.50	8.37	4.27***
	SD	1.85	1.52	

· $p < .10$, one-tailed test.
* $p < .05$, one-tailed test.
** $p < .01$, one-tailed test.
*** $p < .001$, one-tailed test.

dation of this attribution process, an "interpersonal simulation" (Bem, 1965) was also performed.

An Interpersonal Simulation

In order to provide specific data on the stereotypes individuals hold and the attachment of these stereotypes to high and low performing groups, an "interpersonal simulation" was conducted. As described below, the study provided direct data on the attribution process in addition to replication of the previous experimental findings.

For the interpersonal simulation, 60 students were asked to participate in a study on perceptual accuracy. They were told that a large number of undergraduate business students had previously participated in a group problem-solving study in which measurements were taken of intragroup processes and performance. Subjects were told that the researchers were interested in seeing how accurately individuals could assess intragroup processes based upon a minimal amount of information, and that their assessments would be compared to "true" observational measures of group processes collected over the past year. The "Financial Puzzle Task" (as used in the above experiment) was then thoroughly described to the subjects in both written and oral form. Subsequently, subjects were asked to rate a typical group of business undergraduates who had performed in the lowest (or highest) 20% of all three-man groups. Via random assignment, 30 subjects were asked to rate a high performing group and 30 a low performing group. Efforts were made to keep the rating scales as similar as possible to those used in the previous experiment.

As shown in Table 4 the results of the interpersonal simulation followed closely those of the previous study. High performing groups were perceived to be higher in cohesiveness, total influence, quality and quantity of communication, motivation, and openness to change than low performing groups. As in the previous experiment, interpersonal conflict (i.e., low group cohesiveness) was negatively related to performance, while task conflict tended to be positively associated with performance.[7] Likewise, total influence was perceived to be greater in high rather than low performing groups. However, because persons in the interpersonal simulation did not actually participate in a problem-solving group, total influence was not measured by a combination of the rated influence of self and one's teammates. Instead, total influence was measured by, (1) combining the perceived influence scores for the "most influential" and "least influential" persons in the group, (2) by simply asking subjects to rate the influence of each group member. By either of these methods, total influence appeared to be positively associated with group performance.

CONCLUSIONS

The data of the true experiment and the interpersonal simulation, together, provide strong evidence for the attribution effect. The similarity of results from these two studies demonstrates that mere knowledge of performance may cause an individual to attribute one set of characteristics to a high performing group and a different set of characteristics to a low performing group. Supported by these data, the attribution effect thus constitutes a very plausible interpretation of correlations linking perceived group characteristics to work group performance. Moreover, though not yet specifically tested,

---

[7] Table 4 shows a combined task conflict score since, in the interpersonal simulation, the two indicators of task conflict were significantly intercorrelated. In contrast, Table 2 did not show a combined task conflict score since, in the earlier experiment, the two indicators of this variable were not significantly intercorrelated.

this same attribution process may underlie many correlations between self-report data on individual characteristics (e.g., attitudes, perceived role conflict and ambiguity, perceived effort) and individual performance data, as well as many correlations between self-report data on organizational variables (e.g., openness, conflict, goal orientation, climate) and organizational performance data. In sum, the process by which individuals attribute the "causes" of performance may have important implications for the conduct of organizational research.

From the data presented here, the attribution effect can be viewed as potentially more threatening to the interpretation of correlational findings than the simple reversal of causal sequences. As noted by Lowin and Craig (1968) and Farris and Lim (1969), an assumed direction of causation may be incorrect since performance can affect actual interpersonal behavior. However, actual reversals in causation do not always occur and often it is possible for the researcher to discount the probability of their occurrence on logical and theoretical grounds. In essence, the more intuitively obvious or plausible a particular causal sequence is, the safer it is for researchers to discount its actual reversal. In direct contrast, the attribution interpretation posits that organizational participants possess theories of performance just as do organizational researchers. Thus, the more intuitively obvious or plausible a theory of organizational behavior is, the more likely it is for a correlation between self-report data and performance to be threatened by an attribution interpretation. Since there are no doubt a greater number of obvious than nonobvious findings in organizational research, the attribution effect may therefore be a greater threat to cross-sectional findings than actual reversals in causal order.

The attribution effect posited here is not unrelated to the notion of demand characteristics developed by experimental social psychologists (see Orne, 1962; Weber & Cook, 1972). Demand characteristics refer to the process by which experimental subjects may attempt to confirm a researcher's theoretical hypothesis by providing supporting empirical data. Although demand characteristics were originally conceived as a potential threat to the interpretation of experimental data, they are also applicable, like the attribution effect, to survey methodology. If a respondent can easily guess the researcher's hypothesis, any empirically derived relationship between two theoretical variables may be artifactual. The crucial element of demand characteristics, of course, is that the researcher's hypothesis be known or so obvious that most respondents will guess it correctly. In contrast, the attribution effect makes no such assumption. Instead of having to guess the *researcher's* hypothesis, it may only be necessary (as shown in the experiments above) that the majority of the respondents possess their *own* hypotheses linking individual, group, or organizational characteristics to performance.[8]

---

[8] It could be argued that the experimental results presented here are, themselves, products of demand characteristics—that subjects attempted to confirm this experimenter's *a priori* hypotheses. Although it is impossible to totally disconfirm this alternative interpretation, it does not appear to be as plausible an explanation of the data as the attribution effect. Two factors decrease the likelihood of demand characteristics' accounting for the data presented here: (1) Since no hypotheses were related to the subjects, they would have had to guess the purpose of the study in *two quite different* experimental settings; (2) Subjects who participated in these studies did so in order to satisfy a course requirement of another university instructor. These subjects would be less motivated to confirm the experimenter's hypotheses than would subjects who were purely voluntary participants (see Rosenthal & Rosnow, 1969).

Although the attribution effect is a more parsimonious explanation of the present data

Clearly, a major problem still facing the field of organizational behavior is a dearth of firm causal findings. The results of this study, together with previous experiments on the effects of performance, underscore the need for methods more conducive to causal inference. Three primary solutions to this dilemma have already been posited, but not yet widely adopted. First, by conducting longitudinal studies using cross-lag correlation procedures (Pelz & Andrews, 1964; Vroom, 1967) there can be an improvement in our knowledge of causal order. (It should be noted, however, that the use of cross-lag correlation techniques implies equal time lags in the causal links $X_{11} \rightarrow Y_{12} \rightarrow$ and $Y_{11} \rightarrow X_{12}$). Second, by conducting true and (strong) quasi-experiments within organiza-

tions, we may be able to increase the internal validity of our findings without unduly sacrificing external validity (Campbell & Stanley, 1963; Cook & Campbell, 1975). Both as consultants to planned organizational changes and as documenters of naturally occurring organizational changes (Staw, 1974), there are many opportunities to obtain data from which causal inference may be drawn. Third, it may be possible to combine constructively the advantages of laboratory and field methods in the investigation of organizational processes (McGrath, 1964; Evan, 1971). By coordinating laboratory and field studies (e.g., in terms of chosen variables and measurement instruments) the resultant findings could be high in both internal and external validity.

---

than demand characteristics, it would be extremely difficult to devise an experiment which, in testing the attribution effect, would totally control for demand characteristics. For example, one might design a study in which subjects are specifically informed that the experimenter is testing a hypothesis which is the *opposite* of what most persons believe. This design would eliminate demand characteristics but might also severely weaken the test of the attribution effect, since *subjects'* initial theories of performance would probably be shaken by the conflicting information. Thus, providing an experimental context in which no research hypotheses are particularly salient (as in the present experiments) may be as close to an ideal test of the attribution effect as is currently feasible.

REFERENCES

Bem, D. J. "An Experimental Analysis of Self-persuasion." *Journal of Experimental Social Psychology*, 1965, *1*, 199–218.

Bem, D. J. "Self-perception: The Dependent Variable of Human Performance." *Organizational Behavior and Human Performance*, 1967, 2, 105–121.

Bem, D. J. "Self-perception Theory." In L. Berkowitz (Ed.), *Advances in Experimental Social Psychology*. Vol. 6. New York: Academic Press, 1972, pp. 1–62.

Bruner, J. S. & Taguiri, A. "The Perception of People." In G. Lindzey (Ed.), *Handbook of Social Psychology*, 1954.

Calder, B. J. & Staw, B. M. "The Interaction of Intrinsic and Extrinsic Motivation:

Some Methodological Notes." *Journal of Personality and Social Psychology,* 1975, *31,* 76–80. (a)

Calder, B. J. & Staw, B. M. "The Self-perception of Intrinsic and Extrinsic Motivation." *Journal of Personality and Social Psychology,* April, 1975. (b)

Campbell, A. & Katona, G. "The Sample Survey: A Technique for Social Science Research." In L. Festinger and D. Katz (Eds.), *Research Methods in the Behavioral Sciences.* New York: Holt, Rinehart, and Winston, 1953.

Cook, T. D. & Campbell, D. T. "The Design and Conduct of Quasi-experiments and True Experiments in Field Settings." In M. D. Dunnette (Ed.), *Handbook of In-*

dustrial and Organizational Research, Chicago: Rand McNally, 1975.

Deci, E. L. "Effects of Externally Mediated Rewards on Intrinsic Motivation." *Journal of Personality and Social Psychology,* 1971, *18,* 105–115.

Evan, W. M. "Conflict and Performance in R & D Organizations." *Industrial Management Review,* 1965, *7,* 37–45; Also reprinted in B. L. Hinton and H. J. Reitz (Eds.), *Groups and Organizations.* Belmont, California: Wadsworth, 1971.

Farris, G. F. & Lim, F. G. "Effects of Performance on Leadership, Cohesiveness, Influence, Satisfaction, and Subsequent Performance." *Journal of Applied Psychology,* 1969, *53,* 490–497.

Galbraith, J. & Cummings, L. L. "An Empirical Investigation of the Motivational Determinants of Task Performance: Interactive Effects between Instrumentality-Valence and Motivation-ability." *Organizational Behavior and Human Performance,* 1967, *2,* 237–257.

Heider, F. *The Psychology of Interpersonal Relations.* New York: Wiley, 1968.

Jones, E. E. & Davis, K. E. "From Acts to Dispositions: The Attribution Process in Person Perception." In L. Berkowitz (Ed.), *Advances in Experimental Social Psychology.* Vol. 2. New York: Academic Press, 1965.

Jones, E. E., Davis, K. E., & Gergen, K. E. "Role Playing Variations and their Informational Value for Person Perception." *Journal of Abnormal and Social Psychology,* 1961, *63,* 302–310.

Jones, E. E. & Harris, V. A. "The Attribution of Attitudes." *Journal of Experimental Social Psychology,* 1967, *3,* 1–24.

Kelley, H. H. *Attribution in Social Interaction.* Morristown, New Jersey: General Learning Press, 1971.

Kelley, H. H. "The Processes of Causal Attribution." *American Psychologist,* 1973, *28,* 107–128.

Lazarsfeld, P. F. & Menzel, H. "On the Rela-

tion between Individual and Collective Properties." In A. Etzioni (Ed.), *A Sociological Reader on Complex Organizations.* New York: Holt, Rinehart and Winston, 1969.

Likert, R. "Measuring Organizational Performance." *Harvard Business Review,* March–April, 1958.

Likert, R. *New Patterns of Management.* New York: McGraw-Hill, 1961.

Likert, R. *Human Organization: Its Management and Value.* New York: McGraw-Hill, 1967.

Lowin, A. & Craig, J. R. "The Influence of Level of Performance on Managerial Style: An Experimental Object-lesson in the Ambiguity of Correlational Data." *Organizational Behavior and Human Performance,* 1968, *3,* 440–458.

Maier, N. R. F., Solem, A. R., & Maier, A. "Supervisory and Executive Development: A Manual for Role Playing." New York: Wiley, 1957.

McGrath, J. "Toward a 'Theory of Method' for Research on Organizations." In W. W. Cooper, H. J. Leavitt, and M. W. Shelly II (Eds.), *New Perspectives in Organizational Research.* New York: Wiley, 1964.

Nisbett, R. E. & Valins, S. *Perceiving the Causes of One's Own Behavior.* Morristown, New Jersey: General Learning Press, 1971.

Orne, M. T. "On the Social Psychology of the Psychological Experiment: With Particular Reference to Demand Characteristics and their Implications." *American Psychologist,* 1962, *17,* 776–783.

Pelz, D. C. & Andrews, F. M. "Detecting Causal Priorities in Panel Study Data." *American Sociological Review,* 1964, *29,* 836–848.

Rosenthal, R. & Rosnow, R. L. "The Volunteer Subject." In R. Rosenthal and R. L. Rosnow (Eds.) *Artifact in Behavior Research.* New York: Academic Press, 1969.

Schachter, S. & Singer, J. E. "Cognitive, Social and Physiological Determinants of Emotional State." *Psychological Review,* 1962, *69,* 379–399.

Smith, C. G. & Tannenbaum, A. S. "Organizational Control Structure: A Comparative Analysis." *Human Relations,* 1963, *16,* 299–316.

Staw, B. M. "Notes Toward a Theory of Intrinsic and Extrinsic Motivation," paper presented at *Eastern Psychological Association,* 1974. (a)

Staw, B. M. "The Attitudinal and Behavioral Consequences of Changing a Major Organization Reward: A Natural Field Experiment." *Journal of Personality and Social Psychology,* 1974, *29,* 742–751. (b)

Staw, B. M. *The Psychology of Intrinsic and Extrinsic Motivation.* Morristown, New Jersey: General Learning Press, 1975.

Strickland, L. H. "Surveillance and Trust." *Journal of Personality,* 1958, *26,* 200–215.

Tannenbaum, A. S. "Control in Organizations: Individual and Organizational Performance." *Administrative Science Quarterly,* 1962, *7,* 236–257.

Tannenbaum, A. S. *Control in Organizations.* New York: McGraw-Hill, 1968.

Vroom, F. H. "A Comparison of Static and Dynamic Correlational Methods in the Study of Organizations." *Organizational Behavior and Human Performance,* 1966, *1,* 55–70.

Weber, S. J. and Cook, T. D. "Subject Effects in Laboratory Research: An Examination of Subject Roles, Demand Characteristics, and Valid Inference." *Psychological Bulletin.* 1972, *77,* 273–295.

Weiner, B., Frieze, I., Kukla, A., Reed, L., Rest, S., & Rosenbaum, R. M. In E. E. Jones, D. E. Kanouse, H. H. Kelley, R. E. Nisbett, S. Valins and B. Weiner (Eds.), *Attribution: Perceiving the Causes of Behavior.* Morristown, New Jersey: General Learning Press, 1971.

Received: December 11, 1973

Using Simulation for Leadership and Management Research: Through the Looking Glass[1]

Morgan W. McCall, Jr.
Michael M. Lombardo

INTRODUCTION

And the young biologists tearing off pieces of their subject, tatters of the life forms, like sharks tearing out hunks of a dead horse, looking at them, tossing them away. This is neither a good nor a bad method; it is simply the one of our time. [30, p. 61].

This passage from *The Log from the Sea of Cortez* reflects the contrast between modern research methods and the almost leisurely pace of Darwin's cruises aboard the Beagle. Armed with questionnaires and high speed computers, organizational researchers run the risk of generating tatters and hunks of phenomena. While months or years of observation is unlikely to return as a dominant method in organizational research, more has been lost than the sound of the wind in the rigging. Precision methods allow zeroing-in on specific pieces, presuming that the researcher knows what to look for. These methods are particularly keen when we need to focus in, but something is missing when we try to focus out. Then making sense of the pieces is a bit like rebuilding Humpty Dumpty. This paper will suggest that simulation, designed to mirror the environment

and allowing free behavior within it, represents a viable compromise between unhurried, naturalistic observation and more tightly controlled research methods.

All simulations have inherent limitations. There are always artifacts, there are always pieces of reality left out. Simulation pros and cons have been explored at length (see, for example, [7], [27], [34], and [37]) and continuing that debate is not the purpose here. Rather than rehash what has already been said, this paper provides a concrete example of how a person-centered simulation, designed inductively from organizational events, can be used as a research tool in the study of leadership and managerial behavior in complex organizations.

THE ORIGINS OF LOOKING GLASS, INC.

There is more than adequate confusion about the definition of leadership and how, if at all, it differs from management. Some (e.g., [11]) have argued that leadership transcends the formal role; that is, it is something more than the exercise of the authority

---

[1] Reproduced by permission of *Management Science*, 1982, 28, 533–549.

vested in a management position. Others (e.g., [20]) have argued that leadership is but one of many roles that managers must play. To add to the ambiguity, much of the research based on conceptual views of leadership as a social influence process distinct from headship has frequently limited its operational expression to formal leadership role incumbents (e.g., foremen and their direct reports). Other research, truer to the social influence definition, has used ad hoc groups of students doing simple tasks, obviously raising questions as to what analogs, if any, there may be to organizational settings.

Our position on definitional issues is that they may be a red herring. As currently debated, there probably can be no satisfactory resolution: There is truth in all positions. The real question, then, is what we want to learn about, and for us that means understanding how and why people in leadership roles in formal organizations are more or less effective. The answer probably involves both the exercise of interpersonal influence beyond formal responsibility and the ways in which formal responsibilities are carried out. Data, rather than debate, should clarify the issue. We chose, then, to simulate the complex environment surrounding formal leaders in hopes that observing their behavior might clarify our concepts. In short, this paper will use the terms leadership and management synonymously while hoping that the simulation itself will generate the conceptual questions we ought to be asking.

The reasons for developing Looking Glass, a simulation of managerial work in a complex organization, are best summarized by Karl Weick [36, p. 60]:

> What worries me is that some of the least important realities about leaders are being accorded some of the largest amounts of attention. I think we need to spend more time watching leaders "on line," whether that line is simulated or real. We have to put ourselves in a better position to watch leaders make do, let it pass, improvise, make inferences,

scramble, and all the other things that leaders do during their *days between* more visible moments of glory.

We felt that the accumulated research on leadership was too atomistic and left out too much of the whole. Some characteristics of leadership research and the corresponding hopes for the simulation are summarized below:

Traditional Leadership Research	Hopes for LGI Research
Leader-Subordinate Focus	Leader-Organization Focus
Work Group Outcomes	Individual, Business Unit, and Organization
2–5 Styles of Behavior	Broad Range of Behavior
Immediate Situation	Organizational & Environmental Context
Ambiguous Results	Better Questions
Survey Methods	Multiple Methods
Ignore Work Activity Patterns	Preserve Work Activity Patterns

To use Looking Glass as an example of how simulation can contribute to research on leadership, we will begin by describing briefly the simulation itself. Subsequent sections of this paper will give examples of research issues (a) built into the simulation, (b) that occur naturally, and (c) that can be generated by controlled intervention. The final sections will deal with measurement strategies appropriate to simulation and with validity questions.

LOOKING GLASS: AN OVERVIEW

Looking Glass was developed from September 1, 1976, to August 31, 1979, under support from the Office of Naval Research and the Center for Creative Leadership [17]. Based on extensive field interviews with executives, site visits, and technical and business publications, Looking Glass is a 6-hour simulation of a moderate-sized ($200 million in sales) manufacturing corporation.' In each standardized run 20 participants are assigned to 20 top management roles ranging from President to Plant Manager and spanning three divisions (see Figure 1). Their task: to run the company for a day in any way they want.

The simulation begins the evening before the run with a series of events designed to familiarize participants with the company. During this session, participants and staff are introduced, a slide show explaining the company is shown, participants are assigned roles and spend some time in their offices, and job descriptions and annual reports are distributed.

The following morning Looking Glass opens for business. Each participant spends the first 45 minutes at his or her desk reviewing an in-basket containing today's mail. The in-baskets contain an average of 32 incoming items ranging from the trivial (e.g., a wine sales advertisement) to the significant (e.g., cost figures on plant expansion).

After the first 45 minutes, the telephone system is turned on, and the managers are free to call meetings, send memos, place phone calls, etc. Using memo or phone, participants can contact anyone inside or outside the company.

The development of Looking Glass insured that a wide range of management problems and issues exist in the company. These total about 160, and participants are free to deal with them (or ignore them) as they see fit. These problems and issues cover many areas, including finance, personnel, law, production, sales, R & D, government regulations, etc. Examples of the issues include:

- an opportunity to acquire a new plant,
- deciding what to do with a plant that has lost money the last few years,
- pollution and discrimination problems,
- supply shortages,

- production capacity limits,
- a lawsuit with a major customer,
- competition with foreign manufacturers,
- technological innovation and obsolescence.

Each of the three divisions in Looking Glass faces a different external environment. The Advanced Products Division (APD) manufactures products for the electronics and communications industries and exists in an unstable, highly volatile business environment. The Commerical Glass Division (CGD) makes light bulb casings and flat glass, and faces a reasonably stable, predictable environment characterized by high-volume, low-margin products, and well established customer relations. The Industrial Glass Division (IGD) faces an environment containing both unstable and stable components because it makes products varying from auto glass (relatively stable) to space craft windows (highly unstable).

While some simulations of this general type exist, most have been used primarily for training. The potential of such simulations for research has barely been tapped. The results of studies using simulation to look at information processing [26], international relations [8], police communications and stress [4], and military decision making [23] indicate that it can indeed be a powerful tool.

Whereas the simulations cited above focus on crisis situations (e.g., the outbreak of World War I), Looking Glass is aimed at typical, day-to-day behavior. It therefore addresses a variety of issues, and multiple measurement strategies can be used with it.

There are several features of this simulation that increase its potential for research. First is its inductive base. The events participants face were adapted from actual events experienced by executives who reviewed with us the activities recorded in their calendars on what they considered a typical day.

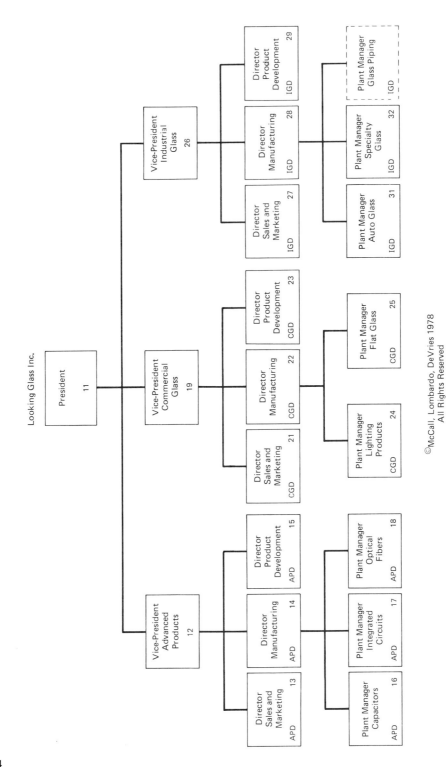

Looking Glass Inc.

©McCall, Lombardo, DeVries 1978
All Rights Reserved

Figure 1. LGI Organizational Chart

The organization faces environmental and structural challenges described by managers involved in that business. In short, the reality of managerial life rather than theoretical representations of that reality is mirrored in Looking Glass.

Second, the people who run Looking Glass (in its research uses) are practicing managers (sometimes intact teams). They are assigned to managerial roles according to their relative hierarchical standing in their real organization, thus preserving authority and status differences as a real part of the simulation.

Third, even though only 20 of Looking Glass's managers are present in the simulation, any other insider or outsider can be contacted by phone or memo. Additional information is available to managers via standard response procedures handled by the staff. Managers whose Looking Glass subordinates are not present can contact them if they choose to do so.

Fourth, Looking Glass is a powerful training tool and is used by several organizations for that purpose in conjunction with the research program.[2] This makes feasible the use of large numbers of managers as participants, and also provides them with incentive for taking the simulation seriously. In addition, it ensures an ever-growing data base containing norm data on a variety of process and outcome measures.

All of these features enhance the possibility that the behavior exhibited in Looking Glass is related to real managerial job behavior. Exploring this relationship empirically should shed light not only on leadership but also on the limits of simulation tools.

The next sections examine: (a) a series of research questions that were designed-in, (b) phenomena that occur naturally because the complexity of real organizations was preserved, (c) possible research interventions, and (d) measurement techniques.

BUILT-IN RESEARCH ISSUES

While many leadership models involve situational contingencies, "situation" is usually defined by a handful of variables embedded in or immediately adjacent to the leader's work group (e.g., leader position power, group task structure, etc.). Some work, however, has shown that the nature of an organization's external environment (e.g., its stability or complexity) affects a variety of structural factors and internal processes (see [29] for a review of such studies). It has been suggested [14] that the nature of the environment determines which leadership style will be most effective. Unfortunately, little evidence is available on this issue, and even less is known about which or

---

[2] Leadership / management training lies basically outside the scope of this paper, but a few comments about LGI's use as a training vehicle are relevant. Three corporations have added training modules to Looking Glass; these range from 1 to 2½ days in length. Although each organizational training effort is adapted to a particular organization's needs, the programs share some common elements: (a) focus on the nature of the managerial job—roles and competencies, (b) emphasis on individual self-development, and (c) preservation of the confidentiality of behavior and data generated by participants.

Since Looking Glass is somewhat of a managerial mirror, dozens of training designs are possible. Some of the most apparent ones include using the simulation as a tool for diagnosing intact groups, a team-building tool for newly formed groups, a realistic job preview for prospective managers, a "safe" way to pilot organizational interventions, and as a stimulus for designing work units to more effectively meet the demands of varying environments.

Another educational use of Looking Glass is through university graduate programs. Although any use is speculative at this time, three university MBA programs are interested in integrating the simulation into financial planning, policy, and organizational behavior curricula.

how environmental factors might directly influence a leader's behavior. It is not even clear that the objective characteristics of the environment are as important as leader *perceptions* of the outside world.

Few researchers use the same operational definitions to describe organizational environments (see, for example, [5], [12], [25], [32], amd [33]). Given this ambiguity, the environmental variation of Looking Glass was designed on the basis of field interviews, expert descriptions of the glass industry, and business publications. The environments reflect reality, and even if they do not reflect precisely a particular theoretical framework, they are conceptually similar to Duncan's Model [5].

To examine relationships between environmental uncertainty and leader behavior, each of Looking Glass's three divisions was designed to face a different environment. Conceptually, the environment of the Advanced Products Division is the most uncertain, while that of Commercial Glass is most certain. Industrial Glass falls between the two:

Uncertain/Complex   Certain/Complex

Much of the literature classifies environments along a simple-complex dimension by distinguishing the number of elements the organization must face. The Looking Glass research indicated that simple environments may be an anachronism. Modern organizations consist of complexity facing complexity. Where organizations apparently differ is in the hostile or benign nature of their environments and the degree to which they can be predicted. The major elements used to create this variation in Looking Glass include the nature and diversity of customers and competitors, the sophistication and likelihood of change in technologies, the predictability of future markets, financial stability, etc. A few of these elements are summarized in Figure 2.

Each division is structured in the same way and contains the primary functions necessary (sales / marketing, manufacturing, product development) to independent operation. Since positions, hierarchical levels, and responsibilities are constant across divisions, a classic case of misfit between structure and environment is created. Numerous researchers (unfortunately using different operational definitions of structure and environment) have found that the structure of effective organizations "fits" the environment in which they function (e.g., [12]). Bureaucratic structures, for example, should be more effective in stable environments. Looking Glass permits researchers to look closely at the processes involved as the three divisions confront the problems generated by their environments. Unless structural changes are made by participants, the best fitting division should consistently perform better than the others.

The internal structure of Looking Glass can be changed from divisional to functional. This manipulation represents a tremendous advantage of simulation. Crucial experiments around the fit hypothesis can be conducted precisely because the environmental elements are controlled while structural elements are manipulated. (In real organizations such control and manipulation is impossible.) Further, the actual behavioral effects of different structures and fits can be observed. This is true both within and across runs.

There is research indicating that level of management has direct effects on leader behavior [22]. Looking Glass has a fixed hierarchy containing four top management levels. Each run of the simulation generates data on one President, three Vice-Presidents, nine Directors, and seven Plant Managers. The lowest simulated position, Plant Manager, is an executive slot carrying with it responsibility for a multimillion dollar manufacturing plant. The formal authority of each position is loosely described in the job description and represents a deliberate effort to keep actual authority somewhat fuzzy. Each

	Advanced Products	Industrial Glass	Commercial Glass
Customers	high percentage military, many independents and smaller customers	customers respond to consumer taste, military contracts	a few large customers of long standing
Technology	fast-changing, highly sophisticated	part stable, part exotic	relatively stable, straightforward
Markets	feast and famine, largely unpredictable	both stable and volatile	primarily slow, steady growth—quite predictable
Competition	many competitors, often vicious and fast-changing	mixed	few competitors, relationships well extablished

Figure 2.   Some Environmental Differences among Looking Glass Divisions.

manager has responsibility for all legal, financial, and personnel decisions in his or her part of the organization (e.g., the Director of Product Development is responsible for all those activities in Product Development). The bias, therefore, is toward a decentralized management structure with three profit centers. Delegation of authority in the simulation flows naturally from practices in the participants' back-home organizations. Where customary practice is for many decisions to be made at the top, that practice is reflected in Looking Glass.

Preliminary observations indicate that authority and division environments interact; it is possible to watch changes in management style over a simulation run. For example, APD's turbulent environment can produce more decentralized management and more ad hoc decision making, even when the back-home organization is quite bureaucratic. This contrasts sharply wtih CGD (the table division) which tends either to become more centralized and less participatory or to move into a team-oriented style [13]. The behavioral effects of hierarchical level seem to depend both on the nature of the environment confronted and on the way that environment is perceived. Managers see APD as it is—volatile—and behave like a crew fighting 40 randomly leaping fires. In contrast, CGD managers diverge sharply in their perceptions of their environment. Some view it as stable and behave bureaucratically; others see it as a dying division and focus on new products and image in an

attempt to breathe some life into an organizational albatross.

The fuzziness of authority in Looking Glass permits the participants to define for themselves the limits of personal action. From a research point of view, this process can be observed as it plays out over the course of the simulation. Hypotheses about the relationships among hierarchy, environment, technology, and power distributions can be generated or the impact of formal authority manipulated by modifying job descriptions to create more or less authority at different levels of the hierarchy.

Because Looking Glass contains a variety of management functions and levels that are identical across divisions, the impact of position on leader behavior can be examined. The fact that environments and technologies differ across divisions permits tests of the main effect of position on power and influence development.

A nagging question in the social sciences is whether the person or the situation is the primary causal agent in behavior. For behavior in organizations, Looking Glass may eventually shed some light on that issue. Each run of the simulation involves 20 individuals, six substantively different positions, four hierarchical levels, and three environments. By systematically collecting data on individual characteristics (such as cognitive complexity or leadership style) and on various performance measures, it will be possible eventually to look at percentages of performance variance contributed by individuals and by aspects of their situations. In spite of the limitations on simulations and the complexity of these data, Looking Glass is a unique vehicle for exploring this critical issue. Results thus far are fragmentary, but suggest that environmental differences and position power account for hefty chunks of the variance.

In summary, simulation is an excellent research vehicle for many organizational issues because variables of interest can be built-in. Looking Glass contains adequate variety in terms of environmental differences, level, and function to permit observation of some major organizational phenomena. The researcher knows exactly how the system stands at the start: Each run of Looking Glass is a true replication.

NATURALLY OCCURRING PHENOMENA

In many respects, studying Looking Glass presents the same challenges as studying a real organization. Looking Glass is simpler, there are fewer members, and many more variables are controlled than is the case in real organizations. But it is still a purist's nightmare in that virtually every variable—just as in a real organization—is confounded. Worse yet, the artifacts of a simulation cannot be identified precisely, much less separated from the "real" effects. This is both a weakness and an advantage. The weakness is that *definitive* statements regarding the impact of any *one* variable can never be made on the basis of data generated by Looking Glass. This is why one should emphasize its role as a stimulus for asking questions, generating hypotheses, and collecting data that can be verified using other methods. The advantage, however, is that moderate control permits the observation of leadership as it plays out in a complex and realistic context. Most of the processes of interest to organizational researchers can be observed as they unfold over 6 hours. Sev-

eral such processes are briefly discussed below:

Coupling

Weick [35] and others have discussed the notion that open systems theory needs refinement. They argue that the interrelatedness of open components (coupling) is not a given, but is itself a variable. Organizations can vary from tightly coupled to loosely coupled. Because of the environmental and structural control in Looking Glass, it is possible to observe and measure the process of coupling. A division, for example, may remain autonomous or become highly interdependent. The same is true of departments within divisions. By classifying the outcomes of each run, factors influencing tight vs. loose coupling and the impact of tight vs. loose coupling on performance can be explored.

Information Processing and Decision Making

How does a manager, embedded in a complex environment and struggling with a job that is fast paced and fragmented, figure out what the relevant cause and effect relationships are? Research on cognitive complexity and human information processing [26] suggests that individuals vary considerably in their ability to discriminate among and integrate pieces of information. This, no doubt, is one element contributing to a manager's operational map of cause and effect relationships. Because the information inputs to the simulation are controlled, it is possible to capture the cognitive maps individuals develop, how they vary, and the impact of the variation.

Whether or not implicit cognitive maps can be made explicit, Looking Glass is a fertile vehicle for exploring decision making under uncertainty. Inputs to the participants cover an array of issues (from nuisances to tactical and strategic problems) and vary in their difficulty, magnitude, and interdependence. While a great deal of research has productively tackled individual decision making on relatively discrete problems (e.g., [28]), Looking Glass confronts managers with a variety of problem types in the context of the other activities comprising managerial work. This permits research on how decisions get made in the never discrete world of the manager: (a) how problems get recognized or ignored, (b) the process of problem definition, (c) the search for and integration of information, (d) how solutions are generated and examined, (e) what action is taken or not taken, and (f) in some cases, the impact of the decision. As important, it is also possible to watch solutions search for problems [3], to examine the juggling of multiple problems and priorities, and to observe the effects of people, politics, interruptions, and other factors on the process of decision making.

Power and Influence

Looking Glass, like most organizations, quickly develops power and influence patterns. Many issues involving these concepts remain unresolved [16], and the simulation provides a relatively unique setting to examine some of them. Participants can, with some consensus, identify who had the most influence in Looking Glass. Preliminary data indicate that perceptions of power are influenced by level in the hierarchy, access to information, and types of problems confronted [17], [19]. Hopefully, Looking Glass will eventually shed some new light on how power gets where it ends up, the effects it has, and which of the many views of the concept most parsimoniously explains the process.

Organizational Climate

A major theme in organizational research in recent years has been the issue of climate (e.g., see [24])—that elusive "something" that reflects a tone, a meaning, unique to an organization. Surveys indicate that climate is a correlate of a number of outcome variables, but little is known about how a climate forms. In runs of Looking Glass, data were collected on a subset of items from the Survey of Organizations [31]. These data indicate that the simulated organization does form a climate by the end of a run, that participants can describe that climate on standard questionnaires, and that there is sufficient variation across runs and within divisions to permit meaningful analysis [19]. Looking Glass has potential for shedding light on how technological and environmental factors, various leadership actions, organizational performance, and interdependence affect climate formation.

Manager's Use of Structure

Managers constantly make structural changes in their organizations. These can be as simple as altering a reporting relationship or as complex as a major departmental reorganization. In spite of the prevalence of structural changes, they have seldom received attention in the leadership research.

Looking Glass presents managers with numerous opportunities to alter the structure of the organization. These include issues like the role of product development, potential plant mergers, and redesigning structure through acquisition or divestiture. By watching how managers react to such problems and initiate their own structural interventions, it may be possible to understand the place of organizational design in leadership behavior.

The list of phenomena that occur during a simulation run could go on. The point is that a rich and complex simulation will produce a vast array of behaviors of interest to organizational researchers. The moderate control of simulation, coupled with its reality base, make interpretation of the behavior more straightforward than it typically is in the field.

INTERVENTIONS

The strength of the laboratory experiment is the control made possible by systematically varying the variable of interest while holding other things constant It is then possible to draw cause and effect conclusions. While not as rigorous as the traditional laboratory experiment, a simulation like Looking Glass can offer many of the same benefits without sacrificing face validity or contextual richness. As examples of experimental uses of simulation, consider sample manipulations, introduction of crises, and presetting managerial strategy.

By varying samples across runs, an almost limitless number of comparisons can be made. For instance, what do inexperienced managers do that experienced managers don't? To explore that question, the researcher might run Looking Glass several times, alternating groups of experienced and inexperienced managers.

What differentiates intact work teams from stranger groups? Which are more efficient, creative, effective? Why? What happens when a new management team is formed? Intact work groups may "get down to business" faster and virtually ignore interpersonal issues. Stranger groups may spend more time floundering in priorities, be more democratic (at least at first), and be more focused on interpersonal relationships.

Other sample manipulations could include high-potential vs. average managers (what do they *do* differently, other than succeed or not?), role reversals, varying proportions of males and females, etc. What effect does a manager's background have? Why not use samples or subsamples from different companies, divisions, functions, or levels?

Sample manipulations in the simulation can provide researchers with a close look at the behavioral differences between groups. The initial stimuli are identical, a condition almost impossible to replicate in the field. Looking Glass has already been adapted for use with British managers, permitting cross-cultural behavior comparisons.

No major crises (except those generated by the participants themselves) are designed into Looking Glass. But a researcher may be interested in the effects of a crisis on organizational processes—a condition hard to create experimentally in an ongoing organization. Looking Glass can be subjected to such an intervention and is long enough to establish a pre-intervention base rate. In one pretest run, a crisis was created by a phone call to the President from a newspaper reporter about a possible materials shortage in one plant (there was such a threat in one Plant Manager's in-basket, but it had been ignored). The organization immediately mobilized around that "problem," even though it was objectively a minor issue. Miscellaneous information was forced together by various managers to create a coherent picture, and many myths were founded on the spot. The intriguing organizational reaction to the intervention suggests that Looking Glass is a fertile resource for generating hypotheses about the formation and resolution of crises, as well as about the impact of crises on managerial behavior.

Another kind of intervention might be to leave a critical role open to observe how potential candidates jockey for position, how work gets absorbed by remaining managers, or how the rest of the organization helps out or exploits the situation. As an example of this latter issue, the research might focus on the problem of capital investment. Each division has needs, but there are limited resources. If a division Vice-President leaves the company, what happens to the divison he or she represents?

Another aspect of succession could be explored, not by actually creating a vacancy, but by introducing rumors of plans for reorganization, impending vacancies, or layoffs. Such manipulations would allow observers to see how behavior is affected by rumors and perhaps examine the forces that exaggerate or subdue rumor effects.

Another set of experimental interventions might involve presetting strategies for Looking Glass managers. It is risky to try out various managerial strategies in real organizations, particularly if those strategies are creative (and the consequences unknown) or if failure would be costly. Many strategic decisions can be modeled with computers to estimate their effects, but little is known about the behavioral impacts of strategic choice. Looking Glass might represent a vehicle for exploring those questions. One way to do this would be to "indoctrinate" the President and the Vice-Presidents prior to the simulation run. Across runs, economic strategies might be varied so that one group sought to maximize profit, another sales, another growth. Each simulation would generate data on the effects of the chosen strategy on the behavior of the other managers, political processes, decision making, problem finding, politicking, etc. Other data might be collected on how organization climate is affected by strategic choice, which departments or divisions gain the most influence, or how operations at lower levels change.

One intriguing use of Looking Glass would be to refine ambiguous concepts, such as politics. To do this, the researcher might give the participants the goal of behaving as politically as possible—of managing in such a way as to produce the highest degree of political behavior in the organization. One hypothesis might be that political activity is more detectable and more destructive in a stable division (CGD) than it is in a division facing a turbulent environment (APD). If the environment is unpredictable, decision making is probably a political process because predictions are a "best guess." As ambiguity increases, thereby obscuring cause and effect relationships surrounding managerial action, it should become harder to detect political motivations.

Other manipulations of managerial strategy include asking the participants to behave as ineffectively as possible, or requiring all managers to participate in all decisions (or subjecting all decisions to a vote).

Different managerial strategies can be set in the different divisions. A complex example would be to look at environment/organization fit in several different ways by contrasting structure with leadership style. As it now stands, Looking Glass's three divisions face different environments but are structured in the same way. One might begin by having all managers in APD use participatory styles while all in CGD are autocratic. These could then be reversed, testing the hypothesis that democratic style is more effective in turbulent environments, while autocratic styles are more effective in stable environments (with structures held constant). Then the experimenter might want to vary the structures in the division, putting a more organic design in APD and keeping CGD bureaucratic. These could then be reversed to test a structural as opposed to a leadership effect on performance.

In summary, complex simulations like Looking Glass can be used as a "research playground" by serving as a testing ground for ideas and hunches. Where a real organization might resist an intervention because of its possible consequences, Looking Glass does not care if a theory makes sense. Interventions that survive a simulated test are not proven, but subsequent field tests have a better chance as a result of possible refinements.

MEASUREMENT IN A SIMULATION

The how and what of measurement should be determined by the research question rather than by the research method. Free simulation of the type described here permits a larger choice of measurement strategies than is typically possible in either field or pure laboratory studies. Listed below are measurement strategies that have been or could be used successfully with Looking Glass:

Observation

Up to nine observers have been used in a given run of the simulation. Depending on the primary research questions involved, observers can be used to collect structured observations or time-sampled data, or can be used anthropologically.

If the behavior to be observed is specific and defined a priori, structured observation is clearly appropriate. Two to three observers (familiar with both the division materials and the dimensions they are to observe) may be assigned to specific roles or to sample all of the roles on a scheduled basis. One variation is to assign one observer to attend all meetings while other observers time-sample behavior.

Because the behavior of participants is not controlled, observers cannot predict what issues will be tackled, when (if at all) meetings will be held, etc. Inevitably, a lot of useful data will be lost. If the major research aim is to follow specific problems through the simulation, time sampling is risky. A better strategy is to assign observers to the role where the problem first appears, with the mandate to follow the problem wherever it goes.

Refining concepts is often a tough proposition in organizational research, and Looking Glass is a good forum for initiating the process. If moving from common sense or intuition to specific definitions is the research goal, anthropological methods can be used. Take, for example, the objective of refining the concept "politics." An observer might be told to write down every incident that might be construed as political (using no specific definition). After a simulation run, these notes are reviewed by the research team and some general parameters established. During the next run, the observer again looks for political behavior, but this time certain events have been eliminated, others targeted. The results are reviewed, further honing is done, and the process is repeated until an operational concept is produced.

Unobtrusive Measures

Participants leave traces of their activities that can be tapped by unobtrusive measures. These include memos they send, phone calls they make, and the information they request from nonlive roles or outsiders. Materials can be collected after each run, and later classified in a variety of ways.

A record of information requests is a valuable data source. Participants can place calls to outsiders or to insiders who are not "live." Staff members deal with these requests (there is a manual of standard responses) and note the topic. These notes indicate the problems receiving a lot of attention during the simulation.

Looking Glass also contains some built-in measures. For example, several participants are due performance appraisals, a number of awards are distributed, and some vacancies are filled. How these are handled yields information about evaluation processes within the company.

Self-Report

Standard self-report measures are appropriate for use after Looking Glass, although standard questionnaires may have to be adapted (e.g., not all participants in Looking Glass have "live" subordinates; in a run only seven participants could answer questions about subordinate behavior).

Simulation is particularly suited to stimulated recall techniques. Looking Glass is complex and participants are involved in many things over the course of 6 hours. The accuracy of their self-reports will be enhanced if a stimulus like a specific memo or a videotape clip is used in conjunction with a specific question.

Peer Ratings

Participants are able to describe or rate each other's behavior on a variety of dimensions (particularly on interpersonal dimensions).

These assessments can be accurate (e.g., [9]) and efficiently collected. By studying the problems in a division and examining the organization chart, it is possible to predict with some accuracy who will interact most with whom. Since the simulation does not force interaction, however, researchers should be careful not to require ratings by peers who have not observed the target person's behavior.

Individual or Group Interviews

In exchange for participation in Looking Glass, a training sequence for the managers was provided. Part of this, the divisional debrief, gathered all members of a division to discuss the decisions they made during the simulation. In this group setting it was possible to record participant perceptions and divisional priorities and reconstruct the decision process from recognition to disposition. Some groups focused entirely on operational problems, while others listed interpersonal or process issues. Some groups were tactical, others strategic. With sufficient structure, "group interview" techniques can generate a lot of data on how things were done.

Pretest Questionnaires and Archival Data

A variety of measures can be collected prior to the simulation, subject only to the patience of the participants. For example, if the research is to explore relationships between cognitive style and managerial behavior, one or several cognitive measures might be administered beforehand.

At a minimum, basic background data such as current position, level, and time with the company should be collected so that sample characteristics can be described. However, participants should not be deluged with an extensive battery of tests prior to the simulation because it may create apprehension, alter their behavior, or magnify the obtrusiveness of the research.

Other outside measures may be readily available and not require participant time. Performance appraisals, promotion histories, and the like may be useful. Other data might be gathered through peer or subordinate surveys (see [21] for a review of such surveys).

Mechanical Records

Many simulations lend themselves to video or audio-taping. A complex simulation like Looking Glass, however, makes *selective* taping imperative. The amount of behavior generated by 20 people over a 6-hour period is mind-boggling. On the other hand, prescheduled meetings (there are a few in Looking Glass), addresses, and phone calls are easily recorded. Too much equipment (for example, a portable video camera) can be obtrusive and is not recommended unless the site is specifically designed to keep it out of the way.

Assessment Center Methods

Looking Glass, or any other simulation not validated specifically for the purpose, should not be used to make selection or promotion decisions. For research purposes, however, assessment center measurement strategies can be useful. For example, each participant works through an in-basket. Written responses could be scored in a standardized way (there will be some psychometric problems since the content of each in-basket is different).

Another example is the use of observers to "case conference" individual or divisional performance. Especially since specific problems are hard to follow as they flow through a division, pooling observations is a useful device for evaluating decision processes.

For additional ideas, the reader is referred to overview articles on assessment center methods by MacKinnon [15] and Howard [10].

Norms and Expert Judgments

An enormous advantage of simulation is the constancy of problems. Since it always starts in the same place, Looking Glass can be seen as a replicated case study with extensive norm tables [19]. Further, outside experts can study specific problems facing the corporation and their judgments can form performance criteria independent of consensus norms.

In summary, almost all measurement methods suitable in either lab or field can be applied to a complex simulation like Looking Glass. This can be a real advantage when multiple method designs are needed to examine a particular research question. Perhaps more important, Looking Glass, or something like it, is a near perfect setting for developing and/or comparing measurement strategies. In that sense, simulation can be a psychometric playground—and it does not use up field settings.

ON VALIDITY AND PRACTICALITY

This paper was not intended to highlight the shortcomings of simulation. Laboratory studies and, by implication, simulations, suffer from a long list of obvious methodological maladies. There are, however, three major questions about simulation that should be addressed here:

- Is simulation valid?
- Is it too impractical to use?
- Do participants see it as a game?

Is It Valid?[3]

Whether a simulation is valid is an empirical question that depends upon the use to which the simulation is put. In Campbell and Stan-

ley [1] terms, methods that smack of the laboratory are often internally valid, but on tenuous grounds when it comes to external validity. In principle, however, a simulation is no harder to validate (and in many ways easier) than a paper and pencil test.

The first step in validating Looking Glass, for example, was taken during its development. The content of the simulation was developed from intensive field interviews with high-level managers about a typical day. Two hundred problems and activities were distilled from field interview notes, then independently clustered by the interviewers. After discussions, 12 categories of problems/activities emerged (e.g., resource allocation, ceremonial, structural) that are similar to Mintzberg's [20] managerial roles.

The interviews were integrated with observations from plant and site visits, extensive reading in business and technical publications from the glass industry, long discussions with consultants from glass companies, and field trials with executives from many industries. In addition, all runs of Looking Glass (after the first two) have been with managers who, during the training period following the simulation, have had ample opportunity to comment on its realism (or lack thereof). The results of these procedures contribute clearly to face validity, and a strong case for content validity can also be made.

A second content validation effort with Looking Glass was the implementation of random time sampling during simulation runs. Some evidence of validity exists if the activity patterns of managers during a simulation run are similar to the patterns found by diary and observational studies done with managers in the field settings [19].

Evidence of construct validity exists if phenomena generally found in field studies

---

[3] Research on the content and construct validity of Looking Glass is reported in McCall and Lombardo [18]. Based on time sampled observational data from 10 standardized runs, the results generally support the validity of the simulation.

of organizational behavior also appear in the simulated organization. Data were collected on information flow, decision making, climate, and power distributions. If the findings are similar to what already exists in the literature, construct validity [6] may be demonstrated.

Finally, it is possible to assess the concurrent predictive validity of Looking Glass by following the design of assessmennt center validation. A study currently being designed will bank performance data from the simulation and track career progress of participants over a period of years.

The data are in on the content validity of Looking Glass, and data pertinent to the other types of validity are under analysis as of this writing. Whether or not this simulation survives these tests, experience shows that complex simulation can be (and should be) subjected to empirical validation procedures similar to those appropriate for other research tools.

Is It Practical?

Complex simulations are demanding, time consuming, and expensive. Looking Glass took 3 years to develop and cost several hundred thousand dollars. Each research run of Looking Glass involves 20 managers, 3 trainers, 2 controllers, at least 2½ days (including debrief time), enough space to accommodate 20 separate work areas, and a 22-line telephone system. Compared to survey or lab study methods, it is less practical. But if the research goal is to learn something about managerial behavior in a complex and realistic organizational setting, it is eminently practical. The key to this practicality is its use as a management development tool that can be placed in numerous organizations and ensure continuous replications.

In a recent review of research on organizational effectiveness, John Campbell concluded that typical research approaches to that topic have not and are not likely to

achieve the appropriate level of understanding. His remarks are worth noting:

> What then can one do? There are really only two choices: (1) carefully done simulation studies, and (2) very intensive and very thorough case studies. Saying this is painful, especially since it completely violates the basic precepts of my own training gained in the midwestern empirical dust bowl. Nevertheless, using the organization as the unit of analysis forces us into such a situation. [2, p. 54]

So is simulation practical? For many important research questions, it had better be.

Is It a Game?

There is no doubt that for some participants a simulation—even a realistic one—is a game. On the other hand, for some people working in an organization is a game. People who have used simulations or participated in them know how involving they can be. Odds are managers will take a realistic simulation of their jobs more seriously than they would a questionnaire. But there is no hard answer to the question, only anecdotal data. During the 23 runs of Looking Glass only a handful of managers have stepped out of role, even during the lunch period. The overwhelming pattern is one of brief business lunches complete with sheaves of memos; less often, participants skip lunch or take it back to their desks. If one accepts the adage that behavior does not lie, it is difficult to imagine why managers from the same organization would discuss Looking Glass problems over lunch (or in the rest rooms) when that would be a natural opportunity to discuss their own problems.

Games are often characterized by play and outright silliness. This was seldom observed; rather most of the indications were that if Looking Glass is a game, managers see it as a serious one. We have noted, however, that participants who are not managers are more game-like in their approach. Perhaps the view that simulations are "just games" reflects more about the participants (usually students) than about simulation per se.

CONCLUSIONS

This paper has attempted to show that carefully designed simulations using managers as participants can be extremely flexible and important tools in the research repertoire because research issues (a) can be designed-in, (b) occur naturally, or (c) are possible via interventions. Further, complex simulations are amenable to multiple measurement techniques, and their validity can be examined empirically.

For research on leadership, these features are critical. Simulation represents one way to enrich our understanding by broadening the focus beyond leader-group relationships and by breaking out of the survey-methodology rut.

It seems only fitting to conclude this paper on a note of caution. Clearly, the purpose here was to encourage researchers to design simulations carefully and to use them more. The assumption was that simulation has received enough bad press and everyone already knows its inherent limitations. It bears repeating that simulation is only one tool for research and that it should be used in combination with other methods. Its main strength well may be its ability to generate new questions and preliminary data on them. No matter how carefully designed, a simulation can never be the reality. It can only reflect it.[4]

[4] In a project as extensive as the development of Looking Glass, literally hundreds of people have been involved. It is impossible to acknowledge all of them. David DeVries and Susan Rice played critical roles in the design of Looking Glass. Mitzi Ellis, Josie Clapp, Alice Warren, Norma Kay, Mildred Dohm, and Jane Swanson put considerable effort into getting this manuscript together.

An earlier version of this manuscript appeared in the first volume of the Looking Glass Operational Manuals [17].

Looking Glass is available for research and training purposes. We encourage individuals or organizations interested in pursuing collaborative research and training efforts to contact Dr. Michael Lombardo, Center for Creative Leadership, P.O. Box P-1, Greensboro, North Carolina 27402, for additional information.

REFERENCES

1. Campbell, D. and Stanley, J. *Experimental and Quasi-experimental Designs for Research,* Rand McNally, Chicago, Ill., 1963.

2. Campbell, J. "On the Nature of Organizational Effectiveness," in P. Goodman, J. Pennings, and Associates, *New Perspectives on Organizational Effectiveness,* Jossey-Bass, Washington, 1977, pp. 13–55.

3. Cohen, M. D. and March, J. G. *Leadership and Ambiguity: The American College President,* McGraw-Hill, New York, 1974.

4. Drabek, T. E. *Laboratory Simulation of a Police Communications System Under Stress,* Ohio State University, College of Administrative Science, Columbus, Ohio, 1969.

5. Duncan, R. "Characteristics of Organizational Environments and Perceived Environmental Uncertainty," *Administrative Science Quarterly,* Vol. 17, No. 3 (September 1972), pp. 313–327.

6. Dunnette, M. "Basic Attributes of Individuals in Relation to Behavior in Organizations," in M. Dunnette (ed.), *Handbook of Industrial and Organizational Psychology,* Rand McNally, Chicago, Ill., 1976, pp. 506–511.

7. Fromkin, H. L. and Streufert, S. "Laboratory Experimentation," in M. D. Dunnette (ed.), *Handbook of Industrial and Organizational Psychology*, Rand McNally, Chicago, Ill., 1976, pp. 415–465.

8. Guetzkow, H. A. "A Decade of Life with the Internation Simulation," in R. G. Stogdill (ed.), *The Process of Model-Building in the Behavioral Sciences*, Ohio State University Press, Columbus, Ohio, 1971, pp. 31–53.

9. Hollander, E. P. "The Reliability of Peer Nominations under Various Conditions of Administration," *J. Appl. Psychology*, Vol. 41, No. 2 (April 1957), pp. 85–90.

10. Howard, A., "An Assessment of Assessment Centers," *Acad. Management J.*, Vol. 17, No. 1 (March 1974), pp. 115–134.

11. Katz, D. and Kahn, R. L. *The Social Psychology of Organizations*, Wiley, New York, 1966.

12. Lawrence, P. R. and Lorsch, J. W. *Organization and Environment: Managing Differentiation and Integration*, Harvard Business School, Boston, Mass., 1967.

13. Lombardo, M. M. "Environmental Impacts on a Simulated Organization," paper presented in M. W. McCall, Jr. (chair), *Leadership in Context: Issues of Organization Design and Environment*, Joint National Meeting TIMS/ORSA, New Orleans, May 1979.

14. Lorsch, J. W. and Morse, J. J. *Organizations and Their Members: A Contingency Approach*, Harper & Row, New York, 1974.

15. MacKinnon, D. W. "An Overview of Assessment Centers," Tech. Rep. No. 1, Center for Creative Leadership, Greensboro, N.C., 1975.

16. McCall, M. W., Jr. "Power, Authority, and Influence," in S. Kerr (ed.), *Organizational Behavior*, Grid, Columbus, Ohio, 1979, pp. 185–206.

17. ——— and Lombardo, M. M. "Looking Glass, Inc.: An Organizational Simulation," Tech. Rep. No. 12, Center for Creative Leadership, Greensboro, N.C., 1978.

18. ——— and ———, "Looking Glass, Inc.: The First Three Years," Tech. Rep. No. 13, Center for Creative Leadership, Greensboro, N.C., 1979.

19. ———, ——— and Rice, S. "Looking Glass, Inc.: Norm Tables," Operational Manual No. 7, Center for Creative Leadership, Greensboro, N.C., 1979.

20. Mintzberg, H. *The Nature of Managerial Work*, Harper & Row, New York, 1973.

21. Morrison, A. M., McCall, M. W., Jr. and DeVries, D. L. "Feedback to Managers: A Comprehensive Review of Twenty-Four Instruments," Tech. Rep. No. 8, Center for Creative Leadership, Greensboro, N.C., 1978.

22. Nealy, S. M. and Fiedler, F. E. "Leadership Functions of Middle Managers," *Psychological Bull.*, Vol. 70, No. 5 (November 1968), pp. 313–329.

23. Olmstead, J. A., Cleary, F. K., Lackey, L. L. and Salter, J. A. "Development of Leadership Assessment Simulations," HumRRO Tech. Rep. 13–21, Human Resources Research Organization, Alexandria, Va., September 1973. (NTIS No. AD-772 990).

24. Payne, R. and Pugh, D. S. "Organizational Structure and Climate," in M. D. Dunnette (ed.), *Handbook of Industrial and Organizational Psychology*, Rand McNally, Chicago, Ill., 1976, pp. 1125–1173.

25. Pugh, D. S., Hickson, D. J., Hinings, C. R. and Turner, C. "The Context of Organizational Structures," *Admin. Sci. Quart.*, Vol. 14, No. 1 (March 1969), pp. 91–114.

26. Schroder, H. M., Driver, M. J. and Streufert, S. *Human Information Processing: Individual and Group Functioning in Complex Social Situations*, Holt, Rinehart & Winston, New York, 1967.

27. Schultz, R. L. and Sullivan, E. M. "Developments in Simulation in Social and Administrative Science," in H. Guetzkow, P. Kotler, and R. L. Schultz (eds.),

Simulation in Social and Administrative Science: Overviews and Case-Examples, Prentice-Hall, Englewood Cliffs, N.J., 1972, pp. 3–47.

28. Slovic, P. "Psychological Study of Human Judgments: Implications for Investment Decision Making," *J. Finance*, Vol. 27, No. 4 (September 1972), pp. 779–799.

29. Steers, R. M. *Organizational Effectiveness: A Behavioral View*, Goodyear, Santa Monica, Calif., 1977.

30. Steinbeck, J. *Log from the Sea of Cortez*, Viking, New York, 1962.

31. Taylor, J. C. and Bowers, D. G. *Survey of Organizations: A Machine-Scored Standardized Questionnaire Instrument*, University of Michigan, Institute for Social Research, Ann Arbor, 1972.

32. Terreberry, S. "The Evolution of Organization Environments," *Admin. Sci. Quart.*, Vol. 12, No. 4 (March 1968), pp. 590–613.

33. Thompson, J. D. *Organizations in Action*, McGraw-Hill, New York, 1967.

34. Weick, K. E. "Laboratory Experimentation with Organizations," in J. G. March (ed.), *Handbook of Organizations*, Rand McNally, Chicago, Ill., 1965, pp. 194–260.

35. ———, "Educational Organizations as Loosely Coupled Systems," *Admin. Sci. Quart.*, Vol. 21, No. 1 (March 1976), pp. 1–19.

36. ———, "The Spines of Leaders," in M. W. McCall, Jr. and M. M. Lombardo (eds.), *Leadership: Where Else Can We Go?* Duke University Press, Durham, N.C., 1978, pp. 37–61.

37. Zelditch, M., Jr. and Hopkins, T. K. "Laboratory Experiments with Organizations," in A. Etzioni (ed.), *Complex Organizations: A Sociological Reader*, Holt, Rinehart & Winston, New York, 1961, pp. 464–478.

Quantitative Field Research

In contrast to the laboratory-based and simulated organizational research discussed in Chapter 4, this chapter focuses on field research carried out in actual organizations. Laboratory and field research are both useful in their own right, but both are constrained to some degree by the settings in which they take place. Laboratory research permits a greater degree of control over contextual factors which allows the determination of causation, but it is limited to some extent in terms of the generalizability to real work settings because of the artificial nature of the laboratory. Field research typically permits a lesser degree of contextual control, but generalizability is not as limited.

Field experiments can provide high degrees of both internal and external validity and thus provide an opportunity to carefully examine organizational behavior phenomena in context. Some of the issues involved in the planning and conduct of field experiments are discussed by Stanley Seashore in the first article in this chapter. Seashore discusses the characteristics of field experiments and provides illustrations of his points through an examination of three well-executed field experiments: one examining the effects of level of decision on work perform-

ance, one investigating the impact of survey feedback on employee attitudes and morale, and the third concerning the effects of change implementation (e.g., supervisory training, structural changes in organziation) on work behavior and attitudes of employees. Seashore also mentions some of the difficulties one can encounter with field experiments.

Many organizational research opportunities do not provide the experimenter with the latitude to manipulate an independent variable or to ensure that employees are randomly assigned to treatment and control groups (such as in a training program). Yet, there may still be an interest in determining what influence was exerted, if any, by some organizational intervention. This concern has become even more critical in organizations today, in both the public and private sectors, that are being forced to cost-justify their programs and systematically demonstrate the effectiveness of a program to ensure its continued support. It is concerning these types of instances, where rigorous experimental control cannot be exercised, that Evans discusses the usefulness of "patchup" designs in the second article in this chapter. Issues concerning threats to internal and external validity are examined as are data interpretation concerns. Such patch-up or quasi-experimental research designs are quite useful and appropriate for the evaluation of new programs and other organizational interventions.

While the first two articles in this chapter are conceptual pieces, presenting discussions of different types of field research design, the remaining six articles provide empirical examples of either field experiments, quasi-experimental designs, or nonexperimental field studies. In the process, several imporant statistical and data-analytic tools are mentioned and effectively illustrated.

The first empirical piece, by Woodman and Sherwood, is a field experiment which examines the effects of a team development intervention on performance and attitudes. The study contains some interesting features that are instructive for the student of research methods. It examines multiple dependent variables (both affective and behavioral) and thus provides an opportunity to examine the effects of the intervention on several outcomes simultaneously, using multivariate analysis of variance. The study incorporates the advantages of both laboratory and field research by retaining the control of the laboratory and the realism (and external validity) of the setting. Because it represents a true experiment, the authors discuss some potential problems, for example demand characteristics, that may serve to influence the results.

Smith's article investigates the relationship between work attitudes and attendance at work of managerial personnel following a major snowstorm. Smith capitalizes on an opportunity to conduct a naturally occurring quasi-experiment. The study demonstrates an unusually strong attitude-behavior relationship and is elegant in its simplicity relative to design and data analysis.

The article by Blackburn and Cummings effectively illustrates the application of a data-analytic technique, multidimensional scaling (MDS), that tends to be widely used in other disciplines (such as marketing) but which has received limited use in the organizational sciences. MDS is used to identify dimensions of work unit structure from a cognitive perspective. Thus, the situation's meaning is defined by participants in the situation rather than being imposed by the researcher, thereby minimizing research bias.

A limitation of most nonexperimental field research is the determination of cause and effect, since data collection takes place cross-sectionally at a single point in time permitting, at best, statements of covariation between or among variables. The use of longitudinal field research, where data are collected at more than one point in time, helps to establish causal priorities, even though statements concerning true causation must still be tempered. The articles by Kimberly and by Organ address such concerns. Kimberly uses two studies as examples to illustrate problems and concerns involved in longitudinal research. He focuses on the temporal dimension of data aggregation and discusses issues involved in the frequency of data collection over time, the potential problems of aggregating data from different time periods which might differ qualitatively, as well as the problem of individuals changing at different rates. Kimberly argues in favor of more longitudinal research since it has implications for better theory construction and the development of a more informed understanding of organizational phenomena.

The Organ article examines trends in job satisfaction in the labor force over a nearly 30 year period. Five potential causal models of job satisfaction are proposed and subjected to analysis using data collected over time. The Simon-Blalock evaluation technique was used for data analysis and testing of the alternative models. The results eliminated three of the models from consideration, as they were not supported by the data. Some advantages of the Organ study are that it proposes several viable models and relies on archival data and nonreactive measures in studying job satisfaction.

The final article in this chapter, written by Schuster, is interesting because it combines several of the features of organizational field research already discussed and incorporates a relatively new type of data analysis technique. The study investigates the effects of union-management cooperative programs on productivity and employment, focusing on programs implemented at nine different plants over a period of four to five years. The study utilizes a stratified, multiple group, interrupted-time-series design and involves measurement of outcome variables before and after the intervention is introduced. In order to effectively analyze the change in the pattern of data in the time series, the autoregressive, integrative moving averages (ARIMA) technique was used, which is just beginning to be applied to organizational data. The study also incorporates qualitative data obtained from interviews and archival data.

SUGGESTIONS FOR FURTHER READING

Bunker, K. A., & Cohen, S. L. "The Rigors of Training Evaluation: A Discussion and Field Demonstration." *Personnel Psychology*, 1977, *30*, 525–541.

Coch, L., & French, J. R. P. "Overcoming Resistance to Change." *Human Relations*, 1948, *1*, 512–532.

Griffin, R. W., "Technological and Social Processes in Task Redesign: A Field Experiment." *Administrative Science Quarterly*, 1983, *28*, 184–200.

Lawler, E. E. "Adaptive Experiments: An Approach to Organizational Behavior Research." *Academy of Management Review*, 1977, *2*, 576–585.

Lawler, E. E., III., & Hackman, J. R. "Impact of Employee Participation in the Development of Pay Incentive Plans: A Field Experiment." *Journal of Applied Psychology*, 1969, *53*, 467–471.

Miller, D., & Friesen, P. H. "The Longitudinal Analysis of Organizations: A Methodological Perspective." *Management Science*, 1982, *28*, 1013–1034.

Morse, N. C., & Reimer, E. "The Experimental Change of a Major Organizational Variable." *Journal of Abnormal and Social Psychology*, 1956, *52*, 120–129.

Oldham, G. R., & Brass, D. J. "Employee Reactions to an Open-Plan Office: A Naturally Occuring Quasi-Experiment." *Administrative Science Quarterly*, 1979, *24*, 267–284.

Stagner, R., & Eflal, B. "Internal Union Dynamics During a Strike: A Quasi-Experimental Study." *Journal of Applied Psychology*, 1982, *67*, 37–44.

Staw, B. M. "Attitudinal and Behavioral Consequences of Changing a Major Organizational Reward: A Natural Field Experiment." *Journal of Personality and Social Psychology*, 1974, *29*, 742–751.

Field Experiments with Formal Organizations[1]

Stanley E. Seashore

A recent task of describing a field experiment concerning organizational structure and process (11) has led us to make a review of some other studies of a similar kind, and to formulate some general thoughts on the dilemmas and strategies in such research. This article is a first rough attempt at organizing these thoughts. It seems worth doing because: a) few people have had any direct experience in conducting field experiments with complex organizations, b) with increasing financial and methodological resources we are likely to see more work of this kind, and c) compared with experiments of other kinds, certain issues of strategy and method become of crucial importance and deserve examination.

Let us first state the reference of discourse. We will consider here experiments done in natural settings where the experiment is incidental to the main purposes of the oranizations. We will consider as a formal organization any relatively stable social system that is complex in the sense of including two or more component groups coordinated through two or more hierarchical levels of leadership. What constitutes an experiment is less easy to state. Obviously, there are alternative designs and a contin-

uum of conformance with ideal experimental design. Let us settle, for the moment, on minimum criteria of: a) definable and measurable change in organizational environment, structure, or process, b) some means for quantification of variables, and c) some provision for testing a causal hypotheses through the method of difference.

These definitions exempt from consideration *simulation experiments* (such as the work of Sidney and Beatrice Rome with a computer model of an organization), *case studies* (such as the Tavistock Institute's work at the Glacier metals factory), *correlational* studies (such as those of the Survey Research Center done in many organizations), and most *ex post facto comparison studies* (such as the work of Mann and Hoffman comparing two power plants with differing degrees of automation). These are all highly productive and valuable classes of research effort, but they are not experiments even by our suggested minimal standards. Also excluded from discussion are the many *group experiments* that have been conducted within organizations (such a the classic Hawthorne Test Room and Harwood Rate Change experiments). Exclusion is on the grounds that such field experiments concern

---

[1] Reproduced by permission of the Society for Applied Anthropology, *Human Organization*, 1964, 23, 164, 170.

Some of the work leading to this paper was supported by a grant from the Air Force Office of Scientific Research, Contract AF 49 (638)—1032.

small groups rather than larger, more complex social organizations, and that the location of the subject groups within complex organizations is, in such cases, only incidental to the purposes, design and conduct of the work.

The reader will recognize that these exclusions are arbitrary, and have no purpose other than to narrow attention to the special problems that arise or become accentuated when one attempts field studies of relatively large and complex organizational units with methods that approach those of classical experimental design.

WHY EXPERIMENTS?

The justification for conducting experiments must rest on grounds of effectiveness and efficiency in generating information and testing hypotheses. The advantages must be sufficient to offset the added costs, which may be great. Two considerations seem relevant.

It is difficult to establish unequivocally a causal relationship between variables without a controlled experiment spanning the period of change in both variables. Organizational theory is becoming sufficiently complex and sophisticated to bring to the fore issues of causality. Therefore, on certain theoretical issues, no other research approach is effective.

The second consideration is one of efficiency and economy. A single well-designed experiment can, in principle, produce information of such unequivocal nature that it outweighs any number of case studies or demonstrations.[2]

Other reasons one might invoke to justify attempts to use the experimental method are of a different order. For example, an experiment in a natural setting with real organizations is likely to produce results that seem acceptable and persuasive to action-oriented people and therefore to encourage application of the results.

Literature on the Methodology of Field Experiments

The otherwise rich literature on methodology of research on human social behavior is barren when it comes to experiments with formal organizations. The two primary works in the field from the early Fifties (4, 6) contain sections on experimental design and on field procedures, but no special reference to experiments with formal organizations, and only one example is mentioned—possibly the only one that existed at the time. A later book by Argyle (2) includes an excellent critical review of methodological designs and principles, arguing strongly for the use of experimental methods, but has no reference to the special case of experiments with formal organizations. Etzioni's recent collection of articles (3) similarly is void of examples or discussion in this area.

A scanning of five recent major works on research design in the behavioral sciences uncovered not a single example of experimental work with formal human organizations, and no reference to the problems of conducting such research in field settings.

The picture looks very different when one turns from sources that focus on experimental design to those that focus on field re-

---

[2] An example of the failure of nonexperimental method comes to mind. Marriott's review (9) of the research on the efficacy of incentive payment plans in raising individual and organizational work performance led to the conclusion that, in spite of many hundreds of successful introductions of incentive pay plans, one cannot know whether the reported effects are produced by the pay plans or by other concomitant factors. There have been a total of three experiments on the matter, but all were done about thirty years ago and all involved N's of less than ten individuals. The amount of useful information from this vast amount of work is remarkably small.

search methods generally. Here one finds a rich fund of example and analytic discussion of procedures for obtaining information about complex social organizations, for inducing change in organizations, and for drawing tentative conclusions from field data. There are numerous reports of anthropological methods in the study of formal organizations, descriptions of participant-observer techniques and of survey techniques, and the like (1). All these have great merit and are highly relevant to the conduct of field experiments, but do not deal systematically with the special problems of experimental design in conjunction with these methods.

Dimensions for Describing and Evaluating Experiments

A general and inclusive set of dimensions for describing and evaluating field experimental designs would be a very long and complicated one, and probably not very useful at the present time. However, some dimensions of evident importance can be suggested as a start:

CHOICE OF POPULATIONS Number and size of organizational units; pre-experimental homogeneity and differences as to membership, structure, function; provision for control populations and for contrasting or variable treatment of experimental units; provision for control of potential confounding variables through randomization, purposive selection, measurement, and statistical treatment of population variables not part of the theory.

APPROACH TO CHANGE Natural vs. purposeful change; if purposeful, is the point-of-change at the level of individual members, general organizational policy, internal structure and process, or in the organizations' environment?

VARIABLES FOR MANIPULATION OR MEASUREMENT Are the point-of-change variables part of the theory? How many independent variables are there and what are the provisions for testing their relationship? How many are

the dependent variables, and do they include both internal and output variables? What causal chains and interactions are implied if not specified by the design?

LEVEL OF THEORY Does the theory refer to institutional, organizational, social psychological, or psychological phenomena? What is the level of abstraction on a continuum from the highly specific and restricted to the highly general and universal?

DURATION IN TIME.

ANALYSIS PLAN Assessment of results through before-after comparisons, through difference between experimental and control units, through analysis of variance, etc. Is analysis at the individual, the group, or the organizational level?

EXAMPLES OF EXPERIMENTS WITH FORMAL ORGANIZATIONS

The total number of research ventures that might be reasonably considered to be field experiments with formal organizations is very small, perhaps from five to ten, depending upon how generous one chooses to be in tolerating deviations from ideal experimental conditions. None of these fulfills the canons of experimental design to the degree ordinarily expected in laboratory or field experiments on small groups. One must view them as rather primitive, pioneering ventures. Three of the better examples are summarized briefly here.

Experiment I concerns the relationship between level of decision-making in an organization and the effectiveness of work performance (10). The population included four parallel divisions (about 500 employees) of a large business firm, all performing similar clerical work under similar conditions. Data on work force composition, past performance, and the like were used to estimate and maximize pre-experimental homogeneity. Divisions were paired for contrasting experimental treatment. The experimental changes involved policy clarification and change, training of individual supervisors and employees, alteration of certain organizational structures and processes. These actions were intended to produce contrasting effects on the independent variable, and measurements were obtained to confirm the success of the change program. Dependent variables included both variables descriptive of internal organizational processes and state and also output variables such as cost of production and member satisfaction. The theory was at the level of social-psychology, in the sense of treating the psychological consequences of social structure and processes. The experimental period extended over a full year, with measurements before and after, and with active change program intervention conducted during the six months preceding the experimental period. Results: increasing the amount of involvement in decision-making of rank and file employees led to reduced cost of work performance, increased employee satisfaction, and increased sense of responsibility for work performance. Increasing the amount of involvement in decision-making by higher-level staff and supervisors also reduced cost of work performance, but otherwise led to reduced employee satisfaction, a lowering of individual responsibility for production, and other similar changes.

Experiment II concerns the feedback of employee attitude survey data as a means for inducing beneficial changes in the attitudes and morale of employees. The population included six departments (about 1,000 employees) of the accounting division of a large utility firm, with two departments serving as control units and four having differential amounts of change treatment. The method and amount of feedback activity was voluntary for each department and hence the experimental units were self-selected. The several departments were of varying size and membership composition, and performed somewhat different functions. The experimental change program was a combination

of natural and purposeful procedures; the units electing to undertake the feedback of survey data did so to the extent possible in ways that expressed their normal policies and work processes but the managers and supervisors received coaching and counseling in feedback procedures and encouragement toward extensive and intensive use of the process. Higher-level management support was obtained to legitimize the experiment. The point of change therefore was internal to the organizatioin, and included policy clarification and change, as well as individual training and alteration of organizational process.

The independent variable was the amount of feedback activity over a one-year span of time and the dependent variables represented numerous aspects of employee satisfaction and morale, treated as separate variables and also summed to obtain an overall index of attitudes favorable to the achievement of the organization's goals. The theory underlying the experiment was social-psychological in character and assumed that unspecified but adaptive changes in the attitudes and overt behavior of supervisors were the principal intervening variables. The elements of the theory were not differentiated or measured separately in the experimental plan. The experiment had a total duration of four years, including two pre-experimental measurements of dependent variables (to set base rates), an active feedback period of about one year followed by a year of time, and a final measurement after the fourth year. Analysis consisted of the comparison of experimental and control departments on the dependent variables at the end of the period, and also before-after change measurements for each department. Results: the amount of the improvements in employee attitudes and "morale" were roughly proportional to the amount of effort allocated to the feedback process.[3]

Experiment III concerns the induction

---

[3] This study was conducted by Floyd Mann. See (8) pages 101–108 for a summary description of this study.

of change in four variables central to Likert's management theory (7) and the consequences with respect to output criteria of work efficiency, waste, absence, and employee satisfaction. The population included five production departments (about 500 employees) of a packaging materials firm. One of the experimental departments was selected by the research team, two others volunteered for experimental change treatment, and the remaining two were used as control units. The departments varied in size and in productive function but were similar in composition of force, and exposure to a common plantwide policy and history. The change procedures included policy change to legitimize the experiment and to permit certain structural changes in the organization, training of supervisory and staff people, and changes in various organizational processes concerning communications and decision-making. The change program was intended to induce in the experimental units: a) more employee involvement in decision-making, b) more use of work groups as a medium for organizational activity, c) more supportiveness in supervisor-employee relationships, and d) more mutual interaction and influence within work groups. Measurements before and after the change program in both experimental and control units confirmed the successful induction of the desired changes. Criterion variables were also measured before, at one point during, and again after the change period. The change program extended over a three year period. The theory was social-psychological in character, and (for purposes of this experiment) treated the independent variables as a set, not attempting to differentiate their separate effects. The dependent variables were treated separately. Assessment of results provided for before-after comparisons for each unit, and for comparison of experimental and control departments before and again after the experimental period. Results: changes in the four independent variables are associated with increased employee satisfaction, reduction in waste, increase in productive efficiency, and dampening of a trend toward increased absenteeism.

SOME DILEMMAS IN EXPERIMENTAL DESIGN

The design and conduct of field experiments with formal organizations involve the same methodological, theoretical, and ethical considerations that apply to any research with human subjects, but some are particularly bothersome. Some comments follow on several dillemmas that are apparent from a review of the experiments that have been reported thus far.

Control vs. representativeness

The most common forms of organization tend to be exactly those most difficult to perform experiments upon. Experiment I, above, achieved a fairly high degree of control over unknown confounding variables by restricting its scope to four parallel divisions matched in a number of respects. Experiment III, by contrast, involved a much more commonly prevailing situation with organizational units differing in a number of respects (size, population mix, nature of work, etc.) in such a way as to leave some question whether the experimental results derived from the experimental variables or from other unknown sources. The added precision of Experiment I must be weighed against the possibility that its results derive from some feature of the restricted and exceptional population. There are at least two guides toward resolving this dilemma. Until more is known about confounding factors in field experiments there is great merit in emphasizing control through the selection of an initially homogeneous population. Those choosing to emphasize representativeness might well compensate for loss of homogeneity by using a larger number of cases, thus allowing randomization of some intruding variables. No experiment known to us so far has an N of organizational units greater than six.

Short-term vs. Long-term Experiments

Of five cases of field experiments with formal organizations which have been examined most closely, three required a span or time (years not months) considerably greater than originally intended, and this permitted the intrusion of personnel changes, technological changes, and other events that may well have confounded the results. The problem appears to be that significant changes in organizational structure and process come about rather slowly; at the same time, the longer an experiment continues in a natural organization, the more likely that there will be some loss of control over experimental conditions. In Experiment III, for example, some organizational units present at the beginning of the experiment simply disappeared under the press of technological change in the course of a three-year change program, and there also took place a considerable but normal turnover of membership in the experimental units. The advantages of short-term experimental plans are very great, but rest upon having powerful change methods and upon excluding variables not subject to change in a short time. Long-term experimental plans permit the utilization of natural changes and changes induced with less risk of stressful side-effects which might themselves introduce confounding effects.

Small, Explicit Theories vs. Global, Syndromatic Theories

Theoretical development, especially during early years of experimentation, is likely to be optimized to the extent that experiments focus upon small segments of organizational theory and deal precisely with a limited number of variables having a high degree of generality. This assertion argues for experiments designed around small, explicit theories (but, note that these may be small

theories about large phenomena). On the other hand, preliminary theory testing is likely to be accomplished more easily on a global or syndromatic basis. Natural organizations function not in segments but as totalities, and it is likely that larger theoretical systems, necessarily coupled with reduced precision of conceptualization and measurement, are needed to capture the main phenomena that occur. All of the experiments examined by the writer chose the latter course, and in translating theory into design ended by making large and risky assumptions about the interrelations among the elements of theory and by using syndromatic assessments. Experiment II, for example, by-passed entirely the details of its theory and measured only the change input, and also the output at the level of individual behavior. Experiment III deliberately treated as a syndrome four independent variables which in theory are separate and not of the same order; this forceable simplification of theory can be justified only on grounds of experimental expediency. The researcher's choice in this dilemma may well be based on grounds of convenience or esthetics until enough progress is made to permit some better judgment of relative effectiveness of the two approaches.

Massive vs. Controlled Change

The dilemma here arises from the conflict between the need to obtain change great enough to sustain measurement while at the same time preserving the possibility of differentiating among change sources and avoiding unintended and uncontrolled change. The experiments conducted thus far appear without exception to have called into play virtually all of the change resources available to the experimenters, and none has attempted to separate in analysis the effects of different sources of kinds of change activities. This dilemma is the counterpart, at the level of change induction, of the preceding point regarding specificity of theory. One known experiment was initially designed to differentiate among three change strategies, but this feature of the initial design failed of realization. Considering the difficulty of inducing a significant intentional change in organizational process, it appears likely that the first successful attempts to differentiate and control the sources of change will take the form of "natural" experiments (which exploit powerful singular events and conditions) or changes induced through modifications of organizational environment and/or formal structure (which require less direct intervention within the organizations).

Near vs. Distant Criteria

Organizational theories of the dynamic variety all involve chains of causal linkages between variables. The differentiation between independent and dependent variables accordingly becomes arbitrary except for their relative position in the causal sequence. One man's independent variable is another's criterion. The dilemma for the designer of experiments lies in weighing the advantages of near and distant criteria. His theoretical interests press toward criteria of organizational structure or process that are presumed to be immediately dependent upon his independent variables; at the same time his concerns for enlarging the conceptual scheme press toward criteria representing the output of the organizational system. The first choice maximizes his chances of getting significant relationships and is more likely to illuminate and add precision to this theory. The second choice offers the important gain of proving some link between his independent variables and the ultimate criteria by which the organizations are judged by society. Of the three examples given earlier, all involved output or distant criteria, and Experiment I also provided for assessment of certain near criteria. An example may be needed to clarify the point: a researcher changing the number of hierarchical levels in his experimental organizations might use a near dependent vari-

able such as change in communication rates within the organizations, or he might choose to use a distant criterion such as change in productivity rates. In principle, of course, one can account for all elements in the theoretically specified causal chains, together with their interactions, but this would be a truly formidable and presently impossible task.

Self- vs. Independent Selection of Subjects

A problem that has not been treated as yet in any experimental investigation on organizations, but which needs attention concerns the consequences of self-selection of the subject organizations. The dilemma for the researcher is to balance the advantages of working with organizations that are accessible and compliant against the hazard that these qualities may themselves interfere with control and representativeness in the research operations. Having a manager willing to expose his organization to experimentation is hardly a typical organizational condition, and implies that the outcome may be prejudiced in unforeseen ways. The same dilemma arises in experiments with individuals and small groups, but in a less disruptive degree.

Scientific vs. Ethical and Practical Considerations

All of the organizational experiments reported thus far involved a degree of collaboration between the subjects and the researchers which is greater than commonly holds for other experiments with human subjects. This collaboration typically includes a rather great financial investment by the subjects with some corresponding expectation of benefit, and the scale of the work means that any harm that inadvertently may be incurred will affect many people. It is the nature of the useful experiments that they tend to go beyond our confident knowledge and established experimental skills, with consequent risk, and in the case of organizational experiments these risks are on a large scale. The course of experimentally induced changes is not likely to remain in the immediate control of the experimenter, and he must depend upon many others who may misunderstand or take advantage of the experimental situation. A protection is often available in the way of making the design and conduct of the experiment a truly collaborative matter with responsibility for consequences located in ways compatible with the structure of the organization, but this in turn limits the change program to matters known to and understood by the participants. A few instances are on record where organizations or members have been harmed by organizational-level intervention for research purposes, and more are bound to occur if experimentation proceeds in a vigorous and venturesome way.

RESEARCH STRATEGIES

At this primitive stage of development in experimentation with formal organizations it is probably desirable to emphasize simplicity of design and opportunism in execution as guides to research strategy. Some suggestions follows:

Search for Optimum Research Sites

This writer is much impressed by the difficulties of establishing control over variables which are not components of the research design. The practical approach will ordinarily involve a deliberate search for subject organizations which are stable in their environment, technology, and membership,[4] and which are accessible in large numbers. Homogeneity of subject organizations has evident advantage; large N's allow randomization, matching or sampling techniques for

removal of some potentially confounding effects. Where will such populations be found? Mainly in activities relatively uncomplicated by changing machine technology (e.g., sales, service, government, education, etc.) and in fields having very large parent organizations with many similar decentralized field units (e.g., armed forces, large corporations, communities, government agencies, etc.).

Availability of Criterion Data

In instances when the research design rests upon hard criteria of organizational performance, a great value must be placed on locating subject organizations that offer reliable differences in performance. Since high reliability and comparability of organizational performance criteria are *very* rare, it is likely that other considerations in choice of research site will yield to this essential one, or else the research designs will need to be modified in ways to avoid the problem entirely. The chief way to avoid the problem is to settle for criteria of organizational structure and process, rather than criteria of organizational output; these are often relatively easy to measure, are less contaminated, and for many theoretical purposes equally or even more useful than the hard criteria.

Induction of Change

A general principle of experimental design is to avoid introducing any changes in conditions other than those absolutely essential for obtaining the desired modification of the independent variables. The organizational experiments reported so far have all involved a rather large amount of loosely-controlled intervention by outside change agents, and this risks the introduction of "Hawthorne effects" and other effects not accounted for in the design. There appears to be great merit in designs which introduce changes in ways that involve little or no contact between ex-

---

[4] Unless, of course, these enter directly into the experimental design.

perimenter and subject organization. How is this likely to be managed? a) Through policy and structural changes introduced via persuasion at the top levels of the organizations, b) by intervention into allocative processes (e.g., assignment of funds, people, tasks) which purposefully affect the subject organizations without direct intervention into the organizations themselves, c) by altering the environment of the subject organizations.[5]

Pre-experimental Assessment of Confounding Variables

One way of coming to terms with potentially confounding conditions is to make in advance a realistic assessment of what they are and then to provide some control through population selection or statistical adjustment of the experimental variables. To do this appears to require a more thorough scouting and preparatory operation than is typically done, and in any case it is a procedure dependent on the insight and judgment of the experimenters rather than upon replicable methods. An ideal situation would be that in which the subject organizations (or others like them) were subjected to a series of preliminary investigations allowing the research team to become intimately familiar with the total situation and thus to have a chance, at least, of knowing the surroundings of the experiment. In Experiment II, described earlier, this was done, and the experiment itself followed after several years of prior research within the organization. In Experiment III, there was a full year of preliminary scouting, but crucial factors were overlooked which later revealed their potency in disrupting the experimental plan. A useful guide in this preliminary work would be the formulation of explicit conditional assumptions implied by the proposed research design, so that points of hazard can more readily be discerned and treated.

Skills in Change Induction

Some variables of importance in organizational theory present special problems with respect to the introduction of purposeful change and probably have to be dealt with through direct and intensive interventions. An example would be a variable such as consideration (a variable referring to a style of supervisory behavior believed to be conditioned by the actor's organizational climate) which has its variance sources in individual personality, local group norms, and formal organizational policy, as well as in the climate and traditions of the organization (5). To attempt to change such a variable experimentally through indirect, sanitary means would probably require a great span of time and considerable uncertainty of outcome. To change it directly through intervention by change agents at the personal contact level is also difficult (failures have been reported) but is known to be feasible. To accommodate the requirements of both experimental change and practical application ventures, there is likely to arise a new professional group devoted to change agentry, different in important respects from their professional colleagues in the fields of training and management consulting. The researcher himself is not likely to have the qualifications or time to perform this essential research function, and in the interests of objectivity he probably should not be involved in it. For such practical reasons, the research plans in field experiments should in many cases provide

---

[5] Alteration of the environment or allocative processes of organizations may at first seem an impossible accomplishment for a researcher, but consider these hypothetical possibilities as examples: Through home-office intervention, field (subject) organizations would be subjected temporarily to different degrees of work overload; through home-office intervention some subject units and not others could be subjected to conditions of inter-unit competition or cooperation.

for some kind of division of labor between those who do the theoretical, analytic, and interpretive work, on the one hand, and those who engage in active and personal interventions in the subject organizations.

Creating New Organizations

One potential means for avoiding many of the foregoing problems has, to our knowledge, never been tried. This is the procedure of linking an experimental plan with the growth of an organization in such a way that new organizational units may be designed from their initiation with contrasting characteristics that permit testing of theoretical propositions. Some lucky researcher will one day be permitted to impose such a plan upon, say, the formation of 100 new welfare agencies, retail outlets, or military units.[6]

Utilization of Natural Change

A prime practical problem in experiments with larger organizations is the induction of a change that is sufficiently great to permit hypothesis-testing even after the consequences of the change are dampened and confounded by the unavoidable surrounding noise. This calls for an enhanced alertness on the part of both researchers and organization managers so that instances of impending natural change can be exploited. In this manner the experimenter may have the use of change events far greater (for reasons of competence and ethics) than those he could introduce on his own initiative. However, optimum use of such situations requires advance knowledge in order that population controls and pre-measures may be instituted.

REFERENCES

1. Adams, R. N. and J. J. Preiss (eds.), *Human Organization Research*, Dorsey, Homewood, Ill. 1960.

2. Argyle, M. *The Scientific Study of Social Behavior*, Philosophical Library, New York, 1957.

3. Etzioni, A., *Complex Organizations: A Sociological Reader*, Holt-Rinehart-Winston, New York, 1961.

4. Festinger, L. and D. Katz, (eds.), *Research Methods in the Behavioral Sciences*, Dryden Press, New York, 1953.

5. Fleishmann, E. A. "Leadership Climate, Human Relations Training and Supervisory Behavior," *Personnel Psychology*, VI, (1953) 205–222.

6. Jahoda, M., M. Deutch, and S. Cook, *Research Methods in Social Relations*, Dryden Press, New York, 1951.

7. Likert, R. *New Patterns of Management*, McGraw-Hill, New York, 1961.

8. Likert, R. and S. Hayes, (eds.), *Some Applications of Behavioral Research*, UNESCO, New York, 1957.

9. Marriott, R., *Incentive Payment Systems*, Staples Press, London, 1957.

10. Morse, N. and E. Reimer, "The Experimental Change of a Major Organizational Variable," *J. Abnormal and Social Psychology*, LII 1956, 120–129.

11. Seashore, S. E. and D. G. Bowers, *Changing the Structure and Functioning of an Organization*, Survey Research Center, Ann Arbor, 1963.

---

[6] This paper has excluded consideration of laboratory experiments, which may involve creation of new complex organizations and may in degree of realism approach field conditions. An example is described in "Experiment on Bureaucratic Authority," by William M. Evan and Morris Zelditch, Jr., *American Sociological Review*, XXVI, (1961), 883–893.

Opportunistic Organizational Research:
The Role of Patch-up Designs[1]

Martin G. Evans

Campbell and Stanley (3), in their penetrating analysis of a variety of experimental and quasi-experimental research designs for the evaluation of change in natural settings, identify a number of factors that may obscure or, more worryingly, create the illusion of a change. These are of two types: internal factors that limit one's confidence in the study, and external factors that limit generalization to other situations or populations.

Internal factors include (a) history—the impact of contemporary events on subjects in addition to the experimentally induced attempt to create a change; (b) maturation—changes in the subject due to the subject's own natural development (perhaps a more worrying phenomenon in educational research on students than in organizational research, where we can expect subjects to have attained a steady state of maturity); (c) testing—the first administration of a test may affect the responses to a second set of administered tests, i.e., pretest confounds the post-test; (d) instrumentation—the meaning of the instrument may change over time; (e) statistical regression—the movement of extreme groups toward the mean. In other words, groups that score poorly on the first administration of a test are likely to have as one component of their low score an error term that depresses their score. On a subsequent administration of the test, this error term is likely to be zero or such as to enhance the score; hence the group score "regresses" toward the overall mean. A similar argument holds for high scoring groups; (f) selection—biases caused by assigning groups with different characteristics to experimental and control groups; (g) experimental mortality—the differential subject attrition from different conditions over time; (h) interaction between some of the above variables, i.e., selection-maturation.

Threats to external validity include (i) test-treatment interaction. Change is caused not by the experimental change alone but by change accompanied by pretesting, which sensitizes individuals and either makes them receptive to or innoculates (9) them against the change; (j) selection-treatment interaction; (k) the effects of the experimental setting, i.e., the Hawthorne effect that knowledge by a subject that he is part of an

[1] Early discussion with A. M. Pettigrew helped bring these issues to a focus. The author wishes to thank S. Hamilton, R. J. House, H. E. McCandless, and D. A. Ondrack for their comments on this paper.

Reproduced by permission of the *Academy of Management Journal*, 1975, *18*, 98–108.

Group A	O_1	O_2	O_3	X	O_4		O_5	
Group B	O_1	O_2	O_3		O_4	X	O_5	
Group C	O_1	O_2	O_3		O_4		O_5	X

Figure 1.   Design of Data Collection

Source: Brown (1).
O = Observation.
X = Experimental Induction.

experiment may create sensitivity to change that would not be present in routine administrative settings; (1) multiple treatment interference—the interaction between several experimental treatments. This could be extended to include history-treatment interactions.

In order to control for these threats, Campbell and Stanley (3) suggest several desiderata in the design of quasi-experiments:

1. Quasi-experiments should include control or comparison groups. Whenever possible, assignment to experimental and comparison groups should be randomized.

2. Before and after measures should be taken, preferably within only half of the experimental and control groups to control for testing-treatment interaction.

3. Time series data should be gathered as this lessens the obtrusiveness of the instruments and reduces the effects of instrumentation and test-treatment interaction.

PROBLEMS IN RESEARCH DESIGN

In research on organizational change it is often difficult to adopt designs of research that even approximate the realistic criteria of Campbell and Stanley.

1. It is virtually impossible to obtain random assignment of subjects, work groups, or organizational units to control vs. experimental conditions. The organization rather than the researcher usually is the arbiter of such decisions, which are often based upon the receptivity of the administrators of particular sites.

2. Often this type of research is an opportunistic process. One finds out about an organizational experiment and "parachutes in" to find out about its impact as best one can.

The purist might argue that, given these constraints, research studies on organizations should not be attempted. The argument here is that they *should* be; "patch-up" designs should be developed which represent combinations of the Campbell and Stanley designs and which, in combination, meet the Campbell and Stanley criteria. This point is well made by Brown (1). He uses the lagged time series design as outlined in Figure 1. A similar design has been employed by Golembiewski et al. (6). Brown argues:

> The combination of two "quasi-experimental" designs—"The Time series" and "the Non-Equivalent control group"—does eliminate most alternative explanations. The time series design, for example leaves the influence of historical events external to the [experimental induction] unaccounted for in explaining any change. But such an event would be expected to influence the comparison group also, even if the comparison group is in some ways dissimilar. In the same fashion, the Time-series design compensates for the weaknesses of the Non-Equivalent Control Group design" (1, p. 703).

One must be aware of possible similarities and differences between the experimental and control groups. It is argued below that potential differential effects of history on the two groups need checking through the questions asked and the investigator's knowledge of the situation.

Experimental	O_1	X	O_2					(a)
Comparison	O_1		O_2					
Experimental	O_1	X	O_2	R*				(b)
		X	O_2	R*				
Comparison	O_1		O_2	R*				
			O_2	R*				
Experimental	O_1	XX	O_2				R*	(c)
			O_2				R*	
	O_1		O_2		X	O_3	R*	
					X	O_3	R*	
Comparison	O_1		O_2			O_3	R*	
			O_2			O_3	R*	
						O_3	R*	

Figure 2.   Experimental Diagram in the Blake Grid Study

Source: Maxwell and Evans (8).
* Randomization within experimental and control treatments.

PATCH-UP DESIGNS

This author has recently been involved in two studies in which an opportunity existed to try to evaluate organizational changes. In both studies, for different reasons, full experimental control could not be exerted, and patch-up designs for specific validity threats had to be developed.

The Blake Grid Evaluation

As part of a larger project (7), an attempt was made to evaluate the impact of the second phase of the introduction of the Blake Grid. This phase is designed to enhance the effectiveness of the behavior of management work groups (8). For the organization studied, (a) pretest data were available, and (b) comparison groups were obtainable from a segment of the organization which was not undergoing the Grid. However, assignment of groups to the experimental and comparison conditions was based on organizational needs rather than on research needs.

The first attempt at a research design was therefore the "Non-Equivalent Control Group Design." See Figure 2, section (a). This design has several threats to validity.

Internal threats include:

Regression—i.e., ineffective groups may be getting the experimental treatment and may therefore exhibit a gain on the tests of interest merely because of the change in direction of the error term's impact.

Selection—i.e., it is possible that the experimental and control groups differ at the start; thus any changes may be masked by this difference.

Selection/maturation interaction—as the groups differ at the start, part of this difference may be in their learning ability or in their familiarity with the organization setting. Again, these differences could mask or enhance changes.

External threats to validity include:

Testing/treatment interaction—here it may be argued that the cause of the change is not simply the experimental induction but the induction accompanied by the pretest, which has sensitized the individual to the concepts introduced by the Grid.

Selection/treatment interaction—in this case the different assignation of groups may interact with the type of experimental induction. In other words, any change observed in the experimental group might be due not to the experimental induction alone but to the induction coupled with the particular kind of group/people who receive it.

Experimental setting—here the group getting the Grid may have known that they were supposed to change and this knowledge helped bring about the appropriate change. This threat also exists when observers know which group gets which treatment (10).

In the study under consideration the modification to the design was to assign individuals in the experimental and comparison groups to two conditions, pretesting and no pretesting, so that the design has the form of Figure 2 section (*b*). Thus within each condition (experimental and comparison) there is a Campbell and Stanley "Separate-Sample Pre-Test—Post-Test Design." Such a design has the following problems in its pure form; i.e., these problems exist *within* each condition.

Within each condition, internal threats include:

History—each subsection experiences the same historical events.

Maturation—the two subsections, being selected at random within a condition, experience similar rates of maturation. If the experimental subsections alone were examined, this could not be ruled out as a cause of the change.

Instrumentation—the standards of evidence required by the interviewer may shift from the first time period to the second, which could account for the observed change within each condition, experimental and control.

No external threats exist. However, it is in combination that such a design shows its strength:

Testing-treatment interaction, selection-treatment interaction, and possible time experimental effect are ruled out of consideration as potential contribu-

tions to change by splitting each group (experimental and comparison) randomly in half and giving only one-half the pretest.

History, maturation, and instrumentation are ruled out through the use of the comparison group.

Thus this design leaves only three potential reasons for misinterpreting the causes of an observed change:

(a) Selection

(b) Regression

(c) Selection-maturation interaction

These problems were not recognized or discussed in the Maxwell and Evans (8) paper. How might they have been controlled? The answer lies in the Brown (1) design. As participation in Phase 2 by work groups is spread out over a six-month period, the experimental group could have been further divided into two subgroups and the design outlined in Figure 2, section (*c*), utilized. The threats from selection, its interaction, and regression would then have been eliminated by comparing the untreated with the treated experimental groups at Time 2. Of course, one must pick up the comparison group at O_3 to check for history between Time 2 and Time 3.

A design outlined by Vaught (11) is similar to this in spirit, though the control is on experimental treatment rather than on testing/treatment interaction.

The Flexible Working Hours Study

This research was designed to attempt to evaluate the impact of a flexible working hours scheme on the job attitudes and satisfaction of clerical workers in a large British insurance company (5). Here there was a major disadvantage in that no pretest measures were obtainable. This is not unusual in organizational research. Management often asks for an evaluation after the experimental

	X	O_1	O_2	O_3	X	O_4	O_5	
Experimental	X	O						(a)
Comparison		O						
Experimental	X	O_1	O_2	O_3				(b)
Comparison		O_1	O_2	O_3				(c)
Experimental	X	O_1	O_2	O_3				
	X		O_2	O_3				
	X			O_3				
Comparison		O_1	O_2	O_3				
			O_2	O_3				
				O_3				
Experimental	X	O_1	O_2	O_3		O_4	O_5	(d)
	X		O_2	O_3		O_4	O_5	
	X			O_3		O_4	O_5	
Comparison		O_1	O_2	O_3	X	O_4	O_5	
			O_2	O_3	X	O_4	O_5	
				O_3	X	O_4	O_5	
					X	O_4	O_5	

Figure 3. Designs for the Flexible Hours Study

induction has been carried out, thus putting one squarely into Campbell and Stanley's pre-experimental situation. Can anything be retrieved from such a situation? With a patch-up design, some insights can be gained.

Since a comparison group (an office on traditional hours) was available, a minimum design, as outlined in Figure 3, section (a) was followed. This design was subject to the following limitations:

Internal—Maturation
Selection
Mortality
Interaction of selection and maturation

External—Interaction of selection and treatment
Experimental Setting

To patch-up this design (a process that is still in progress) several steps were taken:

1. Instead of a single post-measure, a series of three was taken for both the comparison and experimental groups. This provides one with the post-indicators, half a multiple-time series design as in Figure 3, section (b). It yields control over history in addition to that provided by the comparison group; it gives

an opportunity to detect a sleeper effect, i.e., a delayed impact of the experimental indicators, which a single time series cannot do; and it serves as a control on mortality and maturation. However, there still are problems with testing effects and test-treatment interaction.

2. The experimental and control groups had increasing numbers of testees over the three periods, as in Figure 3, section (c). This permits control of effects due to testing and testing-treatment interactions. The problem of selection remains.

3. The final step (which is now in the process of execution) allows testing for the selection effect. The comparison group has been transformed into an experimental group, and further time series data are being generated. The continued examination of the experimental group allows the monitoring of any future effects of history and effects of experimental setting. A similar process has been carried out in a number of other studies (e.g., 4).

DATA INTERPRETATION

The potential differences in interpretation of data from these designs are dramatically illustrated by an examination of some of

TABLE 1
Attitude Measures for Experimental and Control Groups in the Flexible Working Hours Study

		T_1 (December)		T_2 (January)	T_3 (March)
Satisfaction with:[a]				*f	
Using one's capabilities at work	E[b]	1.85		1.64	1.50
	C[c]	1.96		2.04	2.09
Using one's capabilities in leisure activities				*d	
	E	0.91	*[e]	0.59	0.58
	C	0.98		0.93	0.62
				*	
Social satisfaction at work	E	−0.44[g]		0.00	0.01
	C	0.96		0.80	0.61
		*		*	*

[a] Satisfaction is the difference between aspiration and attainment, so the smaller the numerical score, the higher the satisfaction.
[b] E = experimental group
[c] C = comparison group
[d] Asterisks in column below the mean scores indicate that the difference between Experimental and Control groups is significant.
[e] Asterisks between columns indicate that there is a significant change between the scores at two adjacent time periods (December to January or January to March).
[f] Asterisks in a line between the Dec. and March columns indicate that a change from Dec. to March is significant.
[g] A negative score means that people receive more gratification of this need than they aspire to.

the data from the flexible working hours study.

The first question involves testing effects or testing/treatment interaction effects. A preliminary analysis of the data showed that for both experimental and comparison groups there are no differences at the second observation period between those who were tested at period one and those who were not tested. Subsequent to this, an examination of the different information derived from the designs presented in sections (a) and (b) of Figure 3 is possible. Table 1 contains data for several dimensions of attitude examined one and one-half months, three months, and five months after the change occurred. These data are presented for illustrative purposes only. Trends in the data can be examined even though not all the differences are significant. Levels of significance are presented to allow those interested in the substantive data to draw proper conclusions.

Satisfaction with using one's capabilities at work would depend on certain circumstances:

1. If the organization had just been examined at T_1, it would have been concluded that the change had no effect.

2. If the organization had been examined at T_2 or T_3 only, it would have been concluded that there was a difference between the experimental and comparison groups. However, there are several alternative explanations for these differences:

   a) They existed between the groups prior to the change—a selection effect.

   b) They may have been caused by a regression effect. The experimental group may have changed to a more normal state because it was originally dissatisfied.

   c) They may have been caused by the experimental change.

3. If the organization had been examined at T_2 and T_3, then only causes (a) and (c) above remain; if the regression effect were operating, differences due to

this effect would not remain stable from T_2 to T_3.

4. An examination of T_1, T_2, and T_3 would result in cause (a) being ruled out; thus cause (c) is the only remaining plausible explanation. In fact, these data indicate that there is a sleeper effect. The impact of the change on this satisfaction dimension occurs only after three months.

Satisfaction with using capabilities in leisure activities would be determined as follows:

1. By examining T_1 or T_3 alone, one would have concluded that the change had had no effect.

2. By examining T_2 alone, one would have observed differences between the experimental and control groups in favor of the former. However, the three possible interpretations of selection, regression, and true change all would have been tenable.

3. An examination of all the data would lead to the conclusion that satisfaction in both experimental and comparison groups is increasing over time. The change is lagged one period for the comparison group and does not quite reach statistical significance. This suggests that something other than the change has caused this phenomenon. As all data showing this pattern dealt with attitudes toward leisure activity, it may be that a seasonal phenomenon has been uncovered.

Determination of satisfaction with social relationships at work also depends on which data are examined:

1. If the organization had been examined at T_1 or T_2 or T_3 alone, differences between experimental and comparison groups would have been observed. Again

the three interpretations (regression, selection, true change) would have been tenable.

2. Examination of all the data rules out the possibility of regression as a cause, because such a difference would not be stable over time. However, with these data, the possibility of a selection effect cannot be ruled out. In fact, prior to the experimental induction, organizational informants stated that the experimental and control groups differed on this dimension. If all the data took this form, it would not be possible to rule out selection as a cause. This represents a weakness in the post-test only design. However, this weakness occurs only for this data configuration.

Alternative Explanations

In addition to the design controls outlined above, Campbell (2) suggests other methods for improving the chances of currently identifying a real change and rejecting obvious changes:

Try to identify potential rival hypotheses prior to the execution of the research and then incorporate procedures and questions to control for them. Serendipitously this was done in the Flexible Hours study. During the course of the investigation two historical events occurred that potentially, either alone or in interaction with the treatment, might have affected satisfaction:

1. The British Government introduced and modified a pay and prices policy during the course of the exercise. This affected the comparison and experimental groups equally.

2. The organization, between the second and third observation, announced that over the next five years there were to be wide ranging changes in the location of the offices, involving a devolution from London. This had primary impact on the comparison group and a lesser impact

upon the experimental group, in which only two departments were to move.

The results of the study showed that satisfaction with job security declined slightly in the experimental group, but there was a marked downward shift for the comparison group. Although neither trend was significant over time within either group, the comparison and experimental groups differed significantly at T_3 in satisfaction with security, the comparison group being worse off in this regard.

These data, and the differential impact of these historical changes on the control and comparison groups, emphasize the importance of knowing the differences between the two groups in terms of their organization setting so one can be sensitive to potentially confounding events and the possibility of history-selection interaction.

In the use of multiple measures in organizational settings "trace" data often exist in documentary forms. In the type of study discussed here, such data can be used to triangulate the attitudinal data reported, and provide (as in the flexible working hours study) a true before and after study. In the studies reported, data of this sort were not used, but in hindsight should have been. The types of data are listed here to suggest alternative approaches to future investigators:

1. *Blake Grid Study*

   a) Frequency of meetings—after the Grid phase II experience, the number would be expected to increase and then stabilize.

   b) Duration of meetings—after phase II, the length of meetings should increase as people grappled with the problems of planning and critiquing their activity; as they became practiced in these behaviors, meetings should then be shorter.

   c) Absence and turnover of subordinates—if the Grid experience is as-

sumed to generalize from peer relations to supervisory/subordinate relationships, it might (tentatively) be expected that subordinates would have lowered turnover and absenteeism.

2. *Flexible Working Hours Study*

   a) Measures of productivity—if the scheme is designed to improve performance by providing people with increased control over their work, controlling the closure of their work, etc., greater productivity should show up in performance. It had been hoped that there would be before and after data of this kind to use in the study. However, an examination of the data revealed that other technological changes had occurred differentially in different parts of the organization. Therefore, such a comparison was infeasible.

   b) Absences and turnover—if flexible working hours results in improved employee satisfaction, this should be reflected in reduced absenteeism (i.e., in addition to the free flexible day off) and reduced turnover.

   c) Quality of potential hires—if the scheme creates an attractive image of the organization in the labor market, the quality of job applicants should increase. This can be checked by examining qualifications—experience, training, etc.

   d) Traffic flow—a check on whether people altered their behavior could have been made through a census of traffic flow to the office. Two questions are involved:

      1) Did people vary their arrival/departure times?

      2) Were car pools more difficult to form? This question would imply more differences in arrival/departure times. There were some

unobtrusive data bearing on the latter question. The number of cars to be accommodated on the company parking lots rose drastically.

e) Leisure activity—it was expected that shopping patterns might change, with people doing shopping during days off from work, at distant supermarkets, rather than on the way to and from work at more expensive local shops. Sales data could have been acquired from local shops. The local pub was said to be less crowded now at lunchtime as people hurried back to work to build up credit hours.

CONCLUSION

All organizational researchers face the problems outlined above. The purpose here has been to suggest that the use of quasi-experimental designs allows one to make unequivocal inferences about whether an observed change is due to an experimental induction or to spurious causes. The use of several designs in the research plan allows the investigator to arrange for the strength of one to compensate for the weaknesses in the other. Additionally, by careful thought about potential alternative hypotheses, it is possible to test for these during the course of the study. This ad hoc patching is the lot of all engaged in organizational research.

REFERENCES

1. Brown, L. D. "Research Action: Organizational Feedback, Understanding, and Change," *Journal of Applied Behavioural Science,* Vol. 8 (1972), 697–711.

2. Campbell, D. T. "Reforms as Experiments," *American Psychologist*, Vol. 24 (1969), 409–429.

3. Campbell, D. T., and J. C. Stanley. *Experimental and Quasi-Experimental Designs for Research* (Chicago, Ill.: Rand-McNally, 1966).

4. Coch, L., and J. R. P. French. "Overcoming Resistance to Change," *Human Relations,* Vol. 1 (1948), 512–533.

5. Evans, M. G., and B. Partridge. "Flextime: Its Impact on Job Attitudes and Behaviour (Working Paper, London Graduate School of Business, England).

6. Golembiewski, R. T., R. Munzenrider, A. Blumberg, S. B. Carrigan, and W. R. Mead. "Changing Climate in a Complex Organization: Interactions Between a Learning Design and an Environment,"

Academy of Management Journal, Vol. 14 (1971), 465–481.

7. Maxwell, S. R. "Change with the Managerial Grid," in M. R. Hecht (Ed.), *Management Development in Change* (Toronto: Faculty of Management Studies, 1973).

8. Maxwell, S. R., and M. G. Evans. "An Evaluation of Organizational Development: Three Phases of the Managerial Grid," *Journal of Business Administration,* Vol. 5, No. 1 (1973), 21–35.

9. McGuire, W. J. "Inducing Resistance to Persuasion: Some Contemporary Approaches," in L. Berkowitz (Ed.), *Advances in Experimental Social Psychology* (New York: Academic Press, 1964).

10. Rosenthal, R. *Experimenter Effects in Behavioral Research* (New York: Appleton Century Crofts, 1966).

11. Vaught, R. S. "A Semi-Experimental Design," *Psychological Bulletin,* Vol. 81 (1974), 126–129.

Effects of Team Development Intervention: A Field Experiment[1]

Richard W. Woodman

John J. Sherwood

Team development or team building occupies a central position in organization development methodology (Alderfer, 1977; French & Bell, 1978; Beer, 1976). Following French, Bell, and Zawacki (1978) a team development intervention, as used in this study, consists of problem diagnosis and problem-solving meetings with the use of a consultant or facilitator. Meetings focus on the collection of data about problems and issues facing a work group, feedback of the data, identification of problems and setting priorities, and action planning.

Simply stated, a team development intervention is designed to improve the effectiveness of a work group. Research studies have often reported positive outcomes stemming from team development activities. Among the positive outcomes are improvements in performance (e.g., Beckhard & Lake, 1971; Blake, Mouton, Barnes & Greiner, 1964; Bragg & Andrews, 1973; Kimberly & Nielsen, 1975; Luke, Block, Davey & Averch, 1973; Marrow, Bowers & Seashore, 1967; Nadler & Pecorella, 1975); increases in the amount of participation and involvement (e.g., Bragg & Andrews, 1973; Brown,

Aram & Bachner, 1974; Friedlander, 1967; Nadler & Pecorella, 1975; Schmuck, Runkel & Langmeyer, 1969); improvements in organizational climate (e.g., Bigelow, 1971; Fosmire, Keutzer & Diller, 1971; Golembiewski, 1972; Luke et al., 1973); and increases in participant satisfaction (e.g., Hand, Estafen & Sims, 1975; Hautaluoma & Gavin, 1975; Kimberly & Nielsen, 1975; Marrow et al., 1967; Schmuck, Murray, Smith, Schwartz & Runkel, 1975). The above studies have been extensively reviewed elsewhere (Woodman, 1978; Woodman & Sherwood, 1980).

Reviewing the research evidence on team development interventions, Friedlander and Brown (1974) concluded that despite the flawed research designs, there is convergent evidence that team development activities affect participation attitudes and sometimes behavior. That conclusion seems consistent with the literature reviewed by Woodman (1978) although a note of caution should be added. Even though almost all of the published studies report generally positive outcomes, the overall internal validity of available research is not impressive in terms of drawing specific conclusions about team

[1] Reproduced by special permission from *The Journal of Applied Behavioral Science,* 1980, *16,* 211–227, copyright 1980, NTL Institute.

development. Evaluation of team development effects has often suffered from small sample sizes and the absence of control groups. Even when groups have been withheld from the experimental treatment as controls in an organizational setting, a lack of random assignment of persons to groups and/or groups to conditions commonly renders the research design quasi-experimental at best (i.e., falling into Campbell and Stanley's [1966] nonequivalent control group category).

There is a clear need for more rigorous research designs in studies evaluating team development interventions. Despite this need, the researcher faces an acute dilemma in attempting to apply rigorous methodology to an evaluation of OD programs. Just as much current research suffers from methodological weaknesses, the application of more rigorous designs carries with it constraints which may affect the generalizability of any results. This is not unlike the dilemma traditionally faced in laboratory vs. field research in the behavioral sciences.

The research setting utilized in this study was selected to incorporate advantages of both laboratory and field experimentation. The setting retains much of the control of the laboratory yet provides greater external validity because subjects work in traditioned groups. In particular, this research was designed to provide greater control and statistical power than has been prevalent in research on team development to date. The problems in generalizability created by a rigorous research design illustrate the trade-offs involved in attempting to apply sophisticated research methods to organization development evaluations.

METHOD

Experimental Setting

The subjects of this field experiment were 169 males and 23 females enrolled in an introductory engineering survey course at Purdue University. Participation in the experiment was voluntary.

Students in the course are routinely assigned to work groups to perform a series of engineering survey projects requiring group effort. Since performance on the projects was included in the final course grade, it was anticipated that interdependence, motivation, and involvement would be high in contrast to *ad hoc* groups formed in traditional laboratory experiments to work on simulated activities for a short time.

Experimental Design

Subjects were randomly assigned to one of 67 three- or four-person work groups. Work groups in turn were randomly assigned to one of three treatment or control conditions. Groups in Condition #1 received a team development intervention. Condition #2 was a placebo treatment: the presence of an outside observer at appropriate times as the group performed its activities. Groups in Condition #3 were neither observed nor participated in any team development activities. All groups received a posttest. This experimental design is a "posttest-only control group" design (Campbell & Stanley, 1966) with Condition #2 added to test for possible Hawthorne effects.

Procedure

The life of work groups was six weeks, and students were assigned one group project per week. Two team development interventions were conducted during the fourth and fifth weeks. Posttest measurement was taken during the week following completion of the final group project. After the posttest, subjects were debriefed and the purposes of the research fully explained.

Experimental Conditions

THE TEAM DEVELOPMENT INTERVENTION. The team development intervention undertaken in this study followed an action research model of data gathering, feedback, and action planning. The intervention activities were highly structured and focused at all times on task-related issues in order to enhance relevance and reduce interpersonal threat. In terms of Beer's (1976) typology, the intervention fit the goal-setting, problem-solving model of team development.

Team development sessions were held with 22 of the 67 work groups included in the study. Each of these groups were assigned a consultant—doctoral students majoring in either organizational behavior or counseling. Five consultants were employed, and each worked with at least four groups.

Two team development sessions were held one week apart. The first session focused on gathering information from the work group. After a brief introduciton, the facilitator led a discussion aimed at identifying and clarifying individual and group goals within the context of the surveying course. The discussion served as a springboard to focus the group's attention on its process— that is, how group members worked together. Each member of the group completed a 32-item questionnaire identifying behavior which helped or hindered the effectiveness of the group in accomplishing its objectives.

Information from this questionnaire provided the agenda for the second team-building session. The consultant provided a summary of the data from the instrument to the members of the work group. That information was shared, discussed, and clarified in order to serve as the basis for action planning by the group. Action planning focused on how the group might better perform its task—what things members could do differently in order to be more effective and how these changes could be implemented. The second team development session ended with a brief questionnaire evaluating the effectiveness of the consultant.

THE OBSERVER (PLACEBO) TREATMENT. Observers were assigned to 23 of the 67 groups to measure any impact stemming from their presence and attendant feelings about being included in a study, having someone pay attention to one's work, and so on.

THE NO-TREATMENT CONTROL GROUPS. For comparison purposes, 22 work groups received no treatment. Involvement of these groups in the study was limited to the posttest questionnaire described below.

Measures

Effects of the team development intervention were measured on performance, perceived problem-solving effectiveness, participation, goal consensus, perceived learning, and satisfaction. With the exception of performance, all measures were included on the posttest questionnaire.

PERFORMANCE MEASURE. Performance of the work groups was measured by grades on the surveying problems. (It was the belief both of the researchers and the course instructors that grades on the two field projects following team development, while important to the individuals involved, were unlikely to make an important difference in the final course grade.)

AFFECTIVE MEASURES. The posttest questionnaire contained 33 items divided into six 9-point Likert scales. While the measures were developed specifically for this research, some individual items, phrases, common themes, and ideas were derived from and need to be credited to a variety of sources (Alderfer, 1972; Friedlander, 1966; Gibb, 1977; Hackman & Oldham, 1974; Likert, 1967; Schmuck & Runkel, 1972; Taylor & Bowers, 1972).

Problem-solving Effectiveness:

A six-item scale was used to measure the problem-solving effectiveness of the surveying party as perceived by members of the group. Representative item: *To what extent has your group performed successfully on the surveying problems?* The internal consistency reliability of the composite measure was .90 (Cronbach, 1951; Nunnally, 1978).

Participation:

The level of perceived involvement and participation in the surveying problems by members of the work group was indexed by a six-item scale. Representative item: *To what extent have all members of your group "pulled their own weight"?* The internal consistency reliability of the participation measure was .92.

Goal Consensus:

Four items were used to assess the perceived degree of agreement on group goals. Representative item: *To what extent do you believe members of your group have the same goals when working on the surveying problems?* Coefficient alpha was .90.

Learning:

The amount of perceived learning by members of the group was measured by a five-item scale. Representative item: *To what extent does working with your group on the surveying problems provide the opportunity to learn new things?* Internal consistency reliability was .82.

Satisfaction with Performance:

A five-item measure was used to index satisfaction of group members with group performance. Representative item: *To what extent do persons in your group maintain high standards of performance?* Internal consistency reliability was .92.

Satisfaction with Group:

The group members' general satisfaction with other members of their group was assessed by a seven-item composite. Representative item: *To what extent do you enjoy being with the members of your group?* Coefficient alpha was .91.

HYPOTHESES

Hypothesis 1

1. *Performance will be higher for work groups receiving the team development intervention than for groups which do not.*

Hypotheses 2–7

Individuals in work groups receiving the team development intervention will, when compared to individuals in groups which do not receive the treatment:

2. *perceive their group as being more effective;*
3. *report higher levels of participation and involvement;*
4. *express greater agreement on group goals;*
5. *perceive themselves and their group as having learned more;*
6. *express greater satisfaction with their group's performance; and*
7. *express greater satisfaction with their group.*

RESULTS

Hypothesis testing proceeded in three phases: (1) univariate tests (ANOVA) on the performance outcomes; (2) multivariate testing (MANOVA) on the six self-report dependent measures; and (3) ANOVAs for each dependent measure as follow-ups to the MANOVA results.

Performance

The surveying parties completed six projects during the course of this study, the last two of which were done after the intervention. An analysis of variance revealed no differences in performance for Problems 1 through 4 across conditions of the experiment prior to the team development intervention. To a certain extent, this indicates the success of random assignment in terms of ability to perform the task. No significant performance differences, however, existed following the intervention whether Problems 5 and 6 were analyzed separately or together. Thus, the hypothesis of superior performance by work groups exposed to team development activities was not supported. The implications of this result are explored below.

TABLE I
Multivariate Analysis of Variance—Posttest Dependent Measures*

	Test of Roots	dF HYP	dfERROR	F**	p<	Canonical Correlations
Individual-Level Data (N = 192)	1 through 2	12	368	2.398	.005	.305
	2 through 2	5	184	2.016	.078	.228
Group-Level Data (N = 67)	1 through 2	12	118	1.972	.033	.454
	2 through 2	5	59	1.712	.146	.355

* Problem-solving effectiveness, participation, goal consensus, perceived learning, satisfaction with performance, satisfaction with group.
** The statistical test for this analysis was Wilks's lambda criterion using Rao's approximate F-test.

The MANOVA

A multivariate analysis of variance was performed on the six affective dependent measures included on the posttest: perceived problem-solving effectiveness, participation, goal consensus, perceived learning, satisfaction with performance, and satisfaction with group. In effect, this MANOVA was used to test an unstated null hypothesis that there were no significant differences among conditions in terms of mean scores on the posttest scales.[2]

The results of this 2×3 MANOVA are presented in Table 1. There was a significant multivariate effect on the set of six dependent measures, $F(12, 368) = 2.398$, $p<.005$. Technically, this means that the three (one for each condition of the experiment) population mean vectors, each composed of the six dependent variable means, cannot be assumed to be equal. Thus, the null hypothesis of no significant differences in responses across the conditions of the experiment was rejected.

The above analysis was conducted using individual-level data ($N = 192$). In addition, a 1×3 MANOVA was performed using group mean responses ($N = 67$). All groups were weighted equally in this analysis regardless of the number of members. Variations in group size were not confounded with experimental conditions. Again, analyzed at the group level, there was a significant multivariate effect on this set of dependent measures, $F(12, 118) = 1.972$, $p<.033$ (see Table 1).

Univariate Tests of the Hypotheses

Following the finding of significant differences from the MANOVA, the next step in the analysis was to ascertain the contribution of each dependent variable to the multivariate effect. The evidence of this multivariate effect suggests the use of ANOVA for hypothesis testing (Finn, 1974; Spector, 1977). The results of one-way (1×3) ANOVAs are presented in Table 2.

PROBLEM-SOLVING EFFECTIVENESS. Individuals in the intervention condition perceived their group as more effective than individuals in the observer or control groups, $F(2, 189) = 3.148$, $p<.045$. Fisher's least-significant-difference test indicated that Condition #1 (intervention groups) was significantly different ($p<.05$) from Condition #3 (control groups) but not from Condition #2 (observer groups). There was no significant difference between Conditions #2 and #3.

[2] Items, means, standard deviations, and intercorrelations of the measures used in this study are available from the authors on request.

TABLE 2
One-Way Analysis of Variance—Posttest Dependent Measures

Dependent Variable	Individual-Level Data F(2, 189)	p<	Group-Level Data F(2, 64)	p<
Problem-Solving Effectiveness	3.148	.045	1.455	.241
Participation	5.699	.004	4.559	.014
Goal Consensus	2.478	.087	2.273	.111
Perceived Learning	.496	.610	.706	.498
Satisfaction With Performance	1.724	.181	.760	.472
Satisfaction With Group	.756	.471	.570	.569

PARTICIPATION. Individuals in the intervention groups reported higher levels of participation than individuals in observer or control groups. This difference was statistically significant across conditions. $F(2, 189) = 5.699$, $p < .004$. Using Fisher's least-significant-difference test revealed that Condition #1 was significantly different from Conditions #2 and #3 ($p < .05$). There was no difference between Conditions #2 and #3.

GOAL CONSENSUS. Individuals in the intervention groups expressed greater agreement on group goals than individuals in observer or control groups. This difference, however, did not reach acceptable statistical significance, $F(2, 189) = 2.478$, $p < .087$. Brown et al. (1974) also reported no increase in agreement on goals following a team development intervention. To demonstrate statistically significant change in goal consensus would seem to require a more focused effort than was present in this research.

There were no statistically significant differences among conditions of the experiment in terms of perceived learning, satisfaction with group performance, or general satisfaction with the work group.

In sum, univariate F-ratios indicated that Hypotheses 2 and 3 were supported; Hypotheses 4, 5, 6, and 7 were not supported. *Post hoc* multiple-range tests revealed no statistical differences between observer groups and control groups on any measure.

Additional one-way ANOVAs were performed on each of the dependent measures using group-level data, and the results are also summarized in Table 2. With the loss of statistical power using this analysis, the only significant differences exist for participation, $F(2, 64) = 4.559$, $p < .014$. As with analysis of individual-level data, the strongest effects of the team development intervention were registered on the participation measure.

DISCUSSION

Performance

Team development appears to have had no impact on the performance of these work groups insofar as performance was reflected by grades received on the surveying problems. The interpretation of this outcome, however, must be treated cautiously. Using grades from a course as an index of performance is more analogous to using performance appraisal results in industry than it is to an evaluation of outcomes using "hard" productivity data. Like many performance appraisal systems, the grade index used in this research suffered from a restriction in range with grades strongly skewed toward the high end of the scale. Also, a low variability in these grades made it correspondingly more difficult to demonstrate performance differences.

When OD is well (i.e., strongly) done but poorly evaluated, we are faced with internal validity problems: Did the intervention truly make a difference in performance, satisfaction, climate, or whatever? Was it better than doing nothing at all? On the other hand, when OD is evaluated rigorously, this may have an unintended consequence of destroying its effectiveness, and thus we are left with weak interventions strongly measured. The team development of this study clearly fits in the latter category which severely limits the generalizability of performance results to other settings. How then might we account for improvements on other indices from such a relatively "weak" treatment?

Despite the presence of a consultant with the desire to improve the group's functioning, decisions for action planning were ultimately the responsibility of the group. That is, a decision by a group to continue in the same fashion as before the intervention was viewed as a legitimate outcome of team development. Approximately ⅓ of the surveying parties chose not to try to increase their effectiveness either because information gathering and sharing revealed no issues or problems of any significance, or because costs of solving a problem appeared greater than the perceived benefits from its solution. To the extent that groups chose not to attempt to improve performance, performance differences across conditions of the experiment were less likely to occur. Also, to the extent that groups purposely chose actions which reduced group effectiveness in order to meet other goals, peformance differences were less likely. (There was both empirical and anecdotal evidence that groups valued certain behaviors and outcomes more than "making grades.") It would appear, however, that these same decisions did not reduce differences on the affective measures. For example, having gone through the process of team building, a group may experience, and thus report, greater participation regardless of the specific actions taken or not taken following the experience. Performance outcomes or any objective measures of changed behavior may have been more sensitive to the action-planning process and subsequent follow-up than were measures of affective reactions.

Affective Dependent Measures

Mean scores for five of the six dependent affective measures were higher for intervention groups than for groups in other conditions. This result, bolstered by the finding of a significant F-ratio from the MANOVA, indicates that positive affect was associated with the intervention.

EFFECTIVENESS. The finding of perceptions of increased effectiveness is particularly interesting in light of the observation that surveying parties apparently were not more effective in terms of grades. One possible explanation for this discrepancy is that the process of team building with its open sharing of concerns and issues, identification of problems, and planning to solve these problems, colors the perceptions of group members so that they feel greater confidence in the problem-solving skills of the group. This is, of course, *exactly* what team development is designed to do, along with actually improving the problem-solving ability of the team. It is likely that, over time, discrepancies between perceived and actual effectiveness following team building in organizational settings would disappear because of feedback from external sources.

PARTICIPATION. The finding of increased levels of perceived participation following team development was the strongest single effect among the variables examined and replicates results of numerous studies. The validity of studies reporting increased participation following team building is relatively strong when compared to the general body of research concerning team development (cf., Woodman & Sherwood, 1980). These studies, coupled with the true experimental design used here, support the expectation that improvement in participation is a likely outcome of team development efforts. This is a particularly important finding in light of the values associated with collaborative behavior and the assumptions underlying many organization development programs (i.e., participation by interested parties is necessary to affect and sustain meaningful change).

PERCEIVED LEARNING. It is apparent that the intervention had no impact on perceived learning during the surveying problems. Clearly, an impact on learning was not a direct target for change during the team-building experience, but rather an improvement that might conceivably accompany improved group effectiveness. This hypothesis was exploratory and was based more on the desire for this outcome rather than on established theory. We considered it important for the research to support and be consistent with the educational objectives of the course.

SATISFACTION. While individuals in the team development condition scored higher on both measures of satisfaction than individuals in other groups, these differences were not statistically significant. Based on the significant multivariate effects, the present research might be construed as being consistent with literature reporting improved attitudes and climate following team development. Given the generally positive affective reactions, it is unclear why specific satisfaction measures remained unchanged after the intervention. The lack of impact on the measure of satisfaction with performance was easier to understand than the paucity of results in terms of satisfaction with one's group. Satisfaction with performance was significantly correlated ($r = .34$, $p<.01$) with the performance index which was unchanged by the team development experience. The lack of expected results in terms of general satisfaction with one's group is more puzzling. One possible explanation is that the intervention touched only a small portion of the work life of these groups; and therefore, the intervention was overshadowed by other impressions and evaluations of group members.

VALIDITY OF THE MEASURES. As reported, the internal consistency reliabilities of the measures constructed for this research were high. Also, some convergent and discriminant validity evidence exists from the study and pilot work using these measures (Woodman, 1978). One additional measurement issue, however, needs to be explored. Within the context of this research, what is the practical significance of a statistically significant result? For example, the mean difference in participation scores on a 9-point Likert scale between intervention groups (M = 7.58) and control groups (M = 6.84) was .74. The question is then, does this represent a meaningful as well as statistical difference? (Statistically the difference was highly significant, $p<.004$.) The goal of team development is, of course, not to produce statistically significant results but rather to produce substantively meaningful change. In this regard the following comparison should be borne in mind. When team development is conducted in organizational settings, it typically is a much longer process than in this research. For example, Argyris (1965) had five team-building meetings rather than the two conducted here; Schmuck et al. (1969) used six full days; and Fosmire et al. (1971) two weeks. In comparison, the amount of team development in this study might be considered ridiculously short. The fact that statistically significant results emerged from this abbreviated treatment suggests that stronger results could be expected from more comprehensive efforts and argues that the effects (i.e., on perceived effectiveness and participation) are of practical as well as statistical significance.

Sources of Invalidity

The posttest-only control group design, along with random assignment of both individuals and groups into this design, controlled for many potential threats to the internal validity of the experiment (Campbell & Stanley,

1966). In addition, there were no statistically significant differences on the performance index or on any of the six dependent affective measures between the placebo condition and the control condition; thus, the Hawthorne effect did not appear to be a plausible explanation for any changes.

Space does not permit a detailed discussion of the specific procedural steps and manipulation checks on the posttest used to deal with threats to validity not controlled directly by the experimental design (cf., Cook & Campbell, 1976). Compensatory treatment effects, contamination effects, resentment effects, and differential mortality, however, did not appear to be serious problems based on information gathered following the experiment.

A demand characteristic stemming from the nature of team development could influence self-report measures; that is, participants in team development could be led to expect that their experience would result in greater effectiveness, participation, goal agreement, satisfaction, or whatever. This expectation in turn could become a self-fulfilling prophecy on posttest measures with subjects responding more favorably as a result of their prior expectations rather than as a result of actual improvements in the work group. Measured expectations of changes in group behavior, however, were higher immediately following the team-building experience than were later assessments of actual change. This suggests that expectation effects per se did not account for more positive responses on posttest items.

In general, demand characteristics often represent a serious threat to the external validity of an OD intervention. As a matter of course, the process of team development raises certain expectations and/or "demands" certain behavior on the part of participants. The question becomes: Do these demands and expectations represent a confound or do they represent part of the treatment? To the extent that a specific intervention demands certain behavior, then perhaps the generality of any results is reduced. However, to the extent that a demand is in reality part of the treatment, then generality may be sustained by appropriate replication of this treatment. It is not clear, within the context of an OD intervention, whether or not traditional research concerns such as expectation effects, Hawthorne effects, or other demand characteristics are, in all cases, confounds.

Concluding Comments

IMPLICATIONS FOR RESEARCH. The successful use of this setting supports the contention that organization development interventions can be meaningfully investigated in a rigorously experimental fashion. The study also illustrates the possibilities and benefits as well as the limitations of using true experimental design in field research. Field experimentation is a methodology of great potential which has been underutilized in research on OD (King, Sherwood & Manning, 1978).

Demonstrating measurable improvements in performance is likely to be more difficult in most settings than measuring changes in perceptions and attitudes. The selection of performance criteria appears to be a particularly critical issue for any research where group members are not working for pay to produce a quantifiable product. If research in academic settings is to be applicable to other organizational environments, ways must be found to identify stronger analogues for industrial performance criteria. A corollary issue is whether we can expect to generalize OD effects in work settings to more artificial environments in order to examine them under controlled conditions. So, the generalizability issue cuts both ways.

In this research greater insight could have been gained into the impact of team building on performance if we had recorded which groups made specific plans to improve their effectiveness and which did not. Anytime work groups are free to decide their own actions, the researcher would be advised to gather data on those decisions.

IMPLICATIONS FOR PRACTICE.   In the broadest sense, the findings from this research are consistent with much of the empirical literature on team building. That is, team development is more likely to result in attitudinal changes than in changes in behavior. Improvements in performance seem to be situation-specific, suggesting that the practitioner needs to pay careful attention to the dynamics of the setting. At the very least the practitioner needs to be aware of the relative difficulty in demonstrating changes in behavior as opposed to changes in attitudes.

The strong effect of the intervention on perceptions of participation in the group suggests that team building may be particularly useful as a technique for increasing involvement and participation in a group's activities. This research also suggests that the action-planning phase of team development may be critical in terms of performance outcomes. Management may be uncomfortable with a technique which allows a work group to decide on its own not to establish an objective, solve a problem, or strive for a goal. The decision to do nothing toward improvement, even when the need for change has been recognized, is itself a research question of some significance.

LIMITATIONS OF THE STUDY.   Limitations on the generalizability of these findings to other settings should be re-emphasized. While this setting was chosen partly because of its strengths in generalizability in comparison to a laboratory experiment, there are still some obvious differences between groups of college students working within a course structure and groups in other work settings. Most specifically, the generalizability of these findings is constrained by:

1. the short work life of the groups,
2. the use of a shorter, less involved (and hence, weaker) intervention than is typical of most OD efforts,
3. imposition of the intervention on the participants (despite its voluntary nature) in the sense that the needs of the experiment rather than needs of the group determined the treatment.
4. the small size of the groups used in the study (triads, in particular, are sometimes less stable than larger groups), and
5. the random assignment of individuals to work groups. (While this randomization enhanced *internal* validity, it perhaps lessens the probability of forming effective groups. More importantly, it reduces the generality of findings to actual work settings where groups are formed by other methods.)

STRENGTHS OF THE STUDY.   The setting of the research is both a strength and a weakness. The needs of the experiment did not require any deviation from the basic course structure. This helped to minimize demand characteristics which often accompany the placing of subjects in a nonroutine experimental setting. The setting allowed the use of true experimental design with random assignment of treatment and controls which is often difficult to achieve in field research. Because of the experimental design employed, a Hawthorne effect may reasonably be excluded as an explanation of results. Many other threats to validity have been either measured and ruled out or controlled by the procedure employed. While the results were limited, the rigor of the experimental design allows these results to be attributed, with some confidence, to the effects of the team development intervention.

Team development seems destined to continue to play an important role in organizational settings, and may possibly be used to bridge the gap between human processal and technostructural approaches to change. As needs for improvement in the quality of working life and more effective design of work become more intense (Woodman & Sherwood, 1977), evaluations of the efficacy of particular approaches to restructuring the way work is performed likewise take on added importance.

REFERENCES

Alderfer, C. P. *Existence, Relatedness, and Growth: Human Needs in Organizational Settings.* New York: Free Press, 1972.

Alderfer, C. P. "Organization Development." In M. R. Rosenzweig & L. W. Porter (Eds.), *Annual Review of Psychology,* 1977, 28, 197–223.

Argyris, C. *Organization and Innovation.* Homewood, Ill.: Irwin-Dorsey, 1965.

Beckhard, R., & Lake, D. G. "Short- and Long-range Effects of a Team Development Effort." In H. Hornstein, B. Bunker, W. Burke, M. Grindes, & R. Lewicki (Eds.), *Social Intervention: A Behavioral Science Approach.* New York: Free Press, 1971. Pp. 421–439.

Beer, M. "The Technology of Organization Development." In M. D. Dunnette (Ed.), *Handbook of Industrial and Organizational Psychology.* Chicago: Rand McNally, 1976, Pp. 937–993.

Bigelow, R. C. "Changing Classroom Interaction Through Organization Development." In R. A. Schmuck & M. B. Miles (Eds.), *Organization Development in Schools.* Palo Alto, Calif.: National Press Books, 1971. Pp. 71–85.

Blake, R. R., Mouton, J. S., Barnes, L. S., & Greiner, L. E. "Breakthrough in Organization Development. *Harvard Business Review,* 1964, 42 (6), 133–138.

Bragg, J. E., & Andrews, J. R. "Participative Decision Making: An Experimental Study in a Hospital." *Journal of Applied Behavioral Science,* 1973, 9, 727–735.

Brown, L. D., Aram, J. D., & Bachner, D. J. "Interorganizational Information Sharing: A Successful Intervention that Failed." *Journal of Applied Behavioral Science,* 1974, 10, 533–554.

Campbell, D. T., & Stanley, J. C. *Experimental and Quasi-experimental Designs for Research.* Chicago: Rand McNally, 1966.

Cook, T. D., & Campbell, D. T. "The Design and Conduct of Quasi-experiments and True Experiments in Field Settings." In M. D. Dunnette (Ed.), *Handbook of Industrial and Organizational Psychol-ogy.* Chicago: Rand McNally, 1976. Pp. 223–326.

Cronbach, L. J. "Coefficient Alpha and the Internal Structure of Tests." *Psychometrika,* 1951, 16, 297–334.

Finn, J. D. *A General Model for Multivariate Analysis.* New York: Holt, Rinehart & Winston, 1974.

Fosmire, F., Keutzer, C., & Diller, R. "Starting Up a New Senior High School." In R. A. Schmuck, & M. R. Miles (Eds.), *Organization Development in Schools.* Palo Alto, Calif.: National Press Books, 1971. Pp. 87–112.

French, W. L., & Bell, C. H. *Organization Development: Behavioral Science Interventions for Organizations Improvement.* (2nd. ed.). Englewood Cliffs, N.J.: Prentice-Hall, 1978.

French, W. L., Bell, C. H., & Zawacki, R. A. *Organization Development: Theory, Practice, and Research.* Dallas: Business Publications, Inc., 1978.

Friedlander, F. "Performance and Interactional Dimensions of Organizational Work Groups." *Journal of Applied Psychology,* 1966, 50, 257–265.

Friedlander, F. "The Impact of Organizational Training Laboratories Upon the Effectiveness and Interaction of Ongoing Work Groups." *Personnel Psychology,* 1967, 20, 289–307.

Friedlander, F., & Brown, L. D. "Organization Development." In M. R. Rosenzweig, & L. W. Porter (Eds.), *Annual Review of Psychology,* 1974, 25, 313–341.

Gibb, J. R. "TORI Group Self-diagnosis Scale." In J. E. Jones & J. W. Pfeiffer (Eds.). *The 1977 Annual Handbook for Group Facilitators.* La Jolla, Calif.: University Associates, 1977. Pp. 75–81.

Golembiewski, R. T. *Renewing Organizations: The Laboratory Approach to Planned Change.* Itasca, Ill.: Peacock, 1972.

Hackman, J. R., & Oldham, G. R. *The Job Diagnostic Survey: An Instrument for the Diagnosis of Jobs and the Evaluation* of *Job Redesign Projects*. Technical Report No. 4, Department of Administrative Sciences, Yale University, 1974.

Hand, H. H., Estafen, B. D., & Sims, H. P. "How Effective is Data Survey and Feedback as a Technique of Organization Development? An Experiment." *Journal of Applied Behavioral Science*, 1975, *11*, 333–347.

Hautaluoma, J. E., & Gavin, J. F. "Effects of Organizational Diagnosis and Intervention on Blue-collar 'Blues.' " *Journal of Applied Behavioral Science*, 1975, *11*, 475–496.

Kimberly, J. R., & Nielsen, W. R. "Organization Development and Change in Organizational Performance." *Administrative Science Quarterly*, 1975, *20*, 191–206.

King, D. C., Sherwood, J. J., & Manning, M. R. *OD's Research Base: How to Expand and Utilize it*. Paper presented at the OD 78 Conference of Current Theory, Practice, and Research. San Francisco, March 16–17, 1978.

Likert, R. *The Human Organization*. New York: McGraw-Hill, 1967.

Luke, R. A., Block, P., Davey, J. M., & Averch, V. R. "A Structural Approach to Organizational Change." *Journal of Applied Behavioral Science*, 1973, *9*, 611–635.

Marrow, A. J., Bowers, D. G., & Seashore, S. E. *Management by Participation*. New York: Harper & Row, 1967.

Nadler, D. A., & Pecorella, P. A. "Differential Effects of Multiple Interventions in an Organization." *Journal of Applied Behavioral Science*, 1975, *11*, 348–366.

Nunnally, J. C. *Psychometric Theory* (2nd ed.). New York: McGraw-Hill, 1978.

Schmuck, R. A., Murray, D., Smith, M. A., Schwartz, M., & Runkel, M. *Consultation for Innovative Schools: OD for Multiunit Structure*. Eugene, Ore.: Center for Educational Policy and Management, 1975.

Schmuck, R. A., & Runkel, P. J. *Handbook of Organization Development in Schools*. Center for the Advanced Study of Educational Administration, University of Oregon, 1972.

Schmuck, R. A., Runkel, P. J., & Langmeyer, D. "Improving Organizational Problem Solving in a School Faculty." *Journal of Applied Behavioral Science*, 1969, *5*, 455–482.

Spector, P. E. "What To Do with Significant Multivariate Effects in Multivariate Analyses of Variance." *Journal of Applied Psychology*, 1977, *62*, 158–163.

Taylor, J., & Bowers, D. *Survey of Organizations*. Ann Arbor: Institute for Social Research, University of Michigan, 1972.

Woodman, R. W. *Effects of Team Development Intervention: A Field Experiment*. Unpublished doctoral dissertation, Purdue University, 1978.

Woodman, R. W., & Sherwood, J. J. "A Comprehensive Look at Job Design." *Personnel Journal*, 1977, *56*, 384–390, 418.

Woodman, R. W., & Sherwood, J. J. "The Role of Team Development in Organizational Effectiveness. A Critical Review." *Psychological Bulletin*, 1980, *88*, 166–186.

Work Attitudes as Predictors of Attendance on a Specific Day[1]

Frank J. Smith

Past reviews of literature dealing with the relationship between job satisfaction and such work-related behavior as job performance, turnover, and absenteeism have noted the extreme variation in findings, but have tended to conclude that job satisfaction and job withdrawal behavior are inversely related, while performance has a low and inconsistent relationship to satisfaction (Brayfield & Crockett, 1955; Herzberg, Mausner, Peterson, & Capwell, 1957; Katzell, 1957; Porter & Steers, 1973).

The seemingly inconsistent nature of many of the results has been treated differently by different investigators. The most frequent approach involves the attempt to identify variables that might moderate the performance satisfaction relationship and help explain the previous findings. Examples can be seen in review by Schwab and Cummings (1970). Still others have taken a view that performance and job withdrawal behavior are different phenomena and that the job satisfaction/job performance relationship is quite different than that between job satisfaction and job withdrawal. Lawler and Porter (1967), for example, argue that while job

satisfaction has the power to influence both absenteeism and turnover, it can best be seen as being caused by job performance rather than being the cause of it.

Herman (1973), on the other hand, contends that work attitudes can be seen as predictive of either type of work-related behavior as long as such behavior is under the control of individual workers. She also points out that many of the studies relating satisfaction and performance were carried out under situational constraints that may have so limited performance variance as to insure low correlational results.

The present study is in line with Herman's (1973) reasoning, though it deals with only one aspect of the discussion, namely, attendance (the converse of absenteeism). While this work-related behavior is usually the result of an individual's decision that is often under his or her control, it should be noted that even in this instance a number of conditions exist that often confound the actual relationship of attendance to work-related attitudes. For example, the availability of alternatives to work attendance, the financial or social penalties asso-

[1] The author would like to thank Charles L. Hulin for his many helpful suggestions regarding this paper. The author would also like to thank William Ashley, Cheryl Johnson, and Barry Raben for their efforts in collecting much of the data.

Reproduced by permission of the *Journal of Applied Psychology*, 1977, 62, 16–19.

ciated with absenteeism, and simply the effort required in attending work may all influence the attendance decision but may be relatively unrelated to attitudes toward work. Because almost all of the studies reported have been carried out among hourly paid employees, the influence of financial penalty for absenteeism has been present, yet rarely accounted for or even acknowledged. As Porter and Steers (1973) have noted, only in the case of permissive illness pay programs would this penalizing factor be insignificant. It should also be noted that absenteeism over any given period is often relatively slight and is so widely distributed among employees as to be insignificant.

The present study takes advantage of a naturally occurring situation, which is particularly free of some of the confounding conditions mentioned. It also involves behavior requiring considerable effort. While it examines the relationship between attitudes and attendance within narrow time periods, it does so in a situation in which the extent of the behavior within and its variance across the groups studied were of sufficient magnitude to be organizationally significant.

Specifically, the study investigates the relationship between attitudes and attendance on a particular day among groups of managerial personnel, all of whom were located in a single headquarters building of a large merchandising corporation. The observation of attendance occurred on the day following an unexpected and severe snowstorm that greatly hampered the city's transportation system. Because the storm happened to occur shortly after a complete organizational survey of the entire managerial group, it was possible to relate the work attitudes surveyed to attendance.

Since occasional absenteeism by managerial people is not subject to financial penalty and is relatively free of social and

work-group pressure, it can be viewed as being under the general control of the individual. Moreover, attendance following a crippling snowstorm is unique in that the decision to attend is not only under individual control but requires considerable personal effort.

It would be predicted, following Herman (1973), that job satisfaction and job attendance would be positively correlated on the day following the snowstorm but that on any randomly chosen day, the correlation would be low or zero.

METHOD

The attitude measures used were part of a larger organizational survey carried out among all members of the company's headquarters staff. The development of these scales and their validity is described by Smith[2] and additional validity data is presented by Hulin (1966), Dunham (1975), and Dunham and Smith (1977). Multiple-response items that were designed to meet the Guttman criteria and that assess attitudes toward six work-related areas were measured by the following scales: Supervision, Kind of Work, Amount of Work, Career Future and Security, Financial Rewards, and Company Identification.

Sample

The primary sample consisted of 3,010 salaried employees in the company's Chicago headquarters building. Employees performed a mixture of administrative, professional, and technical functions. All job levels below that of the president were involved in the study.

A comparison sample consisted of the 340 salaried members of the company's New

---

[2] Smith, F. J. *Problems and trends in the operational use of employe attitude measurements.* Paper presented at the 70th Annual convention of the American Psychological Association, St. Louis, Missouri, August 1962.

York headquarters office where no storm had occurred. Though the sample is much smaller in number, the job functions and levels included in it are practically identical with those in Chicago.

Procedure

The attitudinal data were collected in November and December of 1974. Since the survey was administered anonymously, subjects were identified only in terms of large functionally related groupings. (The Men's Store, for example, consisted of a large group of men and women working in related merchandise departments.) A total of 27 functional groupings in Chicago and 13 in New York were used in this study. The sample sizes within each unit ranged from 59 to 228 in Chicago and from 28 to 48 in New York.

The attendance data were collected by personnel-department representatives who were not aware of the study's design or intent. Since attendance data are not systematically collected for salaried people, a special effort was made to determine the extent of, and the specific reasons for, nonattendance. Moreover, nonattendance was carefully defined to reflect voluntary absence on only the day studied. Thus, subjects who were absent because of out-of-town travel, were on vacation, or were ill prior to the storm were not counted. Group attendance percentages were computed by dividing the number of people attending by those who reasonably could have attended on the days in question. Thus, the measure obtained here was considerably refined.

For each departmental grouping in Chicago and New York, the percentage of attendance, as defined, was computed. The Chicago distribution, the primary research sample, was unimodal and appeared free of noticeable skew. The average score for each department grouping on each of the six attitude scales was also computed, and Pearson product-moment correlation coefficients

were then computed between these two sets of data.

The satisfaction and attendance data collected on the New York sample were for comparison purposes only. They allow for a comparison prediction of attendance on what amounts to a random day. Since no storms had occurred in New York on the day studied, no greater effort was required in attending work than on any other day and pressures to attend represented the situation normally encountered.

RESULTS

On April 3, 1975, the day after the storm, attendance ranged from 97% to 39% in Chicago ($mdn = 70\%$). In New York, where no storm occurred, attendance was much higher, ranging from 100% to 89% ($mdn = 96\%$).

Table 1 presents the correlational data for both locations. As can be seen, the storm-related attendance in Chicago is significantly correlated with all six attitude measures and, in the case of three scales, is highly significant. It should be noted, however, that only the extreme differences among these correlations are significant. Thus, the correlation between attendance and the Career Future

TABLE 1

Correlations Between Job-Satisfaction Levels and Attendance Levels on Individual Days for the Chicago and New York Groups

Scale	Chicago[a] (n = 27)	New York[b] (n = 13)
Supervision	.54**	.12
Amount of Work	.36*	.01
Kind of Work	.37*	.06
Financial Rewards	.46**	.11
Career Future	.60**	.14
Company Identification	.42*	.02

* $p < .05$, one-tailed test.
** $p < .01$, one-tailed test.
[a] Group following storm, April 1975.
[b] Group, April 1975.

scale was significantly higher than was that between attendance and either the Kind of Work or the Amount of Work scale, $t(24) = 2.02$, $p < .05$ (one-tailed); $t(24) = 1.73$, $p < .05$ (one-tailed).

While the comparison analysis in the New York sample is limited by the small sample (13 department groupings) and the extreme restriction in range of the attendance rates, the small variance in attendance does represent a typical attendance pattern for managers in these functional units. None of the correlations is significant. There appears to be no relationship, on a specific day, between attitudes and attendance.

DISCUSSION

While the situation studied was fortuitous in nature, it did present an opportunity to study behavior that was free of several situational constraints. Within the limitations of the setting, it does appear that job-related attitudes measures can predict job behavior when that behavior is substantially under the control of the employee. This finding is consistent with the point of view expressed by Herman (1973).

The present results also suggest that the behavior predicted should involve considerable effort and should be of sufficient magnitude to be worthy of study. Thus, in the present study, the extent of variation in attendance behavior (ranging from 39% to 97%) and the effort it involved were of considerable magnitude for the Chicago group. For the New York group, these conditions were lacking, and the attempt to predict attendance in such a case seems almost frivolous but was necessary to provide a baseline.

The findings also indicated that attitudes toward certain work aspects are significantly more highly correlated with attendance than others. This emphasizes the importance of looking at these scales separately. When viewed this way, they provide the basis for some insight into the possible specific precursors of absenteeism.

While the present study is of a one-shot nature with only a modest chance of realistic replication, it does point to the value of taking advantage of naturally occurring events that offer a glimpse of behavior in which several obscuring influences have been removed, a condition ordinarily achieved only in laboratory settings.

REFERENCES

Brayfield, A. H., & Crockett, W. H. "Employee Attitudes and Employee Performance." *Psychological Bulletin*, 1955, 52, 396–424.

Dunham, R. B. *Affective Responses to Task Characteristics: The Role of Organizational Function.* Unpublished doctoral dissertation. University of Illinois, 1975.

Dunham, R. B., & Smith, F. J. "Validation of the Index of Organizational Reactions with the Job Descriptive Index, the Minnesota Satisfaction Questionnaire, and Faces Scales." *Academy of Management Journal*, 1977, 20, 420–432.

Herman, J. B. "Are Situational Contingencies Limiting Job Attitude Job Performance Relationships?" *Organizational Behavior and Human Performance*, 1973, 10, 208–224.

Herzberg, F., Mausner, B., Peterson, R. O., & Capwell, D. F. *Job Attitudes: Review of Research and Opinion.* Pittsburgh, Pa.: Psychological Service of Pittsburgh, 1957.

Hulin, C. L. "The Effects of Community Characteristics on Measures of Job Satisfaction." *Journal of Applied Psychology*, 1966, 50, 185–192.

Katzell, R. A. "Industrial Psychology." *Annual Review of Psychology,* 1957, *8,* 237–268.

Lawler, E. E., III, & Porter, L. W. "The Effect of Performance on Job Satisfaction." *Industrial Relations,* 1967, *7,* 20–28.

Porter, L. W., & Steers, R. M. "Organizational, Work, and Personal Factors in Employee Turnover and Absenteeism." *Psychological Bulletin,* 1973, *80,* 151–176.

Schwab, D. P., & Cummings, L. L. "Theories of Performance and Satisfaction: A Review." *Industrial Relations,* 1970, *9,* 408–430.

Received April 7, 1976

Cognitions of Work Unit Structure[1]

Richard Blackburn
Larry L. Cummings

The impetus for this study of cognitions of structural dimensionality developed from two concerns. The first was the authors' general concern with the apparent domination in organizational research of a perspective that has been variously labeled "rational" (Benson, 1977), "social factist" (Pondy & Boje, 1976) and "functionalist" (Morgan, 1980). This research paradigm has led to the treatment of organizational characteristics (i.e., structure, technology, etc.) as objective realities "capable of being measured, described, and included as elements in causal explanations" (Pondy & Boje, 1976, p. 20). Such an approach has provided a wealth of organizational knowledge. It will be argued shortly, however, that an alternative perspective exists that can provide equally valuable information.

The second concern was with the theoretical and empirical underpinnings of the early work on the dimensionality of structure. This concern evolved from perceptions of the premature acceptance by many organizational analysts of a limited but operationalized set of structural dimensions for use in empirical research. Also, it seemed apparent

that some were willing to suggest that closure could now be achieved concerning the probable domain of structural dimensionality (Child, 1974; Hall, 1978; Van de Ven, 1976).

The purpose of the research reported here is to consider an alternative and complementary research perspective in the analysis of organizations and to present a methodology designed in the spirit of the alternative paradigm. The intent is to reexamine the question of structural dimensionality from a cognitive rather than a deterministic perspective.

AN ALTERNATIVE APPROACH

Much of the research conducted in the organizational sciences has been dominated by what Pondy and Boje (1976) contend is a "social factist" paradigm (Ritzer, 1975). This perspective encourages researchers to view participants as "metering devices" capable only of responding to interviews or questionnaires (Pondy & Boje, 1976, p. 12). Constructs so measured are assumed comprehensible and relevant to the participant with the researcher simply assessing partici-

[1] This research is based on the first author's dissertation conducted at the University of Wisconsin-Madison (1980). The authors would like to thank Randall B. Dunham, Kim Cameron, M. Susan Taylor, and Ron Serlin for their helpful comments during the preparation of this manuscript. Financial support for conducting this research was provided by the Richard D. Irwin Foundation, the Graduate School at the University of Wisconsin-Madison, and the School of Business Administration at the University of North Carolina at Chapel Hill.

Reproduced by permission of the *Academy of Management Journal*, 1982, 25, 836–854.

pant perceptions of the extent to which a construct exists in the work setting.

The dominance of this perspective is clearly visible in the major investigations of structural dimensionality (Child, 1972; Holdaway, Newberry, Hickson & Heron, 1975; Pugh, Hickson, Hinings, & Turner, 1968; Reimann, 1973). In each of these studies individuals responded to a set of a priori defined structural variables. These responses then were factor analyzed to reveal a number of "structural dimensions."

The four studies identified above have been subject to criticism on both empirical and conceptual grounds. For instance, McKelvey (1975) criticized the work of Pugh et al. (1968) (and by inference the attempted replications) for inappropriate sampling procedures, inadequate sample sizes given the nature of the multivariate statistical procedures employed, and an incomplete discussion of the criteria used in the selection and interpretation of the component solutions. Blackburn (1982) identifies a serious conceptual problem with these studies. The problem concerns Pugh et al.'s initial imposition of conceptual constraints on the potential outcomes of the multivariate analyses. By limiting the "primary" structure dimensions to those of an essentially Weberian model, the researchers limited the possible dimensional outcome. James and Jones (1976) and Schwab (1980) caution that such an approach immediately constrains the number and type of dimensions measured, as well as the underlying components that could result from any data reduction technique.

Using the research perspective of the social factist and its heavy reliance on researcher specified measures, some underlying structural dimensions may remain unidentified because they were not elements of the original research framework. As Karmel and Egan argue,

> It is not enough to hypothesize the existence of certain dimensions, . . . and then build instruments which depend on the validity of

the initial assumptions about dimensionality (1976, p. 323).

Recently a number of authors have suggested that what is needed in the organizational sciences in general (and, it could be added, in structure research in particular) is an alternative perspective to the investigation of organizational phenomena (Morgan, 1980; Pondy & Mitroff, 1979). One alternative is what Ritzer (1975) calls the "social definitionist" perspective. Rather than focusing on objective facts gathered from organizational "metering devices," the definitionist focuses on participants' definitions of the work environment as the research interest. From a social definitionist perspective, organizational members become actively involved in defining, describing, and/or enacting their work environment. Pondy and Boje (1976) apply Ritzer's paradigmatic conceptualization to organizational theory by advocating the elevation of the "definitionist" paradigm to a position of *parity* with the factist perspective.

What follows, then, is a discussion of an empirical procedure designed to satisfy the critics of past dimensional research *and* the advocates of greater participant involvement in construct definition. It should be noted that what is reported may not necessarily be a better approach to dimensionalizing structure. It is, however, an alternative and a complementary approach by which fresh insights into this phenomenon can be obtained. The research is couched in more rigorous empirical procedures than might appeal to the classic ethnomethodologist. Nevertheless, it is believed to be sufficiently nonpositivistic to satisfy the definitionist desire to allow participants to determine "the meaning in a situation to those involved in it, rather than imposing, a priori, the researcher's meaning" (Pondy & Boje, 1976, p. 10).

Determination of an individual's meaning about structure could be made in two ways. One could adopt a strict definitionist perspective and simply *ask* individuals to define those characteristics they use to describe the structures of particular entities. However, this process assumes (1) that participants are able to recall and verbalize those characteristics; (2) that clarifications of responses would not result in the "priming" of respondents by the researcher; and (3) that analysis and interpretation of results would not be unduly contaminated by researcher biases.

Alternatively, one could use a modified procedure designed in the spirit of the social definitionist perspective but more empirically rigorous than the typical phenomenological approach. This methodology is multidimensional scaling (MDS). This technique seems eminently appropriate if one is willing to assume that the structures of organizations or work units consist of a set of possible structural attributes. It also must be assumed that for any individual in an organization only a limited number of these attributes will be salient when the individual considers the structure of an organization or work unit. That is, only certain of these attributes will influence an individual's perceptions of structure. These attributes could be thought of as cognitive dimensions of structure.

The use of MDS in the organizational sciences has been limited. Three recent studies have investigated the dimensions of perceived *social* structure within a research laboratory (Jones & Young, 1972), a business school (Salancik, Calder, Rowland, Leblebici, & Conway, 1975), and a psychology department (Kaman, Shikiar, & Hautaluoma, 1979). In each of these studies, measures of association between various entities were analyzed and physical representations (often called "maps" or "solutions") were generated such that distances between entities in any solution were monotonically related to the measures of association used as input data. These solutions were interpreted to be the organizational social structure as perceived by participants. The dimensions underlying a particular representation can be viewed as cognitive dimensions of the social structure.

The present research provides a work unit analogue to organizational social structure by arraying work units (rather than individuals) in a perceptual space common to respondents. Such a space will be defined by those dimensions used by participants to describe or define work unit structure. Hence, these dimensions become the cognitive dimensions of work unit structure.

MDS provides a means by which these salient dimensions can be recovered and identified. In doing so, MDS allows the attributes of structure to emerge via the scaling process as opposed to being specified a priori by the researcher (Guzzo, 1979). Thus, it is extremely useful for identifying the dimensionality of a construct in a manner relatively free of researcher bias.

METHOD

Sample

The sample was drawn from a population of 260 full time exempt and nonexempt employees of a production/distribution facility in a major metropolitan area of the upper-Midwest. Impending contract negotiations and operational considerations prevented union employees and members of one functional department ($N=40$) from participating. Of the 220 employees available, 180 (82 percent) provided usable survey results. The sample included employees from across hierarchical levels, functional units, and operating shifts. A brief summary of some key demographic variables is presented in Table 1.

Procedure

All participants completed a 2-part survey administered by the first author to groups of 5 to 20 employees on company time. Each

TABLE 1
Sample Demographics

Demographic Variable	Respondent Sample
Age—modal range	35–39 years
Sex	61% male, 39% female
Average educational level	Completed 2 years post-secondary education
Tenure with the firm—modal range	9–12 years
Salary classification	42% exempt, 58% non-exempt

session lasted about 90 minutes. Employees were guaranteed both anonymity and confidentiality of their responses.

Part 1 of the survey contained the MDS task. To provide the required input, 17 work units were selected for evaluation. Two criteria were used in selecting these units: (1) the desire to include units from across all functional areas and (2) the desire to insure participant familiarity with most of the units selected. Those units chosen represented about 75 percent of all identifiable work units in the organization, and they ranged in size from 5 to 150 employees. The names used in the data collection were those that a group of key organizational members indicated would be the titles most likely used by employees when discussing the work units.

Work units, rather than organizations, were chosen for research purposes to increase the probability of participant familiarity with the entities in the MDS task. As Pierce, Dunham, and Blackburn (1979) note, there is considerable conceptual and empirical evidence to suggest that work units, like organizations, have a multidimensional structure that can range from mechanistic to organic.

On a 9-point rating scale (1—very similar, to 9—very dissimilar), participants responded to the following instructions: "For each pair, please circle the number which best indicates the extent to which you feel each of the units in the pair is similar or dissimilar to the other on the basis of the way you think the units are *structured.*"

During actual data collection one-half of the sample was randomly assigned to a condition in which the MDS instructions merely requested comparisons based on "unit structure." Respondents were free to define and dimensionalize structure in any manner deemed appropriate. The remaining half of the respondents were provided with a series of definitions of structure on which to base their comparisons. These definitions represented a cross-section of definitions that have appeared in recent articles and textbooks. A number of definitions were included in an attempt to provide a broad and, it was hoped, unbiased perspective of the construct. It is argued that the definitions neither defined nor delimited the dimensions that individuals could use to make their comparisons. Rather, the definitions served to focus the respondent's thinking and allow the salient structural dimensions to evolve based on a concept that might be present in the mind of the respondent but whose dimensions cannot be adequately verbalized. Whether or not the two conditions would provide different results was treated as an empirical question. Comparative analysis of the input data indicated strong similarity between the two conditions. Thus data were combined into a single sample for all MDS analyses.

Respondents made 144 paired comparisons. This number reflects all possible pairs of 17 units (136) *plus* 8 comparisons presented in reverse order of the initial presentation (i.e., Unit A vs. Unit B *and* Unit B vs. Unit A). These reversed pairs were included to test the stability of responses within the measurement instrument. Comparisons were presented randomly on each survey page, and pages were randomly ordered within each questionnaire.

Respondents also were asked to rate their relative familiarity with each unit compared (1—very unfamiliar, to 7—very familiar) and their confidence in being able to make the comparisons on the basis of unit structure (1—no confidence, to 7—very confident). In the last section of part 1 respondents were given the opportunity to state in their own words the unit characteristics that they had used in making the paired comparisons. To prevent contamination across parts of the survey, part 1 was collected prior to the distribution of part 2.

The open-ended question concluding part 1 and two sections of part 2 were specifically included to provide information for later use in the interpretation of the dimensions revealed in the MDS analysis. The extent to which traditional structural dimensions might accurately represent characteristics used by individuals in describing work unit structures was of interest. Thus, specific opportunity was provided respondents to indicate the relative importance of a set of traditional characteristics in making the comparisons. These characteristics included elements previously described in the literature as dimensions of structure. Respondents used a 7-point scale (1—very unimportant, to 7—very important) to rate the importance of the number of (1) employees in a unit (size); (2) different jobs in a unit (complexity); (3) standard operating procedures in a unit (standardization); (4) *written* rules, policies, or procedures in a unit (formalization); (5) decisions made outside of a unit (centralization); and (6) supervisors in a unit.

Respondents used the same scale to rate the importance of (1) unit performance; (2) satisfaction/climate within a unit; and (3) the nature of the unit's product/service in the comparison process. Importance of these three attributes would suggest the extent to which individuals dimensionalized structure with characteristics not traditionally thought of as structural. In particular, the unit satisfaction and climate scales were included for two reasons. First, in the formative stages of this research it was suggested that perceptions of unit satisfaction/climate would dom-

inate any cognitive map of structure that was identified. It was considered appropriate to examine this contention empirically. Second, there is evidence in the research on cognitions of social structures among individuals that an evaluative dimension is usually present (Kim & Rosenberg, 1980). It was of particular interest to examine whether similar results would occur in a work unit analogue to this individual research. For example, would units described as extremely formalized be evaluated in a positive/negative manner?

In the second section of part 2, employees were asked to describe their perceptions of each of the 17 work units using the same list of a priori characteristics. These descriptions were collected using bipolar adjective scales (i.e., large-small, many-few different jobs, etc.). It should be emphasized that these ratings were made after the comparison judgments. The actual influence of the characteristics on a cognitive model of structure can be judged only by examining the MDS results.

Measures of unit structural characteristics also were obtained from unit supervisors. This information was collected using an adaptation of the Pugh et al. (1968) instrument and included measures of standardization, specialization, formalization, centralization, complexity, and stratification.

Four weeks after the initial data collection, a retest of both employees and supervisors was conducted. Five randomly selected supervisors again completed the supervisor questionnaire, and a random sample of 30 employees who had participated in the first survey completed a shortened version. The only difference between the two employee surveys was a reduction in the number of paired comparisons. This reduction was achieved by randomly choosing 9 of the original 17 units for inclusion in the retest. Included were 40 paired comparisons, all possible pairs (36) plus 4 comparisons in reversed order.

ANALYSES

MDS Solutions

The KYST multidimensional scaling program was used in this research. Described as a fairly robust, nonmetric, data reduction algorithm (Nunnally, 1978), KYST utilizes as input data the *mean* similarity ratings (averaged over all participants) for each paired comparison. The data are used to construct a spatial representation of the perceived similarity of the units compared. Units placed close together or far apart in an array were perceived as very similar or very dissimilar.

KYST uses an iterative procedure to array the units in various dimensional spaces until the "best" spatial representation of the original similarity data is achieved. The goodness-of-fit between the graphical solution and the original mean comparison ratings is represented by an index known as "stress." A stress value is calculated for each iteration in a particular set of dimensions. Iterations cease when the incremental stress improvement is sufficiently small. The result of this analysis is a physical representation of the map, within which participants place work units on the basis of their cognitions of work unit structure.

The location of work units along the dimension underlying an MDS solution can be compared to the participant ratings of unit structures along the unit characteristics presented in part 2 of the survey. This information allows for the assessment of congruence, if any, between the dimensions used by participants to define work unit structures and those dimensions that comprise the traditional domain of the construct.

Dimension Identification/Interpretation

The first of two major analytical tasks is the identification of the *number* of dimensions in the solution that stress values indicate "best" represents the input data. A perfect fit of "n" units could be achieved in $n - 1$ dimensions, with a stress value of zero. However, the dimensions likely would be difficult to interpret and would not represent a parsimonious description of the domain of structure. Thus, the goal of the MDS identification process is to recover that set of dimensions for which (1) stress values indicate good dimensional resolution; (2) dimension interpretation is straightforward; and (3) no clearer interpretation occurs in higher dimensional solutions (Karmel & Egan, 1976).

The second and more complex of the MDS tasks is the interpretation of the identified dimensional solution. To provide a complete interpretation of the underlying map dimensions, a variety of interpretive procedures was employed. The rationale behind the use of multiple procedures was the desire to identify fully the variable(s) that has (have) a systematic relationship with the positions of the work units along the various dimensions in the MDS configuration.

As "the easiest and most commonly used interpretive procedure" (Kruskal & Wish, 1978, p. 36), multiple regression was initially used to evaluate which of the rated structural characteristics, if any, might be appropriate interpretations of the cognitive structure dimensions produced by the MDS analysis. The regression procedure treats each of the various unit characteristics as "dependent variables" and the configuration coordinates for each unit as the "independent variables."

For each of the 17 units, mean ratings on each of the unit characteristics were regressed over the solution coordinates for that unit. The result is a weighted combination of the coordinates that best "explains" a particular characteristic. Significant ($p < .05$) regression coefficients within significant ($p < .05$) regression equations suggest that the dependent variable in an equation may be an appropriate interpretation for the dimension with the significant coefficients.

Regression analyses are preferred over

simple correlational procedures. Although the latter represent the strength of association between sets of variables, the former provide the direction of the least squares line that maximizes the multiple correlation. This directionality adds interpretive information lacking in the correlational approach.

In addition to the regression analyses, two qualitative procedures were used in the interpretive process. These included analyses of the importance ratings and content analysis of responses to the open-ended question seeking personal bases of comparisons.

RESULTS

Quality of Input Data

A number of procedures were used to assure that input data were of sufficient quality to warrant further analyses. Based on a 7-point scale (1—very unfamiliar, to 7—very familiar), mean familiarity scores for each unit ranged from 3.70 to 4.37 (x=4.06; SD=2.03). Of the sample, 70 percent had average familiarity scores of 3.5 or greater, indicating that respondents were moderately familiar with the units compared. When respondents were divided into three subsamples ($n\cong60$ each), by definition reflecting low, medium, and high familiarity with the units compared, analyses for each sample indicated that increased familiarity with the units results in slightly better resolution of the input data by the MDS procedure. However, comparative analyses of the three maps indicated that they are virtually identical. Although some members of the organization have been labeled as having low familiarity with the units compared, the level evidently was sufficient to allow meaningful comparisons between the many units.

Respondents also indicated their confidence in being able to make the comparative judgments on the basis of unit structure on a bipolar scale (1—not at all confident, to 7—very confident). The average confidence rating was 4.04 (SD=2.01). Respondents reported moderate levels of confidence in their ability to make comparisons on the basis of unit structure.

These moderate values need not cause concern unless the MDS solution suggests that the input data were randomly generated by respondents. It is assumed that individual perceptions of necessity are based on incomplete information and that constructs other than structure may influence employee perceptions of that construct.

Stability of comparative judgments within the MDS task was evaluated by examining the ratings of the eight reversed pairs. Mean differences between the pairs presented in both directions were not significant (p =.05), and the correlation between the two sets of ratings was .85 (p =.05). These results suggest excellent stability in the comparison judgments despite the rather tedious nature of the task.

Stability of judgments over the 4-week period between test and retest indicated good agreement between the 36 comparisons at two points in time. Mean differences ranged from .01 to 1.11, with none significantly different (p =.05). The Pearson product-moment correlation between these two sets of mean comparative judgments was .81 (p =.05).

The Appropriate MDS Solution

Four different MDS solutions were generated for preliminary examination. These arrays were constructed in solution spaces of from two to five dimensions. Each of the four MDS solutions yielded stress values indicating that the configuration had been developed on the basis of nonrandom data. Apparently the employees in this organization utilized some systematic cognitive map of work unit structures when making comparative judgments. Relative stress values did not indicate a preferred solution, and choosing the solution for interpretation involved a trade-off between the desire for solution parsimony and dimensional interpretability.

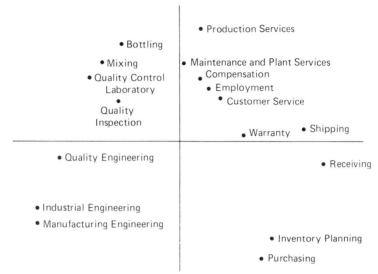

Figure 1. MDS Configuration: Dimension 3 (X-Axis) Versus Dimension 4 (Y-Axis)

Two considerations led to the decision to interpret the five dimension solution. First, previous literature had suggested that the domain of structural dimensions may be large. James and Jones (1976) concluded that there were at least seven dimensions in the domain. Champion (1975) suggested that eight dimensions should be included, and Montanari (1978) proposed at least 16 possible structural dimensions. Given the authors' wish to maximize information gained about possible cognitive dimensions of structure, the 5-dimension solution seemed the likely candidate for interpretation.

A second consideration involved the extent to which the lower dimension solutions were contained in the 5-dimension outcome. Comparative analysis indicated that as the dimensionality of the solution space increases, dimensions from the previous solutions are maintained and new orthogonal dimensions are generated. Choosing the 5-dimensional solution for interpretation provides all of the information present in the other solutions plus one additional dimension.

Space limitations preclude the presentation of the 10 2-dimensional plots that arise from a 5-dimension solution. For illustrative purposes, however, a plot of Dimension 3 by Dimension 4 is presented in Figure 1. The rationale for selecting these particular dimensions will become apparent.

Despite the selection of the 5-dimension solution for interpretation, it should be noted that no pretense is made that this solution contains all of the underlying dimensions of structure. Other dimensions may exist but may have gone undetected because of lack of unit variation along a particular dimension or the inability of the methodology to recover additional dimensions.

Interpretation of Dimensions

As indicated above, ratings of unit characteristics were collected from employees and unit supervisors. Archival information also was collected on unit size (FTE), average supervisory span of control, number of unit levels, and unit complexity (number of different job titles). Perceptions of unit satisfaction and unit climate also were used in the analyses. All of these characteristics were re-

TABLE 2
Multiple Regression Results: Unit Characteristics and MDS Dimension Coordinates

Unit Characteristics	Dimension Coefficients					R	Shrinkage R
	1	2	3	4	5		
Size (P[a])	.572[b]					.79*	.70
Centralization (P)	−.755				.352	.85*	.80
Complexity (P)	−.484	.402				.80*	.71
Climate (P)	−.608	.516				.81*	.73
Satisfaction (P)	−.529	.492				.80*	.72
Size (A[c])					.642	.81*	.73

[a] P = Perceptual measures.
[b] Dimension coefficients are beta weights, and only weights significant at $p < .05$ are reported.
[c] A = Archival measure.
* $p < .05$

gressed over the appropriate solution coordinates. Table 2 contains a summary of the results of this procedure. The table presents only those unit characteristics that when regressed over the MDS configuration yielded significant multiple correlations *and* significant standardized regression coefficients.

Two points must be made. First, although all of the different unit characteristics were analyzed by the regression technique, only those reported in Table 2 satisfied the significance criteria. Second, none of the unit characteristics satisfied the criteria for Dimensions 3 and 4.

Given the relatively small number of observations (17) for a series of regression equations with 5 independent variables, the table also contains values for Nunnally's (1978) "shrinkage factor *R*." Examination of the results in the table suggests that three of the five solution dimensions can be interpreted by the regression procedure.

DIMENSION 1. The first dimension represents a general bureaucratic/affective dimension including such characteristics as size (reported by the supervisor), and employee perceptions of centralization, complexity, satisfaction, and climate.

DIMENSION 2. The affective characteristics appear by themselves as the primary elements of the second dimension. Apparently, to individuals in the organization, "structure" generates a cognitive map that includes an affective component.

DIMENSION 5. The objective size of the unit taken from company records appears to dominate at least one dimension along which individuals define the structure of work units. In previous structure literature, size has been classified as both a contextual and a structural variable. For this sample of employees the actual size of the unit does provide a unique dimension underlying the cognitive map of the work unit structure.

Although three of the five dimensions were initially interpreted by the regression procedure, these results suggest that none of the unit characteristics would be appropriate interpretations of the third and fourth dimensions in the MDS solution. To interpret the underlying dimensions as completely as possible, two qualitative procedures were employed to interpret the third and fourth dimensions. These procedures may also provide confirmatory evidence for the regression interpretations of the first, second, and fifth dimensions.

The first of the qualitative procedures required an examination of the *relative importance* ratings assigned by respondents to those unit characteristics used in the regression analyses. Table 3 presents the rank-ordering of these characteristics based on mean importance ratings averaged over all

TABLE 3

Rank-Order Importance of a Priori Structural, Affective, and Performance Characteristics in MDS Paired Comparisons

Unit Characteristics	Mean Importance Rating	% of Respondents Indicating Medium to High Importance
Unit's product/service	5.56	89.8
Performance level	4.67	73.4
Standardization	4.01	62.9
Number of levels	3.83	58.2
Centralization	3.81	59.3
Complexity	3.78	57.1
Satisfaction in unit	3.63	49.2
Formalization	3.60	50.8
Number of supervisors	3.34	47.5
Size of units	3.23	45.2

respondents. Also included in the table is the percentage of respondents who considered a particular characteristic of at least moderate importance (responses of four or greater) in making the comparisons.

Nontraditional structural characteristics were ranked of first and second importance by respondents. In particular, type of unit product/service received a mean importance rating of 5.56, with 89.8 percent of the respondents indicating that the characteristic was of medium to high importance in making the structural comparisons. Unit performance level was of medium to high importance to 73.4 percent of the sample, with a mean importance rating of 4.67. Because neither unit product nor unit performance yielded significant regression results, both could be considered as candidates for either of the remaining dimensions. A similar statement could be made about perceived unit standardization.

It should be noted that the characteristics rated may reflect only a subset of the characteristics actually used by respondents. Also, because these characteristics were supplied by the researcher, respondents may have inflated their actual importance in the comparisons. It may have been assumed that such factors would not have been included for rating if they were unimportant.

The MDS task allowed participants to define implicitly their cognitive dimensions of work unit structure. The regression procedure and the relative importance analyses limited the interpretation of these dimensions to the a priori set of unit characteristics. To this point in the research a social definitionist data collection process has been combined with an admittedly social factist approach to dimensional interpretation.

The final interpretive procedure comes closer to what the pure social definitionist would likely consider an acceptable interpretive methodology. By examining individual responses to the open-ended survey question asking for a list of factors used in making the comparative judgments, it may be possible to provide interpretations of Dimensions 3 and 4 as well as to assess informally the viability of those interpretations made earlier.

A content analysis of responses to this question is presented in Table 4. The table presents, in rank-order of frequency of mention, eight general categories of unit characteristics identified by at least 8 percent of the respondents. Also included are sample comments from each category. Both similarities and differences were found among the most frequently listed content areas, the regression results, and the relative importance ratings.

The most apparent difference is the ap-

TABLE 4
Rank-Order of Content Areas Used in Making MDS Paired Comparison
(Including Sample Comments)

Characteristics	% of Respondents Citing Characteristics[a]
Interdependency/interrelationship	27
How they are related	
Does the work move between them?	
Relationship between units	
Unit/product/service/function	25
What they do	
What they make	
Unit personnel	20
Number of union workers	
Union vs. nonprofessionals	
Professionals vs. Nonprofessionals	
Dominant unit technology	20
Type of work done	
How they do the job	
Their production process	
Unit administrative structure	10
Span of control	
Decision-making location	
Line vs. staff	9.5
Unit satisfaction/climate	9
Unit morale or satisfaction	
Managerial style	
Personality of unit	
Size	8

[a] Total percentage exceeds 100 because multiple responses were possible.

pearance of a factor identified as the extent of "interdependence" of a unit with other work units. The identification of unit interrelationships as a possible structural dimension is intriguing. Although unit interaction has not been a frequent member of a priori structural domains, a number of authors have labeled this characteristic as a potential dimension of structure (Indik, 1968; James & Jones, 1976; Sells, 1963).

The categories of unit product/service, unit personnel, and dominant unit technology are closely related to the unit function characteristic previously identified as important to respondents. The acceptability of unit function as a dimension in the cognitive map of structure gains additional support from these results.

The remaining content areas reflect structural characteristics previously identi-fied in the regression procedure. The administrative structure category included such responses as location of decision making, span-of-control, and number and kinds of different jobs. The satisfaction/climate category included such responses as morale, climate, managerial styles, and overall unit attitude. These results provide additional validity evidence for both of the preceding interpretive procedures.

These procedures also suggest the following possible interpretations for Dimensions 3 and 4: unit function, unit interrelationships, unit performance, and unit standardization. The latter two characteristics did not appear as significant interpretations in the regression analyses, nor were they mentioned in response to the open-ended questions. Therefore, they may not be as viable interpretations as are the two former characteristics. Unit function appeared as a possible interpretation in both qualitative procedures, and the presence of unit interrelationships in the content analysis supports the salience of this characteristic to respondents. Figure 1 presents the array of the 17 work units along the third and fourth dimensions of the MDS solution. With some minor discrepancies in particular unit locations, the function and interaction labels seem appropriate dimension interpretations.

DIMENSION 3.   Units vary along the third dimension on the basis of *locus of unit interaction*. Units are arrayed from those interacting within the organization to those interacting with constituencies external to the organization. At one extreme of Dimension 3 are the engineering units with interactions limited to elements of the production process. At the other extreme of the dimension are those units that interact with publics (customers, sales representatives, transportation agencies, etc.) external to the organization.

DIMENSION 4.   Along the fourth dimension the units are ordered on the basis of *unit function*. The basic production units (production services, bottling, mixing, maintenance) are clustered at the top of the dimension, followed by personnel functions (compensation and employment), engineering functions and, finally, acquisition functions.

DISCUSSION

The research presented here was designed from an alternative approach to organizational research. Rather than positing the existence of certain structural dimensions a priori, and then soliciting participant responses on scales measuring those dimensions, the authors recovered the structural dimensions of a cognitive map by which participants define work unit structures. This research assumed that the descriptions individuals make of the structures of work units are related to cognitions of those structures. It was assumed further that these descriptions can be meaningfully organized into some cognitive schema (Calder & Schurr, 1981). Finally, it was assumed that a representation of this cognitive orientation could be recovered and interpreted using a multidimensional scaling procedure. The results reported provide substantial evidence that such assumptions are valid, and that such maps do exist.

Based on similarity ratings of unit structures, as MDS analysis considered the nature of the cognitions of work unit structures within an organization. The results of the analyses suggest that MDS provides a viable method for recovering such cognitions. As such, it provides an empirically rigorous procedure for allowing individuals to define salient aspects of their work environment. Various interpretive procedures indicated that five cognitive dimensions of structure could be labeled: bureaucratic, affective, locus of unit interaction, unit function, and objective size.

As a participant-centered alternative to the traditional structure domains, the results presented here represent an apparent synthesis of much of that earlier work. Rather than identifying independent bureaucratic characteristics, such as centralization and complexity, these traditional dimensions of structure were perceived by participants as collectively representing some general bureaucratic profile of a unit structure. From an individual perspective, the results of this research would appear to support Child's contention that "the bureaucratic concept is still useful for describing *one aspect of structure*" (1974, p. 247, emphasis added).

Two of the other cognitive dimensions previously have been labeled dimensions of structure, though not as frequently as the Weberian characteristics. Locus of unit interaction and unit size appear in structural domains identified by James and Jones (1976). It is of note that size of the work unit appears in a cognitive domain of work unit structure. It more frequently has been considered an element of unit context. Although respondents did not consciously rate size as an important factor in making their paired comparisons, the apparent influence of size (or some covariate of size) was sufficiently marked to suggest its inclusion in the MDS solution.

Unit function and locus of interaction seem to be related to the nature of work unit technology, another well-known contextual variable. Unit function and unit interactions likely will be determined by organizational or work unit technologies. The relationship between technology and structure has long been debated at the organizational level of analysis. Results presented here would suggest that some type of relationship exists at the individual level, such that perceptions of technology influence dimensions along which unit structures are perceived and differentiated. The conceptual distinction that is made between technology and structure at the organizational level is somewhat blurred at the cognitive level.

These results should prompt a continued consideration of Sathe's (1978) suggestions concerning the possible existence of two general structures within organizations and (by inference) within work units. Sathe labels the formal structure designed and imposed by top management as a *design* structure. Because these design structures tend to be rigid and unchanging, a structure emerges to cope with day-to-day operational requirements. This *emergent* structure is sufficiently flexible to meet the varying demands of changing work conditions.

The cognitive domain isolated above contains elements from both design and emergent structures. The bureaucratic and size dimensions appear to reflect elements of Sathe's design structure, and unit function and locus of interaction reflect elements of an emergent structure to the extent that day-to-day activities are facilitated by func-

tion and interaction. From the individual's perspective, Sathe's distinction seems valid, as dimensions from both structures determine the nature of structural cognitions.

The presence of the affective characteristics in two of the map dimensions prompts several comments. First, although a purely affective dimension was recovered, it clearly did not dominate the cognitive map, as had been suggested. Second, the results suggest that one can, indeed, generalize from the findings based on maps of individual social structures to the maps based on work unit structures. Although the second dimension was clearly affective in nature, the results for the first dimension indicate a possible reflection of individual evaluation of the specific bureaucratic characteristics salient to the respondents.

Given these results, it could be argued that respondents knew as much (or more) about perceived affective differences between units as about structural differences. In the absence of knowledge about unit structure, the basis for comparison ratings became perceptions of work unit satisfaction/climate. It also might be argued that affect could be related to some unidentified structural dimension, or that the dimension represents a generalized affective response to a generalized interpretation of structure. Finally, the affective dimension could be the result of the nonstructure variance that individuals perceive between work units. Whatever the rationale, the results strongly support the inclusion of an affective dimension in the cognitive map.

Limitations and Implications

Although the intent of this research was to reduce the a priori imposition of systematic constraints on research outcomes, certain limitations do remain. This work was conducted within a single organization, reducing the generalizability of the results. The limitation of data collection to a single organization may have restricted both possible variance in work unit structure and employee perceptions of those structures.

Research constraints were imposed on the a priori characteristics provided for the judgments of relative importance and unit descriptions. A more comprehensive listing of unit characteristics may have provided different results. However, the validity of the dimensional interpretations is increased to the extent that support for the regression results was provided by the other interpretive procedures.

Given these limitations, the most pressing research needs are those directed at reducing or eliminating these shortcomings. Replications of this research in organizations of different type and context would be appropriate. Beyond replications it seems appropriate to investigate the extent to which the dimensions identified here actually exhaust the domain of possible dimensions.

From an individual perspective, examination could be made of differences in individual cognitive maps as they compare to an aggregate map. Also of possible investigation is the impact, if any, of differing structural cognitions on individual behaviors and attitudes in an organizational setting.

At the organizational level, the cognitive orientation of elite decision makers as input into organizational decision making in general and structural alignment in particular recently has received attention (Anderson & Paine, 1975; Bobbitt & Ford, 1980; Child, 1972; Hage & Dewar, 1973; Montanari, 1978). Sensitivity by top management to differing cognitions of structure within the organization could greatly influence the success of organizational change strategies. An examination of the relative congruence between elite cognitions and cognitions of other organizational participants becomes a matter of research and applied interest.

CONCLUSION

There is little doubt that the debate over the research efficacy of various research paradigms will continue. The present research was undertaken in the belief that such debate can prove beneficial to the organizational sciences. The choice of structural dimensionality as the vehicle of presenting an alternative research approach yielded a conceptualization of the construct distinct from that traditionally presented.

It is contended that differing approaches need not be perceived as competitive. Rather, a complementary perspective must be adopted through which a more complete picture of organizational functioning might be drawn. It is argued that the exploration of organizational questions from a variety of perspectives is a valuable process and useful in the evolution of the science of organizations. Thus,

> The challenge is not to decide upon superior methods. The challenge is to embrace diverse methods that pursue several realities, and to distinguish quality in each (Daft, 1980, p. 633).

REFERENCES

Anderson, C. R., & Paine, F. T. "Managerial Perceptions and Strategic Behavior." *Academy of Management Journal*, 1975, *18*, 811–823.

Benson, J. K. "Innovation and Crisis in Organizational Analysis." *The Sociological Quarterly*, 1977, *18*, 3–16.

Blackburn, R. S. "Dimensions of Structure: A Review and Reappraisal." *Academy of Management Review*, 1982, *1*, 59–66.

Bobbitt, H. R., Jr., & Ford, J. D. "Decisionmaker Choice as a Determinant of Organizational Structure." *Academy of Management Review*, 1980, *5*, 13–23.

Calder, B. J., & Schurr, P. H. "Attitudinal Processes in Organizations." In L. L.

Cummings & B. M. Staw (Eds.), *Research in Organizational Behavior* (Vol. 3). Greenwich, Conn.: JA1 Press, 1981, 283–302.

Champion, D. J. *The Sociology of Organizations.* New York: McGraw-Hill, 1975.

Child, J. "Organizational Structure and Strategies of Control: A Replication of the Aston Study." *Administrative Science Quarterly,* 1972, *17,* 163–176.

Child, J. "Comments on Reimann and Mansfield's 'Bureaucracy.'" *Administrative Science Quarterly,* 1974, *19,* 247–250.

Daft, R. L. The Evolution of Organizational Analysis, 1959–1979. *Administrative Science Quarterly,* 1980, *25,* 623–636.

Guzzo, R. A. "Types of Rewards, Cognitions, and Work Motivation." *Academy of Management Review,* 1979, *4,* 215–224.

Hage, J., & Dewar, R. "Elite Values versus Organizational Structure in Predicting Innovation." *Administrative Science Quarterly,* 1973, *18,* 279–290.

Hall, R. H. *Organizations: Structure and Process.* 2nd ed. Englewood Cliffs, N.J.: Prentice-Hall, 1978.

Holdaway, E. A., Newberry, J. F., Hickson, D. J., & Heron, R. P. "Dimensions of Organizations in Complex Societies: The Educational Sector." *Administrative Science Quarterly,* 1975, *20,* 37–58.

Indik, B. P. "The Scope of the Problem and Some Suggestions Toward a Solution." In B. P. Indik & F. K. Berren (Eds.), *People, Groups and Organizations.* New York: Teachers College Press, 1968, 3–26.

James, L. R., & Jones, A. P. "Organizational Structure: A Review of Structural Dimensions and their Conceptual Relationships with Individual Attitudes and Behavior." *Organizational Behavior and Human Performance,* 1976, *16,* 74–113.

Jones, L. E., & Young, F. W. "Structure of a Social Environment: Longitudinal Individual Scaling of an Intact Group." *Journal of Personality and Social Psychology,* 1972, *24,* 108–121.

Kaman, V., Shikiar, R., & Hautaluoma, J. "Perceived Social Structure, Role, and Communication Patterns in an Organization." *Journal of Vocational Behavior,* 1979, *15,* 265–276.

Karmel, B., & Egan, D. M. "Managerial Performance: A New Look at Underlying Dimensionality." *Organizational Behavior and Human Performance,* 1976, *15,* 322–334.

Kim, M. P., & Rosenberg, S. "Comparison of Two Structural Models of Implicit Personality Theory." *Journal of Personality and Social Psychology,* 1980, *38,* 375–389.

Kruskal, J. B., & Wish, M. *Multidimensional Scaling.* Sage University paper series on quantitative applications in the social sciences, 07-011. Beverly Hills: Sage Publications, 1978.

McKelvey, W. "Guidelines for the Empirical Classification of Organizations." *Administrative Science Quarterly,* 1975, *20,* 509–525.

Montanari, J. R. "Operationalizing Strategic Choice." In J. H. Jackson & C. P. Morgan (Eds.), *Organizational Theory: A Macro Perspective for Management.* Englewood Cliffs, N.J.: Prentice-Hall, Inc., 1978, 286–298.

Morgan, G. Paradigms, Metaphors, and Puzzle Solving in Organization Theory." *Administrative Science Quarterly,* 1980, *25,* 605–622.

Nunnally, J. C. *Psychometric Theory.* 2nd ed. *New York:* McGraw-Hill, 1978.

Pierce, J., Dunham, R. B., & Blackburn, R. "Social Systems Structure, Job Design, and Growth Need Strength: A Test of a Congruency Model." *Academy of Management Journal,* 1979, *22,* 223–240.

Pondy, L. R., & Boje, D. M. "Bringing the Mind Back in: Paradigm Development as a Frontier Problem in Organization Theory." Unpublished paper, Department of Business Administration, University of Illinois, 1976.

Pondy, L. R., & Mitroff, I. I. "Beyond Open System Models of Organization." In B. Staw (Ed.), *Research in Organizational Behavior* (Vol. 1). Greenwich, Conn.: Jal Press, 1979, 3–39.

Pugh, D. S., Hickson, D. J., Hinings, C. R., & Turner, C. "Dimensions of Organizational Structure." *Administrative Science Quarterly*, 1968, *13*, 65–105.

Reimann, B. "On the Dimensions of Bureaucratic Structure." *Administrative Science Quarterly*, 1973, *18*, 462–476.

Ritzer, G. "Sociology: A Multiple Paradigm Science." *The American Sociologist*, 1975, *10*, 156–167.

Salancik, G. R., Calder, B. J., Rowland, K. M., Leblebici, H., & Conway, M. "Leadership as an Outcome of Social Structure and Process: A Multidimensional Analysis." In J. Hunt & L. Larson (Eds.), *Leadership Frontiers*. Kent, Ohio: Kent State University Press, 1975, 81–101.

Sathe, V. J. "Institutional versus Questionnaire Measures of Organizational Structure." *Academy of Management Journal*, 1978, *21*, 227–238.

Schwab, D. "Construct Validity in Organizational Behavior." In B. Staw & L. L. Cummings (Eds.), *Research in Organizational Behavior* (Vol. 2). Greenwich, Conn.: JAI Press, 1980, 3–44.

Sells, J. B. "An Interactionist Looks at the Environment." *American Psychologist*, 1963, *18*, 696–702.

Van de Ven, A. H. "A Framework for Organization Assessment." *Academy of Management Review*, 1976, *1*, 64–78.

Data Aggregation in Organizational Research: The Temporal Dimension[1]

John R. Kimberly

INTRODUCTION

Aggregation is an issue in all forms of social science research where the attributes of individual units of analysis are combined empirically and used to make descriptive statements about or test hypotheses regarding the attributes of collectivities or where individual-level relationships are inferred from data on collectivities. In the analysis of organizations, where the interest may lie at multiple levels—individual, group, organizational, and/or institutional—the issues as usually defined are particularly evident. Tendencies for cross-level inference abound. How valid is it, for example, to define structure in terms of summated individual perceptions? Or to define leadership style in terms of averaged subordinate ratings?

These issues have been recognized and their implications have been discussed in detail by others (e.g. Hannan 1971; Firebaugh 1978). Generally unacknowledged, however, are the kinds of issues that *time* poses for data aggregation in organizational research. These issues, of course, are particularly salient in longitudinal organizational research where the researcher must confront time and its effects directly.

The purpose of this paper is first to dis-cuss briefly the concept of 'organizational time' and then to identify, discuss, and illustrate three aggregation issues with examples drawn from the author's own experiences in designing and executing longitudinal research. An earlier article addressed some general design issues (Kimberly 1976). The article, by contrast, focuses solely on aggregation problems.

DAYS, WEEKS, MONTHS, YEARS, AND ORGANIZATIONS

Clocks and calendars record the passage of time and lend a certain stability and predictability to life. The sun rises and sets, seasons come and go, and years pass, creating a psychological sense of continuity and symmetry in human life. But what about organizational life? Is there an isomorphism between calendar time and organizational time? Should research designs which attempt to capture the dynamics of organizational evolution rely on calendar time as a basis for decisions about sampling, data collection, and analysis? If so, what are the appropriate units—hours, days, weeks, years? Or are there rhythms and cycles in organizational life which require rethinking how time and its passage should

---

[1] Reproduced by permission of *Organization Studies*, 1980, *1*, 367–377.

An earlier version of the article was presented at the American Psychological Association Symposium on Data Aggregation in Organizational Research, Toronto, September, 1978.

be conceptualized? Is it enough, for example, to control for organizational age in calendar time in the comparative analysis of structure or should we think about alternatives?

When researchers move towards longitudinal designs, they are likely at least to become aware of the conceptual problem. Pugh and Hickson (1976:1), for example, observed that "Longitudinal studies struggle to describe change against the calendar, without knowing if the variations are major, or are misleading oscillations within longer cycles of larger trends which cannot be seen." But as yet, there has been little public discussion of the theoretical implications of these observations. By focusing on problems in data aggregation which arise in longitudinal organizational research, it is hoped that this article will begin to stimulate serious discussion on a whole range of theoretical and methodological issues which inevitably arise in this sort of research.

Three aggregation problems will be discussed. The *interval* problem involves the question of how frequently what kind of data on what kind of variables should be collected in organizational research. The *differential period problem* arises when data in a given study are aggregated for quite different time periods. The consequences of this design problem are rarely explored. The *morphogenetic problem* has to do with the fact that organizations and the people in them rarely hold still and generally change at different rates in many directions. Each of these problems is easily overlooked in cross-sectional research. The need to deal with them in an explicit, theoretically meaningful fashion becomes readily apparent, however, when longitudinal research is undertaken.

THE INTERVAL PROBLEM

The difference between longitudinal and cross-sectional research is not unlike the difference between motion picture photography and still photography. In the case of still photography, the photographer captures all of the components of the particular setting which are visible at a moment in time. The photo enables one to describe and perhaps measure the relationships among the components of the setting at that point in time. However, on the basis of that one photo alone, one has no idea about how stable those relationships are or how they have evolved. A motion picture, by contrast, presents a dynamic view of the interrelationships among the components. By watching a motion picture, one can tell how relationships have changed over time and perhaps be in a better position to predict how they will change in the future.

A motion picture, however, is nothing more than a collection of still pictures. One of the critical elements in motion picture photography is what intervals should occur between the still pictures that together create motion. If intervals are too long, the result is a jerky, bumpy, and uneven film. If the intervals are too short, the result is inefficiency. There is an analogous problem in moving from cross-sectional to longitudinal research. How frequently should the researcher intervene to gather data? This question has two parts. First, the nature of the phenomena being observed may help define a strategy. If one is interested in changes in worker attitudes, for example, and one has a theory about attitude change which contains time-contingent propositions, then frequency of intervention may be very clear—say three equally spaced times over the course of a year. However, if one is interested in changes in organizational structure it might be that, depending on one's theoretical perspective, the data collection intervals would be less frequent.

Theory about the organizational phenomena may thus help set some parameters. But other factors intrude as well. If the intervals are too long, critical incidents or critical variability may be missed. The effects of a brief but potent externally or internally induced disruption may be overlooked and mistakenly attributed to measured rather than unmeasured variables. But frequent intervention may be both inefficient and counterproductive. It may be inefficient in the sense that just as much could be learned about the phenomena of interest at lower cost by less frequent data collection. To illustrate with an example from another realm, how frequently should a national census be undertaken? This is a costly enterprise, and one would not want to do it more frequently than necessary to capture the basic demographic trends of interest.

Data collection which is too frequent can also be counterproductive. Respondents may become unwilling to provide valid data if they see the effect as an unwarranted imposition on their own time and energy, thus jeopardizing the overall quality of the research. This is also clearly a consideration in the census example noted above.

THE DIFFERENTIAL PERIOD PROBLEM

The differential period problem is common in cross-sectional research and is exacerbated in longitudinal research. Simply put, it has to do with the fact that researchers often aggregate various measures in the same study over different periods of time. Typically, for example, 'hard' performance measures are aggregated for relatively long periods of time, say one year, whereas individual data, such as attitudes and perceptions, are aggregated for relatively short or unspecified periods of time.

The problem here is that the researcher is in a position of trying to predict some dependent variable on the basis of data collected on a set of independent variables for a variety of time periods. Performance, which has been aggregated over time, is being predicted on the basis of independent variables, the values of which reflect aggregation for shorter (or frequently unspecified) time periods. This means, in many cases, that past

performance is predicted on the basis of current behaviours, attitudes, or perceptions. Although the reverse may be feasible, that is, current behaviours, attitudes, or perceptions can be predicted on the basis of past performance, this is another issue.

To illustrate, consider a recent study of the relationship between salespersons' use of a management information system and their attitudes towards it (Robey 1979). A sample of salespersons was sent a questionnaire asking them about their attitudes towards the system which was then used to predict actual system use. System use, however, was defined in terms of a salesperson's behaviour over a 15-month period prior to the study. Performance (use) was aggregated over 15 months and was predicted by attitudes at a particular point in time subsequent to the time period for which the data on use were aggregated. As this study demonstrates, the differential period problem is intimately tied to efforts to infer causality. One has to be careful in aggregating data on dependent and independent variables to align time periods over which they have been aggregated. Otherwise, as noted above, one can be in the uncomfortable position of predicting past behaviour on the basis of present attitudes.

The basic point is that researchers should pay closer attention to the relationships among the time periods for which their data are aggregated. Choices of time periods should be made explicitly, for they have important theoretical implications. Unfortunately, in both cross-sectional and longitudinal research, these implications are often overlooked.

THE MORPHOGENETIC PROBLEM

As frustrating as it may be to many organizational researchers, the fact is that most organizations simply do not remain static. The analytical problem which this motion creates would be relatively trivial if the question were simply whether an organization is staying still or moving. Unfortunately, the problem is much more complex, for various components of most organizations are always changing at various rates and for various reasons. The reason for change may be largely outside the organization's control, such as the imposition of national regulations or changes in levels of activity in the national economy. Alternatively, certain changes may be the direct result of deliberate organizational actions, such as a major reorganization or the development of a new department. Similar complexity is found at the individual level. Changes in the behaviour of individual organizational members may be primarily under the control of the organization or they may have their origins in factors in the personal lives of those individuals over which the organization itself has very little, if any, control. Thus, the stable, unchanging organization is very much the exception rather than the rule.

For those carrying out research in or on organizations the fact of organizational morphogenesis has profound consequences which have been little appreciated in our literature. Perhaps the most significant issue is the fact that within any given time period, the values of some variables may be relatively stable while the values of others change relatively dramatically. Cross-sectional research designs are hopelessly inadequate vehicles for capturing the dynamic quality of organizational life. One has no idea whatsoever in a cross-sectional design which of the variables included may have relatively stable values, which may be changing, what the direction of change is, and at what rate change is occurring. The result is that interpretations of the findings are inevitably problematic. It may well be that one of the underlying reasons why the findings of much organizational research are ambiguous, inconsistent, and occasionally contradictory is that researchers have not yet begun to deal with the fact of morphogenesis.

THE RESEARCH SETTINGS

To illustrate the three problems concretely, examples will be drawn from two research projects in which the author has been involved. One is a study of hospital adoption of innovations in medical technology. Detailed descriptions of this study are available elsewhere (Gordon, Kimberly, and MacEachron 1975; Moch 1976; Moch and Morse 1977; Kimberly 1978). This large-scale survey of hospitals was designed to examine the relationship between organizational structure and innovation, and thus most of the variables included in the study were structural in nature. Among them, for example, were measures of centralization of authority, structural differentiation, technological complexity, and size. The learnings about longitudinal research evolved as we contemplated doing a follow-up survey to determine what kinds of changes had occurred in patterns of innovation adoption.

The second study concerned the birth and early development of a new and innovative school of medicine. In contrast to the hospital study, the medical school study was designed to focus heavily on process, and was a comprehensive effort to monitor several aspects of the school's functioning as an organization in order to understand the course of its development (Kimberly, Counte, and Dickinson 1972). As part of this effort, models of performance developed in industrial settings were adapted and used to predict performance by students in medical school. A number of indices of student behaviour and attitudes were developed to facilitate this effort. Students were interviewed in both a structured and an unstructured fashion at several points during the semester and were also administered certain paper and pencil instruments. In addition, a substantial amount of data was gathered from them prior to their enrollment in the school, and extensive efforts were made to follow-up on them once they had left. The study was carried out over a period of four years, providing a variety of kinds of data over many time periods which could be used to help to explain performance.

There is an interesting difference between the two studies which should be mentioned briefly. The design of the hospital study was strongly influenced by the dominant methodological and theoretical approaches implicit in much of the comparative organizational research carried out in the 1960s and early 1970s. It began as a survey of a number of different hospitals at a particular point in time, and as the possibility of moving towards a longitudinal design was considered, the kinds of questions that arose were ones which were based on the assumption that another survey at a later point in time was the appropriate next step. Included in the initial survey, of course, were some very old, some relatively young, and some middle-aged organizations.

The medical school study, however, was carried out in an organization which was brand new. Its structure was emerging. Its culture was emerging. An elaborate set of norms and values was emerging. It was in no sense a 'mature' organization, and as the researchers watched the school develop, they became sensitive to a number of issues which most researchers who generally intervene in organizations which have already acquired an identity and developed a history are not constrained to think about. Certain things which in the context of the hospital study were nonproblematic became highly problematic in the context of the medical school study. The rhythms and periodicities of organizational life in the medical school helped create a context of meaning for observed behaviours, and structure was seen to emerge as a response to choices and contingencies, both internal and external (Kimberly and Evanisko 1979). And most important of all, the limitations of cross-sectional research became all too apparent (Kimberly 1979).

EXAMPLES OF THE INTERVAL PROBLEM

The interval problem is illustrated, in the case of the hospital study by the question of how long the researchers should wait before undertaking a second survey. Many factors, of course, influenced that decision but key among these was a concern with what a reasonable time interval might be to insure that variation in the phenomena of interest would have occurred. Was it likely, for example, that patterns of innovation adoption would change significantly in the course of two, three, or five years? By waiting too long, might other influences, such as governmental legislation, which were not present in the first survey have an effect? How might such changes affect our study?

In the case of the medical school study, the question was how frequently to gather data from the students, the faculty, the administrators, and the associated physicians. The initial strategy formulated was based primarily on a combination of embryonic theory and a heavy dose of pragmatism. We decided to interview students formally four times during the school year and to gather supplementary questionnaire data at the beginning and at the end of the year. Faculty were to be interviewed three times per year, physicians twice, and administrators weekly. Theoretically, we believed that it was important to monitor developments in the school as closely as possible and that to do so required contact with all of the actors as frequently as possible. Pragmatically, we believed that it would not be possible to interview physicians more than twice a year because of demands on their time. The weekly administrator interviews were set up initially because we wanted to track administrative strategy particularly closely. The administration was willing to cooperate initially because they believed that it would be helpful to them to reflect regularly on what they had accomplished and what their problems were. We believed that faculty would agree to be interviewed three times during the year because each of them was an integral part of the evolving organization and there would be some learning in the process for them. Finally, we wanted to examine the effects of the new school on student performance and hoped that students would be receptive to being under a microscope themselves. Having the support of the school's administration, we believed that students would be cooperative.

Our data collection plans were complex, extensive, and, we believed, well thought out. It did not take us long to learn, however, that as the organization evolved, intervals other than those we had established were more appropriate. Two aspects of the interval problem were particularly noteworthy. First, our plans had to be scaled down. Although initial enthusiasm for our research was high on everyone's part, and remained generally high during the entire first year, we realized that we could not rely on such extensive cooperation in succeeding years. It was unlikely that faculty, students, and administrators would be willing to spend as much time with us as we might have wished. Thus, we were forced to ask ourselves what intervals were both *appropriate* and *feasible* given what we were trying to learn and given that we wanted to stay with the system for a number of years. Second, we became acutely aware of the *timing* issue. Given that our efforts should be scaled down, when should data be collected? Certain features of the system itself helped answer this question. We learned quickly that it was in no one's interest to try to collect data from students two weeks prior to and at least one week following exams of any sort. We also learned that for most students their first six weeks at the school was an intensive socialization experience, and that it was advisable to interview them during this period, when many of their attitudinal and behavioural patterns were being powerfully shaped. We learned that faculty were much more receptive to inter-

views early and late in the school year than any time during the middle as a consequence of their own work loads on both the research and teaching fronts. And finally, we learned that there was no really good time to interview administrators. The day-to-day pressures of managing the school, particularly the finances, tended to overwhelm early perceptions of the benefits of regular reflection. Our weekly interviews became monthly, and we had to struggle to keep to the monthly schedule. All of these things were learned as we lived with the system and became attuned to how it was evolving.

EXAMPLES OF THE DIFFERENTIAL PERIOD PROBLEM

The differential period problem is well illustrated by the original design of the hospital study. In that design, the dependent variable, aggregated adoption behavior, reflected behaviors that occurred some time in the past, yet current structural characteristics were used to predict it. This procedure requires the assumption that structure is relatively invariant through time, an assumption which is certainly open to question. By moving to a longitudinal design, we would be able to address this problem, at least in part.

The medical school study, however, was deliberately designed to deal with the problem. Measures of dependent and independent variables were made at multiple points in time, enabling the researchers to determine precisely what time periods were being used as a basis for aggregating which variables and subsequently to take this information into account in the analyses. For example, one of the dependent variables we were interested in was student performance. We were also interested in examining the old satisfaction/performance relation in a nonindustrial setting. By gathering performance data at three different points during the year, by collecting programme satisfaction data aggregated over periods prior and subsequent to exams, by gathering data on other relevant variables such as patterns of sociometric contact with other students, levels of effort made, and personal life satisfaction for similar time periods, and by adding data on aptitudes and abilities, we were able to build relatively complex models of performance in which causal priority was able to be sensibly established because the differential period problem had been explicitly addressed.

CONFRONTING THE MORPHOGENETIC PROBLEM

The morphogenetic problem is illustrated by the contrasting designs of the two studies. The original design of the hospital study essentially assumed 'away' morphogenesis. The design of the medical school study, however, was consciously oriented to the fact of morphogenesis. By emphasizing adaptability, that design was able to capture some aspects of morphogenesis, but not without substantial costs in terms of the analytical problems associated with changed instrumentation and obvious threats to external validity as it is traditionally defined.

PROBLEM SOLUTION: SOME MODEST PROPOSALS

How solvable are the three problems? The examples presented above contain the seeds of certain solutions. To begin to solve the interval problem, researchers need to ask what processes they are interested in explaining and what chance there is that the phenomena will unfold in a particular time frame. Answers to these questions must come from a theoretical perspective on the phenomena of interest, and often such a perspective can only be developed after having become highly familiar with the nature of the research context itself. The differential period problem is certainly solvable, as is illustrated

by the design of the medical school study. However, it requires that researchers both explicitly recognize the problem in the first place and develop designs for dealing with it in the second.

To begin to deal effectively with the morphogenetic problem, researchers need to begin to work on two related fronts. First, more creativity is needed at the level of theory construction. The fact that variables change at different rates in different periods of time needs to be taken into account in constructing theories of organizational behavior. At the same time, research strategies which are compatible with the fact of morphogenesis need to be developed. To me, this means spending a great deal more time in the field learning about the organizations that we are attempting to understand. Attempts to capture context need to be defined as legitimate if not central elements of the scientific enterprise. By developing quasi-clinical, quasi-intuitive understandings of the tone and texture of the organizations that are the subject of research, it may be possible for researchers to create a context of meaning for those data which are collected. Enough familiarity, for example, with the periodicity and rhythms in the activities of a particular organization or set of organizations may be gained so that interpretation of data becomes straightforward rather than hopelessly confused. To illustrate, simply knowing when and how frequently pay day occurs may provide some important insights into fluctuation in rates of absenteeism. Or knowing when and under what conditions performance evaluations are made may help explain fluctuations in levels of productivity.

In the medical school study, for example, it was found that the distribution of effort devoted to studying by students over the course of the academic year was predictable on the basis of when examinations occurred. A finding which surprises absolutely no one who has spent any time around an institution of higher education, but a finding which may generalize, in its broad implications, to other settings. One need go no further than budget cycles in the federal government or model changeovers in the automotive industry to find potential analogies. The point is that researchers ought perhaps to assume that in most settings under most conditions performance is noncontinuous and is subject to peaks and troughs which may, in the aggregate, be predictable on the basis of characteristics of the organizational system. In other words, focusing on means and variances in performance may be forcing a sort of continuity on the phenomenon of interest which does not combine well with certain realities of the system. The way in which the data are aggregated contains some built-in assumptions about the phenomenon which may well be questionable.

The issue which organizational morphogenesis raises is a difficult one indeed. There is obviously a trade-off between the strategy of becoming intimately familiar with the context of particular organizations, on the one hand, and trying to build general theories of organizational behaviour, on the other. Ours is not the business of creating theories of particular organizations, to be sure. However, my own view is that in the rush to create general theories, we have lost sight of some important dimensions of organizational behaviour. This may well help to account for the lack of richness which characterizes much of our theorizing.

SUMMARY

The central point of this article is that the temporal dimension of data aggregation problems in organizational research has generally been neglected. Although most researchers only signal the need for longitudinal research as they discuss the future research directions suggested by their own cross-sectional work, I am optimistic that longitudinal research will slowly become more widespread. As it does, researchers will have to deal with the issue of organizational time in general and the temporal dimension of data aggregation problems in particular. I have pointed out three specific aggregation problems, the interval problem, the differential period problem, and the morphogenetic problem, more to illustrate some of the kinds of issues that are involved rather than to cover them exhaustively. My hope is that as more and more researchers become aware of these issues and as they begin to reflect creatively on them, the sophistication and quality of much organizational research will be enhanced.

REFERENCES

Firebaugh, G. "A Rule for Inferring Individual-level Relationships from Aggregate Data." *American Sociological Review*, 1978, *43*, 557–572.

Gordon, G., Kimberly, J. R., & MacEachron, A. "Some Considerations in the Design of Problem-solving Research on the Diffusion of Medical Technology" in *The Management of Health Care*. W. J. Abernathy, A. Sheldon, C. K. Prahalad (eds.). Cambridge: Ballinger, 1975.

Hannan, M. T. *Aggregation and Disaggregation in Sociology.* Lexington, Mass.: Heath-Lexington, 1971.

Kimberly, J. R. "Issues in the Design of Longitudinal Organizational Research." *Sociological Methods and Research*, 1976, *4*, 321–347.

Kimberly, J. R. "Hospital Adoption of Innovation: the Role of Integration into External Informational Environments."

Journal of Health and Social Behavior, 1978, *19,* 361–373.

Kimberly, J. R. "Issues in the Creation of Organizations: Initiation, Innovation, and Institutionalization." *Academy of Management Journal,* 1979, *22,* 437–457.

Kimberly, J. R., Counte, M. A., & Dickinson R. O. "Design for Process Research on Change in Medical Education." *Proceedings; Eleventh Annual Conference on Research in Medical Education,* 1972, *11,* 26–31.

Kimberly, J. R., & Evanisko, M. J. "Organizational Technology, Structure and Size: a Developmental View" in *Organizational Behavior.* S. Kerr (ed.). Columbus: Grid, 1979.

Moch, M. "Structure and Organizational Resource Allocation." *Administrative Science Quarterly,* 1976, *21,* 661–674.

Moch, M., & Morse E. V. "Size, Centralization, and Organizational Adoption of Innovations." *American Sociological Review,* 1977, *42,* 716–725.

Pugh, D. S., & Hickson D. J. *Organizational Structure in its Context: the Aston Programme 1.* Farnborough, Eng.: Saxon House, 1976.

Roby, D. "User Attitudes and Management Information System Use." *Academy of Management Journal,* 1979, *22,* 527–538.

Inferences About Trends in Labor Force Satisfaction: A Causal-Correlational Analysis[1]

Dennis W. Organ

The trend of job satisfaction in the labor force is a matter which has provoked intense discussion and controversy in recent years. On the one hand, some accounts (e.g., Gooding, 1972; Sheppard & Herrick, 1972) argue that labor force satisfaction has declined over time and that since the beginning of the 1960s there has been a widespread increase in the alienation and disenchantment of workers from their jobs. Smith, Roberts, and Hulin (1976) found evidence from a sample of over 98,000 employees from 132 branches of a merchandise distribution firm suggesting that satisfaction with job aspects other than pay and type of work declined slightly from 1963 to 1972. On the other hand, the longest running series of national opinion polls concerning job satisfaction—those conducted by Gallup (1972)—suggest that the percentage of respondents expressing dissatisfaction with their jobs remained quite stable at about 10 percent over the years 1963–71 and that if any change has occurred since the 1940s, it is in the direction of increased prevalence of job satisfaction. A number of smaller scale job opinion surveys reviewed by Herzberg et al. (1955) in the mid-1950s found that the

proportion of respondents expressing dissatisfaction was consistently in the neighborhood of 13 percent; national surveys by the University of Michigan's Survey Research Center in 1969 and 1972 found 14 and 11 percent, respectively, expressing negative attitudes toward work (Quinn & Shepard, 1974).

Critics argue, however, that results obtained by opinion polls cannot be taken at face value. Such studies force the respondent to answer one question (e.g., "Is your work satisfying?" or "In general, would you say that you are reasonably well satisfied with your present job?") with a categorical, unqualified "Yes" or "No." According to Blauner (1960), this type of methodology ignores the cultural and psychological pressures on workers to exaggerate the degree of actual satisfaction; the measure, in other words, is reactive due to the socially undesirable properties of a negative response. Others (e.g., *Work in America*, 1973) contend that polls such as Gallup's report as "satisfied" those who are really only saying that they accept the need to work but expect little satisfaction from it. This criticism, however, would seem to pose little rele-

[1] Reproduced by permission of the *Academy of Management Journal*, 1977, 20, 510–19. Portions of this paper were presented at the 1977 Midwest Academy of Management meetings.

vance for inferences about *trends,* since the bias would presumably be essentially constant across time.

Those who argue that labor force satisfaction has been declining point to behavioral indices as supporting their claims. Sheppard and Herrick (1972) note that absenteeism doubled in the automobile industry between 1960 and 1970 and that "turnover rates are climbing" (p. 3). Indeed, data from Bureau of Labor Statistics sources (1976) show that the average monthly quit rate among firms sampled increased from 1.2 percent in 1961 to 2.7 in 1969. However, two parallel trends in the 1960s that are atypical of the longer postwar era must be borne in mind in interpreting the rising quit rate through that period: (1) The rate of unemployment dropped steadily from 6.7 percent to 3.5 as the combination of Kennedy-Johnson fiscal policies and Vietnam War-induced demand produced the longest sustained economic expansion since World War II; and (2) the nation's labor force, having reached an age peak in the late 1950s, became steadily younger through the 1960s to the present time with the influx of particpants under age 25 arising from the "baby boom" of the immediate postwar years.

Armknecht and Early (1972) have shown that changes in the quit rate are quite sensitive to changes in the rate of net new hires, for the labor force as a whole over time as well as cross-sectionally by industry grouping. Porter and Steers (1973) reviewed a number of studies which had demonstrated a strong, negative relationship between age and turnover. Thus, if labor force satisfaction had remained constant, both of the above factors would still have contributed to higher quit rates in the 1960s, thus rendering quit rate *per se* somewhat equivocal as an indicator of job attitudes in the labor force. Lower unemployment would probably have increased absenteeism also; firms would have been drawing greater numbers of marginal workers into their ranks,

there would have been more restraint against disciplining or releasing workers for excessive absenteeism, and overtime pay would have made occasional lost wages due to absenteeism more tolerable.

However, the positive relationship generally found between age and job satisfaction (Herzberg et al., 1955; Quinn & Shepard, 1972; Hunt & Saul, 1975) suggests that a younger work force, other things constant, would on the whole be a less satisfied one. Moreover, both Sheppard and Herrick (1972) and *Work in America* (1973) gave special attention to the "new breed" of younger worker swelling the ranks of the labor market as one who has different and greater expectations of work than either older workers of today or younger workers of previous generations and one who reacts more militantly to employers' failures to meet these expectations.

Taking all of these considerations together, the question remains: What has been the national trend of job satisfaction in the labor force over time? Given the fact that level of job satisfaction has been amply documented as a predictor of quit rate (Porter & Steers, 1973), it is possible to compare and evaluate a number of causal models which treat satisfaction as an unmeasured variable and posit alternative paths through which secular trends could have determined the level of quit rate in the labor force. Blalock (1964) has shown how such a method, testing the partial correlations predicted by various models, can enable one to draw inferences concerning unmeasured variables. The analysis which follows, therefore, seeks to capitalize on the demonstrated relationship between satisfaction and turnover at the microlevel (individual or group) in order to use quit rate as an indicator of job attitudes in the labor force over time. This analysis is, of course, predicated on the aforementioned premise that other variables (i.e., age of labor force and unemployment) also affect quit rate in the labor force.

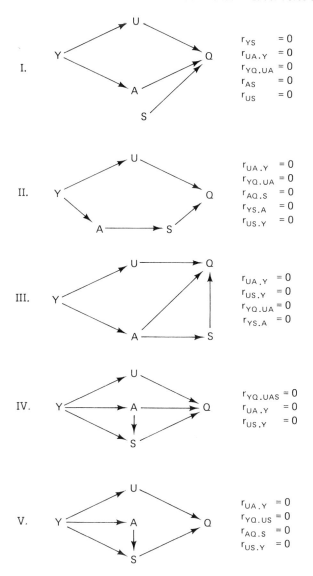

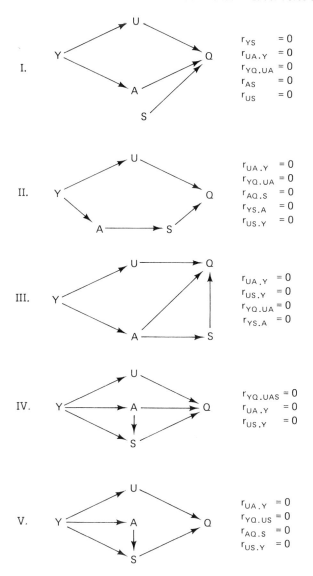

^aY: year (1947 = 1); U: unemployment rate; A: average age of labor force; S: job satisfaction; Q: quit rate.

Figure 1.   Causal Models of Satisfaction Trends Predictions[a]

FIVE PLAUSIBLE MODELS

Figure 1 depicts what would appear, a priori, as the most plausible alternative models. All models have in common the assumption that quit rate (Q) is partially determined by level of unemployment (U) and by level of job satisfaction (S, the unmeasured variable), that level of unemployment and average age (A) of the labor force have changed over the years (Y), that U and A are independent of each other save for their mutual dependence on Y, and that U and S are likewise independent.

One could argue that U and S are positively related: As unemployment increases, job holders reevaluate their work more positively in the light of the alternatives. Even if this were the case, however, it would not vitiate the conclusions drawn from the analysis below, since the assumption is constant across all five causal models. The major effect of the assumption (to the extent it is invalid) is to overstate the portion of variance in quit rate uniquely attributable to unemployment level over and above any indirect effect of U on Q by way of S.

Conceptually, the models differ substantially in other respects. Model I assumes that population or institutional changes over the years have had no direct effect on S; it also assumes that A and S are unrelated, with independent effects on Q. The latter assumption (unrelatedness of A and S) is somewhat dubious in that all known surveys of job opinions (Herzberg et al., 1955; Sheppard & Herrick, 1972; Quinn & Shepard, 1974) have shown greater satisfaction among workers over 30 than those under 30; young workers perenially contain among their ranks the highest incidence of expressed dissatisfaction. However, it is conceptually plausible that such a relationship might not hold true for changes in the age structure of the labor force *as a whole* over time. While age is positively related to job satisfaction in a cross-sectional sense, the job satisfaction of the entire labor force—those in every age group—could increase or decrease over time, hence greater satisfaction as a function of some other variables changing over time could conceivably offset the otherwise negative impact of greater percentages of young workers.

Model II states that changes over time have had no impact on satisfaction except for the indirect (and temporary) effect produced by a younger labor force. This in turn has had an effect on Q funneled completely through lower S.

Model III makes an additional assumption, that a younger labor force leads to higher Q, over and above that predicted from the fact that younger workers tend to be less satisfied. In other words, even satisfied younger workers are more mobile, more likely to be in the dynamic stages of their careers, and have more decision points facing them.

While Models I, II, and III differ conceptually among themselves in some respects, they are identical with respect to predicted partial correlations involving measured variables. All predict partial correlations between U and A, controlling for Y, and between Y and Q controlling for U and A, equal to zero. To the extent that either or both predictions are not supported, all three models must be rejected.

Model IV argues that whatever temporal trends have occurred in S are not solely due to changes in A but also result from other changes, e.g., greater salience of higher-order needs not met by job dimensions, greater expectations, decreasing opportunities for achievement, changes in job characteristics, and so on.

Finally, Model V posits the same secular trends as IV except that, like II, it assumes the effect of A on Q to be totally through S.

Models IV and V are identical with respect to predicted partial correlations among measured variables. What distinguishes both of them from the first three is the fact that neither one predicts the correlation between year and quit rate to vanish when controlling for both age and unemployment. On the other hand, like the previous models, they both do predict a partial correlation between unemployment and age to fall to zero when controlling for year.

It is obvious that these models do not exhaust the probable sets of relationships among the variables, inasmuch as they take no note of such influences as changing occupational mix, changing educational levels, or other structural changes in the economy. Nor do the models take into account changes in real income, styles of supervision, working conditions, legislation, and the like. Thus, all of the models admittedly oversimplify a complex set of relationships. However, some of these factors probably underly changes in measured variables, such as U; others could be regarded as a residual set of forces which could be designated as "X," affecting satisfaction independently of U or A and thus positioned on the causal arrow between Y and S. In such cases, the prediction equations would remain the same. Nevertheless, to the extent that these omitted variables *confound* the relationships between measured variables in the models, the latter unjustifiably sweep a great deal of complexity under the rug.

All of these models are recursive—they rule out reciprocal causation—and potentially lend themselves to the Simon-Blalock (Simon, 1957; Blalock, 1964) mode of evaluation using partial correlations. Some of the predicted partial correlations involve S, which of course cannot be directly tested since it is taken as an unmeasured variable. However, partial correlations involving other variables do permit a test which could eliminate some of the models.

Assumptions

Some assumptions underlying the use of the Simon-Blalock method should be made explicit. First, the models, as noted above, are recursive. If, for example, there were strong reason to believe that variations in quit rate importantly affected unemployment (i.e., that variance in "frictional unemployment" represents a significant part of the variance in total unemployment rate), the models would not justify the proposed method of analysis. Secondly, the models assume linear relationships among the variables, which may not be valid. For example, the relationship between age and satisfaction is more properly described as curvilinear, although sufficiently monotonic so that the assumption of linearity seems not unreasonable. Third, it is assumed that measurement relia-

bility and validity of the variables are reasonably high. The usual assumptions underlying use of multivariate regression techniques, such as homoscedasticity and no error of measurement in independent variables, also apply. With respect to unmeasured variables, Blalock (1964) asserts that "one should avoid complex indicators that are related in unknown ways to a given underlying variable" (p. 164). To the extent that quit rate is related in a more complex manner to satisfaction and/or other unmeasured variables than is represented here, the utility of the analysis is questioned.

METHOD

Data for rate of unemployment and average monthly quit rate for the years 1947–75 and April 1976 were gathered from the 1976 edition of *Historical Statistics of the United States* and recent issues of *Employment and Earnings*, a monthly Bureau of Labor Statistics (BLS) publication. Quit rate data are based on sampling statistics collected by BLS from over 38,000 manufacturing establishments employing over ten million workers. The entire work force numbers approximately 80 million, only a portion of which is in manufacturing; thus, it must be kept in mind that BLS quit rate data may not be representative of the nation's entire labor force. Firms sampled by BLS tend to be the larger ones and not characterized by marked seasonality of employment. Quits are defined as terminations of employment initiated by employees, including unauthorized absences greater than one week but excluding those due to work stoppages. Unemployment data, like monthly quit rate data, were taken as averages for each year in question to smooth over seasonal fluctuations within a year.

Average age of the labor force for the years in question was estimated by consulting the sources cited above as well as past isues of the *Statistical Abstract of the United States* for numbers or proportions of the

TABLE 1
Analysis of Relationships Among Year, Unemployment, Average Age of Labor Force, and Quit Rate

Zero-Order Intercorrelations (n = 30):

	1	2	3	4
1. Year (1947 = 1)	1.00	.42**	−.50***	−.29*
2. Unemployment rate		1.00	−.23	−.69***
3. Average age of labor force			1.00	−.39**
4. Quit rate				1.00

Partial Correlations: Prediction Equations

Variables	Variable(s) Controlled	Partial r
Unemployment and age	Year	−.03
Year and quit rate	Unemployment and age	−.64***

Other Partial Correlations

Variables	Variable Controlled	Partial r
Year and quit rate	Unemployment	−.002
Age and quit rate	Unemployment	−.77***
Unemployment and quit rate	Age	−.87
Year and quit rate	Age	−.67**

Quit Rate Variance Accounted for

	Multiple R	R^2	Increase in R^2	F
By unemployment	.69***	.47	.47	24.9***
By unemployment, and age	.89***	.87	.32	40.2***
By unemployment, age, and year	.93***	.87	.08	17.7***

  * $p < .10$
 ** $p < .05$
*** $p < .01$

labor force in various age categories (16–24, 25–34, 35–44, 45–54, 55–64, 65 and older). The midpoint of each age interval was weighted by the number or proportion of workers contained therein (for the 65 and older category, a midpoint of 66.5 was arbitrarily used) and the products were either summed (when original data were in percent) or summed and divided by total labor force size.

RESULT

The matrix of zero-order correlations and pertinent partial correlations appears in Table 1. It is worth noting in the zero-order correlations that, for the post-war period as a whole, quits have actually tended to decline over time, despite the increase from 1960 to 1969. Also of interest is that rate of unemployment is by far the best single predictor of quit rate, by itself accounting for 47 percent of the variance.

Partial Correlations

The partial correlation between year and quit rate, holding unemployment constant, is −.002. Taken alone, this finding could suggest either that (1) neither changes in age of labor force nor other trends have influenced satisfaction and consequent quit rate or (2) that age changes have had some effect on S and Q, but this has been balanced by other trends. However, the partial correlation between age of labor force and quit rate, holding unemployment constant, is $-.77$ $(p < .01)$, supporting the assumption that a trend (underway since the late 1950s) toward a younger labor force has had the effect of increasing the quit rate—either directly, indirectly through lower job satisfaction, or both.

The second-order partial correlation between year and quits, holding both unemployment and age of labor force constant, is $-.64$ $(p < .01)$. This finding forces one to reject models I, II, and III, since those all predict $r_{YQ \cdot UA} = 0$. Interestingly, however, this second-order partial r is not only large and significant but *negative*: It argues that, if unemployment and age had been held constant over the years, the quit rate would have declined over this period more rapidly than it in fact did. This, in turn, suggests that other trends occurring over time acted to increase satisfaction, but these effects were canceled out during the 1960s by continually declining unemployment rates and a reduction over time in the mean age of the work force.

The essence of the analysis thus far, then, is that labor force satisfaction does not show any long-term trend toward changes in job attitudes over the period 1947–76. Controlling for unemployment—the only cause of quit rate not also related to satisfaction in the models (except I, where age is assumed to be unrelated to satisfaction)—the relationship between year and quit rate is essentially nil. To the extent that higher unemployment tends to increase the satisfaction of those who hold jobs, the inference would be that job satisfaction has actually increased to some extent over the period as a whole. However, even the overall stability otherwise inferred appears to mask two trends: one, certain developments (which cannot be precisely delineated here but might include greater earnings, increased

job security, better physical work environments, and so on) coincident with the time period which would have brought about higher levels of labor force satisfaction; the other, the offsetting increases in the proportion of workers in younger age groups—who, as noted earlier, tend to be the least satisfied.

The two remaining models, IV and V, are both consistent with predicted partial correlations. Path analysis would show that model V, however, would require a path coefficient of absolute value between .77 and 1.00 for the effect of satisfaction on quits in order to be consistent with the findings that $r_{AQ \cdot U} = -.77$. It is difficult to assess the plausibility of that path coefficient being so great. While some studies (e.g., Hulin, 1966, 1968) suggest lower values, they have presented analysis at the individual level, whereas aggregative analyses such as the present one would typically yield higher values. The choice between IV and V would, at present, seem to hinge on the dubious validity of the assumption in V that increased turnover among younger workers is solely attributable to their lower job satisfaction.

The findings of this analysis suggesting stability of labor force satisfaction over the post-war era could mask a curvilinear trend composed of steadily increased satisfaction up to the early 1960s, counterbalanced by a declining trend afterwards. A second analysis, therefore, was carried out for the years 1961–76. Again, unemployment showed the highest correlation with quit rate ($r = -.72$, versus $-.69$ for the entire post-war period). However, a problem encountered was that, over the more recent period, age of labor force correlates negatively and virtually perfectly with year ($r = -.98$). Thus $r_{YQ \cdot U}$ and $r_{AQ \cdot U}$ were virtually identical (.91 and .92, respectively), and the second order partial $r_{YQ \cdot UA}$ is of necessity quite low ($-.16$). In any case, the inference would remain that if an inflection point in job satisfaction were reached in the early 1960s, concurrent changes in age structure of the labor force were probably the underlying factor.

DISCUSSION

Projections in the 1975 *Statistical Abstract* show that the proportion of the population aged 18–24 will peak around 1980 and subsequently decline, and the group aged 25–34 will diminish relative to others around 1985. Thus, we can expect the labor force to become gradually older in the 1980s, and if other factors affecting attitudes hold roughly constant, demographics alone should lead to higher levels of job satisfaction in the labor force in the next decade.

This assertion is, of course, predicted on the validity of either model IV or V as assessed by the foregoing analysis. Actually, all that has been accomplished is to reject three other models and find no immediate evidence for rejection of the other two. Other plausible models remain which could be formulated, specifically those which would explicitly take into account various other structural changes in the economy and labor force not identified here. Hopefully, future research will be directed not only at polling or monitoring the state of labor force satisfaction, but will consider causal models of the type offered above as an aid to systematic diagnosis and forecasting of temporal trends in job attitudes. Otherwise, either short-run declines in such attitudes may precipitate premature crash programs, or temporary increases may give undue cause for complacency.

REFERENCES

1. Armknecht, P. A., & Early, J. F. "Quits in Manufacturing: A Study of Their Causes," *Monthly Labor Review,* Vol. 95, No. 11 (1972), 31–37.

2. Blalock, H. M., Jr. *Causal Inferences in Nonexperimental Research,* (Chapel Hill, N.C.: University of North Carolina Press, 1964).

3. Blauner, R. "Work Satisfaction and Industrial Trends in Modern Society," in W. Galenson and S. M. Lipset (Eds.), *Labor and Trade Unionism,* (New York: Wiley, 1960), 340–354.

4. Gallup, G. H. *The Gallup Poll,* (New York: Random House, 1972).

5. Gooding, J. *The Job Revolution,* (New York: Walker, 1972).

6. Herzberg, F., Mausner, B., Peterson, R., & Capwell, D. *Job Attitudes: Review of Research and Opinion,* (Pittsburgh, PA: Psychological Services of Pittsburgh, 1955).

7. Hulin, C. L. "Job Satisfaction and Turnover in a Female Clerical Population," *Journal of Applied Psychology,* Vol. 50 (1966), 280–285.

8. Hulin, C. L. "Effects of Changes in Job Satisfaction Levels on Employee Turnover," *Journal of Applied Psychology,* Vol. 52 (1968), 122–126.

9. Hunt, J. W., & Saul, P. N. "The Relationship of Age, Tenure, and Job Satisfaction in Males and Females," *Academy of Management Journal,* Vol. 18 (1975), 690–702.

10. Porter, L. W., & Steers, R. M. "Organizational, Work, and Personal Factors in Employee Turnover and Absenteeism," *Psychological Bulletin,* Vol. 80 (1973), 151–176.

11. Quinn, R. P., & Shepard, L. J. *The 1972–73 Quality of Employment Survey,* (Ann Arbor, Mich.: Survey Research Center, University of Michigan, 1974).

12. Sheppard, H. L., & Herrick, N. Q. *Where Have All the Robots Gone?* (New York: Free Press, 1972).

13. Simon, H. A. *Models of Man* (New York: Wiley, 1957).

14. Smith, F., Roberts, K. H., and Hulin, C. L. "Ten-Year Job Satisfaction Trends in a Stable Organization," *Academy of Management Journal,* Vol. 19 (1976), 462–469.

15. U.S. Bureau of the Census. *Historical Statistics of the United States: Colonial Times to 1970, Bicentennial Edition,* Part 1 (Washington, D.C., 1975).

16. U.S. Bureau of the Census. *Statistical Abstract of the United States,* 84th–96th Editions (Washington, D.C., 1963–75).

17. U.S. Department of Labor, Bureau of Labor Statistics. *Employment and Earnings,* Vol. 22, No. 12 (1976), 101, 127–131.

18. *Work in America,* Report of a Special Task Force to the Securetary of Health, Education, and Welfare (Cambridge, Mass.: MIT Press, 1973).

The Impact of Union-Management Cooperation on Productivity and Employment*

Michael Schuster

Research on organizational change and experimentation in unionized settings is much needed.[1] During the last ten years, the declining growth rate of productivity has led to several cooperative attempts to increase organizational effectiveness. Although some of this activity is novel, much of it is not:[2] productivity programs such as Scanlon and Rucker plans[3] and union-management efforts such as health and safety committees, production committees, and productivity bargaining have long histories.[4] Yet there has been surprisingly little empirical research on such endeavors. This paper addresses that gap in the literature by first presenting a research design for evaluating cooperative union-management programs and then applying that design to estimate the impact of nine such programs on productivity and employment.

RECENT DEVELOPMENTS

During the 1970s, there was an increase in cooperative union-management activities to

* This research was supported by a grant from the Employment and Training Administration, U.S. Department of Labor. Helpful comments on earlier drafts of this paper were provided by James Dworkin. Susan Rhodes. Milton Derber, and Christopher Miller.

Reprinted, with permission, from *Industrial and Labor Relations Review*, Vol. 36, No. 3 (April 1983), pp 415–30. © 1983 by Cornell University.

[1] Thomas Kochan, "Labor Management Relations Research Priorities for the 1980s," final report to the Secretary of Labor (Washington, D.C.: U.S. Department of Labor, 1980).

[2] There is no single volume that presents the complete history of union-management cooperation, but three excellent references are James J. Healy, ed., *Creative Collective Bargaining* (Englewood Cliffs, N.J.: Prentice-Hall, 1965); Clinton S. Golden and Virginia Parker, *Causes of Industrial Peace Under Collective Bargaining* (New York: Harper and Row, 1953); and Arie Shirom, "Cooperation and Adjustment to Technological Change: A Study of Joint Management Union Committees," unpublished Ph.D. thesis (Madison, Wis.: University of Wisonsin, 1968).

[3] For a recent study of the Scanlon Plan, see J. K. White, "The Scanlon Plan: Causes and Correlates of Success," *Academy of Management Journal*, Vol. 22, No. 2 (June 1979), pp. 292–312. For a brief description of Rucker Plans, see Carl Hegel, ed., *The Encyclopedia of Management*, 2d ed. (New York: Van Nostrand Reinhold, 1973), pp. 895–900.

[4] A discussion of union-management safety committees may be found in Mary V. Kleeck, *Miners and Management* (New York: Russell Sage Foundation, 1934). Productivity bargaining is discussed in Industrial Relations Research Association, *Collective Bargaining and Productivity* (Madison, Wis.: IRRA, 1975).

improve productivity and the quality of work life. Although exhibiting much variation, these efforts most commonly took the form of plantwide productivity-sharing plans, labor-management committees, and work-redesign projects.[5] The recent increase in these activities resulted from (1) the rise in foreign and domestic competition, which required firms to become more efficient to remain competitive; (2) an increased desire on the part of several employers and union leaders to encourage workers to become more involved in their jobs; and (3) the work of the now defunct National Center for Productivity and Quality of Working Life.

The importance of these efforts was reflected in the enactment of the Labor-Management Cooperation Act of 1978. This act was designed to encourage cooperative union-management ventures "to improve communication, . . . explore new and innovative joint approaches to achieving organizational effectiveness," permit greater worker participation, and eliminate economic conditions that limit the competitive ability and economic growth of a plant, region, or industry. The Act empowered the Federal Mediation and Conciliation Service to provide financial and other assistance to aid companies and unions in this process.[6]

One of the more unusual formats for cooperation that developed during this period was the areawide labor-management committee.[7] Although several communities, such as Toledo, Ohio and Louisville, Kentucky, had developed these committees as early as the mid-1940s, it was the success of the Jamestown, New York Committee in 1972 that drew particular attention in recent years. An additional twenty-odd committees have emerged since 1972, including three in large metropolitan areas: Buffalo, Philadelphia, and St. Louis.

Additional evidence of the upswing in cooperative labor-management activity may be found in the increase in the number of joint safety committees. The Bureau of National Affairs reported that in its 1979 survey of collective bargaining agreements, 43 percent contained provisions establishing such committees, compared to 31 percent in 1970 and 39 percent in 1975.[8]

Similarly, in a recent study of twenty-six sites with labor-management committees in Illinois, Derber and Flanigan found that a majority of the committees had been established in the 1970s. Moreover, five were found to be revitalized efforts of earlier years.[9] Although there is no way of determining whether there has been a marked increase in the number of Scanlon, Rucker, and Improshare plans and of quality-of-work-life projects, this seems likely from the recent attention provided such plans in the popular press, combined with indications that they have spread outside their traditional base in manufacturing into the service and public sectors.

Paradoxically, this increase in cooperative activity came at a time when relations between labor and management at the national level were strained as a result of the defeats of the Common Situs Picketing and

---

[5] National Center for Productivity and Quality of Working Life, *Recent Initiatives in Labor-Management Cooperation* (Washington, D.C.: Superintendent of Documents, 1978).

[6] 29 U.S.C. 175(a).

[7] John J. Popular, "Perspective: Area Labor-Management Committees," unpublished conference paper, "Symposium on Area Labor-Management Committees," Cornell University, July 21–25, 1980.

[8] Bureau of National Affairs, *Basic Patterns in Union Contracts*, 9th ed. (Washington, D.C.: BNA, 1979), p. 110.

[9] Milton Derber and Kevin Flanigan, *A Survey of Joint Labor-Management Cooperation Committees in Unionized Private Enterprises in the State of Illinois, 1979*, report to the U.S. Department of Labor (Washington, D.C.: USDOL, 1980).

Labor Law Reform bills.[10] Although an exploration of this apparent contradiction is beyond the scope of this article, it would seem that the harsh economic environment facing many firms in the 1970s provided the stimulus to shape local relationships in a direction independent from that pursued by national organizations.

PREVIOUS RESEARCH

Most of the research on union-management cooperation has tended to be descriptive of the types of bargaining relationships that may form within a cooperative bargaining relationships;[11] the opportunities and difficulties the parties face in a cooperative relationship;[12] and the detailed experience of one or another cooperative relationship.[13] Only in recent years have researchers attempted to conduct empirical investigations. These have included studies of union leaders' attitudes toward cooperative programs;[14] employee reponses to the Scanlon Plan;[15] and specific quality-of-work-life interventions.[16]

Two previous studies have highlighted

[10] See Richard Prosten, "The Longest Season: Union Organizing in the Last Decade, a/k/a How Come One Team Has to Play With Its Shoelaces Tied Together?" Industrial Relations Research Association, *Proceedings of The Thirty-First Annual Meeting, Chicago, August 29–31, 1978* (Madison, Wis.: IRRA, 1979), pp. 240–49, as well as other papers presented at that session.

[11] Excellent examples of this research are Robert Dubin, "Union-Management Co-operation and Productivity," *Industrial and Labor Relations Review*, Vol. 2, No. 2 (January 1949), pp. 195–209; Frederick H. Harbison and John R. Coleman, *Goals and Strategy in Collective Bargaining* (New York: Harper & Row, 1951); and Sumner H. Slichter, James J. Healy, and E. Robert Livernash, *The Impact of Collective Bargaining on Management* (Washington, D.C.: The Brookings Institution, 1960).

[12] By far the best example of this research is George Strauss and Leonard R. Sayles, "The Scanlon Plan: Some Organizational Problems," *Human Organization*, Vol. 16, No. 3 (Fall 1957), pp. 15–22. Also see George P. Shultz, "Worker Participation on Production Problems: A Discussion of Experience with the Scanlon Plan," *Personnel*, Vol. 28, No. 3 (November 1951), pp. 201–11.

[13] Examples of such case studies are Harold E. Brooks, "The Armour Automation Committee Experience," Industrial Relations Research Association, *Proceedings of the Twenty-First Annual Winter Meeting, Chicago, December 28–30, 1968* (Madison, Wis.: IRRA, 1970), pp. 137–43; Thomas Q. Gilson and Myron E. Lefcowitz, "A Plant-wide Productivity Bonus in a Small Factory: Study of an Unsuccessful Case," *Industrial and Labor Relations Review*, Vol. 10, No. 2 (January 1957), pp. 284–96; Robert B. Gray, "The Scanlon Plan—A Case Study," *British Journal of Industrial Relations*, Vol. 9, No. 3 (November 1971), pp. 291–313; and Wayne L. Horvitz, "The II WU-PMA Mechanization and Modernization Agreement," Industrial Relations Research Association, *Proceedings of the Twenty-First Annual Meeting, Chicago, December 28–30, 1968*, pp. 144–51.

[14] Lee Dyer, David B. Lipsky, and Thomas A. Kochan, "Union Attitudes Toward Management Cooperation," *Industrial Relations*, Vol. 16, No. 2 (May 1977), pp. 163–72; and Alan M. Ponak and C. R. P. Fraser, "Union Activists' Support for Joint Programs," *Industrial Relations*, Vol. 18, No. 2 (Spring 1977), pp. 197–209.

[15] See, for example, Robert A. Ruh, Raymond G. Johnson, and M. P. Scontino, "The Scanlon Plan: Participation in Decision-Making and Job Attitudes," *Journal of Industrial and Organizational Psychology*, Vol. 1, No. 1 (Spring 1973), pp. 36–45.

[16] Paul S. Goodman, *Assessing Organizational Change: The Rushton Quality of Work Experiment* (New York: Wiley, 1979); and Barry A. Macy, "The Bolivar Quality of Work Life Program: A Longitudinal Behavioral and Performance Assessment, Industrial Relations Research Association, *Proceedings of the Thirty-Second Annual Meeting, Atlanta, December 28–30, 1979* (Madison, Wis.: IRRA, 1980), pp. 83–93.

the methodological obstacles associated with research on union-management cooperation: lack of adequate records, the frequent inability or unwillingness of the parties to provide performance data, and the short duration of many programs or studies.[17] In the present study, those problems were alleviated by the author's attempts to gain a high level of cooperation at each research site. Extensive longitudinal data were obtained on the two key variables, plus several others, and minutes of meetings and other documentation from the cooperative program were also solicited.

The theoretical basis of this study is Kochan and Dyer's model of organizational change, which is based, in turn, on an integration of the organizational change and industrial relations literatures.[18] Their model sets forth the factors and conditions they believe lead to: the initial consideration of a cooperative venture by a union and an employer; the parties' selection of a specific change program; and the maintenance over time of the parties' commitment to cooperation.

RESEARCH DESIGN

Selection of the design

This field study employed both qualitative and quantitative techniques to evaluate the operation and effectiveness of union-management programs. The qualitative methods included extensive interviewing and examination of appropriate documents and records. The results of this portion of the research produced lengthy case studies, which will be reported elsewhere; some of this information will be used here, however, to enrich the quantitative analysis.

A stratified, multiple-group, single-intervention, interrupted-time-series design[19] augmented the basic case-study methodology. An interrupted-time-series design involves measurement of an outcome variable before and after a treatment or intervention is introduced. If the intervention has had an effect, it will be indicated by a change in the pattern of the data in the time series.[20]

In this study, the intervention point was the formal date marking the beginning of the cooperative labor-management endeavor. Interrupted-time-series designs are particularly appropriate for studies in which "measurement is unobtrusive and the respondents are not reacting to multiple testings."[21] The present research measured output per hour and level of employment—both of which can be measured unobtrusively.[22]

The research design employed for this analysis has all the attributes of the interrupted-time-series design plus the use of

---

[17] Thomas K. Kochan, Lee Dyer, and David B. Lipsky, *The Effectiveness of Union-Management Safety and Health Committees* (Kalamazoo, Mich.: W. E. Upjohn Institute for Employment Research, 1977); and White, "The Scanlon Plan."

[18] Thomas A. Kochan and Lee Dyer, "A Model of Organizational Change in the Context of Union-Management Relations," *Journal of Applied Behavioral Science*, Vol. 12, No. 1 (Spring 1976), pp. 59–78.

[19] Gene V. Glass, Victor L. Willson, John M. Gottman, *Design and Analysis of Time Series Experiments* (Boulder, Colo.: Colorado Associated University Press, 1975).

[20] See Donald T. Campbell and Julian C. Stanley, *Experimental and Quasi-Experimental Designs for Research* (Chicago: Rand McNally, 1963); and Thomas D. Cook and Donald T. Campbell, *The Design and Conduct of Quasi-Experiments and True Experiments in Field Settings*, in Marvin Dunnette, ed., *Handbook of Industrial and Organizational Psychology* (Chicago: Rand McNally, 1976).

[21] Cook and Campbell, *Design and Conduct*, p. 274.

[22] Eugene J. Webb, Donald T. Campbell, Richard D. Schwartz, and Lee Sechrest, *Unobtrusive Measures: Nonreactive Research in the Social Sciences* (Chicago: Rand McNally, 1966).

multiple experimental units, each of which is distinguished by some feature. In this study, the distinguishing feature was the type of union-management program in each plant: Scanlon Plan, Rucker Plan, or plant-wide committee.

There are two principal strengths of a multiple-group, single-intervention design. The design permits an examination of the pervasiveness of an intervention effect across different groups, and it can lead to the development of a typology of the reactions of different groups in one type of intervention.[23] In the present study, however, the groups (or plants or "experimental units") remained largely the same; it was the type of intervention that differed.

In addition, this research improved in several other ways on the methodology usually employed in such studies. First, the measures of effectiveness (output per hour and level of employment) were calculated at monthly instead of the usual quarterly or yearly intervals. Second, qualitative data were collected to determine whether other factors unrelated to the intervention were at work. Of particular concern was the possibility of coincidental increases in capital investment; but this issue did not materialize, since none of the ten firms studied reported significant increases in capital investment as a cause of productivity improvements. At four of the sites, documentary evidence substantiated this apparent lack of investment; many of the other sites were experiencing economic difficulties that precluded any investment of this nature. Also, many of the sites experienced such abrupt changes in productivity after the introduction of a cooperative plan that other explanations, such as capital investment, were not plausible. Finally, by using a four- to five-year time frame, this study controlled to some extent for other influences on productivity and employment,

such as seasonal and other short-run changes in demand.

Site Selection

Firms with labor-management productivity programs were selected from lists compiled in the 1977 and 1978 *Directory of Labor-Management Committees.*[24] In response to a letter of inquiry mailed during February and March 1978 and again in February 1979, thirty firms agreed to participate in the project. After preliminary investigations, ten sites were selected.

The choice of the ten sites was based on an assessment of the resources available to complete the project. In particular, limiting the sample to ten firms permitted the investigator to obtain and maintain the level of cooperation needed from each site to make the project a success. In addition, the sites were selected on the basis of accessibility, commonality of production, and variation in the type of cooperative program.

The investigator guaranteed the parties at each research site that he would attempt to maintain the utmost confidentiality in interviewing and collecting data from the participants. In spite of this guarantee, the parties at one site, after having engaged in most of the evaluation process, belatedly refused to provide productivity and employment data; and therefore this site had to be dropped from the study.

Table 1 presents several characteristics of the nine sites studied. All nine are manufacturing plants in the private sector, and all but one are subsidiaries of larger corporations. The range of bargaining-unit size, 129–1,200, makes this a sample of small- to medium-sized plants. Finally, the technology of the sites was relatively uniform; as measured by a Woodward scale,[25] all were characterized as mass-production operations.

[23] Glass, Willson, and Gottman, *Design and Analysis*, pp. 23–25 and 39–40.

[24] National Center for Productivity and Quality of Working Life, *Directory of Labor-Management Committees* (Washington, D.C.: Superintendent of Documents, 1977 and 1978).

[25] Joan Woodward, *Industrial Organization: Theory and Practice* (London: Oxford University Press, 1965), p. 39.

TABLE 1
Selected Characteristics of Research Sites.

Site	Product Produced	SIC Number	Bargaining-Unit Size	Employee Characteristics				Type of Cooperative Program
				Age Distribution			Percent Female	
				Under 30	30–55	Over 55		
1	Abrasive Cutting Wheels	3291	160	17%	68%	20%	17%	Scanlon Plan
2	Jet Engine Parts	3722	890	10%	70%	20%	16%	Scanlon Plan
3	Steel Casters	3429	129	40%	40%	20%	40%	Scanlon Plan
4	Steel Shelves	2542	150	47%	35%	23%	0%	Scanlon Plan
5	Steel Chain	3496	450	15%	70%	15%	44%	Rocker Plan
6	Roller Chain	3566	241	20%	40%	40%	44%	Rocker Plan
7	Automotive Components	3694	500	10%	70%	20%	20%	Plantwide Committee
8	Fabricated Steel	331	1,200	40%	25%	35%	3%	Plantwide Committees
9	Ball Bearings	3562	699	40%	30%	30%	35%	Plantwide Committees

Data and measurement

The descriptive data for this study were collected through on-site interviews, using a structured interview schedule adapted from the instrument used by Kochan, Dyer, and Lipsky in their study of safety committees.[26] The schedule was augmented by examination of documents, records, and the minutes of meetings related to the programs. Follow-up visits were made to six of the research sites and extensive telephone conversations and mail correspondence were carried out for the others. Archival data were used to assess the impact of the labor-management programs on the two dependent variables analyzed here—productivity and employment.

Productivity was defined as employee output per hour and was calculated on a monthly basis.[27] Few difficulties were encountered with the measurement of labor input; in most cases, this was simply the total number of hours worked each month. Output was then more difficult to measure. If the plant or firm under study produced only one product, or if several products were produced but each required roughly equivalent labor input, no measurement difficulties existed. If different products were produced and required unequal amounts of labor input, a weighted output index was called for. This study found, however, that most firms do not have an accurate measure of their productivity. At only one site was the firm's measurement capability sufficiently sophisticated to permit anything but a rough estimate of output per hour. Further, the parties at three of the sites failed to keep data

---

[26] Kochan, Dyer, and Lipsky, *The Effectiveness of Union-Management Safety and Health Committees.*

[27] For the methods used, see Leon Greenberg, *A Practical Guide to Productivity Measurement* (Washington, D.C.: Bureau of National Affairs, 1973); and U.S. Department of Labor, Bureau of Labor Statistics, *BLS Handbook of Methods, Bulletin 1910* (Washington, D.C.: GPO, 1976).

that would have permitted even a crude estimate of output per hour. For those sites, financial measures of output were employed,
similar to those used by Puckett.[28]

In most cases, monthly employment was
measured by the average number of workers
employed during the week of the twelfth day
of the month. As with the measurement of
productivity, however, some deviation in the
research design had to be made. Two firms
provided employment data for the last week
of each month and one provided only average
annual employment figures. Employment
was considered stable when its change from
one period to another was not statistically
significant.

Time-series analysis was used to measure changes in productivity and employment within each firm studied. It is
important to stress that only within-site comparisons were made. For a host of reasons,
including the dissimilarity of production
methods among the firms and the use of different productivity measures among the
sites, it was impossible to make comparisons
across the nine sites. Changes in productivity and employment within sites are appropriate measures of program effectiveness, however, since these measures reflect
program goals. In order to control for industry trends, an analysis was made of employment data for the industries of which the
nine plants are a part and for the same
time frames as those used to analyze the
sites.[29]

Data Analysis

The time-series data on productivity and employment were analyzed by fitting regression
lines before and after the initiation of the cooperative programs (interventions) and by
examining changes in the parameters (slope
and intercept). Unfortunately, time-series
data are not appropriate for ordinary least
squares analysis, which requires the error
terms to be independent. That condition is
generally not present in serial data, which
tend to be correlated; any observation in a
time-series, that is, may be predicted to some
degree by the observations immediately preceding it or from previous random shocks.
There are methods for compensating for this
problem, however, that allow the data to be
subjected to conventional least squares analysis. Those methods, known as ARIMA
models (autoregressive, integrative, moving
averages), were developed by Box and Jenkins,[30] and were adopted for interrupted
time-series analysis by Glass, Willson, and
Gottman. Their methods and computer software were utilized in this research.[31]

The analysis compared the actual time-
series data on employment and productivity
in the post-intervention period to the results
that would have been expected from the pre-
intervention observations. A statistically significant change in level (intercept) thus indicates an abrupt change in productivity or
employment, whereas a statistically significant change in drift (slope) indicates a shift

[28] Elbridge S. Puckett, "Productivity Achievments—A Measure of Success," in Fred G.
Lesieur, *The Scanlon Plan: A Frontier in Labor-Management Cooperation* (Cambridge, Mass.:
The MIT Press, 1958), pp. 109–17. In one case (Site One), the measure of productivity used
was *(sales value of production)* / *(hours worked)*; in a second case (Site Three), *(sales value
of production, adjusted for price increases)* / *(hours worked)*; in the third case (Site Four),
(sales value of production) / *(labor costs)*.

[29] The data were for three- and four-digit SIC industries. U.S. Department of Labor, Bureau of Labor Statistics, *Employment and Earnings, United States, 1909–78, Bulletin
1312–11* (Washington, D.C.: GPO, 1979).

[30] George F. P. Box and Gwilyn M. Jenkins, *Time-Series Analysis: Forecasting and Control* (San Francisco: Holden Day, 1970).

[31] Glass, Willson, and Gottman, *Design and Analysis.*

in the trend over time of productivity and employment. Yet another possible result is an abrupt upward shift in level, followed by a gradual decline in the drift; that result might demonstrate that the intervention had an initial effect but then began to lose its potency.[32]

To increase the sensitivity of the test, every effort was made to ensure that there was a sufficient number of data points and that the data points extended over a reasonable time period. The data were plotted on a monthly basis, thereby generating approximately 22 to 65 points; and in all but one case, this was considered to be within an acceptable range.[33] The use of the four-to-five-year time frame—two years before and two after the inception of the cooperative program—should account for all possible patterns of variation.

As was noted earlier, the point of intervention was considered to be the date of the program's official inception. Two of the sites had programs of longer duration than the others and were evaluated on the basis of their continued effectiveness. In these situations, the effective date of the most recent (at the time of this study) colletive bargaining agreement was treated as the intervention point. This date was chosen because in both cases the parties reaffirmed their commitment to the cooperative effort by contractual agreement, when either the union or the company could have ended the program at that point.

Limitations

A number of potential limitations associated with this research should be briefly noted. Limitations due to the research design include the possibility that unmeasured variables influenced productivity and employment; the selection of sites only in manufacturing and with relatively small work forces; and the unpredictable effects of self-selection by firms agreeing to participate in the study.

Additional limitations include the small number of sites studied (although no other empirical study has included as many); the relatively short length (22 to 65 months) of the time-series design; and the questionable accuracy of the firms' data, in particular, the broad measures of productivity. As noted above, only a basic measure of productivity could be utilized because of the relatively unsophisticated methods of record keeping maintained by most of the firms. Changes in either the quality or mix of production could have affected the productivity measure, either positively or negatively. Qualitative data were collected to insure against this potential ambiguity, however.[34]

RESULTS AND ANALYSIS

This section presents for each research site the results of the analysis of productivity and employment data, along with brief vignettes containing the highlights of the cooperative activity. The section begins with an analysis of the experience with Scanlon and Rucker productivity-sharing plans (Sites One through Six) and continues with an analysis of the experience with labor-management committees (Sites Seven through Nine).

Table 2 reports the productivity and employment experience of the nine sites. The table contains point estimates of the level

---

[32] A complete discussion of the possible intervention effects is contained in Cook and Campbell, *Design and Conduct,* pp. 227–46.

[33] Glass, Willson, and Gottman, *Design and Analysis,* p. 112.

[34] At each site, interview questions were posed as to the stability of the firm's production mix over time. The respondents reported little or no major changes in the mix of products over the relevant period.

TABLE 2
Productivity and Employment Data for the Nine Sites.
(*t*-statistics in parentheses)

Site	Level	Level Change	Drift	Drift Change
Site One				
Productivity	19.94	6.89	0.07	−0.05
(N = 58, d.f. = 54)	(30.97)	(814***)	(1.70)	(−0.97)
Site Two				
Productivity: Manufacturing	.92	.40	0.03	0.02
(N = 65, d.f. = 61)	(4.81)	(209*)	(.81)	(0.66)
Productivity: Repair	3.59	0.49	−0.06	0.06
(N = 65, d.f. = 61)	(15.88)	(1.56)	(−5.15)	(3.38***)
Employment	105.81	1.21	−0.08	−0.09
(N = 61, d.f. = 57)	(26.84)	(0.31)	(−0.06)	(−0.05)
Site Three				
Productivity	64.25	6.20	−0.35	.68
(N = 54, d.f. = 50)	(19.28)	(1.47)	(−1.43)	(2.35*)
Employment	96.95	−3.61	2.97	−0.52
(N = 50, d.f. = 46)	(15.69)	(−0.59)	(2.40)	(−0.31)
Site Four				
Productivity	3.80	−0.39	0.00	0.01
(N = 52, d.f. = 48)	(19.25)	(−1.50)	(0.34)	(0.65)
Employment	122.81	−6.79	1.21	−0.74
(N = 51, d.f. = 47)	(14.22)	(−0.76)	(1.68)	(−0.62)
Site Five				
Productivity	12.92	1.94	0.05	−0.15
(N = 52, d.f. = 48)	(14.72)	(1.90*)	(0.75)	(−1.71*)
Employment	624.72	12.58	−6.21	8.52
(N = 60, d.f. = 56)	(28.97)	(0.58)	(−1.35)	(1.31)
Site Six				
Productivity	3.37	0.98	0.01	0.00
(N = 58, d.f. = 54)	(24.16)	(4.99***)	(0.66)	(0.14)
Employment	413.67	8.46	−3.91	2.43
(N = 55, d.f. = 53)	(46.74)	(0.96)	(−1.91)	(0.98)
Site Seven				
Employment	576.08	−170.97	9.65	−17.59
(N = 48, d.f. = 44)	(37.65)	(−8.59***)	(9.44)	(−12.15***)
Site Eight				
Productivity	66.05	−0.95	−0.21	0.03
(N = 48, d.f. = 44)	(23.95)	(−0.21)	(−1.40)	(0.07)
Employment	138.87	1.39	−1.12	1.84
(N = 48, d.f. = 44)	(18.06)	(0.18)	(0.78)	(0.76)
Site Nine				
Productivity	18.52	0.75	−0.41	0.34
(N = 22, d.f. = 18)	(35.18)	(1.09)	(−2.92)	(2.57*)
Employment	815.24	−13.78	−8.48	9.33
(N = 39, d.f. = 35)	(47.89)	(−0.80)	(−1.74)	(1.18)

* p < .05.
*** p < .001.

and drift of the time-series data at time $T = 0$ and also associated t-statistics. Estimation of the post-intervention change in level and drift, with associated t-statistics, permits analysis of the impact of the cooperative union-management effort. Because of space considerations, the results of the statistical analysis of the industry data have been omitted. In general, however, the employment experience at the plant and industry level displayed similar patterns.

SITE ONE

Site One instituted a Scanlon Plan as a last effort to save the plant from a corporate decision to close it in 1971 for economic reasons. Through a series of hastily arranged, tripartite negotiations (among management, labor, and state government), terms were reached under which management would continue to operate the plant. Two of these terms were union pledges to effect a substantial increase in productivity and to end negotiated work standards. In return, management agreed to contract language that precluded the layoff of workers as a result of suggestions flowing from the Scanlon committees.

Results

This site's experience was analyzed for the period January 1969 to December 1973, with the intervention point being March 1971, the start of the Scanlon Plan. As Table 2 indicates, there was an abrupt rise in productivity to a higher and statistically significant level following the introduction of the Scanlon Plan. For the first three years of the Plan, bonuses averaged 1.0 percent, 4.4 percent, and 9.3 percent of employee earnings. Although the firm was unable to provide monthly employment data, thus precluding statistical analysis, annual data were provided. There had been a layoff of 20 percent of the bargaining unit's members in the six months before the institution of the Plan, but employment stabilized after its introduction.

Analysis

This is a classic case of union-management cooperation to save the business and in turn save the jobs of union members. Scanlon enthusiasts have claimed that productivity can "go through the roof." Although this is unlikely to be a universal result, this firm certainly experienced a marked increase in productivity, along with no further reduction in employment. In subsequent years, the Scanlon Plan continued to be successful in this plant, and ten years following its installation, the program remained active.

SITE TWO

Site Two's Scanlon Plan began as the result of management's desire to create an improved workplace environment. Top management was committed to a program of employee participation that would improve communications and encourage better job performance; the Scanlon Plan instituted reflected this commitment. The company and the union created 26 production committees, as well as a 24-member committee to screen suggestions. Opportunities were created to permit employees who were not selected as members of these committees to participate in them. First-line supervision was encouraged, trained, and expected to take a leading role in the implementation and operation of the production committees. In the first three and a half years of the Scanlon Plan, 1,884 suggestions were submitted, of which 70 percent were accepted and 7 percent were still under investigation at the time of this study. In the first three years of the plan, bonuses averaged 5.6, 6.8, and 6.6 percent of earnings, respectively.

Results

The productivity and employment data for Site Two were analyzed for the periods January 1973 to December 1977 and December 1972 to December 1977, respectively, with the intervention occurring in May 1975. Although there was only one Scanlon Plan, one bargaining unit, and one plant location, management, with the exception of several staff functions (such as industrial relations), was organized into two separate operating divisions. Production varied significantly between these divisions, with the larger engaged in parts manufacturing and the smaller involved in repair and service. For this reason, productivity was measured separately for each.

Table 2 shows that productivity increased significantly in the manufacturing division following introduction of the plan. Over time, there was a positive, although not statistically significant, upward trend in productivity. The productivity analysis for the repair division reveals that the increase was more gradual, as indicated by the change in drift. Employment remained stable, with almost no change in the level or the drift.

Analysis

The experience under this Scanlon Plan demonstrates that internal, noneconomic factors can be a sufficiently powerful stimulus to induce effective union-management cooperation. A critical factor in the success of this Scanlon Plan is the commitment of top management to employee involvement in the daily and long-range operation of the company. This commitment has manifested itself in the creation of an environment and structure to produce the desired outcome. Also important has been the maintenance of a sense of equity by virtue of the payment to employees of bonuses stemming from productivity increases.

SITE THREE

Site Three's Scanlon Plan resulted from compromises struck by the company and the union in collective bargaining. The company had first proposed the institution of an individual incentive system to cover only the hourly employees who constituted the bargaining unit. The union rejected this proposal and proposed instead the development of a Scanlon Plan that would cover all employees in the company. Although the management preferred a different group-incentive plan, it finally agreed to the Scanlon Plan.

The plan followed the traditional Scanlon design, with a suggestion system, four Production Committees, and one Screening Committee. The bonus formula included hourly, clerical, and salaried employees. An analysis of the minutes of Screening Committee meetings indicated that most of its deliberations concerned suggestions submitted by the Production Committees. In contrast to the experience of the other firms studied, there was almost no discussion of long-range or environmental issues.

In the first year of the plan, bonuses averaging 4.8 percent of employee earnings were paid in nine of the thirteen possible bonus periods; in the second year, ten bonuses were paid, averaging 3.4 percent; and in the third year, two bonuses averaged only .02 percent. Only in the first year was there an end-of-the-year surplus in the reserve (5.5 percent). In the last year of the plan (1979), the plan paid only one bonus of 2.5 percent.

In July 1979, management unilaterally withdrew office and salaried employees from the calculation of the bonus, claiming that any bonus that was being earned was the result of efforts by those groups. This action altered the basis upon which the bonus was calculated and raised the spectre of management's manipulating the administration of the bonus formula. In fact, following six more bonus periods without positive results, the union exercised its right to terminate the plan upon 30 days' notice, thus ending the program.

Results

The productivity and employment experience of Site Three was analyzed for the periods January 1975 to December 1979 and January 1974 to December 1979, respectively, with the intervention occurring in December 1976. There was a positive, although not statistically significant, increase in productivity following the introduction of the plan. On the other hand, over time, a downward drift in productivity was reversed and shifted upward to a statistically significant degree. Employment remained unchanged and tended to follow an upward industry pattern.

Analysis

The Scanlon Plan at Site Three appears to have been moderately successful in improving productivity. The demise of the plan after three years exemplifies the effects of deviation from traditional principles of implementing Scanlon Plans. First, a Scanlon Plan is much more than an incentive system; it is a different philosophy of conducting an organization's operations.[35] This essential aspect of the plan was missing here. Decision-making authority was never truly placed in the hands of the Production Committees, as approximately 40 percent of their suggestions were referred to the Screening Committee. Also, the Screening Committee itself concentrated on those suggestions and never became a vehicle for the discussion between the company and the union of broader subjects. The separation of the office and salaried work force from the bonus formula

provides additional evidence that this management had not completely accepted the Scanlon philosophy, which stresses the need for the entire organization to work together. Finally, the adjustment of the bonus in midyear, for factors other than extensive technological or financial reasons, seriously undermined the sense of organizational equity needed to facilitate the cooperative process.

SITE FOUR

Site Four was the only family-operated firm in the study. The Scanlon Plan at this site is one of the oldest in the United States, having been established in 1955. The plan was first suggested by the union in 1952, and in contrast with the many other plans instituted during the same era to improve the economic solvency of firms, it was designed to improve relations between the company and the union, to resolve existing problems, and as a financial incentive. The inclusion of this site in the study permitted consideration of the factors contributing to the longterm institution of a Scanlon Plan.

The plan at Site Four calls for five Production Committees and one Screening Committee, which continue to meet monthly and semimonthly, respectively. Interestingly, the semimonthly meetings of the Screening Committee have separate meeting agendas. One brief meeting each month is used to review the bonus system, and the other, more detailed meeting is used to review suggestions and discuss plant problems and long-range issues. Unlike many other suggestion systems that tend to dissipate over time, the system at Site Four has remained vibrant. During the period 1976–79, the annual suggestion rate was 1.5 to 3.0 suggestions per employee each year. Finally,

---

[35] Carl F. Frost, John H. Wakely, and Robert A. Ruh, *The Scanlon Plan for Organization Development: Identity, Participation, and Equity* (East Lansing: Michigan State University Press, 1974).

bonuses paid under the plan were frequent and substantial. Over a 52-month period (from January 1975 to May 1979), bonuses were paid 46 times, with seven payments in excess of 20 percent of employee earnings. These bonuses averaged 10.9, 8.7, 10.8, and 10.8 percent, respectively, in the first four years of that period, and 13.8 percent in the last third of a year.

Results

Productivity and employment were analyzed for the periods January 1975 to April 1979 and March 1975 to May 1979, respectively. The intervention point was the reaffirmation of the plan by virtue of its continuation following the close of contract negotiations in January 1977. In examining plans of long duration, one would not expect abrupt level changes in performance to take place in later years, and none did in Site Four. Productivity and employment tended to be stable, although the direction of the t-statistics for both level changes were negative. This can be explained by a severe drop in economic activity experienced by the firm through the first five months of 1977. The trend in productivity was modestly positive, whereas the trend in employment was slightly downward.

Analysis

As was expected, continuation of the Scanlon Plan after twenty years did not produce a dramatic increase in productivity. Nevertheless, a plan of such long duration is notable. Although some might suggest that the chief cause of the plan's continuity is its payout of large bonuses,[36] other factors appear to have also contributed. Employees' identification with the family owners, along with a strong union and company commitment to the Scanlon concept of a respect for the ability of all organization members to contribute to

the success of the organization, provides a more complete explanation.

SITES FIVE AND SIX

Sites Five and Six are plants within the same division of a large industrial conglomerate. In the analysis of their productivity and employment experience, they are treated separately. The plants are geographically separated by 45 miles; they have separate sets of managers; their employees are represented by different locals of the same international union, each of which bargains a separate collective bargaining agreement; and the plants manufacture different products. At the same time, however, there were some common features associated with the invocation and operation of both plans that can be presented simultaneously.

Eight years prior to the institution of the Rucker Plan, the company and the unions had agreed to eliminate the plants' previous incentive systems. During the 1970s, both plants were being adversely affected by foreign competition. The Rucker Plan was thereby introduced to improve productivity (and the firm's competitive position), to provide additional rewards for employees' efforts (the company had taken a firm stance in bargaining with the union on wages), and to improve communications.

The overall structure of both Rucker Plans was the same. Each had a suggestion system, two employee committees, and a bonus formula. Under Rucker Plans, employees submit suggestions to an Idea Coordinator. The Idea Coordinator pursues the suggestion with appropriate managerial personnel and then responds to the employee.

The employee committees were of two kinds: production and steering. Composed primarily of rank-and-file workers, the Production Committees reviewed all sugges-

---

[36] A. J. Geare suggests this relationship in "Productivity from Scanlon-type Plans," *Academy of Management Review,* Vol. 1, No. 3 (July 1976), pp. 99–108.

tions (accepted and rejected) and discussed such in-plant problems as quality, materials, and pricing. At Site Five, employees were elected to serve on the committee for three-month periods, whereas at Site Six, employees were chosen by management with the approval of the union for six-month intervals. The Screening Committees, composed of top union and company officials, addressed questions similar to those above, but also considered more significant matters, such as market and general economic conditions, pricing decisions, product design, the introduction of new products, and the bonus calculations.

The bonus formula was based on the relationship between bargaining-unit payroll costs and production value. Production value was calculated by subtracting defective goods returned and costs of materials, supplies, and services from the sale value of goods sold. At Site Five, this relationship was determined to be 37.74 percent; at Site Six, it was 40.91 percent. Although, as will be seen below, there were substantial increases in productivity, almost no bonuses were paid at either site. This was due to a divisional management decision not to raise prices. This decision, at a time of rapidly rising costs for materials, supplies, and services, eliminated most of the potential bonus.[37]

Results

The productivity and employment data for Site Five were analyzed for the periods January 1975 to April 1979 and January 1974 to December 1978, respectively. The intervention point was July 1976, when the Rucker Plan was instituted. The results idicate that employment was stable, showing a slight positive increase in level and a somewhat larger, but not statistically significant, upward drift. The more interesting finding is

that the level of productivity increased but that the trend was negative. This would indicate that the plan initially had a positive effect, which later dissipated rather quickly. In 1976, there were three bonuses paid of 13.2, 28.6, and 37.4 cents per hour. After that no bonuses were paid.

At Site Six, productivity and employment were analyzed for the periods January 1974 to October 1978 and January 1974 to March 1979, respectively, with the intervention point being July 1976. The productivity improvement that occurred was quite pronounced. There was an abrupt upward shift in the level of productivity followed by a stable trend. Following the introduction of the plan, employment also increased slightly, in a trend similar to that in the industry.

The bonuses paid at Site Six were larger than those at Site Five, but they were not paid regularly. In 1976, no bonuses were paid; in 1977, there were two months of 14.8 and 56.8 cents per hour; and in 1978, two bonuses of 46.8 and 33.4 cents per hour, with an end-of-the-year bonus of 2.79 cents per hour. Although some reduction in suggestions might have been expected at both sites, the suggestion programs, which had initially been quite active, experienced a steady decline and became mostly inactive. Finally, just prior to the third anniversary of the Rucker Plan, four-month strikes took place at both plants during the renegotiation of the collective bargaining agreement. The failure of the plan to pay consistent bonuses was a key factor in these prolonged disputes.

Analysis

In the Kochan-Dyer model of organizational change in unionized settings, an important factor in institutionalizing union-management cooperation over time is the equitable distribution of benefits stemming from the

---

[37] Production value is sensitive to price increases; that is, unless prices for goods sold, the cost of materials and supplies, and payroll costs increase in roughly the same proportion, as they did in the base period in this case, the bonus will not increase in step with productivity.

endeavor. Equity was not present in this situation. At the outset, the Rucker Plan was strongly supported by the employees at both sites. As a result of the plan's failure to pay a bonus consistently, however, interest waned. A good indication of this was the decline in the effectiveness of the suggestion program. At Site Five, the decline in productivity that followed on the heels of an initially significant improvement also lends support to the Kochan-Dyer theory.

Of greater concern, however, is the lack of control workers have concerning their earnings in these group productivity-sharing plans. (This problem is not limited solely to Rucker Plans.) In these two cases, worker productivity increased, yet additional earnings were not forthcoming. Management's ability to affect the bonus in a nonmanipulative manner, by not raising prices during a period of rising costs, highlights the fact that workers may not be in control of their destinies in these situations.

SITE SEVEN

Site Seven, the first of three sites with labor-management committees to be examined, was a victim of lost tariff protection and foreign competition. As late as 1966, the firm employed 1,700 persons and was the major employer in its community. As a result of its loss of protection from competition, the corporation moved the plant's largest product line out of the country, reducing employment to 1,000. The major loss of jobs, and further economic threats posed by a highly competitive industry, induced the company and the union to hold a series of informal discussion to identify potential solutions. These discussions, in turn, led to formal meetings in which management warned that a complete plant closing was possible and that a wage reduction was necessary to ensure the economic viability of the plant.

In subsequent negotiations, the union agreed contractually to a one-year morato-rium on all wage increases. In addition, the parties agreed to create a high-level Joint Management-Labor Study Committee (JMLSC) "to investigate solutions to productivity and employee utilization problems." These solutions were to be generated by a "constructive new approach." Unfortunately, shortly after these negotiations, corporate management, over the strong objection of the plant manager, instituted a 5 percent pay increase for salaried personnel. This action clouded in an atmosphere of distrust the developing cooperative relationship between the company and the union.

The joint committee met twelve times in 1973 and six times through December 1974, but analysis of minutes and other relevant documents indicates that only animosity resulted. Most of the JMLSC's deliberations centered on which constituency was to bear responsibility for the poor economic position of the plant. Following the last meeting, the parties mutually agreed to allow the committee to die out, with the caveat that they would meet again if either side had an issue to discuss. Although the JMLSC continued to be part of the collective bargaining agreement, neither side had called a meeting in over five years.

Results

This site provided only employment data; the firm was unwilling to provide its productivity data in a manner that could be properly analyzed for this research. The employment experience, however, does permit several lessons to be drawn from the case, thus warranting its inclusion here. The employment data were analyzed for the period November 1970 to October 1974, with the intervention point being the start of the JMLSC in November 1972. The results show a statistically significant reduction in employment following the inception of the committee. Moreover, in contrast to the other sites in this research, Site Seven's experience was dramatically different from that of the industry at large. While employment was falling sharply throughout the industry, there was a steady upward trend at this plant.

Analysis

The failure of this joint committee to have an effect on the participants should come as no surprise. Merely creating a structure for co-operation without first bringing about a change of attitude will not result in meaningful union-management cooperation. Co-operation is a fragile creature—difficult to build and easily destroyed. It is quite possible that union-management efforts such as these require the participation of a skilled neutral to create an environment in which difficult problems may be effectively addressed. Finally, this case should serve as evidence of the limitations of cooperative union-management solutions. Creation of a committee, even assuming it were to be successful, probably would not have resulted in major shifts in the fortunes of this firm, due to environmental factors well beyond its control.

SITE EIGHT

Site Eight's union-management relationship follows the pattern set in Big Steel. Contained within its collective bargaining agreement are nine union-management committees, ranging in responsibilities from ones for civil rights and alcoholism to ones for employment security and productivity. Taken together, the nine committees have many of the elements of a productivity and quality-of-worklife program. The main focus for this study was on the Employment Security and Productivity Committee, despite the fact that this committee never met because neither side appeared willing to address seriously the productivity issue. This failure was unfortunate, since under the collective bargaining agreement, the ESP committee had been given a sizable mandate. The com-

mittee was to operate in an advisory capacity and meet no less often than once a month. The committee was to have a series of functions, including advising plant management on means of improving productivity and stimulating growth; promoting orderly and peaceful relations with employees; and achieving uninterrupted operations in the plant. In addition, either the plant manager or the local union president could suggest topics for consideration at meetings. Both sides also committed themselves to promoting the use of domestic steel.

Results

Both the productivity and employment data were analyzed for the period January 1975 to December 1978, with the intervention point being August 1977. Since the committee structure had been introduced over time, the intervention point used was the reaffirmation of the committees by continuing them in the 1977 collective agreement. Reflecting the general downturn in the U.S. economy at the time, productivity remained approximately the same over the period, and employment also remained stable.

Analysis

It would be naive to argue that the committee system generally, or the Employment Security and Productivity Committee in particular, had any impact on the experience of this firm. Clearly, a committee that never meets should have little or no impact on the productive process at the workplace. The experience at this site provides other evidence on the process of change, however.

In the Kochan-Dyer model, an important factor inducing change is a strong stimulus. Clearly, an insufficient stimulus existed to create commitment on the part of the union or the company in this case. The case also further demonstrates the futility of attempting to impose change externally. Unfortunately, rather than acknowledging this failure and selecting a different course of action, the parties once again, at the national level, recently created an even more elaborate system of local union-management cooperation and employee participation.[38]

SITE NINE

Site Nine demonstrates the fragile nature of union-management cooperation and the difficulty of employing scientific research designs in its evaluation. The parties at this site created a high-level committee called the Union-Management Study Group on Productivity and Quality of Worklife. The committee's mission was to examine problems associated with "productivity improvement," "quality of worklife," "reward pay systems," and "human relations" and had as its mandate (as stipulated in a memorandum of understanding between the parties):

> To develop relations that encourage teamwork and understanding between people; to provide an honest, open communication system that promotes a sense of responsibility, pride, satisfaction, and recognition for achievement.

At the outset, group meetings were held to develop and maintain open lines of communication between the committee and employees on the shop floor. Consultants from the company, union, and academia were employed to facilitate the work of the committee. Initially, several modest improvements in working conditions were implemented. After three months, seven subcommittees for different locations in the plant were in place. Other activities undertaken at the same time included group-process training, visits to other companies, and the development of an experimental work-redesign

project. The last effort was rejected by the employees involved, because of their concern about its potential implications for job security.

In spite of that rejection, the final product of the committee's work was a recommended addition to the collective bargaining agreement in which the company and the union agreed to begin to redesign the work process around production teams and to institute a work-group or plantwide productivity-sharing plan. Each work group would have the right to terminate the plan after a "reasonable" trial period, and no worker or group of workers would lose pay or seniority as a result of the plan. This proposal was defeated by a vote of the union's membership: 129 in favor and 540 opposed.

Results

Productivity and employment were analyzed for the periods June 1975 to March 1977 and January 1974 to March 1977, respectively. The intervention occurred in January 1976, when the Study Group was formed. Because the period of this analysis was so short, some additional productivity data following the end of the plan were used to diagnose the ARIMA model. Only seven productivity observations were available for the pre-intervention period because of differences over the period in methods of record keeping. Consistency in data measurement over a time series is an essential prerequisite for this research design. Caution should therefore be taken in interpreting these results. Productivity increased slightly following introduction of the committee, but it did exhibit a statistically significant positive trend. Employment, which had followed a declining pattern throughout the industry, also began to rise slightly.

---

[38] Labor Cools It with Big Steel," *Business Week*, April 28, 1980, pp. 26–27; and John Hoerr, "Beyond Bargaining: Unions and Bosses Try Trust," *Business Week*, May 5, 1980, p. 43.

Analysis

This coopeative effort failed for several reasons. There was a dispute among the union's leadership as to the merits of the program, one leader having resigned from the committee. Kochan and Dyer have suggested that if coalitions develop to block the cooperative venture, gaining an initial commitment will be less likely.[39] The evidence from this case supports their contention. Interviews with company and union officials consistently indicated that the consultants had pushed the parties too quickly and may have failed to account for internal union politics. Finally, supervision was not directly involved in the program. In spite of a positive trend in productivity, causal inferences from the operation of the committee would be inappropriate.

CONCLUSIONS

In contrast to most previous research on union-management cooperation, this study has shown that a scientific research design and performance measures can be utilized to assess the effectiveness of such programs. This strategy is optimized by complementing it with traditional forms of qualitative analysis.

Because of the small number of firms investigated and the relatively short periods of time analyzed, the results of this study must be considered preliminary. It is nevertheless suggestive that of the nine sites studied, four experienced statistically significant abrupt positive changes in productivity, and two others demonstrated statistically significant positive trends. Employment remained stable in eight cases and dropped significantly in only one; in most instances, employment tended to follow the industry pattern.

A major finding of this study has been to document the diversity of patterns in the practice of union-management cooperation. Support was also found for several propositions in the Kochan-Dyer model. For example, cooperation requires a stimulus to change a traditional bargaining relationship; in the present study, cooperation was stimulated by the dire financial position of one company and by adverse competitive conditions in several others. Additional stimuli were provided by factors internal to the firm, including a desire to upgrade the workplace environment, improve communication, and replace or supplement an existing compensation program. One site (Eight) demonstrated that cooperation could not be imposed by actors external to the immediate union-management relationship. Yet another site (Nine) provided evidenced of the ability of coalitions to block the permanent installation of a cooperative effort.

The importance of preserving organizational equity as a condition for maintaining cooperative endeavors must not be underestimated. Several cooperative efforts resulted in very few bonus payments. In three cases, management was able to "adjust" or "manipulate" the formula: in one instance, this was accomplished by redefining the labor ratio; in the other two, management failed to raise prices during an inflationary period.

In other cases, the frequent disbursement of bonuses appeared to provide the requisite sense of organizational equity to maintain commitment over time. At the same time, however, it should not be assumed that the potential for earning a bonus will be sufficient in itself to ensure the success of a cooperative endeavor. Key management and supervisory personnel must share the goals of the cooperative effort and be willing to share their authority to make decisions. Similarly, cooperative union-management endeavors must take into account the political realities within unions; in particular, care should be taken that union leaders are not perceived as co-opted by managers or

---

[39] Kochan and Dyer, "A Model of Organizational Change," pp. 68–69.

external consultants, as was the case at Site Nine.

The experience at Site Seven suggests that many union and employer representatives will need assistance in developing the proper attitudes for moving toward more cooperative stategies. In this respect, recognition must be given to the differences between unionized and nonunion settings when devising change strategies. Finally, neutrals and consultants must not only offer the parties a wide array of behavioral science training, but, as Site Nine shows, they must also be thoroughly skilled in the mechanics and implications of the collective bargaining agreement.[40]

---

[40] One of the great benefits to be derived from the area labor-management committee is its ability to provide this kind of expertise.

Qualitative Research
Methods

FIVE

In recent years, organizational researchers have been quite impressed with "numbers," as one can quickly infer from an inspection of the quantitative/statistical orientation of most reported research in the organizational science journals. This orientation can most likely be traced to the belief that quantitative research is somehow more scientific than research which relies on qualitative data. For this reason, it tends to be the orientation emphasized in most research methods courses provided during graduate training.

Clearly, there are trade-offs created by an exclusive focus on either quantitative or qualitative research methods. Studies involving large samples and sophisticated statistical analyses seem to provide an appearance of objectivity and high generalizability of the findings to other settings and samples. What is sacrificed, presumably, is a more in-depth and informed understanding of the phenomenon under investigation. Qualitative research, on the other hand, provides a highly detailed and richer account of the topic under investigation, but one which does not necessarily have a high degree of generalizability.

Indeed, both types of research orientations have their strengths and limitations.

Optimally, therefore, researchers should seek to capture aspects of both orientations. Such combined approaches should serve not only to enrich the nature of the research itself, but also to provide more confident statements concerning the validity of observed relationships. The use of multiple methods and the convergence of results across methods permits stronger statements concerning true effects and helps to circumvent potential problems of method variance or methodological artifact.

The opening article by Mintzberg highlights the "stream of decisions" in an extended program of important research. Mintzberg defends exploratory research, which is often denigrated for reflecting such characteristics as lack of formal hypotheses, post hoc analyses, and capitalization on chance findings. He further suggests that an obsession with statistical rigor may obscure rather than illuminate, or may yield insignificant (in the practical sense) results. The use of anecdotal data to complement systematic data is also highlighted as an important aid in theory building.

Levine's analysis of the Watergate investigation illustrates the utility of searching other fields for interesting and useful alternative methods. Washington Post reporters Bernstein and Woodward began with a theory, then enlarged its scope as they immersed themselves in their investigation. They exhibited great tenacity and creativity in their use of a variety of evidence-gathering techniques. Numerous topics in their story have analogs in organizational research: the use of evidence; formal and informal controls; alternative hypotheses (see Platt, Chapter 1); responsibility to the public (see, for example, the piece about ethics by Mirvis and Seashore in Chapter 6 of this book); the role of the editorial review process; the working relationship of the research team. Their story also conveys the curiosity, puzzlement of new facts, and the spurring on of incomplete understanding which can characterize an exciting research program.

Webb and Weick give us a reminder of the widely-read yet seldom heeded book, *Unobtrusive Measures* (Webb, Campbell, Schwartz, & Sechrest, 1966). Like some other writers, including those in this section of the book, they argue for more multimethod inquiry. Too many researchers "satisfice" in their data collection strategies; the field must "add variety to inquiry that registers a greater proportion of the variety in ongoing organizations." As one example, the effects of deadlines are analyzed via unobtrusive measures in a wide array of contexts, including applications to graduate school, the New York Stock Exchange, and the National Football League. Such "playfulness" could help to "reshuffle thinking about traditional organizational topics and introduce nontraditional topics . . . to the field."

The article by Luthans and Davis is based on Gordon Allport's nomothetic/idiographic distinction and the observation that almost all organizational research is nomothetic. The authors discuss the importance of assumptions upon which research is based. They also highlight the utility of single case experimental designs, which have been used extensively in behaviorism laboratory paradigms but not by many organizational researchers. Subjects can be used as their "own controls," as opposed to the usual creation of separate control groups. Luthans and Davis point out the advantages of this approach with respect to internal and external validities, its major weakness (generalizability), and the solution to this weakness (replications; see Lykken in Chapter 1). In addition, they indicate some problems of inferential statistics and the usefulness of visually inspecting data (Fields, Chapter 2). Other discussions in their paper are similarly consistent with the "qualitative" research movement.

The final reading, by Jick, merges the "complementary camps" of "qualitative" and "quantitative" methods. Interviews, surveys, archival records, and other techniques are used to converge on the effects of a merger on employees. Jick suggests that this triangulation provides not only a form of cross-validation but more, in that each method can uncover unique as well as common variance. Jick's results were mostly consistent. Discrepancies, though, become not a need for defensive reconciliation, but instead opportunities for enriching the explanation.

SUGGESTIONS FOR FURTHER READINGS

Bouchard, T. J. "Field Research Methods: Interviewing, Questionnaires, Participant Observation, Systematic Observation, Unobtrusive Measures." In M. D. Dunnette (ed.), *Handbook of Industrial and Organizational Psychology.* Chicago: Rand McNally, 1976.

Garfinkel, H. *Studies in Ethnomethodology.* Englewood Cliffs, NJ: Prentice-Hall, 1967.

Jauch, L. R., Osborn, R. N., & Martin, T. N. "Structural Content Analysis of Cases: A Complementary Method for Organizational Research." *Academy of Management Review,* 1980, *5,* 517–525.

Light, D. "Surface Data and Deep Structure: Observing the Organization of Professional Training." *Administrative Science Quarterly,* 1979, *24,* 551–559.

Morgan, G., & Smircich, L. "The Case for Qualitative Research." *Academy of Management Review,* 1980, *5,* 491–500.

Piore, M. J. "Qualitative Research Techniques in Economics." *Administrative Science Quarterly,* 1979, *24,* 560–569.

Van Maanen, J. "Observations on the Making of Policemen." *Human Organization,* 1973, *32,* 407–418.

Van Maanen, J., Dabbs, J. M., & Faulkner, R. R. *Varieties of Qualitative Research.* Beverly Hills, CA: Sage, 1982.

Webb, E. J., Campbell, D. J., Schwartz, R. D., & Sechrest, L. *Unobtrusive Measures: Nonreactive Research in the Social Sciences,* Chicago: Rand McNally, 1966.

Whyte, W. F. *Street Corner Society.* Chicago: University of Chicago Press, 1955.

An Emerging Strategy of "Direct" Research[1]

Henry Mintzberg

For about eight years now, a group of us at McGill University's Faculty of Management has been researching the process of strategy formation. Defining a strategy as a pattern in a stream of decisions, our central theme has been the contrast between "deliberate" strategies, that is, patterns intended before being realized, and "emergent" strategies, patterns realized despite or in the absence of intentions. Emergent strategies are rather common in organizations, or, more to the point, almost all strategies seem to be in some part at least, emergent. To quote that expression so popular on posters these days, "Life is a journey, not a destination."

In this article I will describe my journey into research, to step back from the stream of decisions concerning my own research since I began a doctoral dissertation in 1966, and to discuss the patterns—the themes or strategies—that appear. In retrospect, some seem more deliberate to me, others more emergent, but in general they appear to represent a blending of the two. The point I wish to make is that these themes form their own strategy of research, one that I would like to contrast with a more conventional strategy of research that seems to have dominated our field.

A word on the data base. I have been involved in three major research projects these past 13 years (and since three do not a sharp

pattern make, the title refers to an emerg*ing* rather than an emerg*ent* strategy). First was my doctoral dissertation, a study of the work of five managers through structured observation (Mintzberg, 1973). Essentially, I watched what each did for a week, and recorded it systematically—in terms of who they worked with, when, where, for how long, and for what purpose. These data were used to induce a set of characteristics and of roles of managerial work. Second, over the course of some years, teams of MBA students were sent out to study local organizations; one assignment was to take a single strategic decision and to describe the steps the organization had gone through from the very first stimulus to the authorization of the final choice. From these reports, we selected the 25 most complete and inferred a structure of the "unstructured" decision process (Mintzberg, Raisinghani, and Théorêt, 1976). Our third project, mentioned in the opening of this paper, involves the study of organizational strategies through the tracing of patterns in streams of decisions over periods of 30 or more years. This is a large project, at the present time involving a number of months of on-site research in each organization. We first spend a good deal of time reading whatever historical documents we can find, in order to develop thorough chronologies of decisions in various strategy

[1] *Administrative Science Quarterly*, 1979, 24, 582–589.

areas. Then we switch to interviews to fill in the gaps in the decision chronologies and to probe into the reasons for breaks in the patterns (i.e., for strategic changes). We have so far completed five of these studies (Mintzberg, 1978, reports on the earliest phase of this research), and five more are now underway (in addition to about 15 similar but shorter studies carried out by MBA students as part of their team work). Two other projects, while not based on our own research, form part of the data base of this paper. These are attempts to synthesize the empirical literature in two areas—organizational structuring and power. These efforts have led to two books (Mintzberg, 1979, 1983), both revolving around the notion of configurations, or ideal types of many dimensions.

This paper focuses on seven basic themes each of which underlies to a greater or lesser degree these various research activities.

THE RESEARCH HAS BEEN AS PURELY DESCRIPTIVE AS WE HAVE BEEN ABLE TO MAKE IT

This hardly seems unusual in organization theory. But most of the work has been concentrated in the policy area, where prescription has been the norm for a long time. Moreover, one could argue that much of the "descriptive" research about organizations has set out to prove some prescription, for example that a participative managerial style is more effective than an autocratic one.

The orientation to as pure a form of description as possible has, I believe, enabled us to raise doubts about a good deal of accepted wisdom: to be able to say that managerial work observed has more to do with interruption, action orientation, and verbal communication than with coordinating and controlling; to say that diagnosis and timing count more in strategic decision making than the choice of an alternative from a

given set; to say that strategy formation is better understood as a discontinuous, adaptive process than a formally planned one. The little boy in the Hans Christian Andersen story, who said that the emperor wore no clothes, has always served as a kind of model to me. This is not to imply that our work so exposes the manager; in fact, I believe it clothes him in more elegant garments. It is the literature of management that often emerges as naked, since much of what it says becomes transparent when held up to the scrutiny of descriptive research.

THE RESEARCH HAS RELIED ON SIMPLE—IN A SENSE, INELEGANT—METHODOLOGIES

The field of organization theory has, I believe, paid dearly for the obsession with rigor in the choice of methodology. Too many of the results have been significant only in the statistical sense of the word. In our work, we have always found that simpler, more direct methodologies have yielded more useful results. Like sitting down in a manager's office and watching what he does. Or tracing the flow of decisions in an organization.

What, for example, is wrong with samples of one? Why should researchers have to apologize for them? Should Piaget apologize for studying his own children, a physicist for splitting only one atom? A doctoral student I know was not allowed to observe managers because of the "problem" of sample size. He was required to measure what managers did through questionnaires, despite ample evidence in the literature that managers are poor estimators of their own time allocation (e.g., Burns, 1954; Horne and Lupton, 1965; Harper, 1968). Was it better to have less valid data that were statistically significant?

Given that we have one hundred people each prepared to do a year of research, we should ask ourselves whether we are better off to have each study 100 organizations, giving us superficial data on ten thousand, or each study one, giving us in-depth data on one hundred. The choice obviously depends on what is to be studied. But it should not preclude the small sample, which has often proved superior.

THE RESEARCH HAS BEEN AS PURELY INDUCTIVE AS POSSIBLE

Our doctoral students get a dose of Popper (1968) in their research methodology course. Popper bypasses induction as not part of the logic of scientific inquiry, and the students emerge from the course—like many elsewhere—believing that somehow induction is not a valid part of science. I stand with Selye (1964) in concluding that, while deduction certainly is a part of science, it is the less interesting, less challenging part. It is discovery that attracts me to this business, not the checking out of what we think we already know.

I see two essential steps in inductive research. The first is *detective work,* the tracking down of patterns, consistencies. One searches through a phenomenon looking for order, following one lead to another. But the process itself is not neat.

> Even in the nineteenth century, celebrated discoveries were often achieved enigmatically, Kekuly tortuously arrived at his theory of the benzene molecule; Davy blundered onto the anesthetic properties of nitrous oxide; Perkin's failure to produce synthetic quinine circuitously revealed aniline dyes; and Ehrlich tried 606 times before he succeeded in compounding salvarsan in 1910 (Dalton, 1959: 273).

The second step in induction is the *creative leap.* Selye cites a list of "intellectual immoralities" published by a well-known physiology department. Number 4 read "Generalizing beyond one's data." He quotes approvingly a commentator who asked whether it would not have been more correct to word Number 4: "Not generalizing beyond one's data" (1964: 228). The fact is that there would be no interesting hypothesis to test if no one ever generalized beyond his or her data. Every theory requires that creative leap, however small, that breaking away from the expected to describe something new. There is no one-to-one correspondence between data and theory. The data do not generate the theory—only researchers do that—any more than the theory can be *proved* true in terms of the data. All theories are false, because all abstract from data and simplify the world they purport to describe. Our choice, then, is not between true and false theories so much as between more and less useful theories. And usefulness, to repeat, stems from detective work well done, followed by creative leaps in relevant directions.

Call this research "exploratory" if you like, just so long as you do not use the term in a condescending sense: "OK, kid, we'll let you get away with it this time, but don't let us catch you doing it again." No matter what the state of the field, whether it is new or mature, all of its interesting research explores. Indeed, it seems that the more deeply we probe into this field of organizations, the more complex we find it to be, and the more we need to fall back on so-called exploratory, as opposed to "rigorous," research methodologies.

To take one case of good exploration and a small leap, a young doctoral student in France went into the company in that country that was reputed to be most advanced in its long-range planning procedures (in a country that takes its planning dogma very seriously). He was there to document those procedures, the "right" way to plan. But he was a good enough detective to realize quickly that all was not what it seemed on the surface. So he began to poke around. And with small creative leaps he produced some interesting conclusions, for example, that planning really served as a tool by which top management centralized power (Sarrazin, 1977–78). Peripheral vision, poking around in relevant places, a good dose of cre-

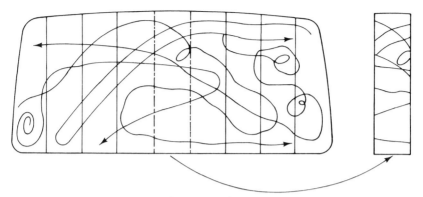

Figure 1. Slicing up the organization.

ativity—that is what makes good research, and always has, in all fields.

Why do we let our doctoral students be guided by mechanical methodologies into banal research? Weick (1974: 487) quotes Somerset Maugham: "She plunged into a sea of platitudes, and with the powerful breast stroke of a channel swimmer made her confident way toward the white cliffs of the obvious." Why not, instead, throw them into the sea of complexity, the sea of the big questions, to find out if they can swim at all, if they can collect data as effective detectives, and if they are capable of even small leaps of creativity. If not, perhaps they have chosen the wrong profession.

THE RESEARCH HAS, NEVERTHELESS, BEEN SYSTEMATIC IN NATURE

I do not mean to offer license to fish at random in that sea. No matter how small our sample or what our interest, we have always tried to go into organizations with a well-defined focus—to collect specific kinds of data systematically. In one study we wanted to know who contacts the manager, how, for how long, and why; in the second we were interested in the sequence of steps used in making certain key decisions; in the third, we are after chronologies of decision in various strategic areas. Those are the "hard"

data of our research, and they have been crucial in all of our studies.

THE RESEARCH HAS MEASURED IN REAL ORGANIZATIONAL TERMS

Systematic does not mean detached. Probably the greatest impediment to theory building in the study of organizations has been research that violates the organization, that forces it into abstract categories that have nothing to do with how it functions. My favorite analogy is of an organization rich in flows and processes, as implied in the Figure, kind of like a marble cake. Then along comes a researcher with a machine much like those used to slice bread. In goes the organization and out come the cross-sectional slices. The researcher then holds up one of them, shown to the right in the Figure, and tries to figure out what it is he or she is seeing. "Hmmmm . . . what have we here? The amount of control is 4.2, the complexity of environment, 3.6." What does it mean to measure the "amount of control" in an organization, or the "complexity" of its environment? Some of these concepts may be useful in describing organizations in theory, but that does not mean we can plug them into our research holus-bolus as measures. As soon as the researcher insists on forcing the organization into abstract categories—into his terms instead of its own—he is reduced to using perceptual measures, which often distort the reality. The researcher intent on generating a direct measure of amount of control or of complexity of environment can only ask people what they believe, on seven-point scales or the like. He gets answers, all right, ready for the computer; what he does not get is any idea of what he has measured. (What does "amount of control" mean anyway?[2]) The result is sterile description, of organizations as categories of abstract variables instead of flesh-and-blood processes. And theory building becomes impossible. Far from functioning like detectives, "In touching up dead data with false colors, [social scientists] function much like morticians" (Orlans, 1975: 109).

If someone is interested in studying perceptions, then by all means let him study perceptions. But let him not study perceptions if it is control or complexity he is after. There is no doubt that "the perceptions of the chief executive are important in understanding why organizations are structured as they are" (Pfeffer and Leblebici, 1973–74: 273). But that does not justify researchers—these and many others—in drawing conclusions about how the "environment," as opposed to the "perception of the environment," affects structure.

Measuring in real organizational terms means first of all getting out into the field, into real organizations. Questionnaires often won't do. Nor will laboratory simulations, at least not in policy research. The individual or group psychologist can bring the phenomenon he is studying into his laboratory holus-bolus; the *organization* theorist cannot. What is the use of describing a reality that has been invented? The evidence of our research—of interruptions and soft data and

information overload—suggests that we do not yet understand enough about organizations to simulate their functioning in the laboratory. It is their inherent complexity and dynamic nature that characterize phenomena such as policy making. Simplification squeezes out the very thing on which the research should focus.

Measuring in real organizational terms means measuring things that really happen in organizations, as they experience them. To draw on our research, it means measuring the proportion of letters sent by customers or the number of new stores opened in a given year. It is the job of the researcher to abstract from the particular to the general, to develop concepts from his measurements in the field. I believe the researcher shirks his responsibility when he expects the manager to do the abstracting, to decide how complex is the environment (or even what complexity means). Managers do not think about complex environments; they think about new discoveries in plastics, about the problems of getting the R&D people to work with those in marketing, about how a proposed piece of legislation will affect sales.

My favorite anecdote in this regard concerns Peter Travis, an Australian and one of the world's great potters. He was approached by a researcher who wanted to study the creative process. The researcher proposed to elicit protocols from Travis as he worked. They tried that, but got nowhere. Travis felt he could not verbalize about the creative process; he had to demonstrate it visually. So he proposed to make a bowl on his wheel, then another, then another, and continue until he had a thousand pots. He might make ten alike and then vary the rim on the eleventh. By the twentieth he might modify the shape, and by the one-hundredth he might not feel

---

[2] A number of studies in management policy have sought correlations of performance and amount of planning—to show that planning pays. But what exactly is the definition of planning in the context of actual strategy formation? The answer to that question requires intensive research on decision-making processes, as in the research in France cited earlier, not a few measures on questionnaires or the counting up of a bunch of formal documents that management may never look at.

like making bowls at all but instead decide to form bottles. One form would lead to another so that by the one-thousandth pot Travis would have a visual record of the creative process. The researcher could then come in and describe it. (Travis apparently really intends to carry out his side of the bargain. The best part of the story is that Travis, in recounting, thought that his proposal was so "obvious." One thousand pots. "How else would you study creativity?" It seems that we need creative minds to study creativity. And complex minds to study complexity. Too bad Peter Travis didn't choose to become a management researcher. But then again, which doctoral program would have let him in?)

THE RESEARCH, IN ITS INTENSIVE NATURE, HAS ENSURED THAT SYSTEMATIC DATA ARE SUPPORTED BY ANECDOTAL DATA

More and more we feel the need to be on site, and to be there long enough to be able to understand what is going on. (We began with a week and are now spending months and even years.) For while systematic data create the foundation for our theories, it is the anecdotal data that enable us to do the building. Theory building seems to require rich description, the richness that comes from anecdote. We uncover all kinds of relationships in our "hard" data, but it is only through the use of this "soft" data that we are able to "explain" them, and explanation is, of course, the purpose of research. I believe that the researcher who never goes near the water, who collects quantitative data from a distance without anecdote to support them, will always have difficulty explaining interesting relationships (although he may uncover them). Perhaps this has something to do with how our minds work. Those creative leaps seem to come from our subconscious mental processes, our intuition (e.g., Hadamard, 1949). And intuition

apparently requires the "sense" of things—how they feel, smell, "seem." We need to be "in touch." Increasingly in our research, we are impressed by the importance of phenomena that cannot be measured—by the impact of an organization's history and its ideology on its current strategy, by the role that personality and intuition play in decision making. To miss this in research is to miss the very lifeblood of the organization. And missed it is in research that by its very design precludes the collection of anecdotal information.

THE RESEARCH HAS SOUGHT TO SYNTHESIZE, TO INTEGRATE DIVERSE ELEMENTS INTO CONFIGURATIONS OF IDEAL OR PURE TYPES

Organizations intermingle a great many elements in their functioning. Researchers who focus on two variables at a time—who catch what someone has called "the economists' plague": holding all other things constant—seem to cloud issues almost as often as they clarify them. Consider the unending debates about size and administrative ratio or bureaucracy and centralization. Literally, the more that has been published, the more confused the issues have become (and I apologize for this bivariate hypothesis). We shall never have closure so long as we pretend that other things can be held constant. We live in a world of dynamic systems. (A colleague of mine claims that everything in the world correlates with everything else at 0.30) Organizations also experience all kinds of lags and discontinuities. For example, because structural change often follows strategic change (Chandler, 1962; Stopford and Wells, 1972; Rumelt, 1974), it is somewhat a matter of luck whether a two-variable cross-sectional study manages to capture the structure that reflects today's situation—which it typically measures—or yesterday's, which it typically does not. And the presence of discontinuities (e.g., Woodward, 1965, about structure as a function of technology; Klatzky, 1970, about A/P as a function of size) plays havoc with these conventional approaches.

We can also question whether the human brain prefers to think in terms of continuous and bivariate relationships, or searches for another kind of order, characterized by clusters or configurations, ideal or pure types. We seem to put diverse elements together into various envelopes. The word "democracy," for example, seems to be captured less by some scale of freedom than by a configuration of elements—a free press, due process, elected officials, and so on. Likewise I believe that we prefer to understand our organizations in terms of pure types—configurations of many elements.

But to generate those configurations, I have more faith in typologies than taxonomies, if I understand correctly how these terms are used. In other words, while I believe we need empirical data to generate our categories—systematic data reinforced by a good deal of anecdote—I do not expect them to come from mechanical data reduction techniques. It is pattern recognition we are after, in the form of those creative leaps, and I believe that human, not electronic, brains are most capable of achieving those leaps.

To conclude, these seven characteristics underlie the research we have been doing these past 13 years. Together they seem to form their own configuration: research based on description and induction instead of implicit or explicit prescription and deduction; reliance on simple, inelegant, as opposed to "rigorous" methods of data collection; the measurement of many elements in real organizational terms, supported by anecdote, instead of few variables in perceptual terms from a distance; and the synthesis of these elements into clusters, instead of the analysis of pairs of variables as continuous relationships. We might call this strategy, for want of a better term, "direct research."

REFERENCES

Burns, Tom "The Directions of Activity and Communication in a Departmental Executive Group." *Human Relations,* 1954, 7, 73–97.

Chandler, Alfred D. *Strategy and Structure.* Cambridge, MA: MIT Press, 1962.

Dalton, M. *Men Who Manage.* New York: Wiley, 1959.

Hadamard, J. S. *Psychology of Invention in the Mathematical Field.* Princeton, Princeton University Press, 1949.

Harper, W. K. "Executive Time: A Corporation's Most Valuable, Scarce and Irrecoverable Resource." DBA thesis, Graduate School of Business Administration, Harvard University, 1968.

Horne, J. H., & Lupton, T. "The Work Activities of 'Middle' Managers—an Exploratory Study." *Journal of Management Studies,* 1965, 2, 14–33.

Klatzky, S. P. "Relationship of Organizational size to Complexity and Coordination." *Administrative Science Quarterly,* 1970, 15, 428–438.

Mintzberg, Henry *The Nature of Managerial Work,* New York: Harper & Row, 1973. "Patterns in Strategy Formation." *Management Science,* 1978, 24, 934–948. *The Structuring of Organizations.* Englewood Cliffs, NJ: Prentice-Hall, 1979. *Power In and Around Organizations.* Englewood Cliffs, NJ: Prentice-Hall, 1983.

Mintzberg, Henry, Duru Raisinghani, and André Théorêt "The Structure of 'Unstructured' Decision Processes." *Administrative Science Quarterly,* 1976, 21, 246–275.

Orlans, H. "Neutrality and Advocacy in Policy Research." *Policy Sciences,* 1975, 6, 107–119.

Pfeffer, Jeffrey, and Huseyin Leblebici "The Effect of Competition on Some Dimensions of Organizational Structure." *Social Forces*, 1973–74, 52, 268–279.

Popper, K. R. *The Logic of Scientific Discovery*. New York: Harper & Row, 1968.

Rumelt, R. P. *Strategy, Structure, and Economic Performance*. Boston: Division of Research, Graduate School of Business Administration, Harvard University, 1974.

Sarrazin, J. "Decentralized Planning in a Large French Company: An Interpretative study." *International Studies of Management and Organization*, 1977–78, 7, 37–59.

Selye, Hans *From Dream to Discovery: On Being a Scientist*. New York: McGraw-Hill, 1964.

Stopford, J. M., & Wells, L. T. *Managing the Multinational Enterprise: Organization of the Firm and Ownership of the Subsidiaries*. New York: Basic Books, 1972.

Weick, Karl E. "Amendments to Organizational Theorizing." *Academy of Management Journal*, 1974, 17, 487–502.

Woodward, Joan *Industrial Organization: Theory and Practice*. London: Oxford University Press, 1965.

Investigative Reporting as a Research Method[1]

An Analysis of Bernstein and Woodward's All the President's Men

Murray Levine

Bernstein and Woodward's (1974) development of the Watergate story was more than muckraking. It gave us an unparalleled view of people in power and of governmental structures through which political power was exercised and restrained. Watergate raised the national consciousness about the potential misuse of power and introduced concepts (e.g., cover-up) that have served to guide our understanding of behavior in governmental and political organizations and, by extension, in other formal organizations as well.

The authors developed the story by using investigative reporting methods, very well described in *All the President's Men*. Investigative reporting deserves analysis as a research method. Existing textbooks (e.g., Anderson & Benjaminson, 1976) tend to be how-to-do-it treatises with little analysis of the methods themselves. While Bernstein and Woodward's (1974) book is superbly written, dramatic, and highly absorbing, it includes no reflection on the methods themselves.

Investigative reporting has much in common with qualitative and clinical research in the social and psychological sciences (see Balaban, 1973, 1978; Bogdan & Taylor, 1975; Diesing, 1971; Douglas, 1976; Erikson, 1964; Waelder, 1960; Whyte, 1955). The various treatises on the subject of qualitative research include defenses of that approach in relation to the predominant quantitative and experimental methodologies (e.g., Cronbach, 1975; Giorgi, 1970; Makkreel, 1975; Truzzi, 1974; Campbell, Note 1). These works contain many insights, much wisdom, and sophisticated analyses of the nature of social science and its methods. However, the qualitative approach still has an uncertain methodological status and is denigrated by some as little more than a useful art form. Bernstein and Woodward's work deserves the accolade of art, but there was, in addition, a distinct method of their approach. By making that method explicit, we may develop some further insight into qualitative research approaches.

Investigative reporting is a search for

[1] The author wishes to thank David I. Levine for his capable criticism and careful editing of an earlier draft of this article.

Reprinted by permission of *American Psychologist*, 1980, 35, 626–638.

evidence to justify publication of a story; many forms of evidence are described in the book's pages. In addition to evidence obtained through interviews and documents, the authors used evidence similar to that used by clinicians—their own emotions, the emotions of others, and details of language (see Erikson, 1964; Waelder, 1960). Douglas (1976) has pointed out that the evidence in qualitative research and in the law (e.g., Clearly, 1972) is similar in nature to the evidence people commonly use in coming to understand their social worlds. What, then, distinguishes professional research?

The self-conscious emphasis on controlled and disciplined observation and inference distinguishes the professional researcher from the ordinary citizen. There are distinctive controls in the researcher's work, if control is defined as a probe of the limits of inferences that can reasonably be drawn from any set of observations (Group for the Advancement of Psychiatry, 1959). Control means more than an emphasis on reliability (e.g., confirmation by two or more sources). In telling the fascinating inside story, Bernstein and Woodward provide unusual insights into the many controls that the journalistic enterprise introduces into the investigative process.

Watergate required a theory to make sense of the mass of disconnected pieces of information and indeed to guide the subsequent investigation. From the beginning, Bernstein and Woodward operated with a more or less explicit theory, the scope of which enlarged as the investigation proceeded. The theory that Bernstein and Woodward used in their investigation can be considered similar in structure and function to the models used in modern science (Harré & Secord, 1972; Hesse, 1966). A model is a concrete image of how some set of structures and processes might act to produce a particular phenomenon. Bernstein and Woodward explained Watergate by showing how it happened, and in the process they provided a theoretically useful model of

the corruption of power. We now have a concept and an image—Watergate—which allows us to raise the question of whether or not we are dealing with another Watergate when we encounter a new set of phenomena that requires explanation and understanding. Moreover, the model has implications for testable action in the real world, since it enables us to consider legislation and other controls over power.

Every human enterprise unfolds within a social context that shapes it. The social organization and culture of newspapers and that of the typical settings in which clinical and social researchers work are quite different. These differences are important in understanding to what extent investigative reporting methods can be transposed or adapted to the social science enterprise. Many factors limit the degree to which investigative reporting methods can be useful in the context of social science or clinical research. However, in the use of evidence, in the use of formal and informal controls, and in the need for theory and models to guide the inquiry, investigative reporting has, I contend, much in common with qualitative approaches in social and clinical research. In the following sections, I shall examine the Bernstein and Woodward (1974) book in an effort to illustrate this thesis and to systematize our understanding of qualitative methods.

EVIDENCE

Investigative journalism is a search for evidence to justify the publication of a story about an event or a set of events. Ethical and legal considerations, and the journalists' shared cultural need for statements grounded in fact, require that investigative reporters document the details of a story with reliable evidence. Some evidence, though useful in guiding the investigator, is not sufficiently objective or reliable to be useful in documenting the story. Published stories are usually warranted only by evidence (e.g., documents, statements of participants in the events) with greater probative value. However, both hard and soft evidence are interwoven in the investigative process.

Documents and Records

"Rosenfeld [an editor] always felt better whan he knew that somewhere, no matter how inaccessible, there was a piece of paper that could support a story" (Bernstein & Woodward, 1974, p. 90). The pieces of paper were many and varied. They consisted of private documents (e.g., address books, p. 24) as well as public and quasipublic records (e.g., library slips, pp. 32–33; records of long-distance telephone calls, p. 39; bank records, p. 39; credit-card records, p. 127; bills, p. 243; and cancelled checks, p. 43). The search for documents is based on the premise that all of us leave records of our presence, our movements, and our associations in this complex society. The usefulness of records is limited by their accessibility, by the investigator's knowledge about their location and the kinds of information different records contain, and by the imaginativeness with which records and documents may be used for a variety of investigative purposes.

Reconstruction of the organizational structure of the Committee to Re-elect the President (CRP) from its telephone roster (Bernstein & Woodward, 1974, p. 60; see also p. 286) was one of the most ingenious uses of a public document. The reconstruction provided leads to informants and, more important, enabled the reporters to ascertain who had responsibility for decisions. A variety of other documents and records linked people and events, provided background for understanding specific events, and furnished leads to other evidence. Historians and lawyers are much more familiar with the use, and the pitfalls in the use, of documentary evidence than social scientists and clinical researchers are (Barzun, 1974; Winks,

1968), but documents can illuminate social science problems when used appropriately (A. Levine & M. Levine, 1977; M. Levine, 1979).

That documents may be of use to social scientists is one conclusion, but the cultural norms and ethics governing access to documents are quite different for social scientists and for journalists. The difference may be gleaned from Anderson and Benjaminson's (1976) classification of records:

> There are three kinds of records. There are those the law entitles the public to see, those the law prohibits the public from seeing, and those not mentioned by the law. Good investigators do not admit the existence of a category of records they will never see. As far as they are concerned, the only important distinctions among the three kinds of records involve the methods best suited to getting them and the relative difficulty in doing so. (p. 39)

Some journalists believe that their public mission allows them to obtain access to information by any means short of committing a crime; they may be willing to skirt even that line as well (see Bernstein & Woodward, 1974, pp. 232–236; 248–250). Differences between investigative journalists and social scientists in terms of professional culture, ethical principles, and legal constraints (e.g., New York State Public Health Law, Article 24A; 42 USC. 289; CFR Title 45, Part 46) may limit the adaptability of investigative methods for social scientists, although Douglas (1976) holds an opposite opinion.

Informants and Interview Data

The testimony of participants in events constitutes primary data for investigative reporters as well as for lawyers and social scientists. Interviewees may have been direct participants, or they may have indirect knowledge through conversations with participants or through personal observation of some of the activities. Bernstein and Woodward also used informants to provide general information on the culture, habits, values, styles, practices, and reputations of individuals and organizations. Such background information was crucial in helping the reporters understand other evidence, in providing them additional leads, and in assuring them that they were moving in the right direction.

The peculiar conditions of interviewing required that the reporters vary their methods of obtaining and recording the interview data. Standardized procedures and standardized interview protocols would have made no sense at all. The reporters had some idea of what each informant might provide, but information was often unexpected. Moreover, different interviewing techniques were required for cooperative or noncooperative interviewees. Of particular interest was the technique of confronting reluctant interviewees with adverse information requiring comment, confirmation, or denial. The response to this confrontational approach sometimes yielded still further data of importance.

In a situation as complex as Watergate, few knew the whole story. The reporters had to develop it by gathering information from numerous informants and then coordinating, correlating, and cross-checking what different individuals with access to the same material said, fitting together pieces much as one might fit the pieces of a jigsaw puzzle together. Contradictions from different sources were treated not as proof of unreliability, but as additional information.

Informants' Networks

In building the story, the two reporters assumed that everyone was part of a social network and that members of that network could provide information about other members and their relationships. For example, when Bernstein first learned of the burglary, he spoke to anyone at the Watergate complex he could reach—desk clerks, bellmen, maids, and waiters (Bernstein & Woodward,

1974, pp. 14–15). To learn more about McCord, the reporters checked a roster of 15 people who served with McCord in an army unit (see also pp. 54, 61, 286, 333). Sometimes such dragnet searches proved fruitless (p. 55). Sometimes the source for building a network was found in personal documents. Thus by checking every name and telephone number found in the burglars' address books, the reporters found a connection to Howard Hunt in the White House (pp. 23–24).

Much of the investigation assumed that in any social enterprise people were connected to each other for a purpose. By determining the nature of their transactions, one could begin to understand the complex of issues. The first clue was frequently an indication of some business or some acquaintance between the parties (e.g., Bernstein & Woodward, 1974, pp. 30, 44–45, 131, 157, 159). When Donald Segretti emerged as an important figure in the "dirty tricks" campaign, the reporters again began with a dragnet network of acquaintances and soon were able to trace links of friendship between Segretti and a number of White House and CRP figures (pp. 130–131). They also uncovered the "rat fucking" practiced by Segretti, Chapin, and Ziegler, who had known each other in college. Chapin and Ziegler later worked on Nixon's political campaign in California under Haldeman's direction and then joined an advertising agency where Haldeman was vice-president (p. 131).

Investigators' Networks

The reporters' own networks were of crucial importance in providing information. Woodward's "Deep Throat" was a long-time acquaintance with whom he had spent many evenings prior to Watergate discussing power and politics in government (Bernstein & Woodward, 1974, p. 136). Many friends in and out of government and a number of other reporters offered information (e.g., pp.

23, 34, 131, 142). Once it became known that they were interested in the story, Bernstein and Woodward received information from a variety of volunteer informants. Some sources were considered suspect, or at least the information had to be treated carefully because the parties were known to have vested interests (p. 153). Unsolicited tips from the general public had to be checked out. These were less helpful than one might otherwise believe (p. 117), although sometimes such leads did produce useful data (pp. 290–293).

Credibility of Informants

An investigative reporter must assess the reliability of informants and interviewees. The nature of an informant's position, his or her reputation, and the reporters' previous experience with that person were important in assessing information. Moreover, the informants' demeanor and emotional state provided further clues to the validity or meaning of what they revealed. Witness demeanor and witness credibility are important issues in the law of evidence. Testimony in open court is required in part so that a jury can observe a witness's demeanor (Cleary, 1972, pp. 582, 602).

Woodward relied a great deal on his informant Deep Throat, who was in a position to have important information, and who never said anything that was incorrect (Bernstein & Woodward, 1974, p. 75). Deep Throat's manner of conducting himself was important. "He was dispassionate and seemed committed to the best version of the obtainable truth" (p. 137). Similarly, Woodward, who had not met Hugh Sloan before, was impressed by Sloan's care and his unwillingness to mention the names of persons he had no reason to think had done anything wrong. The detail an informant could provide added to the credibility of his or her story. Shipley, who named Segretti, had notes showing dates, times, places, and people involved in events (p. 119).

Beyond an informant's demeanor and position, it was sometimes necessary to assure an informant's credibility in other ways. Woodward, for example, made a dozen telephone calls to other attorneys and to the local bar association to assure himself and his editor of one informant's personal reputation (p. 161; see also p. 329). In other instances the reporters used other knowledge they had to judge the reliability of a source of information (pp. 306, 365). An informant's position and relationship to others were important. "Sloan was devoted to Stans. . . . Sloan hesitated. He was trying to plead Stans' case and instead was getting him in deeper" (p. 99). Sometimes the reporters had to be concerned about attacks on their own credibility from informants who might deliberately give them false information (p. 211; see also p. 358).

Nonverbal Communication

Nonverbal communication was almost as critical as verbal communication, not only in helping the investigators assess the information they received from informants but also in providing clues to the state of the system they were studying. It was important, in understanding the story and the stakes involved, to appreciate the emotional states of their informants (Bernstein & Woodward, 1974, pp. 46, 48, 61, 79, 80, 91, 104, 181, 211, 295, 325).

> What information the reporters were getting at this time came in bits and pieces, almost always from people who did not want to discuss the matter. Their fright, more than anything else, was persuading Bernstein and Woodward that the stakes were higher than they originally perceived. Indeed, they too were unsettled by the reactions to their visits. (Bernstein & Woodward, 1974, p. 62)

An informant's affect, especially taken in relation to other information, provided revealing clues, sometimes pointing to other data and sometimes confirming previous information. When Woodward asked McGregor about Liddy, McGregor angrily told a story that another informant had said would be used as a cover story (pp. 48–49). The unexpected anger was a clue supporting the belief that the cover story was false.

Informant's emotions read in context helped to elaborate the meanings of statements and events. When Bernstein was discussing "dirty tricks" with a Justice Department attorney, the man became outraged. His affect impressed Bernstein because it was uncharacteristic, an additional clue that the White House staff was violating all accepted standards of political conduct (p. 134).

An informant's affect influenced the degree of conviction the reporters felt in the validity of a report. Sometimes the feeling tone aroused suspicion of lies or concealment. In other instances the tone was a clue to the importance of the issue, or it raised questions about causes. In their sensitivity to the emotional states of their interviewees, the reporters shared much with clinicians.

There are distinct lessons here suggesting the amount of information that is lost when subjects fill out questionnaires and are not seen in person as they tell their stories in their own words. The data may be soft or subjective, but the perceived emotional state of an informant provides critical information for clinicians as well as for investigative reporters.

Details of Language

Investigative reporters as well as clinicians are sensitive to the details of subjective reports and pay careful attention to the language and context of communications. In some instances unsolicited comments raised questions, as when White House press aide Clawson denied something no one had asked him about directly (Bernstein & Woodward, 1974, p. 25; see also p. 163). In some instances, apparent denials of published stories contained hidden confirmations.

Nixon's early statement denied that anyone "presently employed" in the White House had anything to do with the burglary (p. 59; see also pp. 73, 108–109, 146, 150). A source who usually denied incorrect stories might confirm a story simply by remaining silent when asked (p. 179).

Public figures are apparently reluctant to tell outright lies, but they are not beyond making statements and using words that attempt to conceal the truth. Woodward at one point confronted Kissinger with the information that Kissinger had personally authorized wiretaps. Because Kissinger used the words "almost never" and "almost inconceivable" Woodward felt Kissinger's angry comments were not denials (pp. 345–346; see also pp. 175, 356).

The context of communications can also provide important information beyond the words involved. When a story broke about the President's appointments secretary, Ziegler, Dole, and McGregor used similar language in their rebuttals. The reporters and their editors took the concerted response as a sign that the counterattacks were probably ordered by the President, or at least made with his knowledge and consent (Bernstein & Woodward, 1974, pp. 172–173; see also pp. 62, 212).

Much of what the reporters used as evidence in directing their inquiries would be classified as hearsay, or not of sufficient probative value to be admissible in a trial court, although it would be admitted before a grand jury, which has a broader investigative role. While every such clue was useful in shaping the story, professional discipline demanded more evidence for confirmation before a piece was submitted for publication.

Some Limits of Clinical Evidence

Accuracy was critical in pursuing the Watergate story. If the reporters proved incorrect in one of their assertions, they and their newspaper would be vulnerable to libel suits. More important, their reputations within their own organization and profession would have been damaged, and potential sources would have been reluctant to provide them with information in the future. To a remarkable degree the reporters were accurate, as subsequent events demonstrated. However, at one critical point they appeared to have made an error, which temporarily damaged their credibility and certainly damaged their confidence. The error was caused in part by their reliance on the sort of indirect communications just described.

The reporters had strong reasons to believe that H. R. Haldeman, Nixon's top aide, not only was among the people who controlled the secret espionage fund but may well have been a key culprit. Although there was good reason to suspect Haldeman, the reporters knew enough about how he operated to understand that he would have preserved "deniability." They needed some very direct evidence to tie him to the Watergate events. In an interview with Hugh Sloan, Bernstein tried to get him to confirm Haldeman's role, because Sloan knew who authorized expenditures from the secret fund. Sloan refused to do so in straight-forward fashion, but he conceded as much in a roundabout way. Later, in an attempt to confirm that Sloan had testified under oath to the grand jury that Haldeman was the person in control of the fund, Bernstein interviewed an FBI agent. The agent agreed with Bernstein's assertion that Sloan had testified to Haldeman's involvement under oath to the grand jury. The agent, however, agreed it was *John* Haldeman who had been implicated. Although Bernstein rechecked, the slip was to prove ominous for the particular story. Bernstein attempted to obtain confirmation from another source, a Justice Department lawyer, who refused to give any direct information but agreed to use a complex set of signals. After the story was printed, it developed that the lawyer had misunderstood the code and had signaled exactly the opposite of what Bernstein thought he had meant.

The investigators knew something was wrong when a White House press secretary issued an unequivocal denial that Sloan had named Haldeman before the grand jury, and Sloan's attorney confirmed the denial. In analyzing their error, Bernstein and Woodward (1974) found that they had relied too strongly on indirect evidence and inference:

> They had assumed too much. Persuaded by their sources, and by their own deductions that Haldeman loomed behind "Watergate," they had grasped a slim reed—the secret fund. . . . But they had taken short cuts once they themselves had come to be convinced that Haldeman controlled the fund. They had heard what they wanted to hear. (pp. 217–218)

Tracing their errors, they realized that they had not questioned Sloan closely enough, that they had depended on an FBI agent whose reliability was not known to them, and that the indirect codes for confirmation with the attorney left too much room for misunderstanding. They were right in their assumption that Haldeman had controlled the fund, but wrong in their belief that the statement had been made to the grand jury. They had opened themselves to questions about their accuracy.

Inferences drawn from indirect evidence and from an informant's demeanor are not always correct, especially in the absence of other evidence (e.g., Bernstein & Woodward, 1974, pp. 167–168). Despite subjective certainty and clarity, hunches and inferences must not be confused with evidence and certainly ought not to be weighed heavily in the absence of other evidence.

Field Interviewing

The problems of interviewing in the highly charged atmosphere of Watergate required the reporters to use every bit of information, including what they could glean from details of language and emotions. Many of the persons who were approached were willing to be interviewed. Others set conditions. Some would only give partial information or hints or would only confirm information the reporters already had. The reporters used a confrontational technique with hostile interviewees in an effort to elicit spontaneous responses because these might be the only information the interview would produce. These special circumstances placed a premium on flexibility and on maintaining rapport. The reporters had to exercise self-control and make sensitive use of their own emotional states as part of the interview process.

The reporters frequently called people they didn't know. Many were reluctant to respond (see Bernstein & Woodward, 1974, p. 84), and some were rude. After working hard to see Martha Mitchell, Woodward had to be content to talk with her while a vacuum cleaner was going (pp. 96–98). Another interviewee seemed more interested in the Sunday afternoon football game on television than in talking (p. 166). An acquaintance of Woodward's hung up on him (p. 24).

Although they always identified themselves as reporters, Bernstein and Woodward often had to sell themselves as human beings, to look for some way of appealing to potential interviewees, of obtaining a person's sympathy, or of helping the person to find some rationalization for participating (p. 26). The rapport-building process often required extensive social conversation before getting on the important subject matter. Because the interviews were sensitive, the reporters often took no notes as they delicately worked around the edges of the subject (p. 62). However, Bernstein once played on a reluctant interviewee's curiosity by using a notebook to help make her more accepting of the interview (p. 67). Some respondents made the interview into a guessing game, forcing the reporters to act as if they knew more than they did.

The interview process required great sensitivity to the respondent's motivations and feelings. A nervous interviewee would insist that everything be off the record (p. 26). A fearful bookkeeper who didn't want to be accused of giving out anyone's name used initials, but only after arriving at a tacit agreement that she would confirm or deny information to try to help her bosses, Sloan and Stans, whom she respected (see also p. 87). When Segretti expressed annoyance at the media, Bernstein and his colleague Meyers "calculatedly dumped on the opposition" (Bernstein & Woodward, 1974, p. 227; see also p. 271).

The reporters were aware that shifts in an interviewee's mood might have been simulated for effect. When Woodward confronted Kissinger about his role in ordering wiretaps, Kissinger replied cagily. At other points he responded angrily to Woodward's interrogation and accused Woodward of trapping him into talking. Woodward felt "Kissinger had an effective way of moving back and forth from anger to tranquility" (Bernstein & Woodward, 1974, p. 345).

The reporters not only had to deal with others' aggression toward them, they themselves had to be aggressive in obtaining information (see pp. 49, 91, 94, 114, 193, 214, 254, 288–289, 292, 358–360, 361). Sometimes their own expression of anger was spontaneous and intuitive, but at other times it was calculated (see pp. 42, 55–56, 72–73). At one point, Woodward felt it necessary to confront Deep Throat because he was not forthcoming.

> He told Deep Throat both of them were playing a chicken shit game—Deep Throat for pretending to himself that he never fed Woodward primary information, and Woodward for chewing up tidbits like a rat under a picnic table that didn't have the guts to go after the main dish. (Bernstein & Woodward, 1974, p. 141)

On another occasion, Bernstein decided to try to get information by deliberately angering his informant (p. 184). Woodward pressured a 20-year-old college student by questioning the student's ethics in agreeing to do political spying (pp. 290–292).

The pressures on the reporters, and their belief that they had a right to information from others, sometimes led them to overreact and to act out (pp. 213–216) Many of the interview situations touched the two reporters' emotions deeply and required great self-control on their part lest their judgment or their relationship with the interviewee be affected. When the reporters received information they were seeking or information they found startling, it was necessary for them to remain calm so that no obvious emotions would interfere with the ongoing interview (pp. 44–45, 54, 71, 100, 102, 138, 180, 182, 212, 251, 337).

Bernstein's telephone interview with John Mitchell is a prime example. He called for comment on the story that Mitchell had controlled the secret political espionage fund while he was Attorney General. For Bernstein, the only constant in the interview had been his "adrenal feeling" as he "perceived the excruciating depths of Mitchell's hurt" (Bernstein & Woodward, 1974, pp. 109–110). Later Bernstein found himself in an agitated state, unable to hit the proper keys as he was typing out the conversation based on his notes. After another interview, during which he had drunk large quantities of coffee and had been excited by the information he had received, Bernstein found it difficult to keep the information straight (p. 71; see also pp. 211–212).

Because they cajoled, pressured, entreated, and confronted (e.g., pp. 49, 80, 148), the two reporters sometimes felt inner conflict, as when Bernstein obtained confidential records from a source in a credit bureau, although he personally felt the records ought to remain private. Nowhere was the conflict between the requirements of their role and their personal feelings more clearly revealed than in their relationship with Hugh Sloan. They both liked Sloan, but they felt as if they were "using" him. The reporters described themselves as feeling like "vul-

tures" because Sloan was having a difficult time in his personal life while they were becoming famous.

In one sense, it seemed as if the reporters felt less responsibility for the well-being of the persons involved than they did for the story. However, both of them were acutely aware of the impact their stories had on those who figured in them, especially if the information was adverse (e.g., pp. 89, 116, 148). Incidents revealing hurt to others were sobering and added to Bernstein and Woodward's sense of need for care, self-control, and self-awareness.

The circumstances of interviews ranged from meticulously planned to most informal. Some took place in homes and offices, but other interviews were held in underground parking garages, in airplanes, in taxicabs, on doorsteps, in restaurants, and on park benches. The interviews took place at all hours of the day and night, whether they were conducted in person or by telephone. Many interviews were with total strangers, but in others the reporters took advantage of friends and casual acquaintances. Sometimes they went back to sources over and over again, to obtain new information or to recheck information. They returned delicately, knowing that what they had printed might have changed the relationship. In other instances it was obvious to all that there was an adversary relationship if not outright animosity, and since they had to be in contact with each other, both parties had to deal with their anger.

The wide variety of people and circumstances, the profound emotions, the uncertainties of the situation, the difficulties of getting information, and the extremely high stakes—all these exacerbated the problems of remaining oriented toward the facts. In clinical settings, controls for the clinician's emotional involvement are provided by the attempt to achieve insight through personal therapy and by supervision. There are analogous patterns in investigative reporting. The reporters were both helped and hindered by the controls and supports that are involved in working for a newspaper and working as a team. It is to an examination of these controls and supports that I now turn.

CONTROLS, SUPPORTS, AND THE SOCIAL SYSTEM OF THE NEWSPAPER

Given the ambiguities of evidence, the difficulties in obtaining evidence, a newspaper's responsibility to the public, and the stakes involved for the targets of its stories and for the newspaper itself, a newspaper requires controls. The major control is through the editorial review process. The editorial review process played a highly significant role in the development of the Watergate story.

Editorial Review

The editors performed a number of functions in addition to assigning the reporters to stories and approving the final copy. The several editors served in roles similar to that of the cross-examiner recommended for use in social science field studies (M. Levine, 1974). When Bernstein and Woodward discovered that Hunt had been reading material on Chappaquiddick, the metropolitan editor, Rosenfeld, was enthusiastic about the story, but he took it to the executive editor, Bradlee, for clearance. Bradlee functioned much as an editorial reviewer would in a journal. He criticized the sufficiency of the available evidence to support the inference the reporters wanted to draw, and he interrogated them about the credibility of one of their sources. Concluding that the evidence was insufficient to support certain assertions, Bradlee revised the story before authorizing its publication and did not place it on the front page (Bernstein & Woodward, 1974, pp. 33–34).

When they first determined that an intelligence fund within CRP had been used to make payments to the burglars, the reporters realized that they had information from but one source. Conferring with two editors, they decided to soften the statement in print. Eventually they evolved an unwritten rule that a charge of criminal misconduct would not be used unless there were at least two confirming sources (p. 81). The editors helped form this rule, which was intended to guarantee the reliability of information, and acted to control the precision of the inferences they were willing to print.

Metropolitan editor Rosenfeld's forte as a cross-examiner was locating holes in proposed stories. Not only did he carefully examine what the reporters wrote, but he passed them questions to be used with sources and demanded to be kept closely informed on all developments. Rosenfeld did not approve a story for publication until he had interrogated his reporters (pp. 93–94).

Whenever Bernstein and Woodward reported details about the involvement of high officials in the Watergate financing, Bradlee reviewed the story and asked if they were absolutely certain of the facts. Once they were able to reassure him, Bradlee approved publication, even though the reporters did not yet have the full account. As managers of a daily newspaper, the editors could not wait for a definitive account but had to approve significant pieces of the larger story as the pieces could be confirmed, not unlike journal editors who publish disconnected studies and leave it to others to put the separate articles into a coherent theoretical structure (Bernstein & Woodward, 1974, pp. 105–106, 135).

The editors were cautious about the language they permitted in each story. They were very concerned that they not be accused of bias. The image of neutrality was important (pp. 174, 205). The editorial staff also exercised a certain amount of control and provided support to see that ethically proper procedures were followed (pp. 107, 111, 112, 215, 216, 229, 289, 306). To some extent they were concerned because of their potential liability in a libel suit. That liability would extend throughout the newspaper's hierarchy.

Editorial control through cross-examination could fail to serve its intended purpose, as was discovered in the error in the story about Haldeman and the grand jury. Before the story was printed, "Bradlee served as prosecutor, demanding to know exactly what each source had said" (Bernstein & Woodward, 1974, p. 203). It was only after he had satisfied himself and had obtained the recommendation of the other editors that Bradlee approved the story. Even after Bradlee approved, another editor, Simons, asked the reporters to try to find another source before printing it. Simons and Rosenfeld repeatedly asked the reporters for assurances that the story was accurate and well documented (p. 204).

Despite all the precautions and the fact that the reporters had four sources, the details of the story proved to be in error. Neither they nor their editors had caught the problem (p. 218). Their position was no different from that of a social scientist whose experiment is published after it has undergone editorial review and for which another investigator later discovers an artifact accounting for the results.

The Research Team as a Control

In addition to editorial review, the reporters' partnership provided another level of control. At first, Bernstein and Woodward were reluctant to work together because they were so different tempermentally and stylistically. However, they soon discovered that their differences, although requiring accommodation, provided distinct advantages. They acted as critics of each other, one providing the brake for the other's enthusiasm. To strengthen their working relationship, they evolved a rule that gave either one veto power over any story they were to run. If one of them felt the story was not solidly grounded, they did not use it, sometimes even after they had obtained editorial approval (Bernstein & Woodward, 1974, pp.

135–136, 165, 182, 202, 273–274). This rule allowed both men to attend seriously to their own intuitions and, at the same time, spurred them to make more certain of the factual bases for their stories.

The Organizational Structure of the Newspaper

The organizational structure of a newspaper provides a variety of supports to deal with fast-breaking stories. Reporters do not have fixed assignments but can be assigned as needed. They do not work regular shifts but, instead, work as professionals, keeping their own hours, governed primarily by publication deadlines. Thus, Bernstein and Woodward were available to cover stories at all hours of the day or night and on weekends. The resources of the newspaper were such that a reporter could fly to Miami or to California in pursuit of a lead, sometimes at a moment's notice, as when Bernstein followed the Watergate burglars and their attorney into a taxicab and then onto an airplane in order to be able to talk to them about their guilty pleas (Bernstein & Woodward, 1974, p. 258). The newspaper could hire temporary help anywhere in the country to pursue assignments, such as reporter Meyers who waited for days for Segretti to return to his apartment (p. 127ff).

The competitive nature of the newspaper business drove the reporters to continued effort, and in this the attitude of their editors was a clear factor. The editors continued to press them for more material (pp. 153, 224–225). For example, when the *Los Angeles Times* published an important story that they had been after, Bradlee said little about it, but his manner showed that he was unhappy about having been scooped. "I can't kick ass for getting scooped, but I do let it be known that I feel let down and that I hate it. Don't forget that I hate it" (Bernstein & Woodward, 1974, p. 115).

The pressure to get one particular story culminated in an effort of dubious ethics, skirting the borders of illegality. Woodward had a tip that a grand juror was sufficiently angry that she was willing to talk. The newspaper's legal counsel advised that the burden of keeping the oath of secrecy of grand jury proceedings is placed on the juror. Although it was not illegal to ask such a person questions, the reporter would be pressing the juror to violate the law. When the issue of interviewing the jurors came up at an editorial conference, private doubts about the ethics of the procedure went unstated, but the reporters agreed to ask their questions without mentioning the grand jury and/or the interviewee's participation in it.

The tactic backfired. One of the jurors told the prosecutor, who informed Judge Sirica (pp. 232–237). The episode caused the reporters much anguish and embarrassment, for they realized that they had allowed expediency to overcome principles, exposing others to arrest and punishment (pp. 247–251).

Competiton With Other Newspapers

In any scientific endeavor, there is usually a community of scientists working on the same or similar problems who provide social controls beyond the experimental controls. As each group obtains its findings, they are published, providing new information and new leads to the other teams. Other laboratories will examine the data critically and may attempt to replicate or confirm the findings, then reporting their results in later publications. The analogue exists in journalism.

Even in the early phase of Watergate, other newspapers followed the story and added pieces to the developing picture. For example, when the New York Times published a story listing telephone calls made

from Barker's Miami phone to CRP in Washington, Bernstein used a source within the telephone company to confirm the finding. The source led him to the Miami District Attorney's office, which, in turn, led him to evidence of an illegal campaign contribution (Bernstein & Woodward, 1974, p. 36ff). Other examples can be provided of one team confirming the findings of another and then building on those findings (see pp. 113–115, 151, 166, 174, 175, 283, 287–288, 324–325).[2]

Confirmation was important for other reasons. After the Post's story on Haldeman had been shown to be incorrect in certain details, the reporters' credibility was severely challenged. A New York Times story confirming the existence of a secret CRP fund, and showing that $900,000 in cash disbursements had been made from the fund, restored their position considerably (p. 219). Confirmation provided protection because prestigious and powerful members of the press backed their efforts (p. 259).

An interesting insight into the attitudes and relationships among competitive investigators can be gleaned from the account of a dinner meeting with Seymour Hersh of the New York Times. The reporters discussed the case in general, discussed their own viewpoints, and exchanged impressions of the principals, but they did not exchange information that would reveal their current investigative approaches. Hersh even held back the details of the story that was to be published the next morning (Bernstein & Woodward, 1974, p. 312). Such secretiveness extends beyond normal experience in informal exchanges with colleagues, but it resembles the attitudes displayed by Watson and Crick in The Double Helix (Watson, 1968).

---

[2] The reporters' attempt to independently replicate the Watergate story—in the sense of finding their own evidence, then interviewing the same informants from a different perspective—provided important social controls for the formal investigations as well. While there is no direct evidence on this point, their efforts were probably critical in moving the Justice Department to do its job and in moving the Senate Select Committee to make a more thorough investigation as well. In effect, the presence of an independent and competing investigative team served a control function analogous to that of a community of scientists working on the same scientific problem.

Success and Failure of Social Control

It is clear that the editorial process is a source of control. It is a conservative influence in that the burden of proof is placed on the reporter to convince the editor, and the editor tests the proof by cross-examining the reporter. The organizational structure of the newspaper facilitates the investigative process by providing resources, support, and protection against outside pressure. By the same token, the newspaper can act to limit the independence of the investigative reporter in protection of its own interests.

Although care is exercised to ensure accuracy, the pressures of competition and of a daily production schedule may lead to error in publication. Newspaper reports are subject to error because of an editor's enthusiasm or biases, or for other organizational reasons. However, publication itself becomes part of the corrective process because other investigators covering the story will confirm or disconfirm it. Thus, in investigative reporting, as in science, the more powerful control is not the research design but the social control inherent in independent review, criticism, and attempts at replication of the reported observations.

THE ROLE OF THEORY

It is a truism that facts have no meaning outside of a context that gives them meaning. The process of theory building is a process of infinite approximation, or the inductive development of a modifiable hypothesis or schema (Diesing, 1971; Makkreel, 1975). The provisional assumptions underlying the investigation take form in the investigator's freely roaming imagination.

Theory, or schema, played a key role at every step in the Watergate investigation. The need for an explanation frequently arose not because of some fact per se, but because the fact represented something intriguing or puzzling, sometimes simply on an intuitive basis and sometimes because previous expectations about how the world was constructed were not met. The puzzlement and interest generated by an observation that did not make sense propelled the investigation until an explanation arose that did. The Watergate burglary itself made no sense as a piece of political espionage, and its ties to the White House and other events made no sense until the "Plumbers'" operation was uncovered. That, in turn, made sense only in the context of the particular conceptions of power that were shared in the culture of those surrounding Nixon.

The pages of *All the President's Men* are filled with events that piqued the reporters' curiosity or gave them a feeling of incomplete understanding and a need for further investigation. There are at least thirty references to circumstances that Bernstein and Woodward described as not making sense, either because there was some departure from a norm in the events that did occur, or because things that ought to have happened did not. In a great number of instances their emotional reactions were stronger than mere curiosity. Sometimes they described themselves as "baffled" or "perplexed." At other times they were "unsettled" by people's reactions to them and were "amazed," "shocked," "stunned," or "unnerved" by information, descriptions, or actions that departed from their expectations. It was these subjective reactions that powered their need for explanation.

Within the first few days after the burglary, Bernstein, acting on the basis of his surprise that an informant close to the administration spoke with "scorn and derision" of the people surrounding Nixon (Bernstein & Woodward, 1974, p. 29), wrote a five-page memo detailing the "Chotiner Theory." His editor, interest aroused by the speculation, encouraged him to pursue it (p. 30). This particular theory proved incorrect, but it was the catalyst necessary to launch and to guide an investigation.

One of the editors, Sussman, was described by the reporters as a theoretician at heart. Deeply interested in the Watergate puzzle, Sussman kept careful track of every detail and made the intellectual effort to put the pieces together at every opportunity. He served not as a cross-examiner of data but as a source of questions. Moreover, Sussman used a historical model, the Teapot Dome scandal, as a guide for his own thinking and as a source of hypotheses.

The need for explanations led to a search for facts to provide them (pp. 56, 179, 278, 298–299). The idea of a massive cover-up had come to Bernstein well before he had the facts available to support publication of the story (p. 91). Proof of the theory that the White House had been heavily involved in political espionage was necessary to account for the seeming senselessness of the Watergate burglary taken by itself (p. 118).

Information was accumulated in bits and pieces. Some of it was not direct evidence but, rather, was information about the personality and character of given actors. Informants helped the reporters understand the culture and social organization of the Nixon administration. Combined with more specific pieces of evidence, this information supported an early story pointing to massive political espionage and sabotage, directed by the White House, as a partial explanation of the Watergate burglary, an event that otherwise made no sense.

Bernstein and Woodward (1974) admitted the initial story was "interpretive—risky" (p. 150). "The story was based on strains of evidence, statements from numerous sources, deduction, a partial understanding of what the White House was doing, the reporters' familiarity with the 'switchblade mentality' of the President's men, and disparate pieces of information the reporters had been accumulating for months" (pp. 150–151). In a great deal of what Bernstein and Woodward did, it appeared necessary to suspend faith in the constructs they held, and to work to overcome their feelings of awe of the Presidency and their disbelief that public officials could

act as they did. It was the development of new concepts that allowed the investigation to proceed, even though the new concepts came slowly and required modification of existing concepts.

The reporters were constantly developing alternative hypotheses to account for information they received and interpreting its implications. When the story first broke, an editor suggested it might not be political espionage but just a case of some "crazy Cubans" (p. 16). Indeed, the idea that the burglary might be the work of Republicans seemed highly implausible at first. One alternative interpretation was that the reporters were being deliberately misled or set up in some way (p. 90). The suspicion of a setup caused them to hold publication of the story of the White House taping system, even though they had some advance information about it, because they feared the tapes might have been manufactured or recorded in such a way as to be self-serving (p. 363).

THEORY AND INVESTIGATION IN THE SOCIAL SCIENCES

Though it has long been an aim in the social sciences to develop encompassing theory, and though we honor such giants as Freud, Marx, Weber, Durkheim, and Hull for their theories, some critics contend that grand, abstract theories obscure rather than clarify. Indeed, as thoughtful a quantitatively oriented social scientist as Cronbach (1975) has come to believe that it is not possible to develop laws in the social sciences that will hold generally because of the problem of higher order interactions. And, in point of fact, John Stuart Mill (1843/1965) anticipated this view more than 100 years ago by despairing of ever developing a precise social science, except perhaps in economics, because the complexity of the social world did not permit precise formulation and testing of hypotheses. Cronbach argues that the role of the social scientist is not to develop grand theory but to pin down the contemporary facts and, in common with colleagues in the humanities, to attempt to develop explanations and interpretations that make sense of the contemporary world.

In comparing investigative reporting with social science, I am struck by the fact that investigative reporters make it their business to immerse themselves in their stories, personally getting as close as possible to the events and trying to find the human interest elements of the stories. Social scientists who endeavor to develop theory prefer to construct measures that have the merit of abstracting the essence from circumstances; however, such measures also remove the researcher from direct contact with the phenomena of interest. Questionnaires and attitude scales that force individuals to respond in abstract terms provide the social scientist with abstractions rather than with close representations of the experiences themselves.

Representations of feelings and meanings provide the basis for our understanding of each other and of the social world (Makkreel, 1975), but are often inappropriate and less than useful in our attempts to understand the physical world. Modern abstract theoretical statements reduce such meaning–feeling variables to a minimum. That ultimate abstraction, the mathematical formula, eliminates such considerations entirely. A beautiful example of how abstract concepts entirely eliminate meaning–feeling statements from scientific discourse is provided by Lévi-Strauss when he quotes the zoologist Hediger describing his first encounter with a dolphin:

"Flippy was no fish, and when he looked at you with twinkling eyes from a distance of less than two feet, you had to stifle the question as to whether it was in fact an animal. So new, strange and extremely weird was this creature, that one was tempted to consider it as some kind of bewitched being. But the zoologist's brain kept on associating it with cold fact, painful in this connection, that it was known to science by the dull name, *Tursiops truncatus.*" (Lévi-Strauss, 1962/1966, p. 38)

It may be useful to eliminate meanings and feelings from equations reflecting relations among nonhuman subjects. Certainly much of our intellectual effort in the social sciences is modeled on forms useful in the physical sciences. However, the advantages of an abstract, quantitative approach may paradoxically result in considerable disadvantage when it comes to aiding our understanding of the human condition.

Investigative reporting, participant–observer research, and research deriving from clinical interaction—all of these approaches have the distinct advantage of bringing us close to the phenomena of interest. Such methods are faulty when subject to no discipline. What I have tried to point out here is that investigative reporting does have a discipline to it in that its results are grounded in evidence whose reliability is probed in a number of ways. The inference process is also limited by social controls. The method requires theory to guide investigation, and it can result in concepts or models that have significance beyond the unique events for which they were developed.

There are a number of strands in contemporary social science[3] that lead toward a

---

[3] London (1961, 1974, 1975, 1977) has tried to develop both a philosophy of method and a system of discipline for dealing with data derived from direct human experience, using observers who were participants in events. His use of a novelist to make dramatic sense of experience (London, 1974) has not received the attention it deserves. Kvale (1976) has pointed out that meanings are psychology's data and has described some of the difficulties and advantages of working with meanings as data. Campbell (Note 1) also believes that the quantitative and the qualitative necessarily complement each other in the research enterprise. Harré and Secord (1972) have called for an anthropomorphic social psychology. They too are interested in the direct human experience of events as the key to finding explanatory concepts.

renewed interest in, and acceptance of, clinical and qualitative methods. We can understand these methods better by observing how skilled investigators use them, and to that end, Bernstein and Woodward have provided us with an exceptionally useful document. I hope that other investigators will similarly provide us with a careful record of their own approaches so that a teachable, disciplined method of doing field research, case studies, and clinical research may emerge.

REFERENCES NOTE

1. Campbell, D. T. *Qualitative Knowing in Action Research* (Kurt Lewin Award Address, Society for the Psychological Study of Social Issues). Paper presented at the meeting of the American Psychological Association, New Orleans, August 1974.

REFERENCES

Anderson, D., & Benjaminson, P. *Investigative Reporting.* Bloomington: Indiana University Press, 1976.

Balaban, R. M. "The Contribution of Participant Observation to the Study of Process in Program Evaluation." *International Journal of Mental Health*, 1973, 2, 59–70.

Balaban, R. M. "Participant Observation—Rediscovering a Research Method." In L. Goldman (Ed.), *Research Methods for Counselors.* New York: Wiley, 1978.

Barzun, J. M. *Clio and the Doctors: Psychohistory, Quanto-history and History.* Chicago: University of Chicago Press, 1974.

Bernstein, C., & Woodward, B. *All the President's Men.* New York: Warner Books, 1974. (Paperback)

Bogdan, R., & Taylor, S. J. *Introduction to Qualitative Research Methods.* New York: Wiley, 1975.

Cleary, E. W. (Ed.). *McCormick on Evidence.* St. Paul, Minn.: West, 1972.

Cronbach, L. J. "Beyond the Two Disciplines of Psychology. *American Psychologist*, 1975, 30, 116–127.

Diesing, P. *Patterns of Discovery in the Social Sciences.* Chicago: Aldine-Atherton, 1971.

Douglas, J. D. *Investigative Social Research.* Beverly Hills, Calif.: Sage, 1976.

Erikson, E. H. *Insight and Responsibility.* New York: Norton, 1964.

Giorgi, A. *Psychology as a Human Science.* New York: Harper & Row, 1970.

Group for the Advancement of Psychiatry. *Some Observations on Controls in Psychiatric Research* (Report No. 42). New York: Author, 1959.

Harré, R., & Secord, P. F. *The Explanation of Social Behavior.* Oxford, England: Blackwell, 1972.

Hesse, M. B. *Models and Analogies in Science.* Notre Dame, Ind.: Notre Dame University Press, 1966.

Kvale, S. "Meanings as Data and Human Technology." *Scandinavian Journal of Psychology*, 1976, 17, 171–180.

Levine, A., & Levine, M. "The Social Context of Evaluative Research: A Case Study." *Evaluation Quarterly*, 1977, 1, 515–542.

Levine, M. "Scientific Method and the Adversary Model: Some Preliminary Thoughts." *American Psychologist*, 1974, 29, 661–677.

Levine, M. Congress (and evaluators) ought to pay more attention to history. *American Journal of Community Psychology*, 1979, 7, 1–17.

Levi-Strauss, C. *The Savage Mind.* London: Weidenfeld & Nicclson, 1966. (Originally published, 1962.)

London, I. D. "Respondent-evaluation Applied to Quotational Analysis: A Case Study." *Psychological Reports*, 19961, *9*, 615–621.

London, I. D. "The Revenge of Heaven: A Brief Methodological Account." *Psychological Reports*, 1974, *34*, 1023–1030.

London, I. D. "Interviewing in Sinology: Observations on and its Meaning for Social Sciences." *Psychological Reports*, 1975, *36*, 683–691.

London, I. D. "Convergent and Divergent Amplification and its Meaning for Social Sciences." *Psychological Reports*, 1977, *41*, 111–123.

Makkreel, R. A. *Dilthey: Philosopher of the Human Studies*. Princeton, N.J.: Princeton University Press, 1975.

Mill, J. S. *On the Logic of the Moral Sciences*. Indianapolis, Ind.: Bobbs-Merrill, 1965. (Originally published, 1843.)

Truzzi, M. (Ed.). *Verstehen: Subjective Understanding in the Social Sciences*. Reading, Mass.: Addison-Wesley, 1974.

Waelder, R. *Basic Theory of Psychoanalysis*. New York: International Universities Press, 1960.

Watson, J. D. *The Double Helix*. New York: Atheneum, 1968.

Whyte, W. F. *Street Corner Society*. Chicago: University of Chicago Press, 1955.

Winks, R. W. (Ed.). *The Historian as Detective: Essays on Evidence*. New York: Harper & Row, 1968.

Unobtrusive Measures in Organizational Theory: A Reminder[1]

Eugene Webb

Karl E. Weick

The purpose of this article is to review and tighten the relationship between unobtrusive measures (Webb et al., 1966) and organizational inquiry and, in the process, to remind investigators that these measures continue to be workable, credible components of multimethod inquiry.

The object of interest is found in this illustration:

> You know, I am really stupid. For years I have looked for the perfect pencil. I have found very good ones, but never the perfect one. And all the time it was not the pencils but me. A pencil that is all right some days is no good another day. For example, yesterday I used a special pencil soft and fine and it floated over the paper just wonderfully. So this morning I tried the same kind. And they crack on me. Points break and all hell is let loose. This is the day when I am stabbing the paper. So today I need a harder pencil at least for a while. I am using some that are #2 & ⅜. I have my plastic tray you know and in it three kinds of pencils for hard writing days and soft writing days. Only sometimes it changes in the middle of the day, but at least I am equipped for it. I have also some super-soft pencils which I do not use very often because I must feel as delicate as a rose pedal to use them. And I am not often that way. But when I do have such moments I am prepared. It is always well to be prepared. Pencils are a great expense to me and I hope you know it. I buy them four dozen at a time. When in my nor-mal writing position the metal of the pencil eraser touches my hand, I retire that pencil (Steinbeck, 1969: 35–36).

The recent enthusiasm for variations on Murphy's Law has produced marvelous exhibits of unobtrusive measures (Faber, 1979):

1. The more sophisticated the equipment, the bigger the adjustment department needed (p. 34);
2. The quality of food and service is inversely proportional to the captivity of the clientele (p. 37);
3. The quality of food in a restaurant is in inverse proportion to the number of semicolons and exclamation marks on the menu (p. 38);
4. You can tell how bad the musical is by how many times the chorus yells hooray (p 46);
5. The number of agency people required to shoot a commercial on location is in direct proportion to the mean temperature of the location (p. 50);
6. The length of a country's national anthem is inversely proportional to the importance of the country (p. 71);
7. In war, victory goes to those armies whose leaders' uniforms are least impressive (p. 112).

If we think of organizational inquiry as involving three steps—design, data collection,

---

[1] Reproduced by permission of *Administrative Science Quarterly*, 1979, 24, 650–659.

and analysis—an assessment of the field will show that there has been a substantial increase in the complexity and requisite variety of design (e.g., Cook and Campbell, 1979) and analysis (Tukey, 1977). But there has not been a corresponding increase in the complexity of data-collection techniques. Data collection in organizational inquiry is characterized by satisficing, and people who value unobtrusive measures are restless in the face of that conclusion.

The term unobtrusive measures has become something of a ceremonial citation that signifies sympathy toward multimethod inquiry, triangulation, playfulness in data collection, outcroppings as measures, and alternatives to self-report. The search for alternatives to self-report directly joins unobtrusive measures to current issues in organizational inquiry. While investigators regularly detail the limits of self-report they also regularly say that despite these limits, the methods are good enough. They acknowledge that self-report involves small ideas generated by overly surveyed people that are overinterpreted, yet they continue to collect such data. This contradiction originates in several places.

Self-report also remains the dominant style of measurement because investigators have dealt continually with articulate populations. Less articulate populations, because they had neither time nor interest nor talent to work with self-report measures, are underrepresented in organizational research. Self-report measures seem to be used with higher levels of organizations, unobtrusive measures such as turnover with lower level portions of organizations such as the assembly line. In the latter case, the usage of unobtrusive measures seems to allow investigators to avoid talking to people and finding out what really goes on and what work is really like. If self-reports were extended downward, and unobtrusive measures upward, inquiry should become more valid as well as more interesting.

Finally, self-reports persist partly because the field relies heavily on cognitive concepts, concepts that are more readily operationalized by talk than by other traces.

Unobtrusive measures seem to be associated with and induce a different set toward data collection than is true for self-report measures. Some characteristics of this set are implicit in earlier discussions by Palmer and McGuire (1973). Bouchard (1976), Sechrest (1976), and Webb and Elsworth (1976); this article makes six of these characteristics explicit.

INVESTIGATORS CONSTRUCT AND IMPOSE MULTIPLE INDICES THAT CONVERGE

The concern with multiples turns on the fact that it takes multiples of some form to capture and preserve multiples in the phenomenon of interest (i.e., organizations). These sensing multiples can be multiple hypotheses (people who use unobtrusive measures are convinced it is as important to develop banks of hypotheses as banks of data), multiple theoretical degrees of freedom (Campbell, 1975), multiple indicators, and multiple methods. The person concerned with multiples faces the question that if organizations are complex, does that mean that many different complex methods should be directed simultaneously at the phenomenon of interest or that many different indices within a single method (e.g., a battery of unobtrusive measures) should be used? In either case the intention is to match the variety of the source with variety in the sensing device that is applied to it (e.g., Weick, 1979: 188–193).

The tight coupling between multiples and unobtrusive measures, however, sometimes works against adoption of this procedure. Some people avoid using unobtrusive measures because they assume you can use them *only if* you also use a multimethod battery. And since a multimethod battery is complex and time consuming, to avoid it is to avoid unobtrusive measures. People may also avoid unobtrusive measures because they feel they add little information to that gained from other methods in a multimethod inquiry. Or unobtrusive measures are avoided because, when used in combination with other measures, the fact of multiplicity increases the likelihood that the resulting data will be inconsistent. To avoid the difficult task of interpreting contradictions, people avoid multiple measures.

INVESTIGATORS ASSUME THAT NOISE IS RARE

People who use unobtrusive measures think in terms of a signal-to-noise ratio, but tend to be generous in their definition of signal. The person using unobtrusive measures presumes that most of the world contains informative indicators and that it is silly to ignore outcroppings because they seem nonserious, untraditional, or puzzling. The image of a signal-to-noise ratio reminds people that they reject much information that is available, that the definition of what is signal and what is noise is variable, and that there will be dross in any observational setting.

An example of an unobtrusive measure is the number of bar transactions in Chicago's O'Hare airport before and after an air tragedy. It exemplifies the signal-to-noise ratio in the sense that those bar transactions do not involve just purchases of hard liquor. Nonalcoholic beverages, snacks, cigarettes, sweets, aspirin, and remedies for upset stomachs are also requested on those checks. To some investigators those "extras" are a nuisance whereas those who are sympathetic toward unobtrusive measures see no reason to assume a priori that such extras are meaningless as indicators of shifts in anxiety. Unobtrusive measures buy a lot of dirty details.

To some that is their strength, to others it is their greatest liability.

INVESTIGATORS BELIEVE IN AMORTIZATION

Unobtrusive measures are sometimes viewed as flawed because they are generated outside of the investigator's direct control. If an investigator manufactures data by the means of an experiment or an interview then those data are thought to be more scientific than if the data were manufactured by someone else and were picked up opportunisitcally by the investigator. The way to preserve this point is to argue that "hard scientists don't believe in amortization." Hard science seems to be based on the premise that there can be only a single purpose for data and that the investigator should be the one who designs and defines that purpose and creates the universe so that it is ideal for scientific purposes. Data created for other purposes are seen as neither scientific nor hard. People who favor unobtrusive measures find that stance counterproductive and naive.

INVESTIGATORS FIND FOOLISHNESS FUNCTIONAL

Unobtrusive measures have come to be associated with a light-hearted, playful stance toward the world in data collection. This stance furthers science in several ways. If the same event, for example, is regarded as both absurd and serious then more of it is likely to be seen because, in fact, it contains both qualities. Foolish interludes generate novel inputs and permit people to recognize and break the singular focus toward a problem in which they had persisted. Foolish interludes disconfirm assumptions thereby creating interest (Davis, 1971), put distance between the observer and the phenomenon, sustain morale, recruit interest in the topic, aid retention, facilitate the content and process of free association, expose assumptions, forestall criticism that degenerates into cynicism, offset the preoccupation with rational models that is characteristic of organizational inquiry, and insert topics into inquiry (e.g., managing as Chinese baseball in Siu, 1978) that wouldn't be acknowledged or accepted if introduced in a more straightforward manner.

Enthusiasts for unobtrusive measures can be openly playful, which means that they can be playful with vigor, which means they can extract all of the benefits that flow from humor when it is done well. Playfulness becomes more exhibitionistic, less constructive, and more artful the more it is done hesitantly, self-consciously, and apologetically. Playfulness is risky among colleagues hardened to cute experiments, clever concepts, and artful prose. But to compromise playfulness with seriousness is to engage in neither and to offend enthusiasts of both.

INVESTIGATORS PONDER THE VARIANCE RATHER THAN THE MEAN

People who use unobtrusive measures presume that the variance is at least as interesting as the mean and typically more so. For people interested in organizations, the key question is, how do you get low variation? If individual differences are so abundant, then how can it be that for some populations in some settings, there is so little difference visible? This is the kind of question that lends itself to unobtrusive measures and it is the kind of question that interests people who use unobtrusive measures to understand organizations. For example, many theories of power are conspiratorial (e.g., Pfeffer, 1977) and one of the best indicators of conspiratorial power is a lack of variance. Governance of Washington, often said to be insensitive yet consistent, can be indexed by the fact that much of the district's governance is done by people who have zip codes clustered in areas *outside* the district (Washington, 1967). The unobtrusive measure of similarity of zip code (low variance) when the expectation is a higher variance suggests the presence of organizing and pattern where none was suspected.

INVESTIGATORS USE EXPECTANCY AS A CONTROL

Expectancies are the controls of both common sense and science; surprise is an indicator of the abuse of expectancies. What people don't do, who isn't in a network, practices that weren't made, are data and they become data because of the a priori expectations that existed. Thus, sophisticated and successful use of unobtrusive measures requires that investigators lay out in advance what they expect to find so that the surprise when they don't find it is visible and documented. Everyone, for example, appoints a chairman for meetings, especially when those meetings are consequential. However, given this expectancy as a control, the fact that Kennedy didn't appoint a chairman of the deliberations on the Cuban Missile Crisis becomes an indicator of added interest. To identify an omission and to judge its significance is to have an elaborated set of expectancies readily at hand. Enthusiasts for unobtrusive measures tend to be eclectics, and one reason for this is the presence among eclectics of wide-ranging sets of expectancies, some of which become disconfirmed and attract attention no matter what the organizational event.

DEADLINES: UNOBTRUSIVE MEASURES AT WORK

As an example of a phenomenon articulated and studied by a family of investigations—some direct, some unobtrusive—we can consider work on the effect of deadlines. The history of the word deadline shows it to be grounded in an engagingly attractive organization control mechanism. Its nineteenth-century beginning was as a line drawn in the soil around a group of prisoners. Anyone stepping outside that line significantly shortened his life span. Currently, deadlines are less noxious. They serve as general control devices for both individuals and organizations, signaling the seasons of some organizations and setting a rhythm for the activities of the organization's members.

The characteristics of that rhythm setting were the concern of a group of students at the Stanford Business School in the early 1970s. The group converged around Hull's marvelously simple idea: the goal gradient hypothesis. Hull (1934) had proposed that the approach velocity of a hungry rat increases exponentially as it nears a food source.

To explore that idea in naturalistic settings, both observational and archival approaches were used. The first check on Hull's hypothesis was a failure. The Minneapolis airport, and its long escalator, provided the setting for the informal test: do people accelerate speed (i.e., begin walking on the escalator) as the end of the ride nears? Does the density distribution look related to the goal gradient? A wasted 45 minutes showed no cross-species support for Hull's finding with rats. People started walking at all points on the ride, even after one partialled out the "how-many-in-front" effect.

But in the spirit of measures (and don't give up the hypothesis) thinking, the goal gradient generality was tested by two organizational deadline investigations. The first (Jerrell, 1973) looked at the rate of applications to the Stanford Graduate School of Business. The second (Glenn, 1974) examined the "makeup" rate of incompletes in the School of Education at Stanford. Both archival checks showed support for the proposition that organizational deadlines do indeed appear to pull behavior from relevant populations.

In the business school study, Jerrell noted that two deadlines existed for applications; the first, if one applied for financial aid, and the second, for admission independent of financial questions. Plotting the rate of applications against these two deadline dates, Jerrell found a nicely scalloped curve. The applications slant up exponentially as the first deadline is approached, drop off and then start the exponential rise to the second and last deadline.

Glenn showed similar curves when students make up incomplete grades. The institution establishes a quarterly deadline to file the incompleted work and the behavioral activity curve races up in frequency as each deadline nears and then falls away as it passes. The patterns detected by Jerrell and Glenn were replicated over several years.

Lest one feel this to be an unduly limited probing—one limited to the unreal world of the academy and its occupants—the field of inquiry was extended to two very real-world settings: the New York Stock Exchange and the National Football League. Using available records, Grauer (1973) traced the intraday trading volume of the Big Board. Was the approaching final bell for trading associated with trading volume? Grauer found the expected pattern. Trading was heavy in the early hours (as overnight orders were executed), dipped in midday, and then escalated as the closing bell neared—simple support for the deadline effect.

This support was strengthened by asking what happened in the pattern of trading when the New York Stock Exchange extended its closing time from 3:00 to 3:30. The answer is that nothing happened. When the closing time was 3:00, the last two hours showed escalating trading. When the closing time was 3:30, again the last two hours showed escalating trading; the activity curve simply shifted half a notch to the right. The closing bell was the marker, the magnetic draw, not the economic variables of the hour. Grauer also demonstrated that the gradient of the end-of-day trading slope was greater on Friday than on other days. With two days of no trading ahead, Friday's closing bell had a particularly potent pull. (It should be noted that this is a pattern analysis independent of the absolute number of shares traded.)

Grauer took advantage of another naturally-generated time variable. Because of the inability of brokerage houses to process orders, the New York Stock Exchange closed on Wednesdays for a while in 1969—thus moving to a four-day trading week. He had observed the Friday difference: end-of-day trading was higher with the prospect of two days of non-trading. But what now happens to the *shape* of the trading curve on Tuesdays? With no trading on Wednesday, does the deadline effect become more pronounced? The simple answer is yes. A second-difference analysis shows the end-of-day trading slopes steeper for four-day work week Tuesdays than for five-day work week Tuesdays.

In this allegedly most rational of worlds, trading on the Big Board, the deadline gradient effect was observed for individual day trading and for end-of-sequence (work week) trading.

Yet another natural occurrence of deadline behavior is on the football field. In his pilot study for a provocative dissertation on play-calling behavior, Fischer (1973) used archival records to track the number of plays executed per quarter in professional football games. The deadline characteristic is slightly different from that found in the stock market investigation. The market closes at 3:30 EST, but a football game ends when 60 minutes of elaborately calculated playing time has expired. Now rank those quarters in order of the mean number of plays executed by both teams. A subtle student of football (and/or an advanced cost-benefit analyst) might have predicted Fischer's findings. In order of frequency of total plays executed: Quarter 2 > Quarter 4 > Quarter 3 = Quarter 1.

By the nature of the rules of American football, the second and fourth quarters are deadline quarters, while the first and third quarters are not. Possession of the ball is unaffected by the end of the first and third quarters. So the data support the general notion that a deadline promotes higher activity. That the mean number of plays is greater in the second quarter than in the fourth quarter, illustrates that a deadline can be both a friend and a foe. For the team leading in points during the fourth quarter, there is a strong disincentive to execute plays, the goal being one of letting time expire while one is still ahead. The losing team does all it can to accelerate the rate of play as it attempts to catch up. Toward the end of the second quarter, there is no such strategy divergence. Both teams would like to run plays and make points before the closing of the half. Thus, the greatest number of plays is in the second quarter.

In a less playful vein, there is Weiner's (1973) study of the effect of an imposed deadline on organizational decision making. Weiner examined the properties of the desegregation actions of the San Francisco United School District. Working within a garbage can model (Cohen, March, and Olsen, 1972) Weiner traced the appearance of the desegregation issue, the lack of decisive action, and the final organizational move triggered by a judge's mandate—a 50-day deadline by which a desegregation plan was to be submitted. Students of the theory of organized anarchies might attempt a prediction of organizational processes before consulting Weiner's study as a genuine tumbling garbage can at work.

We conclude this discussion of deadline research with two studies, neither of which is unobtrusive, but both of which are within the same research group. Dowling (1973) was interested in cultural differences in time perception and exploited the available subject pool of foreign students at Stanford as subjects. Using a questionnaire approach, he asked about time behavior in one's home country. How late can one be for work without being "too" late? How much time must pass beyond the scheduled start of a concert before it is "late starting"? What time would one appear at the restaurant for a 12:15 lunch date? Dowling showed a cultural difference, with Northern Europeans stating that they adhere more closely to time cues. One must keep all of this in perspective, however. Dowling plugged the notion of role into his questioning and asked what time one would show up for a 12:15 lunch if one person were a prospective employer and the other were a prospective employee. It will surprise few readers to learn that there was a difference in reported punctuality; the potential employee is reported to arrive earlier.

Arvedson (1974) has conducted the most thorough investigation of deadline effects. He studied the effect of setting various deadlines for the solution of an anagram and the influence of suggesting to subjects that the allocated time was short or long. This factorial study is studded with interesting findings about deadlines, but two are of particular note here. One relates to the property of deadlines that keeps people working, the other to the success rate when subjects think they have a short or long deadline.

Arvedson ran 51 subjects in a control condition in which no time deadline was mentioned. Six of these 51 nondeadline subjects gave up and said they could not solve the anagram; only one of the 157 subjects who had a deadline gave up. They may not have solved the problem but they were still working. Whatever else it may do, the deadline has an energizing function.

A second finding is that performance rate is greater when people are led to believe that they have a "long" versus a "short" time to do the job. When a constant eight minutes was available to work the anagram problem, 42 percent of those who were told their time was "short" completed the task. For those told they had a "long" time to do the task, 55 percent completed the job. A deadline, as in eight minutes to do a job, is not a deadline; it depends on the social refer-

ence. It should surprise no student of organizations that a labeling exercise, even if false, of what is an appropriate criterion of time in which to do a job has an effect.

CONTROL: UNOBTRUSIVE MEASURES AT WORK

Unobtrusive measures can both reshuffle thinking about traditional organizational topics and introduce nontraditional topics such as deadlines to the field. To illustrate how traditional themes are reopened when measured unobtrusively, consider the issue of control. Organizations are effective to the extent that they control variation in the actions of their employees by constraints and comparisons. This key principle of organizational theory has been explored primarily by asking who has muscle and how is that muscle exhibited? Efforts at control leave other traces, however, and our purpose here is to list some of these.

Control is indexed most literally by how easy it is to get into and out of the physical plant of the organization. Organizations concerned with trade secrets (e.g., toy manufacturers) have fewer entrances to their premises than do less concerned organizations. More constraint is visible when calls go through a central switchboard rather than directly to the people being contacted, when home phone numbers are not given out by office switchboard operators, when background checks become more extensive, when the number of master keys in circulation decreases and the number of gradations in the master key system increase, and when "security risks" are defined more broadly. Written documents index control in such ways as explicit discussions of control in annual reports, coercive elements in employee handbooks, and in the thickness of procedure manuals distributed by headquarters to branch organizations as well as the degree to which those manuals have been thumbed and marked. If, for example, Lufthansa employees in North America receive manuals that are four inches thick while the desks of Air France employees contain manuals only one-half inch thick, we can infer the presence of differences in contraint. Discretionary behaviors provide unobtrusive measures of control. The amount of money people allocate before they are subject to review is sensitive to differences in constraint. As a variant, one could ask, "How much money does it take to get the attention of the provost at Cornell, the Secretary of the Army, the president of Bechtel?" While these sums are diagnostic in their own right, all such figures will have exceptions (e.g., the Secretary wants to know about *all* allocations involving programs for women) and these exceptions are clues to the political realities faced by such people.

Structural traces reveal control emphases. Organizational charts identify nominal controls and who figures in whose plans to bypass an immediate superior and get a wider hearing. The labels on organizational charts represent efforts to control expectations, requests, and accountability. The presence of oversight committees represents an effort to reduce the power of outsiders and to increase the diversity of views considered. Formal arrangements to bypass portions of an organizational chart, as when managers are required to go to their subordinate's subordinates to get input for any major decision, represent an effort to reduce the effects of filtering and to discover bad news before it becomes a disaster.

As noted earlier, low variance signifies the potential presence of control and this low variance can meaningfully range across items as diverse as dress, wall trappings, names, departments through which interdepartmental mail envelopes have previously circulated, zip codes of residence, time of arrival or departure, sports preferences, seating at meetings, format of daily calendar, jewelry, formality of telephone greeting, etc. These measures, all of which are obvious, tend to be overlooked in favor of what people say about the control they exert and receive.

Since that talk may itself be controlled in such a way that crucial phenomena are selectively inattended and/or represented in innocuous images, cross-checking by other less influenceable measures is especially crucial (Edwards, 1979).

CONCLUSION

Our reconsideration of unobtrusive measures suggests that, for organizational questions, ceremonial citation should be turned into substance. Heavy prior reliance on self-report has excluded crucial populations from organizational inquiry, postponed cross-checking of propositions, inflated the apparent consequentiality of minor irritations in the workplace, and imposed a homogeneity of method which raises the prospect that the findings of the field are method-specific. Further development and application of unobtrusive measures should offset the tendency to satisfice in data collection and should add variety to inquiry that registers a greater proportion of the variety in ongoing organizations (Daft and Wiginton, 1979). The provocativeness of that registry is evident in a final illustration which comes from a description by Lazard (1946: 168) of the psychological consequences of living for two years under an assumed name in occupied France to avoid being arrested by the Germans.

> I have already said that I was friendly with the priest in the neighboring village whom I had taken into my confidence. I asked him one day what he thought of an existence which placed one constantly under a deliberate lie. He knew what I meant and replied that as far as he was concerned it was of no importance theologically, that the only truth was that due to God. I stayed more than an hour with him, speaking of a thousand things. When I was leaving, the woman (who had some suspicions about my identity) entered by the garden. He said to me, "Wait five minutes in that little room on the side there before coming out. It will be better if you are not seen now. After such a conversation as we have had there sometimes remain on the face things which one would prefer to hide."

References

Arvedson, L. A. "Deadlines and Organizational Behavior: A Laboratory Investigation of the Effect of Deadlines on Individual Task Performance." Doctoral dissertation proposal, Graduate School of Business, Stanford University, 1974.

Bouchard, T. J. "Unobtrusive Measures: An Inventory of Uses." *Sociological Methods and Research,* 1976, 4, 267–300.

Campbell, D. T. "Degrees of Freedom and the Case Study." *Comparative Political Studies,* 1975, 8, 178–193.

Cohen, Michael D., James G. March, and Johan P. Olsen "A Garbage Can Model of Organizational Choice." *Administrative Science Quarterly,* 1972, 17, 1–25.

Cook, T. D., & Campbell, D. T. *Quasi-Experimentation: Design and Analysis Issues for Field Settings.* Chicago: Rand McNally, 1979.

Daft, R. L., & Wiginton, J. C. "Language and Organization." *Academy of Management Review,* 1979, 4, 179–192.

David, M. S. "That's Interesting: Towards a Phenomenology of Sociology and a Sociology of Phenomenology." *Philosophy of Social Science,* 1971, 1, 309–344.

Dowling, J. B. "The Social Context of Time Behavior." Unpublished manuscript, Graduate School of Business, Stanford University, 1973.

Edwards, R. *Contested Terrain.* New York: Basic, 1979.

Faber, H. *The Book of Laws.* New York: Times, 1979.

Fischer, P. C. "A Report on the Influence of Deadlines on the Behavior of the Professional Football Team." Unpublished manuscript, Graduate School of Business, Stanford University, 1973.

Glenn, J. R. "Presidential Time Allocation in American Colleges and Universities." Doctoral dissertation proposal, Graduate School of Business, Stanford University, 1974.

Grauer, F. L. "On Deadline effects: Intraday Trading Volume on the New York Stock Exchange." In E. J. Webb (ed.), Papers for the March 1973 Deadline Conference. Unpublished manuscript, Graduate School of Business, Stanford University, 1973.

Hull, C. L. "The Rat's Speed-of-locomotion Gradient in the Approach to Food." *Journal of Comparative Psychology,* 1934, 7, 393–422.

Jerrell, S. L. "Goal Gradient Illustration: MBA Admission Applications." In E. J. Webb (ed.), Papers for the March 1973 Deadline Conference. Unpublished manuscript, Graduate School of Business, Stanford University, 1973.

Lazard, D. "Two Years Under a False Name." *Journal of Abnormal and Social Psychology,* 1946, 41, 161–168.

Palmer, J., & McGuire, F. L. "The Use of Unobtrusive Measures in Mental Health Research." *Journal of Consulting and Clinical Psychology,* 1973, 40, 431–436.

Parmenter, R. *The Awakened Eye.* Middletown, CT.: Wesleyan, 1968.

Pfeffer, Jeffrey "Power and Resource Allocation in Organizations." In Barry M. Staw and Gerald R. Salancik (eds.), *New Directions in Organizational Behavior:* 235–265. Chicago: St. Clair, 1977.

Sechrest, L. "Another Look at Unobtrusive Measures." In H. W. Sinaiko and L. A. Broedling (eds.), *Perspectives on Attitude Assessment: Surveys and Their Alternatives:* 94–107. Champaign, IL.: Pendleton, 1976.

Siu, R. G. H. "Management and the Art of Chinese Baseball." *Sloan Management Review,* Spring: 1978, 83–89.

Steinbeck, John *Journal of a Novel.* New York: Viking, 1969.

Tukey, J. W. *Exploratory Data Analysis.* Reading, MA.: Addison-Wesley, 1977.

Washburn, W. E. "Power in Washington: A Zip-coded Directory." *Washington Post, Potomac Magazine,* 1967, 132, 48–54.

Webb, E. J., Campbell, D. T., Schwartz, R.

D., & Sechrest, L. *Unobtrusive Measures.* Chicago: Rand McNally, 1966.

Webb, E. J., & Ellsworth, P. C. "On Nature and Knowing." In H. W. Sinaiko and L. A. Broedling (eds.), *Perspectives on Attitude Assessment: Surveys and their Alternatives:* 223–238. Champaign, IL.: Pendleton, 1976.

Weick, Karl E. *The Social Psychology of Organizing,* 2d ed. Reading, MA.: Addison-Wesley, 1979.

Weiner, S. S. "Deadlines and School Desegregation in San Francisco." In E. J. Webb (ed.), Papers for the March 1973 Deadline Conference: unpublished manuscript, Graduate School of Business, Stanford University, 1973.

An Idiographic Approach to Organizational Behavior Research: The Use of Single Case Experimental Designs and Direct Measures[1]

Fred Luthans

Tim R. V. Davis

More than 40 years ago Gordon Allport introduced the terms *idiographic* and *nomothetic* to represent two perspectives and methodologies for doing research in psychology. He borrowed the terms from the neo-Kantian philosopher Windelband and defined them as follows:

> The nomothetic approach . . . seek only general laws and employ only those procedures admitted by the exact sciences. Psychology in the main has been striving to make of itself a completely nomothetic discipline. The idiographic sciences . . . endeavor to understand some *particular* event in nature or in society. A psychology of individuality would be essentially idiographic (1937, p. 22).

Allport's purpose was to remind psychologists of the time that they were going down the path of group-centered nomothetic research and were ignoring the individual-centered idiographic perspective. This observation produced a spark for controversy and debate in psychology over the ensuing years

(Beck, 1953; Endler, 1973; Falk, 1956; Harris, 1980; Holt, 1962; Skaggs, 1945). Except for some related concerns surrounding quantitative versus qualitative research (Argyris, 1979; Behling, 1980; Mintzberg, 1979; Morgan & Smircich, 1980; Van Maanen, 1979) and what Evered and Louis (1981) label "inquiry from the inside" and "inquiry from the outside" that very recently have surfaced in the literature, the idiographic versus nomothetic controversy has not really been evident over the years in the field of organizational behavior.

The nomothetic versus idiographic approaches currently are not a "hot" methodological issue in the organizational behavior field because, like in Allport's time, there is almost a singular preoccupation with the nomothetic approach. With but a few exceptions—for example, Dalton (1959), Mintzberg (1973), Pettigrew (1973), Van Maanen (1973)—there is a notable absence of what could be labeled as idiographic research reported in the organizational behav-

[1] The research program leading to this paper was supported in part by Organizational Effectivness Research Group, Office of Naval Research (Code 442), under Contract No. N00014-80-C-0554; NR 170-913 (Fred Luthans, principal investigator).

ior literature. In the field's rush for scientific respectability, the traditional case study design generally has been degraded and excluded for not being scientific enough. From a scientific perspective this may be justified. Not justified is the exclusion (or perhaps it is unawareness) of some potentially powerful causal experimental designs (e.g., intensive single case experimental designs) and direct methods (e.g., systematic participant observation) that can flow from and be compatible with an idiographic perspective.

The purpose of this paper is not to polarize the field of organizational behavior into a classic idiographic versus nomothetic debate. There already is enough controversy in areas such as motivation and leadership and, as Evered and Louis have noted, "the idiographic/nomothetic dichotomy has been dysfunctional for the development of the social sciences, because it carries the presumption that only nomothetic research can yield general laws" (1981, p. 391). Instead of this dichotomy, the perpective taken here is that both nomothesis and idiography have a place and can contribute to our knowledge of organizational behavior. Even when Allport made the original distinction he vainly tried to point out that the two approaches were "overlapping and contributing to one another" and that "a complete study of the individual will embrace both approaches" (1937, p. 22). This conciliatory message, of course, generally fell on deaf ears, and the same may happen here. The position taken here is that research in organizational behavior needs to proceed both from the idiographic to the nomothetic and from the nomothetic to the idiographic and not just from the nomothetic approach alone. For instance, it is felt that a strong argument for better understanding of organizational behavior can be made by intensive study of one or a few cases of real employees interacting in real organizations before attempting to study a large number of subjects across controlled and standardized environments. Once again, however, it is not suggested that

the nomothetic approach be dropped or deemphasized. Rather, as Allport saw it years ago, there is a need for both approaches, and going back and forth from one to the other may yield the best results for the field of organizational behavior.

The concern here is that the idiographic perspective and some of its possible accompanying designs and methods have somehow been lost or misunderstood in the development of the field of organizational behavior. The purpose of this paper is to bring an understanding of the need for an idiographic perspective and to describe and analyze some designs and methods that can be used systematically and intensively to study single cases in naturally occurring situations.

ASSUMPTIONS OF NOMOTHESIS AND IDIOGRAPHY

Recently there has been some interest and concern about the underlying assumptions of social science knowledge in general and organizational inquiry in particular. Burrell and Morgan, for example, divide the ontology, epistemology, human nature, and methodology assumptions into subjective-objective dimensions. In particular, the subjectivist approach to social science includes a nominalism assumption for ontology, an antipositivism assumption for epistemology, a voluntarism assumption of human nature, and, importantly, an idiographic assumption for methodology. The objectivist approach, on the other hand, assumes a realistic ontology, a positivist epistemology, deterministic human nature, and a nomothetic methodology. Thus, in this classification scheme idiographic represents a subjectivist approach to social science methodology, and nomothetic represents an objectivist approach to social science methodology.

More specifically, Burrell and Morgan state that the idiographic approach is based on the view that one can only understand the social world by obtaining first-hand knowledge of the subject under investigation. It thus places considerable stress upon getting close to one's subject and . . . emphasizes the analysis of the subjective accounts which one generates by "getting inside" situations and involving oneself in the everyday flow of life—the detailed analysis of the insights generated by such encounters with one's subject and the insights revealed in impressionistic accounts found in diaries, biographies and journalistic records (1979, p. 6).

In other words, this is a "subjective" approach to methodology according to Burrell and Morgan or what Evered and Louis (1981) would call "inquiry from the inside," and it depends on what has become known as "qualitative" data gathering techniques. The nomothetic approach to methodology, according to Burrell and Morgan, is

> basing research upon systematic protocol and technique. It is epitomised in the approach and methods employed in the natural sciences . . . It is preoccupied with the construction of scientific tests and the use of quantitative techniques for the analysis of data. Surveys, questionnaires, personality tests and standardized research instruments of all kinds are prominent among the tools which comprise nomothetic methodology (1979, pp. 6–7).

Nomothesis

Although qualitative methodologies have very recently been given attention in the field of organizational behavior (for example, the December 1979 issue of *Administrative Science Quarterly* is devoted entirely to qualitative methodology, and some recent sessions of the Academy of Management meetings have been devoted to the issue of qualitative versus quantitative research), quantitative methodologies have unquestionably dominated. "Good" research in organizational behavior (and probably more accurately the *only* research allowed in the most respected journals) has tried to follow the widely accepted criteria for internal and external validity (Campbell & Stanley, 1966; Cook & Campbell, 1976, 1979). Sophisticated inferential statistics are used to analyze the data, test hypotheses, and draw conclusions. This dominant form of research is almost a pure nomothetic approach.

Control *group* experimental designs that depend on representative sampling from the population and make random assignments to the experimental and control *groups* and then make *group* comparisons on the statistical analysis obviously are a group-centered, nomothetic approach to research. In this highly popular approach, individual behavior is *averaged,* environmental conditions are controlled and standardized as much as possible, and the person-environment *interaction* generally is ignored. Usually, highly abstract variables in organizational behavior (e.g., leadership, motivational or attitudinal states, and job design or organizational structural variables) are isolated for analysis over a large enough N to give appropriate statistical power. This dominant approach is not designed for, nor is it particularly effective in, the systematic analysis of holistic interactions of real people in real organizations.

Policy Research

Some may argue that although idiographic research is not being done in the mainstream of the organizational behavior field, it is being done in the so-called "policy" area of management. The research of Mintzberg in particular (Mintzberg 1973, 1978; Mintzberg, Raisinghani, & Theoret, 1976) does represent an idiographic approach. Although some policy researchers are following the innovative lead of Mintzberg—for example, Sarrazin (1977–78)—most of the others seem to be following a nomothetic approach. For example, recognized policy researchers such as Schendel and Cooper stress the need for and use of nomothetically-based quantitative models for business strategy. See Hatten, Schendel, and Cooper, (1978). Overall, however, it is probably true that policy research and to an extent more sociologically-based macro-oriented organizational theory concerns (Cowney & Ireland, 1979) have recognized the need for and have to date used an idiographic research approach more so than has the psychologically-based, micro-oriented organizational behavior field.

The "Sameness" Assumption

Although Burrell and Morgan (1979) or Evered and Louis (1981) recognize the subjective/inside and objective/outside philosophy of science assumptions for idiographic and nomothetic methodologies, perhaps even more important to the understanding and the actual conduct of research on organizational behavior are the theoretical assumptions that are made. For example, the nomothetic approach is appropriate and necessary for certain research questions in organizational behavior given certain theoretic assumptions. By the same token, for other research questions under other theoretic assumptions, the nomothetic approach becomes less useful and an idiographic approach seems needed. Marceil (1977) notes that the "true nomothetic" stance would be using a method of selective examination of many subjects under the theoretic assumption that individuals are more similar than different.

This sameness theoretic or "average is beautiful" assumption of nomothesis goes way back to the Belgian astronomer Adolphe Quetelet. He asserted that human traits followed a normal curve, and that nature strove to produce the "average" person but failed for various reasons, resulting in errors or variations in traits that grouped around the average (Stilson, 1966). As Hersen and Barlow note:

> If nature were "striving" to produce the average man, but failed due to various accidents, then the average, in this view, was obviously the ideal. Where nature failed, however, man could pick up the pieces, account for the

errors, and estimate the average man through statistical techniques (1976, p. 5).

In other words, the averaging approach has a great deal of popular appeal to the researcher because it assumes that variability or error can be accounted for or averaged out in a group. The catch to this logic is that there is no such thing as an average individual. As Kurt Lewin noted almost 50 years ago, "the only situations which should be grouped for statistical treatment are those which have the individual rats or for the individual [human subjects] the same psychological structure and only for such period of time as this structure exists" (1933, p. 328).

Not only the basic averaging assumption of nomothesis but also the popular statistical techniques flowing out of this approach can be questioned. For example, Marceil makes the following observation of the currently widely used factor analysis technique:

> The R technique [correlational technique associated with factor analysis] involves the correlation of the results obtained from many persons taking two (or more) tests on one occasion. The goal of this correlational procedure is to determine which test items cluster together across individuals, the implication being that such clusters represent functional entities. Whether these clusters are the actual factors hypothesized by factor analytic theory or are merely statistical quirks is not known (1977, p. 1050).

Not only factor analysis, but the commonly used control group experimental designs and the accompanying multivariate statistical techniques in general fall under the theoretic assumption of sameness and the methodologic assumption of controlled examination of many subjects.

An alternative (and some would argue opposing) set of assumptions more in line with an idiographic approach is not being given attention in the field of organizational behavior. Specifically, an alternative methodologic assumption based on intensive examination of one or a few cases under the theoretic assumption of dynamic interactionism is, with the few possible exceptions that have already been noted, missing in the organizational behavior literature. These alternative underlying assumptions suggest the need to explore further the theoretical foundation of organizational behavior and the feasibility of alternative methodologies of research.

AN INTERACTIVE THEORETICAL FOUNDATION

An increasing number of psychologists are questioning the "sameness" assumption and are proposing the alternative *interaction* notion. This is not new. Pioneering behavioral scientists such as Georg Simmel (1950), George Herbert Mead (1934) and Kurt Lewin (1951) recognized an interactionist framework long ago, and others such as Sells (1963) have been proponents for a long time. But the ideas of interactional psychology have surfaced in the literature with renewed enthusiasm (Ekehammar, 1974; Magnusson & Endler, 1977; Terborg, Richardson, & Pritchard, 1980).

The Person-Situation

One of the leading spokespersons for the movement away from concentrating on abstract general variables in situation-free environments to examine person-situation interactions in naturalistic settings has been the personality theorist/researcher Walter Mischel (1973, 1976). Mischel (1973) states that the emphasis should shift (1) from attempting to compare and generalize about what different individuals "are like" to an assessment of what they *do* behaviorally and cognitively—in relation to the psychological conditions in which they do it; (2) from describing situation-free people with broad trait objectives to analyzing the specific interactions between conditions and the cognitions and behaviors of interest. In other

words, with the first point Mischel is questioning the sameness theoretic assumption taken by the nomothetic approach, and with the second point he questions the standardized, "situation-free" assumption made when using nomothetic designs and methods.

By definition organizational behavior is not situation free. Organizational participants do not operate in a highly controlled, standardized environment. In a recent article Mintzberg forcefully points out:

> We shall never have closure so long as we pretend that other things can be held constant. We live in a world of dynamic systems. (A colleague of mine claims that everything in the world correlates with everything else at 0.3) ... it is somewhat a matter of luck whether a two-variable cross sectional study manages to capture the structure that reflects today's situations—which it typically measures—or yesterday's, which it typically does not (1979, p. 588).

What has been missing in organizational behavior is the theoretic assumption recognized by the interactional psychologists that both people and situations vary and that the behavior of a particular person in a particular situation is a result of the joint characteristics of both (Terborg et al., 1980).

An Interactive Perspective

Over a decade ago John Campbell and his colleagues (Campbell, Dunnette, Lawler, & Weick, 1970) in their comprehensive review of research on managerial behavior and performance concluded that an "interactional" or "interactionist" perspective was needed. In organizing the literature on managerial behavior up to that time they identified three categories of variables—person (individual trait characteristics), process (behavior description variables), and product (outcome variables). They were critical of these three variables being studied separately and concluded that "all three must be considered concurrently, and the effects and moderating influences of different organizational environments must be included as well" (Campbell et al., 1970, p. 12).

This recognition for an interactive perspective for organizational behavior also has been made by a few others. For example, see Roberts, Hulin, and Rousseau (1978) for an overall interactive framework that proposes organizational behavior to be a function of the characteristics of the responding unit, the characteristics of the environment in which the unit operates, and the interaction of unit and environmental characteristics. But they all stop short of carrying this theoretic assumption to its logical conclusion. They do not provide a clear account of guidelines for *how* these variables can be examined interactively. They do not suggest methodologic designs or methods to do interactive research. For example, after calling for an interactive perspective, Roberts, Hulin, and Rousseau lament that

> New methodological models are clearly needed to take into account the summary nature of variables, their relative attachment to particular units of analysis, and their causal reciprocity. No entirely adequate solutions to the measurement problems introduced here have been developed (1978, p. 99).

They also defend and advocate the use of nomothetic studies and discount the use of single case studies to test hypotheses.

> If generalization from nomothetic studies proves invalid, the damage caused by conducting such research is inexpensively repaired. Information about single organizations can always be drawn from compiled data gathered in a nomothetic study, through disaggregation. The opposite is usually not possible.... Case studies should be used to generate hypotheses, not to test them (1978, p. 69).

Social Learning B-P-E Interaction

Most recently social learning theory has been proposed as a theoretical foundation for organizational behavior (Davis & Luthans,

1980). Borrowing from Bandura's (1976, 1977) notion of reciprocal determinism, the social learning theoretic assumes a continuous, dynamic interaction among the person (including internal cognitions and traits), the environment, and the behavior itself. This social learning approach goes one dimension beyond the person-environment interaction and adds the behavior itself as an interactive variable. Unlike the earlier Campbell et al., (1970) or Roberts et al. (1978) interactive proposals, this behaviorally oriented behavior-person-environment or simple B-P-E interactive notion from social learning theory does suggest some proven research designs and methods for helping determine the nature of causal reciprocity and the meaningful testing of hypotheses.

An interactive theoretic such as B-P-E from social learning does not fit the nomothetic mold for group-centered designs and methods in standardized environments. Instead, intensive analysis of single cases in natural environments is called for. Qualitative methodologies are an obvious answer. However, the problem with the commonly used impressionistic accounts of qualitative research is that they do not provide causal conclusions or meaningful testing of specific hypotheses. On the other hand, single case experimental designs have been used by behavioral researchers for intensive study of subelements of partial B-P-E interactions or the holistic B-P-E interactive dynamic in naturalistic settings. For example, see Komaki, Waddell, and Pearce (1977). In addition, unlike the qualitative methods used in idiographic research, the single case experimental designs and systematic observation methods can lead to causal conclusions and be used to test specific hypotheses.

SINGLE CASE EXPERIMENTAL DESIGNS

Single case experimental designs first of all must be distinguished from the so-called "case" approach used in clinical psychology, sociology, and business policy and strategy. Whereas all make an intensive analysis of one or a few cases, the traditional case approach used in these other applications is not an experiment. In other words, in traditional case analysis an independent variable(s) is not manipulated to determine its causal effect on a dependent variable(s). By the same token, the single case *experimental* design should be evaluated against the standards for internal and external validity that are used for pure or quasiexperimental control group designs commonly used in nomothetic research.

Background

Single case experimental designs certainly are not new. They have a long history in experimental psychology. For example, the famous studies by Pavlov used single subject experimental designs and, of course, Skinner (1953) is on record as stating that he would much prefer a study with a thousand replications of a single subject than one study of a thousand subjects in order to understand human behavior. Only recently, however, have single case experimental designs been developed for use in applied settings. The works of Sidman (1960), Allport (1962), Dukes (1965), Baer, Wolf, and Risley (1968), Bergin and Strupp (1970), Lazarus and Davison (1971), Kazdin (1973), and, especially, Hersen and Barlow (1976) have contributed to the development of workable single case experimental designs that can be adapted to research of interactive organizational behavior in natural settings.

Reversals or ABAB Designs

The specific designs that have evolved out of the above cited development are commonly called reversals (or ABAB) and multiple baseline designs. Briefly, summarized, the reversal or ABAB design is performed as follows:

(A) First a baseline measure is obtained on the dependent variable. This is usually some type of individual (or even group) dependent variable measure.

(B) After the baseline is obtained, an intervention is made (the independent variable) and the dependent variable is measured (usually through systematic observation) until the change stabilizes.

(A) At this point of stabilization the intervention is withdrawn and base-line conditions are reestablished. In other words a reversal is attempted.

(B) Once the dependent variable measure stabilizes under the baseline conditions, then the intervention is made again and the impact is measured.

The major advantage of this reversal design is that the subjects serve as their own controls. Thus, the problems of intersubject variability that plagues the popular control group experimental group experimental designs is eliminated. The major drawback is that it assumes that the dependent variable being measured is capable of being reversed when the intervention is withdrawn and baseline conditions are reestablished. To overcome this potential problem, the multiple baseline design can be employed.

Multiple Baseline Designs

Briefly summarized, the steps of the multiple baseline design are as follows:

1. Baseline data are obtained on two or more dependent variables. (These dependent measures, usually obtained by systematic observation, could be gathered on individuals, groups, or even situations.)

2. The intervention (independent variable) then is made on one of the dependent variables, but baseline conditions are maintained on the other(s), and the impact is measured.

3. Once the dependent variable has stabilized after the intervention, the next dependent variable receives the intervention and the impact is measured.

4. These staggered interventions continue until all the dependent variables are brought under the intervention.

This multiple baseline design eliminates the practical problems of attempting to reverse a dependent variable but makes the assumption of noninterdependence of the dependent variables.

An Example

Although these single case designs may be viewed in opposition to the between-group comparison designs used in the nomothetic approach, both have their strengths and weaknesses that make them suited or unsuited to the particular research problem at hand. Two studies by Komaki et al. (1977) clearly demonstrate how such single case designs can be successfully applied to organizational behavior research.

Their first study involved the analysis of the performance behavior of an attendant in the gameroom store in the downtown area of a metropolitan city. It illustrates the use of the reversal or ABAB single case experimental design. This design was adaptable to the idiographic study of an employee, environment, behavior, interactive dynamic in a natural setting and provided powerful evidence for concluding that there was a causal relationship between the independent variable and the dependent variable. The subject acted as his own "control," and the research was grounded in the organizational setting in which the individual behavior actually took place. In a second study the researchers analyzed the behavior of two clerks in a neighborhood grocery store. Instead of the reversal, this latter study utilized a multiple baseline design. The controlling influence of the intervention on three dependent vari-

ables offers convincing evidence that the independent variable did indeed cause the change in the dependent variables.

A few other organizational behavior studies also have demonstrated the applicability of reversals (Gupton & Le Bow, 1971; Kreitner & Golab, 1978; Luthans & Bond, 1977; Luthans & Davis, 1979; Luthans & Maris, 1979; Marholin & Gray, 1976) and multiple baseline designs (Kreitner, Reif, & Morris, 1977; Lamal & Benfield, 1978; Luthans & Davis, 1979; Van Ness & Luthans, 1979). In other words, although considerably more studies need to be done in the future, already there is some evidence that idiographic research of interactive organizational behavior in real settings can be done effectively by single case experimental designs.

Internal and External Validities

In a separate comprehensive analysis, Komaki (1977) has shown clearly that the threats to internal validity in experimentation identified by Campbell and Stanley (1966) either are ruled out by the procedures adopted in reversal and multiple baseline designs or do not present a major problem. The additional potential threats to internal validity later noted by Cook and Campbell (1976) are not covered by the Komaki analysis—that is, diffusion or imitation of the treatment, compensatory equalization of treatment, compensatory rivalry, resentful demoralization of respondents receiving less desirable treatments, and local history—also can be ruled out by these designs because they do not utilize a control group, which mainly contributes to these additional threats.

Some of the major threats to external validity identified by Campbell and Stanley (1966) and Cook and Campbell (1976, 1979) such as the interactive effects of testing, the reactive effects of experimental arrangements, and the effects of multiple-treatment interferences also are of no major problem. But other factors, such as *demand characteristics, experimenter effects,* and *expectations,* are a potential problem in single case designs as they are, at least to some degree, in all research and need to be carefully considered. The main argument against single case designs is the weakness that this approach shares with most group comparison research: the problem of generalizing the findings to a given population.

Most contemporary researchers in organizational behavior would argue that a sample of only one or two individuals or cases/groups makes any attempts to generalize the finding unreasonable. However, as Edgington points out:

> The belief that you cannot statistically generalize to a population of individuals on the basis of measurements from only one subject is certainly correct. However, it is also correct that you cannot statistically generalize to a population from which you have not taken a random sample, and this fact rules out statistical generalization to a population (at least to a population of some importance) for virtually all psychological experiments, those with large samples or small (1967, p. 195).

The major solution to this generalization problem, as Skinner (1953) first recognized and Hersen and Barlow (1976) have more recently emphasized, is replication. Like all research findings, those obtained by single case designs need to be tested in a variety of settings under a variety of conditions. Replication will allow the researchers to generalize realistically from one setting to another with some degree of confidence.

Judgmental External Validity

It also must be remembered that external validity is a judgmental process, not, as it is often portrayed, a binary (yes or no) decision. Because it is judgmental, specific criteria for assessing the generalizability of replicated single-case studies can be developed and used. For example, Kennedy (1979) suggests the following evaluative criteria for the attributes of the sample cases: (1) wide range of attributes across the sample cases; (2) many common attributes between sample case(s) and the population of interest; (3) few unique attributes in the sample case(s); and (4) relevance of attributes. She also suggests the following evaluative criteria for attributes of the treatment in judging external validity: (1) wide range of treatment attributes across replications, (2) common patterns of treatment outcomes across sample cases; and (3) common treatment functions across cases.

The above criteria for assessing the external validity of single case studies still depend on replication. However, Kennedy (1979) also makes the point that even without replication the judgment of generalizability could be shifted to the user of the case data rather than the researchers who produce the data. This is what is done in legal and clinical generalizations. However, in order to generalize meaningfully from one case to another, the user must have full, rich information. That is, an intense, in-depth case analysis is needed. To the extent that the information is there, single case studies may prove to be more valuable to management practitioners than nomothetically oriented group studies because, as Kennedy (1979) points out, group comparisons may not generalize to individual cases. It is these individual, single cases that practitioners must deal with on a day to day basis.

Statistical Analysis

The role played by inferential statistics should be examined, and visual inspection of the data should not be ruled out. Group-centered research designs, of course, greatly depend on inferential statistics. Statistics serve as the gatekeepers for inferring causality in nomothetic research. However, as Cook and Campbell point out: "Unfortunately, they are fallible gatekeepers even when they are properly used, and they fail to detect both true and false patterns of covariation" (1976, p. 225). They then propose a taxonomy of threats to what they call statistical conclusion validity. This validity can be improved by watching for statistical power, fishing and the error rate problem, reliability of measures, reliability of treatment implementation, random irrelevances in the experimental setting, and random heterogeneity of respondents. Such attention recognizes some potential problems and gets away from the blind acceptance of statistical conclusions in experimental research.

Because of the limitations of inferential statistics, some single case researchers build a case for the exclusive use of careful graphing of data and visual analysis methods. See Kratochwill (1978) for papers that take this position. Others suggest and use both conventional (e.g., modified analysis of variance models) and more specialized (e.g., time series analysis) statistical analysis techniques. Kazdin (1976) gives a comprehensive overview of the statistical techniques that can be used in single case experimental designs. Once again, however, a polarized, mutually exclusive either-or situation has tended to develop. Nomothetic research depends on and almost exclusively uses inferential statistics. Because this approach dominates the field of organizational behavior, too often the outcome is that all research must use inferential statistical analysis to be accepted. Idiographic research, on the other hand, which depends on qualitative data in general and much more on descriptive statistics and simple visual inspection of quantitative data in particular, may be, out-of-hand, deemed to be unacceptable. Yet, as has been stressed throughout this paper, such polarization is dangerous and unwarranted. As Elashoff and Thoresen state:

> doctrinaire positions that unequivocally advocate just one strategy and condemn others (e.g., all experiments require randomized groups or applied time-series data must avoid any inferential statistics) do far more harm than good. Any statistical method, descriptive

or inferential, serves as a tool that may or may not be useful, depending on the task at hand. . . . Statistical and visual methods should be partners in the analytic endeavor (1978, pp. 290–291).

DATA COLLECTION

As noted earlier, nomothetic research, because of its assumptions, has depended largely on self-report surveys, questionnaires, and interviews as data gathering techniques. For example, Martinko and Carter (1979) found that practically all the studies reported in the *Academy of Management Journal* in a recent 10-year period used questionnaires, self-reports, and interviews as the data collection procedure. There is growing recognition that these methods have severe problems. For example, the reactivity and obtrusiveness of self-reports and questionnaires is well documented (Webb, Campbell, Schwartz, & Sechrest, 1966), as are the social desirability biases (Arnold & Feldman, 1981; Golembiewski & Munzenrider, 1975). In addition, there is a host of practical problems in administering questionnaires (Petry & Quackenbush, 1974) as well as psychometric problems such as anonymity, language, and external response sets. Even though the widely accepted standardized questionnaires used in organizational behavior research may have acceptable reliabilities, they have been found to have questionable construct validity (Schreisheim & Kerr, 1977; Schreisheim, Bannister, & Money, 1979). Interviews also are widely used as a data gathering technique, but they generally are recognized to have even more problems than self-report surveys and standardized questionnaires (Schwab, 1969; Valenzi & Andrews, 1973).

Despite the recognized problems with self-report surveys, standardized questionnaires and interviews, their use continues unabated. Mintzberg (1979) tells of a doctoral student who was not allowed to observe managers because of the "problem" of sample size. He was required to measure what managers did through questionnaires, despite ample evidence in the literature—for example, Harper (1968)—that managers are poor estimators of their own time allocation. Mintzberg asks the question: "Was it better to have less valid data that were statistically significant?"

Obviously, for researchers under pressure to publish and operate with limited resources, it is much easier to ask (via questionnaires or interviews) than it is to observe. In addition, of course, when abstract constructs such as motivation or perceptions are the unit of analysis for the research, indirect measures are required. On the other hand, when dynamic B-P-E interactions are the unit of analysis, then qualitative methods in general and observational measures in particular become required. As Kerlinger points out, "Observations must be used when the variables of research studies are interactive and interpersonal in nature" (1973, p. 554).

Qualitative methods are not as precisely defined and identifiable as are quantitative methods, but rather, as Van Maanen explains, "is at best an umbrella term covering an array of interpretive techniques which seek to describe, decode, translate, and otherwise come to terms with the meaning, not the frequency, of certain more or less naturally occurring phenomena in the social world" (1979, p. 520). Most qualitative researchers (Sanday, 1979) use direct techniques such as observation. However, some do not. Bruyn (1967) explains that in some phenomenological studies the researcher may not enter the actual setting but instead may examine symbolic meanings as they constitute themselves in human consciousness. If the intensive, single case experimental design is used to analyze interactive organizational behavior in natural settings, then observational measures can become an especially useful data gathering technique (Bijou, Peterson, & Ault, 1968).

Observation, however, is not the only measurement technique available for idiographic research. For example, a number of behavioral (Johnston, Duncan, Monroe, Stephenson, & Stoerzinger, 1978) and unobtrusive (Webb & Weick, 1979; Webb et al., 1966) measures found in today's organizations, as well as other qualitative impressions derived from diaries or archival records, could be profitably employed. In addition, quantitative methods could be used in combination with observation and other qualitative methods to produce as much and as reliable data as are possible. Once again, the position taken here is that the key to advancing knowledge in organizational behavior is not to exclude any measurement techniques (those normally associated with nomothetic or idiographic research) but instead to draw from all techniques in a multiple measures approach (Jick, 1979; Lockwood & Luthans, 1980).

A FINAL WORD

This paper has suggested that an idiographic approach with its accompanying designs and methods may be used profitably in researching organizational behavior. Presently, the study of organizational behavior depends largely on a comparison of the group and/or average individual under highly controlled, standardized environments because of the popular nomothetic control group experimental designs, inferential statistical analysis, and the self-report, questionnaire, and interview methods of data collection. This approach, of course, is appropriate and necessary under the theoretic assumption that people basically are the same and operate in a constant environment. However, under an interactive theoretic assumption of behavior-person-environment (B-P-E), that is, the holistic interaction of the behavior itself, the person, and the naturalistic environment, idiography takes on special importance as a methodological approach. In particular, the idiographic approach may be used profitably in combination with the more commonly used nomothetic approach. For example, first the idiographic perspective would be used to gain an in-depth understanding and explanation. This then may be followed by the more traditional nomothetic approach.

Although the designs and methods of the nomothetic approach are well known to organizational behavior researchers, designs and methods adaptable to idiographic research are not. Central to an idiographic approach to interactive organizational behavior studies in natural settings that intends to examine and make causal conclusions and test specific hypotheses are intensive single case experimental designs and direct methods such as systematic participant observation. When understood and on close examination, these designs and methods hold up as well (and

some idiographic researchers would argue better) to the same evaluative criteria for scientific research that currently are being used by nomothetically based researchers. However, the purpose of this paper was not to pit one research perspective and methodology against another. Instead, it was to point out, and learn about, another approach to research on organizational behavior. This purpose perhaps is best expressed in a conversation that reportedly took place between two famous psychologists. Edward Tolman stated: "I know I should be more idiographic in my research, but I just don't know how to be," and Gordon Allport replied: "Let's learn!" (Hersen & Barlow, 1976, p. xiii). This conversation seems very relevant to the field of organizational behavior today.

REFERENCES

Allport, G. W. *Personality: A Psychological Interpretation.* New York: Holt, 1937.

Allport, G. W. "The General and the Unique in Psychological Science." *Journal of Personality,* 1962, *30,* 405–422.

Argyris, C. "Using Qualitative Data to Test Theories." *Administrative Science Quarterly,* 1979, *24,* 672–679.

Arnold, H. J., & Feldman, D. C. "Social Desirability Response Bias in Self-report Choice Situations." *Academy of Management Journal,* 1981, *24,* 377–385.

Baer, D. M., Wolf, M. M., & Risley, T. R. "Some Current Dimensions of Applied Behavior Analysis." *Journal of Applied Behavior Analysis,* 1968, *1,* 91–97.

Bandura, A. "Social Learning Theory." In J. T. Spence, R. C. Carson, & J. W. Thibaut (Eds.), *Behavioral Approaches to Therapy.* Morristown, N.J.: General Learning Press, 1976, pp. 1–46.

Bandura, A. *Social Learning Theory.* Englewood Cliffs, N.J.: Prentice-Hall, 1977.

Beck, S. J. "The Science of Personality: Nomothetic or Idiographic?" *The Psychological Review,* 1953, *60,* 353–359.

Behling, O. "The Case of the Natural Science Model for Research in Organizational Behavior and Organization Theory." *Academy of Management Review,* 1980, *5,* 483–490.

Bergin, A. E., & Strupp, H. H. "New Directions in Psychotherapy Research." *Journal of Abnormal Psychology,* 1970, *76,* 13–26.

Bijou, S. W., Peterson, R. F., & Ault, M. H. "A Method to Integrate Descriptive and Experimental Field Studies at the Level of Data and Empirical Concepts." *Journal of Applied Behavior Analysis,* 1968, *1,* 175–191.

Bruyn, S. T. "The New Empiricists: The Participant Observer and Phenomenologist." *Sociology and Social Research,* 1967, *51,* 317–322.

Burrell, G., & Morgan, G. *Sociological Paradigms and Organisational Analysis.* London: Heinemann, 1979.

Campbell, D. T., & Stanley, J. C. *Experimental and Quasi-experimental Designs for Research.* Chicago: Rand McNally, 1966.

Campbell, J. P., Dunnette, M. D., Lawler,

E. E., & Weick, K. E. *Managerial Behavior*. New York: McGraw-Hill, 1970.

Cook, T. D., & Campbell, D. T. "The Design and Conduct of Quasi-experiments and True Experiments in Field Settings." In M. D. Dunnette (Ed.), *Handbook of Industrial and Organizational Psychology*. Chicago: Rand McNally, 1976, 223–326.

Cook, T. D., & Campbell, D. T. *Quasi-experimentation: Design and Analysis Issues for Field Settings*. Chicago: Rand McNally, 1979.

Dalton M. *Men who Manage*. New York: Wiley, 1959.

Davis, T. R. V., & Luthans, F. "A Social Learning Approach to Organizational Behavior." *Academy of Management Review*, 1980, 5, 281–290.

Downey, H. K., & Ireland, D. Quantitative versus Qualitative: Environmental Assessment in Organizational Studies." *Administrative Science Quarterly*, 1979, 24, 630–637.

Dukes, W. F. N = 1. *Psychological Bulletin*, 1965, 64, 74–79.

Edgington, E. S. "Statistical Inference from N = 1 Experiments." *Journal of Psychology*, 1967, 65, 195–199.

Ekehammar, B. "Interactionism in Personality from a Historical Perspective." *Psychological Bulletin*, 1974, 81, 1026–1048.

Elashoff, J. D., & Thoresen, C. E. "Choosing a Statistical Method for Analysis of an Intensive Experiment." In T. R. Kratochwill (Ed.), *Single Subject Research: Strategies for Evaluating Change*. New York: Academic Press, 1978, 287–311.

Endler, N. S. "The Person versus the Situation—A Pseudo Issue? A Response to Alker." *Journal of Personality*, 1973, 41, 287–303.

Evered, R., & Louis, M. R. "Alternative Perspectives in the Organizational Sciences: 'Inquiry from the Inside' and 'Inquiry from the Outside.' " *Academy of Management Review*, 1981, 6, 385–395.

Falk, J. L. "Issues Distinguishing Idiographic from Nomothetic Approaches to Personality Theory." *Psychological Review*, 1956, 63, 53–62.

Golembiewski, R. T., & Munzenrider, R. "Social Desirability as an Intervening Variable in Interpreting Organizational Development Effects." *Journal of Applied Behavioral Science*, 1975, 11, 317–332.

Gupton, T., & Le Bow, M. D. "Behavior Management in a Large Industrial Firm." *Behavior Theory*, 1971, 2, 78–82.

Harper, W. K. *Executive Time: A Corporation's Most Valuable, Scarce, and Irrecoverable Resource*. Unpublished doctoral dissertation, Harvard University, 1968.

Harris, J. G. "Nomovalidation and Idiovalidation: A Quest for the True Personality of People." *American Psychologist*, 1980, 35, 729–744.

Hatten, K. J., Schendel, D. E., & Cooper, A. C. "A Strategic Model of the U.S. Brewing Industry: 1952–1971." *Academy of Management Journal*, 1978, 21, 592–610.

Hersen, M., & Barlow, D. H. *Single Case Experimental Designs: Strategies for Studying Behavior change*. New York: Pergamon, 1976.

Holt, R. "Individuality and Generalization in the Psychology of Personality." *Journal of Personality*, 1962, 30, 377–404.

Jick, T. D. "Mixing Qualitative and Quantitative Methods: Triangulation in Action." *Administrative Science Quarterly*, 1979, 24, 602–611.

Johnston, J. M., Duncan, P. K. Monroe, C., Stephenson, H., Stoerzinger, A. "Tactics and Benefits of Behavioral Measurement in Business." *Journal of Organizational Behavior Management*, 1978, 1, 164–178.

Kazdin, A. E. "Methodological and Assessment Considerations in Evaluating Reinforcement Programs in Applied Settings." *Journal of Applied Behavioral Analysis*, 1973, 6, 517–531.

Kazdin, A. E. "Statistical Analyses for Single-case Experimental Designs." In M. Hersen & D. H. Barlow, *Single Case Experimental Designs*. New York: Pergamon, 1976, 265–316.

Kennedy, M. M. "Generalizing from Single Case Studies." *Evaluation Quarterly*, 1979, 3, 661–678.

Kerlinger, F. N. *Foundations of Behavioral Research.* New York: Holt, 1973.

Komaki, J. "Alternative Evaluation Strategies in Work Settings: Reversal and Multiple-baseline Designs." *Journal of Organizational Behavior Management,* 1977, *1,* 53–77.

Komaki, J., Waddell, W. M., & Pearce, M. G. "The Applied Behavior Analysis Approach and Individual Employees: Improving Performance in Two Small Businesses." *Organizational Behavior and Human Performance,* 1977, *19,* 337–352.

Kratochwill, T. R. (Ed.). *Single Subject Research: Strategies for Evaluating Change.* New York: Academic Press, 1978.

Kreitner, R., & Golab, M. "Increasing the Rate of Salesperson Telephone Calls with a Monetary Refund." *Journal of Organizational Behavior Management,* 1978, *1,* 192–195.

Kreitner, R., Reif, W. E., & Morris, M. "Measuring the Impact of Feedback on the Performance of Mental Health Technicians." *Journal of Organizational Behavior Management,* 1977, *1,* 105–109.

Lamal, P. A., & Benfield, A. "The Effects of Self-Monitoring on Job Tardiness and Percent of Time Spent Working." *Journal of Organizational Behavior Management,* 1978, *1,* 142–149.

Lazarus, A. A., & Davison, G. C. "Clinical Innovation in Research and Practice." In A. E. Bergin, & S. L. Garfield (Eds.), *Handbook of Psychotherapy and Behavior Change: An Empirical Analysis.* New York: Wiley, 1971, 196–213.

Lewin, K. "Vectors, Cognitive Processes and Mr. Tolman's Criticisms." *Journal of General Psychology,* 1933, *8,* 318–345.

Lewin, K. "Formalization and Progress in Psychology." In D. Cartwright (Ed.), *Field Theory in Social Science.* New York: Harper, 1951, 1–29.

Lockwood, D. L., & Luthans, F. "Multiple Measures to Assess the Impact of Organization Development Interventions." In *The 1980 Annual Handbook for Group Facilitators.* San Diego: University Associates, 1980, 233–245.

Luthans, F., & Bond, K. M. "The Use of Reversal Designs in Organizational Behavior Research." In R. L. Taylor, M. J. O'Connell, R. A. Zawacki, & D. D. Warrick (Eds.), *Academy of Management Proceedings,* 1977, 86–90.

Luthans, F., & Davis, T. R. V. "Behavioral Self-management—The Missing Link in Managerial Effectiveness." *Organizational Dynamics,* Summer 1979, 42–60.

Luthans, F., & Maris, T. L. "Evaluating Personnel Programs through the Reversal Technique." *Personnel Journal,* 1979, *58,* 692–697.

Magnusson, D., & Endler, N. S. "Interactional Psychology: Present Status and Future Prospects." In D. Magnusson & N. S. Endler (Eds.), *Personality at the Crossroads: Current Issues in Interactional Psychology.* Hillsdale, N.J.: Erlbaum, 1977, 3–31.

Marceil, J. C. "Implicit Dimensions of Idiography and Nomothesis: A Reformulation." *American Psychologist,* 1977, *32,* 1046–1055.

Marholin, D., & Gray, D. "Effects of Group Response-cost Procedures on Cash Shortages in a Small Business." *Journal of Applied Behavior Analysis,* 1976, *9,* 25–30.

Martinko, M. J., & Carter, N. "A Critical Evaluation of Methodology in Organizational Research." In E. L. Miller (Ed.), *Proceedings of the 22nd Annual Conference of the Midwest Academy of Management,* 1979, 321–326.

Mead, G. H. *Mind, Self and Society.* Chicago: University of Chicago Press, 1934.

Mintzberg, H. *The Nature of Managerial Work.* New York: Harper & Row, 1973.

Mintzberg, H. "Patterns in Strategy Formation." *Management Science,* 1978, *24,* 934–948.

Mintzberg, H. "An Emerging Strategy of 'Direct' Research." *Administrative Science Quarterly,* 1979, *24,* 582–589.

Mintzberg, H., Raisinghani, D., & Theoret, A. "The Structuring of 'unstructured' Decision Processes." *Administrative Science Quarterly,* 1976, *21,* 246–275.

Mischel, W. "Toward a Cognitive Reconceptualization of Personality." *Psychological Review*, 1973, 80, 284–302.

Mischel, W. *Introduction to Personality.* 2nd ed. New York: Holt, Rinehart & Winston, 1976.

Morgan, G., & Smircich, L. "The Case for Qualitative Research." *Academy of Management Review*, 1980, 5, 491–500.

Petry, G. H., & Quackenbush, S. F. "The Conservation of the Questionnaire as a Research Resource." *Business Horizons*, August 1974, 43–47.

Pettigrew, A. M. *The Politics of Organizational Decision-making.* London: Tavistock, 1973.

Roberts, K. H., Hulin, C. L., & Rousseau, D. M. *Developing an Interdisciplinary Science of Organizations.* San Francisco: Jossey-Bass, 1978.

Sanday, P. R. "The Ethnographic Paradigm(s)." *Administrative Science Quarterly*, 1979, 24, 527–538.

Sarrazin, J. "Decentralized Planning in a Large French Company: An Interpretative Study." *International Studies of Management and Organization*, 1977–78, 7, 37–59.

Schreisheim, C. A., & Kerr, S. "Theories and Measures of Leadership: A Critical Appraisal of Current and Future Directions." In J. G. Hunt & L. L. Larson (Eds.), *Leadership: The Cutting Edge.* Carbondale, Ill.: Southern Illinois University Press, 1977, 9–45.

Schreisheim, C. A., Bannister, B. D., & Money, W. H. "Psychometric Properties of the LPC Scale: An Extension of Rice's Review." *Academy of Management Review*, 1979, 4, 287–290.

Schwab, D. P. "Why Interview? A Critique." *Personnel Journal*, 1969, 48, 126–129.

Sells, S. B. "An Interactionist Looks at the Environment." *American Psychologist*, 1963, 18, 696–702.

Sidman, M. *Tactics of Scientific Research: Evaluating Experimental Data in Psychology.* New York: Basic Books, 1960.

Simmel, G. "The Sociology of Georg Simmel." In K. H. Wolff (Ed.), *The Sociology of Georg Simmel.* Glencoe, Ill.: Free Press, 1950, 3–424.

Skaggs, E. B. "Personalistic Psychology as a Science." *Psychological Review*, 1945, 52, 234–238.

Skinner, B. F. *Science and Human Behavior.* New York: Free Press, 1953.

Stilson, D. W. *Probability and Statistics in Psychological Research and Theory.* San Francisco: Holden-Day, 1966.

Terborg, J. R., Richardson, P., & Pritchard, R. D. "Person-situation Effects in the Prediction of Performance: An Investigation of Ability, Self-esteem, and Reward Contingencies." *Journal of Applied Psychology*, 1980, 65, 574–583.

Valenzi, E., & Andrews, I. R. "Individual Differences in the Decision Process of Employment Interviewers." *Journal of Applied Psychology*, 1973, 58, 49–53.

Van Maanen, J. "Observations on the Making of Policemen." *Human Organizations*, 1973, 32, 407–418.

Van Maanen, J. "Reclaiming Qualitative Methods for Organizational Research: A Preface." *Administrative Science Quarterly*, 1979, 24, 520–526.

Van Ness, P. W., & Luthans, F. "Multiple Baseline Designs: An Alternative Strategy for Organizational Behavior Research." In E. L. Miller (Ed.), *Proceedings of the 22nd Annual Conference of the Midwest Academy of Management*, 1979, 336–350.

Webb, E., & Weick, K. E. "Unobtrusive Measures in Organization Theory: A Reminder." *Administrative Science Quarterly*, 1979, 24, 650–659.

Webb, E. J., Campbell, D. T., Schwartz, R. D., & Sechrest, L. *Unobtrusive Measures: Non Reactive Research in the Social Sciences.* Chicago: Rand McNally, 1966.

Mixing Qualitative and Quantitative Methods: Triangulation in Action[1]

Todd D. Jick

There is a distinct tradition in the literature on social science research methods that advocates the use of multiple methods. This form of research strategy is usually described as one of convergent methodology, multimethod/multitrait (Campbell and Fiske, 1959), convergent validation or, what has been called "triangulation" (Webb et al., 1966). These various notions share the concept that qualitative and quantitative methods should be viewed as complementary rather than as rival camps. In fact, most textbooks underscore the desirability of mixing methods given the strengths and weaknesses found in single method designs.

Yet those who most strongly advocate triangulation (e.g., Webb et al., 1966; Smith, 1975; Denzin, 1978) fail to indicate how this prescribed triangulation is actually performed and accomplished. Graduate training usually prepares us to use one method or another as appropriate and preferred, but not to combine methods effectively. And even those who use multiple methods do not generally explain their "technique" in sufficient detail to indicate exactly how convergent data are collected and interpreted.

WHAT IS TRIANGULATION?

Triangulation is broadly defined by Denzin (1978: 291) as "the combination of methodologies in the study of the same phenomenon." The triangulation metaphor is from navigation and military strategy that use multiple reference points to locate an object's exact position (Smith, 1975: 273). Given basic principles of geometry, multiple viewpoints allow for greater accuracy. Similarly, organizational researchers can improve the accuracy of their judgments by collecting different kinds of data bearing on the same phenomenon.

In the social sciences, the use of triangulation can be traced back to Campbell and Fiske[2] (1959) who developed the idea of "multiple operationism." They argued that more than one method should be used in the validation process to ensure that the variance reflected that of the trait and not of the method. Thus, the convergence or agreement between two methods ". . . enhances our belief that the results are valid and not a methodological artifact" (Bouchard, 1976: 268).

---

[1] The author is indebted to Dafna Izraeli for helpful comments and criticisms of an earlier version of this paper.

Reproduced by permission of the *Administrative Science Quarterly*, 1979, 24, 602–611.

[2] Webb et al. (1963: 3) list other sources from the 1950s, but Campbell and Fiske's article is most often cited elsewhere in the literature.

This kind of triangulation is labeled by Denzin (1978: 302) as the "between (or across) methods" type, and represents the most popular use of triangulation. It is largely a vehicle for cross validation when two or more distinct methods are found to be congruent and yield comparable data. For organizational researchers, this would involve the use of multiple methods to examine the same dimension of a research problem. For example, the effectiveness of a leader may be studied by interviewing the leader, observing his or her behavior, and evaluating performance records. The focus always remains that of the leader's effectiveness but the mode of data collection varies. Multiple and independent measures, if they reach the same conclusions, provide a more certain portrayal of the leadership phenomenon.

Triangulation can have other meanings and uses as well. There is the "within-method" kind (Denzin, 1978: 301) which uses multiple techniques within a given method to collect and interpret data. For quantitative methods such as survey research, this can take the form of multiple scales or indices focused on the same construct. For qualitative methods such as participant observation, this can be reflected in "multiple comparison groups" (Glaser and Strauss, 1965: 7) to develop more confidence in the emergent theory. In short, "within-method" triangulation essentially involves cross-checking for internal consistency or reliability while "between-method" triangulation tests the degree of external validity.

Blending and integrating a variety of data and methods, as triangulation demands, may be seen on a continuum that ranges from simple to complex designs (Figure). Scaling, that is, the quantification of qualitative measures, would be at the simple end. Smith (1975: 273) concluded that scaling is only a "primitive triangulatory device." It

does not effectively force a mix of independent methods, neither does it reflect fundamentally diverse observations nor varieties of triangulated data. Another primitive form of triangulation often found in organizational research is the parenthetical, even somewhat patronizing, use of field observations to strengthen statistical results. For example, a hypothetical study of job satisfaction among employees might revolve around a significant chi-square result demonstrating deep discontent. To support the results, it might be noted that a strike occurred earlier that year. But, we are likely not informed about the intensity, dynamics, meaning, and aftermath of the strike. Thus, important qualitative data had been insufficiently integrated with quantitative findings.

A somewhat more sophisticated triangulation design, already discussed, would be the "within-methods" strategy for testing reliability. The limitations of this approach lie in the use of only one method. As Denzin noted (1978: 301–302), "observers delude themselves into believing that five different variations of the same method generate five distinct varieties of triangulated data. But the flaws that arise using one method remain. . . ." Next in the continuum is the conventional form, the "between methods" approach designed for convergent validation. The use of complementary methods is generally thought to lead to more valid results, as noted. It is currently the archetype of triangulation strategies.

Triangulation, however, can be something other than scaling, reliability, and convergent validation. It can also capture a more complete, *holistic,* and contextual portrayal of the unit(s) under study. That is, beyond the analysis of overlapping variance, the use of multiple measures may also uncover some unique variance which otherwise may have been neglected by single methods. It is here

Scaling . . . . . Reliability . . . . . Convergent Validation . . . . . Holistic (or Contextual) Description . . . . .

Simple Design   Complex Design

Figure 1.   A continuum of triangulation design.

that qualitative methods, in particular, can play an especially prominent role by eliciting data and suggesting conclusions to which other methods would be blind. Elements of the context are illuminated. In this sense, triangulation may be used not only to examine the same phenomenon from multiple perspectives but also to enrich our understanding by allowing for new or deeper dimensions to emerge.

In all the various triangulation designs one basic assumption is buried. The effectiveness of triangulation rests on the premise that the weaknesses in each single method will be compensated by the counter-balancing strengths of another. That is, it is assumed that multiple and independent measures do not share the same weaknesses or potential for bias (Rohner, 1977: 134). Although it has always been observed that each method has assets and liabilities, triangulation purports to exploit the assets and neutralize, rather than compound, the liabilities.

Perhaps the most prevalent attempts to use triangulation have been reflected in efforts to integrate fieldwork and survey methods. The viability and necessity of such linkages have been advocated by various social scientists (e.g., Vidich and Shapiro, 1955; Reiss, 1968; McCall and Simmons, 1969; Spindler, 1970; Diesing, 1971; Sieber, 1973). They all argue that quantitative methods can make important contributions to fieldwork, and vice versa.

Thus, researchers using qualitative methodology are encouraged to systematize observations, to utilize sampling techniques, and to develop quantifiable schemes for coding complex data sets. As Vidich and Shapiro (1955: 31) wrote, "Without the survey data, the observer could only make reasonable guesses about his area of ignorance in the effort to reduce bias." Survey research may also contribute to greater confidence in the generalizability of results.

Conversely, quantitative-oriented re-searchers are encouraged to exploit "the potentialities of social observation" (Reiss, 1968: 360). Among other assets, field methods can contribute to survey analysis with respect to the validation of results, the interpretation of statistical relationships, and the clarification of puzzling findings (Sieber, 1973: 1345). Thus, informants can be utilized during the course of quantitative research (Campbell, 1955) and "holistic interpretation" (i.e., context variables) can be used to shed light on quantitative data (Diesing, 1971: 171). More implicitly, the very selection of a research site is typically a function of qualitative data as is the process of building and pretesting a survey instrument.

Diesing (1971: 5) boldly concluded that the variety of combinations is so great that survey research and fieldwork are better viewed as two ends of a continuum rather than as two distinct kinds of methods. Yet, research designs that extensively integrate both fieldwork (e.g., participant observation) and survey research are rare. Moreover, journals tend to specialize by methodology thus encouraging purity of method.

Fortunately, there are some exceptions to be found. Some particularly good examples of combining methods include LaPiere's (1934) seminal investigation of the relationship between attitudes and behavior, Reiss' study of police and citizen transactions (1968: 355), Sales' (1973) study of authoritarianism, Van Maanen's (1975) data on police socialization, and the studies described in, or modeled after, Webb et al. (1966). Furthermore, it is probable that the triangulation approach is embedded in many doctoral theses that, when packaged into articles, tend to highlight only the quantitative methods. Thus the triangulation model is not new. However, this model of research and its advantages have not been appreciated. In this respect, it would be helpful to articulate and describe its usage.

AN ILLUSTRATION OF HOW TRIANGULATION WORKS

The triangulation strategy was used in a study I conducted on the effects of a merger on employees (Jick, 1979). Early interviews suggested that employees were intensely anxious in this state of flux, especially concerning their job security. One focus of the research was to document and examine the sources and symptoms of anxiety, the individuals experiencing it, and its impact on the functioning of the newly merging organization.

How have anxiety and its dynamics in an organization been measured? Marshall and Cooper (1979: 86) noted, for example, that there is no one generally agreed way of measuring stress manifestations. On the basis of past research, there are several alternative techniques one could use: (a) Ask the person directly, (b) Ask the person indirectly (e.g., projective tests), (c) Ask someone who interacts with the person, and (d) Observe systematically the person's behavior or (e) Measure physiological symptoms. Predictably, each of these strategies has both strengths and weaknesses. Most of the limitations revolve around the likelihood of high demand characteristics and considerable obstacles in the measurement process.

Given high demand characteristics in the study of anxiety and the potential pitfalls in each method, the most appropriate research strategy was deemed to be triangulation. No single method was sufficient and thus a design evolved that utilized a combination of methods. Data were collected over a period of 14 months which incorporated multiple viewpoints and approaches: both feelings and behaviors, direct and indirect reports, obtrusive and unobtrusive observation. Methods were wide-ranging enough to tap a variety of anxiety dimensions.

The research "package" used in the investigation of the dynamics of anxiety and job insecurity included many standard features. Surveys were distributed to a random sample of employees. They contained a combination of standard and new indices related to stresses and strains. To complement these data, a subsample was selected for the purposes of semistructured, probing interviews. The survey also contained items related to the symptoms of anxiety as well as projective meaures. These were developed to be indirect, nonthreatening techniques. In addition to self-reports, interviews were conducted with supervisors and coworkers to record their observations of employees' anxiety.

Another set of methods, somewhat less conventional, proved to be especially fruitful. Predominantly qualitative in nature, they were based on unobtrusive and nonparticipant observation as well as archival materials. For example, one of the merging organizations housed an archives library, which contained a variety of files, books, and organization memorabilia from its 100-year history. It also contained a comprehensive set of newspaper clippings that cited the organization and the merger, as well as a broad variety of internal memos to employees. This was indeed a rich data source.

The development of unobtrusive measures tends to be far more unorthodox and innovative than most research methods. Perhaps the most instructive unobtrusive measure in this case was a kind of anxiety "thermometer." The idea emerged because of certain fortuitous circumstances in that a further research opportunity was found in the archives. The archivist mentioned that employees were frequently using the files. When asked why, he said that they came to compare recent news reports and memos (regarding the organization's future) with past pronouncements. Since recent information tended to be ambiguous, if not contradictory, the files provided an opportunity to review materials systematically. Most employees were apparently seeking information to relieve their anxiety about the uncertain shape of things to come.

Hence these visits to the archives were

treated as expressions of employee anxiety, a thermometer of anxiety level in the organization. The search for information seemed to represent an attempt to reduce uncertainty. It was hypothesized that the more people who visited the archives to use the files, the higher the anxiety level. Thus emerged an effort to track the pattern of visits. The archivist consented to record the number of archive users along with some supplementary data on the visitors such as age, work location, and the amount of time spent at the files.

The pattern of archive usage was then compared with data culled from ongoing interviews, the cross-sectional survey, and other unobtrusive techniques. These other measures also tracked anxiety-related behavior, as for example, (a) archival data on turnover and absenteeism trends and (b) a content analysis of rumors, news stories, and hospital events reflecting to the flow of "shocks" to which employees were subjected.

It should be underscored that the quantitative results were used largely to supplement the qualitative data, rather than the reverse which is far more common in organizational research. The surveys became more meaningful when interpreted in light of critical qualitative information just as other statistics were most useful when compared with content analyses or interview results. Triangulation, in this respect, can lead to a prominent role for qualitative evidence (just as it also should assure a continuing role for quantitative data).

PUTTING IT ALL TOGETHER: IS THERE CONVERGENCE?

These various techniques and instruments generated a rather rich and comprehensive picture of anxiety and job insecurity (Greenhalgh and Jick, 1979; Jick, 1979). Self-reports, interviews, and coworker observations reflected a range of perceptions—some qualitatively described while others quantitatively represented. In turn, behavioral and objective data collected through archival sources and unobtrusive measures complemented the other data.

It is a delicate exercise to decide whether or not results have converged. In theory, a multiple confirmation of findings may appear routine. If there is congruence, it presumably is apparent. In practice, though, there are few guidelines for systematically ordering eclectic data in order to determine congruence or validity. For example, should all components of a multimethod approach be weighted equally, that is, is all the evidence equally useful? If not, then it is not clear on what basis the data should be weighted, aside from personal preference. Given the differing nature of multimethod results, the determination is likely to be subjective. While statistical tests can be applied to a particular method, there are no formal tests to discriminate between methods to judge their applicability. The concept of "significant differences" when applied to qualitatively judged differences does not readily compare with the statistical tests which also demonstrate "significant differences."

The various methods together produced largely consistent and convergent results. Archival and interview data indicated a strong relation between high turnover rates and job insecurity/anxiety while survey data showed a parallel relation between expressed propensity to leave and job insecurity.[3] These findings were formed on the basis of telephone interviews with employees who quit, personal interviews with their former supervisors, significant correlations found in survey data with a large random sample of employees, and the clear pattern seen between lay-off rumors reported in news stories and turnover statistics. Not only were the

---

[3] For specific results and data tables, see Jick (1979).

within-methods comparisons consistent, but there was also consistency in between-methods comparisons. Thus, the sociometric charting results of archive visits were congruent with the expressed anxiety reported in surveys and interviews. Both sets of results confirmed which events tended to be most anxiety producing and under what conditions anxiety was reduced. Thus, different measures of the same construct were shown to yield similar results (Phillips, 1971: 19).

There were also some surprises and discrepancies in the multimethod results which led to unexpected findings. When different measures yield dissimilar results, they demand that the researcher reconcile the differences somehow. In fact, divergence can often turn out to be an opportunity for enriching the explanation.

For example, in my study, those most stressed (according to surveys of self-reports) were least likely to visit the archive's news files (according to sociometric data), *contrary* to what was hypothesized. That is, while the survey showed that the group reporting the most anxiety were the least educated and least professionally mobile in terms of job skills, these low-skilled employees were underrepresented at the archive's library. One method produced results which predicted manifestations of anxiety but a second method failed to confirm the prediction. However, further interviews and observations—still other qualitative methods—helped to reconcile the disagreement by suggesting that the poorly educated employees tended to rely more on oral communication (e.g., close informal grapevines) than written documents. This interpretation resulted then from the divergent findings based on sociometric data, nonparticipant observations at work and outside work, and open-ended interviewing.

In seeking explanations for divergent results, the researcher may uncover unexpected results or unseen contextual factors. In one instance, interview data helped to suggest a relation between job insecurity/anxiety and certain attitudinal symptoms. Survey results, however, indicated that while employees at the site of the central organization were less insecure in their jobs than employees at the satellite site the magnitude of symptoms was the reverse. That is, the "victors" reported more symptoms than the "vanquished." But further interviewing and an analysis of field notes showed that the more severe symptoms reflected unique sources of anxiety at the central organization. Fieldwork and survey results were thus compatible as a variety of previously unconsidered contextual factors were brought to light.

The process of compiling research material based on multimethods is useful whether there is convergence or not. Where there is convergence, confidence in the results grows considerably. Findings are no longer attributable to a method artifact. However, where divergent results emerge, alternative, and likely more complex, explanations are generated. In my investigation of anxiety, triangulation allowed for more confidence interpretations, for both testing and developing hypotheses, and for more unpredicted and context-related findings.

Overall, the triangulating investigator is left to search for a logical pattern in mixed-method results. His or her claim to validity rests on a judgment, or as Weiss (1968: 349) calls it, "a capacity to organize materials within a plausible framework." One begins to view the researcher as builder and creator, piecing together many pieces of a complex puzzle into a coherent whole. It is in this respect that the firsthand knowledge drawn from qualitative methods can become critical. While one can rely on certain scientific conventions (e.g., scaling, control groups, etc.) for maximizing the credibility of one's findings, the researcher using triangulation is likely to rely still more on a "feel" of the situation. This intuition and firsthand knowledge drawn from the multiple vantage points is centrally reflected in the interpretation process. Glaser and Strauss' (1965: 8) observation about fieldworkers summarizes this point of how triangulated investigations seem to be crystallized:

> The fieldworker knows that he knows, not only because he's been there in the field and because of his careful verifications of hypotheses, but because "in his bones" he feels the worth of his final analysis.

THE "QUALITY" IN TRIANGULATION

Triangulation provides researchers with several important opportunities. First it allows researchers to be more confident of their results. This is the overall strength of the multi-method design. Triangulation can play many other constructive roles as well. It can stimulate the creation of inventive methods, new ways of capturing a problem to balance with conventional data-collection methods. In my study, this was illustrated by the development of an anxiety "thermometer," which unobtrusively measured changes in anxiety level.

Triangulation may also help to uncover the deviant or off-quadrant dimension of a phenomenon. Different viewpoints are likely to produce some elements which do not fit a theory or model. Thus, old theories are refashioned or new theories developed. Moreover, as was pointed out, divergent results from multimethods can lead to an enriched explanation of the research problem.

The use of multimethods can also lead to a synthesis or integration of theories. In this sense, methodological triangulation closely parallels theoretical triangulation (Denzin, 1978: 295); that is, efforts to bring diverse theories to bear on a common problem (e.g., LeVine and Campbell, 1972; Marris, 1975). Finally, triangulation may also serve as the critical test, by virtue of its comprehensiveness, for competing theories.

A thread linking all of these benefits is the important part played by qualitative methods in triangulation. The researcher is likely to sustain a profitable closeness to the situation which allows greater sensitivity to the multiple sources of data. Qualitative data and analysis function as the glue that cements the interpretation of multimethod results. In one respect, qualitative data are used as the critical counter-point to quantitative methods. In another respect, the analysis benefits from the perceptions drawn from personal experiences and firsthand observations. Thus enters the artful researcher who uses the qualitative data to enrich and brighten the portrait. Finally, the convergent approach utilizes qualitative methods to illuminate "behavior in context" (Cronbach, 1975) where situational factors play a prominent role. In sum, triangulation, which prominently involves qualitative methods, can potentially generate what anthropologists call "holistic work" or "thick description." As Weiss concluded, "Qualitative data are apt to be superior to quantitative data in density of information, vividness, and clarity of meaning—characteristics more important in holistic work, than precision and reproducibility" (1968: 344–345).

The triangulation strategy is not without some shortcomings. First of all, replication is exceedingly difficult. Replication has been largely absent from most organizational research, but it is usually considered to be a necessary step in scientific progress. Replicating a mixed-methods package, including idiosyncratic techniques, is a nearly impossible task and not likely to become a popular exercise. Qualitative methods, in particular, are problematic to replicate. Second, while it may be rather obvious, multimethods are of no use with the "wrong" question. If the research is not clearly focused theoretically or conceptually, all the methods in the world will not produce a satisfactory outcome. Similarly, triangulation should not be used to legitimate a dominant, personally preferred method. That is, if either quantitative or qualitative methods become mere window dressing for the other, then the design is inadequate or biased. Each method should be represented in a significant way. This does however raise the question of whether the various instruments may be viewed as equally sensitive to the phenomenon being studied. One method may, in fact, be stronger or more appropriate but this needs to be carefully justified and made explicit. Otherwise, the purpose of triangulation is subverted.

Triangulation is a strategy that may not be suitable for all research purposes. Various constraints (e.g., time costs) may prevent its effective use. Nevertheless, triangulation has vital strengths and encourages productive research. It heightens qualitative methods to their deserved prominence and, at the same time, demonstrates that quanti-

tative methods can and should be utilized in complementary fashion. Above all, triangulation demands creativity from its user—ingenuity in collecting data and insightful interpretation of data. It responds to a foreboding observation suggested by one sociologist (Phillips, 1971: 175):

> We simply cannot afford to continue to engage in the same kinds of sterile, unproductive, unimaginative investigations which have long characterized most . . . research.

In this sense, triangulation is not an end in itself and not simply a fine-tuning of our research instruments. Rather, it can stimulate us to better define and analyze problems in organizational research.

REFERENCES

Becker, H. S., & Geer, B. "Participant Observation and Interviewing: A Comparison." *Human Organization*, 1957, *16*, 28–32.

Bouchard, T. J., Jr. "Unobtrusive Measures: An Inventory of Uses." *Sociological Methods and Research*, 1976, *4*, 267–300.

Campbell, D. T. "The Informant in Quantitative Research." *American Journal of Sociology*, 1955, *60*, 339–342.

Campbell, D. T., & Fiske, D. W. "Convergent and Discriminant Validation by the Multitrait-Multimethod Matrix." *Psychological Bulletin*, 1959, *56*, 81–105.

Cronbach, L. J. "Beyond the Two Disciplines of Scientific Psychology." *American Psychologist*, 1975, *30*, 116–127.

Denzin, N. K. *The Research Act*, 2d ed. New York: McGraw-Hill, 1978.

Diesing, P. *Patterns of Discovery in the Social Sciences*. Chicago: Aldine-Atherton, 1971.

Glaser, B. G., & Strauss, A. L. "Discovery of Substantive Theory: A Basic Strategy Underlying Qualitative Research."

American Behavioral Scientist, 1965, *8*, 5–12.

Greenhalgh, L. & Jick, T. D. "The Relationship between Job Security and Turnover and its Differential Effects on Employee Quality Level." Paper presented to Academy of Management conference, Atlanta, Georgia, 1979.

Jick, T. D. "Process and Impacts of a Merger: Individual and Organizational Perspectives." Doctoral dissertation, New York State School of Industrial and Labor Relations, Cornell University, 1979.

LaPiere, R. T. "Attitudes vs. Actions." *Social Forces*, 1934, *13*, 230–237.

LeVine, R. A., & Campbell, D. T. *Ethnocentrism, Theories of Conflict, Ethnic Attitudes, and Group Behavior*. New York: Wiley, 1972.

Marris, P. *Loss and Change*. Garden City: Anchor Books-Doubleday, 1975.

Marshall, J. & Cooper, C. "Work Experiences of Middle and Senior Managers: The Pressures and Satisfactions." *Management International Review*, 1979, *19*, 81–96.

McCall, G. J., & Simmons, J. L. eds. *Issues in Participant Observation: A Text and Reader.* Reading, MA: Addison-Wesley, 1969.

Phillips, D. L. *Knowledge from What?: Theories and Methods in Social Research.* Chicago: Rand McNally, 1971.

Reiss, A. J. "Stuff and Nonsense about Social Surveys and Observation." In Howard Becker, Blanche Geer, David Riesman, and Robert Weiss (eds.), *Institutions and the Person:* 351–367. Chicago: Aldine, 1968.

Rohner, R. P. "Advantages of the Comparative Method of Anthropology." *Behavior Science Research.* 1977, *12*, 117–144.

Sales, S. M. "Threat as a Factor in Authoritarianism: An Analysis of Archival Data." *Journal of Personality and Social Psychology*, 1973, *28*, 44–57.

Sieber, S. D. "The Integration of Fieldwork and Survey Methods." *American Journal of Sociology*, 1973, *78*, 1335–1359.

Smith, H. W. *Strategies of Social Research:* *The Methodological Imagination.* Englewood Cliffs, NJ: Prentice Hall, 1975.

Spindler, G. D., ed. *Being an Anthropologist.* New York: Holt, Rinehart and Winston, 1970.

Van Maanen, J. "Police Socialization. A Longitudinal Examination of Job Attitudes in an Urban Police Department." *Administrative Science Quarterly*, 1975, *20*, 207–228.

Vidich, A. J., & Shapiro, G. "A comparison of Participant Observation and Survey Data." *American Sociological Review*, 1955, *20*, 28–33.

Webb, E. J., Campbell, D. T., Schwartz, R. D., & Sechrest, L. *Unobtrusive Measures: Nonreactive Research in the Social Sciences.* Chicago: Rand McNally, 1966.

Weiss, R. S. "Issues in Holistic Research." In Howard S. Becker, Blanche Geer, David Riesman, and Robert Weiss (eds.), *Institutions and the Person:* 342–350. Chicago: Aldine, 1968.

Some Final Thoughts

SIX

Our final section steers away from issues of research design and technical skill development. In moving beyond the foundations of conceiving and implementing single projects or grander-scale programmatic research efforts, the articles in this section present viewpoints that serve to broaden or challenge any single-minded perspective of the research process.

To be sure, the book has to this point provided a rich array of assumptions, concepts, techniques, and choice points that are truly suggestive of the breadth of opportunity in the conduct of organizational research. Nonetheless, many scientists, through habit, convenience and efficiency, or conscientious choice, become locked into more or less unchanging approaches to their research. We hope the quality and variety of prior readings has provided an indication of the range of interesting and useful options; we believe the ideas offered in the following readings will help ensure that a greater number of perspectives and approaches will in fact be explored.

In this spirit, three concluding readings are offered. The first raises the issue of ethics in the conduct of organizational research, thereby bringing a crucial perspective to consider in tandem with the technical decisions which typically seem to get most of the attention in research endeavors. The second article provides a humorous yet thought-provoking statement about the levels of rigor, control, and objectivity in our approaches to science. The third piece also asks us to take a hard look at ourselves and paves the way for open minds and new approaches to research in the future.

The ethics article is by Mirvis and Seashore, who raise a number of key ethical questions and illustrate various ethical dilemmas researchers may confront. Because multiple roles are being performed, issues of personal values, confidentiality, dissemination of information, and others are raised with respect to the conflicting expectations of various stakeholder and participant groups in the study. A case example provides useful insights for the clarification and resolution of uncertainties and conflicts that arise throughout the process. At the very least, the article serves to raise some consciousness about the importance of ethical considerations.

We couldn't resist including Woodman's tongue-in-check glossary of research terms. The seriousness in the humor allows an en-

373

joyment of the piece at two levels. Beneath the humor is a reminder that we should view our field, ourselves, and our studies with a humble realization of their imperfections and fallibilities. Further, the implication is made that even rigorous concepts and plans can be implemented shoddily, thereby covering up some degree of slippage and thus, nonrigor. Cutting corners in planning and execution is a satisficing rather than maximizing decision mode.

Daft's concluding piece provides an eloquent epilogue. He gives a warning against becoming too narrowly captivated by techniques that are newly discovered, such as in graduate school (or this book!). He further issues a challenge for new learning, for taking chances and making mistakes on the road to good scholarship. In so doing, Daft conveys the excitement of research and the rich availability of "sufficient puzzlements to last for a productive career." In short, there is much to look forward to.

Suggestions for Further Reading

Bobko, P. "Concerning the Non-Application of Human Motivation Theories in Organizational Settings." *Academy of Management Review*, 1978, 3, 906–909.

Beyer, J. M., & Trice, H. M. "The Utilization Process: A Conceptual Framework and Synthesis of Empirical Findings." *Administrative Science Quarterly*, 1982, 27, 591–622.

Hakel, M. D., Sorcher, M., Beer, M., & Moses, J. L. *Making it Happen: Designing Research with Implementation in Mind*. Beverly Hills, CA: Sage, 1982.

Hunter, J. E., Schmidt, F. L., & Jackson, G. B. *Meta-Analysis: Cumulating Research Findings Across Studies*. Beverly Hills, CA: Sage, 1982.

McGrath, J. E., Martin, J., & Kulka, R. A. *Judgment Calls in Research*. Beverly Hills, CA: Sage, 1982.

Pinder, C. C. "Concerning the Application of Human Motivation Theories in Organizational Settings." *Academy of Management Review*, 1977, 2, 384–397.

U.S. Department of Health, Education, and Welfare. *The Institutional Guide to DHEW Policy on Protection of Human Subjects*. Washington, D.C.: U.S. Government Printing Office, 1971.

U.S. Office of the Federal Register. "The Final Regulations Amending Basic HHS Policy for the Protection of Human Research Subjects." *Federal Register*, 1981, 46, 8366–8392.

Walton, R. E., & Warwick, D. P. "The Ethics of Organization Development." *Journal of Applied Behavioral Science*, 1973, 9, 681–698.

Wilson, D. W., & Donnerstein, E. "Legal and Ethical Aspects of Nonreactive Social Psychological Research: An Excursion into the Public Mind." *American Psychologist*, 1976, 31, 765–773.

Being Ethical in Organizational Research[1]

Philip H. Mirvis

Stanley E. Seashore

When social and behavioral scientists leave their laboratory, clinical practice, or survey center to conduct research in organizations, they are not fully prepared for the challenge of being ethical. The ethical problems encountered in these real-life settings take on unique and disconcerting features arising from the fact of social organization. In these cases researchers are dealing with a social system composed of people who have positions in a hierarchy and who, in their collective identity as an organization, also have relationships with supporters, consumers, government, unions, and other public institutions. As a result, researchers cannot approach participants in the study as independent individuals because they behave within an interdependent framework of rights and responsibilities. Nor can they invoke existing distinctive guidelines for dealing with employees, managers, clients, or sponsors because all have overlapping interests that are sometimes in conflict. Finally, they cannot single-handedly manage the ethical dilemmas that arise because they are a weak force in a field of powerful ones, with only limited means for ensuring moral action or for redressing moral lapses. Questions are raised for researchers of their responsibilities, not only to individuals but also to the social system that encompasses them, for according to law and to custom, to harm a living system is analogous to harming a person. Consider some of the questions in a field experiment recently conducted in branches of a large metropolitan bank.

RESEARCH IN ORGANIZATIONS: SOME ETHICAL QUESTIONS

In this study, there was developed an information system that would gather financial, behavioral, and attitudinal data (from records and directly from employees) and return it periodically to work groups for problem solving and decision making. In presenting this idea, the social scientists asserted for themselves a role of "action researchers," where *action* meant working with a task force of bank employees to operationalize and implement the program, and

[1] The authors would like to thank Joan E. Sieber, Edward E. Lawler III, J. Richard Hackman, Robert L. Kahn, Daniel Katz, Robert D. Caplan, and anonymous reviewers for their helpful comments.

Reprinted by permission of the *American Psychologist,* 1979, *34,* 766–780.

research entailed evaluating the information system's effect on employees' participation and work performance.

Is it ethical in a case such as this to implement a change program that promotes one set of values, processes, and goals at the expense of others? One manager welcomed the information system because it enabled him "to involve everyone in the management of the branch"; another resented it because "it took management ... out of [my] hands." In proposing the system, the researchers chose an action role that was contrary to the detached and dispassionate posture recommended by many in their profession. In fulfilling this action role they counseled some managers on the effective use of the information and confronted others over its ineffective use. One manager felt this helped him "get off my fanny"; another felt it was "shoved down [my] throat."

What is the meaning of voluntary consent, confidentiality, and privacy in the case of persons whose employment contract stipulates the participation in studies, revelation of personal data, and inspection of behavior, all as simply "part of the job"? In this instance, several managers wanted to participate in the study, and others asked not to be involved. In the research design, branches were matched according to size, location, and other factors in such a way that some eager managers were assigned an inactive part and reluctant others were "persuaded" to join in. Steps were taken to protect the privacy of managers and the confidentiality of data collected for the information system. One manager reported, however, that he was not sure his data wouldn't be seen by "the boys downtown [top management]." When it was discovered that an official had "asked" a manager to see the reports for his branch, neither were the researchers so assured.

Under what conditions are the benefits greater than the risks of providing (or withholding) experimental treatments, descriptive data, or evaluative interpretation that could be used to improve an organization,

hire or fire its members, or influence their welfare on the job? One manager used the information to guide weekly problem-solving meetings, to improve customer service, and to promote employee development. The supervisor in the branch said it gave them a "common tool to concentrate on as a group." Another manager used the information to identify "uncooperative" employees and force their resignation or transfer; for those who remained, he used it to explain "why we have to do certain things." The supervisor said the system gave the manager a tool to "rake people over the coals." She found it hard to cope with the stress and "not carry it home in the evening."

There are few moral principles that can be applied to these situations. Those that address the values, processes, and goals of research programs merely acknowledge the power implicit in hierarchy, in the researcher's sponsorship, and in vested interests in organizations. Those that provide for voluntary consent, confidentiality, and privacy ignore that organizations necessarily are, in part, systems of compliance, coercion, and public accountability. Those that ensure a favorable balance of benefits and risks assume the researcher is able, with confidence, to specify and control the activities and consequences of a study and is immune from co-optation over its course. Furthermore, in organizational research, the usual protective strategies of debriefing or care of participants cannot be effectively invoked. Yet in comparison with other research, the impact, whether for good or evil, may be magnified in intensity and scope.

To address the ethical problems in organizational research, therefore, we propose that the researcher needs to consider his or her relationships not only with the participants in the study but also with their roles as employees, managers, members of an organization, and members of society. This article relies on role theory and its related concepts to describe ethical dilemmas that arise in organizational research and to propose means to moderate them. Role concepts bridge personal and institutional behavior by representing both the requirements that social systems have for their members and the personal identity that members invest in the social system. Viewed as *role systems* (Katz & Kahn, 1978), organizations can be seen as sets of relations among people that are maintained, in part, by the role expectations the people have for one another. When communicated, these expectations delimit the behavior of members of the organization and their rights and responsibilities with respect to others in their role system.

A researcher studying an organization also assumes a role and forms role relations with others in the organization. He or she communicates role expectations to them and is the recipient of their communications. In this article we take the view that most of the ethical concerns in organizational research arise from the conjuncture of these roles. In the first sections, we develop this perspective by describing the roles and by examining the sources of role ambiguity and conflict in a research effort. This affords the reader concepts for analyzing ethical dilemmas in organizational research. It provides to practicing researchers guidelines for clarifying their roles, anticipating role conflicts, and responding to them through policy and planning decisions.

Ethical decision making, however, is embedded in action; its essence in organizational research is considered choice among alternative courses in action where the interests of all parties have been clarified and the risks and gains have been openly and mutually evaluated. Thus, the responsibility of the ethical decision maker is not merely to impose predetermined roles on the research participants; it is *to create new roles* that are mutually clarified and compatible and, in creating them, *to affirm general ethical norms governing human research*. In later sections of this article we explicate this view by describing ethical norms in research and by presenting a case example of multiple research relationships where the participants invoked them to jointly address the role pressures they encountered in an ethical and productive way.

Throughout this article it is our contention that most ethical dilemmas in organizational research arise not from personal immorality but from the researcher's becoming entangled in a network of multiple roles and in the conflicting expectations derived from them. Thus, the challenge of being ethical lies not simply in the application of moral prescriptions but in the process of creating and maintaining research relationships in which to address and moderate ethical dilemmas that are not and cannot be covered by prescription. We conclude by proposing that research training and a code of ethics be developed that are compatible with this perspective. In offering these proposals, we look ahead to a future for organizational research in which the risks of ethical conflict increase but in which the institutional, professional, and personal benefits of acting ethically increase as well.

ROLES AND ORGANIZATIONAL RESEARCH

When entering a large organization, social scientists encounter a complex, established role system that regulates relationships among individuals and groups. Moreover, they bring to the setting their own existing role relations with colleagues, their profession, their home institution, and the sponsors and users of their research. Their relationship with the host organization can be represented as an intersection of these two role systems. Behavior in this new, combined system is influenced in some respects by the previous history, norms, and role relations in each subsystem, and in some respects by the new dynamics of the research effort. Figure 1 depicts a common form of this intersection. It shows the relationship between the researcher and the participants,

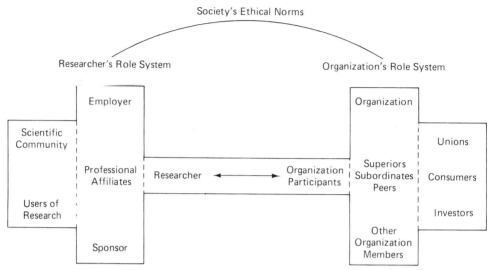

Figure 1. Research role systems.

each nested within their immediate role systems, which are in turn nested within a larger social system, the society, and its attendant ethical norms.

New roles and role relations are created at the region of intersection through the exchange of role communications. This process can be either aided or impeded by the initial role expectations of the parties. All cultures, whether societies or formal organizations, provide standard role models that can be tentatively invoked and tested for their applicability to new situations. Yet in the case of organizational research, sponsors may hold one set of expectations for the researcher, the home institution may hold another, and since few organizations have established role models for researchers, factions in the organization may hold still other expectations. On first encounter, the itinerant researcher is likely to be confronted with a wildly disparate array of role messages, all derived from different sets of culturally established role models. Only rarely will they all be compatible. Thus, the researcher's task is not simply *role taking* but also *role making* (Graen, 1976).

Pictured in this way, role definition can be seen as a personal, interpersonal, and organizational process in which individuals' responses to themselves, to one another, and to one another's roles can bring about the formation of clear and compatible or, alternatively, unclear and incompatible role definitions. In this light, the problems encountered by the researchers in the bank study described above can be reconsidered.

In that study, one set of role expectations came from reference groups and role models in the researcher's own "back-home" role system. As members of a profession, the researchers accepted responsibilities to solicit the informed and voluntary consent of the participants and, as action researchers, assumed such added responsibilities as involving employees in the joint design of the project and consulting with managers in its use to solve problems participatively. They explained to the organization the necessity and implications of such a role.

Nevertheless, from the beginning, both managers and employees tried to fit the researchers into established role models already familiar to the firm. Top management, for example, viewed the researchers as "off-beat" (academic) but inexpensive consultants (the study was externally funded) whose job was to demonstrate a way in which branch morale and performance could be improved. Hence they felt justified in "persuading" managers to participate and in "asking" to review the confidential reports in one branch where such a gesture from the "boys downtown" might stimulate further improvement. Following the formation of the task force and the empowerment of lower level personnel, in contrast, many employees began to see the researchers as partisans providing them a means with which to communicate their ideas and frustrations directly to management. In one branch they were emboldened to resist a branch manager's decision, taking control, in the manager's words, "out of my hands." Some managers responded by sharing their control, but another powerful bloc portrayed the researchers as "outsiders" attempting to wrest their power away from them. One manager therefore used the data to reassert his power, isolate "uncooperative" employees and remove them, and "rattle the [teller] cages" of those who remained. The personnel manager, a key stakeholder, made wary by the research team's funding from the U.S. Department of Labor, feared the sponsor might be in a position to spur employee initiatives toward unionism; by the end of the study he credited the researchers with harnessing employees' energies and thus, not coincidentally, diverting them from union drives.

Even in such a relatively simple situation, the social scientists' roles were defined, redefined, confused, and ultimately brought into conflict with other roles. As events unfolded, there were powerful pressures and incentives for the researchers to adopt the role preferred by one or another of the participant or stakeholder groups. In this study, as in others, the competing role expectations produced an ethical dilemma: The researchers' responsibility to increase em-

ployee participation (required by the research design and approved by all levels of management) was in direct conflict with their responsibility not to diminish the standing of those managers who were unable or unwilling to work participatively with their staffs. As it happened, those branches in which the managers used the new information system participatively showed improvements in morale and teller performance, training, and turnover. In contrast, in branches where managers did not use the data participatively, employees felt disillusioned and behaved accordingly: Morale declined and turnover increased, in many cases well above preexperimental levels (Nadler, Mirvis, & Cammann, 1976).

This consequence, and many others that arise in organizational research, can be traced to the process of role definition, clarification, and resolution of conflict. It is our thesis that when social scientists, as members of one role system, and organization members, as members of another, begin a research effort, the ethical problems must be anticipated, diagnosed, and treated in light of this intersection of role systems, and resolved through collaborative effort and appeal to common, transcendent goals.

ROLE AMBIGUITY IN ORGANIZATIONAL RESEARCH

One notable characteristic of established organizations is the pervasive and detailed understanding the members have of one another's roles. This understanding is, for the most part, sustained, reinforced, or modified through acts or interactions that indirectly convey role-defining and role-maintaining meanings. There is not much explicit talk about roles; there is thus little facility for the purposeful design of novel roles, such as those of organizational researchers. It is not surprising, then, to find the first stages of a research project, like those in any process of new role definition, to be marked by misunderstanding and uncertainty.

The first source of role ambiguity in an organizational study is the uncertainty over which persons and groups should be considered a part of the research effort. During the first weeks of a project, the researcher's contact is often limited to a few people in key functional areas and to those in general management or administration. At the same time, there are others in the organization who have legitimate concerns about the study. The task of the researcher is to identify these parties and initiate role communications with them. Included among them are people and groups participating in the study and, when its scope warrants, other stakeholders such as union officials and those in other work areas who will be affected by the results. In most instances those parties at interest are readily identifiable as legitimate senders and receivers of role messages. Less well identified are those who do not or cannot effectively communicate their expectations and those who are unknowingly excluded.

There are many reasons why individuals and groups with significant interests at stake may remain excluded from an organizational research project. Characteristics of the researcher such as age, sex, race, or background may disincline some parties from coming forward to present their interests. The formation of a research team or of an in-house liaison group that attempts to match its own composition with that of major organizational groups can increase the likelihood that the researchers will be able to identify and respond to the interests of these parties (Berg, 1977). Conflict between hierarchical or functional groups may also lead one group to exclude themselves or to be excluded from a study. One of the present authors, Seashore, was engaged by top officials of a large firm to conduct an action research project and only belatedly discovered that there was within the firm an established social scientist whose interests were pertinent to the study

but who had been unilaterally excluded by others. As the project developed, it became clear that such exclusion was unwarranted; however, invitations for inclusion were perceived as co-optation, and efforts to restructure the fractured role system proved unavailing. The social scientists were caught at the disjunctive borders of different role systems, at first without full cognizance of one another, and then with means foreclosed for creating compatible role relations. In such instances, it is incumbent on the researcher to be alert to and openly examine the potential harm associated with such exclusion and, at a minimum, to establish contact with the excluded parties to clarify the aims and intentions of the study. The failure to do so invites coercion or co-optation of or by the excluded and poses unanticipatable risks to the researcher and the participants.

Merely identifying the parties to a research effort does not clarify the part they are to play in the study. A second source of role ambiguity is the uncertainty the researcher and the participants have about one another's roles and role responsibilities. In order to seek clarification of the researcher's role, for example, organization members may focus selectively on different role messages. They may respond to the researcher's employer, sponsor, and other cues from the researcher's role set. In addition, they may generalize from past experiences or from the folklore that surrounds them. A team of researchers from the Institute for Social Research (ISR) recently conducted a survey of employees in a division of a large service organization. Ten years previously a similar survey had been conducted by other members of the Institute, but with inadequate provision by the management for feedback of the data throughout the division. As a belated consequence, some employees initially refused to cooperate with a new group of "rip-off artists." Even after a decade, the role definition derived from this earlier study, remembered by some and transmitted to others, rose to haunt the researchers in their efforts to define a new role.

The researcher's observed behavior may in time provide the ultimate source of role information to the participants. Until then, imputed role stereotypes still have to be overcome. It is commonplace, for example, for a researcher who enters an organization through management to be seen initially as their agent. In the same way, those following in the steps of engineers may be assigned the role of "time-and-motion experts," and those working through the personnel department are sometimes assumed to be "corporate shrinks." Seldom does the researcher's behavior conform to the negative aspects of such stereotypes. Nevertheless, assigning the researcher a stereotyped role can lead to a self-fulfilling prophecy. It is thus incumbent on researchers to communicate, clearly, explicitly, and by behavioral example, their intended role definitions. As a corollary, they must also clarify their roles to themselves.

There are many roles that social scientists can assume in organizational research, and each implies the use of particular means toward intended ends. Researchers may, for example, be entering an organization to study it unobtrusively, to intervene in it experimentally, to help it, or to accomplish some combination of these objectives. Through these means they may be there to study problems, diagnose them, or ameliorate them. Clarification of the choice of role helps the researcher to distinguish his or her own role responsibilities and the anticipatable risks and benefits that follow from the choice of means and ends. An open role clarification, moreover, provides a basis for which to consider what unintended consequences might follow from the choice of one as opposed to another role (Michael & Mirvis, 1977).

In addition, an open role clarification helps to distinguish the coordinate role responsibilities of the participants. The organization members, too, need to determine whether they are to be passive subjects, active participants in a change program, uninvolved observers in the role system, or clients who should expect to receive specific benefits. Organizational field studies, like those in the laboratory, have their demand characteristics. Participants often have to guess at the researchers' intentions and define their own roles accordingly as subservients, colleagues, accomplices, or saboteurs. It is incumbent on researchers to limit the guesswork by working closely with the participants to define their respective roles and to arrive at mutually understood (if not always initial or preferred) role definitions. The failure to do so may leave unclear the full range of risks and benefits in a study and may leave unidentified the interests and existing role requirements of some of the participants. One way of clarifying roles is through the negotiation of a research "contract" that identifies the interests of the researcher and the participants and that explicates, in the best way possible, the rights and responsibilities of their respective roles.

The final source of role ambiguity in a research project is the uncertainty over the role of other stakeholders in both the researcher's and the organization's role systems. It is quite common, for example, for organization members to question an academic's motivations in helping them or to suspect collusion between them and their sponsors. Indeed, it seems quite incredible to many people in organizations that anyone would laboriously gather information for its own intrinsic interest, without intent to employ it in trade or in self-serving action. Yet if organization members often err in imputing such malevolence to the researcher, researchers err in seeing organization members as participants without outside interest. More often than might be suspected from research reports, organization members co-opt researchers and exploit their activity or results for personal or organizational gain. Thus in clarifying roles, it is also important to clarify role relations to other stakeholders in the role system. Through stakeholders' ties to the researcher or the participants, such parties may gain access to confidential data or subvert the intended aims of the project to further their own. Moreover, they are likely to succeed unless their role in the project is foreseen and clarified. For researchers, the ethical consequences that follow from being duped may be equal to those from willful deception.

ROLE CONFLICTS IN ORGANIZATIONAL RESEARCH

Ethical dilemmas often arise not because roles are unclear but because they are clearly in conflict. Whether individual, as in the case of foremen in their roles as supervisors of hourly employees and as subordinates of first-line management, or institutional, as in the case of union and management or manufacturing and inspection functions, role conflict is a prevalent fact of organizational life. Academic researchers are well aware of role conflict, too, because the role demands of teaching are often incompatible with those of research and public service.

In a field research project, social scientists occupy a boundary position and receive role-defining messages not only from persons in their own role system but also from the participants and stakeholders in the organization. This greatly enlarges the sources of legitimate role communications. It also increases the likelihood of role conflict between the researcher and the participants and the researcher and various stakeholders. Consider such conflict in a research project in which Seashore collected confidential data from and about managers in an organization regarding their leadership style, effectiveness, personal health, and family. Late in the study, the president of the firm, faced with a crucial decision, asked the researcher for a private opinion about the promotional qualifications of one of these managers. The researcher felt ethically committed to his as-

surances of confidentiality and to opinions based on confidential data, and declined to comment even though he believed the information would benefit an individual he admired and judged to be of very high managerial potential. The president considered it unethical of the researcher to withhold information about a very "public" person in a position normally exposed to scrutiny.

Whose sense of ethical behavior should prevail? The researcher's professional role gave priority to privacy and confidentiality; the president's to the use of all information of benefit to the firm. Shortly thereafter, the person in question saw fit "voluntarily" to resign—a loser in some subterranean combat in which there was no chance for compromise between roles respectful of private and of organizational interests.

Role conflict may also exist between participants, between participants and stakeholders, and between stakeholders themselves with regard to a research project. This kind of conflict faced Mirvis and a colleague when they requested research collaboration from a business firm and one member of the board of directors objected because he did not want the firm to be a "guinea pig" for a study funded by a government agency. Upon discussing his concerns, it was discovered that he feared the study, a social audit, would result in the unintended consequence of legislation by the agency mandating social reporting. The researchers assured him this was not their intent nor that of the funding agency and included this assurance in their funding request. Imagine the shock when, in meeting with representatives from the agency, they discovered that some officials hoped to implement such audits nationally. In objecting to this, the researchers told the representatives quite explicitly that this was not their own intent and that, moreover, they had offered their assurances to the host organization on the matter. Whether or not that objection or the attitude from which it arose contributed to the funding decision is indeterminate. In any case, the agency withdrew its support.

Role conflicts can also arise from within a researcher, a participant, or a stakeholder. An example is seen in the case of one participant, a top manager in an organization in which there was general assent to an arrangement under which all feedback of research information would be to a designated committee that would "own" the data and would have full control over its internal distribution and use. The manager appreciated the merit of this arrangement because it clarified responsibilities and powers on an unaccustomed matter and was intended to forestall potential role conflicts and ethical quandaries for several parties, including himself and the research team. Soon thereafter, the same manager, for a plausible reason, firmly demanded that some of the research material be provided directly to himself before it became accessible to the committee. In his view, the inherent responsibilities and rights of a plant manager superseded the specifically designed protective role system he had helped to create. What can, should, or must the research team do in such a circumstance?

There is simply no way to escape such role conflicts in organizational research. The more conflict, and the more parties that hold conflicting expectations, the more stressful the situation becomes. At some point, researchers (like their subjects) are "damned if they do and damned if they don't" and suffer the role strains associated with this situation.

These strains become painfully personal when researchers experience role conflict within themselves. Such a personal role conflict relatively new to social science has come forward in recent years, now that social scientists are seen as professionals offering valuable services. Physicians, lawyers, and clinical psychologists, for example, assert the ethical principle that they are obliged to serve, if they can, any and all clients in need who so request. Social scientists, formerly protected by the public presumption of their incompetence or irrelevance (not to mention the high principle of academic freedom), have been spared such an ethical demand. This may be changing. Seashore, for example, was scolded sharply for ethical malfeasance when he declined to be engaged in research for a certain organization, for the reason that he did not personally value the organization's purposes. Others may be inclined to adopt a role in which they seek to change the organization and its mission.

To cope with the role pressures emanating from several parties, from a single individual, or from within, the researcher must anticipate them. Research role conflicts are predictable, for example, when working with groups already in conflict. It is therefore important for the researcher to clarify his or her role with respect to labor and management, supervisors and subordinates, competing departments, and public versus private interests. Similarly, it is important to clarify the nature of research roles with anxious employees and with trapped administrators, who themselves may hold conflicting expectations. Finally, it is important that the researcher clarify his or her stance with respect to research and action, for much of that conflict is internal to the researcher who must favor one or else compromise both (Seashore, 1976).

Besides clarifying roles, it is incumbent on the researcher to build role relations with the participants and stakeholders and between them. In this way he or she can provide for the joint and collaborative examination of the intended means and ends of the research and for the unintended consequences, can establish procedures for the acknowledgment and resolution of role conflicts, and can negotiate his or her role such that it is mutually compatible with the roles and role relations in the organization. This raises an important distinction between the ethical implications of role ambiguity and of role conflict. Ambiguity, in all instances, is potentially accessible to moderation by the researcher and the parties involved, limited mainly by the time and energy available and by the occasional agreement that some ambiguity is preferable to premature clarity. Role conflict, in contrast, is sometimes unmanageable except by incorporating such conflict into the research relationships themselves. Thus, creating a role that is mutually compatible with the role system of the host organization does not necessarily imply equal concern for all competing interests. One form of compatibility is to take sides openly and then, with the full cognizance of the other side, to behave accordingly. This carries with it the implication that the researcher may be denied access to complete and valid data from some of the participants or be unable to counter efforts to discredit or sabotage the research. It must be recognized that ideals of impartiality and scientific validity themselves have ethical implications. These values can be realized only in the study of organizations where all parties honor them above others, or else in the conduct of trivial research. Thus, having clarified roles and built role relations, it is incumbent on the researcher to clarify the ethical basis of the research and to openly examine value conflicts in the research relationships.

ETHICAL NORMS IN ORGANIZATIONAL RESEARCH

So far we have detailed, in the language of role theory, some of the inevitable sources of ambiguity and conflict that can and often do create ethical dilemmas for the organizational researcher. Fortunately, there exist superordinate ethical and social norms that serve to dampen the adverse consequences of these dilemmas and facilitate the achievement of research objectives with a tolerable balance of risk and gain. However ill defined these norms may seem to be, a social system places limits on the actions that may be taken by individuals acting in their roles and

advances standards to be upheld that protect its members and ensure the system's own survival. Regardless of role pressures and the benefits to be gained from acting otherwise, social behavior is governed by some widely shared norms regarding freedom, self-determination, democracy, due process, equity, and so on.

Thus, much as roles differentiate the parties in a research effort and carry distinctive expectations, shared norms embody general expectations and bind the parties together. When studying an organization, researchers encounter the norms of their own role system, of the host organization, and of the larger society, some of which have legal standing. These norms form the ethical basis for the research, not just because they are lawful or even based on accepted moral principles, but also because they apply to the demands of concrete situations.

The norms of the parties in an organizational study are in some respects more protective and constraining than in, say, a laboratory experiment. It is usually the case in organizations, for example, that when members accede to the organization the power to make policies and to institute procedures, they expect honest and equitable treatment in return. This provides an ethical basis for the organization's decision to sponsor a research study, whether the intention is to benefit its members directly or to contribute to the society's storehouse of knowledge, from which its members derive indirect benefits. It implies that the organization will inform its members of the aims and intent of the study and solicit their voluntary consent when they are to participate directly in it. Should the organization abuse that power, however, the researchers, asserting a norm of self-determination, may be justified in openly seeking to empower employees or in terminating the study (Laue & Cormick, 1978). Similarly, should the researcher prove incapable or incompetent, the organization, asserting a norm of due process, may be justified in terminating the research effort (Bermant & Warwick, 1978).

There are in place, too, some institutional structures to enforce these norms. Institutional review boards, in evaluating proposed projects, are increasingly involving social scientists and knowledgeable lay persons who are familiar with the exacerbated questions posed by organizational research. Organizations are formulating research policies and expecting researchers to be well versed in the risks and benefits associated with their work. Researchers themselves are undertaking peer reviews. In one study, two researchers from the ISR devised a plan for the longitudinal analysis of data that required the designation of organizational units for comparison on grounds that were, in part, a matter of subjective judgment. The analytic outcome was deemed implausible by some individuals qualified to have an opinion. The norms of the research community then required an independent inquiry to review data sources, analytic decisions, and possible sources of error. As it happened, no errors were detected, but community norms regarding respect for data were properly asserted as a matter of ethical responsibility.

There are occasions, however, when the norms governing research relations are unclear and must be clarified in the context of those relations. For example, organizations collect a myriad of data about employees, some of which is reported to government, shareholders, and managers, and some of which is held in private. In seeking access to such data for research purposes, Mirvis has informed employees but has not solicited their specific consent when examining data that are public or broadly accessible. He has, however, sought consent when the data are confidential, as in the case of personnel files, or private, as in the case of employees' opinions measured through a survey or interview. As common as this practice may be, it should also be common practice to affirm the norms with the organization and to establish their common interpretation.

There are occasions, too, when the applicable norms are in conflict. In an evaluation effort recently completed, the researchers discovered that the special personal relationship of the (unaffiliated) change agent with an employee contributed significantly to the failure of the intervention. Asserting a norm of scientific candor and completeness, the researchers felt an obligation to report this feature of the findings to the scientific community. At the same time, publication would have embarrassed the change agent and potentially threatened a fellow professional's future. In addition, the reputation of the organization member involved might also have suffered. Thus, the researchers faced a dilemma in which their normative responsibilities to the scientific community were at odds with the protective norms that governed their research relationship with the participants. They resolved the matter by discussing it with the change agent and then camouflaging the nature of the relationship in public reports, deleting documentation and falsifying information that might have led to the parties' identification. In their judgment (and consistent with their values) the risk to individual welfare outweighed the benefits of an accurate account of events.

In cases where one set of ethical norms is in conflict with another, the researcher has the responsibility to invoke the additional norm that the conflict be confronted openly, fully, and honestly. This is not to say that all parties' values will be (or should be) honored in its resolution. It does imply that they will be represented and asserts that the conflict be settled by reason and reciprocity rather than by the preemptive use of power or the selfish reversion to personal whim.

The norm of reciprocity can govern any research relationships that are extended in time and that bring roles and norms into conflict. To establish it, the task of the ethical researcher is not only to create a research role and establish its attendant norms, it is also to build open working relationships with the parties at interest such that the ethical dilemmas that do arise can be examined with reciprocal interest for each other's interests and values.

DEFINING AND CLARIFYING ROLES AND RESOLVING ROLE CONFLICTS: A CASE EXAMPLE

We have proposed that forms of organizational research pose ethical problems that lie beyond the scope of the current canons of ethical treatment of clients and research subjects and cannot be confronted effectively or ethically by a researcher guided only by their prescriptions. The reasons for this can be traced to the complexity of the role systems in which the participants and the researchers are immersed. Such problems, however, can be anticipated from awareness of these impinging rule systems, and this anticipation can also guide forward planning and action to the end of avoiding, moderating, or productively resolving them when they do arise.

Although this view may be widely acceptable in the abstract, its application is another matter. There has not yet emerged a sufficient body of shared experience, tested procedure, or institutionalized practice to make application easy. There are in progress, however, events that hold promise for clarification and instructive example. Social scientists are increasingly reporting not only their research theories, methods, and results, but also their treatment of ethical matters. Examples include analyses of researcher and client relations in organizations (Argyris, 1970), the recent collection of candid reports of failures by organizational change agents and project directors (Mirvis & Berg, 1977), and research cases analyzed in terms of role relations (Klein, 1976). With the accumulation of such cases and analyses, social scientists will have available a more experiential and less speculative codification of ethical issues and appropriate response strategies.

The authors, along with colleagues, have been engaged for several years in a research program in which an explicit effort is being made to anticipate ethical issues that arise from role relationships and to create social structures, shared norms, and decision processes capable of coping with them. Since the work is still in progress, it is premature to attempt a detailed description and evaluation of these efforts to act ethically, but mention of some of the strategies employed is pertinent here. The points mentioned are not offered as tested prescriptions, to be emulated by others, but only as an interim report on efforts to find workable approaches to the choice of ethical actions.

The research program is concerned with the conduct of demonstration projects aimed at improving effectiveness and the quality of working life in both private- and public-sector organizations (Drexler & Lawler, 1977). Certain features of the set of field studies need to be mentioned. First, the typical case involves a longitudinal assessment of the progress and outcomes of organizational change programs undertaken by a joint labor–management committee composed of representatives from management and from employees or their unions, and aided by external consultants. The committee's charge is to review problems and change opportunities and to help initiate actions and solutions. The duration of their efforts, lasting a period of at least three years, makes inevitable changes in circumstances, personnel, and roles that can be neither planned nor anticipated by the assessment team. Second, the typical case presents an impressive, if not appalling, array of intersecting role systems, each with legitimate interests to be accommodated; these involve the firm's management, the unions, the external consultants, research funding agencies, a third-party agency to coordinate activities at the site, and a team of ISR staff members. Finally, the ISR team is authorized to observe events over the period, to obtain such data and measurements as they see fit, and to make a public report describing and appraising the outcomes. Such a provision for independent evaluation and public reporting is not unprecedented, but it is rare in organizational life.

The general strategy employed to address the potential ethical issues has involved (a) initial efforts to define roles; (b) early attempts to clarify roles and to reach agreements, in writing, defining the interests of the several parties, along with their role responsibilities; (c) anticipating possible sources of role conflict and responding to them through policies and decision-making procedures; and (d) providing for the resolution of remaining conflicts through collaborative effort, review of research relationships, and continuous legitimation of the ethical basis of the research. A few examples will illustrate the steps taken to clarify roles and build role relations and the agreements negotiated to affirm ethical norms in a novel set of role relations.

Defining Roles in a Quality-of-Work-Life Project

- The joint committee will be composed of equal numbers of representatives chosen by the management and by the union.
- The external consultants will be selected by the committee, will work under the direction of the committee, and will agree to an independent evaluation.
- ISR representatives will serve as the independent evaluators and will be permitted to attend, take notes, and review documents pertinent to committee meetings.

Clarifying Roles and Role Relations

- All participation by members of the organization in committee meetings will be voluntary.
- The management and the union assure that no member of the organization will suffer loss of or reduction in pay, loss of or reduction in benefits, or be suspended or terminated, as a result of activities stemming from the project.
- Either management or the union may terminate the project and agreements associated with it, for any reason, upon 24 hours notice.
- The management will provide to ISR personnel such operating and fiscal information from its records as is needed for the evaluation of the project; ISR will hold confidential all such information except as release is authorized by the management.
- The personal provision of information to ISR from organization members shall be voluntary and under assurance that the privacy and anonymity of informants will be maintained.

Responding to Potential Role Conflict

- The joint committee will be empowered to direct the project and will decide for itself its internal rules for decision making [all have chosen to decide by consensus].
- The committee shall not take any action that violates, abrogates, or extends the union–management contract unless authorized through the normal negotiation process.
- ISR will review its instruments and evaluation plans with the joint committee and will be responsive to their suggestions and criticisms.
- All visits to the project site by representatives of the external sponsors, the coordinating agency, or the ISR team will be subject to the consent and conditions provided by the joint committee.
- ISR will provide factual information from its records to the committee, and only to the committee, upon request, but will not provide opinions, interpreta-

tions, or recommendations based on those data; the control over the dissemination and use of the data will rest with the committee.

- The external consultants will have no privileged access to ISR's research data.

- During the course of the project, ISR will not make public any information concerning the project without the consent of the joint committee, except for information previously made public by others.

- Following completion of the project, any public reports by ISR will be subject to review and consent by the management, by the unions, and by the consultants as to factual matters and as to the release of previously confidential information, but not as to opinions and interpretations made by ISR staff.

Such agreements seem excessively legalistic and rigid when abstracted from their context. Each of the provisions negotiated in agreements at the start and throughout the projects affirms ethical norms binding on clients and researchers—norms such as those pertaining to protection of participants' welfare, preservation of scientific interests, avoidance of coercion, minimization of risk, and the like. It is significant that under such terms, the achievement of ethical solutions to operational problems is plainly a matter of concern to all the parties, not only a matter of the researcher's judgment. In all instances, the provisions were elaborated through discussions or through the precedent of earlier, specific actions. In many cases, the original specifications were altered by informal agreement to meet the necessities of unanticipated conditions. Such role contracts have been applied not as inflexible credos but as a reminder of original intentions to conduct research ethically.

The reader should not assume that all this attention and effort has resulted in unqualified success in the management of ethical dilemmas. The approach has been successful, so far, in the sense that the research requirements have been met and the researchers' role has been tolerated in all places, even honored in some, despite the stresses that accompany organizational change programs. Nevertheless, if mention were made of all ethical dilemmas encountered and painfully resolved or tolerated in some fashion, they would form a long list in which co-optation of the researchers undermined scientific interests and mutual distrust brought the participants' interests into conflict with the evaluation role. At sites where these pressures were managed more effectively, the strategies of the researchers, broadly speaking, were to work with the other parties to maintain the integrity of the evaluation role and to fulfill their mutual responsibilities to ensure that the research was conducted ethically.

Table 1 provides a summary of these and the more general strategies for clarifying ambiguous roles and resolving role conflicts in organizational research. Implementing these strategies is indeed a challenging undertaking. Yet if the ethical norms on which they are based are unduly slighted, then research in organizations could not be done ethically, effectively, or at all.

LOOKING AHEAD

The social science research profession, like other professions, faces a near future of turmoil: Ethical norms are in flux, we are becoming less encapsulated in environments of our own making, and we will more often work on issues of concern beyond our disciplinary interests. Yet to look closely at the role and normative conflicts in future research not only ensures the discovery of ethical dilemmas but also makes them more salient and vexing.

This can, of course, lead to paralysis as the increasing attention to analyzing risks and benefits, obtaining consent, and managing role relations takes precious time and energy away from research. Becoming fix-

TABLE I

Strategies for Addressing Ethical Dilemmas in Organizational Research

Source	Strategy	Ethical norm
Role ambiguity		Anticipating coercion or co-optation of or by uninvolved parties, researcher, participants, and stakeholders; examining risks and benefits; identifying personal, professional, scientific, organizational, job-holder, and stakeholder interests
Regarding which persons or groups are part of the research	Creating an in-house research group composed of all parties implicated directly or indirectly in the study	
Regarding the researcher's role	Communicating clearly, explicitly, and by example the intended role; clarifying the intended means and ends; examining potential unintended consequences; providing for informed participation	
Regarding the participants' roles	Clarifying role responsibilities and rights; providing for informed consent and voluntary participation; establishing procedures to ensure anonymity, confidentiality, job security, and entitlements; providing for redress of grievances and unilateral termination of the research	
Regarding the stakeholders' roles	Clarifying role responsibilities and rights; establishing procedures to ensure participants' anonymity, confidentiality, job security, and entitlements	
Role conflict		Avoiding coercion of or by uninvolved parties, researcher, participants, and stakeholders; acting with knowledge of risks and benefits; representing personal, professional, scientific, organizational, job-holder, and stakeholder interests through collaborative effort and commitment to ethical basis of the research
Between researcher and participants, between researcher and stakeholders, within researcher	Creating and building role relations, providing for joint examination of intended means and ends and potential unintended consequences, establishing procedures for resolution of conflict through joint effort within established ethical norms	
Between participants, between stakeholders, between participants and stakeholders, within participant or stakeholder	Organizing full role system, providing for collaborative examination of intended means and ends and potential unintended consequences, establishing procedures for resolution of conflict through collaborative effort within established ethical norms	
Ambiguous or conflicting norms		Establishing ethical basis of research
Within or between researcher, participants, and stakeholders	Clarifying ethical norms for research, providing for collaborative examination of unclear or incompatible norms, establishing procedures for resolution of value conflicts through collaborative effort	

ated on ethics itself has ethical consequences. As Benne (1959) noted, "Making valid distinctions between neurotic anxieties and ethical concerns is a 'learned' rather than a 'natural' ability" (p. 66). Thus it is not simply a matter for researchers to "behave ethically," for as we have sought to show, ethical action does not follow from good intentions alone. Instead it is incumbent on researchers and organizational participants to learn how to conduct research ethically. The social science community recognizes this need. When Seashore began his research career, there was great naiveté about ethical consequences in organizational research. Today, as Mirvis begins his, naiveté itself is unethical.

One place to begin to address ethics in organizational research is in the pre- and in-service training of social scientists. A body of knowledge is already being developed to help identify the roles and role responsibilities of organizational consultants (Benne, 1959), organizational development practitioners (Walton & Warwick, 1973), group trainers (Glidewell, 1978), and evaluation researchers (Sieber & Sanders, 1978). The normative values that govern research relations have become the subject of study (Warwick & Kelman, 1973). In the same vein, social scientists are addressing their role in the larger society (Gouldner, 1962) and the social and political consequences of their research activities (Guskin & Chesler, 1973). All of this heightens awareness of the ethical conflicts in research and also creates a climate in which to learn to conduct research ethically.

To further this purpose, we would suggest that social scientists more often apply their knowledge of social organization to their own research activities. Their knowledge of roles and role relations, for example, could be used to define their roles as researchers and to diagnose the ethical problems that are faced in a research effort. Similarly, their methods of policy analysis and contingency planning could be applied

to address the foreseeable conflicts and to respond to the second- and third-order consequences of the research. Finally, their knowledge of the intra- and interpersonal skills of organizing could be used to help build role relations in order to cope with uncertainty about risks and benefits and to manage the ethical dilemmas that arise.

Among the several social and behavioral science disciplines, psychologists have the most richly developed and documented ethical guidelines, as well as institutionalized agencies for surveillance of practice and resolution of public complaints. The current documents of the American Psychological Association (1963, 1967, 1973, 1975), however, have evolved largely from clinical and counseling practice, from research with unorganized subjects, and from a preoccupation with collegial relationships; they do not adequately address the issues that arise in the context of organizational settings. The other social science disciplinary groups have even more rudimentary ethical provisos and generally lack organizational mechanisms for the accumulation of experience, codification of issues, and exposure of cases to the healing properties of light, air, and public debate. None of these disciplinary groups, as far as we know, offers any effective guidance for the in-service training and supervision of organizational researchers or practitioners (Alderfer & Berg, 1977). Most important, no explicit counsel is given to researchers regarding their responsibilities to work closely with members in the organization to anticipate, prepare for, and openly confront the role conflicts and normative differences that precipitate ethical dilemmas in organizational research.

Up to this point, there have been no systematic efforts to formulate ethical guidelines specific to organizational research. Stone (1978) has identified a potpourri of ethical questions researchers face in every study; others, notably Argyris (1970), have examined one or more ethical questions in depth. But now, as researchers' roles become increasingly differentiated, research relations increasingly tangled, and the consequences of "unethical" behavior increasingly dire, the need for common concepts for analyzing ethical dilemmas and common principles for resolving them becomes pressing. There should be arrangements for the public airing of ethical dilemmas, presentation of rationales for choosing a course of action, and derivation of general principles. Preparation of a casebook on ethical standards for organizational researchers would be a good next step along the way.

Such a casebook would deal with familiar generic issues but would treat them in the context of organizational research. Among the specific questions would be the following: (a) How can the anonymity of organizations and the privacy of individuals be appropriately respected when they occupy social roles that are inherently, or even legally, exposed to scrutiny and in which the distinction between personal and public interest is obscure? (b) What is the meaning of voluntary consent, given that organizations are open systems and countless individuals may be indirectly implicated in research? (c) What is the meaning of informed consent when organizational processes are set in motion and take on their own dynamics without anyone knowing, with confidence, the outcomes? (d) How can principles of confidentiality be operationalized when it is not obvious who or what social entity "owns" the information? Examining these and related issues with attorneys, ethicists, union representatives, managers, and other interested citizens would add a diversity of viewpoints and would provide the basis for a common ethical code.

As researchers reflect on and act within their roles, one ethical principle of the American Psychological Association must surely apply. That is the first principle, that the researcher is personally responsible for the ethics of the research effort. The Milgram (1965) studies showed vividly how people can behave unethically because of their role in a social setting. Surely, as researchers we often behave like Milgram's subjects, letting social habits and coercions supersede our personal values. One aim in applying role theory to the conduct of research is to enable researchers to look critically at their own roles and role relations. We believe that by analyzing research relations in terms of roles and the norms that govern them, researchers shed light on their ethical dilemmas. Likewise, by contemplating these dilemmas, they also shed light on their choice of roles.

That phrase *choice of roles* sharpens the view we advocate, for it implies that there exists in any situation an array of alternative roles that can potentially satisfy ethical criteria. But the phrase does not imply that the ethical researcher need only choose a role and then hold to its prescriptions. The thrust of our argument is directly contrary, for we believe that roles are not "taken"; they are conferred on people and affirmed or modified through assertion, negotiation, and consensus. In a relatively brief, simple, contrived, and power-imbalanced relationship, as in the medical model of professional behavior in relation to a client, the professional may gain instant acceptance of his or her own choice of roles; but a social scientist studying an organization can do so only by choosing a role so innocuous that no other roles are significantly implicated or by identifying with a powerful group of supporters capable of insulating him or her from the normal role-forming obligations.

At the beginning of this article, we proposed that ethical choice is embedded in action and that its essence is the considered choice among alternative courses of action where the interests of all parties have been clarified and the risks and gains have been openly and mutually evaluated. Those who, from a distance, judge this or that role model to be unethical are strangers to the problems of field research in organizations. We have described our own research, our own moral choices, and have proposed role theory as a means for understanding ethical quandaries encountered in organizational research. When conducting such a study, the researcher is immersed in action and can only fitfully guide it with abstract moral reflection. Role theory, to be relevant to ethical decision making, must be useful in action. We believe it can be applied to research in organizations, but we have come to the conclusion that although it cannot be prescriptive as to the *content* of the researcher's role, it can be prescriptive as to the *processes* that can lead to a tolerable (and temporary) consensus among all interested parties regarding a moral course of action. This view does not lessen the researcher's personal responsibility for his or her choice of role or role behavior. On the contrary, it requires that

social scientists choose and fulfill an acceptable public role or leave the scene.

Neither organizational nor research roles are biological, but they do seem to have built-in survival mechanisms. They perpetuate order in the research relationship and, within that order, perpetuate themselves. This can lead to the presumption that following current ethical role prescriptions, including those presented here, is an assurance of ethical conduct. But ethics are not inherent in role behavior. Just the reverse: Ethical conduct in research requires criticism of roles, norms, and the institutions that sustain them. To be ethical, then, we must be critical of our roles in institutions, the norms that govern these roles, and the institutions themselves. This critique can inform ethical decision making. It can also free us to conduct research ethically.

References

Alderfer, C. P., & Berg, D. N. "Organization Development: The Profession and the Practitioner." In P. H. Mirvis & D. N. Berg (Eds.), *Failures in Organizational Development and Change.* New York: Wiley-Interscience, 1977.

American Psychological Association. *Ethical Standards of Psychologists.* Washington, D.C.: Author, 1963.

American Psychological Association. *Casebook on Ethical Standards of Psychologists.* Washington, D.C.: Author, 1967.

American Psychological Association. *Ethical Principles in the Conduct of Research with Human Participants.* Washington, D.C.: Author, 1973.

American Psychological Association. *Standards for Providers of Psychological Services.* Washington, D.C.: Author, 1975.

Argyris, C. *Intervention Theory and Method.* Reading, Mass.: Addison-Wesley, 1970.

Benne, K. D. "Some Ethical Problems in Group and Organizational Consultation." *Journal of Social Issues,* 1959, *15*(2), 60–67.

Berg, D. N. "Failure at Entry." In P. H. Mirvis & D. N. Berg (Eds.), *Failures in Organizational Development and Change.* New York: Wiley-Interscience, 1977.

Bermant, G., & Warwick, D. P. "The Ethics of Social Intervention: Power, Freedom, and Accountability." In G. Bermant, H. C. Kelman, & D. P. Warwick (Eds.), *The Ethics of Social Intervention.* Washington, D.C.: Hemisphere, 1978.

Drexler, J. A., Jr., & Lawler, E. E., III. "A Union–management Cooperative Project to Improve the Quality of Work Life." *Journal of Applied Behavioral Science,* 1977, *13*, 373–387.

Glidewell, J. C. "Ethical Issues In and Around Encounter Groups." In G. Bermant, H. C. Kelman, & D. P. Warwick (Eds.), *The Ethics of Social Intervention.* Washington, D.C.: Hemisphere, 1978.

Gouldner, A. W. "Anti-minotaur: The Myth of a Value-free Sociology." *Social Problems,* 1962, *9*, 199–213.

Graen, G. "Role Making Processes in Organizations." In M. D. Dunnette (Ed.), *Handbook of Industrial and Organizational Psychology.* Chicago: Rand McNally, 1976.

Guskin, A. E., & Chesler, M. A. "Partisan Diagnosis of Social Problems." In G. Zaltman (Ed.), *Processes and Phenomena of Social Change.* New York: Oxford University Press, 1973.

Katz, D., & Kahn, R. L. *The Social Psychology of Organization* (2nd ed.). New York: Wiley, 1978.

Klein, L. *A Social Scientist in Industry.* New York: Halsted Press/Wiley, 1976.

Laue, J., & Cormick, G. "The Ethics of Intervention in Community Disputes." In G. Bermant, H. C. Kelman, & D. P. Warwick (Eds.), *The Ethics of Social Intervention.* Washington, D.C.: Hemisphere, 1978.

Michael, D. N., & Mirvis, P. H. "Changing, erring, and Learning." In P. H. Mirvis & D. N. Berg (Eds.), *Failures in Organizational Development and Change.* New York: Wiley-Interscience, 1977.

Milgram, S. "Some Conditions of Obedience and Disobedience to Authority." *Human Relations,* 1965, *18,* 57–76.

Mirvis, P. H., & Berg, D. N. (Eds.). *Failures in Organizational Development and Change.* New York: Wiley-Interscience, 1977.

Nadler, D. A., Mirvis, P. H., & Cammann, C. "The Ongoing Feedback System: Experimenting with a New Managerial Tool." *Organizational Dynamics,* 1976, *4,* 63–80.

Seashore, S. E. "The Design of Action Research." In A. W. Clark (Ed.), *Experimenting with Organizational Life: The Action Research Approach.* New York: Plenum Press, 1976.

Sieber, J. E., & Sanders, N. "Ethical Problems in Program Evaluation: Roles, not Models." *Evaluation and Program Planning,* 1978, *1,* 117–120.

Stone, E. *Research Methods in Organizational Behavior.* Santa Monica, Calif.: Goodyear, 1978.

Walton, R. E., & Warwick, D. P. "The Ethics of Organization Development." *Journal of Applied Behavioral Science,* 193, 9, 681–698.

Warwick, D. P., & Kelman, H. C. "Ethical Issues in Social Intervention." In G. Zaltman (Ed.), *Processes and Phenomena of Social Change.* New York: Wiley-Interscience, 1973.

A Devil's Dictionary of Behavioral Science Research Terms[1]

Richard W. Woodman

Writing around the turn of the century, Ambrose Bierce remarked that "to apologize is to lay the foundation for a future offense." In that spirit, to those who may perceive the following as imperfectly respectful of the seriousness of our endeavors, an apology is offered in advance.

It is hoped that these definitions contain just enough truth to make us uncomfortable. Not taking ourselves too seriously helps to retain a sense of perspective, reminds us of the fallibility always present in human endeavors, and thus may serve to strengthen our sometimes feeble attempts at science.

ARTIFACT   The only true fact in an experiment.

BIAS   The sugar in the gas tank of measurement. There are many sources of bias, which may be roughly categorized as (a) uncontrollable, and (b) unknown.

CONTROL GROUP   A group having some vague resemblance to an experimental group. In the ideal control group, neither flood, fire, nor famine will cause any change in criterion scores.

CORRELATIONAL STUDY   The last two words of the phrase, "It is only a . . ."

DECEPTION EXPERIMENT   An experiment in which the researcher is pleased to believe that the true nature of the situation is unknown to the participants. Typically the only parties deceived are the funding agency and the journal editor.

DEMAND CHARACTERISTICS   Unintended situational or experimenter effects. Not to be confused with verbal and non-verbal cues provided by the experimenter to define the parameters of acceptable behavior during the course of an experiment.

DOUBLE-BLIND EXPERIMENT   An experiment in which the chief researcher believes he is fooling both the subject and the lab assistant. Often accompanied by a belief in the tooth fairy.

EVALUATION APPREHENSION   An unreasonable fear developed by subjects as a result of an experimental situation. This fear would appear to be catching as it often affects the experimenter as well, particularly around the time tenure decisions are made.

EVALUATION RESEARCH   Research conducted in an organization having a surplus of cash. Acceptance of the findings is de-

---

[1] With apologies to Ambrose Bierce

Reproduced by permission of the *Academy of Management Review,* 1979, 4, 93–94.

pendent upon the congruence between the reality and the dream.

EXPERIMENTER EFFECTS   All the effects in an experiment.

EX POST FACTO DESIGN   A research design growing out of a consulting contract.

FIELD EXPERIMENT   An experiment which should have been done in the laboratory.

HOMOGENEITY OF VARIANCE   An assumption commonly made, frequently violated, and never tested. It does not seem to matter.

HYPOTHESIS   A prediction based on theory formulated after an experiment is performed designed to account for the ludicrous series of events which have taken place.

LABORATORY EXPERIMENT   An experiment more appropriately suited for field research.

LEVEL OF SIGNIFICANCE   An imaginary dividing line between causal effects and chance. The level of significance serves as a guide for the experimenter in terms of how many replications must be performed before chance falls his or her way.

LINEAR MODEL   An assumption concerning the nature of reality applied unquestioningly to every relationship as though God had determined that truth must always run in straight lines.

MANIPULATION CHECK   A handy device which allows the researcher to dispose of data from subjects who stubbornly refuse to conform to the experimenter's perception of reality.

METHODOLOGICALLY UNSOUND   Using methodology with which I am unfamiliar.

NON-EQUIVALENT CONTROL GROUP   A control group.

NULL HYPOTHESIS   The type of hypothesis used by a pessimist.

ONE-SHOT CASE STUDY   The scientific equivalent of the four-leaf clover, from which it

is concluded all clover possesses four leaves and is sometimes green.

PARTICIPANT OBSERVATION   A method of gathering data somewhat analogous in degree of objectivity to taking notes while playing outside linebacker.

PLACEBO   The sugar pill of research, often used to discourage a mysterious Mr. Hawthorne from making an untimely appearance. In the South, pronounced place-bo.

POSTTEST   A measurement made too late.

PRETEST   A measurement made too early.

QUASI-EXPERIMENTAL DESIGN   Experimental design.

RANDOMIZATION   The assignment of subjects to conditions in an experiment according to some preconceived plan. Randomness like chastity is more often claimed than maintained.

RELIABLE   Sometimes capable of giving the same results.

REPEATED MEASURES   Placing the dice in the cup for another throw.

REPLICATION   Lightning striking twice in the same place. Replication is a particularly hazardous undertaking for the fledgling experimenter due to the undesirable consequences of failing to reproduce the results of a well-known colleague.

REVIEWER'S NOTE   A rejection slip based upon literature and theories in vogue during the period the reviewer was studying for his or her Ph.D.

SAMPLE   A unique collection of subjects having virtually no chance of being representative of the population from which it was drawn. This shortcoming is trivial and is generally ignored.

STATISTICAL ANALYSIS   Mysterious, sometimes bizarre, manipulations performed upon the collected data of an experiment in order to obscure the fact that the results have no generalizable meaning for humanity. Commonly, computers are used, lending an additional air of unreality to the proceedings.

SUBJECT   Mankind's equivalent of the white rat. A victim of science.

TESTS OF SIGNIFICANCE   A ritual performed by worshippers of a Diety known as the "God of Significant Differences." The failure of this illustrious Personage to appear in the results of an experiment, even after painstaking observance of the proper rites, has been known to occasion attacks of acute temptation.

UNOBTRUSIVE   MEASURES   Experimental techniques of unclear origin having something to do with worn tiles. Observing madam in her bath without bringing forth screams.

VALIDITY   There are many types of validity. The distinctions among them are boring. Suffice it to say validity issues may be summarized as being chiefly remarkable for the unfair, unrealistic constraints which they place upon the creativity and imagination of the researcher.

VOLUNTEER SUBJECT   A college sophomore who, of his or her own free will, is allowed to choose between participating in an experiment or failing a course.

Learning the Craft of Organizational Research[1]

Richard L. Daft

What research techniques can be used to obtain significant new knowledge about organizations? Many of us would answer by referring to what has become known as the natural science model of research (Behling, 1980; Popper, 1964). The natural science model is typically associated with good research in organization textbooks (Behling, 1980), and is exemplified by precise definition, objective data collection, systematic procedures, and replicable findings. A milestone in the use of systematic procedures in organization studies was Campbell and Stanley's (1963) work on experimental design. The natural science model is sometimes called quantitative research (Morgan & Smircich, 1980). This approach assumes that social reality is a concrete, measurable phenomenon. Advocates of this approach stress the importance of reliability, validity, and accurate measurement before research outcomes can contribute to knowledge.

Others of us would answer that significant new knowledge about organizations is the result of qualitative procedures. Qualitative research is concerned with the meaning rather than the measurement of organizational phenomena. Qualitative research techniques were highlighted in a special issue of *Administrative Science Quarterly* (Van Maanen, 1979). Organizations are assumed to be enormously complex social systems that cannot be effectively studied with the same techniques used to study physical or biological systems (Daft & Wiginton, 1979; Pondy & Mitroff, 1979). Qualitative research procedures assume that organization realities are not concrete, but are the projection of human imagination (Morgan & Smircich, 1980). Those who prefer qualitative research techniques argue that direct involvement in organizations and the use of human senses to interpret organization phenomena are necessary for discovering new knowledge.

A few of us would suggest yet a third answer. This answer would not make the distinction between natural science and qualitative research techniques as separate avenues to significant research outcomes. Organizations are complex, multidimensional entities. A range of techniques can be adopted to effectively pursue a range of research topics (Daft, 1980). Indeed, qualitative and quantitative approaches can be used side by side, as in the natural sciences. The qualitative (our terminology) method of "direct observation" (Mintzberg, 1979) is similar to watching cell matter under an electron microscope or sending Voyager II out for a first hand look at Saturn. The qualitative notion of "organizational stimulation" (Salancik, 1979) is similar to feeding large doses of artificial sweeteners to mice or treating cell cultures with chemicals to observe the response. Perhaps at a superficial level, research in the natural and social sciences seems to call for different approaches. But in

---

[1] Reprinted by permission of the *Academy of Management Review*, 1983, 8, 53 9-546.

many ways research in these fields is similar. In his address to the American Psychological Association, Oppenheimer (1956) proposed that we are all in this together, facing similar problems, suffering the same human limitations, trying to probe into the apparent randomness of a vastly complicated physical and social world to see patterns and make sense of it.

What techniques can be used to obtain significant new knowledge about organizations? Those who do not answer in quantitative or qualitative terms would argue that significant new knowledge is the outcome of something deeper. Research involves basic attitudes and ways of thinking. Research is a craft. Like other crafts, activities are not analyzable (Perrow, 1967). Cause-effect relationships are not clear. Unexpected problems appear. Procedures are not available to describe each aspect of research activity. The learning of craft skills may take years of trial and error. Through practice we learn how to ask research questions, how to conduct research projects, and what to strive for when writing a research article. Significant research, then, is the outcome of a way of thinking we can call craftsmanship.

The dilemma for the field of organization studies is that the technical, methodological aspects of the research process are taught to aspiring scholars in graduate school. A professor once told several of us as students, "You will need at least 5 years to outgrow the effect of your dissertations." At the time we could not appreciate the meaning behind what the professor said. We were captivated by the power of newly discovered research methods. Elegant and sophisticated techniques went into the design of our dissertations. What was there to possibly outgrow?

What many of us discover after graduate school is that research techniques taught in graduate school are not enough. Only the formal side of the research process can be effectively transmitted through textbooks and the classroom. We cannot learn to perform significant research by following a textbook

anymore than we can learn to be good writers by studying the rules of grammar. In one sense, significant research requires new learning beyond what we learned in graduate school. As a craft, research is interesting, exciting, and satisfying. The challenge for researchers is to get beyond sheer techniques, whether quantitative or qualitative, to interject the craft attitude into the research process. The purpose of this paper is to explore more fully those elements that make up the craft part of the research process.

THE RESEARCH CRAFT

The following material sketches seven elements that form a tentative framework of research craftsmanship. The use of these elements by organizational researchers is briefly explained and contrasted with the formal, prescriptive approach to research frequently taught in graduate school.

Build in Plenty of Room for Error and Surprise

Training for the study of organizations, as most of us experienced it, reflected a rather traditional approach to scientific analysis. We learned about scientific rigor, experimental control, planning, and the anticipation and removal of uncertainties that could upset the research blueprint. The research challenge was to plan the work so that it would come out as predicted.

The problem, of course, is that this approach assumes investigators know a substantial amount about the phenomenon under investigation. Knowledge beforehand makes for clean, tidy, hypothesis testing research, but the knowledge return will typically be small. If we have a good idea about what the research answer will be, if we understand the phenomenon well enough to predict and control what happens, why bother to ask the question? If we are to acquire knowledge that is really new, then we don't know the answer in advance. The significant discoveries, the good science, require us to go beyond the safe certainty of precision in design.

Lewis Thomas (1974) said that good basic research needs a high degree of uncertainty at the outset, otherwise the investigator has not chosen an important problem. We should start with incomplete facts, ambiguity, and plan experiments on the basis of probability, even bare hunch, rather than certainty. Then look for surprise. Quality of work is measured by intensity of surprise. The greater the astonishment, the greater the new knowledge about the world.

Those of us in organizational behavior and theory often seem to have it backward. Books on research design, courses on research methodology, and comments from journal referees lead me to believe that many investigators desire absence of surprise in their research. Hard logic and previous evidence should justify every step. A journal referee once insisted "you can't use that hypothesis because there is no previous evidence to support it." A successful project is one in which everything comes out as predicted.

The myth that successful research comes out as predicted, probably more than anything else, restricts the discovery of new knowledge in our discipline. Reviews of landmark studies in the behavioral and organizational sciences indicate that they tended to be loosly done (Daft & Wiginton, 1979; MacKenzie & House, 1978). The significant studies often approached the problem as an open-ended question to be answered rather than as a hypothesis to be tested (Lundberg, 1976).

The notion of building uncertainty into research has been a big discovery for me. It is okay to ask research questions without the answer in advance. In one sense, all scientific progress is due to errors and deviations. New knowledge surprises us, changes how we see things. If our experiments are per-

fectly designed and the results come out as expected, then they are probably a waste of time. We must take chances; we must make mistakes to be good scholars.

Research Is Storytelling

In graduate school we learned that research procedures include designing a project, collecting data, counting things up, looking for relationships, testing hypotheses, and reporting the findings in a journal article. These steps are certainly necessary in an empirical science.

The craft side of research is not like this at all. Research is storytelling. The scientific method is more like guesswork, the making up and revising of stories. By storytelling, I mean explaining what the data mean, using data to describe how organizations work. Stories are theories. Theory need not be formal or complex. Theories simply explain why. The "why" is important, and we should be creative and ruthless in pursuit of it (Weick, 1974). The why, not the data, is the contribution to knowledge.

Data collection and analysis are integral parts of the research process, but they are intermediate points between an initial hunch and the final story about the organizational world. Data do not stand alone. So many papers miss the essential point of research. Data are treated like so many playing cards to be shuffled, reshuffled, and dealt around. Research is often viewed as if it is naming the game and calculating the probability of each hand. Emphasis on method and calculation misses what the data represent. Human behavior and processes in organization are what we care about. The data alone are not enough, no matter how sophisticated the techniques for collection and analysis.

Geologists, for example, are storytellers (McPhee, 1981). They take observations from outcroppings, roadcuts, tunnels, maps, and drillings. These are geological datapoints, which are collected and analyzed rigorously. But geologists do not report only the data. They use the data to construct wonderful stories about geological history. They describe the appearance of lakes and oceans, the wearing down of mountains, and the ecological systems of animals and plants that inhabited the earth. These stories provide insight and understanding about the earth's history. Geologists make up stories and continue to revise and elaborate the stories with subsequent research projects. In much the same way, craftsmen in organization research use data to tell stories about the behavior and processes within organizations.

Design Research as a Poem, Not as a Novel

The logic of research, as I learned it, was to reach out for more variables whenever possible. Multivariate analysis was one key to success, and still seems to be. Most review papers recommend that future studies incorporate additional variables as the path to uncovering true relationships and greater understanding. Journal referees enjoy pointing out how operationalization of additional variables would make a study better, perhaps even publishable. To the extent that variables represent characters in a story, then the approach often recommended would result in a novel, with many characters, a complex plot and almost infinite relationships.

I no longer accept this approach. Poetry seems to have greater applicability to organizational research. By poetry, I mean a research design that includes only a few, perhaps two, three, or four variables. But they have to hang together in a meaning unit, a coherent framework of sorts, that explains some aspect of organizations. A research poem must also have depth. The meaning unit must take a deep slice into organizations and convey a rich conceptualization to others.

These two ingredients—a few variables that form a coherent whole and depth of meaning—constitute an ideal research framework. Most of the significant ideas in our field are poems. Theory X and Theory Y is a poem. So is the notion of differentiation and integration. For me, Perrow's dimensions of task analyzability and variety constitute a poem. *Organizations in Action* is a book of poetry. Thompson (1967) expressed several important models in simple two-variable contingency tables.

The thread common to all of these concepts is simplicity in the sense of only a couple of key variables, but the ideas hang together in a unit to explain some dimension of organization. The ideas have depth. Differentiation and integration summarize a cluster of behaviors that may be found in organizations. The concepts have layers of meaning that enable us to understand a complex notion in a single thought, much like a metaphor. The concepts have roots that run deep into organizations.

Human organizations are enormously complex, so how is it possible to understand them with simple models? Two reasons. First, good research doesn't try to answer all questions about an issue. It doesn't pretend to. The best research provides an utterly imperfect model of organization reality. One goal of research is simply to understand a tiny piece of organizational reality. The insights provided by a simple model can be used to raise new questions for future research. Second, Simon (1981) argued we don't have to measure system complexity to model it. Everything in organizations may be related to everything else (Boulding, 1956; Pondy & Mitroff, 1979), but a model of two or three key variables can still be accurate. The model provides a basis for a deeper story. A hundred variables may be involved, but substantial insights about organization relationships can be uncovered from an assessment of a few key dimensions.

Writing poetry in organizational research is extremely difficult. Successful poems can be the result of genius, or chance. This does not imply that every study should be limited to a small number of variables, only that we should not expect a large number of variables to produce great insights. We can strive for simplicity in our research. Simplicity means fundamental, not trivial. We should not let the addition of variables substitute for thinking carefully about organizations or for searching out key dimensions.

Research Decisions Are Not Linear

If any activity should be characterized by rational, logical decision processes, it would certainly be empirical research. The rational model begins with a carefully formulated research problem based upon a thorough literature review. Next the research design and methods are chosen. Some sort of triangulation may be possible. Data are collected and analyzed, and the results are used to support or confirm specific hypotheses.

The craft decision process is much more random and messy. After evaluating research decision processes, Martin (1981) proposed that the garbage can model served as a better description of a random, chancy process. Campbell, Daft and Hulin (1982), based on retrospective interviews with prominent organizational scholars, discovered that most significant research did not follow the rational model. The original decision to undertake a project resulted from the simultaneous convergence of several events, such as the discovery of a new research technique, the availability of a research site, and the appearance of a new idea. The investigator spontaneously grabbed the opportunity. The Campbell, et al. interviews also found that when research decisions were rational and linear, the research findings tended to be less significant. Research undertaken as a logical next step tended to produce outcomes that were routine and dull.

Another side to the decision making process concerns intuition and feelings. If the rational research model can be characterized as left brain activity, then many research decisions are made in the nonlinear area of the right brain. The Campbell, et al. (1982) study found that investigators cared about their research. They felt passion for their studies. Investigators couldn't explain it but the significant studies felt good from the beginning. Mitroff (1972) reported that research objectivity among the scientists he studied was a myth. Scientists are not free of bias, opinions, or convictions. They care deeply about their work and have a stake in the outcome (Watson, 1968).

Another nonlinear attribute by which a research project can be judged is beauty. Kaplan (1964) proposed that esthetic quality is one way of validating a theory. "A scientist sometimes needs the courage, not only of his convictions, but also of his esthetic sensibilities" (1964, p. 319). Mintzberg wrote that if an idea is not beautiful, then perhaps it will not be useful either (1982). The decision to undertake a study is based upon a symmetrical hanging togetherness that pleases the beholder. The right brain has an important role in the craft side of the research process. Significant research is not a logical next step, is not the outcome of a strategic plan, is not calculable. The best time to undertake a research project is when the investigator suddenly realizes, "What a lovely idea!"

Relate Ideas to Common Sense

We have all heard or used the argument that research ideas are on the frontier of organizational knowledge. The concepts may not make sense to those not involved with the research, especially managers. The evaluation of our findings must be objective. We learn to distrust gut reactions and other indicators of common sense. As scientists we expect to seek a higher proof.

Perhaps there is some truth to this idea because the common sense of laymen and scientists may differ (Davis, 1971). On the other hand, I have gradually come to realize that common sense—of both the investigator and his colleagues—is the best test, the ultimate test, of our theories. I am beginning to understand what Oppenheimer (1958, p. 129) meant when he said, "Science is the adaptation of common sense." Scientists simply look for aspects of experience not visible in daily life by using instruments such as telescopes or questionnaires. Oppenheimer went on to say, "We come from common sense, we work for a long time, and we give back to common sense refined, original and strange notions that enrich what we know. We come to new things in science with what we already know." C. Wright Mills (1955) found it essential to integrate what he was doing intellectually with what he was doing as a person. To trust one's own experience, Mills said, is the mark of a mature scholar. In a sense, we cannot deal with new scholarly findings except on the basis of the familiar and old-fashioned.

One way to embrace common sense is to use analogy and metaphor in our scientific descriptions. Huff (1978) writes that metaphor makes the strange familiar, and allows recognition and learning that links an idea to previous experience. Metaphor and analogy provide a vehicle for relating new ideas to what we already know. Without this linkage the new idea has little value, little impact, and provides no means to elaborate upon previous experience.

Other fields, especially the natural sciences, make use of analogies (Dreistadt, 1968). Analogies are not perfect representations in any sense, but they provide a basis to make the new familiar. Oppenheimer (1956) argued that we cannot be surprised at a discovery unless we have a view of how it ought to be. A recent paper argued that biological metaphors of organizations are inadequate (Keeley, 1980). Of course they are inadequate, all analogies are. But biological and other types of analogies still help us communicate the essence of new ideas.

The final point about common sense concerns the notion of proof. Ultimate proof of an idea or theory is its acceptability to our common sense. An important test of validity is liking an idea, feeling right about it, being able to use it to throw light on a previously hidden aspect of organization. Objective proof seldom will exist somewhere outside ourselves that will demonstrate correctness or validity. No statistical test will do this for us; no amount of replication will make acceptable an idea that doesn't square with experience. Even if the organization reality we study is hard and objective, we aren't. We cannot obtain knowledge independent of our own judgment and social construction (Morgan & Smircich, 1980).

The notion of differentiation and integration in organizations is an example of concepts that are useful to experience although they are not provable in objective fashion (Lawrence & Lorsch, 1967). The scientific measurement of these concepts has been challenged (Tosi, Aldag & Storey, 1973), yet the ideas continue to flourish because they are useful and acceptable to students and managers of organizations. These ideas make sense at a deeper, nonstatistical level.

Learn about Organizations First-hand

This idea seems so obvious that I am reluctant to state it as part of the research craft, but it is not stressed in many Ph.D. programs. Organizations are so rich that anyone who actually observes them, who goes out for a look around, will find sufficient puzzlements to last for a productive career. For some reason, direct contact with organizations, first-hand learning, is not given high value. Collecting data is stressed, and so is running correlations and reporting statistical coefficients. As I reviewed numerous papers, it became painfully clear that many authors have never seen or witnessed the phenomena about which they write. Authors cannot give an example to illustrate a point. They have an enormously difficult time thinking beneath the correlation coefficients to discuss what the coefficients represent in terms of organizational activities and processes. Authors typically report very thin descriptions of a large number of relationships, never touching the why of the correlations, only dealing with the fact that variable Y is related to variable Z, as if that constituted everything.

The difficulty that many authors have developing interesting and insightful theories about organization is probably explained by a lack of experience with organizations. G. R. Grice admonished his students who were trying to understand animal learning, "No matter how much research money you may have, or how many assistants you may hire, always handle your own rat" (Hackman, 1982). If those of us in organization studies would handle our own rats, the supply of important research problems and new theoretical insights could be quickly increased.

Organization studies is an empirical science. Mintzberg's strategy of direct research on managers (1973) and decision making (1976) illustrates how powerful first-hand knowledge can be. If we look, really look, at our subject of study, we can't help but see things that will inform us about organizations. Staying in one's office and mailing out questionnaires may have the appearance of research, but often it reduces the opportunity to learn about organizations.

One of the unexpected discoveries from interviews with leading scholars by Campbell, et al (1982) was the importance of real world contacts. Significant studies often began through direct contact with organizations—perhaps a training session with managers, a consulting job, or a puzzlement encounter during field interviews. On the other hand, studies which turned out to be less significant were not originated in organizations. These studies originated in more academic fashion, from one's university office, perhaps based upon a journal article and the perceived opportunity to make a small modification that would yield a quick publication.

Arm-chair theorizing and other forms of non-contact with organization can also be helpful, especially if the ideas probe into organizational ideas in a speculative way and provide a fresh perspective to guide empirical research. But even arm-chair theories have to be informed by contact with organizations somewhere along the way. Contact either in the form of visits and observations or perhaps through descriptive case analyses provides the intellectual raw material for useful theory.

Many Colleagues in Our Discipline Really Care about Quality Research and New Knowledge

The need to publish articles becomes apparent to most of us during graduate training. Many, many people in our field seem preoccupied with the idea of publication. They do whatever is necessary to have a paper published and will send it to any conference or seminar or journal to get publication credit. In the worst cases, people cut up their data or trade authorships to increase the number of publications listed on their resume.

So much of our career progress is based on publication that attention gets distracted from the content of our articles. In a publication environment, failure to publish means failure in an academic career; hence a large proportion of us are seduced into this process without realizing there is another game to be played. There are fewer players at the other table, but there is a serious research game being played out right now in organization and management theory. There are many colleagues who count the content of a paper first and publication second. Among these scholars, an unpublished working paper will have impact if it adds to the developing knowledge base. A working paper can influence the thinking and research of others. Formal publication is anti-climactic. Individuals can be known by their ideas, not by the number of publications.

I cannot specify the boundaries of this research orientation, or identify very precisely the players, only that the game is played, and that I have experienced the thrill of sitting at the table. The concern for content is a welcome haven from the publication wars, and far more productive. The machine gun fire of referee criticism is replaced by positive words of encouragement and support. The bombshells of journal rejection are replaced by collegial advice, intellectual exchange, and a desire to get to the truth. Interchanges with senior scholars that did not have publication as their ultimate goal had a profound impact on my intellectual development. Publication is a fact of life for all of us. We all feel the pressure. But there is tremendous support within our discipline for high quality empirical and theoretical work. We don't have to do mindless research if we choose not to, and publication will take care of itself.

CONCLUSION

What research techniques can be used to achieve significant new knowledge about organizations? The answer proposed here is that formal research techniques—either quantitative or qualitative—as taught in graduate school are not sufficient. Significant research grows out of experience and mastery of the attitude and frame of mind that make up the research craft. The research craft is enhanced by respect for error and surprise, storytelling, research poetry, emotion, common sense, first-hand learning, and research colleagues.

The elements of the research craft described above are neither fixed nor complete. Every scholar can add characteristics that help lead to significant outcomes in his or her own research. Scholars can progress through their own stages of learning and de-

velop their own guidelines. The important thing is that the craft perspective be mastered and used to build upon the techniques of science taught in graduate school.

What worries me is that many of us seem to have never discovered or acknowledged the craft aspects of scholarship. Formal techniques and method dominate in most manuscripts and journal articles that I read. The authors act as if there is only a single approach, which includes measurement precision, perfect prediction, dispassionate analysis, and many variables. Authors often eschew real organizations, storytelling and common sense.

How can we facilitate the learning of research methods to include craft characteristics? We can convey to our students that research is a craft as well as an exercise in methodology. Formal techniques are easy to teach in the classroom, while the craft attitude and way of thinking are learned through experience. We can tell students there is an uncertain, emotional, human side of research, and research that incorporates these properties can be science at its best. Even more important, we can experiment with these elements in our own research and show them to students first hand. A great scholar like Kurt Lewin used apprenticeship to pass the research craft to his students (Marrow, 1969). By showing students how to design studies on the basis of anticipated surprise, beauty, first-hand experience, emotion, and storytelling, we can be role models for the kinds of things that go into significant research. We can ask students to learn formal research techniques in class, and then invite them to join us in the research adventure.

References

Behling, O. "The Case for the Natural Science Model for Research in Organizational Behavior and Organizational Theory." *Academy of Management Review*, 1980, 5, 483–490.

Boulding, K. E. "General Systems Theory: The Skeleton of Science." *Management Science*, 1956, 2, 197–207.

Campbell, D. T., & Stanley, J. C. *Experimental and Quasi-Experimental Design for*

Research. Chicago: Rand McNally, 1963.

Campbell, J. T., Daft, R. L., & Hulin, C. L. *The Generation and Development of Research Problems in the Study of Behavior in Organizations.* New York: Sage, 1982.

Daft, R. L. "The Evolution of Organization Analysis in *ASQ: 1959–1979.*" *Administrative Science Quarterly,* 1980, 25, 623–636.

Daft, R. L., & Wiginton, J. "Language and Organization." *Academy of Management Review,* 1979, 4, 179–191.

Davis, M. S. "That's Interesting: Toward a Phenomenology of Sociology and a Sociology of Phenomenology," *Philosophy of Social Science,* 1979, 1, 309–344.

Dreistadt, R. "An Analysis of the Use of Analogies and Metaphors in Science." *The Journal of Psychology,* 1968, 68, 97–116.

Hackman, J. R. Personal communication, 1982.

Huff, A. S. "Evocative Metaphors." Paper presented to the Third Annual Workshop on Organizational Design, 1978.

Kaplan, A. *The Conduct of Inquiry.* San Francisco: Chandler Publishing Company, 1964.

Keeley, M. "Organizational Analogy: A Comparison of Organismic and Social Contract Models." *Administrative Science Quarterly,* 1980, 25, 337–362.

Lawrence, P. R., & Lorsch, P. *Organization and Environment.* Cambridge, Mass.: Harvard University Press, 1967.

Lundberg, C. C. "Hypothesis Creation in Organizational Behavior Research." *Academy of Management Review,* 1976, 1, 5–12.

Mackenzie, K. D., & House, R. "Paradigm Development in the Social Sciences: A Proposed Research Strategy." *Academy of Management Review,* 1978, 3, 7–23.

McPhee, J. A. *Basin and Range.* New York: Farrar, Straus, Giroux, 1981.

Marrow, A. J. *The Practical Theorist: The Life and Work of Kurt Lewin.* New York: Basic Books, 1969.

Martin, J. "A Garbage Can Model of the Research Process." Paper presented at the Conference on Methodological Innovation in Studying Organizations. Greensboro, North Carolina, August, 1980.

Mills, C. W. *On Intellectual Craftsmanship.* Milwaukee: University of Wisconsin Library, Mimeo, 1955.

Mintzberg, H. *The Nature of Managerial Work.* New York: Harper & Row, 1973.

Mintzberg, H. "An Emerging Strategy of 'Direct' Research." *Administrative Science Quarterly,* 1979, 24, 582–589.

Mintzberg, H. "If You're Not Serving Bill and Barbara, Then You're Not Leadership." In J. G. Hunt, U. Sekaran, and C. A. Schreisheim (eds.) *Leadership: Beyond Establishment Views.* Carbondale, IL: Southern Illinois University Press, 1982, 239–259.

Mintzberg, H., Raisinghani, D., & Theoret, A. "The Structure of Unstructured Decision Processes." *Administrative Science Quarterly,* 1976, 21, 246–276.

Mitroff, I. I. "The Myth of Objectivity of Why Science Needs a New Psychology of Science." *Management Science,* 1972, 18, B613–B618.

Morgan, G., & Smircich, L. "The Case for Qualitative Research." *Academy of Management Review,* 1980, 5, 491–500.

Oppenheimer, R. "Analogy in Science." *The American Psychologist,* 1956, 11, 127–135.

Perrow, C. "A Framework for Comparative Organizational Analysis." *American Sociological Review,* 1967, 32, 194–208.

Pondy, L. R., & Mitroff, I. I. "Beyond Open Systems Models of Organization." In Barry M. Staw (ed.) *Research in Organizational Behavior.* Greenwich, Conn.: JAI Press, 1978, 3–39.

Popper, K. R. *The Poverty of Historicism.* New York: Harper Torchbooks, 1964.

Salancik, G. R. "Field Stimulation for Organization Behavior Research." *Administrative Science Quarterly,* 1979, 24, 638–649.

Simon, H. *The Science of the Artificial.* Cambridge, MA: MIT Press, 1981.

Thomas, L. *The Lives of a Cell: Notes of a Biology Watcher.* New York: Viking Press, 1974.

Thompson, J. D. *Organizations in Action.* New York: McGraw-Hill, 1974.

Tosi, H., Aldag, R., & Storey, R. "On the Measurement of the Environment: An Assessment of the Lawrence and Lorsch Environmental Uncertainty Questionnaire." *Administrative Science Quarterly,* 1973, *18,* 27–36.

Van Maanen, J. "Reclaiming Qualitative Methods for Organizational Research: A Preface." *Administrative Science Quarterly,* 1979, *24,* 520–526.

Watson, J. D. *The Double Helix: A Personal Account of the Discovery of the Structure of DNA.* New York: Atheneum, 1968.

Weick, K. E. "Amendments to Organizational Theorizing." *Academy of Management Journal,* 1974, *17,* 487–502.

Index